Personality Theories, Research, & Assessment

Personality Theories, Research, & Assessment

By
Raymond J. Corsini
Anthony J. Marsella
University of Hawaii at Manoa

and Contributors

F.E. PEACOCK PUBLISHERS, INC. ITASCA, ILLINOIS 60143

Copyright ©1983
F.E. Peacock Publishers, Inc.
All rights reserved
Library of Congress
Catalog Card No. 82-061261
ISBN 0-87581-288-0
Printed in the U.S.A.
Third Printing, 1986

To
    Anne Anastasi
      Edgar Borgatta
   and
       George Guthrie
       William Lebra

for their support and encouragement

A great thorough-going man does not confine himself to one school, but combines many schools, as well as reads and listens to the arguments of many predecessors.

KUO HSI

Contents

List of Contributors

ANSBACHER, HEINZ L., Ph.D.
Emeritus Professor
Department of Psychology
University of Vermont
Burlington, Vermont

CORSINI, RAYMOND J., Ph.D.
Private Practice, Clinical Psychology
Senior Counselor, Family Education Centers
Honolulu, Hawaii

GIOVACCHINI, PETER L., M.D.
Private Practice, Psychoanalysis
Clinical Professor
Department of Psychiatry
University of Illinois
Chicago, Illinois

HOLDSTOCK, T. L., Ph.D.
Senior Lecturer
Department of Psychology
University of Witwatersrand
Johannesburg, South Africa

KOBASA, SUZANNE C., Ph.D.
Lecturer
Department of Behavioral Sciences
University of Chicago
Chicago, Illinois

LUNDIN, ROBERT W., Ph.D.
Professor and Chairperson
Department of Psychology
University of The South
Sewanee, Tennessee

MADDI, SALVATORE, R., Ph.D.
Professor
Department of Behavioral Sciences
University of Chicago
Chicago, Illinois

MADURO, RENALDO J., Ph.D.
Private Practice, Jungian Psychoanalysis
Associate Professor
School of Medicine
University of California
San Francisco, California

MARSELLA, ANTHONY J., Ph.D.
Professor
Department of Psychology
University of Hawaii at Manoa
Honolulu, Hawaii

PEDERSEN, PAUL B., Ph.D.
Professor
Department of Education
Syracuse University
Syracuse, New York

ROGERS, CARL R., Ph.D.
Resident Fellow
Center for the Study of the Person
La Jolla, California

SECHREST, LEE J., Ph.D.
Professor
Department of Psychology
University of Michigan
Ann Arbor, Michigan

SHONTZ, FRANKLIN C., Ph.D.
Professor
Department of Psychology
University of Kansas
Lawrence, Kansas

WHEELWRIGHT, JOSEPH B., M.D.
Professor Emeritus
Department of Psychiatry
University of California
San Francisco, California

YANG, ALAN K., Ph.D.
Assistant Professor
Department of Psychology
California Polytechnic State University
San Luis Obispo, California

ZIFERSTEIN, ISIDORE, M.D.
Private Practice, Psychiatry
Clinical Professor
Department of Psychiatry
University of California
Los Angeles, California

Preface

PERSONALITY THEORIES, RESEARCH, AND ASSESSMENT contains 15 chapters divided into five sections: One, FOUNDATIONS; Two, THEORIES; Three, THEORETICAL ORIENTATIONS; Four, ASSESSMENT; and Five, RESEARCH.

Section One discusses historical origins and issues as well as contemporary issues.

Section Two provides coverage of classical and contemporary personality theories. A unique feature of this section is that every theory is discussed according to a common outline containing the following elements: Introduction, History, Assertions, Applications, Validation, and Prospects. This format permits a comparative perspective since the chapters can be read "horizontally" (i.e., across topics) and "vertically" (i.e., across theorists).

Section Three covers four important orientations in personality theory: Existentialism, Constitutionalism, Soviet Theory, and Asian Theory. These orientations represent major perspectives on the topic of personality rather than the work of a single individual. Once again, a common outline is used to facilitate comparison of the orientations.

Section Four contains a chapter on personality assessment which reviews a number of objective and subjective approaches to the topic. In addition, it offers the reader an overview of the issues, methods, and tactics involved in personality assessment.

Section Five includes two chapters on personality research. The first discusses the issues, approaches, and new directions in personality research; the second offers an overview of three popular research topics: anxiety, aggression, and locus of control.

In brief, we believe this text provides a comprehensive, detailed, and balanced view of the field of personality.

We wish to express our deep appreciation to a number of people involved in the production of this edition including Tom LaMarre, college editor of F. E. Peacock Publishers, Inc., Ms. Alida Labrie, for compiling the glossary, Ms. Rene Kuroiwa and Ms. Satoko Lincoln, for typing and, of course, the many contributors to the volume.

Raymond J. Corsini
Anthony J. Marsella
Honolulu, 1982

SECTION ONE
FOUNDATIONS

CHAPTER I

Conceptual Issues and Historical Considerations

Raymond J. Corsini
and Anthony J. Marsella

No topic is more interesting to people than people. Biographies, autobiographies, histories, novels, plays, and newspapers are about people. Short stories, poems, movies, television commercials and children's books are about people. Peter Rabbit, Br'er Fox, Mickey Mouse, and the Little Engine That Could are humans in animal or machine disguise. Of all courses in college, the most popular are those that deal with people. Our interest about ourselves and others is boundless and endless. And yet, despite this enormous and constant interest, despite the novels and plays and books about people, at this point in history there still is no generally accepted, comprehensive, uniform understanding of human nature.

There are many personality theories, some extremely complex and some simple and clear, some old and new, each intending to explain how we develop our unique personalities and how we maintain them.

The curious layman learns of the theories of the original big three, Sigmund Freud, Alfred Adler, and Carl Jung, and reads about the modern theories of Carl Rogers, B. F. Skinner, and George Kelly. He or she wonders about constitutional theories, existential theories, Asian theories, and Soviet theories about the nature of humans. It is logical to ask: Why so many theories? *Why can't they come to some agreements about human nature?*

This book will help answer some of these questions. You will be overwhelmed and confused at first by all the answers given, and then, hopefully, you will be able to see the entire spectrum of theories in a unified and comprehensive manner and begin to understand personality formation and maintenance—how we become and remain ourselves—and why we have so many theories about personality.

TOWARD A DEFINITION OF PERSONALITY

Allport (1937), who collected no fewer than 50 definitions of personality, divided them into five types:

1. *Omnibus.* Any definition that says "sum total" is an omnibus definition.
2. *Arrangement.* A second type of definition arranges personality traits in some orderly manner.
3. *Hierarchical.* This kind of definition believes personality is structured in levels appearing in a fixed order.
4. *Adjustment.* Another definition type views the individual as struggling to find his or her identity, trying to adjust to the world.
5. *Distinctiveness.* This kind of definition stresses the individual's uniqueness.

Allport (1937) defined personality as follows:

> Personality is the dynamic organization within the individual of those psychophysical systems that determine his unique adjustment to the world. (p. 48)

What are these psychophysical systems? To give "something" a name generates the idea that what is named actually exists. For example, in the statement, "Jim has a good deal of intelligence," the word *intelligence* tends to be conceived as something; that is, as some *thing*, otherwise how could one have "a good deal" of it? We hear it in the same way we would hear this sentence: "Jim has a good deal of money." This process whereby abstract words gain meaning is known as reification or hypostatization: making a concept real through naming it. We shall soon give names to a number of concepts and then in a circular manner use them to explain behavior.

Concepts intended to explain something or assumed to exist as entities are knows as *constructs.* They are imaginary and are used on an "as if" basis—*as if* they were real. The word *intelligence* thus represents a construct to explain why some people learn more quickly than others: *because they have a high intelligence.* While it is necessary in personality theory to create and to give names to various concepts, you should always keep in mind that constructs are hypothecated entities but are not real in the sense that your arm or nose is real.

Allport suggested a list of various psychophysical systems within the individual, elements which make up what we call personality.

1. *Temperament.* A temperament is a biologically based, physiological function. Thus, a "temperamental" person may be sensitive, ner-

vous, fast-moving, irritable, and tense because he was "born that way." Some newborn infants are placid, while others are squirmy. We say that the first group has an even temperament, and the second is temperamental. In short, the basic concept of temperament is that it is biologically based.

2. *Trait*. A trait represents a constant or persistent way of behaving. Thus, if an individual tells the truth always, this is an indicator of trait of honesty.

3. *Character*. The semantic problem of personality theory is illustrated by this word. Character can mean about the same as personality, but it can also mean about the same as trait, and it can mean "personality evaluated," as in "He has a good character." Generally, in personality theory, it has this third denotation, and it is used evaluatively, such as "She has a character defect," meaning that she tends to act unethically in certain circumstances.

4. *Mood*. This word represents a general, overriding, sometimes constant and sometimes temporary, emotional state. People who are generally sad or happy, optimistic or pessimistic, have these particular moods. The word *state* more or less means the same as mood. "He is in a bad mood" means that he behaves in an angry, emotional, touchy manner.

5. *Disposition*. This term has a similar meaning to the word *set* in general psychology. It means the tendency of an individual to act in a particular manner. A person who has a happy disposition is likely to see things in a pleasant way; a person with a mean disposition is likely to be cruel or punitive.

6. *Trend*. This term indicates direction. Thus a person may have a tendency to go one way or another. Disposition and trend fit together in the sense that one may be disposed (set) to go in a particular direction (trend).

7. *Habit*. This refers to a persistent mode of behavior generally fixed, constant and automatic.

8. *Attitude*. This term encompasses opinions, views, and dispositions representing a generalized set of values toward classes of objects.

Personality and Values

Psychology is neutral, but psychologists are not. As a science, psychology is not concerned with good or bad, but as a profession, it is certainly tied up with values. This position is quite common for all sciences. A physician who examines under a microscope a parasite that may be harming the patient has no animosity to that particular creature, even though the physician may prescribe medicine as a cure, thereby killing the parasite. The term *normal* is used in one way by the psychologist-as-scientist (normal = average) and in a different way by the psychologist-as-therapist (normal = desirable). The same is true for other evaluative terms about personality, such as good, desirable, pleasant, strong, or impressive. These terms are employed by people who like or dislike certain aspects of certain people, but they do not have constant meanings. In personality theory we will not be concerned about "good" and "bad" personalities and not even about "normality" and "abnormality." We will be simply concerned with how people develop and maintain their personality.

Perspectives

Individuals can be viewed from three perspectives:

1. *Subjectively*—as persons see themselves.
2. *Socially*—as seen by others.
3. *Veridically*—as one really is.

We all strive for veridicality, but no one can ever know if this state of absolute truth is ever reached.

To illustrate, let us take the person about whom more biographies have been written than anyone else: Napoleon Bonaparte. Suppose that Napoleon himself, his wife Josephine, and his Austrian opponent Metternich were asked to use the most appropriate word to describe him relative to the seven characteristics listed in the first column of Table 1–1.

The table shows three different perspectives on one man. Napoleon probably saw his own lifestyle as cautious, while Josephine saw him as daring and Metternich as being secretive. Which view is the more accurate? Not only do we not know, but the answer is never knowable. When we talk about personality of any person, we are always dealing with opinions—not facts. It is not a fact that Napoleon was smart or kind or brave or ambitious

TABLE 1–1. HYPOTHETICAL JUDGMENTS ABOUT NAPOLEON BONAPARTE

Characteristics	NAPOLEON	JOSEPHINE	METTERNICH
LIFESTYLE	Cautious	Daring	Secretive
INTELLIGENCE	Foresighted	Clever	Shrewd
STABILITY	Self-controlled	Jealous	Suspicious
DOMINANCE	Independent	Aggressive	Stubborn
ACTIVITY	Active	Quick	Hasty
SENSITIVITY	Appreciative	Sensitive	Sarcastic
MOOD	Worrying	Excitable	Emotional

or wily, even though everyone might have so agreed. It is not a fact that Lincoln was compassionate or that Washington was truthful or that Roosevelt was energetic.

Imagine the consequences when two sets of personality concepts clash. This explains many conflicts between husbands and wives, children and parents, employees and employers. It explains racial and religious prejudices when personalities of groups of people are identified.

Issues in Personality Theory

Personality theories take up many disputed issues—some going back to the very beginnings of concern about human nature, none of them ever settled.

Below are some important issues:

Responsibility. Suppose someone breaks the law, to what degree is he or she responsible? In most of our states the McNaghten rule applies: People are not responsible for their behavior if they are considered insane, but otherwise they are responsible and if they break the law, they deserve punishment.

Personality theorists assume a variety of attitudes on this issue of responsibility. Some say that the person is completely determined by the environment; he has no choice about his behavior. Others take the biological deterministic position that from the instance of conception the individual's personality is established by heredity, and, consequently, he has no choice. Another deterministic attitude is that the individual's behavior is controlled by environment and heredity—but again he cannot be considered responsible. He has no choice.

These three viewpoints of the individual's powerlessness are rejected in the real world by everyone, including the strictest of theoreticians. One can visualize a professor who accepts theoretically the inability of the individual to make real decisions or to be responsible nevertheless telling a student: "You'd better make up your mind to do some studying, otherwise you'll fail my course."

A fourth general position relative to this issue of responsibility is "soft determinism," which holds that a person does have freedom to make judgments and decisions, and is responsible, but this individual's thinking and behaving are affected and limited by both heredity and environment. A fifth position, generally assumed by the law and by some religions, is that regardless of heredity or environment, all not-insane individuals are fully responsible for their own behaviors, and we all have free will.

Proof. Another important issue in personality theory has to do with proof. There are three general ways of trying to prove any issue. The first is by logic. One may start with what appears to be a valid statement, such as Descartes's famous "I think, therefore I am," and having made this point can go on to further theorizing. So-called armchair philosophers often assume that how they think and feel and act is similar to how all others operate, and so they project themselves as representatives of Mankind.

A second general way of getting proof is to depend on observations of a number of individuals taken one at a time. This clinical method is known technically as the *idiographic* method. Freud is an example of an idiographic therapist who came to general nomothetic conclusions about human nature. He would study an individual thoroughly, and on the basis of all the evidence he would come to conclusions not only about that person but about people in general. His conclusions would be backed also by his own experiences, knowledge of other patients, and readings. Generally speaking, the understandings of human nature given by clinicians such as Freud and Carl Rogers and Albert Ellis come from close attention to individual patients dealt with over a long time.

The third way of getting proof about personality theories is by experimentation. In this procedure many people are observed or tested and conclusions are based on group norms. Allport and Skinner are examples of theorists who validate their contentions on the basis of the *nomothetic* method.

Time.   Theorists differ relative to time emphasis. There are three general positions. Some, such as Freud, generally emphasize the importance of the *past*: one's heredity, one's childhood. Others, such as Ludwig Binswanger, emphasize the importance of the *present*, the immediate moment, the now. Still others, such as Alfred Adler, emphasize the importance of the future, holding that expectation of attainment of goals explains behavior.

An eclectic position might be that people make decisions in the *present* in terms of their expectations for the *future*, affected by their experiences in the *past*, so that the past, the present, and the future are involved to some degree at all times.

Consciousness.   There are three points of view about consciousness. One is that consciousness is a private matter and so it is meaningless and valueless. People should simply be evaluated objectively in terms of behavior, without consideration of what may be in their heads. A second point of view states that personality is really one's consciousness: How one thinks and feels is what personality is all about, since behavior is a consequence of one's thoughts and emotions. A third point of view states that the unconscious is what is really important and that consciousness is only the tip of the personality iceberg.

For a behaviorist such as B. F. Skinner, the concept of consciousness is unimportant in understanding personality; for a commonsense theorist such as Rogers, one's consciousness and self-awareness explain personality; and for a depth theorist such as Carl Jung, the real understanding of personality depends on the unconscious.

Integrity. Some personality theorists see the individual as an indissolvable, single unity. A person is mind-body and not body and mind. Those who assume such unity are *monists*. Those who assume the existence of mind and body are dualists. A *pluralist* might add "soul" and sees the individual as having a body and a mind and a soul.

Learning. One difference between theorists often has to do with how much learning, under what conditions, and what kinds of learning occur, rather than with whether one learns or not. Personality is usually considered by all theorists as modifiable, some in terms of autochtonous processes and some by environmental processes, and some by both internal and external processes.

The Mind. A monist who believes there is only body is impatient with any discussion about "mind." Behaviorists following the original notions of John B. Watson may not deny their own phenomenology or that others have thought and feelings, but they believe that psychology should be the science of behavior; any concern with subjective awareness leads to a dead end and so should simply be disregarded.

Those who do take the mind-body position have a variety of views. One of them is *interactionism*; namely, that the body affects the mind and the mind affects the body. Psychosomatic medicine, for example, is interactionism. Another point of view is *parallelism*, that the mind and body operate in a synchronous manner but do not directly affect one another.

Functions of the Mind. If we accept the existence of mental processes, then it should be possible to make some sort of divisions of the mind. The most common separation is in two parts: cognition and affection. Cognitive or "thinking" functions are remembering, planning, creating, imagining, and so on, and affective or "emotional" functions are feeling, suffering, worrying, and so on.

Balance. Another important concept is whether the person generally tends to inertia or to change. There are a number of terms relative to this issue. *Conation* (an old name for will-want-volition-desire) is the tendency for an individual to move forward, change, modify, develop. Some people see the person as constantly in motion towards goals. Adler and Karen Horney are examples of theorists who feature this aspect. The contrasting position is homeostasis, the ultimate tendency of the individual to remain at rest, to be in balance, to achieve quietude, harmony, equilibrium.

Viewpoint. By viewpoint is meant whether the theorist starts from the "top" or from the "bottom," whether he / she is inductive or deductive in approach. An inductive theorist is generally a reductionist and takes a mechanistic, elementarist view: The individual is composed of parts—organs which, fitted together, make the person. The deductive theorist takes a molar, holistic, *gestalt* type of view about the person, seeing him or her as an indivisible unit operating on the basis of some organizing principle.

Zeitgeist. It is possible that personality theories are a function of the dominant philosophical-political position of one's society, the *Zeitgeist.* Pastore (1949) has shown that psychologists' theories are related to their politicosocial views. Theorists are not necessarily free of the influences of their own environments. They are quite likely to be biased by their sociopolitical views and to present to the world something which they believe to be objectively true but which nonetheless is a distorted personal view.

This social issue has important consequences. All our interactions with people are based on certain conceptualizations of the nature of people. A school staffed and directed by Adlerians would be quite different from one directed by Jungians. A prison operating on the basis of the theory of Allport would be different from one run by Jungians.

In Pastore's research, hereditarians were generally politically conservative, while environmentalists were politically liberal. Those in the hereditarian camp are more likely to espouse a eugenic point of view, while those in the environmental camp will likely take a *euthenic* stance of social issues.

Semantics. One of the major problems of personality theory is the issue of language. There are many difficulties in communication. Here are some of them. (1) *Translations.* Since some of the more important theories, including the first three in this book, were originally written in foreign languages and then translated into English, the issue of proper translation is important. The fact is that in some cases the translation was improper (as, for example, Freud's *Trieb,* by which he meant *drive* but was translated as *instinct*); in some cases an apparently proper translation gives a wrong impression (*Individuale Psychologie* translated into English as *Individual Psychology* gives a completely incorrect impression that Adler's system is about individuals, when the word *Individuale* as used by Adler meant *unitary* or *indivisible*); or in some cases there just is no accurate translation (Adler's term *Gemeinschaftsgefühl* which literally means "a feeling for community" is best, but still inadequately, translated as *social interest.*) (2) *Duplications.* Different theorists may mean the same thing and yet use different words. An example is Freud's *defense mechanism* and Adler's *safeguarding tendency*. (3) *Varying denotations.* The same word may be used by different theorists to have somewhat different meanings. *Transference* to a psychoanalyst means a displacement of affect from one person to another but to an eclectic therapist it may simply mean a strong emotional reaction or attachment by the therapist to patient or vice versa. (4) *Unrecognized commonalities.* In many theories there is implicit the notion of innate growth, or inherited propensity for perfection, or drive to perfection, etc., but this and other concepts are not generally made explicit.

As an examination of the glossary starting on page 670 shows, the special language of personality theory is rather extensive.

Personal Factors.   The question asked earlier: "Why so many theories?" may be answered simply by saying that personality theorists project their own personalities into their views about human nature. Personality theories often seem to be a reflection of the theorist's own personality (Corsini, 1956). Regardless of how much a theorist attempts to be impartial and objective, to verify hypotheses and to be cautious in suggesting theories, most probably personal bias distorts perception. But this is what theories are all about: means for individuals to express opinions based on observations and contemplation.

Every theorist in this book has conducted clinical research and / or objective experimental research and is convinced of the validity of his or her views. One possible explanation for differences in views is that they simply represent different experiences, different awarenesses, different perceptions, and finally, different conclusions from others.

Metrics.   In the history of science, advances often have been a function of metrics: instruments, tools, techniques. The telescope advanced astronomy, the microscope advanced medicine, and the weighing balance advanced chemistry. Also, in the history of science, advances have been a function of classifications. Mendeleev's periodic law and Linnaeus's biological structure permitted students of chemistry and zoology to cooperate in systematic study. Personality researchers and theoreticians badly need objective, valid and reliable instruments and meaningful matrices to measure, to plan and to evaluate.

Extensive work in this area has been done by Raymond B. Cattell and Hans J. Eysenck, J. P. Guilford, and Frederick Thorne. Cattell has been producing prodigious amounts of information in charting the basic traits of personality and in providing objective instruments for the measurement of facets of personality through multivariate research studies.

Our intention in this Introduction is to raise questions, to consider issues, to help you realize that personality theories have important personal and social consequences. They are not "just theories." The theory that you personally will accept is highly likely to be one that fits in with your own world view.

While it is extremely difficult not to take sides and to find some theories more sensible than others, in reading the theories in this book you should be alert to the strong possibility of only reinforcing your present biases. For your personal development and for the sake of science, you should be as neutral and as open-minded as possible for as long as possible, especially regarding views you are likely to reject if they contradict your own position philosophically, socially, or politically.

We have by no means touched on all the important issues involved in personality theories. We could discuss personality theories in relation to religion, to social movements, to history, to science, to politics, to individual growth and still be legitimately within our area of discussion. However, limitations of space and the constraints of the purpose of this book do not make this possible. But, let us examine some other topics of critical importance.

REACHING CONCLUSIONS ABOUT PERSONALITY

Psychology as a science depends on exact information. Psychologists are aware that some things may be so perfectly obvious that there is no need to examine, measure, or prove them. For example, it is perfectly obvious, is it not, that the world is flat and that the sun rotates around a stationary world? How foolish to even question this obvious fact! And yet, this is what scientists do. They want to be *sure*, and they don't want to take even the obvious for granted.

Now, we have a real problem which we want to share with you—and hopefully this will make sense to you. On the one hand, we accept the intelligence, devotion, and good judgment of the various theorists in this book. We see them as good observers and interpreters. But—and this is a big *but*, they *do* differ from one another in important points. So if Freud says one thing and if Adler contradicts him, whom shall we believe? Suppose that Freud has 1,000 followers and Adler only 100. Should we go with the majority? Suppose that Freud has a more lucid style and is a better and more convincing writer; should this be the criterion? How do we, in our search for truth, come to judge one group's opinions against another's? Or—and this will be a more common problem—suppose every single theorist's point of view seems reasonable. We are then in a state of confusion.

All this leads to several conclusions which we wish to share with the readers.

1. One should read sympathetically, and yet critically, the evidence

given us by the various theorists who have come to varying conclusions.

2. Sometimes what happens is relevant to the fable of the blind men and the elephant: each theorist is correct, but he is seeing a different part of the elephant, so that if the theorists do not agree, it does not mean that one is right and the other is wrong, but that they are simply addressing themselves to different problems.

3. One of the many possibilities for different views is that the various people are simply using different words for the same things. So if one points to something and calls it *pasta*, and someone else calls it *spaghetti*, they are both referring to the same thing. But if someone who doesn't know the words hears someone speak of the goodness of *pasta* and someone else praises *spaghetti*, the unknowing listener may think that there is a real difference; and, if the two proponents don't know each other's language, they will believe that they are talking about real differences.

Still another example of problems in research is found in the differences between Hans Eysenck and Raymond Cattell, in their common search for the factors of personality. Both use a complex form of mathematical analysis knows as *factor analysis*, but one uses one form of this method, and the other uses a different form, and so they come up with different answers—and both can be correct at the same time! Using the analogy of language again, if someone points to something and says that this is a *chat*, and someone else points to something and says, "No, it is a *cat*," a person who knows both French and English could say, "You are both right." That is a feline and the French call it a *chat* and the English call it a *cat*."

4. Still another problem has to do with framing of the question. For example, Freud stated what was for him a simple, obvious, and evident fact: human beings have certain innate (instinctual) demands, and society may interfere with these innate needs, such as the expression of sex. This results in a conflict between what nature wants and what society wants—and the result of the conflict is neurosis.

Freud framed the problem in this manner and probably was satisfied, since he could conceptualize nothing except the existence of biology and society. And in terms of this framing of the problem, he came to his various conclusions, and thousands of people who accepted his framing of the problem came to similar conclusions.

Alfred Adler, however, took a quite different view of the total reality. He posited the existence of something else besides biology and society. This new thing was called creativity, something within the individual not determined by biology or by society.

In short, Adler stated that while it is true that biology and society exist and have strong effects, the human person can transcend the limits of these factors, since he or she has the capacity for choice. Consequently we must posit "something" in the person which can make choices, can make decisions, can "overcome" effects of both biology and society.

Thus it is clear that there are many factors involved in reaching conclusions about the accuracy of a given personality theory. And the problem is further complicated by the fact that new evidence is continually being provided about personality from both clinical and laboratory studies. Some of the new evidence is very powerful, and may well shift our entire perspective on personality.

HISTORICAL VIEWS OF HUMAN NATURE AND PERSONALITY

Introduction

All the theorists discussed in the present book belong to the 20th century. Their views reflect not only their own personal predispositions and experiences but also the intellectual trends of the times in which they lived. For example, Freud's theory mirrors four major ideological sources of influence: (1) Victorian concepts of morality; (2) 19th century fascination with biology and physics; (3) romanticist (Rousseauian) notions of society and human nature; and (4) Darwinian assumptions of Mankind's evolution.

Freud lived in a time of Victorian morals, when sexual impulses were greatly repressed, especially among women. For him, this repression represented a major determinant of human behavior, and much of his theory was built around it. Freud also chose to construct his model of the mind in conformity with hydraulic models of energy transformations then in vogue in physics and biology. Freud noted that the mind involved the transformation of life energy (libido) according to principles of hydraulic pressure. Each person had a limited amount of energy, and this was distributed across the different components of the mind: *id*, *ego*, *superego*. If most of the energy (libido) was committed to the *superego*, there would be less energy available for the *id* or *ego*. This was a mechanistic notion of mind in agreement with prevailing views in the biology and physics of the era.

Freud's thinking was also influenced by the romanticist concepts of human nature advanced in the early 18th century by Jean-Jacques Rousseau, who had written, "Mankind is by nature good, it is society which makes him bad." Rousseau's words were the banner cry for social reformers who sought to improve humanity's plight. For Freud, Mankind's essential nature was primarily biological, and not necessarily "good," but, like Rousseau, he viewed society as the villain. Indeed, in his book *Civilization and Its Discontents*, Freud wrote that human beings were doomed to eternal neurosis because everything that they did to strengthen society resulted in greater repression of their basic biological nature.

Lastly, Freud's views were greatly influenced by the writings of Darwin.

Coincidentally, Freud was born only a few years (1856) before Darwin published his revolutionary volume, *The Origin of Species* (1859). But, it is not coincidental that Freud considered human beings to be biological creatures, with basic drives of sex and aggression. For Freud, society was artificially imposed on Mankind's true nature, and this imposition was the source of all forms of human maladjustment and discontent.

These few paragraphs suggest that the times in which we live greatly influence our assumptions about human nature. We exist in a given moment in history when certain ideological forces, known as the *Zeitgeist*, shape our thoughts and perspectives. The theorists discussed in the present book reflect the era in which they lived. By the 20th century, many competing ideologies had roots which could be traced to prior centuries. Some ideologies even had their roots in Greece and Rome. Our contemporary views of human nature have evolved over the course of centuries, and will continue to evolve long into the future. Already, views of human nature have formed around the contemporary concepts of *cybernetics* and *information theory*, an outgrowth of our perception that the mind is a giant computer with input and output modes. We even speak of *programming* the mind.

A valuable purpose for studying history is that it provides a perspective for better understanding the present. Santayana stated, "Those who fail to learn the lessons of the past are doomed to repeat its mistakes." Thus, it is valuable for us to examine past views of human nature, for these can provide us with insights about views which we currently hold in the future. The following paragraphs summarize some of the perspectives on human nature held in the past eras of the Western world.

Ancient Greece

Two basic streams of thought run through Greek philosophy; the natural and the supernatural. The naturalistic viewpoint was championed by Thales (640 B.C. - ?), an Ionian philosopher who introduced astronomy and mathematics to Grecian culture. He suggested that all things were composed of one substance which assumed different forms (i.e., gases, liquids, solids), but possessed only one nature. Even human beings were composed of this one vital substance; as such, they were continuous with trees, animals, oceans, and even rocks. Humans were subject to the same naturalistic laws which governed all things. Thales was the first to write on *physiologia* or the science of nature and he felt that one of the tasks of philosophy was to understand natural laws.

This naturalistic view of human nature also appeared centuries later in the work of Hippocrates (460 B.C. - 377 B.C.), the father of medicine, who argued against evil spirits and supernatural forces as causes of disease. He believed disease was a function of natural forces that could be uncovered with careful study. Hippocrates proposed the *humoral theory* of behavior which suggested that human beings possessed four body humors or fluids: blood, phlegm, yellow bile, and black bile. Imbalances among these humors were responsible for disease. Centuries later, Galen (130–200 A.D.) suggested that characterological orientations or styles were also related to humor imbalance. For example, a predominance of *black bile* produced severe melancholia and an individual who was brooding, moody, and withdrawn. A preponderance of *blood* produced an assertive and forceful person (sanguine personality) who was direct and courageous. In contrast, excessive amounts of *phlegm* produced a phlegmatic character; weak, fragile, and indecisive. Lastly, a preponderance of *yellow bile* resulted in a choleric, irritable, bitter, and resentful individual.

The importance of Hippocrates' work was not the validity of his theory, but rather that he explained human nature according to naturalistic principles agreeing with the Thalian perspective. This perspective remains today, and stands in ready contrast to the mystical or supernatural tradition which also grew out of Greek thought.

Supernatural views of human nature emerged with the work of the philosopher Pythagoras (582 B.C. – 507 B.C.), a highly revered teacher considered by some to be the Greek god, Apollo, in human form. Pythagoras emphasized purification of the body through abstinence and of the mind through study. Students were expected to accept Pythagoras' teachings without question. The curriculum consisted of geometry, arithmetic, astronomy, and music.

Most readers will recognize Pythagoras for his famous theorem in geometry. But, his major contribution in philosophy was the idea that human beings were really something different from other forms of nature because they possessed the capacity for reason. Reason belongs to Man alone.

Pythagoras differentiated human beings from animals and plants. This thinking would later find itself expressed in Aristotle's notions that while all things had a soul, there were different types of souls. Plants possessed a *nutritive* soul, while animals possessed a *sensing* soul. But human beings had a *rational* soul; they could reason, and reason was not subject to natural laws. Thus, human beings were set above naturalistic laws; they were elevated to a new level, and assigned a new nature.

These two streams of thought, the natural and the supernatural, remain today and find their representation in those theories of personality which focus on naturalistic explanations of human behavior (e.g., constitutional, behavioral, trait/type) versus higher order explanations (e.g., phenomenological, existential, humanistic, analytical).

These streams of thought, however, were to yield to a new view of human nature with the onset of the Dark Ages in Western Europe. The fall of the Roman Empire in 200 A.D. brought with it many changes in ideological thought. Basically, ancient knowledge was lost amid the turmoil and strife that overran Europe. In its place, a new explanation emerged—*demonology*.

From 200 A.D. to approximately 1500 A.D., Western European thought was dominated by the Catholic church. Rational understanding disappeared in favor of faith. Human beings were considered weak, corruptible and sinful, susceptible to the forces of evil. Supernatural views dominated these centuries, in the form of devils, demons, witches, and evil spirits. There was a preoccupation with death; life was considered a time of testing for the hereafter.

The retreat from rationality brought omnipresent fear. Faith in whatever the church or its representatives demanded was the only source of refuge. There was hostility toward knowledge; anyone challenging the church's views was considered a heretic. Faith was required for earthly survival and for eternal salvation! Any event unexplainable by Christian dictum was attributed to demons or witches. Life was considered a battleground between the forces of good and the forces of evil. Human nature was base, an evil thing with little redemptive value. This demonic view stood in stark contrast to the perspectives on human nature of ancient Greece and Rome, and was to last almost twice as long. Indeed, this view still survives in various forms today, under the guise of Gothic religious sentiments.

The Renaissance

At the very time when the Dark Ages were flourishing and human beings were considered vile temples of evil and corruption, forces were already being set in motion to end this perspective, launching a new era rooted in the value of temporal experience. The new era was subsequently called the *Renaissance*, a rebirth.

The Renaissance period occurred roughly between 1200 A.D. and 1600 A.D. although no historical era has clear-cut times of onset and demise. The major theme of the Renaissance was the celebration of life—a return to views of human nature which valued human individuality. Optimism replaced pessimism, life replaced death, hope replaced fear, and rationality replaced blind faith.

A number of events stimulated this new view of human nature. For example, the Crusades resulted in the return of ancient knowledge to Western Europe from its sanctuary in the Byzantine monasteries of the Middle East. Printing presses then made this knowledge more accessible. The pursuit of life also rose to new thrusts of inquiry about the nature of the world. Copernicus suggested that the earth revolved around the sun, and was not the center of the universe as had been believed. This greatly reduced mankind's importance in the grand scheme of cosmic events. Anatomists such as Vesalius and DeFabrica probed the structure and function of the human body, offering naturalistic explanations for bodily events that were previously attributed to God, the devil, or both. The assault on authority also occurred in the writings of Shakespeare, who portrayed "kings as villains"; he captured the human flaws of kings and nobles who were previously unassailable. The same effect occurred with the writings of Martin Luther, who challenged the authority of the Catholic Church and of the Pope. The discovery of new lands by Spanish and Portuguese explorers also opened up the Western world to new opportunities for ideological change.

All these events and many others occurred within a short span of time; the result was a new vision of human nature. Though witchcraft and demonology were to continue for 500 more years, it was clear that they would not inherit the future. Humanism as an ideology had emerged as a new and vital force. The torpid past would gradually yield to a future filled with awe at the new world about it.

The Renaissance period represented a new consciousness about the value and worth of the individual. With this view came new products of individual expression, including new forms of art, literature, philosophy, and religion. There was concern for the present. This stood in dramatic contrast to the emphasis on life after death, which characterized the Dark Ages. People became topics of interest and inquiry throughout the arts and the sciences; there was a new emphasis on providing naturalistic explanations of human behavior. Modern-day personality theory was born in ancient Greece, forged in the Renaissance, and polished in the 20th century.

The Enlightenment

Historians termed the era following the Renaissance the *Enlightenment*, or "Age of Reason." It began and developed during the 17th and 18th centuries in Europe, and was characterized by a commitment to rationalism in direct contrast to the blind faith of the Dark Ages. The "new" view of human nature assumed human beings were rational beings capable of perfectability through reason. In describing the Enlightenment, the *New Columbia Encyclopedia* states,

> A rational and scientific approach to religious, social, political, and economic issues promoted a secular view of the world and a general sense of progress and perfectability....Proponents of the Enlightenment agreed on several basic attitudes. With supreme faith in rational man, they sought to discover and to act upon universally valid principles governing humanity, nature, and society. They variously attacked spiritual and scientific authority, dogmatism, intolerance, censorship, and economic and social restraints. (*New Columbia Encyclopedia*, 1975, p. 877)

Within this context, many new perspectives on human nature were formed. For example, John Locke (1632–1704), the famous English philosopher, argued against the concept of innate ideas. He claimed that our mind is blank at birth, a *tabula rasa*; it subsequently acquires ideas through experience from the five senses, and from reflection or rational thought. Other important thinkers of the period with regard to human nature include Thomas Hobbes (1588–1679), David Hume (1711–1776), George Berkeley (1685–1753), Voltaire (1694–1778), Immanuel Kant (1724–1804), and Jean-Jacques Rousseau (1712–1778).

Romanticism: The Age of Rousseau

Will and Ariel Durant, authors of the 10-volume *Story of Civilization*, believed Jean-Jacques Rousseau's influence on Western views of human nature was so pervasive that they assigned his name to an entire historical era and to one of their 10 volumes. Rousseau was a Swiss-French philosopher who was launched into fame when he won an essay contest in 1749 by arguing that "Mankind is by nature good, and it is society which makes him bad." These words became the banner cry for many subsequent social reformers seeking massive social changes in an effort to encourage Mankind's perfectability. Even insanity came to be viewed as a part of the price to be paid for civilized life. Rousseau called for a return to nature—the way of the "noble savage."

Within the context of this viewpoint, anything natural was endowed with virtue, while anything which was a product of civilized minds was endowed with vice and evil. Poetry (e.g., Wordsworth, Keats, Shelley, Byron); political thought (e.g., Thomas Jefferson, Maximilian Robespierre, Karl Marx); philosophy (e.g., Goethe, Immanuel Kant); literature (e.g., Leo Tolstoy, Victor Hugo, Friedrich Schiller): all came to reflect Rousseau's beliefs. Rousseau's thoughts conflicted directly with those of Voltaire and the rationalists.

In contrast to Voltaire, who stood for rationality and science, Rousseau stood for emotion, mysticism, and subjectivity. In describing the romantic movement, Will and Ariel Durant (1967) wrote:

> But what shall we mean by the Romantic movement? The rebellion of feeling against reason, of instinct against intellect, of sentiment against judgment, of the subject against the object, of subjectivism against objectivity, of solitude against society, of imagination against reality, of myth and legend against history, of religion against science, of mysticism against ritual, of poetry and poetic prose against prose and prosaic poetry, of neo-Gothic against neo-Classical art, of the feminine against the masculine, of romantic love against the marriage of convenience, of "nature" and "natural" against civilization and artifice, of emotional expression against conventional restraints, of individual freedom against social

order, of youth against authority, of democracy against aristocracy, of man versus the State—in short, the revolt of the nineteenth century against the eighteenth...(Durant & Durant, 1967, p. 887).

Rousseau provided a new conception of human nature. As one commentator on the times wrote, "He invented nothing, but he set everything on fire."

Evolutionism

In 1858 Charles Darwin (1809–1882) and Alfred Wallace (1823–1913) independently published summaries of their research on evolution. Their efforts launched yet another perspective on human nature, a view in which human beings were considered to be descendants of lower species. This position came to be known as evolutionism, since it suggested humans evolved from more primitive life forms via principles of natural selection (later known as "survival of the fittest").

In many respects, the doctrine of evolutionism brought Western conceptions of human nature back to the point of view held by the ancient Ionian philosophers. It will be recalled that they believed human beings were part of nature, and were subject to the same natural laws as other forms of life. The Ionians never separated Mankind from nature; the two were continuous.

In evolutionism, human beings were once again returned to nature. For Rousseau, humans were by nature "good"; for evolutionists, this value judgment was not made. Rather, humans were placed within the context of lower animal forms and thus were subject to many of the same drives and needs as biological creatures. These creatures instinctively pursued survival through aggression and unbridled sexual activity. The scene was now set for Freud and for the scores of personality theorists who were to follow.

The perspectives on human nature were shaped through the crucible of history: natural, supernatural, rational, societal, biological, and psychological views. These are the same views that remain in modern times, even as we approach the 21st century.

The theories in this book are more detailed presentations of many of the positions we have discussed. They represent the efforts of humanists, clinicians, scientists, and other scholars oriented toward understanding the nature of human nature. Like the views from the past, they too developed within a given historical and cultural *zeitgeist*. A century from now, readers of personality textbooks will look back upon contemporary theorists with the same knowing smile that our faces assume when we read the works of the learned writers of past centuries and eras.

If we place ourselves in the positions of those readers of the 21st century, we can come to see that no single theory of human nature is right or "true."

The theories advanced through the centuries and even those currently in the process of formulation, develop within a given cultural and historical period of time, and of necessity, come to reflect the influences of that period. As cultures change, and as the present becomes the past, the truths which seemed so self-evident often melt away as the simple and erroneous logic of a given era.

Each theory of human nature is like a set of spectacles or glasses which limit our vision to a particular view by virtue of their formula or color. Each theory enables us to see certain aspects of the problem, but none provides the full answer. George Kelly (see Chapter 6) said each theory simply offers a ''range of convenience'' which provides us with a tool for understanding certain aspects of human behavior. No theory is right and no theory is wrong! These are value judgments, not facts.

Different theories of personality offer us the opportunity to view certain aspects of human behavior through the glasses of their promulgators. The reader should examine each of the theories discussed in the present textbook with these thoughts in mind. The theories will provide the reader with many hypotheses about their own behavior and the behavior of others. For some theorists, the evidence they have mounted for their claims may make them more attractive than others. This is natural. But it would be well for the reader to remind him/herself of the current section on historical views of human nature, and the basic conclusion that we now reach: our understanding of human nature is continually evolving and will never achieve final form. The modern theories, which we sometimes hold so blindly, become the myths of our past, frequently subject to ridicule and sighs of disbelief. Each era of time gives rise to views of human nature which reflect the cultural and historical dynamics of that particular time. The themes of the past often remain with us and are subject to new elaborations and extensions; in time, these changes are changed still further. The study of human nature requires the ability to live with uncertainty and doubt. It is these states which are the essence of progress, for they propel us continually into the future in search of better questions. In closing, we say: seek questions, not answers, tolerate uncertainty and doubt, embrace knowledge but do not blindly accept it, be a part of your times but stand apart from them as well.

REFERENCES

Allport, G. *Personality: A psychological interpretation.* New York: Holt, 1937.

Corsini, R. Freud, Rogers, and Moreno. *Group Psychotherapy*, 1956, *9*, 274–281.

Durant, W., & Durant, A. *The story of civilization (Vol. 10).* New York: Simon & Schuster, 1967.

Harris, W., & Levey, J. (Eds.). *The new Columbia encyclopedia.* New York: Columbia University Press, 1975.

Pastore, N. *The nature-nurture controversy.* New York: King's Point, 1949.

SECTION TWO
THEORIES

CHAPTER II

Psychoanalysis

Peter L. Giovacchini

SIGMUND FREUD

Psychoanalysis began as a conceptual system designed to explain certain types of psychopathology. It later developed into a technique of treatment and finally expanded to a theory of personality of both normal and disturbed individuals. It has not, however, achieved the ultimate goal of being a comprehensive general psychology.

Originally developed by Sigmund Freud (1856-1939), psychoanalysis for many years had him as its only proponent. As a result, the theory still has many of his biases. Nevertheless, although still controversial, psychoanalysis is the oldest and most influential of all personality theories.

Psychoanalysis, a depth psychology, views the mind as an entity containing primitive and sophisticated elements, hierarchically ordered. The primitive end of the spectrum has biologically based instincts (known as *id*) striving for expression against more structured reality-based elements (known as *ego*), which strive to make instinctual gratification consonant with internalized moral standards (known as *super-ego*).

Since psychoanalytic theory views psychopathology as a clash of forces within the mind, it is dynamic. Based upon deterministic principles, its foundation depends upon strict causality. The clashing forces within the personality are, for the most part, unconscious but nevertheless have effects on conscious feelings and behavior. An unconscious having effects on conscious (higher) levels of the personality is known as a dynamic unconscious and represents the most fundamental unique hypothesis of psychoanalytic theory.

Psychoanalytic treatment essentially is based upon interpretation by the analyst of unconscious motivations. Because the patient is allowed to verbalize freely (free association), he ascribes certain attributes of infantile feelings and relationships onto the therapist (transference). The classical analyst confines his therapy to the interpretation of the transference.

Today the psychoanalytic method, by focusing upon the structure of the psychic apparatus, in addition to instinctual impulses (Freud considered instincts differently than zoologists and ethologists do), permits a wider range of emotional disorders to be treated psychoanalytically than was the case originally.

Other than the immutability of a few fundamental concepts—such as the dynamic unconscious and working within the transference context—psychoanalysis is far from static. This is due to a unique interplay between learning and research activities and therapeutic application. One augments the other. This interplay not only sheds light upon man's most precious possession, his mind, it also leads to therapeutic innovation aimed at alleviating the misery of many apparently hopeless patients.

INTRODUCTION

In the last century, the fundamental goal of medicine advanced from ameliorating symptoms to extinguishing diseases by eradicating causes. With the introduction of the germ theory of Louis Pasteur and Robert Koch and the discoveries in pathology by such giants as Rudolph Virchow, doctors became hopeful that eventually all diseases would be conquered. Such ideals were founded on a purely organic, physiochemical, materialistic approach.

Patients suffering from emotional problems tended to upset this idyllic outlook, but most investigators did not question the feasibility of searching for organic causes for emotional disturbances. They attributed their lack of knowledge about these disturbances to the fact that adequate methods to discover fundamental physiological causes had not yet been developed. In the late 1800s psychiatrists, then known as alienists, contented themselves for the most part with describing and classifying abnormal behavior. Most were inclined to think in terms of organic, neurological causes for disturbed behavior. This approach was useful for the understanding of certain dementias, and it did lead to insights about the neuroses and psychoses.

An extremely important discovery set dynamic psychiatry back many years. Just when many scientists were beginning to consider emotional problems in terms of intrapsychic factors, Hideyo Noguchi discovered (in 1904) that general paresis, a relatively common disease often characterized by states of grandiosity associated with insanity, was caused by bacteria. What was beginning to be looked upon as a functional psychosis turned out to be syphilis of the brain.

It is interesting to note that the only psychiatrist who ever received a Nobel prize was Julius Wagner von Juaregg for his fever treatment of this same general paresis. These discoveries reinforced the hope that all mental diseases could be explained and treated on a similar organic basis.

In such an environment, Freud discovered psychoanalysis. Psychoanalysis thus emerged because of clinical necessity. Those clinicians consumed by an unrelenting need to understand what was happening within a person's mind rather than just simply controlling behavior needed a conceptual system to restore order to the chaotic confusion that patients presented. Freud generated order where before patients had been viewed as exhibiting meaningless behavior or outright shamming.

Although some analysts have modified Freud's superstructure and some of his metapsychological concepts, the fundamental postulates of psychoanalysis remain unchanged today. Psychoanalysis is a science because it stems from observations made within a consistent frame of reference.

HISTORY

Precursors

Abnormal psychology goes back to Hippocrates. We shall not go into great detail regarding the forerunners of psychoanalysis since this topic has been admirably done by others, including Alexander and Selesnick (1966), Zilboorg and Henry (1941), and in particular, Ellenberger's (1970) scholarly treatise.

Man has always been fascinated by mental aberrations and has usually explained mental phenomena whenever possible. Madness holds a particular fascination for people as do "mental" situations, such as dreams. One need only refer to the Bible or to Herodotus (1952) for examples of explanations of such phenomena.

Some early therapies had rationales aimed at eliminating what were regarded as noxious causes. Most primitive therapies were based on the exorcism of internalized devils. Even though these orientations prevailed centuries ago, one cannot help being reminded of a best seller of the 1970s, *The Exorcist*, which was not universally considered a work of fiction.

Any therapy based upon restoring psychic equilibrium by eliminating causes can be considered a precursor of psychoanalysis. Methods used to achieve such cures have varied from primitive brain surgery (trephining) to torture. Others before Freud used free association, the principal tool of psychoanalysis. Freud apparently was quite familiar with Ludwig Börne, who recommended that one who wished to become a writer should put every thought that occurred to him on paper for three days, without any regard for coherence or relevance (see Jones, 1953). In one of Aristophanes' comedies (Aristophanes, 1955) Socrates instructs a merchant to lie on a couch and uninhibitedly tell him what came to his mind. This episode seems very much like free association. The concept of the unconscious mind had been known for centuries. Reaching into the hidden depths of a person's soul preoccupied poets, philosophers, and physicians, as well as the clergy. Nietzsche (1937) and Spinoza (1952), for example, gave descriptions of the unconscious similar to Freud's, and he acknowledged his debt to them.

In spite of similarities of various earlier procedures and systems of thought, Freud's resolution of causal factors, development of free association, and recognition of unconscious forces were combined in the unique fashion that unequivocally makes him the discoverer of psychoanalysis.

Beginnings

Psychoanalysis, therefore, is the work of a single man, Sigmund Freud. In most other sciences it is usually possible to trace a continuum of development from antiquity to the present, punctuated with moments of deceleration (as in the Dark Ages) or acceleration (as in the 17th century). But Freud's achievement was discontinuous with what had preceded him; in terms of modern physics, it can be considered a quantum jump. Freud worked alone, isolated for many years during a period which he referred to as his "splendid isolation" (Freud, 1914a).

Any great discovery creates opposition, since it disturbs established ways of thought. Freud (1914a) compared the reactions to his work with those experienced by Copernicus and Darwin. He noted that Copernicus's demolition of the geocentric theory threatened man's omnipotence regarding his central position in the universe, and Darwin's theory of evolution shook man's belief in his uniqueness of being specially created by God. Now psychoanalysis postulated that man was not even in control of his mind, because unknown forces within him ruled his behavior.

Freud was born in 1856 in Moravia (now part of Czechoslovakia), but when he was very young his family moved to Vienna. He did very well in school and was repeatedly the first in his class. He showed a great interest for the humanities: history, classical literature, and languages. Some of his early letters are truly remarkable for their erudition and sophistication (Freud, 1969). Nevertheless, he turned to science. It is interesting that at the tender age of 21 the future discoverer of castration anxiety wrote his first article which involved the discovery of the testes of a particular species of eel, an animal whose genitals had not been previously located (see Freud, 1877).

After having graduated with honors from the *gymnasium,* Freud entered medical school. He was not particularly interested in treating patients (Freud, 1925, 1964); his main interest was in research. After graduation he postponed his final clinical training and spent eight years working under the renowned neurophysiologist Ernst Brücke.

His work in Brücke's laboratory was successful, and if he had remained, he might have achieved fame as a neurologist or neurophysiologist. In those days, research scientists were often gentlemen of means who did not rely upon their work for their income, but Freud had to support his family. He had fallen in love and wanted to get married, so following Brücke's advice, he decided to leave the laboratory and make a living by the clinical practice of neurology. The majority of patients who came to a neurologist's office then usually turned out to be psychoneurotics. Because of his scientific background, and perhaps the natural bent of his mind, Freud was not content with the superficial therapies of the time—hydrotherapy, massage, and faradic (electric) stimulation. There was considerable ambivalence about hypnosis, stemming from the ways Mesmer had employed it (Ellenberger, 1970). Freud learned that the great Jean-Martin Charcot was using hypnosis to do marvelous things with hysterical patients in Paris. In his eagerness to learn more about their treatment, Freud spent nearly a year in Paris, attending Charcot's lectures and demonstrations and watching Hippolyte Bernheim hypnotize subjects. These experiences made a profound impression upon him.

Freud learned from Bernheim's experiments on posthypnotic suggestion, that there is a part of the mind, largely unknown to consciousness, which nevertheless has effects upon feelings and behavior. In other words, he formulated the concept of the dynamic unconscious. The concept of the unconscious mind which influences feeling and behavior and can create symptoms is Freud's unique discovery. He now had a basis upon which he could begin to understand what, up to this time, had seemed totally irrational.

Returning to Vienna, Freud met considerable opposition from his colleagues when he tried to make them view hysterical patients from the viewpoint of a dynamic unconscious. Unfortunately, he presented his ideas in terms of unconscious sexual feelings which are capable of producing anxiety (Freud, 1895a, 1895b, 1898). The world was not ready for this viewpoint, and the combination of outraged morality and wounded narcissism which resulted from being told that there were forces within persons over which they had little control created considerable opposition. However, as Ellenberger (1970) points out the medical community was not particularly hostile to Freud. Freud found a sympathetic ear in Josef Breuer, a successful, well-respected Viennese internist. Breuer was treating a patient by hypnosis. He regressed his patient back to a traumatic moment when the symptoms had begun and then, through catharsis (relieving tension by talking freely) and abreaction (emoting), was able to eliminate the symptom.

Freud collaborated with Breuer, and they produced *Studies on Hysteria* (Breuer & Freud, 1895), which Freud believed represented the beginnings of psychoanalysis, a discovery which at first he generously granted to Breuer but later withdrew (Freud, 1914a)—as he should have, since quite clearly the psychoanalytic aspects of this early book were written exclusively by Freud. In any case, after several years, Breuer was glad to dissociate himself from the movement (Jones, 1953).

Current Status

The current acceptance of psychoanalysis varies from country to country, and there have been considerable changes in astonishingly short periods of time. Psychoanalysis is practically nonexistent in Iron Curtain countries. In Vienna, Freud's residence, it was virtually ignored and has only recently become respectable. It received an enthusiastic early reception in England, and after World War II the United States became its strongest bastion. It has also achieved great popularity in Mexico and South America, although the situation is fluid, and rapid changes keep occurring.

After World War II, there was a rush of candidates in the United States to psychoanalytic institutes, and interest in psychoanalysis almost followed a geometric progression. In the 1960s a slow decline in the interest in psychoanalysis began to be noted, as behavior therapy and sensitivity groups emerged and psychopharmacology became popular.

Treatment Perspectives and Applications.   Psychoanalysis as a treatment technique has encompassed a wider range of clinical conditions than the early practitioners anticipated. In addition to treating psychoneuroses, the only clinical entity that Freud finally concluded was amenable to analysis, the psychoanalytic method has been expanded to include the treatment of patients suffering from characterological disorders and some psychoses (Boyer & Giovacchini, 1967; Giovacchini, 1975, 1977).

Freud's model was based upon unconscious forces clashing with higher levels of the personality. His theory was dynamic in that it focused upon conflicting forces which led the ego to defenses against unacceptable feelings and impulses. This process results in symptoms which define the neurosis. This approach has been referred to as id-psychology in contrast to ego-psychology, which emphasizes defects in the structure of the psychic apparatus due to emotional maldevelopment. Id-psychology and ego-psychology complement rather than replace each other.

Psychoanalysis stresses autonomy rather than adjustment or conformity. It belongs neither to the establishment nor to those who rebel against the establishment. Its aim is to widen a person's range of choice, rather than to dictate choice.

However, psychoanalysts have not remained impervious to the surrounding culture. Some analysts believe that the forces underlying movements concerned with the fate of the world should be their concern. The Chicago Institute for Psychoanalysis has opened up a center for psychohistory specifically designed to study national and international problems in terms of psychoanalytic constructs.

The involvement of psychoanalysis in areas other than the treatment of individual patients is prevalent today. This began with Freud, who had a wider viewpoint than the clinical one. He speculated about the development of humans from the primeval horde (Freud, 1913a), the evolution of civilization (Freud, 1930), and the origins and delusional qualities of religion (Freud, 1927). He also did psychoanalytic studies on great men of the past, as well as writing a variety of papers on myths (Freud, 1922), fairy tales (Freud, 1913a), and literary themes (Freud, 1907, 1913b). His monograph on Moses (Freud, 1939) attracted considerable attention and controversy.

Freud envisioned psychoanalysis as a much more encompassing discipline than just a clinical specialty. Today, we have pathobiography and psychohistory. Freud contributed to the former, attempting to explain how Leonardo da Vinci (Freud, 1910) and Dostoevsky (Freud, 1928)—functioned, in terms of their character structure and unconscious motivation.

Psychoanalysis' theoretical system is based upon the concept of the unconscious motivation of the individual, how the mind develops, and the specific modalities a person uses to deal with the external world. How useful the knowledge of such mental processes is for the understanding of global phenomena or groups (see Freud, 1921) is debatable.

ASSERTIONS

Since from the very beginning the chief focus of psychoanalysis has been on patients suffering from emotional disturbances, the mind is studied mainly in the context of psychopathology. To paraphrase Freud, psychoanalysis is "first and foremost" a clinical discipline.

Development

Metapsychology is a term Freud coined in a book dealing with normal behavioral phenomena (Freud, 1901). He was attempting to construct a comprehensive psychology applicable to all mental states. Metapsychology is defined as a system of psychology that views the mind and its development from several different frames of reference simultaneously. Originally, they were topographical, psychodynamic, and psychoeconomic. Today several others have been added, such as the structural, adaptive, and genetic hypotheses.

1.   *The topographical hypothesis views the mind in terms of three systems.*

Freud (1900, 1915d) initially conceptualized the mind as consisting of three systems, the *unconscious,* the *preconscious,* and the *conscious.* The unconscious contains elements which cannot become conscious by volition. They cannot ascend to the level of awareness without special efforts. By contrast, the preconscious, although also unconscious, contains elements (some are referred to as memory traces) which can become conscious by simply directing attention toward them. Consciousness is the agent of the mind which perceives both inner and outer stimuli.

Viewing the unconscious both as an area of the mind and as a quality of mental processes, Freud was able to distinguish between forces easily accessible to conscious control and those rigidly defended against. The topographical hypothesis postulates a tripartite organization where the unconscious and preconscious, both having the attribute of being unconscious, are compared to consciousness. The pathway to consciousness is blocked for the unconscious but remains open (to be more precise, partially open) for the preconscious.

These ideas were quite useful clinically. However, Freud noted some inconsistencies as he made further clinical discoveries. He noted certain impulses were prevented from reaching consciousness. He referred to this as repression and located the repressive process in the higher levels of the mind, those conscious or close to consciousness. Freud also discovered the existence of unconscious guilt in some patients. Guilt is a feeling which, to be experienced, requires the type of organization characteristic of the preconscious and conscious (the unconscious presumably is an inchoate, disorganized system which does not follow the usual rules of logic).

2.   *The mind is composed of the id, ego, and superego.*

To resolve such contradictions, Freud (1923a) constructed the *structural hypothesis.* Here again, he dealt with a tripartite model dividing the mind into the now familiar *id, ego,* and *superego.* The id corresponds to the unconscious of the topographical hypothesis, and the ego includes the preconscious and conscious. The superego is located within the ego, although it dips into the id and makes judgments as to what aspects of the id should be admitted into ego territory.

The principal advantage of the structural hypothesis is that the ego has unconscious as well as conscious attributes. The structural hypothesis also gives greater emphasis to the higher levels of the personality, such as the ego, which can now be conceptualized as a group of subsystems. The topographical hypothesis allows room for expansion and breadth.

Both systems are compatible with hierarchal structuring of the psychic apparatus. In the structural hypothesis, however, it is easier to visualize how the ego or superego "dip" into the id. It must be emphasized that these are descriptions of a model, a way of looking at things. The structural model is an abstraction, but too often it has been looked at in a concrete fashion. The ego and id have been considered actual entities, with specific brain locations (Brenner, 1957). The metaphors of id demons and superego watchmen have even been taken literally (Waelder, 1960).

3. The mind is a dynamic battleground.

One of the aims of psychoanalysis is to explain emotional disturbances. Freud found it useful to view his patients' psyches in terms of clashing forces between various parts of their minds. At first, conflicts were described as struggles between the unconscious. The concept of the dynamic unconscious as a psychic state which cannot easily become conscious and yet can have effects upon consciousness makes it natural for the adoption of the *psychodynamic* viewpoint, which stresses opposing or conflicting vectors.

Something unconscious, usually referred to as an *impulse, need, drive,* or *instinct,* seeks access to consciousness. Inasmuch as the conscious part of the personality (ego) finds this aspect of the unconscious objectionable, it will strive against permitting the impulse to gain its objective. The ego has to serve three masters, according to Freud (1923a)—the id, the superego, and reality.

The structural hypothesis adds dimensions to psychodynamic formulations in this manner. If an unconscious impulse seeking expression offends the psyche's morality by being unacceptable to the superego, which is the site of moral judgments, then it must be defended against. It must be similarly excluded from motility or conscious expression if it is at variance with the demands of the external world.

Basically, the psychodynamic hypothesis views the mental aparatus as a series of interacting forces. The id and the ego conflict with each other when id elements are either not acceptable to the superego or are at variance with reality. Since the psychic apparatus is also conceptualized as consisting of various levels with different degrees of complexity—one end of the spectrum being considered primitive and the other end sophisticated and reality attuned—it would seem inevitable that forces emanating from one level would confict with forces derived from other levels.

4. The mind seeks homeostasis and requires energy.

A model of the psychic apparatus requires concepts that will account for movements within it. Some vitalizing principle must be elucidated to make a conceptual system that deals with living processes comprehensible. Borrowing from Claude Bernard (1949) and thermodynamic theory, Freud postulated a constant low level of energy as the ultimate optimal state of balance for the mind. High energy levels experienced as tension states are painful, according to Freud (1911a). Pleasure results from changing a high energy state to a low energy state, although later, Freud (1920) added that it was the change itself that accounted for pleasure, rather than the low energy level.

The id is the mind's energy reservoir (Freud, 1915d). Instincts reside in the id and, when activated by biological needs such as hunger, push forward toward consciousness. They possess a quantum of energy known as *cathexis.* Inasmuch as instincts have energy, they are referred to as being *cathected*; the greater the cathexis, the more they are energized. The energy of the sexual instincts is called *libido,* although the term has gained a more general connotation and often refers to energy levels in general. There is some confusion here intrinsic to the *psychoeconomic hypothesis,* because Freud did not elaborate on differences in types of energy.

Instincts reach a certain level of cathexis which, if sustained, is experienced as unpleasure or painful. At this point the instinct requires gratification; that is, the need which the instinct represents has to be satisfied. The process of satisfaction is accompanied by a discharge of tension, which also means that the instinct loses its cathexis; it is *decathected.* In essence, Freud's energic theory is a tension-discharge hypothesis, and it was in context with the prevailing hydrodynamic orientation of the physics of his day.

Today, many analysts believe that the psychoeconomic hypothesis is imprecise, not in accord with biological data, and anachronistic. It is considered to be the weakest part of the psychoanalytic theoretical edifice, and many think it should be eliminated. However, rather than weakening the conceptual system by discarding it, some theoreticians believe that modifications will strengthen Freud's model.

5.   *A person's past affects his present.*

Later hypotheses were formulated after Freud, but some certainly were suggested by him. Hartmann (1964), Rapaport (1966), and Erikson (1950) are prominent among those analysts who have contributed extensions of metapsychology.

The *genetic hypothesis* represents an orientation which evaluates the influence of the past upon a person's current adjustment. Although psychoanalytic theory from the very beginning has stressed the importance of infantile experiences, only relatively recently has there been an increased interest in the early years of life. This is due to research projects that collect their data from direct observation of the mother-child relationship rather than from the psychoanalytic treatment of patients which had previously been the chief source of information. In such *longitudinal studies* the child's emotional development is usually followed for years.

How the individual reacts and adjusts to his environment represents a frame of reference called the *adaptive hypothesis,* which is primarily concerned with various systems within the ego responsible for meeting needs in a fashion acceptable to reality. This point of view has become prominent recently because patients today have problems related to defects in these systems or, at least, such defects are more readily recognizable today than in Freud's time.

6. Fundamental motives are instinctual.

Instincts are the basic motivating forces of the psyche, according to psychoanalytic theory. However, the concept of instinct here is different from the one commonly accepted by biologists and ethologists. Freud did not actually use the word *instinct*. He employed the word *Trieb,* which translators reproduced as *instinct.* In German *Instinkt* corresponds more closely to our similar word in English, whereas *Trieb* is more closely related to the word *drive.* Freud was referring to an impetus, an impelling force within the mind which has effects on both psychic equilibrium and development. Freud (1915a) defined instinct (*Trieb*) as a borderland concept between the somatic and the psychic, characterized by its (1) source, (2) aim, and (3) object.

The *source* of instincts emphasizes their organic origin. It consists of the organ system responsible for the excitation that sets the process of forming an instinct in motion. For example, when an organism needs food, certain physiological changes occur. The stomach muscles periodically contract, and these contractions are felt as hunger pangs by the perceptual elements of the mind. The whole organism is driven to gratify its need for food and can be considered as being propelled by an oral drive or instinct. One can draw similar conclusions about the sexual drive, locating the inciting factors in the gonads.

The *aim* of the instinct is to achieve gratification, the fulfillment of a need. According to the psychoeconomic hypothesis, an instinct causes tension, which means it raises the energy level. The organism seeks to lower the energy level to maintain psychic equilibrium, or homeostasis. This process is conceptualized as *instinctual discharge;* that is, the tension created by instinctual forces has to be dissipated by gratifying the instinct. These concepts have been briefly criticized above and will be elaborated upon further.

The *object* of the instinct is simply the product that fulfills the need which the instinct expresses. Food, the breast, the nurturing person can each be considered objects of the oral instinct. Those situations or objects that lead to sexual release are the objects of the sexual instinct. Unlike the biologist's static concept of instincts, Freud's view considers them as undergoing development. Some instincts are more primitive than others. Freud (1905b) postulated a continuum, a progressively structured hierarchy, which describes the course of emotional development.

7. All instincts are basically sexual.

Since Freud believed that all instincts are basically sexual, although his concept of sex extended far beyond genital sexuality, this continuum is known as *psychosexual development*. At the very beginning of life, there is very little psychic organization. The mind consists simply of the id, which is considered an undifferentiated mass (Freud, 1900, 1917a, 1920, 1926a). The id reacts to contacts with the outer world as impingements and constructs a protective outer core (*Reizschutz*) against potentially disruptive stimulation. The progressive structuralization of this core leads to the formation of the ego.

During this early phase, before the construction of the ego, instincts are (as Freud designated) *autoerotic*. They stem from various sources, known as *erogenous zones,* and achieve their gratification through the body. For example, the need to suck is stimulated by physiological tension in the mouth (oral mucosa being the source) and satisfied by sucking of the thumb. These erogenous zones, which involve the mouth, skin, genitals, and thermal and equilibratory systems, are poorly coordinated during the neonatal stage. In a relative sense, they act independently, as if they did not know of the existence of one another. As the psyche gains structure and unity, these autoerotic instincts become subordinated to the *genital zone*. As Freud (1905b) stated, they undergo confluence.

When autoerotic instincts act separately, they are known as part instincts. On their road to genitality, or as psychoanalysts would say toward the state of genital dominance, they traverse through several stages. During the autoerotic phase, there is as yet no ego. Once the ego begins to form, the autoerotic instincts, instead of going directly to the part of the body which gives gratification, now aim themselves toward the ego. This stage is known as *primary narcissism* (Freud, 1914b).

With greater differentiation of the psychic apparatus, the mind begins to have some dawning awareness of the existence of an outer world. This permits distinctions to be made between the inner and outer world. Instincts now can momentarily direct themselves toward the outer world, but since the perception and acceptance of the outer world is still tenuous, they easily retreat back into the ego. Freud (1914b) compared this interaction to the pseudopodia of an amoeba which tentatively extrudes into the environment to seek particles of food and then withdraws back into the cell body. This phenomenon is analogous to what is known as *secondary narcissism*.

    8.   *Sexuality is intimately related to instinctual developments.*

As noted above, Freud (1911b, 1914b) postulated three early phases of instinctual development.

    1. *Autoerotism,* a stage of partial instincts achieving gratification through the body before ego structure has been consolidated.
    2. *Primary narcissism,* a stage where there is a rudimentary ego toward which the instincts direct themselves.

3. *Secondary narcissism,* a stage where distinctions are beginning to be made between the psyche and the outer world, and instincts transiently reach into the external world, only to be pulled back into the ego.

It is germane before proceeding to clarify some issues regarding the role of sexuality in instinct theory. Instinct theory is often referred to as *libido theory,* and this has led many people to believe that Freud was obsessed with the idea of sex. True, Freud did stress sexual factors as being primary causes for the neuroses. From the very beginning, he viewed psychopathology in terms of sexual trauma occurring early in childhood (Breuer & Freud, 1895; Freud, 1896). However, he did not limit sex to just genital excitation. All the component instincts already discussed and those about to be discussed yield pleasure when gratified, and Freud viewed all this pleasure as erotic. Hunger and sex are basic needs, the former being associated with individual survival and the latter with survival of the species. What goes beyond survival involves erotic pleasure. Thus, Freud called the energy of the sexual instincts *libido*, but he had no corresponding term for the instincts of self-preservation.

Freud has been accused of being a pan-sexualist. He argued this against his opponents, but inasmuch as he stressed sexual factors and considered early infantile activity as erotic, there seems to be some merit to the arguments of his adversaries. Later Freud was careful to point out that he was describing *pregenital* sexuality and, in essence, he was emphasizing that there are other types of strivings beyond simply seeking to satisfy basic survival needs. He carefully described the sequential progression of methods of obtaining gratification and linked them with various bodily zones. Insofar as the body and pleasure are involved, he preferred to regard these activities as sexual in a pregenital sense.

9. *There is a series of built-in stages of sexual development.*

Freud (1905a) postulated the existence of an oral sexual phase following the narcissistic stage. The outside world is perceived in terms of *oral satisfaction.* From autoerotic pleasure, the infant begins to recognize the mother's breast as a source of gratification. Oral instincts are the only instincts connected with both survival and erotic pleasure. Sucking is a pleasure in itself and not simply part of an activity that seeks food. Abraham (1921) elaborated upon Freud's descriptions and divided the oral stage into two subphases. The first is a passive phase where the infant just lies back, so to speak, and expects to be fed. This he called the *passive-dependent phase.* It is followed by a phase where the infant aggressively seeks satisfaction of oral needs. The second phase usually occurs around six months of age, at the time of dentition, and is accompanied by aggressive biting. Abraham called this phase the *oral cannabalistic phase.*

The next phase that Freud postulated is the *anal phase,* related to toilet training, occurring usually around 12-16 months. Gratification now refers to sphincter control. Previously, certain impulses could not be subjected to conscious volition. During this phase, the child begins to control the retention and expulsion of feces. Freud felt that the child was becoming preoccupied with preservation and destruction, so he referred to this stage as the *sadistic-anal phase* and called the corresponding instincts anal-sadistic. Freud (1926a) raised the question as to whether these were also sexual instincts and finally concluded that parts of them were. Abraham (1924) also subdivided this stage of psychosexual development into two subphases. He divided the anal phase into passive and aggressive components, the former being concerned with retention and the latter with forcible expulsion.

Following the anal phase comes the *phallic phase,* a relatively later addition to the psycho-sexual scheme of development (Freud, 1923b). The male attaches pride to the penis, an organ which becomes treasured and idealized. Phallic instincts are concerned with ambition and the acquisition of power. This phase created difficulties when considered a stage of normal development, since it is difficult to see where the female fits in this phase. Previous phases were concerned with the gratification of impulses and the maintenance of control. Now, at the genital phase, the child is preoccupied with conflicting feelings *within* his/her psyche. Although during some pregenital phases the child was also concerned with conflicts, these conflicts were between an instinctual wish and a prohibition from the outer world.

10. *Children develop libidinal attitudes toward parents.*

The child's dependence upon his mother acquires additional qualities. The child begins to feel possessive and wants her exclusively. This attitude may have been reinforced by earlier experiences which stimulated rivalry, such as the birth of a sibling. The boy's chief rival is the father, and now we have the famous *Oedipus complex.* The child's possessiveness acquires incestuous overtones. The child has ambivalent feelings toward his father. He is dependent upon him for support and as a source of identification, and so he loves him. But he also fears and hates his father because he stands in his way of possessing his mother. Since the penis is the organ of sexual activity and since his fears of the father's retribution are related to incestuous feelings, the child fears his father will punish him by castrating him. Thus, we have the concept of *castration anxiety.*

Freud devoted less attention to the female Oedipus (Elektra) complex. Rather than being threatened by castration, the little girl fears the loss of love and her development is more difficult because she has to shift her emotional involvement from the mother to the father. Freud's focus was mainly on the development of male sexuality. He investigated female sexuality but, for the most part, he considered women to be mysterious and un-fathomable.

11. The conscience develops in reaction to the Oedipus complex.

This situation seems similar to others seen during earlier stages of psychosexual development in that there is an instinctual wish, this time a genital rather than an oral or anal wish, and an external prohibition, in the form of a castrating father. Now the situation changes. Whereas in previous phases the child defended himself against an external prohibition, during the genital phase the child defends himself against an *internal prohibition*. The child incorporates various elements of his father's personality as he perceives them. These elements have the qualities of moral imperatives and, as an internalized set of rules emphasizing what is forbidden, come to represent what is commonly called conscience, or in freudian terms, *superego*.

Incestuous wishes are repressed at the behest of the superego. Although the child is deprived of a desired relationship with his mother, he is spared the terror of the threat of castration. More accurately, he is spared the pangs and torments of guilt, the reactions to a superego whose harshness would become manifest if incestuous wishes were to emerge from repression.

There are advantages to obeying the superego besides protection from anxiety or guilt. The superego has two faces: "thou shalt" and "thou shalt not." The latter has received primary emphasis, but the former, "thou shalt," becomes the basis of the child's identification with the father. That part of him which admires his father will want to emulate him, and his attitudes about masculinity will be based upon the model his father presents.

Freud (1923a) repeatedly stated that the superego which arises about age four is the heir to the Oedipus complex. The Oedipus complex is then buried and the next several years are designated as the *latency phase,* when the child is seemingly unpreoccupied with sexual matters. During earlier stages prior to the latency period the child's sexual curiosity is intense, reaching a peak around the phallic phase, and his behavior displays this erotic orientation. Infantile masturbation is common. During the latency phase, all elements of infantile sexuality seem to be repressed. The latency phase has been divided into two subphases, early and late. During the former, the child is still grappling with oedipal problems and repressive defenses, and during the latter he concerns himself with adjustments forced upon him because of the biological changes of puberty and the social demands of adolescence (See Bornstein, 1951).

Some analysts (Fenichel, 1945) do not believe the latency period is at all sexually quiescent. They consider that the repression Freud described is far from complete. Undoubtedly social and cultural factors play a significant role in this. The forces which supported repression in Freud's mid-Victorian milieu have been considerably modified. Still, when compared to the next phase, puberty, whatever happens sexually in the latency phase is mild.

12. *Puberty involves a series of sweeping readjustments.*

The next phase, *puberty,* is often, but not always, stormy. Due to hormonal and physiological factors, repressed sexual feelings become greatly intensified. Previous defenses are no longer adequate, and sweeping readjustments are required. These become further complicated because the adolescent cannot regress to earlier dependent infantile states, as might occur during the early latency period. The reactions to these stresses are varied and range from flagrant, rebellious, antisocial and promiscuous behavior to the seeking of ascetic ideals and the pursuit of a monastic life.

Erikson (1950) extends psychosexual development into adulthood and old age. He and others tend to stress cultural factors more than the primarily biological orientation of Freud.

Freud's scheme has been criticized (Horney, 1937) because it overemphasizes biology and minimizes interaction with the environment. Freud has been accused of being a male chauvinist (Ellenberger, 1970), and as one scrutinizes some of his concepts of psychosexual development, such as the phallic phase and the passing of the Oedipus complex in girls (Freud, 1924), there seems to be some merit to the argument. The little girl feels castrated from the beginning, so castration anxiety cannot be the motivating factor which represses incestuous feelings.

13. *There is a death instinct.*

A preceding section described the development of instincts considered sexual. However, Freud always viewed the mind in terms of polarities and so maintained a fundamental dualism. Consequently he had to bring another group of instincts into either apposition or opposition to the sexual instincts. His first instinct theory postulated two classes of instincts, the *ego instincts*, which are self-preservative, and the *sexual instincts*. After much analysis and consideration, he eventually came to his final statement about instincts, in which he posited a *life instinct* (Eros) and a *death instinct* (Thanatos), a duality and polarity which finally contented him. While this concept is intuitively appealing and certainly all-embracing, modern analysts for the most part have been unwilling to go along with it.

Maintenance

Nosology. The various developmental processes discussed above must be placed in proper perspective to be clinically useful. The deviations and distortions that occur throughout the course of emotional maturation are varied in form and have different outcomes.

Although psychoanalysts are more interested in psychic processes than in classification, a diagnostic system had to be erected which went beyond simple description. In the past, clusters of behavioral phenomena and symptoms had been given specific names. Diagnosis was purely descriptive. In underplaying behavioral categorization, psychoanalysis offers the clinician a different method to reach a diagnosis.

Freud had to begin at the beginning because he wanted to use his insights to classify patients. Still, he tried to use well-known labels whenever possible. His excursions into the field of diagnostic formulations were still imprecise; he believed that psychoanalytic treatment could be used for many conditions, even for paranoid patients (see Freud, 1896). Later, he became more discriminative and reserved his method only for psychoneurotic patients.

14. *Some individuals are psychologically normal.*

The first group of patients other than hysterics to be subjected to analytic scrutiny were not considered to have purely psychological problems. They were viewed in terms of dammed-up tension which manifested itself in symptons but which did not achieve mental representation. These were known as the *actual neuroses*. In German, *Aktuell* means topical, in the sense of current. These neuroses, precipitated by events in the outside world, were not due to internal psychological conflicts but were what we now call *situational neuroses*. Freud distinguished between patients with periodic physiological needs that were either being constantly gratified, or that could not be gratified. The former he labeled *neurasthenia*, and the later *anxiety neurosis*. These two entities were distinguished from the *psychoneuroses*.

Neurasthenics suffered from fatigue, weakness, and headaches, in general symptoms that characterize a depleted person. Freud believed that these patients practiced excessive masturbation and that they were drained of energy, since they were discharging sexual energy faster than physiology could build it up. Anxiety neurosis, on the other hand, was considered due to dammed-up accumulated sexual energy which, because of external circumstances, could not be discharged directly. Freud (1895a) thought the periodicity of anxiety attacks was based upon the cyclical buildup of sexual tension. He also postulated that persons who experience enforced sexual abstinence or incomplete sexual satisfaction were likely to develop this neurosis.

Pent-up sexual feelings are transformed into anxiety without reaching higher levels of mentation. This means that the libido does not energize (cathect) memories of sexual gratification which would impel the person to repeat the experience with an appropriate partner. Instead, sexual feelings are discharged by episodic anxiety attacks.

15.   *Psychoneurotic maladjustment falls into two categories:*
      Transference and narcissistic neuroses.

Freud's clinical experience caused him to subdivide the psychoneuroses further, on the basis of his judgment as to which patients would be amenable to psychoanalytic treatment. He divided the psychoneuroses into the transference neuroses and the narcissistic neuroses (Freud, 1915a).

The *transference neuroses* are characterized by their capacity to form transferences, that is, to project infantile feelings onto the psychoanalyst. These patients usually can be analyzed, because transference is the most important and indispensable therapeutic vehicle in psychoanalytic treatment. The transference neuroses are generally considered to be hysteria, phobic states, and obsessive-compulsive neuroses (Freud, 1914b). There have been other classifications included in the transference neuroses, but the above three are always found in diagnostic handbooks.

The *narcissistic neuroses* consist of two entities, depression and the psychoses. Freud did not make major distinctions between the psychoneuroses and the psychoses, and he was inclined to group the depressions into the same category as the psychoses. He first called the latter paraphrenias, and he did not particularly distinguish between schizophrenia, or paranoia, or what in recent times have been called borderline states and characterological disorders. Persons with these conditions, according to Freud, did not form transferences and therefore were untreatable by the psychoanalytic method. The patient's libido was fixated onto his own ego and could not be directed sufficiently toward the analyst, so that a transference could be established. Further experience, however, has proven that even these patients can, indeed, develop transferences (Giovacchini, 1972, 1975).

16.   *The formulation of anxiety theory is crucial to understanding*
      maladjustment.

Anxiety Theory.   The concept of anxiety is fundamental and central in psychoanalytic theory. Freud's concept of anxiety underwent major changes throughout the years. It is easy to group his ideas into two categories referred to as the first and second anxiety theories. The *first anxiety theory,* sometimes known as the toxic or surplus theory, was formulated in 1895 (Freud, 1895a). Anxiety was simply considered deflected libido. Freud believed that sexual tension builds up because of internal hormonal accumulation and by external erotic stimuli. If such feelings are not gratified, they overflow and are discharged as anxiety. Thus anxiety originates in the deeper levels of the personality, the id. Sexual feelings, instead of being perceived by the ego, are directly transformed into anxiety.

In 1926 (Freud, 1926a) anxiety theory was markedly revised. Instead of originating in the id, the origin of anxiety was now located in the ego. When an unacceptable instinctual impulse threatens to break into the sphere of the ego, the ego becomes aware of impending danger. Since the danger is internal, the ego cannot flee from it as from external danger. Instead, it generates anxiety, which acts as a signal to inform the psyche it is being threatened. Anxiety sets in motion various psychic mechanisms designed to protect the ego. These mechanisms, known as defenses, repress the aberrant impulse. This is the *second anxiety theory,* which is also known as the *signal theory.*

Anxiety is distinguished from fear by its consequences, since from a subjective viewpoint both emotions are identical. Fear disappears when one flees from external danger, but one cannot physically escape from anxiety, an internal danger.

17.   *The psyche employs a variety of defenses.*

Defenses and Symptoms.   The ego may use many methods to defend itself against internal dangers. The ultimate aim of all defenses is to achieve repression.

Repression, a mental mechanism, keeps certain impulses and feelings from becoming conscious. A repressed impulse cannot be brought to the surface by conscious effort. *Suppression* of an impulse, on the other hand, means that the impulse can easily be made conscious. A suppressed impulse is deliberately withheld.

Freud (1915c) described two types of repression, primal repression and repression proper. *Primal repression* is the most archaic of the two types. Freud postulated that there are elements within the id that can never reach consciousness. He traced these elements back to the prehistory of Mankind and believed that something our ancestors repressed still resides in a state of primal repression in the id of modern people. There is considerable similarity between these ideas and Jung's primitive archetypes and collective unconscious. The primally repressed core within the id attracts ego elements in some ways (associatively) similar to it. This attraction from within can be compared to a magnet.

By contrast, *secondary repression* is more like a pressure from the outside, an "afterpressure" (*Nachdrangen*), as Freud described it. The impulsion to repression originates in the ego, and the objectionable feeling or impulse is pushed back into the id. If it is associatively related to other repressed elements in the id, then there is a combination of after pressure and the attraction exerted by primal repression.

Secondary repression, a useful clinical concept, helps explain many otherwise incomprehensible phenomena. The concept of primal repression is only of historical interest; it is untestable, inasmuch as it postulates the existence of elements that have never been conscious and never can be conscious. Therefore it is of limited interest scientifically.

Repression is discussed here first because it is a central concept to the theory of defenses. It is both a defense and the aim of defenses. Defenses are mental mechanisms set in motion by anxiety which, in turn, is a response to internal danger. Defenses protect the psyche from being overwhelmed by unconscious impulses perceived as dangerous. The aim of a defense is to rerepress the aberrant impulse which had been repressed and now threatens to reemerge. A defense is a mechanism, an abstract concept. Behavioral manifestations of this postulated mechanism can be observed and are known as character traits or symptoms.

18. Defenses can be arranged in a hierarchy.

Although there are differences of opinion among psychoanalysts regarding the significance of various defenses relative to each other, practically everyone agrees that, as with everything else in psychoanalysis, defenses can be arranged along a hierarchal continuum. There may be some disagreement as to exactly where a particular defense belongs on this continuum, but the principle of a hierarchy is firmly established. There is also some variation as to precisely what the defense mechanisms are. The list in Figure 2-1, therefore, includes only those widely accepted by a majority of clinicians. They are also listed, with the principle of hierarchy in mind, so that the more sophisticated defenses characteristic of a well-structured ego are at the top. Further down the list, the defenses are more primitive and are characteristic of early developmental phases.

Other authors have listed many more defenses, but these are probably the most readily accepted ones (Waelder, 1960). Many of these defenses subsume other more elemental processes. For example, in order to project, the psyche has had to use splitting mechanisms first. That is, in a regressive

---

1. Rationalization
2. Repression
3. Displacement
4. Identification
5. Conversion
6. Isolation or intellectualization
7. Reaction formation or overcompensation
8. Undoing
9. Introjection
10. Projection
11. Denial

FIGURE 2-1.   DEFENSES ARRANGED IN A HIERARCHAL CONTINUUM

fashion, a significant person referred to as an object is split into good and bad objects. The bad object is then projected into the outside world. The study of defenses deals with the interplay between observable data and the preconceived conceptual system. The latter has to be consistent with the data. In this instance, the data fit well with a conceptual system first established in another frame of reference, the stages of psychosexual development.

The most important criterion which determines whether a defense is relatively sophisticated or primitive is the amount of reality testing. Rationalization, at the top end of the spectrum, distorts reality only minimally, whereas denial, at the bottom end, totally disavows reality. A person who uses *rationalization* explains his or her behavior in a socially acceptable manner to maintain self-esteem. For example, say that a student fails an examination. He rationalizes that too many responsibilities did not give him adequate time to study. It could well be that the student was, indeed, overburdened in the fashion he described, so he is dealing with reality elements. His distortion may be slight: he may be magnifying the significance of his responsibilities in bringing about his failure. There also may be other more important reasons for his poor performance. He may have been lazy, or the material may have been too difficult for his ability. He may have felt inadequate to compete with his classmates. There may have been many reasons for his failure, but none was acceptable to him. He chose the least threatening one, and rationalized.

By contrast, *denial* involves a blotting out of reality. The patient who uses this defense does not acknowledge a sector of reality. A mother may continue nursing her dead baby as if he were still alive, or a rejected bride may keep the wedding table intact for years, as occurs in one of Dickens's novels. In not perceiving a segment of reality, gross reality distortion occurs, and for that reason denial is placed at the bottom of the hierarchal list.

Different levels of emotional development are associated with specific defenses. Although psychosexual theory was not constructed with the concept of defense in the foreground, it is conceptually consistent that the more primitive levels of development would have the least developed reality-testing functions. The rationale for the psychosexual theory of development is strengthened when empirically observed defenses can be arranged in a hierarchal continuum on the basis of their reality-testing properties, and this hierarchy is found to be parallel to the developmental hierarchy.

Since defense presupposes conflict, developmental stages must be considered in terms of psychopathological distortions. The hierarchy of defenses can be easily juxtaposed with the hierarchy of psychopathology. Briefly, rationalization is found in a more-or-less normal psyche; repression, displacement, and conversion are typical of hysteria; isolation, reaction formation, and undoing characterize the obsessive-compulsive neurosis; and introjection, depression, projection, and denial characterize paranoid and other psychotic states.

This does not mean that certain defenses are only associated with particular conditions. To allay the anxiety some readers may have, it can be emphasized that we all use these defenses at some time or other. One is not necessarily paranoid just because one uses projection on occasion.

Different psychopathological states are characterized by the preponderant use of particular defenses. If a particular defense has become the chief modality by which a person maintains a balance between the inner world of his psyche and the external world, then it is possible to diagnose a specific type of emotional disorder. Ordinarily, defenses are human attributes called occasionally into play under appropriate circumstances.

Brief descriptions of the other types of defenses and their symptomatic expression follow. To repeat, a defense is simply a mechanism, an abstraction which has no meaning unless considered together with its behavioral manifestations. Various constellations of behavior can be conceptualized in terms of these mechanisms.

Repression has been described first (see Assertion 17) because of its special position as a defense as well as the aim of all defenses. In repression, the unacceptable impulse is pushed out of the ego, and this self-protecting process may involve special mechanisms which cover the whole gamut of defenses. In hysteria, repression can occur without the further aid of defensive portions of the ego. The impulse is simply shut out, a process normally seen when something meaningful or sought after is forgotten, through a lapse of memory. This obliteration of feelings and impulses is less reality oriented than the socially acceptable reasons chosen by a person who rationalizes, and in spite of the fact that the aim of all defenses is to achieve repression, the defense of repression is nevertheless lower on the hierarchal list than rationalization.

Displacement refers to replacing the object of the impulse (usually the person capable of gratifying the impulse) by a substitute object.

Identification is part of normal development as well as a defense. Anna Freud (1936) described how a person takes the character traits of another person and makes them his own. He incorporates someone else's personality to defend himself against unacceptable, usually destructive, feelings toward a particular person, as well as fear of retaliation, which often takes the form of castration anxiety. Anna Freud described the special instance of *identification with the aggressor*. In a situation where one feels a potential victim of another person's aggression, he may identify with that person and behave like the aggressor, to master the terror of his passive helplessness. Anna Freud referred to instances of this sort in concentration camps.

Conversion was one of the first defenses Freud described. Today, examples of conversion are rare, but this defense illustrates qualities characteristic of all defenses. A conflict between a sexual impulse and opposing forces is converted into a somatic dysfunction, a situation typically found in the psychoneurotic entity, conversion hysteria. Thus, conversion refers to the transformation of a psychical impulse into a somatic disturbance. The latter, a symptom, may take many forms, such as paralysis of a limb, areas of anesthesia, blindness, and deafness. The symptom is a symbolic expression of a compromise between the unacceptable impulse and the forces that oppose it. Defenses in general incorporate the very elements being defended against, and this is reflected in the symptom. For example, a hysterical paralysis of the arm may be a symbolic compromise between the wish to masturbate and the prohibition against that wish. The wish, itself, is to some extent gratified by the attention the arm receives from both physicians and the patient. It is manipulated, stroked, examined; it receives considerable attention. To the patient, the arm unconsciously represents the penis. The substitution of the arm for the penis is called an *upward displacement.* This is an example of how a symptom may represent more than one defense—in the above example, conversion and displacement.

19. *Isolation, reaction formation, and undoing are characteristics of obsessive compulsive neuroses.*

In *isolation,* the impulse reaches consciousness but it is deprived of its feelings. Psychoanalysts would say it is decathected, since it loses its cathexis. Without its affect the unacceptable impulse, say a sadistic impulse, is rendered harmless. A defensive maneuver, isolation (often referred to as intellectualization) is an important aspect of normal thinking, and it accounts for the obsessional patient's capacity to deal with seemingly violent or disturbing thoughts in a calm, detached fashion.

Reaction formation, or overcompensation, leads to the repression of the forbidden impulse by replacing it with its opposite. Repressed cruelty is converted into kindness. Like conversion, overcompensation is another example of how the defense incorporates what is being defended against. Frequently, even casual observers recognize intuitively what overcompensating people are defending themselves against. The cloying sweetness of some do-gooders can be devastating and infuriating, because the recipient of such "kindness" can sense the murderous underlying rage. "Killed with kindness" is an apt expression of the situation where a destructive feeling is portrayed by its opposite.

Undoing is another example of a mental mechanism involving the expression of an unacceptable impulse and prohibiting forces. There is a temporal separation between the two. The unacceptable impulse is expressed or acted out by some action, and the prohibitive forces make up or "undo" the previously intended destruction. The latter usually takes the form of a ritual of atonement or expiation. Both the hostile act and the atonement for it may be symbolically disguised. Freud (1909b) offers the following example.

His patient, while walking down a country road, kicks a stone onto the middle of the road. He then reflects that when his beloved's carriage comes down the road it will hit this stone, overturn, and kill her. To undo this potential murder, he now kicks the stone off the road. On reflecting further, he decides this is all very silly, and so he kicks the stone back to the center of the road. He repeats this sequence endlessly.

20. *Introjection and projection position feelings in the internal and external worlds.*

Introjection is in some ways similar to identification. Some aspect of the outer world is internalized for defensive purposes. It differs from identification, however, in that the psyche does not structure the whole personality according to someone else's attributes. Rather, a portion of the external world, usually an ambivalently perceived person, remains circumscribed within the psyche, rather than being amalgamated into various ego systems, as occurs with identification. Freud (1917b) conceptualized such a mechanism when he studied mourning reactions and depressions, conditions in which the loss of a beloved is defended against by preserving and reacting to the memory of that person, who is tenaciously preserved in the psyche.

Projection is the counterpart of introjection; introjective-projective processes are often discussed. Something unacceptable within the self is attributed to, that is, is projected onto, someone else. This is the familiar paranoid orientation where all goodness stays inside and all badness emanates from outside forces and persons.

21. *Sublimation is an adjustment process rather than a defense mechanism.*

No discussion of defenses would be complete without considering *sublimation*. It is an adjustive socializing process, but inasmuch as it does not lead to repression, it is neither defensive nor psychopathological. Sublimation involves the transformation of a sexual instinct into something nonsexual. This process converts what may initially have been antisocial into socially acceptable behavior. The instinctual impulse, although transformed, is nevertheless gratified, or discharged, according to Freud. This does not occur to any significant extent with defenses. The commonly given example of sublimation is that of the artist who sublimates anal impulses to smear feces to painting with a brush and producing beautiful paintings. Sublimation is included in this section because even though technically different from defenses, it resembles reaction formation to the point that there is no sharp line of demarcation between them. It is doubtful whether a sexual instinct can really be gratified by nonsexual activity. Consequently, some analysts (Waelder, 1960) believe that true sublimations do not exist: What seems to be sublimatory behavior is probably reaction formation.

22. The reasons for the choice of neuroses is unknown.

Neurosegenesis refers to the processes involved in the causation of neuroses. The *choice of neurosis* remains as baffling a puzzle as it was in the early days of psychoanalysis. Undoubtedly, to a larger or smaller degree, there is an interplay of constitutional and environmental factors at the bottom of every neurosis or emotional distrubance. Psychoanalysis limits itself to the environmental aspect and how it affects the stability of the mind. The differences between the various neuroses have been discussed briefly above; now they will be focused upon. It will be noted that a neurosis is defined by the chief defenses it utilizes and the level of psychosexual development that has been reached.

23. The neuroses are regressive phenomena.

Presumably, in the psychoneuroses the patient has already reached the phallic level of development. Difficulties are encountered when the patient attempts to resolve the Oedipus complex. Inasmuch as oedipal feelings are traumatically conflicted, the patient regresses to a previous stage of emotional development. In terms of psychic development, he returns to a stage where he was relatively comfortable.

Fixation Point. The fixation point is well described by Freud's analogy of an advancing army. As the army proceeds it captures various garrisons on the way to its final objective. The harder the battle, the more soldiers are required to hold their position. This weakens the advancing army, and if it encounters intense opposition, it retreats back to the position where it left the greatest number of troops behind.

In hysteria, considered the most "advanced" neurosis, the person has practically reached the genital level of development. The conflict is oedipal, and the patient regresses only slightly. This description is purposely tentative because many analysts (Giovacchini, 1972, 1975) believe that this picture is incomplete. In any case, the hysterical patient uses such defenses as repression, identification, displacement, and conversion.

The *obsessive-compulsive person* has regressed to the anal phase and employs isolation, reaction formation, and undoing as chief defensive modalities. The *depressed individual* is regressed to the oral phase and is characterized by introjective defenses. More severely disturbed people—paranoids, schizophrenics, borderline states and those with character disorders—regress to early narcissistic phases and use such primitive defenses as projection, denial, and splitting.

24. Dreams have meaning and purpose.

Dream theory has always been a cornerstone of the psychoanalytic conceptual framework. Psychoanalysts believe that dreams have a rationale and are not simply the breakdown products of a disordered or fatigued mind.

The dream's function is to *preserve sleep,* and each dream represents the *fulfillment of an unconscious wish.*

A dream is formed in the following fashion. Something during the day, usually some incompleted thought or action, is retained in memory. Usually this element is an indifferent or trivial element and is known as the *day residue.* During sleep, due to a lowering of defenses, an unconscious impulse threatens to break through into consciousness and awaken the dreamer. This often occurs with nightmares. The day residue, however, usually has some associative connection with the unconscious impulses; thus, the latter attaches itself to it and, through a variety of mechanisms, becomes transformed into a dream.

The operations of the unconscious are called *primary processes* and are characterized by (1) displacement, (2) condensation or overdetermination and (3) symbolization. These account for the bizarre qualities of many dreams. *Displacement* occurs when the unconscious impulse attaches itself to the day residue. The energy of one is transferred (displaced) to the other. *Condensation* or *overdetermination* refers to several impulses being represented by a single dream element, and *symbolization* calls attention to the use of symbols in dreams.

Dreams are divided into two levels: the *latent dream* refers to the unconscious wish, and the *manifest content* refers to what is remembered or what the dreamer reports. For the dream to progress from the latent to manifest dream stage it must undergo what Freud (1900) called *secondary revision:* the unconscious, turbulent elements of the latent dream have to be pulled together in a sufficiently rational, coherent fashion so that it can be put in a visual and sometimes auditory form. Recent dream research, according to some investigators, seems to contradict some of Freud's assertions and strengthen others. Freud himself discussed certain situations, such as punishment and traumatic dreams, which he believed contradicted some aspects of his thesis.

25.   *The ego is the central focus of clinical concerns.*

The type of patients found in the consultation rooms of current psychoanalysts have little resemblance to the patients described by the pioneers of psychoanalysis. Instead of presenting clear-cut symptoms that can be conceptualized in terms of clashing forces within the mind, they speak of vague dissatisfactions and frequently ruminate about where they fit in society and the purpose of their existence. Consequently, certain aspects of psychoanalytic theory have required further emphasis and development. Since the ego is the organ of the mind which adapts to both the external and internal world and which defines the sense of identity, it had to be examined further. Several schools of ego psychology have developed, but only two have remained effective.

Heinz Hartmann (1964) and his co-workers Ernst Kris and Rudolph Lowenstein, as well as others (mainly in New York), postulated an ego psychology which retained Freud's dualistic instinct theory and energic hypothesis. Hartmann compartmentalized the ego into an *autonomous* part, independent of instinctual forces, and a part that is the outgrowth of instincts. He retained the energic hypothesis and added *neutralized energy* to libidinal and aggressive energy as an extension of Freud's hypothesis that sexual energy is sublimated into nonsexual energy. According to Hartmann, aggressive energy is neutralized into nonaggressive, or neutral, energy.

Winnicott (1958) modified many of Klein's (1948) concepts and combined them with his own. Winnicott has had a substantial following in Great Britian, but an ever-increasing number of analysts in the United States, such as Boyer (Boyer & Giovacchini, 1967), Ekstein (1966), Giovacchini (1972, 1975), Lindon (1967), and Searles (1965) are integrating Winnicott's views with their own. Basically these analysts regard the ego in terms of various subsystems, principally focusing upon the identity system (often known as the self-representation), the integrative system (a coordinating system), and the executive apparatus, which interact with the outer world. No specific energic hypothesis is requried for these concepts. This theoretical orientation enables psychoanalysts to treat a wider range of patients than had previously been thought possible.

APPLICATIONS

Assessment

Methods of evaluating potential patients for psychoanalytic treatment vary. Once Freud had consolidated his treatment approach and technique, he adopted a nondirective attitude. He did not advocate systematic history taking but took a wait-and-see attitude following the patient's verbal material, without preconceived judgments regarding psychopathology or treatability. This established an atmosphere in which the patient experienced maximum freedom to express himself as uninhibitedly as possible.

Today, some psychoanalysts, in conformance with the medical model, resort to a more structured approach. They usually see patients for two to four interviews and take an extensive history. The history of the present problem is chronologically ordered, with special emphasis on life circumstances that can be associated with the exacerbation or remission of symptoms. Then the analyst inquires about the patient's emotional development, paying particular attention to childhood events. Finally, a family history is elicited, with special relevance being given to the personalities and possible emotional disorders of parents. Sibling relationships are also emphasized.

At the same time the psychoanalyst does a mental status examination, noting the patient's appearance, orientation to time and space, appropriateness of affect, and characteristics of stream of thought, as well as the appearance of any special symptoms, such as delusions and hallucinations. This assessment is to determine whether the patient has sufficient ego strength to undergo analysis. The analyst may also interview other members of the family, although this is seldom done with adults. It is frequently done with adolescents and is practically standard procedure with children.

If the analyst has doubts about the feasibility of conducting analysis with a particular patient, he may ask for psychological testing—usually projective tests, especially the Rorschach examination. If the patient seeks psychoanalysis in a clinic or institute, a routine social history is done by a social worker, and the analyst has this information at his or her disposal before seeing the patient.

The analysts with medical training are especially sensitive to the possibility that organic factors may cause or contribute to the clinical picture. They may ask for an independent medical examination to check the possibility of a neurological disorder. Many analysts without medical degrees insist upon a routine physical work-up, and sometimes they consult with a physician when they suspect their patient may be developing symptoms that cannot be explained on a psychological basis.

After having obtained the above information, the analyst will ordinarily conduct a trial analysis. The analyst asks the patient to lie down and begin free associating. He listens to the patient for about two weeks, seeing him four to five times a week to determine whether it is wise to continue.

Freud initially advocated a trial analysis, without such involved examinations. He believed that such an analysis could serve as a therapeutic test to determine whether the patient is analyzable. Today, some analysts (Giovacchini, 1972, 1975, 1977) believe that the complicated investigations outlined above are not only unnecessary but a hindrance to analysis as well. They advocate little history taking and starting analysis as soon as possible. The patient is not told that this is a trial analysis, since the analyst wants to avoid giving the patient the impression that he is on trial. The patient's psychopathology does not have to meet any standards to be treated by the psychoanalytic method. Treatment is simply instituted, and the patient determines whether he wishes to continue.

Treatment

The essence and chief focus of psychoanalysis is the treatment relationship. Its most meaningful discoveries have been in this area. Some superficial aspects of the psychoanalytic interview have undergone modification, but the principles underlying therapeutic strategy have remained remarkably constant.

Psychoanalytic therapy began with hypnosis. Breuer (Breuer & Freud, 1895) hypnotized his famous patient, Anna O., and had her relive the traumatic moments that reputedly were responsible for her symptoms. Inasmuch as the patient discharged pent-up tension and anxiety, this procedure was referred to as *abreaction,* or "chimney sweeping." This was the beginning of the talking cure.

Freud (Breuer & Freud, 1895) replaced hypnosis by pressing his finger on the reclining patient's forehead and having him say anything that came to mind associated with the period of time when his symptoms originated. Through this experience Freud discovered *resistance.* The patient who at one level was anxious to cooperate with the therapist because of his tormenting symptoms would nevertheless withhold material in direct defiance of the instructions he had been given.

Almost simultaneously with the discovery of resistance, Freud recognized another phenomenon which he called *transference.* He noted that patients, especially female patients, formed rather intense positive feelings toward him. Some professed being in love with him. Freud, rather than accepting this as a reaction to his irresistible charm, looked at himself in the mirror and, always the scientist, asked what factors could account for his patient's reactions. He considered such situations as phenomena worthy of study rather than a natural consequence not requiring further explanation.

The patient gradually attributes to the analyst qualities that once belonged to a significant person of his infantile past. Thus, some of his feelings toward the analyst become irrational in view of present-day realities. The ability of the patient to distinguish between this childish orientation and the actual analytic relationship becomes the main therapeutic vehicle. The patient relives his childhood conflicts in the here and now of the analytic interaction, and the recognition by the patient (through the analyst's interpretations) of how his infantile orientation influences his behavior and thinking permits him a greater freedom of choice in his reactions and relations with both the inner world of his psyche and reality.

Transference is the most important therapeutic vehicle as well as the chief obstacle to cure (Freud, 1905a, 1912, 1915b). If the patient's negative transference is too intense, he will attack and defy the analyst, refusing to cooperate. Interpretations will be of no avail, and the patient will cling to his anger, stubbornly resisting any acknowledgment of its infantile origin or transference implications. Erotic transference has a similarly disruptive effect. The patient wants to be loved by the analyst and loses sight of the therapeutic task (Freud, 1915b). The modern therapeutic task can be defined as making the unconscious conscious through the use of tranference interpretations. The analyst uncovers unconscious feelings as the patient allows himself to be fully aware of transference feelings. Gradually the patient begins to recognize how he is distorting his image of the analyst according to needs that originated in childhood.

Psychoanalytic Procedure. The patient is asked to lie down on the couch and to put all of his feelings or thoughts into words. He must not choose what he will say or omit anything because he believes it is trivial, irrelevant, nonsensical, painful, or embarrassing. This is about the only demand the analyst makes of the patient. It is known as the *fundamental rule (Gründregel)*. This process is called *free association.*

Rational behavior and thinking are governed by what psychoanalysts refer to as the *secondary process.* Irrelevant and distracting thoughts are excluded, and behavior is determined by an assessment of needs and of the available and acceptable methods that will satisfy such needs. This is known as *reality testing,* an important aspect of the secondary process, based upon logical principles and organization and realistic judgments.

In psychoanalytic treatment, the patient is asked to give up secondary-process thinking. He is supposed to let what is called the *primary process* dominate, suspending logical operations as much as possible so that his thinking will follow a more primitive course than it previously did. By practicing free association, the patient relives infantile feelings in the transference. These are now subjected to logical scrutiny and reality testing, mediated by higher psychic systems which previously had no influence over such impulses as they remained hidden in the unconscious. In a preceding section this latter process was referred to as maintaining repression through defenses.

The analyst provides a setting where the patient can reveal the most frightening aspects of himself. He does this in a nonanxious atmosphere. Instead of viewing the patient's revelations as frightening human tragedies, the analyst calmly accepts the fact of their occurrence and views them as topics of extreme interest and worthy of inquiry. The patient gradually shares the analyst's perspective and becomes further involved with the infantile within himself, rather than feeling overwhelmed by it. The analytic setting permits the patient to regress with some degree of comfort.

Because of a somewhat relaxed regression (although its manifestations may from time to time be stormy), and the concomitant bringing to the surface of infantile elements, primitive forces within the self are no longer as oppressive or constrictive as previously. Furthermore, often the patient regresses to an ego state which precedes the formation of pathological psychic structures. Having reached such a regressed state, the patient has another chance to develop, this time without the constricting and distorting influences that plagued his initial development.

The knowledge gained about primitive mental states from the study of regressed states has led to a more extensive application of psychoanalytic treatment. Many analysts no longer confine psychoanalytic technique to the treatment of psychoneuroses. Patients suffering more severe emotional conditions, even some psychoses, are now being treated by the psychoanalytic method.

Institutional

Psychoanalysis loses some of its character once it strays outside the consultation room. However, in spite of the opposition it has encountered, its principles have overtly or covertly guided various types of institutions. Three types in particular can be emphasized: (1) child-rearing practices, (2) education, and (3) therapeutic institutions.

Child-Rearing Practices.   In many ways, child-rearing has become institutionalized. There are certain principles and traditions which cannot be ignored if the goal is the approval of society and presumably if optimal results in producing a happy, healthy adult are desired.

The psychoanalytic orientation stood in marked contrast to the rigid behavioristic approach advocated by John B. Watson. The behaviorist arranged everything on a rigid schedule, to introduce the child to order and discipline. A certain amount of frustration was considered to be in the child's best interest. The psychoanalytic approach stresses relating to the child's needs and abandoning any preconceived adult notions about schedules and delay. More specifically, it maintains that the adult should not force the child to move on to a higher development position; the child is to proceed at his own pace. The psychoanalytic position is permissive.

Education.   Psychoanalysis stresses that the child focuses upon various activities at specific stages. His behavior is phase specific. There are appropriate ages for introducing certain learning experiences. Because of attributes characteristic of a particular developmental phase, the child of any given age may be better able to incorporate some aspects of the external world than others. Some teachers have used these ideas in setting up educational programs. Psychoanalysis also stresses autonomy, and educators have tried to integrate this focus in their formats. Usually this has led to less rigid curricula and a tendency toward a permissive outlook.

How successful these attempts have been is an open question. Psychoanalysis does not have a comprehensive learning theory, and until this lack is remedied it seems unlikely that much will be accomplished by psychoanalytic insights in furthering the educational process.

Therapeutic Institutions.   One might expect that psychoanalysis would be influential in mental hospitals. Actually, it has received a mixed reception there. From the psychoanalyst's viewpoint, hospitalization is not a treatment issue. A patient is hospitalized generally for the benefit of the relatives who can no longer stand him. If he is not able to care for himself and requires that someone look after him, hospitalization is custodial rather than psychotherapeutic.

How can the patient's hospitalization be turned to best advantage? Is the hospital simply a place to contain the patient between analytic hours? Bettelheim (1974) constructed a total therapeutic milieu based on psychoanalytic principles at the Orthogenic School of the University of Chicago. Basically, he created a setting tailored as much as possible to the child's needs, reacting to the child's unconscious requests as well as being sensitive to nonverbal communications. Chestnut Lodge in Maryland has a similar philosophy and is probably the only psychoanalytic hospital in the world today. The Menninger Clinic has also hospitalized some patients for psychoanalytic treatment.

Drugs and somatic approaches such as shock therapy are often employed in hospitals. This emphasizes the medical model. The doctor and other staff decide what should be corrected, and then they institute methods to achieve desired changes. In this regard, the patient is not really consulted and remains the passive recipient of authoritative caretaking.

Psychoanalysis in a hospital setting retains some elements of the medical model, inasmuch as it is concerned with the total person. By contrast, it attempts also to foster maximal autonomy. This combination often stimulates considerable resistance among mental health professionals.

Self

Psychoanalysis focuses upon the workings of the mind. The Socratic motto "Know thyself" would be the most appropriate end point of analysis. The world is looked at in terms of subtle and often hidden motivations.

The psychoanalytic frame of reference is empathic. This does not mean that the analyzed person should go around analyzing others, in what is derisively called parlor analysis. To look at and interpret someone else's behavior in terms of unconscious motivation is not the hallmark of a successful analysis. It represents the clumsy fumbling of the insecure amateur.

Analysis should not foster arrogance. There have been analysts and analysands who adopt a superior attitude because they believe they now know all the secrets of the human mind and feel they belong to an exclusive cult. This was especially true during the early days of psychoanalysis, when analysts banded together and isolated themselves, presumably for mutual protection. Their behavior probably was an overcompensation for an experienced vulnerability. Today the situation is much different. Ecclesiastic and esoteric seclusion is not part of the analytic scene. If such accusations, on specific occastions, seem justified, then one is attacking a particular analyst or group and not analysis. These are grotesque distortions of analysis. If anything, analysis should promote tolerance and acceptance, recognizing every man's right to construct his own reality and to choose a lifestyle consonant with his private world. His world may be different, but it is worthy of being respected and understood. The analytic perspective does not seek to manage another's life. It is the polar opposite of those philosophies and therapies designed to control behavior.

In addition to being a theoretical system and a therapeutic technique, psychoanalysis is also a philosophy, a *Weltanschauung*. One's personal psychoanalysis never ends. The analysand may terminate the ritual of analysis by stopping his appointments, but the process continues.

Should everyone be analyzed? This frequently asked question is anti-analytic. The essence of analysis is autonomy. Can autonomy be imposed? Obviously, this is a contradiction. One has to choose for oneself. Some people have made comfortable adjustments to life and seek no further. Some are not curious and do not care to look inward. There are many others whose minds are restless and are admirably suited for the mutually explorative activity that characterizes the patient-analyst relationship.

VALIDATION

Evidence

Psychoanalysis has been attacked as being unscientific (Nagel, 1959), since its theories and hypotheses are not based upon experiments and controlled studies. Its theoretical edifice is considered empty and speculative by some opponents.

For some, the scientific basis of psychoanalysis is dependent upon its therapeutic results. This is related, although not identical, to the belief that a valid hypothesis has to have predictive value. The tenets of a psychoanalysis would be considered part of science if they could predict behavior and therapeutic change. Prediction is equated with therapeutic efficacy.

Scientific explanation and prediction are not necessarily related. The Babylonians, for example, were rather skillful at making predictions, but their explanations for the bases of their predictions were unscientific; they included mysticism and magic.

Still, if psychoanalysis is a method of treatment, then it has a goal; it is attempting to do something similar to other scientists who are confronted with solving problems. The validity of the method is judged by what it accomplishes. However, accomplishments are judged in the same frame of reference as the conceptual foundation of the treatment method.

For example, behavioral change is not relevant to the psychoanalytic treatment process. Behavioral change includes giving up symptoms. The essence of treatment is the formation of insight, verbal or otherwise. The patient learns how infantile patterns are repeated and constantly intrude into current adaptations. They restrict options as to how to relate to the external world as well as to various parts of the self. By being aware of how these childhood orientations are relived in the transference relationship with the therapist, the patient gains some control over what had been inexorable and unconscious forces. Thus, psychoanalytic treatment enhances autonomy and leads to higher levels of psychic integration. How this occurs is explained by concepts that underlie the treatment process such as regression and transference.

The changes that psychoanalysis brings about cannot be measured in terms that would suit the logical positivists because they do not involve levels that can be evaluated operationally. Still, the changes that occur are the inevitable extensions of goals that are both inherent in as well as define the psychoanalytic process.

All analysts can describe patients who have improved tremendously but the improvement is not manifest in quantifiable reactions and behavior or even subjective states of well being. However, these patients have experienced subtle changes indicating increased autonomy. They have developed an attitude of introspection, a psychological mindedness which creates a certain orientation, an openness, toward themselves and others. It can best be compared to a person who has been exposed to an area of science, art or philosophy. He becomes deeply involved, reads all he can, seeks and finds charismatic teachers and makes what he is pursuing and learning part of himself. His self-concept becomes expanded. After these experiences, he is not exactly the same person he was before he pursued this particular course. In many ways, he is still the same person but there have been accretions which have made his world considerably and perhaps immeasurably larger.

Science, according to Max Planck, is based upon two assumptions: (1) there is a real world, and (2) it is knowable (see D'Abro, 1951). Hypotheses are constructed so that parts of the universe which seem chaotic can be understood in a more orderly fashion. Science is based upon a series of abstractions that help explain apparently unrelated data. A better hypothesis applies to a wider range of data. Then, previous hypotheses recede into the background.

Opponents of psychoanalysis point out that psychoanalysis is not based upon controlled experiments (Nagel, 1959). They question the validity of obtaining data from treating patients or relying upon observations. If these factors disqualify psychoanalysis as a science, then astronomy and geology would find themselves in similar straits.

Nagel criticized psychoanalysis because he believed that its hypotheses were not capable of being disproven. He cited the Oedipus complex as an example and did not elaborate what he meant by disproof. In his classic textbook (Cohen & Nagel, 1934), Nagel stated that if a body of data could be better explained by a new hypothesis, then older ones, for pragmatic purposes, were disproven. If the child's feelings toward parents as manifested through dreams and behavior or if the fantasies of patients can be better explained by other hypotheses, then the oedipal hypothesis can be considered no longer useful. Psychoanalysis, as a part of science, is nonjudgmental. It does not deal with right or wrong. Some hypotheses are better than others only if they are more useful (Giovacchini, 1967).

The fundamental hypothesis of psychoanalysis is the *dynamic unconscious*. Other hypotheses can be considered extensions or superstructures of the dynamic unconscious. These secondary hypotheses can be modified or discarded without threatening psychoanalysis. If, however, the concept of the dynamic unconscious were proven invalid, then psychoanalysis would crumble. But the demise of psychoanalysis is highly improbable, since the evidence that supports the concept of the dynamic unconscious stems from more frames of reference than those validating the existence of electricity.

Before enumerating these frames of reference, it is germane to consider again the dynamic unconscious, which postulates the existence of mental processes that cannot spontaneously become conscious. These unconscious elements, Freud claimed, have effects upon conscious behavior without the person being aware of it. This later aspect is novel. Unconscious mental elements were well known since antiquity, but that they could affect so-called rational behavior is Freud's unique discovery and constitutes the essence of psychoanalysis.

The following frames of reference, listed in order of decreasing probability, support the concept of the dynamic unconscious: (1) posthypnotic phenomena, (2) parapraxes, (3) symptoms, and (4) dreams.

Posthypnotic Phenomena. Posthypnotic suggestion furnishes the most elegant evidence to support the validity of the dynamic unconscious. A patient in hypnosis can be given suggestions to behave in a particular manner latter, when he is no longer in a trance. He can be told that he will have no conscious recall of such suggestions. Under hypnosis a person may be told that when awake he is to turn off a lamp when the hypnotist coughs. Following hypnosis, the subject will not consciously know of any connection between the cough and his turning off the light. He may not even be aware that the hypnotist coughed. He may deny that he turned off the light or may rationalize his behavior. When the hypnotist explains that the subject was instructed to behave in the way he did during hypnosis, there may be no recall. It is obvious that the subject responds to a situation of which be consciously knows nothing. This is an example of the dynamic unconscious at work.

Parapraxes.   Slips of the tongue, unusual lapses of memory such as forget-ting familiar names, and other common, inexplicable aberrations of behavior which can be considered the psychopathology of ordinary life are called parapraxes (Freud, 1901). They are also often called Freudian slips. Such behavior often seems irrational, and it is plausible to assume that it emanates from forces within the self of which the person has no conscious awareness. Forgetting something "well known," if that something is later recalled, almost defines the unconscious. The bursting forth of an unin-tended insult is evidence that something relegated to the unconscious can affect one's behavior, in spite of efforts to control revealing such feel-ings. The assumption made about such slips is that what breaks through is a derivative of some element which remains in the unconscious.

Symptoms.   From a rational viewpoint, symptoms make very little sense. During the course of psychoanalytic treatment, the analyst may discover their meaning. Insofar as the patient was not aware of the rationale behind his symptomatic behavior, the motivating forces behind such behavior must reside in the unconscious. The symptom can be understood as a com-promise between an unconscious impulse and the defense against that impulse.

Dreams.   Dreams also have a rationale which can be discovered through free association. Unconscious impulses and defenses against such impulses are regularly encountered in analyzing dreams. In dreams, however, the unconscious wish is more often discernible than is symptomatic behavior, because of the partial relaxation of defenses occurring during sleep. In some dreams, however, distorting forces may make it difficult to arrive at their meaning.

Comparisons

Psychoanalytic theory and treatment are fundamentally different from any other system of psychotherapy. The differences are particularly noteworthy when the objectives of treatment are examined. Most systems of treatment make the assumption that the therapist's reality is better than the patient's. Consequently, their efforts are directed toward altering the patient's behavior to conform to a preestablished reality model. How this is achieved varies with the type of treatment.

Behavioral modification achieves its goals by a system of rewards and punishments. This is fundamentally the same conditioning principle that Ivan Pavlov elucidated at the beginning of the century. This approach, con-crete and mechanistic, totally ignores deeper, inner causes. The person's autonomy is considered a hindrance, because the essence of the behavior modification approach is to manipulate a person into conforming. Some behaviorists apparently do not like the word *conform* and point out they attempt to change behavior that the client wants to change. This implies that the person has freedom of choice. What is ignored is the unconscious. The person's decision is neither spontaneous nor free. He has been coerced into making it because society or his conscience is at variance with his symptomatic behavior. His true motivations are subtle and complex and cannot simply be disposed of by signing a contract, or whatever manipulation the behavioral modification approach contrives.

Transactional analysis has goals similar to behavioral modifications; only the method is different. It takes into account psychoanalytic principles, those concerned with the dynamics of various interpersonal relationships. Beyond this point it parts company with psychoanalysis, because the transactional analyst becomes involved in roleplaying. He pretends to be the mother or father or whatever and then somehow gets the patient to work out some conflict. The method of transactional analysis is as far removed from psychoanalysis as is behavioral modification. It is concerned with reenactment, and even though it is aimed at bringing to the fore infantile relationships, transference, which refers to viewing the analyst in terms of an emotionally significant person of the past, is essentially ignored. The nature of the interaction as a game strategy is stressed, and it is believed this understanding should lead to corrections at the behavioral level. The correction of the transference distortion, however, is impossible because the therapist has adopted a role rather than reflected what the patient has projected onto him.

Client-centered therapy, supposedly nonintrusive, is designed to give the client insight by reflecting back to him what he has said. The fact that expressions such as "reflecting back" are metaphors is unfortunately forgotten. In client-centered therapy the process underlying the metaphor is not even considered, so in a sense this is a therapy primarily based upon a model defined by the idea of mirroring the client's verbal statements and not upon a conceptual system, since client-centered therapy really has no theory. In fact, the use of a conceptual system is decried.

New therapies are springing up every day, involving groups and individuals. To some extent, most of them utilize some psychoanalytic principles. However, *allowing transference to develop, with the aim of increasing the patient's autonomy by extending control over inner primitive forces, is unique to psychoanalysis.*

Psychoanalysis developed from medicine and has retained some superficial elements of the medical model. Some psychoanalysts admit that certain aspects of the medical model are inappropriate to their ultimate goal of enhancing autonomy (Freud, 1926b).

The background of the therapist is important in determinng his orientation. The medical psychoanalyst has the most rigorous and lengthy training

of any profession. He must attend medical school and then put in one year
of internship, usually three years of psychiatric residency, and, on the
average, five years of analysis and supervised training in a psychoanalytic
institute.

Many therapists, in rejecting the medical model, argue that medical
education is unnecessary for the practice of psychoanalysis (Freud, 1926b).
Quite a few analysts agree, but most would like to retain some medical
training in a much modified and abbreviated form. In some cities
arguments about training have led to absurd consequences. In rejecting the
present arduous process of training for psychotherapy, many persons have
rejected all training. In New York City, for example, quite a sizable number
of persons start practicing psychotherapy with little more than a course in
undergraduate psychology. In some instances, they do not even have that.
Frequently, they have been in treatment with someone who represents some
school of psychotherapy. The therapist treats him and then trains him. Such
trainees band together, and a new movement is born.

Obviously, standards of training and competence in psychotherapy have
to be established. This is taking place, but it is a slow process.

PROSPECT

From time to time, the opinion is stated that psychoanalysis is dead. The
course of psychoanalysis has been stormy since its very beginning, but it has
survived.

One must expect dissent when dealing with a topic as sensitive as basic
motivations. To learn there are forces within your mind over which you do
not have complete control and to place yourself in the hands of someone
who claims he or she knows more about you than you do must be threatening. Opposition led to counter-reactions; analysts defended themselves by
withdrawing from their contemporaries. In Freud's day, this meant separation from the psychiatric group. As analysts isolated themselves, they over-
compensated by acting as if they were an elite cult. As the years passed,
others began recognizing some of the exciting ideas in psychoanalytic theory
and became intrigued with the analytic method and philosophy. Gradually,
psychoanalysis became more popular and accepted. The influx of students
seeking training after World War II made psychoanalysts less secretive and
esoteric.

Today, there are several issues which affect psychoanalysis and which
may determine its future course. Rapid and immense changes have occurred
in our society, and psychoanalysis has been caught in the swirl. Many
previous standards and mores have been discarded. What had been considered psychopathology, such as homosexuality, is now called alternate
lifestyles.

Psychoanalysis has been attacked because it has been viewed as a representative of the establishment. Psychoanalysis originated in a mid-Victorian, highly structured conformist culture and was rejected because it was too much at variance with traditional beliefs. Today, its role has been reversed; it is called reactionary and traditional.

Psychoanalysis is said to advocate conformity by a culture that considers itself anticonformist. In truth, psychoanalysis stresses autonomy in a culture that wants to equalize everything and is really frightened of autonomy.

This confusion has led to the emergence of many schools of psychotherapy which, on the surface, seem to be against conformity but which, by manipulating behavior, sometimes takes on an Orwellian, big-brother grotesqueness. There are other motives behind these movements, such as seeking the prestige and economic advantages that psychoanalysts have acquired without the training and sacrifices they underwent.

As psychoanalysts come out of seclusion, they may no longer provoke mystical awe and it may then be possible to make progressive changes that will put psychoanalysis where it belongs, among the other clinical disciplines. The trend is toward moving away from a strict medical model, and this will be reflected in educational practices. Psychoanalytic education will become more available, and present-day institutes will upgrade and modify entrance requirements and curricula.

Psychologists and social workers are now beginning to be given the clinical training formerly reserved only for physicians. The question of a medical background will have to be reevaluated, and perhaps it will prove to be an anachronism—as Freud himself indicated (Freud, 1926b). It is possible that special programs which include some exposure to clinical medicine will be instituted for the training of future lay analysts.

As psychoanalysis becomes less parochial, general attitudes about it should become more relaxed. Then it can be appreciated for what it is. Psychoanalysis is not a religion, a cult, or a fantasy; it is a scientific theory and a clinical technique which attempts to alleviate misery and suffering and to accentuate and bring out the dignity and nobility inherent in every person.

ANNOTATED BIBLIOGRAPHY

Primary Source

Freud, S. *The complete psychological works of Sigmund Freud.* (Standard ed.) London: Hogarth Press, 1952-1974 (24 volumes). This magnificent collection of all of Freud's psychological papers, books, lectures, and monographs is an absolute essential for any person who wishes to understand psychoanalysis in depth. This is a scholarly, annotated collection, each article being preceded by an introduction which places it in its proper perspective and in the context of the development of Freud's ideas. The 24th volume is a comprehensive index which contains considerably more than just the standard subject-author index.

Secondary Sources

Fenichel, O. *The psychoanalytic theory of neuroses.* New York: Norton, 1945.

This relatively long textbook has been a standard reference for many years. Classical psychoanalysis is systematically and accurately represented, and up until the time of its publication, most of the relevant literature is reviewed. This book is being revised to bring it up to date.

Brenner, C. *An elementary textbook of psychoanalysis.* New York: International Universities Press, 1957.

This is a short, concise, excellent textbook for the student who does not want the detailed expositions found in the above works. In spite of its brevity, this book is remarkably lucid.

Giovacchini, P.L. *Psychoanalysis of character disorders.* New York: Jason Aronson Press, 1975.

This book consists of a collection of articles dealing with the theory and treatment of patients suffering from severe psychopathology, a focus which is becoming increasingly prevalent in modern analysis.

Waelder, R. *Basic theory of psychoanalysis.* New York: International Universities Press, 1960.

This is another relatively short, excellent textbook. In addition to examining the technical aspects of psychoanalysis, it briefly concerns itself with some philosophical issues.

Winnicott, D. W. *Collected papers: Through pediatrics to psychoanalysis.* New York: Basic Books, 1958.

This book contains many of the major articles of a prominent leader of the British school. His ideas about psychopathology and treatment are more in accord with present-day psychoanalysts whose focus is mainly ego psychological.

REFERENCES

Abraham, K. The influence of oral erotism on character formation. In *Selected Papers on Psycho-Analysis* (pp. 370-393). London: Hogarth Press, 1948. (Originally published, 1921.)

Abraham, K. A short study of the development of the libido, viewed in the light of mental disorders. In *Selected Papers on Psycho-Analysis* (pp. 418-480). London: Hogarth Press, 1948. (Originally published, 1924.)

Alexander, F., & Selesnick, S. *The history of psychiatry.* New York: Alfred A. Knopf, 1966.

Aristophanes. The plays of Aristophanes. In *Great Books of the Western World.* Chicago: Encyclopaedia Britannica, Inc., 1955.

Bernard, C. *An introduction to the study of experimental medicine.* New York: Henry Schuman, 1949.

Bettelheim, B. *A home for the heart.* New York: Alfred A. Knopf, 1974.

Bornstein, B. On latency. *Psychoanalytic Study of the Child* (Vol. 6, pp. 279-285). New York: International Universities Press, 1951.

Boyer, L. B. & Giovacchini, P. L. *The psychoanalytic treatment of characterological and schizophrenic disorders.* New York: International Science Press, 1967.

Brenner, C. *An elementary textbook of psychoanalysis.* New York: International Universities Press, 1957.

Breuer, J. & Freud, S. *Studies on hysteria.*

Standard edition, *The Complete Works of Sigmund Freud* (Vol. 2). London: Hogarth Press, 1955. (Originally published, 1895.)

Cohen, M. & Nagel, E. *An introduction to logic and scientific method.* New York: Harcourt, Brace, 1934.

D'Abro, A. *The rise of the new physics.* New York: Dover Publications, 1951.

Ekstein, R. *Children of time and space of action and impulse.* New York: Appleton-Century-Crofts, 1966.

Ellenberger, H. *The discovery of the unconscious.* New York: Basic Books, 1970.

Erikson, E. H. *Childhood and society.* New York; W. W. Norton, 1950.

Fenichel, O. *The psychoanalytic theory of neuroses.* New York: W. W. Norton, 1945.

Freud, A. *The ego and the mechanisms of defense.* New York: International Universities Press, 1946. (Originally published, 1936.)

Freud, S. Beobactungen über Gestaltung und Feineren Bau der als Hoden beschriebenen Lappenoragane des Als, S. B. *Akad. Wiss.,* Wien, 1877 III Abt., 75, 15.

Freud, S. *On the grounds for detaching a particular syndrome from neurasthenia under the description "anxiety neurosis."* Standard edition (Vol. 3, pp. 85-119). London: Hogarth Press, 1962. (Originally published, 1895.) (a)

Note: Standard edition refers to the Standard edition of *The Complete Psychological Works of Sigmund Freud,* which consists of 24 volumes. See the Annotated Bibliography above.

Freud, S. *A reply to criticisms of my paper on anxiety neurosis.* Standard edition (Vol. 3, pp. 119-141). London: Hogarth Press, 1962. (Originally published, 1895.) (b)

Freud, S. *Further remarks on the neuropsychoses of defense.* Standard edition (Vol. 3, pp. 157-187). London: Hogarth Press, 1962. (Originally published, 1896.)

Freud, S. *Sexuality in the aetiology of the neuroses.* Standard edition (Vol. 3, pp. 259-287). London: Hogarth Press, 1962. (Originally published, 1898.)

Freud S. *The interpretation of dreams.* Standard edition (Vols. 4 and 5). London: Hogarth Press, 1953. (Originally published, 1900.)

Freud, S. *The psychopathology of everyday life.* Standard edition (Vol. 6). London: Hogarth Press, 1966. (Originally published, 1901.)

Freud, S. *Fragments of an analysis of a case of hysteria.* Standard edition (Vol. 7, pp. 1-123). London: Hogarth Press, 1953. (Originally published, 1905.) (a)

Freud, S. *Three essays on the theory of sexuality.* Standard edition (Vol. 7, pp. 123-247). London: Hogarth Press, 1953. (Originally published, 1905.) (b)

Freud, S. *Delusions and dreams in "Jensen's Gravida."* Standard edition (Vol. 9, pp. 1-97). London: Hogarth Press, 1959. (Originally published, 1907.)

Freud, S. *Notes upon a case of obsessional neurosis.* Standard edition (Vol. 10, pp. 151-319). London: Hogarth Press, 1955. (Originally published, 1909.) (b)

Freud, S. *Leonardo da Vinci and a memory of his childhood.* Standard edition (Vol. 11). London: Hogarth Press, 1957. (Originally published, 1910.)

Freud, S. *Formulations on the two principles of mental functioning.* Standard edition (Vol. 12, pp. 213-227). London: Hogarth Press, 1958. (Originally published, 1911.) (a)

Freud, S. *Psycho-analytic notes on an autobiographical account of a case of paranoia.* Standard edition (Vol. 12, pp. 1-85). London: Hogarth Press, 1958. (Originally published, 1911.) (b)

Freud, S. *The dynamics of transference.* Standard edition (Vol. 12, pp. 97-109). London: Hogarth Press, 1958. (Originally published, 1912.)

Freud, S. *The occurrence in dreams of material from fairy tales.* Standard edition (Vol. 12, pp. 279-289). London: Hogarth Press, 1958. (Originally published, 1913.) (a)

Freud, S. *The theme of three caskets.* Standard edition (Vol. 12, pp. 289-303). London: Hogarth Press, 1958. (Originally published, 1913.) (b)

Freud, S. *On the history of the psycho-analytic movement.* Standard edition (Vol. 14, pp. 1-67). London: Hogarth Press, 1957. (Originally published, 1914.) (a)

Freud, S. *On narcissism: An introduction.* Standard edition (Vol. 14, pp. 67-105). London: Hogarth Press, 1957. (Originally published, 1914.) (b)

Freud, S. *Instincts and their vicissitudes.* Standard edition (Vol. 14, pp. 109-141.) London: Hogarth Press, 1957. (Originally published, 1915.) (a)

Freud, S. *Observations on transference love.* Standard edition (Vol. 12, pp. 157-172). London: Hogarth Press, 1958. (Originally published, 1915.) (b)

Freud, S. *Repression.* Standard edition (Vol. 14, pp. 141-159). London: Hogarth Press, 1957. (Originally published, 1915.) (c)

Freud, S. *The unconscious.* Standard edition (Vol. 14, pp. 159-217). London: Hogarth Press, 1957. (Originally published, 1915.) (d)

Freud, S. *Introductory lectures on psycho-analysis.* Standard edition (Vols. 15 and 16). London: Hogarth Press, 1963. (Originally published, 1917.) (a)

Freud, S. *Mourning and melancholia.* Standard edition (Vol. 14, pp. 237-259). London: Hogarth Press, 1957. (Originally published, 1917.) (b)

Freud, S. *Beyond the pleasure principle.* Standard edition (Vol. 18). London: Hogarth Press, 1955. (Originally published, 1920.)

Freud, S. *Group psychology and analysis of the self.* Standard edition (Vol. 18). London: Hogarth Press, 1955. (Originally published, 1921.)

Freud, S. *Medusa's head.* Standard edition (Vol. 18, pp. 173-178). London: Hogarth Press, 1955. (Originally published, 1922.)

Freud, S. *The ego and the id.* Standard edition (Vol. 19). London: Hogarth Press, 1961. (Originally published, 1923.) (a)

Freud, S. *The infantile genital organization: An interpolation into the theory of sexuality.* Standard edition (Vol. 19, pp. 141-149). London: Hogarth Press, 1961. (Originally published, 1923.) (b)

Freud, S. *The dissolution of the Oedipus complex.* Standard edition (Vol. 19, pp. 173-183). London: Hogarth Press, 1961. (Originally published, 1924.)

Freud, S. *An autobiographical study.* Standard edition (Vol. 20). London: Hogarth Press, 1959. (Originally published, 1925.)

Freud, S. *Inhibitions, symptoms and anxiety.* Standard edition (Vol. 20, pp. 75-173). London: Hogarth Press, 1959. (Originally published, 1926.) (a)

Freud, S. *The question of lay analysis.* Standard edition (Vol. 20). London: Hogarth Press, 1959. (Originally published, 1926.) (b)

Freud, S. *The future of an illusion.* Standard edition (Vol. 21). London: Hogarth Press, 1961. (Originally published, 1927.)

Freud, S. *Dostoevsky and parricide.* Standard edition (Vol. 21, pp. 173-195). London: Hogarth Press, 1961. (Originally published, 1928.)

Freud, S. *Civilization and its discontents.* Standard edition (Vol. 21). London: Hogarth Press, 1961. (Originally published, 1930.)

Freud, S. *Moses and monotheism.* Standard edition (Vol. 23). London: Hogarth Press, 1964. (Originally published, 1939.)

Freud, S. *The origins of psychoanalysis* (M. Bonaparte, A. Freud, & E. Kris, Eds.). New York: Basic Books, 1964.

Freud, S. Some early unpublished letters of

Sigmund Freud. *International Journal of Psycho-Analysis,* 1969, *50*, 419-426.

Giovacchini, P. L. Methodological aspects of psychoanalytic critique. *Bulletin of the Philadelphia Association for Psychoanalysis,* 1967, *17*, 10-26.

Giovacchini, P. L. *Tactics and techniques in psychoanalytic treatment, I.* New York: Science House, 1972.

Giovacchini, P. L. *Psychoanalysis of character disorders.* New York: Jason Aronson Press, 1975.

Giovacchini, P. L. *Psychoanalysis of primitive mental states.* New York: Jason Aronson Press, 1977.

Hartmann, H. *Essays on ego psychology.* New York: International Universities Press, 1964.

Herodotus. *The history of Herodotus.* In *Great Books of the Western World.* Chicago: Encyclopaedia Britannica, Inc., 1952.

Horney, K. *The neurotic personality of our time.* New York: Norton, 1937.

Jones, E. *The life and works of Sigmund Freud, I.* New York: Basic Books, 1953.

Klein, M. *Contributions to psycho-analysis, 1921-1945.* London: Hogarth Press, 1948.

Lindon, J. (Ed.). Panel on regression. *Psychoanalytic Forum,* 1967, *12*, 295-317.

Nagel, E. Methodological issues in psychoanalytic treatment. In S. Hooke (Ed.), *Psychoanalysis, scientific method and philosophy* (pp. 38-57). New York: New York University Press, 1959.

Nietzsche, F. *The philosophy of Nietzsche* (W. Wright, Ed.) New York: Random House, 1937.

Rapaport, D. The structure of psychoanalytic theory. *Psychological Issues,* 5 (2 and 3), 1966.

Searles, H. S. *Collected papers on schizophrenia and related subjects.* New York: International Universities Press, 1965.

Spinoza, B. *The chief works of Benedict de Spinoza.* New York: Dover Publishing Co., 1952.

Waelder, R. *Basic theory of psychoanalysis.* New York: International Universities Press, 1960.

Winnicott, D. *Collected papers: Through pediatrics to psychoanalysis.* New York: Basic Books, 1958.

Zilboorg, G. & Henry, G. *A history of medical psychology.* New York: Norton, 1941.

CHAPTER III

Individual Psychology

Heinz L. Ansbacher

ALFRED ADLER

Individual Psychology is the name Alfred Adler (1870–1937) gave to the personality theory he developed when, after a nine-year association with Sigmund Freud, from 1902 to 1911, he broke with him and established his own school of thought. Adler began lecturing in 1926 in the United States, where he made his home after 1934. He published some 10 books and 300 articles, gave countless public lectures, founded a journal, and headed an organization to further his theory and its applications. Individual Psychology is thus one of the oldest of the modern schools of personality. After a period of relative neglect following Adler's death and World War II, Individual Psychology has since found increasing interest and support.

Unique among personality theories, Individual Psychology has inherent in it a philosophy of humanism, best seen through the essential concept of social interest, which states in effect that human well-being and progress are a function of cooperative behavior. Despite its name, Individual Psychology is a social psychology which considers the concept of an isolated human being to be a meaningless abstraction.

Adler's psychology is:

1. *Holistic*, viewing the individual as an indivisible entity.
2. *Phenomenological*, seeing the person from his unique point of view.
3. *Teleological*, viewing man as pulled by the subjective future rather than pushed by the objective past, creatively striving for goals rather than reacting automatically to events.
4. *Field-theoretical*, considering a person's actions, thoughts, and feelings as transactions with his surrounding world.
5. *Socially oriented*, viewing the individual as not only reacting to society, but also as being a contributing active participant.
6. *Operational* in methodology.

Adlerian psychology stresses consciousness and cognition, responsiblity, meanings, and values. It considers man as creator and essentially captain of his soul secure in his belief he can overcome obstacles. Both behavior and emotions subserve the individual's purpose, of which he may, however, be quite unaware. Behavior follows from cognitive constructs in a logical manner, characterized in the normal individual by reasonableness and in the mentally disturbed by "private intelligence" or "private logic."

Adler's psychology presents itself as a complete and full method of understanding people, and it is used in counseling, psychotherapy, education, and other aspects of human behavior. Adlerian theory, originally developed as an alternative to Freud's theories, stands today validated and can be considered a prototype of most present-day theories of personality and psychotherapy.

INTRODUCTION

When Alfred Adler presented his system of personality and psychopathology he named it *Individual Psychology*. The name presented difficulties from the start because it is easily mistaken for individualistic psychology, whereas it means nearly the opposite.

Meaning of the Name

Adler chose the term *individual* in its Latin meaning of indivisible, for he regarded the person as an indivisible organic unit, in contrast to the view that a person can be meaningfully analyzed into parts. Adler (1912) described the individual as "a unified community in which all parts cooperate for a common purpose" (p. iv, translation modified from the original), suggesting that Individual Psychology is a socially oriented teleological psychology.

This description is a quotation from Rudolf Virchow (1862), the great 19th-century German physician and founder of German social medicine. It is from an essay, "Atoms and Individuals," in which Virchow contrasts the inorganic with the organic world and shows, in opposition to the dominant physicalism of his time, that living phenomena cannot appropriately be reduced to physicochemical principles. Indivisibility is not the most important meaning of *individual*, since this is shared with the term *atom*. The more important meaning is that which differentiates the individual from the atom, namely that the individual is a unified biological *community, cooperating for a common purpose*. If these characteristics are intrinsic to the biological unit, then it should be "natural" for man, the highest form of biology, to realize his biological properties in his social living.

The term *individual*, so understood—as the polar opposite not of *society* but of *atom*—embodies the entire conception of an organismic, humanistic, and teleological approach, in contrast to a mechanistic, reductionistic, and causalistic approach. In this light the name Individual Psychology would appear to have been a most thoughtful choice to express the complete antithesis from the scientific standpoint of Freud's psychoanalysis.

Purpose of the Theory

Adler realized that a theory is not a replication of reality but a human construction, a tool, to be used for a purpose. The purposes of a personality theory may be to conceptualize the development of man in general, to construct postulates to stimulate research, to demonstrate how man's behavior is controlled by internal and external forces as other events in the natural sciences are, and so on.

Adler's primary concern was to construct a theory useful not only to the helping professions but to the largest possible number of people in their process of living. Adler (1927a) wrote: "Only the understanding of human nature by every human being can be the proper goal for the science of human nature" (p. 15). "The understanding of human nature seems to us indispensable to every man" (p. 224). Adler believed he had come close to this goal when he wrote: "There may be more venerable theories of an older academic science. There may be newer, more sophisticated theories. But there is certainly no theory which could bring greater gain to all people" (1964, p. 364 n).

Adler introduced only a minimum of technical terms and constructed his theory in adaptation to what one finds and must deal with in everyday living, while taking into account all the established facts. His criteria were applicability and usefulness.

Philosophy of Science

In matters of the philosophy of science—Adler consistently selected the alternative which would facilitate the improvement of man and which expressed confidence in man. On the issue of *determinism versus free will* Adler took the position that man has sufficient options to make all the difference in the world. As to the *ethical nature of man*, Adler held that man by nature is neither good nor evil but has the potentiality for either. On the *mind-body issue*, he emphasized the ultimate importance of the mind; on the *past-present issue*, the importance of the present, including in the present the conception of the future; and on the *nature-nurture issue*, the importance of nurture, plus, however, man's own creativity.

From his aim that his theory should be practically applicable to life situations, and from his view that life in its sociocultural aspects is continuously evolving, Adler (1930) was satisfied if his theory was applicable to present conditions. "Individual Psychology claims not more for itself than to be taken as a theory which does justice to the present conditions of civilization, and to our present knowledge of man and his psychological condition, and which does so better than other theories" (p. 47).

HISTORY

Precursors

Adler's personality theory is essentially a conceptualization of the nature of man. Of course, man has, throughout the ages, been concerned in philosophy and in literature with constructing the most useful and satisfactory concept of himself to serve as a guiding principle for his conduct. Since Adler's orientation was humanistic rather than mechanistic and physicalistic, he could freely acknowledge his indebtedness to some of these earlier developments. In a general sense he acknowledged his indebtedness to the Bible, the Stoics, and great authors such as Shakespeare, Goethe, and Dostoevsky. In particular, he recognized the following:

Marx. As a young student Adler became interested in socialism and Karl Marx—not his economic and political but the psychological and philosophical aspects. This is reflected in Adler's emphasis on the social nature of man, his creativity, and his ability to influence his circumstances while at the same time being influenced by them. Adler's main dynamics, striving to overcome felt inferiorities, is related to Marx, as is Adler's conviction of the necessity for attaining equal rights for women.

Nietzsche. Adler's inferiority-superiority dynamics was most likely inspired by the dialectics of Nietzsche. Adler (1913) considered him "one of the soaring pillars of our art" (p. 123). "Among all great philosophers...Nietzsche is closest to our way of thinking" (Nunberg & Federn, 1962, p. 358). The great difference—one that makes all the difference in the world—is that Nietzsche's ideal was Superman, whereas Adler's ideal was Fellowman.

Vaihinger. The idea of thought constructs as tools for coping with the problems of life Adler found confirmed in the work of the German philosopher Hans Vaihinger. Adler (1912) wrote: "A fortunate circumstance made me acquainted with Vaihinger's ingenious *Philosophy of 'As If'*, a work in which I found the trains of thought suggested to me by the neurosis set forth as valid for general scientific thought" (p. 30).

Bergson. The idea of memory as purposeful Adler found in the works of the French pragmatist Henri Bergson. Adler (1912) noted in connection with "apperceiving memory" (p. 55), "I have to call attention here to Bergson's fundamental teachings" (p. 56 n). In writing about the goal orientation of the "stream of life," Adler (1920a) added, "I consider it a special honor that in discussing these psychological phenomena I can cite the fundamental theories of Vaihinger and Bergson, in addition to my own findings and views" (p. 245).

Kant. Adler referred to Immanuel Kant for his own important conception that "reason is inseparably connected with social interest" (1956, p. 149). Furthermore, Adler's notion of "common sense" as a criterion of sanity, in contrast to "private intelligence" as one of insanity, can be traced to Kant (Ansbacher, 1965a).

Others. Still other influences on Adler were Ludwig Klages for the importance of nonverbal communication, and Pierre Janet for the concept of neurosis as based on a feeling of insufficiency. Adler also saw certain parallels between his own views and those of G. Stanley Hall, John Dewey, and William James. For some of his organismic concepts he referred to the early anthropological social psychologists Moritz Lazarus and Heymann Steinthal.

Beginnings

Adler was born in 1870 in Vienna, the son of a Jewish merchant. After receiving his M.D. degree from the university there in 1895, he became a practicing physician. In 1902 he was invited by Freud with three others to form the original circle which became the Vienna Psychoanalytic Society. He became president in 1910 but resigned from the society a year later. Freud claimed Adler as a disciple who subsequently defected. Adler (1956) strongly denied this, conceding, however, that he learned a great deal from Freud, although in a negative sense: "I profited by his mistakes" (p. 358).

Early Recognition in the United States. Adler's major work, *The Neurotic Constitution*, appeared in 1912, and his first volume of collected papers, *Heilen und Bilden*, edited with Carl Furtmüller, in 1914. Adler's subsequent acceptance in the United States by important individuals who were also friendly toward Freud was astoundingly rapid.

Among psychiatrists, William Alanson White and Smith Ely Jelliffe, at that time editors and publishers of the *Psychoanalytic Review*, became interested in Adler. White wrote an introduction to *The Neurotic Constitution* which appeared in English translation in 1917, and Jelliffe supplied a translation of Adler's (1907) earlier monograph on organ inferiority which also appeared in 1917. That year also Adler's (1917) original essay on homosexuality was published in English, simultaneously with its German publication.

Among psychologists, G. Stanley Hall, who had invited Freud to the United States in 1909, took an immediate interest in Adler's books and studied them in seminars with his students. This led to an invitation to Adler to give a lecture series in the United States; however, it never took place, undoubtedly due to the outbreak of World War I in August 1914 (Ansbacher, 1971a).

After such early successes, how is the subsequent gradual decline of Adler, which today in turn is being followed by a renaissance of interest, to be explained? Our hypothesis is that Adler's early acclaim rested on an inadequate understanding of his work, due to two factors:

1. Adler was then at the mere beginning of his development of his ideas, whereas the present-day renaissance rests largely on his later writings (1964) and the practical work of the followers he eventually acquired.
2. Adler's psychology was understandably, yet erroneously, taken as a supplement or corrective of psychoanalysis.

Within this framework, Freud's (1914) accusation that Adler's theory "is actually nothing else but psychoanalytic knowledge, which the author...has now labelled as his own by changing the terminology of it" (p. 342), eventually had its impact.

Events in Europe. After the separation from Freud, Adler (1912) introduced the name Individual Psychology and founded the Society for Individual Psychology, at first named Society for Free Psychoanalytic Research. In 1914 he founded the *Zeitschrift für Individualpsychologie*. During World War I Adler served in the Austrian Army as a neuro-psychiatrist. Directly after the war he created a series of child guidance clinics in the Vienna public schools, with the consent of the authorities but on a completely voluntary basis. They were conceived as training seminars for teachers and other interested persons (parents, physicians, social workers, students) and were thus conducted generally before 30 to 50 such persons. By 1927 there were 22 such clinics in Vienna and 20 in the rest of Europe (Freudenberg, 1928). When the Vienna clinics were closed in 1934 by a new reactionary government, there were over 30 of them.

The year 1930 represented a peak, with the Fifth International Congress of Individual Psychology in Berlin. The congress was attended by over 2,000 participants and was reported at length in a leading psychiatric journal (Kankeleit, 1931). The honorary congress committee included Kurt Lewin and Bruno Klopfer. There were then also some 33 local Individual

Psychology organizations, 15 in Germany, 16 in various European countries, and one each in Palestine and the United States.

Later Years. From 1926 on Adler spent increasing portions of the fall and winter in the United States, primarily lecturing but also conducting clinics and a private practice. Among the numerous institutions he lectured at were Columbia University, the New School for Social Research, Harvard University, Wayne University, and the City College of New York. Two years after Adler was appointed visiting professor of medical psychology at Long Island College of Medicine in 1932, he and his wife Raissa took up residence in New York, and in 1935 the *International Journal of Individual Psychology* was founded, with Sydney Roth as publisher. Adler died on a lecture tour in Aberdeen, Scotland, on May 28, 1937, leaving his wife, a son, and two daughters, a third daughter having died before him. His daughter Alexandra and son Kurt are practicing Adlerian psychiatrists in New York City.

There are five biographies of Adler available in English by: Hertha Orgler (1963), psychotherapist and enthusiastic early follower of Adler; Phyllis Bottome (1957), novelist and good friend; Carl Furtmüller (1964), earliest co-worker and friend; Henri F. Ellenberger (1970), psychiatrist and historian, who gives the most scholarly account; and Manes Sperber (1974), novelist and early protégé of Adler, who appraises him quite critically.

Early Disciples. As a founder of societies, periodicals, and guidance centers, and a believer in carrying psychology to the people, Adler had a large number of significant early disciples. We can name only some of these here; for their writings, consult the bibliography of Mosak and Mosak (1975).

Rudolf Dreikurs continued (in Chicago) Adler's method of counseling before a group, systematized the technology of Adlerian counseling and psychotherapy, and succeeded in creating a new generation of Adlerian practitioners. Alexandra Adler and Danica Deutsch founded the first mental hygiene clinic and training institute in New York. Lydia Sicher introduced Adlerian methods on the West Coast. Sofie Lazarsfeld originated Adlerian sexual and marital counseling and wrote several books on the subject. Carl Furtmüller was Adler's original collaborator, even from before the time when they both participated in the Freudian circle. Oskar Spiel and Ferdinand Birnbaum were instrumental in establishing an Adlerian experimental school in Vienna. Erwin Wexberg wrote an early textbook and did some important editing. Herbert Schafer and Eric Weissmann became the deans of Adlerian psychology in France and England, respectively.

Adler was quite determined that Individual Psychology should not be identified with any religion or political party. On these grounds he separated from Fritz Künkel, Rudolf Allers, and Viktor Frankl on the one side, and Otto Rühle, Alice Rühle-Gerstel, and Manes Sperber, on the other. A third category continued functioning in Germany under National Socialism; outstanding among these are Leonhard Seif, founder of the Munich group, who trained a large number of Adlerian psychologists, and also Johannes Neumann.

Current Status

To consider the current status of Adlerian psychology, one must distinguish between the Adlerian movement and the recognition of Adler by the profession and the world at large.

The Adlerian Movement.   The Adlerian movement today numbers several thousand members in the United States, Canada, and European countries, especially Germany. It is composed of psychiatrists, psychologists, social workers, counselors, and educators, as well as lay people who accept the theory and apply the method of Adlerian psychology to family life and personal development. The lay movement received its strongest boost through the work of Dreikurs (1957, 1964).

Organizationally, the movement consists of numerous local societies and many study groups. In the United States the central organization is the American Society of Adlerian Psychology, which holds annual meetings and publishes as its main organ the *Journal of Individual Psychology*, devoted primarily to theoretical and research papers. There are Adlerian training institutes in New York, Chicago, Minneapolis, and other cities. Numerous courses and summer institutes at various colleges and universities are also given. Internationally, there is the International Association of Individual Psychology, founded in Adler's day, which meets every three years. One independent summer institute which has been meeting for several years in Europe and Israel has drawn hundreds of participants from many countries. The movement has in recent years enjoyed a steady growth.

Recognition of Adler.   The recognition of Adler is small in proportion to the validation of his theories. Although in books dealing specifically with personality theories he usually receives adequate consideration, in books on personality in general and other relevant topics he may not be mentioned. Yet his concepts are used widely, although in most cases without attribution. To mention only a few, concepts introduced by Adler include: inferiority feelings, striving for self-esteem, goal orientation, dependency, overprotection, avoidance of responsibility, lifestyle, achievement striving.

This discrepancy between the acceptance and wide use of Adlerian concepts and the prevailing relative lack of recognition of Adler is a paradox which will be dealt with in the last section, "Prospect."

ASSERTIONS

Due to the holistic and purposive-dynamic nature of the theory of Individual Psychology, its assertions do not readily lend themselves to a distinction between processes of development (becoming) and processes of maintenance (being). However, to abide by the requirements of this book, the distinction is made (although with some reluctance) as follows: Of the 17 assertions, the first 5 are placed under the *development* heading and the remainder under *maintenance*. The last assertion is actually developmental in nature, however.

Development

1. Man, like all forms of life, is a unified organism.

This is the most fundamental assertion of Adler. A human differs basically from a mechanism. A mechanism consists of a number of separate parts assembled. An organism starts from one fertilized ovum, and all the parts grow and develop from the original cell.

The individual is not divided against himself. He is not the battleground of conflicting forces. Inner conflicts are really alternatives of choice presented by a given situation derived from man's self-determination. This includes the freedom to make mistakes. Says Adler (1929b): "Rightly understood, the whole of this mental process...is not ambivalence but a dynamic unity. Only if it is not understood as a whole do we see it as two contradictory and warring entities" (p. 87).

Another important consequence of this understanding is that the opposition between conscious and unconscious is done away with. "The conscious and the unconscious [are] not separate and conflicting entities, but complementary and cooperating parts of one and the same reality" (Adler, 1929b, p. 29).

This unity is to be understood also longitudinally, over time. Adler (1912) stated, "We must regard each single life manifestation as if traces of the past, the present and the future, together with the superordinated guiding idea, were present in it at the same time" (p. iv, translation modified).

To regard the individual as a unity has the practical advantage that this corresponds to the way in which one encounters another person in actual life, in friendship, in an employment situation, or in psychotherapy. No matter under what circumstances, all we have before us and all we can deal with is one individual and what he tells us or what we can see that he does. Even when he talks about his past, his present, or his future—it all comes from the present individual and is channeled through and directed from his highest nervous centers. It is all channeled through the individual and expresses his totality, his lifestyle.

2.   *Life is movement, directed toward growth and expansion.*

While a mechanism is inert and needs a driving force to set it in motion, the living organism is always in motion: heartbeat, blood circulation, breathing, brain waves (EEG). The entire metabolism consists of movements which go on without interruption from birth to death. The main dynamic problem thus is understanding not various drives or motives, but the direction and form of the ongoing movement, a view which was also advanced by George Kelly (1955, pp. 34–39). To quote from Adler:

> The most important characteristic of life is motion. . . . The chief characteristic of a movement is. . . direction and, therefore in a psychic movement, a goal. . . . Striving towards a goal. . . . we find everywhere in life. Everything grows "as if" it were striving to overcome all imperfections and achieve perfection. This urge toward perfection we call the goal of overcoming, that is, the striving to overcome. (1964, pp. 85–86)

3.   *Man is endowed with creativity and within limits is self-determined.*

Adler sees the human being as active and as initiator of actions, not as a passive S-R mechanism. Man actively interprets and uses presented stimulus material for his own purposes. In this sense everybody is creative. The criterion is the capacity to formulate, consciously or most often unconsciously, a goal of success for one's endeavors and to develop planful procedures for attaining the goal. Only in the truly feeble-minded is such purposeful creative power absent (Adler, 1964, pp. 46–47).

The presupposition is that man is not completely determined by heredity and environment, but that, once he has come into existence, he develops the capacity of influencing and creating events, as witnessed by the cultural products all around us, beginning with language, which are all human creations.

> The important thing is not what one is born with, but what use one makes of the equipment. . . . As to the influence of the environment, who would claim that the same influences are. . . responded to by any two individuals in the same way? Thus we find it necessary to assume the existence of still another force: the creative power of the individual. (Adler, 1964, pp. 86–87)

The individual's uniqueness ultimately rests in this creative power. Objective biological and social conditions, past and present, provide probabilities, opportunities, and limitations. But they are not directly causal factors in the individual. These are the individual's self-determined goals and purposes.

4.   Human movement is guided by subjective goals.

Adler's basic disagreement with Freud was over his mechanistic and zoomorphic approach to human dynamics. Adler found that many psychologists, like Freud, "present their dogmas disguised in mechanistic or physical similes....a pump handle...a magnet...a sadly harassed animal struggling for the satisfaction of its elementary needs" (1956, p. 92). But human dynamics can be adequately presented and approached only if we make central the fact that man is guided in his actions by his future as he anticipates it and as he wants to effect it. Thus Adler's dynamics became one of final causes. Adler expressed his position most forcefully in the following:

> The most important question of the healthy and the diseased mental life is not whence? but, whither? Only when we know the effective, direction-giving goal of a person may we try to understand his movements...In this whither? the cause is contained. (1956, p. 91)
> Individual Psychology insists on the indispensability of finalism for the understanding of all psychological phenomena. Causes, powers, instincts, impulses, and the like cannot serve as explanatory principles. The final goal alone can. Experiences, traumata, sexual development mechanisms cannot yield an explanation, but the perspective in which these are regarded...which subordinates all life to the final goal, can do so. (1956, p. 92)

5.   Human dynamics involve a goal and a starting point.

Adler's original dynamic conception was: (1) Inferiority feelings, (2) Goal of superiority, (3) Compensatory movement,—a *bipolar*, dialectical conception, with compensation being an effort to resolve the antithesis. When Adler (Adler & Furtmüller, 1914) soon afterward introduced the concept of "masculine protest," he specified these three factors as follows: "(a) traits evaluated as feminine, (b) wanting to be a real man, (c) compromise formation between *a* and *b*" (p. 90).

Adler gave up the concept of drive in favor of "masculine protest" and striving, because he did not want to express himself in terms of a mechanistic natural science, but rather in social science terms. *Drive* is a mechanistic concept: machines are driven, have drives (overdrives, drive shafts, etc.). But *protest*, as well as *striving*, are human concepts; machines neither protest nor strive.

Typical for a mechanistic concept, a drive is *unipolar*, that is, it is simply an applied force and nothing else. It is a *demonstrative*, positivistic conception. On the other hand, a protest is a solemn declaration of opinion, usually of dissent or objection, although it may also be an assertion. It is a *bipolar, dialectical* conception regarding which Rychlak (1968) states: "Dialectical terminology presents us with the *most accurate* picture of the fundamental human condition" (p. 255). Instead of "human condition," we would say "how man operates." While Adler soon gave up the broad

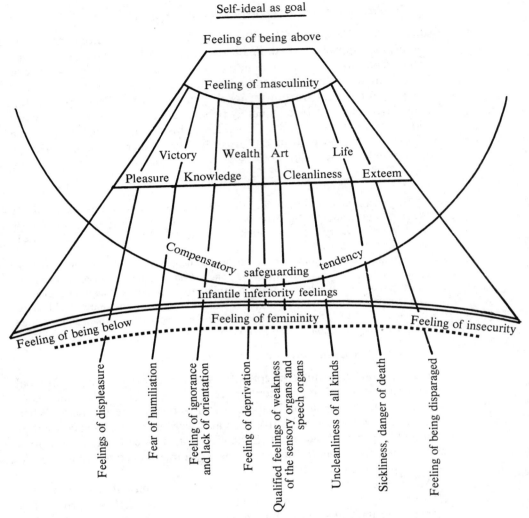

FIGURE 3–1. THE INFERIORITY-SUPERIORITY DYNAMICS

usage of the terms *feminine, masculine,* and *masculine protest,* he retained the dialectical structure and meaning.

This dynamic is expressed by Adler particularly well in the following, where it is also tied in with the concept of the past and the future.

> The future is tied up with our striving and with our goal, while the past represents the state of inferiority or inadequacy which we are trying to overcome. This is why...we should not be astonished if in the cases where we see an inferiority complex we find a superiority complex more or less hidden. On the

other hand, if we inquire into a superiority complex....we can always find a more or less hidden inferiority complex....If we look at things this way, it takes away the apparent paradox of two contradictory tendencies...existing in the same individual....The striving for superiority and the feeling of inferiority are naturally complementary. We should not strive to be superior and to succeed if we did not feel a certain lack in our present condition....The striving for superiority never ceases. It constitutes in fact the mind, the psyche of the individual. (1929c, pp. 27–28)

The naming of the two poles—inferiority feeling and superiority—is, however, meant to convey a more general concept. Adler (1912) illustrated this in the diagram shown in Figure 3–1, which he described as "a preliminary, certainly incomplete schema which corresponds more to the psyche of the neurotic which is given more to abstractions, than to the structure of the sound psyche" (p. 73, translation modified).

It is instructive to tabulate the pairs of opposites given in this diagram, to render a more complete picture of what Adler understood by his bipolar dynamics. Table 3–1 is arranged in the order in which the terms appear in Figure 3–1, starting at the bottom and going from left to right.

Over the years Adler found still other names to describe the general aspired goal of people, such as striving to be a real man, striving for power, or striving for a goal of superiority, success, perfection, or completion—all as subjectively understood. Superiority was the most frequently used description. "It runs parallel to physical growth and is an intrinsic necessity of life itself....All our functions follow its direction. They strive for conquest, security, increase, either in the right or in the wrong direction" (Adler, 1956, p. 103).

TABLE 3–1. ADLER'S DYNAMIC PAIRS OF OPPOSITES

Starting point	*Goal point*
Feelings of:	*Feelings of:*
Displeasure	Pleasure
Humiliation	Victory
Ignorance	Knowledge
Deprivation	Wealth
Weakness of sensory organs and of speech	Art
Uncleanliness	Cleanliness
Sickliness, mortal danger	Life
Disparagement	Esteem
Being below	Being above
Femininity (stereotype)	Masculinity
Insecurity	Safeguards
Infantile inferiority	Self-ideal

Since the striving is so often in the wrong direction, that is, without social interest (see below), the terms *power or superiority* have generally acquired the meaning of power or superiority over others, and the neutral meanings of these terms, such as mastery, competence, and superiority over difficulties in general, have been mostly forgotten. This being the case, we prefer Adler's neutral designation of the two poles as simply minus and plus, as in,

> The impetus from minus to plus never ends....The history of the human race points in the same direction....All [functions] betoken the essence of this eternal melody....Even if anyone wanted to escape...he would still find himself in the general system, striving upward from below. This not only states a fundamental category of thought, a thought construct, but what is more, it represents the fundamental fact of our life. (Adler, 1956, p. 103)

The table of opposites (Table 3-1) indicates some of the particular concrete contents which the minus-to-plus dynamics may take on.

Maintenance

6. *Man lives inextricably in a social world.*

In a holistic theory such as Adler's, man is seen not only as a whole but also as a part of larger wholes. A unified organism, he is also part of social organizations—his family, community, humanity—in the larger context in which he lives. In other words, man as a system is also part of larger systems.

Adler opposed Freud's argument that society is based on individual repression with the question: Which came first, the individual or society? After all, society is formed by individuals, and the individual is unthinkable without cooperation among individuals. The concrete reality is the existence of individuals, while society is an abstraction. The culture into which we are born is the precipitate of the creativity, the contribution, the work of countless thousands of individuals just like ourselves, over thousands of years, all striving from a minus to a plus situation, thus enabling human progress.

The outstanding example of the unity of the individual and the social world is language. On this point Adler (1956) says: "Language...a miracle which distinguishes man from all other creatures...reckons with the social life of man, is its product and, at the same time, its cement." (p. 130). Only by the acquisition of language through social interaction does the growing infant become a person. The self or the lifestyle develops as the individual acquires the ability to communicate and to form concepts with the aid of language.

7. *The important life problems—human relations, sex,*
    occupation—are social problems.

The important problems of human beings are not drive satisfaction. Drives
do not exist to any degree of purity in human beings. They become soon
merged with cultural conceptions and regulations, and the individual's own
ideas as to how a specific need should be met to satisfy his striving for success. Take, for example, hunger. There is an infinite variety of ways, quantitatively and qualitatively, in which various cultures and individuals have
met this need. These arbitrary ways of satisfying hunger become so compelling that they appear to the individual as the only natural and correct way.
The satisfaction of hunger becomes socially and individually determined.

The sexual problem is not so important from the viewpoint of the
satisfaction of a physiological need which, after all, can be met by masturbation. It becomes a great problem precisely because it is additionally and
most importantly a social problem: the situation of two people of different
sexes intimately living and working together demands greater cooperation
than almost any other situation. The successful solution of this problem is
not only of concern for the two individuals involved directly, but through
the procreative function it becomes of general social concern. The sexual
problem is posited by nature through the phenomenon of sexual dimor-
phism, since the species is created in two sexes.

Occupation is set as a problem by the fact that we have to gain our
livelihood on this earth, and it has become an immensely social problem
through the phenomenon of the division of labor.

Adler (1956) describes the general social problem as a continuous necessity "to reckon with others, to adopt ourselves to others, and to interest
ourselves in them" (p. 132). Finally, these three problems are interrelated.
"None...can be solved separately. Each demands a successful approach to
the other two" (p. 131).

8. *Social interest is an aptitude which must be consciously developed.*

Every system of psychology must deal with the fact that the individual lives
in society, is socialized, as well as the problem of human nature in relation
to society. Asch (1952, pp. 324–349) has shown that there are essentially
three views possible about this relationship.

The first view is that man is, by his original nature, entirely selfish. These
selfish tendencies are opposed by society, so that intrinsically a state of conflict exists between individual and society. A favorable resolution requires
repression of the primary tendencies and their sublimation into secondary,
socially acceptable tendencies. Asch calls this the "'private profit' notion of
social relations" (p. 326): The individual engages in social action to be better able to pursue his individual ends.

This is the original behavioristic and Freudian view. Miller and Dollard

(1941) considered social interests a "facade behind wh h the functions of the underlying innate drives are hidden" (p. 14). F ud (1921) stated: "What appears...in the shape of *Gemeingeist, espr de corps*, group spirit, etc., does not belie its derivation from wh t was originally envy....Social justice means that we deny ourselves many things so that others may have to do without them as well" (pp. 87–88).

While from the start Adler did not accept Freud's *concept* of repression, he nevertheless at first expressed himself similarly as far as *structure* was concerned. Considering at that time that inferior organs have important dynamic attributes, Adler (1907) stated that the inferior organ "has to bow under *the yoke of civilization*....In this process, organic instincts are changed, ennobled, psychically molded, and often transformed to their polar opposites—occurrences which are grouped by Freud as 'organic repression'" (p. 57). This position was, of course, completely given up by Adler, although he never renounced it specifically.

The second possible view is that man harbors within himself both innate selfish and social drives whose dominance alternates, depending on the circumstances. Charles Darwin, William McDougall, and W. Trotter are the representatives of such a theory. Man would be in conflict with himself, a struggle between bad and good, the prototype of the dual personality. This view is today quite outdated.

Adler accepted this view briefly in a second stage of his development, writing then of a guiding fiction "of overcoming others" and of a counterfiction which "forces considerations upon the guiding fiction, takes social and ethical demands of the future in account....The harmony of these two fictions...is the sign of mental health" (1956, pp. 143–144). In the same vein he wrote somewhat later, "An overstimulated striving for power either finds its limits in the demands of society and in the admonitions of social interest, which is physiologically and socially founded,...or goes astray" (1956, p. 144). He also spoke of a "blending of social interest with the striving for personal superiority" (1956, pp. 144–145).

The third view, rejecting the first two, leaves man with a unitary dynamic force toward growth plus a positive interest in interacting with the surrounding world, a social interest. This view is shared with Adler by the Gestalt psychologist Solomon Asch. In Asch's (1952) version,

> Social tendencies are an expression of our most basic orientation to the world....We seek the company of others for the same general reason that we seek for the company of things, because we strive to relate ourselves meaningfully to the surroundings. Social interest is an intrinsic part of our extending interest in the surroundings. (p. 334)

Whereas for Asch social interest is apparently wholly innate, in Adler's (1956) final formulation, "Social interest is not inborn, but is an innate potentiality which has to be consciously developed'' (p. 134). By this formulation Adler accomplished several things:

1. The assumption of an innate positive factor for social living is straightforward and logical, considering that all culture has been created by people spontaneously interacting and cooperating with one another.
2. By conceiving of the social factor initially as a potentiality or aptitude, Adler took it out of the dynamic or conative realm and into the cognitive realm. This is required by an organismic, holistic theory which can recognize only one dynamic force, certainly no conflict among opposing forces.
3. By saying the social disposition must be trained, Adler could account for the observation that under unfavorable conditions it is most often underdeveloped.

Additionally, as we shall see below, social interest is characterized by its usefulness. Usefulness in turn is defined by Adler (1929b) as ''in the interests of mankind generally'' (p. 78). Thus, social interest actually means not merely an interest in others, but an *interest in the interests of others*. This distinction is important because the first could be merely for the sake of exploiting others, as a slaveholder may be interested in his slaves or a confidence man in his prey. This is also how Ralph Barton Perry (1954) defined social interest; he wrote that it is an ''interest of one person in the interest or interests of a second person'' (p. 81), the crucial part being that we are not merely interested ''in a second individual where [his] interests are disregarded'' (p. 81). The second person can, of course, be extended into a group and the whole of society.

The original term for social interest, *Gemeinschaftsgefühl*, has offered difficulties to the translators. The following translations have been used: social feeling, community feeling, communal feeling, fellow feeling, sense of solidarity, social sense, communal intuition, community interest, and, finally, social interest. Some have thought the term cannot be translated.

But the difficulty is with the term itself—in any language. It has, in any language, two components: *interest*, referring to a psychological process and its development; and *social*, referring to objects in the outside world toward which the process is directed. The difficulty is that both components denote entire dimensions rather than single referents. Under the next two assertions—based on Ansbacher (1965b, 1968)—we aim to clarify these dimensions and thereby to clarify the meaning of the term.

9. *The social interest concept comprises various psychological processes.*

Adler refers to three different processes which can be arranged into three developmental steps in forming the social interest concept.

1. *Aptitude.* Social interest is an assumed aptitude for cooperation and social living which can be developed through training.
2. *Ability.* When this aptitude has been developed it will find expression in objective abilities or skills of cooperating and contributing, as well as in understanding others and empathizing with them.
3. *Secondary dynamic characteristics.* The developed social aptitude is likely to acquire secondary dynamic characteristics, as abilities generally may do in the form of attitudes and interests. In this form social interest would influence the direction of the basic striving, by becoming part of the goal of success, but be no more in conflict with it than any other interest.

In Table 3-2 the term *social interest* has been analyzed according to its implied developmental sequences and corresponding attributes assigned to them by Adler. These sequences could be shown to exist also for such skills as reading or skiing: Initially aptitudes, they can be developed into skills, and can acquire secondary motivational characteristics.

10. Social interest extends in time and space.

Extension in Space. By "social" Adler refers developmentally to ever-widening circles of actual persons.

> After the mother has succeeded in connecting the child with herself, her next task is to spread his interest towards his father,...the other children of the family, to friends, relatives....She must give the child his first experience of a trustworthy fellow being and then...spread this trust and friendship until it includes the whole of our human society. (1956, p. 373)

But Adler extended the meaning of *Gemeinschaft*, the "social" in social interest, to a variety of other "objects," way beyond what one would expect. *Gemeinschaft* is not limited to the community of men but means general connectedness. Thus Adler stated that "Social interest may extend beyond these boundaries and express itself toward animals, plants, lifeless objects, or finally towards the whole cosmos" (1927a, p. 46). "Social feeling is actually a cosmic feeling, a reflection of the coherence of everything cosmic, which lives in us, which we cannot dismiss entirely, and which gives us the ability to empathize with things which lie outside our body" (1927a, p. 60, new translation). Another time Adler simply equated social interest with "being in harmony with the universe" (1964, p. 43).

Extension in Time. With the concept of social interest serving as a guiding principle in making choices, the ultimate criterion is an ideal society of the future. By the *community* in "community feeling" Adler did not mean "a

TABLE 3–2. ANALYSIS OF TERM *SOCIAL INTEREST* **ACCORDING TO IMPLIED DEVELOPMENTAL STEPS, AND CORRESPONDING ATTRIBUTES**

Developmental Steps	*Corresponding Attributes**
1. Aptitude	Innate potentiality or substratum of social interest (p. 134), for cooperation (p. 135), for contact feeling (p. 295)
2. Ability	
a. Behaviorally	Ability to cooperate (p. 136), relating to others in a useful way (p. 139), contributing to common welfare (p. 155), behaving as part of mankind (p. 156), true compensation for all weaknesses (p. 154)
b. Intellectually	Understanding others (p. 137), empathy (p. 136), reason (p. 149), common sense v. private intelligence (p. 149)
3. Secondary dynamic characteristics	
a. Attitudinally	Evaluative attitude toward life (p. 185), of harmony with the universe (p. 136), feeling at home on this earth (pp. 136 & 155), identification with others (p. 136), feeling of belongingness (p. 138)
b. Motivationally	Interest in others (p. 140), interest in community *sub specie aeternitatis* (p. 142), striving for an ideal community (p. 142), making spontaneous social effort (p. 134)†

*Attributes assigned to developmental steps in social interest by Adler (1956). Page numbers refer to this source.

†These last attributes sharply distinguish social interest from social conformity. They allow for the striving for general betterment which implies changing existing norms rather than conforming to them. Mere conformity "would be nothing other than an exploitation of the accomplishments of the striving of others" (Adler, 1956, p. 107).

private circle of our time, or a larger circle which one should join."

Social interest means...*feeling with the whole, sub specie aeternitatis,* under the aspect of eternity. It means a striving for a form of community...as it could be thought of if mankind had reached the goal of perfection. It is never a present-day community or society, nor a political or religious form. Rather the goal...would have to be a goal which signifies the ideal community of all humanity, the ultimate fulfillment of evolution. (1964, pp. 34-35)

This consideration removes behavior imbued with social interest from mere conformity, or mere "adjustment" to a presently existing group and present standards. Such an adjustment would actually freeze the evolution, the progress, the becoming. It would limit the individual, whereas social interest liberates him from the inadequacies of the present society in his efforts for a better society of the future.

"An adaptation to immediate reality," on the contrary, "would be nothing other than an exploitation of the accomplishments of the striving of others, as the picture of the world of the pampered child demands" (Adler, 1956, p. 107). But the great cooperation and social culture which man needs demand "spontaneous social effort" (Adler, 1929b, p. 31).

Through extension into the future, the concept of social interest not only provides a place for the independent spirit, the nonconformist who contributes to the advancement of mankind; it also makes him the ideally normal man. The criterion is whether the nonconformity is in the ultimate interest of mankind, or whether it is merely a rebellion for personal, private reasons.

11. Social interest is the criterion of mental health.

For Adler the degree of social interest was "the main characteristic of each person" and "involved in all his actions" (1937, p. 774). Furthermore, all desirable traits were subordinated to social interest and nearly all undesirable traits to its lack. Adler said:

> It is almost impossible to exaggerate the value of an increase in social feeling. The mind improves, for intelligence is a communal function. The feeling of worth and value is heightened, giving courage and an optimistic view, and there is a sense of acquiescence in the common advantages and drawbacks of our lot. The individual feels at home in life and feels his existence to be worthwhile just so far as he is useful to others and is overcoming common, instead of private, feelings of inferiority. Not only the ethical nature, but the right attitude in aesthetics, the best understanding of the beautiful and the ugly, will always be founded upon the truest social feeling. (1956, p. 155)

Thus social interest becomes Adler's criterion for mental health. "Social interest is the barometer of the child's normality. The criterion which needs to be watched...is the degree of social interest which the child or the individual manifests" (1956, p. 154).

The idea of social interest and its relationship to mental health, especially in the advancing age, had been expressed by John Stuart Mill, with whom Adler had also other important ideas in common (see Ansbacher, 1968, p. 140 n.). But Adler was not aware of any of this. Mill (1863) wrote:

> When people who are tolerably fortunate in their outward lot do not find in life sufficient enjoyment to make it valuable to them, the cause generally is, caring for nobody but themselves. To those who have neither public nor private affections, the excitements of life are much curtailed, and in any case dwindle in value as the time approaches when all selfish interests must be terminated by death: while those who leave after them objects of personal affection, and especially those who have also cultivated a *fellow-feeling with the collective interests of*

mankind, retain as lively an interest in life on the eve of death as in the vigor of youth and health. (pp. 16–17; italics ours)

12.   *Social interest is operationally defined as social usefulness.*

Adler (1927b) introduced the concept of social usefulness with the comment:

> A person...who does not have a true social feeling...stops, hesitates, fights, escapes, when he comes in a new situation such as kindergarten, school, marriage, friendship. All these are social situations and require social feeling. It is this type that become the criminals, problem children, neurotics and suicides. Striving for superiority [like everybody] and lacking in courage [defined as activity plus social feeling or social interest] they turn from the useful to the useless side. (p. 119)

This was illustrated by Adler with an informal diagram similar to Fig. 3-2.

It is noteworthy that socially useless behavior is described in terms of making a choice in the face of a critical situation, a quite operational definition. In explanation of the choice, Adler asserted:

> There is only one reason for an individual to sidestep to the useless side: the fear of a defeat on the useful side....Since all problems of life require a well-developed social interest and the patient is lacking this in his style of life, he is in a certain sense right to make a detour. (1956, pp. 157–159)

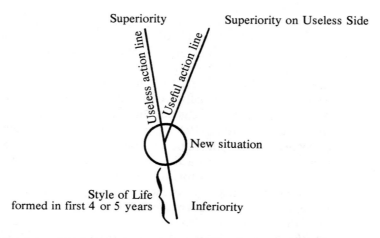

FIGURE 3–2.   DEVIATING TO THE USELESS SIDE IN FACE OF A NEW SITUATION

At the same time Adler published a much more sophisticated version of this diagram, stating that it comprised his entire system. "More than twenty years of work...are reflected in it" (1956, p. 157). This diagram is shown in Fig. 3–3, where the lines and loops represent movements of individuals; the circles, life problems. The small circles stand for children's preliminary problems—friendship, school, relationship to the other sex. The larger circles stand for the three life problems of adulthood—social relations, occupation, and love and marriage. The loops below the small circles stand for turning away from the respective problems and seeking distance. This will occur when the individual, due to underdeveloped social interest, is unprepared for meeting the problem. From lack of courage he will detour and continue his striving on the socially useless side. The horizontal lines from left to right indicate the detouring at the adult level. The striving on the left side is for a commonly useful goal of perfection; that on the right side, for an exaggerated private goal of personal superiority. Such persons are the failures in life.

Artists were for Adler a special case of people who, while retreating from life problems, eventually become eminently useful for humanity through their work. Scholarly activity could probably also be included here.

But no one's choices are always on one side or the other. Hence, in a concrete case it is decisive where a person stands on balance: "The path of the neurotic, etc., and of the problem child runs on both sides of life, although in different degrees" (Adler 1929a, p. 123). This is equally true for the normal person.

13. *The consequences of one's behavior is what counts.*

To serve as a criterion of mental health in a given case, social interest must be empirically validated. Adler's psychology is not only subjective or phenomenological; it is also pragmatic and empirical. When there is a discrepancy between word and deed, the latter counts. Adler held, with the Bible and William James: "By their fruits ye shall know them" (1964, p. 64). Accordingly, socially useful action, that is, action that others may recognize as being in the general interest, is more important than professed social interest. Adler (1926) expressed this very strongly in stating: "It is quite insignificant what a person thinks, feels, or wants by his performance. Only the accord of his action with the requirements of evolution can vindicate him. He creates for the community and for posterity, even if in so doing he considers only his own well-being" (pp. 363–364). Adler (1929c) expressed the same thought again in the following: "The normal man is an individual who lives in society and whose mode of life is so adapted that, *whether he wants it or not*, society derives a certain advantage from his work" (p. 41, italics added).

The neurotic, on the other hand, while he "expects a contribution from the group in which he lives" (Adler, 1956, p. 114), often has the most lofty

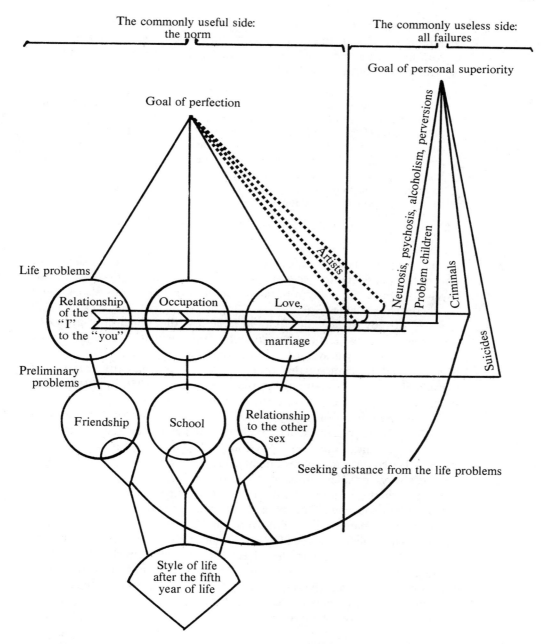

The commonly useful side:
the norm

The commonly useless side:
all failures

Goal of personal superiority

Goal of perfection

Life problems

Relationship of the "I" to the "you"

Occupation

Love, marriage

Artists

Neurosis, psychosis, alcoholism, perversions

Problem children

Criminals

Suicides

Preliminary problems

Friendship

School

Relationship to the other sex

Seeking distance from the life problems

Style of life after the fifth year of life

FIGURE 3–3. OUTLINE OF THE DYNAMICS OF THE NORM AND OF THE FAILURES

After a figure by Kurt A. Adler

social and ethical ideals and daydreams, which may be considered a means of gaining feelings of superiority over others. Adler warned: "We must not be confused by the fact that some neurotics seem to be benevolent and wish to reform the whole world" (1964, p. 60).

> The really important difference of conduct is...that of usefulness and uselessness. By useful I mean in the interests of mankind generally. The most sensible estimate of the value of any activity is its helpfulness to all mankind, present and future, a criterion that applies not only to that which subserves the immediate preservation of life, but also to higher activities such as religion, science, and art. It is true that we cannot always decide what is strictly worth while from this point of view. But [the more] we are guided by the impulse to act usefully...the nearer we approach to true perception. (Adler, 1929b, p. 78)

14. *Activity is, after social interest, the second most important personality trait.*

As the physicist describes movement it involves two variables—space (or direction, and time (or speed), which depends on energy. When the psychologist uses the concept of movement he should logically also account for these two variables.

Adler acknowledged the first variable by the dimension of social usefulness-social uselessness, the *direction* of movement. "As in physics we cannot measure any movement without relating it toward another space, so in Individual Psychology this other space is the social organization of mankind and its supposedly eternal demands" (1956, p. 163). The preceding two assertions have dealt with this dimension.

The second dimension, *energy*, was acknowledged by Adler a few years later through the concept of activity. One would expect degree of activity to be related to the individual's physiological makeup. And indeed Adler notes: "Hereditary and environmental factors play a part" (1964, p. 60). But, as always in Adler, this is modified by the personality, the style of life. It is not a matter of straight causality, but of "probability."

To explain what he means by activity, Adler stated, "A child who runs away from his parents, or a boy who starts a fight in the street, must be credited with a higher degree of activity than a child who likes to sit at home and read a book" (1964, p. 60). Degree of activity is relatively constant throughout life, "corresponding entirely to the constancy of the individual law of movement, i.e., the style of life" (p. 60). Adler believed the recognition of this second personality dimension "opens an entirely new and valuable perspective for psychiatric treatment, education, and prophylaxis" (p. 61).

15. *Social interest and activity imply a two-dimensional personality theory with a fourfold typology.*

With the two movement variables—social interest or usefulness, and activity—Adler advanced a two-dimensional theory of personality structure. Such a conception leads to four personality types when the two dimensions are dichotomized. Adler described the four personality types as follows:

> The first type consists of individuals whose approach to reality shows...a more or less dominant or "ruling" attitude (the "ruling" type)....
>
> A second type—surely the most frequent—expects everything from others and leans on others. I might call it the "getting" type.
>
> A third type is inclined to feel successful by avoiding the solution of problems,...tries to "side-step" problems in an effort thereby to avoid defeat (the "avoiding" type).
>
> The fourth type struggles, to a greater or lesser degree, for a solution of these problems in a way which is useful to others. (1964, p. 68).

As Adler did not name this type we shall name it—the socially useful type. Adler continues:

> In the fourth type...we can always find a certain amount of activity...used for the benefit of others....The first type also has activity, but not enough social interest...this type acts in an unsocial way....They become delinquents, tyrants, sadists....To this type also belong suicides, drug addicts, and alcoholics, whose lesser degree of activity causes them to attack others indirectly. They make attacks upon themselves to hurt others. The second and third types shown even less activity and not much social interest....Their shock results are neuroses and psychoses. (1964, p. 69-70)

This description led us to construct a fourfold table, the results of which are shown in Table 3-3. Only Adler's second, the "getting" type, does not quite fit. But then Adler had the least to say about this type, although he described it as "surely the most frequent."

The process of constructing this table gave rise to two syntheses within Adler's writings which are now incorporated in the table.

1. *The four temperaments.* A few years before describing his activity-social interest typology, Adler discussed the four temperaments of Hippocrates (1956, pp. 169-171). These are so similar in behavioral content to the four types that we have added them—the sanguine matching the socially useful type; the choleric, the ruling type; the melancholic, the avoiding type; and the phlegmatic, the getting or learning type.

2. *Opinion of the self and the world.* Individual Psychology is behavioral (objective), as well as phenomenological (subjective). The dimensions of activity and social usefulness are objective, with the first referring to the individual and the second to his objective relationship to the world around him. But Adler expressed also a purely phenomenological conception of these two dimensions, "the individual's opinion of himself and of the en-

TABLE 3-3.   SOCIAL INTEREST—ACTIVITY TYPOLOGY

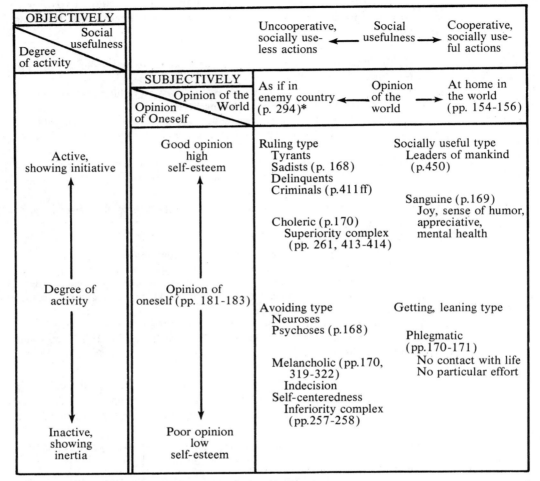

Note: Page references are to Adler (1956).

vironment with which he has to cope'' (1964, p. 24). Connected with a person's law of movement is a specific apperception, ''the way in which man looks at himself and the external world'' (Adler, 1956, p. 182). ''For me there can be no doubt that everyone conducts himself in life from the very beginning of his action as if he had a definite opinion of his strength and his abilities and a clear conception of the difficulty or ease of a problem at hand'' (1956, p. 182), ''without his understanding it or giving himself an account of it'' (1956, p. 195).

In Table 3–3 we have plotted ''opinion of oneself'' along with ''degree of activity'' on the left side of the table, the *y* axis, and ''opinion of the world'' and ''social usefulness'' across the top, the *x* axis.

Adler frequently indicated that activity and opinion of oneself are positively related, as is shown in Table 3–3. Criminals are active and display a good opinion of themselves, "a cheap superiority complex" (1956, pp. 413–414). At the other extreme, "Every neurotic has an inferiority complex" (1956, p. 257) and is also low in activity.

Regarding social usefulness and opinion of the world reflecting one another, we can cite: "Feeling-at-home is an immediate part of social interest" (Adler, 1956, p. 155), which in turn is evaluated by social usefulness. Among the requirements of a good leader are "a strongly developed social interest" and "an optimistic outlook" (1956, p. 450). On the other hand, the criminals who are active on "the useless side of life" are in conflict with what they consider "this hostile world" (1956, p. 413). In melancholia, or depression in more modern language, Adler sees an "aggressive nature" and a perception that "the preponderant majority of men are hostile" (1956, p. 319). These examples may suffice to make the point.

16. All human functions serve the individual's "law of movement," his lifestyle.

The unit to be studied in psychology is the individual person and his way of living. All the general processes one can observe among people, such as drives, emotions, and cultural experiences, must be understood as subordinated to the individual's unique organization, "his law of movement," his style of life. Upon entering life, a child

> ...is more or less dependent on his own creative power and ability to divine a path....Thus he arrives at his law of movement which aids him after a certain amount of training to attain a style of life, in accordance with which we see the individual thinking, feeling, and acting throughout his whole life. (Adler, 1956, pp. 187–188)

Organic as well as psychological functions are subordinated to the style of life, although both were originally factors in its formation.

> The organic functions are dominated by the style of life. This is notably the case with the lungs, the heart, the stomach, the organs of excretion and the sexual organs. The disturbance of these functions expresses the direction which an individual is taking to attain his goal. I have called these disturbances the organ dialect, or organ jargon, since the organs are revealing in their own most expressive language the intention of the individual totality. (Adler, 1956, p. 156)
> The dialect of the sexual organs is especially expressive. (Adler, 1956, p. 156)
> My questioners often...believe that the sexual impulse is the central motive....Our experience is that the sexual components cannot even be correctly estimated except in relation to the individual's style of life. (Adler, 1956, p. 46)
> We are far from disputing that every mental and bodily function is necessarily conditioned by inherited material, but what we see in all psychic activity is the *use which is made* of this material to attain a certain goal. (Adler, 1956, p. 30)

Such a functional dynamic psychology Adler called "psychology of use," in contrast to a "psychology of possession." In the former all functions as well as all hereditary and environmental influences become "building blocks" for the lifestyle.

17. *Developmental conditions provide probabilities for personality formation.*

A holistic theory of personality has little use for developmental stages, in that they artificially divide the individual life cycle into discrete steps, raising self-fulfilling expectations for the various stages as described. Instead, personality, that is the lifestyle, is seen by Adler (1929b) as emerging gradually, uniquely, and as a whole: "In the first four or five years the child builds up its own prototype...and lays the irrevocable foundation of his style of life" (p. 31). Since Adler stresses man's "free creative power," all influences on the child function only as probabilities, not as "causes."

The great positive factor is a mother, or her equivalent, who fills "the two-fold function of motherhood: to give the child the most complete possible experience of human fellowship, and then to widen it into a life-attitude towards others" (Adler, 1956, p. 372).

Three negative factors threatening the child's development of self-esteem and social interest are:

1. *Organ inferiorities and childhood diseases.* "Such children may easily become self-centered, lose hope of playing a useful part in our common life, and consider themselves humiliated by the world" (Adler, 1956, p. 368).
2. *Pampering.* A pampered child "has been trained to receive without giving.... He has lost his independence and does not know that he can do things for himself" (Adler, 1956, p. 369). His social interest and ultimately his self-esteem are low, which combination makes him prone to failure.
3. *Neglect.* The neglected, hated, or unwanted child "has found society cold to him.... He will be suspicious of others and unable to trust himself.... Many failures in life come from orphans or illegitimate children" (Adler, 1956, pp. 370–371). Such a child strives "to escape and to get at a safe distance from others" (Adler, 1929b, p. 36).

Under all three of these circumstances, the child is more likely to develop a "pampered style of life" (Adler, 1956, pp. 241–242), the actual predisposing condition for failure in life. It is characterized by expecting from others, pressing them into one's service, evading responsibility, blaming circumstances for one's shortcomings, while actually feeling incompetent and insecure. It is, however, not to be attributed to the circumstances. Rather, "the pampered style of life as a living phenomenon is the creation of the child, though its formation is frequently aided by others" (Adler, 1956, p. 242).

For other aspects of lifestyle development, the person's family constellation provides important probabilities. This will be dealt with in the Assessment section below.

APPLICATIONS

Assessment

Adler's methods of personality assessment were aimed at obtaining a conceptualization of the whole person, his lifestyle. Since personality is a unified whole, in theory any judicial sampling of behavior would suffice. Adler asserted: "We can begin wherever we choose: every expression will lead us in the same direction—towards the one motive, the one melody, around which the personality is built. We are provided with a vast store of material. Every word, thought, feeling, or gesture contributes to our understanding" (1956, p. 332). Adler and his followers developed three specific methods of lifestyle assessment: the interpretation of (1) early recollections, (2) the family constellation, and (3) dreams.

Early Recollections. It is a paradox that with a conception of man as largely self-determined and future-oriented, Adler should go into the past to ask for early recollections. The answer is that the Adlerian is not primarily interested in what happened to the individual in the recollection, but how he chose to respond to the situation which he described. The recollection itself is understood as of his choosing. Adler stated categorically:

> There are no chance memories. Out of the incalculable number of impressions which meet an individual, he chooses to remember only those which he feels, however darkly, to have a bearing on his situation. Thus his memories represent his "Story of my life"; a story he repeats to himself to warn him or comfort him, to keep him concentrated on his goal, and to prepare him by means of past experiences, so that he will meet the future with an already tested style of action. (1956, p. 351)

From this viewpoint, it is not important whether or not a given recollection corresponds to the objective facts.

Two early recollections serve as illustrations. Marilyn Monroe, the sensationally successful film star and "sex symbol," always described herself as a poor waif and a victim of circumstances. Eventually she put her career in jeopardy, after three divorces lived a lonely life, and finally committed suicide. She reported the following incident from the age of one, at her grandmother's: "I remember waking up from my nap fighting for my life.

Something was pressed against my face. It could have been a pillow. I fought with all my strength'' (Ansbacher, 1974b, p. 129).

By contrast, Betty Ford, the cheerful, outspoken wife of President Gerald Ford and the mother of an apparently happy family, reports:

> I was either 2 or 3, in my mother's arms on the front porch of our summer cottage by a lake in Michigan. A summer storm was approaching, and my mother—I can still "see" her doing this—pressed me closer to her while saying, over and over again, how nice it was going to be, how beautiful the storm was going to be. To this day I like an approaching storm and dark water and the thunder and lightning. My mother was, of course, terrified of storms, but didn't want me to be, and I'm not. (Agel, 1975)

Family Constellation. Adler (1929c) made certain inferences from a person's birth order as to how he was most likely to have reacted to his ordinal position. A firstborn is for a while like an only child and is then dethroned from that position. Thus oldest children are often conservatives, who feel that those in power should remain there. The second child, on the other hand, "wants to equal" the first. "He does not recognize power, but wants the power to change hands" (p. 91). The youngest child "is in an advantageous position since he can never be dethroned." Regarding such and many further observations on birth order, Adler, however, warned that these are only "tendencies" and that "there is no necessity about them" (p. 92).

As an aid to such investigation, Dreikurs (1967, pp. 87-94) devised an interview guide with the questions: "Who was most different from you? In what respect? Who was most like you? In what respect? What kind of child were you?" This is followed by asking the person to describe other siblings and to identify the highest and lowest ranking sibling on each of 21 attributes. If the person does not include himself in a ranking he is asked to which of the two siblings he is most similar. The attributes include intelligence, school grades, rebelliousness, pleasingness, gregariousness, to name a few. In rationale this method is similar to Kelly's (1955, pp. 219-266) Role Construct Repertory Test, although much simpler.

Dream Interpretation. Adler's method of dream interpretation differs from Freud who considered dreams a disguise for alien thoughts deeply buried in the unconscious. For Freud the dream represented a wish, while for Adler the dream was an intention, a kind of rehearsal, and so had premonitory qualities. For Adler (1956, pp. 357-365) the dream is a metaphorical expression, as in poetry, of thoughts, referring to some actual problem to be faced. The dream metaphors and metaphorical solutions are in line with the person's lifestyle and support it. Adlerian dream interpretation has been well presented by Shulman (1969).

The following account by Ansbacher (1974c, p. 802) may serve as a brief example of Adlerian interpretation. William D. Dement, dream physiologist, reported: "One subject in our laboratory in a single night ran the gamut from being with 'two hippopotamuses in a millpond' through a 'taffy pull in the Soviet Embassy' to 'hearing Handel's *Messiah* sung by a thousand-voice chorus in this beautiful cathedral,' back to 'writing at my desk.'" Dement gave this as an example of "the wildly unpredictable nature of dream content," the "fundamental determinants" of which "remain cloaked in obscurity." However, while specific dream content is unpredictable, due to the dreamer's creativity, it is not unintelligible. In the dreams described above the common denominator is bigness, strength, activity, and a pleasant feeling tone. From this we infer that the dreamer in waking life shows great activity, buoyancy, and optimism, with perhaps some grandiosity and manic traits. He is also a cultured person and interested in music. The dreams sustained his confidence and optimism for the next day's work. When this interpretation was given to Dement he replied: "The individual in question is essentially as you describe him."

Treatment

Adler's conceptualization of mental disorders followed the educational model which considers mental disorders not a disease to be cured, but rather an erroneous way of living, a mistaken lifestyle with mistaken opinions of self and the world and mistaken goals of success, all strongly connected with underdeveloped social interest. Through these mistakes the patient is a "failure" in solving his life problems. That is his disorder.

The purpose of assessment in treatment is to gain a clear conception of the patient's particular mistakes and convey this to the patient so that he may then avoid these mistakes. It is as in sport instruction. In swimming, tennis, or skiing, the pupil does not know why he is not doing better. But the instructor can see exactly the mistakes the pupil makes, in breathing, leg position, or distribution of weight. The instructor makes him aware of his mistakes so that he may avoid them and replace them by the "correct" movements. Adler's (1929b) aim was "to replace the great mistakes by small ones....Big mistakes can produce neuroses, but little mistakes a nearly normal person" (p. 62).

Psychopathology Theory.   In a general way the patient's mistake is that he is striving on the socially useless side, and in a way that makes only "private sense," contrary to "common sense" (Adler, 1956, pp. 150, 253–254). This is usually based on a high goal of personal superiority, compensating for strong inferiority feelings, which precludes the development of social interest. "The striving for personal superiority and the nondevelopment of social interest...are one and the same mistake" (Adler, 1956, pp. 240–241). In consequence, the individual will have difficulty in meeting his life's problems, which in turn makes him fear failure which would "injure his vanity and interfere with his striving for personal superiority" (Adler, 1956, pp. 293–294). This constellation is the "neurotic disposition," later called the pampered lifestyle.

The symptoms are the patient's "arrangements" to serve as excuses for not meeting his life problems, and to protect his self-esteem.

> The life plan of the neurotic demands categorically that if he fails, it should be through someone else's fault and that he should be freed from personal responsibility.... When the individual helps along with his devices, then the entire content of life is permeated by the reassuring, anesthetizing stream of the life-line which safeguards the self-esteem. (Adler, 1956, p. 271)

Adler adds the important principle, "Every neurotic is partly right" (1956, p. 334), in that he met with "traumas" and "frustrations," which can easily be construed as adverse "causes." But he is only "partly right" in that he is not obligated to construe his life in this manner. Others with similar experiences have responded differently.

An individual with a mistaken lifestyle may still go through life without coming to a crisis, as long as his circumstances are so favorable that he is spared any test. For a crisis to develop there must be such a test or a task—"the exogenous factor, the proximity of a task that demands cooperation and fellowship" (Adler, 1956, p. 297).

Individual Therapy

Four phases of Adlerian psychotherapy have been variously described. These are, however, only conceptual categories which in practice may and do freely run into one another and may also be condensed. The phases are:

1. *Establishment and maintenance of a good relationship with the patient.* The therapist presents himself as a trustworthy person and extends social interest to the patient to awaken and develop the patient's social interest. Thereby the therapist also raises the patient's self-esteem and encourages him. "Psychotherapy is an exercise in cooperation and a test of cooperation" (Adler, 1956, p. 340). To this Dreikurs (1967) adds: "Therapeutic cooperation requires an alignment of goals.... What appears as 'resistance' constitutes a discrepancy between the goals of the therapist and those of the patient" (p. 7). An important way to win the patient is to make him feel understood, whereby one also wins his respect. To maintain cooperation one must be tactful and avoid dogmatic statements. Dreikurs

offers interpretations with such phases as "Would you like me to tell you?" or "Could it be?" (p. 60).

2. *Psychological exploration.* The methods presented in the preceding section on assessment are to enable the therapist to gain an understanding of the patient's hidden and presumably erroneous goal and purposes of which the patient may be quite unaware, and thus to conceptualize the patient's lifestyle.

3. *Conveying the therapist's understanding to the patient.* This may also be called giving insight, which is accomplished through interpreting the patient's statements and actions to him. This is what Watzlawick, Weakland, and Fisch (1974) have called reframing, giving the patient a new frame of reference. As to the content of interpretation, the therapist listens dialectically; that is, he asks himself what opposite could be paired with a certain statement. This is in accord with the assumed self-deception of the patient. "While he regards one point, we must look at the other. He looks at his obstacles; we must look at his attempt to protect his fictive superiority and rescue his ambition" (Adler, 1964, p. 199). When the patient speaks of his generosity, the therapist may understand an accusation of stinginess against others. The question, "What would you do if you were well?" (Adler, 1956, p. 332) leads to the interpretation that this may be the exact activity from which the patient is excusing himself by his symptoms.

4. *Reorientation and reeducation.* This is the most important phase in psychotherapy. It uses various forms of confrontations and directives. For example, when a middle-aged man who had been in psychoanalytic treatment brought up his unresolved Oedipus complex, Adler would say: "Look here, what do you want of the old lady?" (Ansbacher, 1965b, p. 347). As mentioned, Adler was a pragmatist. Thus insight on the part of the patient is less important than change in behavior. The criterion of success of treatment is objective: "As soon as the patient can connect himself with his fellow men on an equal and cooperative footing, he is cured" (Adler, 1956, p. 347).

Group Processes and Approaches. Adlerian theory is so keyed to group process that it brings this even into individual therapy, in that "The therapist appears as the representative for the human community" (Dreikurs, 1967, p. 32), the "common sense."

Within the framework of social interest Adlerians have used any form of therapy beyond the one-to-one dyadic mode: multiple psychotherapy, family therapy, outpatient treatment and therapeutic social clubs, psychodrama and action therapy, milieu therapy, conventional group therapy, as well as educational group counseling. For references see Ansbacher (1974c, p. 804). But as Papanek (1961) pointed out, it is understood that the group "be based on healthy social values," else it would merely encourage "socially shared autisms" (p. 188).

Adler originated in his child guidance clinics a form of group approach in which children were treated before a group of observers, the children coming in with, or shortly after, their parents or teachers. The group was at first primarily a training seminar for teachers, but was soon recognized as actually facilitating therapy. By their mere presence and occasional comments, the observers embodied the common sense, as "witnesses" so to speak.

Today this type of treatment is carried on in numerous Family Education Centers. The technique, which has been described by Dreikurs, Corsini, Lowe, and Sonstegard (1959), has become particularly teachable through videotapes of counseling demonstration sessions by Dreikurs (1969, 1971).

Counseling. Any distinction between counseling and psychotherapy is quite arbitrary in Adlerian theory. Dreikurs (1967) talks about the same four phases or steps in counseling as in psychotherapy, but considers counseling "concerned mainly with the acute situation and the solution of immediate problems," while psychotherapy aims more at "a complete re-organization of the individual's life" (p. 258).

Institutional

Of the 10 applications discussed under this heading, the first 6 are practical, while the other 4 are more conceptual or theoretical. The first two, school and family, greatly outdistance the remainder as far as the number of people actually involved is concerned.

School. As early as 1931, Oskar Spiel (1962), together with Ferdinand Birnbaum, applied Adlerian principles in the classroom. The difficult child was considered to be one who himself suffers difficulties. He must be given insight into his goals and mistaken ways of achieving them and led to correct his misconceptions of himself and the world around him. Part of the method was class discussions aimed at self-government, at mutual academic aid among class members, and at understanding the reasons for misbehavior of classmates so as to encourage them and to elicit their cooperation.

Dreikurs (1957, pp. 12–17) advanced this approach by classifying children's problems according to four goals of disturbing behavior and developing ways of identifying these goals and dealing with them.

Family. Adlerian parent education is again best represented by Dreikurs (1964), in a book particularly useful for parent study groups. Averaging 14 members, such groups meet under lay leadership for about 10 sessions, discussing the book's "practical steps in a new direction" (p. viii). The spread of these groups has been phenomenal. One of the techniques recommended is the family council (Dreikurs, Gould, & Corsini, 1974). This is a deliberative body composed of all family members, meeting regularly for the purpose of arriving at a consensus on family problems. Everyone must abide by a decision once it has been reached by consensus. The functions of chairperson and secretary rotate among all family members.

Social Work. Although Adlerian psychology has not yet found its place in American social work as it has in educational guidance and parent education, it would, according to Harold Werner (1967), "provide a theoretical rationale that completely supports the traditions and beliefs of social work" (p. 16). In pre-Hitler Germany, Individual Psychology was apparently widely applied in social work. Hilde Ottenheimer (1959) explains in her review, "Since in social work we are mostly dealing with persons who have lost their community ties, the Adlerian theory was ready-made to determine the remedial measures" (p. 849).

Crime and Delinquency. Adler (1964) was particularly interested in the rehabilitation of criminals. He was, according to Ellenberger (1970), "among the great pioneers of dynamic psychiatry...the only one who wrote something on criminals from his direct experience" (p. 618). Adler hired an ex-convict as his gardener and won in him a lifelong devoted friend (Bottome, 1957, pp. 191–193; Orgler, 1963, pp. 227–239). A follower of Adler, Ernst Papanek, who was director of the Wiltwyck School for Boys, was immortalized by Claude Brown (1965, pp. 84–88, 124–128) through his description of how Papanek brought him back to a useful life.

Work, Industrial Morale, Old Age. If the striving to overcome difficulties, the striving for success, is basic, it is to be expected that, everything else being equal, people's morale would be higher when they are working than when idle. Industrial morale studies have amply confirmed this hypothesis. At the same time, according to Willard Beecher (1955), the principal job of management should be "to set up and maintain conditions that lead to *teamwork*, just as a good therapist would do...where everyone...regards all others as equal," and where "the job is our only boss" (p. 128). The mental hardship in both unemployment and old age is that the person is prevented from contributing and exercising his skills and thus feels useless and diminished in his sense of well-being.

Leadership, Group Morale. A main component of group morale is a common purpose, and a main function of the leader is to formulate the goal and give the group a sense that it can be attained. The question of the personal requirements of leadership was answered by Adler in the following:

A strongly developed social interest is the first. An optimistic outlook and sufficient self-confidence are just as necessary. The leader must be capable of quick action;...he must have ease in making contact with people; and he must possess tact so as not to frustrate the assent of others....He must, in a word, be a real human being who possesses courage and skills. In him becomes realized what other men dream about. (1956, p. 450)

Social Movements. Adler considered racial and other prejudices a form of depreciation tendency, boosting one's own self-esteem by depreciating others. Prejudice as scapegoating provides excuses for one's own inadequacies. Kenneth B. Clark (1967), well-known black psychologist, found that in his work and struggles "the most significant and persistent influence...had been the social dynamic theories of Alfred Adler" (p. 181). Frantz Fanon (1967), a black revolutionary who had studied psychiatry, believed that "Adler will help us to understand the conception of the world held by the man of color" (p. 62).

The prejudice of woman's inferiority takes the same form as other prejudices. Adler (Adler & Furtmüller, 1914) strongly advocated equal rights of the sexes, deploring masculine supremacy as "one of the deepest wounds of our social life" (p. 133). Equality must, however, be "fitted into the natural scheme of things" (Adler, 1929c, p. 67). *Machismo* has for some time been explained in Adlerian terms (Batt, 1969; Ramos, 1962).

Religion. For Adler the idea of God is a concretization of a goal of perfection and greatness in which an entire culture can share. Adler contended that "an unpremised mechanistic position" is "an illusion, inasmuch as it is without goal and direction,...after all, the essence of life" (1956, p. 461). In this respect he considered the religious view far ahead, pointing out, however, that "God cannot be proven scientifically," but "is a gift of faith." The applicability of Adlerian theory to religious concerns was the object of a small symposium (Ansbacher, 1971c).

Literary Criticism. "Every individual," Adler stated, "represents both a unity of personality and the individual fashioning of that unity....But as an artist...he is...an imperfect human being" (1956, p. 177). If real and fictional persons are artistic creations, they both can be similarly approached. The task of Adlerian literary criticism is to understand a given character in his unique style of life, including his goal of success, through seeking the coherence of all his thinking and acting. Adler (1920b) admired the writer's synthesis, "whereas analysis profanes and desecrates" (p. 268, translation modified), and he validated his own thinking against great literary works. Some Adlerian studies have dealt with Camus (Rom, 1960); *Hamlet* (Mairet, 1969); Somerset Maugham, (Burt, 1970); and *The Catcher in the Rye* (Irving, 1976). The numerous studies of an earlier period are included in Kiell (1963) and Mosak and Mosak (1975).

Psychohistory and Psychobiography. One may well say with Jacob Bronowski that all of man's history is a record of the *Ascent of Man*, revealing his incessant striving from a minus to a plus situation, for competence, overcoming difficulties, power. Cruelties were in every case based on the misapplication of power in the interest of personal, ethnic, or class superiority over others; blessings, on its application in the common, the social interest. Although Freudian ideas still dominate psychohistory, as they do literary criticism, the historian Mazlish (1974) notes that since the work of Harold D. Lasswell "Adler's influence...has continued to inspire political scientists and, to a lesser degree, historians as well" (p. 1037). Mazlish refers to the "exemplary" study of Woodrow Wilson by Alexander L. and Juliette George (1956). According to A. L. George (1968), Lasswell's Adlerian-based hypothesis, "power...to overcome low estimates of the self," has had some influence on five studies of political leadership, and "the fruitfulness of Adler's theories...is now widely recognized" (p. 29). Youngdale (1975) presented a "new perspective" on American populism which is "closely linked with...the outlook of Alfred Adler" (p. 45), who stresses "the goal-directed and social quality of human life" (p. 13). Adler himself wrote "On the psychology of Marxism," "Danton, Marat, Robespierre," and gave an interview on Mussolini (Adler, 1964, pp. 313, 405, 320). Other studies are on the Schreber case (Shulman, 1959), the assassins of American presidents (Chaplin, 1970), Ben Franklin (McLaughlin and Ansbacher, 1971), Hitler (Brink, 1975), and Marilyn Monroe (Ansbacher, 1974b, pp. 124–138).

Self

Adler constructed his theory with the intent that every human being should be able to understand it and profit by it. With this in mind he clad his theory mostly in everyday language and selected, from among still-debated basic issues regarding the nature of man, those alternatives that hold the greater promise for man. Such a theory should certainly be suited for self-help and self-improvement of the more "normal" person, although the more neurotic would still require outside help. The large and continuous sale of Adler's *Understanding Human Nature* (1927a), translated in some dozen languages, and others of his books would seem to reflect this self-help aspect.

Self-application among College Students. Some specific information as to what a person may find useful in Adler comes from an informal inquiry among a class of undergraduate students, conducted some time ago by the present writer. The students had taken a course entitled "Personality," with Adler (1956) as text. After the final examination the students ($N = 60$) were asked to write on: "What have you learned in this course which should be of direct help to you in daily life?'' They were assured that they would not be graded on their replies. Three basic assumptions of the theory emerged as particularly helpful: (*a*) human self-determination, (*b*) goal orientation, and (*c*) innate capacity for social interest. These were helpful in supporting existing optimistic views, in providing new encouragement, and in giving meaning to life. A sundry category is made up of such statements as:

> I can attempt to avoid...oversensitivity.
> Striving on the useful side will, I hope, guide many of my actions.
> I hope to employ the principle that more interest in the partner than the self is the only way to have a happy marriage.
> I will understand my role as a teacher more fully...try to prevent any child from being discouraged.

An Early Self-Help Group.   Rühle-Gerstel (1930) recognized three preconditions of therapy: a need for help, insight, and encouragement. Insight may be attained through lectures and books, but courage to change is achieved very rarely by oneself. Here a study group can take the place of the therapist. She reported on a study group which, under her tutelage, read books by Adler and from which she was often absent months at a time. In this group, encouragement was provided in the following ways: "Everybody came to experience his mistakes as average, without a particularly tragic note.... He also experienced much comradeship and sincere effort on his behalf and thereby learned to extend these toward others" (p. 60). "Thus they learned...gradually to laugh at themselves and like themselves. They found the right method not to be hard toward themselves nor to pity themselves, but to be pleasant, helpful and considerate" (p. 61).

Present-Day Study Groups.   The numerous study groups mentioned in the preceding section generally meet under lay leadership, as noted. Thus they can rightfully be noted also in the present section on self-help.

VALIDATION

Three papers have reviewed validation of Adlerian theories. Ansbacher (1947) dealt with the areas of perception, memory, intelligence, mother-child relationship, compensation, organ inferiority, crime and delinquency, the consistency of personality, and human dynamics. Ansbacher (1964) reviewed consensual validation or acknowledgments of Adler's importance in general personality theory, existential psychology and psychiatry, neo-Freudian psychoanalysis, Freudian psychoanalysis, theory of mental health, and anthropology. Ferguson (1968) was concerned with trends in contemporary academic psychology toward Adlerian theory. Her categories were: the active organism, stimulus selection, feedback process, central processes, and expectancy-purpose. This section, sampling the current scene, carries these reviews further with only a minimum of duplication.

Evidence: Consensual Validation

Father of Modern Psychotherapy. Adler's principles are being reiterated by increasing numbers of academic and clinical psychologists, mostly without reference to Adler. Yet this phenomenon represents in fact a far-flung consensual validation. It was best described by Albert Ellis (1970), founder of Rational-Emotive Psychotherapy, in the following:

> Alfred Adler, more even than Freud, is probably the true father of modern psychotherapy. Some of the reasons are: He founded ego psychology, which Freudians only recently discovered. He was one of the first humanistic psychologists. . . . He stressed holism, goal-seeking, and the enormous importance of values in human thinking, emoting, and acting. He correctly saw that sexual drives and behavior, while having great importance in human affairs, are largely the result rather than the cause of man's nonsexual philosophies.
>
> For these and other reasons Adler strongly influenced the work of Sullivan, Horney, Fromm, Rogers, May, Maslow and many other writers on psychotherapy, some of whom are often wrongly called neo-Freudians, when they more correctly could be called neo-Adlerians.
>
> My own system of rational-emotive psychotherapy was profoundly influenced by Adler; and the public demonstrations of psychotherapy which are so often given today by Moreno, the late Perls, Schutz, Dreikurs, Ackerman, myself, and many other therapists also owe much to Adler's pioneering methods.
>
> It is difficult to find any leading therapist today who in some respect does not owe a great debt to the Individual Psychology of Alfred Adler. (pp. 11–12)

Floyd W. Matson (1964), political scientist and humanist, made a similarly strong statement when he wrote:

> The influence of Adler . . . seems in retrospect to have been scarcely less extensive than that of Freud . . . It might even be argued (with conscious heresy) that it was the turn first taken by Adler some fifty years ago which has come to be the "mainstream" of the psychoanalytic movement—and that taken by Freud which has been in fact the "deviation." (p. 194)

Judd Marmor (1972), former president of the American Psychiatric Association, wrote:

> Adler truly deserves to be recognized as one of the most original, creative, and progressive thinkers in the history of modern psychiatry. He must be credited with being the first of the ego-psychologists, and the first psychoanalyst to conceive of human psychology in holistic terms. (p. 153)

Viktor E. Frankl (1970), founder of Logotherapy, says about Adler that what he achieved in opposing Freud

> ...was no less than a Copernican switch. No longer could man be considered as the product, pawn and victim of drives and instincts; on the contrary, drives and instincts form the material that serves man in expression and in action. Beyond this, Alfred Adler may well be regarded as an existential thinker and as a forerunner of the existential-psychiatric movement. (p. 12)

H.L. Minton (1968) comments particularly on Adler's concept of power having found validation. "Several contemporary approaches appear to parallel Adler's final conceptualizations regarding power and social interest" (p. 47), that is, power in the sense of success, effectance, or competence. These are the approaches of R.W. White, H. L. Minton, Kurt Lewin, Fritz Heider, Julian Thibaut, George Kelly, and J. W. Rotter.

Maslow (1970), founder of modern humanistic psychology, sums up briefly in stating, "For me Alfred Adler becomes more and more correct year by year. As the facts come in, they give stronger and stronger support to his image of man." He adds, "In one respect especially the times have not yet caught up with him. I refer to his holistic emphasis." (p. 13)

The Breadth of Adler's System.   Adler always endeavored to show that "Individual Psychology is the heir to all great movements whose aim is the welfare of mankind. Although its scientific foundation obligates it to a certain intransigence, it is eager to receive stimulation from all fields of knowledge and experience, and to return the stimulation" (1956, p. 463). In the same vein Adler (1935) also wanted "every student of Individual Psychology to acquire as full a knowledge of other psychological systems as possible....Any unprejudiced critic must admit that introspectionism, psychoanalysis, functionalism, behaviorism, purposivism, reflexology, and Gestalt psychology have made valuable contributions. But the same must be said of Individual Psychology" (pp. 3–4, translation modified).

This approaches a broad eclecticism from a definite point of view. That Adler realized this can be seen from his immediately following disclaimer: "Thereby we are by no means advocating the weakly (*schwächlich*) eclecticism" (1935, p. 4).

This breadth of Adler's system has best been recognized and supported by Frederick Thorne (1970). Thorne wrote: "The ultimate clinical validation of any theoretical viewpoint...is a function of breadth of phenomena which the system is able to clarify and explain...Adler...receives increasing recognition because more and more of his concepts are found to be relevant and clinically valid" (p. 142). Thorne finds that Adler was concerned "with a much wider range of behavior than Freud, and [was] much more pragmatic than Jung's mysticism" (p. 135). "Adlerian psychology is the only system to have some practical relevance in case handling with mental defectives, social misfits, felons, and maladjusted normals" (p. 142). "Historically it is important to keep the record straight by giving Adler credit for his pioneering in broadening the spectrum of psychological theorizing" (p. 143).

Adler's broadness was also pointed out by Ernest Becker (1963), social scientist, who, going beyond clinical psychology, compared Adler to Dewey in this respect, and believed they both suffered just on that account. "Adler, like Dewey in a sense, suffered both from narrow popularization and from his own broadness: he was either cheapened in the common understanding, or ignored because the reach of his ideas led too far" (p. 83). Becker (1970) praised Adler for setting "a standard for breadth of mind and moral courage without which the science of psychology will remain an idle pastime" (p. 169).

Evidence: Empirical Validation

Comprehensiveness of Theory. Two studies may be offered as empirical validation of sorts of the comprehensiveness of Adler's system.

Farberow and Shneidman (1961, pp. 306–313) asked clinicians of various orientations to appraise in writing one case of attempted suicide from the summary of interviews of the case by a psychiatrist. Subsequently they asked the clinicians to Q-sort into nine normally distributed categories 76 cards, each with a statement to be judged for applicability to the case. The Q-sorts from the six participating clinicians were then subjected to a conventional factor analysis reported by Kelly (1963). The Adlerian judgments showed the highest communality, $h^2 = .74$; followed by the Kellyian, .71; the Sullivanian, .51; the Rogerian, .46; the Freudian, .43; and the Jungian, .39. This would indicate that the Adlerian judgments expressed the consensus of all the judgments better than any of the others.

Taft (1958) submitted the ratings by Hall and Lindzey (1957) of 17 personality theories on 18 dimensions to a cluster analysis. Among other results he found that with regard to "most similarity in factors to the 16 other theories," Adler's theory came first, followed closely by the theories of Freud and H. A. Murray. From this Taft concluded that these three theories "are either very eclectic. . . or have had a major influence on other theories. Let the reader decide for himself."

Two-dimensional Personality Theory. Adler's two-dimensional personality theory has been validated through extensive factor-analytic studies—by J. B. Guilford, R. B. Cattell, H. J. Eysenck and others—of questionnaire returns and ratings. According to Eysenck and Rachman (1965), these studies have led to "almost universal agreement" regarding a two-dimensional theory (pp. 18–22). Although the authors named the two

TABLE 3–4. EMOTIONALITY AND EXTRAVERSION-INTROVERSION TYPOLOGY (EYSENCK & RACHMAN 1965)

	Unstable	*Emotionality*	*Stable*
Extraversion	*Choleric:* active, impulsive, aggressive; psychopaths, delinquents; truants; rude, egocentric		*Sanguine:* leadership; carefree, responsive, outgoing, sociable
Introversion	*Melancholic:* Depressed, anxious, quiet, unsociable, rigid, inferiority feelings, nervousness, obsessive		*Phlegmatic:* passive, careful, thoughtful, controlled, even-tempered, calm

dimensions "emotionality" and "introversion-extraversion," these may be reconciled with Adler's dimensions of social interest and activity.

The Eysenck-Rachman typology is present in Table 3–4. A comparison with Table 3–3 above will show how closely it resembles the Adler typology. Both typologies also embody the four temperaments.

Self-Determination and Mental Health. Freud (1917) prided himself on having shown that "man is not even master in his own house...his own mind" (p. 252). According to Adler, man "is and wants to be the master of his fate" (1956, p. 156). Only the neurotic seeks freedom from personal responsibility (1956, pp. 270–271), blaming all sorts of "objective causes" not under his control for his difficulties, and it is the discouraged individual who has lost "faith in his own mental and physical powers" (1956, p. 400).

Adler's understanding has been validated by a massive body of research on "internal versus external control," initiated by J. B. Rotter (1966) and discussed by H.M. Lefcourt (1966). This has established that it is indeed the disadvantaged and discouraged of all sorts who tend to perceive events as being beyond their personal control, while the others do perceive "events as being a consequence of one's own actions, and thereby, under personal control" (Lefcourt, 1966, p. 186). This applies to retardates and schizophrenics compared to normal peers, to persons with lower mental age compared to those with higher mental age, to delinquents who did not learn information useful for obtaining parole compared to those who did, to blacks and American Indians compared to whites, to lower class compared to middle-class persons, and to blacks not willing to participate in social action compared to those willing (Lefcourt, 1966, p. 189). All this validates Adler's assertion of "normal" as self-determined within limits. According to D.L. Mosher (1968), Adler's influence on Rotter "was heuristically powerful and pervasive" (p. 33).

Seeking Success—Avoiding Failure. Adler considered "the striving for success...inherent in the structure of life" (1964, p. 102). While in discouraged individuals this principle is still valid, success is redefined as avoidance of further failure and defeat. "It is the fear of defeat...which occasions the outbreak of the so-called neurotic symptoms....Psychoses...appear when the patient feels absolutely checkmated, with no hope of going on" (Adler, 1929b, p. 13).

This is supported by research of McReynolds and Guevara, as reported by McReynolds (1968). Schizophrenics, and to a lesser degree neurotics, were indeed found to be "more highly motivated to avoid failure and less strongly motivated to attain success" (p. 157) than normal individuals. The studies by J.W. Atkinson on achievement motivation, as well as the earlier work of Kurt Lewin, both quoted by McReynolds, point in the same direction.

Depreciation Tendency. Adler described the phenomenon of undervaluation of others to raise one's own self-esteem as one of the characteristics of the neurotic striving for success (1956, p. 55). He called this the "depreciation tendency, a tendency analogous to the fable of 'The fox and the sour grapes'" (p. 68). Similar dynamics are expressed in what Jay Haley (1963) has humorously termed "oneupmanship," which he defined as "the art of placing a person 'one-down'" (p. 192).

Research studies relevant to this hypothesis, reviewed by M. R. Goldfried (1963), have led him to conclude: "(*a*) In general, there is a positive relationship between one's attitude toward self and one's attitudes toward others. (*b*) Individuals who are maladjusted [presumably have low self-esteem] tend to have more negative attitudes toward others" (p. 44).

More recently, Teichman and Foa (1972) reported a study specifically designed to test Adler's hypothesis that "the neurotic, to a greater extent than the normal, employs depreciation and accusation of significant others to safeguard his self-esteem" (p. 49). They found the hypothesis confirmed in the United States and in India with regard to one's parents.

Antithetical Thinking. Adler noted: "The neurotically disposed individual has a sharply schematizing, strongly abstracting mode of apperception. Thus he groups...events according to a strictly antithetical schema...and admits no degree in between" (1956, p. 248). This hypothesis has been supported from several sides.

Neuringer (1974) found this hypothesis amply validated in cases of suicide, and acknowledged that Adler saw clearly that "a certain cognitive style determined certain outcomes in a much more powerful way than the experiences themselves" (p. 63). Ryle and Breen (1972) found that neurotics generally "tend to extreme judgments." Teichman (1971) concluded from his data that neurotics "will differentiate among family members more than well-adjusted controls" (p. 75). Berger (1964) observed, in underachieving college students, that they engage indeed in the kind of sharply categorizing thinking which Adler had described as "I must have this or nothing" (1956, p. 190).

Sex-Role Identification. For Adler, "uncertainty of one's sexual role and of one's masculinity" was first among "the typical occasions for the onset of a neurosis and psychosis" (1964, pp. 296-297). Supporting this hypothesis, H. B. Biller (1973) found in his studies that sex-role uncertainty is indeed "a very basic determinant of psychopathology." He praises Adler's astuteness in listing it first among "developmental precursors to psychopathology."

Mother's Influence on Attitude toward Father. Adler described the mother as the child's "bridge to social life" (1956, p. 372), the focal agent in developing his social interest. "After she has succeeded in connecting the child with herself, her next task is to spread his interest towards the father, and this task will prove almost impossible if she herself is not interested in the father" (p. 373). From this, Baxter, Horton, and Wiley (1964) developed the hypothesis that "father identification should be adversely affected by interparental conflict" (p. 167). They found this hypothesis confirmed in a study of 180 male and female college students. More specifically, while males identified significantly more with the father than females, in harmonious homes both sexes identified significantly more with the father than in conflictful homes. This second finding particularly would never have been predicted from a Freudian hypothesis.

Personality of the Criminal. Chaplin (1970), reporting on a study of American presidential assassins, noted that all nine cases fitted Adler's description of the criminal personality. They all were zealots; were socially and physically disadvantaged; had ideas of grandiosity; were loners, unmarried, or failures in marriage; and were unable to work steadily. "Even the cases of the two exceptions.. can be understood in terms of these dynamics. Thus the salient characteristics developed and described...independently of Adlerian theory, confirm it strikingly" (p. 212).

Rebelliousness of the Second-Born. Adler advanced a number of hypotheses on the effect of birth order on personality (p. 46). Research in this area has taken on enormous dimensions, amounting to some 400 publications between 1963 and 1971 (Vockell, Felker, & Miley, 1973). We shall mention here two studies referring to the hypothesis of Adler (1956, pp. 376–382) that second-borns are likely to be rebellious and not to recognize power or authority. Taintor (1970) found among 323 psychiatric diagnoses of Army recruits that 35 percent of the firstborns were diagnosed as neurotic and 37 percent as personality disorders, whereas among second-borns only 10 percent were found to be neurotic and 54 percent, personality disorders. Adler's hypothesis was also supported by LeMay (1968) with college girls referred for misconduct, among whom second-borns were found overrepresented and firstborns underrepresented.

Early Recollections. While early recollections are widely used by Adlerian practitioners in personality appraisal, validating research is still limited. Taylor (1975) reviewed six studies done between 1957 and 1965 and found the evidence in support of early recollections as a clinical tool "far from conclusive, but . . . encouraging" (p. 218). Manaster and King (1973) found that in accordance with Adlerian theory in at least one out of three or four early recollections of male homosexuals, there is a woman seen in a negative light. And Manaster and Perryman (1974) found that a number of early recollection variables differentiated between students in different occupational areas.

Comparisons

In discussing similar systems above, we began by establishing the contrast to Freud's system as an alternative to which Adler's system developed. We shall presently pursue this comparison further by presenting judgments of the relative soundness of the two systems. This will be followed by comparisons with other systems.

Adler's Optimism and Soundness. Shortly after Adler's separation from him, Freud (1914) noted: Based on aggression, "there is no room in the Adlerian system for love . . . , a cheerless view of life" (p. 347). Ironically, further development proved exactly the opposite to be the case; Freud augmented his system with the death instinct or instinct of destruction, while Adler added to his system social interest, which does indeed include love. Today Adler generally is recognized as the optimist, Freud as the pessimist. In the words of Hall and Lindzey (1957), "Adler restored to man a sense of dignity and worth that psychoanalysis had pretty largely destroyed" (p. 125).

More importantly, many recent judgments refer to Adler's greater soundness. Maddi (1968), comparing three models of personality—the psychosocial conflict model (Freud), the actualization fulfillment model, (Rogers), and the perfection fulfillment model (Adler)—concludes that "the Adlerian view is the most sound" and, given a choice among the three, "I would cheerfully choose the latter" (p. 160). Mowrer (1959) wrote: "Adler was probably not so gifted as Freud and was nothing like as brilliant a writer; but he was, it now appears, *sounder*." Ashley Montagu (1970) also stressed Adler's soundness: "When we come to evaulate the overall view of human nature and of man's future, there can, in my opinion, be no doubt of the far greater soundness and hopefulness of Adler's view than of Freud's" (p. 19). And finally a judgment by R. W. White (1957): "Unlike Freud, who struggled relentlessly . . . to secure immortality for his concepts, Adler struggled to secure immortality for his practical wisdom. . . . Now Adler's ideas have gone into the stream of contemporary thought and have become the accepted clinical common sense of our time" (p. 4).

Freud's Unsoundness. Freud's greater unsoundness is founded in his "metapsychology." Adler's original critique referred to Freud's sexual instinct or libido theory, including the concepts of repression and pleasure principle; his mechanistic, elementaristic and reductionistic approach; and the reifications which all this suggests. After Adler's separation, Freud worked these and similar additional concepts into his metapsychology, which consists of (1) the "topography" of id, ego, and superego, and the distinction between unconscious, preconscious, and conscious; (2) the instinct theory, including the psychosexual states of development; and (3) the pleasure principle and repetition compulsion. Today, even many who consider themselves followers of Freud reject these basic assumptions, thereby implicitly validating Adler. We shall give three examples of such rejections.

According to George S. Klein (1973), the Freudian system actually contains two separate and conflicting theories. The first is Freud's metapsychology, which is positivistic, deterministic, reductionistic, and mechanistic. Klein found this incompatible with and "irrelevant" to psychoanalytic practice, where one meets and interprets in terms of "purpose, function, accomplishment," intention, and meaning. This implies a second, teleological rather than causalistic theory, according to which Klein would reconstruct psychoanalysis while completely abandoning the first theory. Ansbacher (1974a) has shown that Klein's arguments are point for point restatements of Adler's original critique of Freud.

Marmor (1973) rejects Freud's sexual theories as not having withstood the test of time. "The postulate of a fluid-like energy coursing through the body...and capable of 'repression' or discharge, simply does not jibe with modern neurophysiology" (p. 86); "Oedipus complex and incest guilt...prove...to be no explanation at all" (p. 88); infantile "incestuous" wishes may be considered as merely "a metaphorical...description" (p. 87). This is exactly what Adler had maintained: the Oedipus complex "must be taken symbolically" (1956, p. 69), as "a figure of speech" (p. 375) of the "pampered child who does not want to give up his mother" (p. 185).

Leon J. Saul (1972) rejects Freud's metapsychology because those who stress it tend to describe patients in mere generalities. He cites a case of guilt feelings in whom two years of psychoanalysis achieved only the interpretation that the guilt "was from masturbation as a child" (p. 11). Saul's new approach "quickly revealed that the guilt stemmed from hostility...derived from...(a) *feelings of inferiority*...because he had been...consistently *overprotected*...and (b) *protest* against all the *responsibility* which he now carried in adult life" (pp. 11–12, italics added). The new interpretation uses entirely Adlerian concepts: inferiority feelings; overprotection, corresponding to Adler's "pamerping"; protest, as in "masculine protest"; and avoidance of responsibility, of which Adler had noted: "The neurotic vehemently resists being removed from his freedom of responsibility" (1956, p. 271).

Other Systems. Compared to the various similar systems described initially, it is to be noted in general that Adler's system was created not by an academic psychologist or a philosopher but by a practitioner with a shrewd sense for the theoretical essentials that would facilitate treatment. Further, it was kept, in terminology and structure, as simple as possible to make it accessible to nonprofessional persons, yet it is in fact most comprehensive, as shown above. Additionally, we want to make two further specific comparisons.

Regarding present-day *humanistic psychology*, it must be noted that with its encounter groups and emphasis on self-actualization it is less rational and cognitive and less socially oriented than Adler's humanism. Kurt Adler (1970) commented on this, "These groups foster mainly catharsis...and very often...overt depreciation of others" (p. 116). O'Connell (1971) found that a poorly led sensitivity group "reinforces the neurotic behavior of the self-centered person" (p. 67), while Papanek (1961) noted the danger of "socially shared autisms" (p. 188) as mentioned above.

On the other hand there are important methodological similarities with modern *behaviorism*, while differences in the concept of man also seem to be diminishing. O'Connell (1973), comparing Adler and Skinner, summarized:

> Both see the movements of an individual toward his goal as the basic psychological reality; both see these movements taking place in a social environment as transactions influenced by the consequences they generate...Both distrust reified terms and emphasize concrete data. Adler's concept of encouragement is a close parallel to reinforcement...Both put feelings in a place of secondary importance,...are favorably disposed to religion,...committed to bringing about a better social order. (p. 93)

There are also numerous systems of psychotherapy bearing considerable similarity to Adler's approach, such as William Glasser's *Reality Therapy*, Eric Berne's *Transactional Analysis*, Frederick Perls' *Gestalt Therapy*, and family therapy as represented by Virginia Satir. But they generally do not have a personality theory of their own.

PROSPECT

The future of Individual Psychology is difficult to predict, for we are confronted with the paradoxical situation mentioned earlier. On the one hand there is the general agreement among those who know Adler—Adlerian or non-Adlerian—that Adler's ideas have been widely accepted. On the other hand there is equal agreement that Adler's ideas have made their way anonymously without due credit to their originator. Munroe (1955) noted that "Adler's fate is like that of Heine, whose little masterpiece *The Lorelei* attained such prompt popularity that when he himself asked a group of people singing it for the name of the author, he was told, 'Why, nobody wrote it—it's a folk song''' (p. 335). Fifteen years later, Ellenberger (1970) still found this story applicable to Adler, in a version referring to Franz Schubert and his *Lieder* (p. 646).

With Adler this situation is extreme. Ellenberger describes in some detail the extent to which Adler has influenced the neo-Freudians, from Edward Kempf to H. S. Sullivan, Karen Horney, Erich Fromm, Thomas French, Clara Thompson, Sandor Rado, Theodore Reik, and Abraham Kardiner, as well as the existentialists Frankl, Binswanger and Sartre; and still others, including Freud (Ellenberger, 1970, pp. 637–645). Ellenberger notes "a collective denial of Adler's work and the systematic attribution of anything coined by him to other authors. We have numerous instances of psychoanalysts picking up some of Adler's most original findings and asserting that they were implicitly contained in Freud's writings, or neglected aspects of Freud's thinking" (p. 645). Rotter (1960) also noted: "Theorists for the last 20 years have been writing books re-expressing many of Adler's concepts without reference to Adler, although sometimes twisting and turning considerably in order to prove that these ideas were accepted by Freud" (p. 383), often "invoking 'neglected aspects' of Freud's writing" (p. 384).

Ellenberger calls this "wide-scale, quiet plagiarism" (1970, p. 646), and believes, "It would not be easy to find another author from whom so much has been borrowed from all sides without acknowledgment than Alfred Adler" (p. 645). Meerloo (1970) admitted, with regard to Adler, that "we are all plagiarists, though we hate to confess it" (p. 14).

When *The Individual Psychology of Alfred Adler*, in which nearly all of Adler's thoughts are recorded with detailed references to the sources, appeared, White (1957) believed, "It will hereafter count as fair play in reviews and criticism to point out that an author's supposedly new ideas come straight from Adler" (p. 3). But this hopeful prediction has not come to pass. Nor has the appearance of Ellenberger's work brought any change. The vigorous Adlerian movement of which we wrote earlier, being essentially on the practical level, has also had little influence on the general literature, although it has undoubtedly been a factor in bringing all of Adler's books into print again, in English as well as in German. Thus it is still not uncommon today that an otherwise well-trained psychologist or psychiatrist will admit he knows little of Adler and never read him in the original, although numerous textbooks on personality theories, specifically, deal with Adler at length and quite adequately.

Ellenberger (1970) attempts to explain this Adler paradox, in comparison to the recognition and prestige conceded to Freud, partly on the basis of their respective personalities. Freud was imposing, well-groomed, lived in the best residential quarter, kept several servants, acquired university titles, was a master of German prose, and the founder of "a science bent on discovering the mysteries of the soul." Adler was unassuming, lived in a more bourgeois residential area with only one servant, was refused a university title, wrote in ordinary style, and promoted a rational, common sense psychology with immediate practical application (p. 647).

Will the situation continue as it is, or will there be a change toward adequate general recognition of Adler? Opinions differ. Interestingly, Adler (1933) was inclined toward the first alternative. He wrote: "Individual Psychology is born of this age and will have a lasting influence on the thought, poetry and dreams of humanity. It will win many adherents who clearly understand its value, and still more who will hardly know the names of its pioneers."

The second alternative, growing recognition of Adler in the future, is discussed by Gardner Murphy (1970). He believes that "There will be more and more recognition and application of the basic Adlerian conception of the need of the living individual to fulfill and complete itself in an environment which can be less competitive and less hostile; less impersonal; more and more genuine and socially meaningful." This view is shared by Sahakian (1970), who believes "The psychology of Adler is due for a...resurgence, owing to a renewed appreciation of the viability of its profundity and originality" (p. 15). Finally, there is the word by Wilder (1970): "The chapter 'Alfred Adler' is not closed yet in the history of mankind" (p. 460).

Our hope is with these last three predictions. A full recognition of Adler would greatly facilitate an understanding of all personality theory and psychotherapy, in addition to what his theory still has to offer on its own, and would thus be of great benefit to all.

ANNOTATED BIBLIOGRAPHY

Primary Sources

Adler, A. *The neurotic constitution: Outlines of a comparative individualistic psychology and psychotherapy* (1912.) Translated by B. Glueck and J. E. Lind. New York: Moffat, Yard, 1917.

This is Adler's most important book, and the only one not based on a series of lectures or a collection of separate papers. In it he developed his inferiority-superiority dynamics, striving for enhancement of self-esteem which in the neurotic takes the form of an exaggerated "masculine protest," where "I want to be a real man," striving for personal power, becomes the guiding fiction. In contrast to the normal guiding fiction, that of the patients is based on an accentuated and

dogmatized antithetical mode of apperception. Unfortunately, the translation is poor, beginning with the title, the correct translation of which would be: "The Nervous Character: Principles of a Comparative Individual Psychology and Psychotherapy."

Adler, A. *The individual psychology of Alfred Adler: A systematic presentation in selections from his writings.* Edited by H. L. and R. R. Ansbacher. New York: Basic Books, 1956.

This is an anthology of all of Adler's writings from 1907 to 1937, designed to make his contributions to theory and practice available in a systematic and authentic form. The first two chapters present Adler's writings between 1907 and 1911, most of which are to date not available anywhere else in English. The six following chapters present Adler's personality theory proper. Chapters 9 to 14 deal with psychopathology, psychotherapy, and personality appraisal; Chapters 15 and 16, with developmental psychology and treatment of the problem child; Chapter 17, with crime and related disorders; Chapter 18, with general life problems; and Chapter 19, with problems of social psychology. The Introduction by the editors compares Adler's theory with other theories.

Adler, A. *Superiority and social interest: A collection of later writings.* Edited by H. L. and R. R. Ansbacher, Evanston, Ill.: Northwestern University Press, 1964.

This second anthology, supplementing the first, presents Adler's significant later writings which had heretofore not appeared in book form. It contains 21 papers by Adler, with 17 dating between 1931 and 1937 and 9 being original translations. Part I deals with general assumptions and principles, Part II with theory of neurosis, Part III with case discussions and techniques of treatment, and Part IV with various psychological disturbances. Part V consists of Adler's essay on religion. Part VI is a biographical essay on Adler by Carl Furtmuller. Part VII is the complete bibliography of Adler's writings.

Adler, A. *The practice and theory of individual psychology* (1920). Translated by P. Radin. Totowa, N.J.: Littlefield, Adams & Co., 1968.

A collection of 28 papers published between 1909 and 1920 covering all important aspects of Adler's theories up to that time. Included are important articles on homosexuality, compulsion neurosis, dream interpretation, the unconscious, depression, prostitution, and wayward children.

Adler, A. *Understanding human nature* (1927). Translated by W. B. Wolfe. New York: Fawcett Premier Books, 1969.

Adler's best selling book; addressed to the general reader, based on popular lectures, and widely translated.

Adler, A. *Problems of neurosis: A book of case histories* (1929). Edited by Philip Mairet. New York: Harper & Row, 1964.

A collection of 37 case discussions interwoven with important theoretical considerations. The book has an introduction by H. L. Ansbacher.

Adler, A. *Social interest: A challenge to mankind* (1933). Translated by John Linton and Richard Vaughan. New York: Capricorn Books, 1964.

This is Adler's last book, presenting his most advanced thinking. Social interest has become the most important concept, and life style has replaced life plan. The German title is *Der Sinn des Lebens*, the translation of which is "The meaning of life." But this could not be used since previously a series of lectures had been published in English entitled *What Life Should Mean to You* (Adler, 1931), which, although very good, has incidentally never been translated into German.

Secondary Sources

Manaster, G. J., & Corsini, R. J. *Individual psychology: Theory & practice.* Itasca, Ill: F. E. Peacock, 1982.

This is the first complete text on Individual Psychology written in English by two editors of the *Journal of Individual Psychology*. Approximately one-half of this book is devoted to theory and the other half to practice. Written in a simple style with many case histories and illustrations, it covers more completely the material in this chapter and in Harold Mosak's chapter in *Current Psychotherapies*.

Mosak, H., & Mosak, B. *A bibliography for Adlerian psychology.* New York: Wiley, 1975.

This is a listing of references for Adlerian psychology in the broadest possible sense. It includes, from Adlerian writers, even their smallest contributions in newsletters and reviews, as well as their papers on non-Adlerian topics, and from non-Adlerian writers, their contributions on topics of Adlerian interest. An item by several authors is entered under each name. In all there are nearly 10,000 entries. These are provided with a subject index of 38 pages.

REFERENCES

Adler, A. *Study of organ inferiority and its physical compensation: A contribution to clinical medicine.* (S. E. Jeliffe, trans.). New York: Nervous and Mental Disease Publication Co., 1917. (Originally published, 1907.)

Adler, A. *The neurotic constitution* (B. Glueck & J. E. Lind, trans.). Introduction by William A. White. Freeport, N.Y.: Books for Libraries, 1972. (Originally published, 1912.)

Adler, A. Der vervöse charakter. In A. Adler & C. Furtmüller (Eds.), *Heilen und bilden* (W. Metzger, Ed.; pp. 123–133). Frankfurt am Main: Fischer Taschenbuch, 1973. (Originally published, 1914.)

Adler, A. The homosexual problem. *Alienist and Neurologist*, 1917, *38*, 268–287.

Adler, A. *Praxis und theorie der Individualpsychologie.* Frankfurt am Main: Fischer Taschenbuch, 1974. (We are referring to the German edition for material not included in the English edition.) (Originally published, 1920.) (a)

Adler, A. *The practice and theory of Individual Psychology.* Totowa, N.J.: Littlefield, Adams, 1969. (Originally published, 1920.) (b)

Adler, A. Marriage as a task. In H. Keyserling (Ed.), *The book of marriage: A new introduction by twenty-four leaders of contemporary thought.* New York: Harcourt, Brace, 1926.

Adler, A. *Understanding human nature.* New York: Fawcett Premier Books, 1969. (Originally published, 1927.) (a)

Adler, A. Individual psychology. *Journal of Abnormal and Social Psychology*, 1927, *22*, 116–122. (b)

Adler, A. *Individualpsychologie in der schule.* Frankfurt am Main: Fischer Taschenbuch, 1973. (Originally published, 1929.) (a)

Adler, A. *Problems of neurosis.* New York: Harper & Row, 1964. (Originally published, 1929.) (b)

Adler, A. *The science of living.* Garden City, N.Y.: Doubleday Anchor Books, 1969. (Originally published, 1929.) (c)

Adler, A. Fundamentals of individual psychology. *Journal of Individual Psychology*, 1970, *26*, 36–49. (Originally published, 1930.)

Adler, A. Vorrede. In R. Dreikurs (Ed.), *Einführung in die Individualpsychologie.* Leipzig: Hirzel, 1933.

Adler, A. Prevention of neurosis. *International Journal of Individual Psychology*, 1935, *14*, 3–12.

Adler, A. *The individual psychology of Alfred Adler: A systematic presentation in selections from his writings* (H. L. & R. R. Ansbacher, Eds.). New York: Basic Books, 1956.

Adler, A. *Superiority and social interest: A collection of later writings* (H. L. & Rowena R. Ansbacher, Eds.). Evanston, Ill.: Northwestern University Press, 1964.

Adler, A., & Furtmüller, C. (Eds.). *Heilen und bilden.* Frankfurt am Main: Fischer Taschenbuch, 1973. (Originally published, 1914.)

Adler, K. A. Adlerian view of the present-day scene. *Journal of Individual Psychology*, 1970, *26*, 113–121.

Agel, J. First memory. *New York Times Magazine*, October 26, 1975, p. 111.

Ansbacher, H. L. Alfred Adler's place in psychology today. *Internationale Zeitschrift für Individualpsychologie*, 1947, *16*, 97–111.

Ansbacher, H. L. The increasing recognition of Adler. In A. Adler, *Superiority and social interest* (pp. 3–19). (H. L. & R. R. Ansbacher, Eds.). Evanston, Ill.: Northwestern University Press, 1964.

Ansbacher, H. L. Sensus privatus versus sensus communis. *Journal of Individual Psychology*, 1965, *21*, 48–50. (a)

Ansbacher, H. L. The structure of Individual Psychology. In B. B. Wolman (Ed.), *Scientific psychology* (pp. 340–364). New York: Basic Books, 1965. (b)

Ansbacher, H. L. The concept of social interest. *Journal of Individual Psychology*, 1968, *24*, 131–149.

Ansbacher, H. L. Alfred Adler and humanistic psychology. *Journal of Humanistic Psychology*, 1971, *11*, 53–63. (a)

Ansbacher, H. L. (Ed.). Religion and individual psychology. *Journal of Individual Psychology*, 1971, *27*, 3–49. (b)

Ansbacher, H. L. The first critique of Freud's metapsychology: An extension of George S. Klein's "Two theories or one?" *Bulletin of the Menninger Clinic*, 1974, *38*, 78–84. (a)

Ansbacher, H. L. Goal-oriented individual Psychology: Alfred Adler's theory. In A. Burton (Ed.), *Operational theories of personality* (pp. 99–142). New York: Brunner/Mazel, 1974. (b)

Ansbacher, H. L. Individual psychology. In S. Arieti (Ed.), *American handbook of psychiatry* (2d ed.), Vol. 1 (pp. 789–808). New York: Basic Books, 1974. (c)

Asch, S. E. *Social psychology*. New York: Prentice-Hall, 1952.

Batt, C. E. Mexican character: An Adlerian interpretation. *Journal of Individual Psychology*, 1969, *25*, 183–201.

Baxter, J. C., Horton, D. L., & Wiley, R. E. Father identification as a function of mother-father relationship. *Journal of Individual Psychology*, 1964, *20*, 167–171.

Becker, E. Adler and the modern world (Review of *Adler's place in psychology* by L. Way). *Journal of Individual Psychology*, 1963, *19*, 83–89.

Becker, E. Tribute to Alfred Adler. *Journal of Individual Psychology*, 1970, *26*, 169.

Beecher, W. Industrial relations in the light of Individual Psychology. *American Journal of Individual Psychology*, 1955, *11*, 123–130.

Berger, E. M. Antithetical thinking in personality problems. *Journal of Individual Psychology*, 1964, *20*, 32–37.

Biller, H. B. Sex-role uncertainty and psychopathology. *Journal of Individual Psychology*, 1973, *29*, 24–25.

Bottome, P. *Alfred Adler: Portrait from life*. New York: Vanguard, 1957.

Brink, T. L. The case of Hitler: an Adlerian perspective of psychohistory. *Journal of Individual Psychology*, 1975, *31*, 23–31.

Brown, C. *Manchild in the promised land*. New York: New American Library, Signet, 1971. (Originally published, 1965.)

Burt, F. D. William Somerset Maugham: An Adlerian interpretation. *Journal of Individual Psychology*, 1970, *26*, 64–82.

Chaplin, J. P. The presidential assassins: A confirmation of Adlerian theory. *Journal of Individual Psychology*, 1970, *26*, 205–212.

Clark, K. B. Implications of Adlerian theory for an understanding of civil rights problems and action. *Journal of Individual Psychology*, 1967, *23*, 181–190.

Dreikurs, R. *Psychology in the classroom*. New York: Harper & Row, 1957.

Dreikurs, R. (with Vicki Soltz). *Children: The challenge*. New York: Duell, Sloan and Pearce, 1964.

Dreikurs, R. *Psychodynamics, psychotherapy, and counseling*. Chicago: Alfred Adler Institute, 1973. (Originally published, 1967.)

Dreikurs, R. *Understanding your children: Study guidebook*. (J. A. & N. M. Peterson, Eds.). Burlington, Vt.: Vermont Educational Television, University of Vermont, 1969.

Dreikurs, R. *Counseling the adolescent: Guidebook*. (J. A. & N. M. Peterson, Eds.). Burlington: Vt.: Vermont Educational Television, University of Vermont, 1971.

Dreikurs, R., Corsini, R. J., Lowe, R., & Sonstegard, M. *Adlerian family counseling: A manual for counseling centers*. Eugene: University of Oregon Press, 1959.

Dreikurs, R., Gould, S., & Corsini, R. J. *Family council*. Chicago: Regnery, 1974.

Ellenberger, H. F. Alfred Adler and Individual Psychology. In *The discovery of the unconscious* (pp. 571–656). New York: Basic Books, 1970.

Ellis, A. Tribute to Alfred Adler, *Journal of Individual Psychology*, 1970, *26*, 11–12.

Eysenck, H. J., & Rachman, S. *The causes and cures of neurosis: An introduction to modern behavior therapy*. London: Routledge and Kegan Paul; San Diego: Knapp, 1965.

Fanon, F. *Black skin; white masks.* New York: Grove Press, 1967.

Farberow, N. L., & Shneidman, E. S. (Eds.). *The cry for help.* New York: McGraw-Hill, 1961.

Ferguson, E. D. Adlerian concepts in contemporary psychology: The changing scene. *Journal of Individual Psychology*, 1968, *24*, 150–156.

Frankl, V. E. Tribute to Alfred Adler. *Journal of Individual Psychology*, 1970, *26*, 12.

Freud, S. On this history of the psychoanalytic movement. In *Collected papers.* Vol. 1 (pp. 287–359). London: Hogarth, 1953. (Originally published, 1914.)

Freud, S. *A general introduction to psychoanalysis.* Garden City, N.Y.: Garden City Publishers, 1943. (Originally published, 1917.)

Freud, S. *Group psychology and the analysis of the ego.* New York: Liveright, 1949. (Originally published, 1921.)

Freudenberg, S. *Erziehungs-und Heilpädagogische Beratungsstellen.* Lepizig: Hirzel, 1928.

Furtmüller, C. Alfred Adler: A biographical essay. In A. Adler, *Superiority and social interest* (pp. 311–393). Evanston, Ill.: Northwestern University Press, 1964.

George, A. L. Power as a compensatory value for political leaders. *Journal of Social Issues*, 1968, *24*, 29–49.

George, A. L., & George, J. L. *Woodrow Wilson and Colonel House.* New York: John Day, 1956.

Goldfried, M. R. Feelings of inferiority and the depreciation of others: A research review and theoretical reformulation. *Journal of Individual Psychology*, 1963, *19*, 27–48.

Haley, J. *Strategies of psychotherapy.* New York: Grune & Stratton, 1963.

Hall, C. S., & Lindzey, G. *Theories of personality.* New York: Wiley, 1957.

Irving, J. *The Catcher in the Rye*: An Adlerian interpretation. *Journal of Individual Psychology*, 1976, *32*, 81–92.

Kankeleit, O. 5. Internationaler Kongress für Individualpsychologie in Berlin, vom 26. bis 28. September 1930. *Archiv für Psychiatrie und Nervenkrankheiten*, 1931, *93*, 261–336.

Kelly, G. A. *The psychology of personal constructs* (Vol. 1). New York: Norton, 1955.

Kelly, G. A. Nonparametric factor analysis of personality theories. *Journal of Individual Psychology*, 1963, *19*, 115–147.

Kiell, N. (Ed.). *Psychoanalysis, psychology and literature: A bibliography.* Madison: University of Wisconsin Press, 1963.

Klein, G. S. Two theories or one? *Bulletin of the Menninger Clinic*, 1973, *37*, 102–132.

Lefcourt, H. M. Belief in personal control: research and implications. *Journal of Individual Psychology.* 1966, *22*, 185–195.

LeMay, M. L. Birth order and college misconduct. *Journal of Individual Psychology*, 1968, *24*, 167–169.

Maddi, S. R. *Personality theories: A comparative analysis.* Homewood, Ill.: Dorsey Press, 1968.

Mairet, P. Hamlet as a study in Individual Psychology. *Journal of Individual Psychology*, 1969, *25*, 71–88.

Manaster, G. J. & King, M. Early recollections of male homosexuals. *Journal of Individual Psychology*, 1973, *29*, 26–33.

Manaster, G. J., & Perryman, T. B. Early recollections and occupational choice. *Journal of Individual Psychology*, 1974, *30*, 232–237.

Marmor, J. Holistic conception, and points of mild issue. *Journal of Individual Psychology*, 1972, *28*, 153–154.

Marmor, J. Freud's sexual theories 70 years later. *Medical World News, Psychiatry*, 1973, 86–88.

Maslow, A. H. Tribute to Alfred Adler. *Journal of Individual Psychology*, 1970, *26*, 13.

Matson, F. W. *The broken image: Man, science and society.* Garden City, N.Y.: Doubleday-Anchor, 1966. (Originally published, 1964.)

Mazlish, B. Psychiatry and history. In S. Arieti (Ed.), *American handbook of psychiatry* (2d ed., Vol. 1, pp. 1034–1045). New York: Basic Books, 1974.

McLaughlin, J. J., & Ansbacher, R. R. Sane Ben Franklin. An Adlerian view of his autobiography. *Journal of Individual*

Psychology, 1971, *27*, 189–207.

McReynolds, P. The motives to attain success and to avoid failure: Historical note. *Journal of Individual Psychology*, 1968, *24*, 157–161.

Meerloo, J. A. M. Tribute to Alfred Adler. *Journal of Individual Psychology*, 1970, *26*, 14.

Mill, J. S. Utilitarianism. In *Utilitarianism, liberty, and representative government* (pp. 1–80). New York: Dutton, 1951. (Originally published, 1863.)

Miller, N. E., & Dollard, J. *Social learning and imitation*. New Haven, Conn.: Yale University Press, 1941.

Minton, H. L. Contemporary concepts of power and Adler's views. *Journal of Individual Psychology*, 1968, *24*, 46–55.

Montagu, A. Social interest and aggression as potentialities. *Journal of Individual Psychology*, 1970, *26*, 17–31.

Mosak, H. H., & Mosak, B. *A bibliography for Adlerian psychology*. New York: Wiley, 1975.

Mosher, D. L. The influence of Adler on Rotter's social learning theory of personality. *Journal of Individual Psychology*, 1968, *24*, 33–45.

Mowrer, O. H. Comments on Trude Weiss-Rosmarin's "Adler's psychology and the Jewish tradition." *Journal of Individual Psychology*, 1959, *15*, 128–129.

Munroe, R. L. *Schools of psychoanalytic thought*. New York: Dryden, 1955.

Murphy, G. Tribute to Alfred Adler, *Journal of Individual Psychology*, 1970, *26*, 14–15.

Neuringer, C. Validation of the cognitive aspects of Adler's theory of suicide. *Journal of Individual Psychology*, 1974, *30*, 59–64.

Nunberg, H., & Federn, E. (Eds.) *Minutes of the Vienna psychoanalytic society, Vol. 1, 1906–1908*. New York: International Universities Press, 1962.

O'Connell, W. E. Sensitivity training and Adlerian theory. *Journal of Individual Psychology*, 1971, *27*, 65–72.

O'Connell, W. E. Social interest in an operant world. *Journal of Individual Psychology*, 1973, *29*, 93. (Abstract)

Orgler, H. *Alfred Adler: The man and his work*. New York: Mentor, 1963.

Ottenheimer, H. Soziale Arbeit. In S. Kaznelson (Ed.), *Juden im Deutschen kulturbereich* (2d ed.; pp. 825–857). Berlin: Jüdischer Verlag, 1959. Quoted by H. L. & R. R. Ansbacher, Editorial review, *Journal of Individual Psychology*, 1973, *29*, 204–209.

Papanek, H. Psychotherapy without insight: Group therapy as milieu therapy. *Journal of Individual Psychology*, 1961, *17*, 184–192.

Perry, R. B. *Realms of value: A critique of human civilization*. Cambridge, Mass.: Harvard University Press, 1954.

Ramos, S. *Profile of man and culture in Mexico*. Austin: University of Texas Press, 1962.

Rom, P. The notion of solidarity in the work of Albert Camus. *Journal of Individual Psychology*, 1960, *16*, 146–150.

Rotter, J. B. Psychotherapy. *Annual Review of Psychology*, 1960, *11*, 381–414.

Rotter, J. B. Generalized expectancies for internal versus external control of reinforcement. *Psychological Monographs*, 1966, *80* (1) Whole No. 609.

Rühle-Gerstel, A. Individualpsychologische autodidaktik. *Internationale Zeitschrift für Individualpsychologie*, 1930, *8*, 52–61.

Rychlak, J. R. *A philosophy of science for personality theory*. Boston: Houghton Mifflin, 1968.

Ryle, A., & Breen, D. Some differences in the personal constructs of neurotics and normal subjects. *British Journal of Psychiatry*, 1972, *120*, 483–489.

Sahakian, W. S. Tribute to Alfred Adler. *Journal of Individual Psychology*, 1970, *26*, 15.

Saul, L. J. *Psychodynamically based psychotherapy*. New York: Science House, 1972.

Shulman, B. H. An Adlerian view. In M. Kramer et al. (Eds.), *Dream psychology and the new biology of dreaming* (pp. 117–137). Springfield, Ill.: Thomas, 1969.

Sperber, M. *Masks of loneliness: Alfred Adler in perspective* (Krishna Winston, trans.).

New York: Macmillan, 1974.

Spiel, O. *Discipline without punishment: An account of a school in action.* London: Faber & Faber, 1962.

Taft, R. A cluster analysis for Hall and Lindzey. *Contemporary Psychology,* 1958, *3,* 143–144.

Taylor, J. A. Early recollections as a projective technique: A review of some recent validation studies. *Journal of Individual Psychology,* 1975, *31,* 213–218.

Teichman, M. Antithetical apperception of family members by neurotics. *Journal of Individual Psychology,* 1971, *27,* 73–75.

Teichman, M., & Foa, U. G. Depreciation and accusation tendencies: Empirical support. *Journal of Individual Psychology,* 1972, *28,* 45–50.

Thorne, F. C. Adler's broad-spectrum concept of man, self-consistency, and unification. *Journal of Individual Psychology,* 1970, *26,* 135–143.

Virchow, R. Atoms and individuals. In (Ed.) L. J. Rather. *Disease, life, and man: Selected essays.* Stanford, Calif.: Stanford University Press, 1958. Pp. 120–141. (Originally published, 1862).

Vockell, E. L., Felker, D. W., & Miley, C. H. Birth order literature 1967–1971: Bibliography and index. *Journal of Individual Psychology,* 1973, *29,* 39–53.

Watzlawick, P., Weakland, J., & Fisch, R. *Change: Principles of problem formation and problem resolution.* New York: Norton, 1974.

Werner, H. D. Adler, Freud, and American social work. *Journal of Individual Psychology,* 1967, *23,* 11–18.

White, R. W. Is Alfred Adler alive today? (Review of *The individual psychology of Alfred Adler,* H. L. & R. R. Ansbacher, Eds.). *Contemporary Psychology,* 1957, *2,* 1–4.

Wilder, J. Alfred Adler in historical perspective. *American Journal of Psychotherapy,* 1970, *24,* 450–460.

Youngdale, J. M. *Populism: A psychohistorical perspective.* Port Washington, N.Y.: Kennikat Press, 1975.

CHAPTER IV

Analytical Psychology

**Renaldo J. Maduro and
Joseph B. Wheelwright**

CARL JUNG

Analytical psychology, a major school of psychoanalytic thought and clinical practice, seeks to understand the structure, psychodynamics, and unfolding of the human psyche. Founded in 1914 by Carl Jung (1875-1961) as a development from, as well as a reaction against, Freud's position, it widens and deepens orthodox Freudian theory.

Current Jungian theory can be seen from three historical perspectives: (1) the point of view of Dr. Jung's original formulations; (2) how classical concepts which distinguish current Jungians from members of other analytical schools have been modified, amplified, or remained unchanged; and (3) the judgments of relatively objective observers in the field of personality studies. In this chapter, each of these three perspectives will be taken into consideration.

We shall discuss nine important emphases of Jungian personality theory:

1. Jung's relatively introverted perspective on unconscious mental processes: his lesser attention to external reality per se than to intrapsychic reality, the complicated interaction of internal objects, archetypal images, complexes, and unconscious fantasies.
2. Jung's discovery and elucidation of the importance of an archetypal or transpersonal layer of the psyche—the collective unconscious.
3. Jung's teleological emphasis on the psyche's spontaneous striving *toward* psychological wholeness and self-realization. This life process is purposive and implies active dialogue between ego-consciousness and a bipolar *psychodynamic self*.
4. Jung's bipolar concept of a self-regulating psyche in which the principle of creative unconscious compensation is at work.

125

5. Analytical psychology's broad definition of psychic energy which does not reduce life to only sex or aggression but includes many other instincts, such as creativity.

6. Jung's stress on personality development throughout normal stages of the life cycle, and on an innate potential or religious instinct for intensified self-actualization, beginning typically with a midlife crisis.

7. Jungian psychology's greater concern for central preoedipal experiences and anxieties involving freedom from the images of the personal and transpersonal mother, than for later developmental issues related to oedipal strivings.

8. Jung's emphasis on the adaptive significance of regression.

9. Jung's discovery and classification of different psychological types—ego attitudes and functions.

INTRODUCTION

Importance of Theories

Humans are distinguished from other primates by a capacity to organize and give meaning to complex symbolic experiences. From time immemorial, all cultures and individuals have created belief systems or theories about how, why, and when individuals and groups behave as they do. Anthropologists use the terms *world view* and *ethos* in reference to how diverse peoples think and feel reality is actually or logically constructed.

Every personality theory, like any culture, has its own world view and ethos: a fundamental character or spirit, which characterizes the beliefs, customs, or practices of a group of adherents, and an integrative set of dominant assumptions which order and classify experiences. For example, a personality theory may or may not highly value the concept of free will. The existence of a world view lends psychological security, meaning, and coherence to everyday life and its activities.

Personality theories seek to explain the natural order of things in terms of the extremes of human behavior and individual differences, but also of typical and universal patterns. Useful theories attempt to construct a reality of the psyche which takes both intrapersonal and interpersonal dynamics into account.

The Unconscious

Underlying theoretical premises are often unconscious and exist as predispositions to behave in certain consistent predictable ways over a long period of time. Thus, the concept of motivation assumes great importance. A comprehensive theory of personality considers unconscious, irrational inner promptings important. The study of personality should not attend only to overt behavior, or what is consciously known; it also should investigate implicit culture. It does not overlook vital consideration of powerful unconscious motivating forces. Personality theories differ in the extent to which they are open to and value unconscious aspects of personality structure, development, and psychodynamics. One may rightly question the validity of any theory which refuses to take the subjective elements of experience into account.

Theories are abstract speculations and by definition tentative, often innovative. A personality theory should never be considered final or closed. If it is to be holistic, practical, and able constantly to generate new hypotheses, it must deal with the following dimensions of human existence: (1) the psychological, conscious and unconscious; (2) the physiological, biological, and constitutional, and (3) the sociocultural context in which personalities develop, grow, and behave.

The Personal Equation

Theoretical systems in psychology cannot escape a founder's own personal psychology. In this sense, every theory is a personal confession. It reflects a subjective bias, even in the very questions it asks. If acknowledged openly and taken seriously into account, this personal bias may prove to be a scientific asset rather than a liability. Jung's term for that bias was "the Personal Equation."

Jung derived his theoretical structure from many sources, not the least of which was his own inner life and self-analysis. He wrote from his own conflictual depths, but also from his extensive work with neurotic, borderline, and psychotic patients. For him the existence of the deep unconscious was central. His work was characterized by scholarly empiricism, drawing objectively on the observation of dreams and other clinical phenomena. Analytical psychology, as put forth by Jung, may also be said to respect the irrational, the intuitive, the teleological, and the parapsychological dimensions of human existence.

HISTORY

Precursors

Jung's intellectual ties and philosophical foundations are more firmly rooted in what Ellenberger (1970) calls "psychiatric Romanticism and philosophy of nature" (p. 657), rather than in the period of the Enlightenment. Jung's thought is related to classical Greek and Latin philosophers, to Protestant theological tradition, and to Asian philosophies. More specifically, it is related to Immanuel Kant, Johann Schiller, Friedrich Nietzsche, Søren Kierkegaard, Johann Wolfgang Goethe, and to the phenomenologists Edward Husserl and Martin Heidegger.

Jung's extended readings included the works of two noted German cultural anthropologists, Adolf Bastian and Leo Frobenius. Bastian promoted the idea that the psychic unity of mankind could explain the occurrence of the same rites, myths, and symbols all over the world better than the concept of diffusion could. Bastian's "elementary ideas" in many ways foreshadow what Jung would later call the "archetypes" and what modern anthropologists would return to study as "natural symbols," once the limitations and fallacies of unilinear social evolutionary theory were put aside. In connection with Jung's lifelong interests in cross-cultural studies, Georg Friedrich Creuzer deserves mention. Creuzer's work explored symbolism among so-called primitive peoples, giving special attention to the interpretation of complex myths and folktales.

Four of Jung's predecessors are particularly important as philosophers of the unconscious: (1) Gottfried Leibnitz, who postulated the concept of an irrational unconscious in the 18th century; (2) Carl Gustav Carus, who distinguished three levels of the unconscious, including a "general" universal one that had creative, compensatory, self-healing functions; (3) Arthur Schopenhauer, who emphasized irrational forces at work in man, principally blind sexual forces that are often repressed; and (4) Eduard von Hartmann, who described three levels of unconscious functioning, including an absolute or universal source of images.

Jung matured intellectually at a time when great changes were taking place in psychiatry and neurology. Many of his contemporaries were innovators, and he benefited from them by personal contacts as well as reading. In addition to Eugen Bleuler, Pierre Janet had great influence on Jung. What Janet studied as "psychological automatism," dual personalities, the "function of synthesis," and "subconscious fixed ideas," Jung later called *complexes*. Theodore Flournoy's study of parapsychology aided Jung in similar scholarly endeavors, and it inspired Jung's early interest in the phenomenon of cryptomnesia. Alfred Binet's two types of intelligence became an integral part of Jung's work on introverted and extraverted types. Finally, Jung incorporated much from Alphonse Maeder's work on the teleological function of dreams. Jung credited and acknowledged his debt to these and many other men who form the backdrop for his intellectual growth and development, including later influences from Sigmund Freud and Alfred Adler.

Beginnings

Jungian psychology can best be understood through an appreciation of the founder's personal background, especially his childhood experiences, which

Jung himself felt were decisive in forming his basic character, scientific attitudes, and psychological interests. From early childhood, Jung was an introvert. In his autobiography (1961) he describes himself as solitary, intellectual, and fascinated by the questions which philosophy, psychology, and theology normally pose.

Because the development of Jung's thought sunk deep roots in philosophical-humanistic soil, the symbolic was just as real to him as the physical. Natural science or rationalism were never enough for him. Jung's fundamental approach to the psyche, based on a coherent humanistic world view, stands at the center of his work throughout his long life, in sharp contrast to Freud's pessimism. Moreover, this difference existed before they collaborated. Jung's relative lack of concern for materialistic and strictly rational interpretations is reflected as early as November 28, 1896, in a talk he gave to fellow medical students at the University of Basel entitled "On the Limits of the Exact Sciences."

Carl Gustav Jung was born on July 26, 1875, in the small village of Kesswil, Switzerland. He was named after an illustrious and unconventional paternal grandfather, a physician who was interested in mental health, philosophy, classical studies, and poetry. Jung's maternal grandparents were renowned Hebrew scholars, theologians of distinction, and interested in parapsychology. Thus many of Jung's later interests, including creativity in old age, were reflected in his kinship identifications.

Jung's father, a poor country pastor of the Swiss Reformed Church, was devoted to intellectual pursuits and the care of his parishioners. Although Jung experienced him as religiously conventional, he was a classical and oriental scholar, and much of the son's erudition and appreciation for these subjects can no doubt be traced to early contact with his father. Jung experienced his father as irritable, ineffectual, and distant, and his childhood was marked by religious conflicts with his father which persisted into adolescence. These disputes usually ended acrimoniously. It is as though Jung wrestled to come to terms with his father's views versus his own personal discovery of a truly religious attitude toward life for most of his career.

Jung's mother was in many ways a more influential person in his life—perhaps ultimately the source of his emphasis on a creative unconscious and man's universal need to free himself from the potentially engulfing "world of the Mothers." In his autobiography (1961), Jung recalls that his mother was perceived as very strong but also as emotionally ambivalent ("dual") and at times weak, disturbed, and depressed.

Jung reports a singularly lonely and often unhappy childhood in which he had to cope with the severe marital problems of his parents. He would often retreat to the attic or some other solitary place to be alone. He was the oldest child and only son, and intimate relationships with a younger sister do not seem to have figured prominently in his life or to have provided much satisfaction.

After completing secondary school studies, Jung chose to study medicine at the University of Basel. This was made possible by a scholarship which his father, soon to pass away, helped his son secure. Jung was a medical student from 1895 to 1901. During that time he distinguished himself academically among fellow students and decided to specialize in psychiatry. To this end he received a position under the tutelage of the famous psychiatrist Eugen Bleuler at the well-known Burghölzli Psychiatric Hospital in Zurich. Soon after this important and creative relationship began, Jung published his medical dissertation in 1902 entitled, "On the Psychology and Pathology of So-called Occult Phenomena." This first publication demonstrates originality and insight. In this earliest paper can be found the seeds of central concepts which would later, when more highly developed, cost him his "orthodox" psychoanalytic standing.

Jung took a leave of absence to study hypnosis with Janet in Paris during the winter of 1902. Upon his return he married, was appointed lecturer in psychiatry at the University of Zurich and, under the influence of Bleuler, resumed his work with patients at Burghölzli, developing psychological tests and measurements, principally his Word Association Test. These experiments added to his rapidly growing fame. Prior to meeting Freud, Jung's position as one of Europe's leading psychiatrists was secure, his private practice was flourishing, and he had already impressed his colleagues as being unusually brilliant.

In 1906 Jung first corresponded with Freud and thereafter took up the cause of psychoanalysis with outstanding vigor. This meant defending Freud and his theories against public and professional outcry, as well as teaching and promulgating the particular orientation of the Zurich school, which always differed somewhat from that of the Viennese inner circle. In the same year Jung visited Freud for the first time in Vienna, his well-known psychoanalytic interpretation of schizophrenic process was published as the *Psychology of Dementia Praecox* (1907). A copy was presented to Freud, who was extremely impressed by it.

The first Freud-Jung meeting ushered in six years of close collaboration in the discovery and development of psychoanalysis. Jung never relinquished his profound admiration for Freud as a person and for his discoveries. The enthusiasm was mutual: Freud considered Jung his "successor" for life and a "crown prince." The nature of this relationship has until recently been known mainly through Freudian accounts, as a result of which Jung's break with Freud was generally viewed as heresy. With the publication of the Freud-Jung letters, the father-son nature of the relationship (Freud was 19 years older than Jung) has been clarified, as well as the fact that Jung had already developed a clear independent orientation to the unconscious which differed significantly from Freud's, even before they met (Adler, 1973; McGuire, 1974).

By 1909 Jung had achieved an international reputation. With Freud, he traveled to the United States to lecture on the controversial science of psychoanalysis at Clark University. Jung was the first president of the International Psychoanalytic Association and managing editor of the very first psychoanalytic journal, the *Jahrbuch*. He lectured extensively on psychoanalysis and taught courses at the University of Zurich.

Although this period is characterized by Jung's passionate involvement, and constant defense of and devotion to Freud, there was from the very start a fundamental misunderstanding. Ellenberger (1970) writes: "Freud wanted disciples who would accept his doctrine without reservation. Bleuler and Jung saw their relationship as a collaboration that left both sides free" (p. 669).

For a time divergencies between Jung and Freud remained unchecked, and Jung continued to champion Freud. However, with Jung's *Symbols of Transformation* (1911) there was a decisive break. In the same year Jung went to New York to lecture on psychoanalysis, declaring that his own version of psychoanalysis was a further development of Freud's ideas. The rift grew wider as Freud's suspicions and anger grew, and when the International Association met in Munich in October of 1913, Jung resigned as president and as editor of the *Jahrbuch*.

There followed six years (1913-19) during which Jung suffered profoundly. Jung describes this obscure period of introversion or creative illness in his autobiography (1961). After this period of intense mental turmoil and self-analysis, Jung emerged with increased strength and creative vigor.

The end of this period is marked by the publication in 1921 of what some consider his most important work, *Psychological Types*.

After 1914, Jung became the founder and leader of his own psychoanalytic school of thought, which he called Analytical Psychology. For the rest of his life he devoted himself to teaching, study, and to his family of five children and a wife, Emma, who became an analyst in her own right. He was a dedicated psychotherapist with a huge practice. Although his later life was characterized by increased interiority, he also took delight and scholarly interest in travel to England, America (the Pueblo Indians), black Africa, and Asia.

Before his death Jung experienced increased world recognition for his creative experimental genius and his courageous pursuit of knowledge in previously unexplained areas of the mind. Jung died in his home at Küsnacht, Zurich, on June 6, 1961, at the age of 85.

Current Status

Jung may be considered one of the most revolutionary and creative thinkers of modern time concerning psychoanalytic theory and related subjects. Although a small group of Jung's students constituted a Psychology Club in

Zurich as early as 1916, Jung himself was not quick to encourage formal Jungian institutions. Until 1946 he remained ambivalent and reluctant about founding training institutes. In the light of an accelerating rediscovery of Jung and his analytic theories today, the increasing number of such organizations reflects greater structure and activity in this area since his death.

The number of Jungian analysts has remained relatively small. In 1981 about 600 certified Jungian analysts belonged to the International Association of Analytical Psychology. At present 18 autonomous Jungian analytic training institutes function in England, France, Germany, Israel, Italy, Switzerland, and the United States. Additional certified analysts belong to smaller societies or are individual members of the international association in at least 20 additional countries, including Australia, Belgium, Brazil, Canada, Finland, India, Japan, Korea, the Netherlands, Sweden, and Venezuela. Training institutes in the United States have joined the National Accreditation Association for Psychoanalysis. Some Jungians belong to the liberal, all-inclusive American Academy of Psychoanalysis, which includes followers of Erich Fromm, Karen Horney, Harry S. Sullivan, and others who share a belief in the validity and importance of the unconscious.

Although training procedures vary widely, the heart of Jungian analytic training everywhere is a lengthy personal-training analysis, plus years (usually four) of didactic seminars, written and oral examinations, controlled case supervision, tutorial work, and, in most places, a clinical dissertation.

Jungian institutes traditionally train duly recognized clinicians at the doctoral level in medicine or clinical psychology (M.D. or Ph.D.), although, as with other schools, clinical social workers and exceptional others complete the trainee picture. From beginning to end, the average length of time invested by an individual in Jungian training amounts to six to eight years. Candidates at various stages of the training process may join the International Association of Jungian Trainees and Newly Qualified Analysts which meets once a year in a different part of the world.

Although Jungian psychology has been taught in major colleges and universities for many years, not until recently does the world seem to have caught up with Jung. Some contemporary interest in Jung is superficial and stems from so-called occult or mystical notions which get confused with Jung's concept of experiences of the self. More significant is the serious attention being given to Jung's ideas which are being rediscovered by psychoanalysts of many schools. In many scientific quarters, the shift has been from Freud to include Jung (cf. Frey-Rohn, 1975).

Particular theoretical emphases characterize Jungian analytical theory. This chapter draws attention to particular aspects of modern depth psychology which seem, in our view, to relate most cogently to selected theoretical emphases or assertions stressed early by Jung and his students. Given the great areas of overlap with basic psychoanalytic theory as developed by pioneers in this field, a comparative approach may prove useful to the student considering an approach to unconscious mental processes which differs, in some respects radically, from so-called orthodox analytical theory. Readers interested in greater in-depth understanding of analytical psychology are referred to the 21 volumes of *The Collected Works of C. G. Jung;* his autobiography, *Memories, Dreams, Reflections; The Library of Analytical Psychology;* the *Journal of Analytical Psychology; Spring, An Annual of Archetypal Thought; Psychological Perspectives;* and other non-English publications dealing with the modern science of analytical psychology available to the scholarly public. The items in the Annotated Bibliography at the end of this chapter are also recommended.

ASSERTIONS

Development

1. *Personality is influenced by potential activation of a collective transpersonal unconscious.*

Jung's general concept of a collective unconscious in which archetypes exist as potential symbols grew out of his practicing the classical psychoanalytic method. In day-to-day analytic work, gradually, his awareness of a deeper transpersonal level of the psyche was sharpened and further corroborated by personal experiences in self-analysis. His understanding of the collective unconscious was rounded out by many years of scholarly research into the basic underlying structures and functions of geographically widespread myths and symbolic motifs. As a result of his own confrontations with unconscious mental processes, distinct part-personalities or categories of human experience which could not be reduced to personal sexual causes presented themselves. He discovered motifs which could not be attributed to individual experiences alone. In Jungian theory, therefore, a critical topographical and structural distinction is made between the personal and the collective unconscious.

Before proceeding to a discussion of psychodynamic maturational processes from a modern Jungian perspective, we will first say something about the structure of the psyche which includes four main entities: (1) a psychodynamic self which includes activities of a personal and a collective unconscious, (2) complexes, (3) the ego, and (4) archetypes. They are defined in the Glossary, and during the course of our discussion they will be clarified further.

2. *Elements unacceptable to the ego are located in the personal unconscious.*

The personal unconscious may be equated roughly with the Freudian "repressed unconscious." Although Jungians do not want to be limited to this concept of the unconscious, Jung's theory locates painful experience, anxiety-laden fantasies, feelings, and thoughts unacceptable to the ego and the superego in the personal unconscious. Here they remain repressed, suppressed, isolated, denied, "forgotten," split off, and dangerously unrecognized by ego-consciousness. Experiences which have never been strong enough to make a significant impression on the ego also exist in this region of the mind, but, like the contents of Freud's preconscious region, they are accessible to consciousness.

During deep analysis, they are remembered, repeated, and can be integrated or worked through, so that large portions of this material may be assimilated and made conscious through confrontation and synthesis. Jung calls this area of the mind the *shadow,* a global term with both personal and transpersonal connotations. In addition to standing for the denied or projected "otherness," the shadow can be considered the archetype of primary evil or moral "badness." The concept of the shadow, however, need not be restricted to evil or to fantasies contrary to superego demands (repressed for the sake of ego ideals); it can refer simply to whatever natural potentials are undeveloped and relatively undifferentiated in the psyche. In this sense the shadow has great value. *Complexes* located in the personal unconscious assume great importance.

3. *Complexes are structured and energized around an archetypal image.*

Jung's free association experiments after the turn of the century drew heavily on the scientific methodology of his day. He had first impressed Freud with his discovery of unconscious affect-toned "complexes" which belong essentially to the personal unconscious. Complexes may be seen as containing archetypal cores (affect-images) which, when activated, draw personal experiences to them. The ego is in constant "dialogue" with the unconscious via its encounters with this inner world of interrelated complexes. Because this dialogue involves fantasy transactions between the ego and complexes which are personal *but rooted in the archetypal psyche,* it is only partially accurate to equate Jung's "personal unconscious" with Freud's repressed unconscious.

The ego is either strengthened or weakened by contact with the unconscious in its encounters with the complexes. The ego may relate to a complex in four different ways: (1) by remaining completely *unconscious* of it, (2) by *identification* or "possession," (3) by *projection,* and (4) by *confrontation* which alone leads to assimilation and growth.

Complexes are always *bipolar* in three senses. First they have both a "negative" and a "positive" valence and are always potentially growth restricting or growth fostering when activated. Second, when activated, a complex always relates structurally to another complex. Complexes are not randomly dispersed in the unconscious. In terms of inner-world relations, for example, the mother complex is paired and interacts with a daughter or son (child) complex, father complex, and so on (Perry, 1970). If a mother complex is predominantly negative, when activated ("tapped") it may overwhelm the ego. The goal of Jungian psychoanalysis would be, in this case, to weaken or depotentiate the negative effect of complexes through analysis of transference and the internalization of a "corrective emotional experience" with a "good" mother-person. During development, the child or adult is constantly "taking in" (introjecting) experiences from contact with significant others, referred to in Jungian theory as "external objects." The individual, simultaneously, puts out (projects) the state of his inner world, his cast of characters, the "internal objects" who inhabit him. External objects taken in and added to an ever-changing sense of inner-world reality, however, are not totally accurate perceptions of external reality. On the contrary, introjections and identifications are altered to some extent by the individual's preexisting complexes, internal objects, archetypal images, and instinctual needs. The structuring (internalization) of an inner world is therefore intricate and subtle, utilizing complicated projective-introjective processes assumed to be operative at birth. Complexes (internal objects) are bipolar in a third important sense. Since they contain archetypal cores, the complexes, like all other archetypal potentialities, are psychosomatic entities. The somatic pole of the complex is rooted in instinctual physical experiences of the body ego/self fueled by the drives, while the other "spiritual" or psychic pole is linked with unconscious and potential fantasy structures in the mind.

The dominant role of complexes as feeling-toned groups of internal objects or representations in the unconscious is a central part of Jungian theory. An understanding of how unconscious complexes are structured, energized (cathected), and developed over time has been greatly augmented by developments in modern internal-object relations theory. The central position given to complexes by Jung has changed little with time. In Jung's words: "The individual representations are combined according to the different laws of association (similarity, coexistence, etc.), but are selected and grouped into larger combinations [fields of interaction] by an affect" (1907, p. 40).

Complexes belong to the basic structure and psychic energy distribution system of the psyche which functions on the principle of energic balance or homeostasis. Jungian analysis seeks to make conscious and to integrate energy contained in the complexes—especially those that promote dissociation and impair the unity of the psyche. A complex can remain autonomous, either because it is totally unconscious and therefore not known to the ego, or because even though it is "known" intellectually, resistances are still great enough to prevent assimilation into consciousness. Complexes, therefore, can remain independent, and be harmful. Jacobi (1959) describes how simple conscious knowledge of a complex's existence may be futile: "the complex's harmful action will continue until we succeed in 'discharging' it, or until the excess of psychic energy stored up in it is transferred to another gradient, that is, until we succeed in assimilating it emotionally" (p. 10).

In therapy, growth-inhibiting complexes must be weakened. The first step in the treatment process is to make complexes conscious and therefore accessible to the synthetic functions of the ego. It is not enough to know about them intellectualy; they must be experienced and lived through in the transference during analysis. Once brought to conscious attention, a complex and its historical development can be understood. This usually occurs only after the analysis of defenses and resistances to such insights has been sufficiently dealt with. Such understanding makes a complex less autonomous, uncontrollable, and compulsive. Correction, disidentification of the ego with a complex, new adaptive behaviors, and transformation are possible once a person is in dialogue with the internal figures that inhabit him. In connection with this process, dream analysis and the helpful collaboration of the analyst are central.

Any general understanding of the archetypes of the collective unconscious begins with an appreciation of the *indivisibility* of the personal and collective aspects of the psyche (cf. Neumann, 1959; Williams, 1963). This indivisibility is perhaps conceptualized most lucidly in terms of how personal-transpersonal elements come together in the formation, building up, activation, or weakening of innumerable complexes in the personal unconscious during the course of normal development.

The personal unconscious is closer structurally to the ego in the psyche than to the collective unconscious. The latter may be seen as an extension of the personal unconscious and outside the comprehension of the ego much of the time. The ego itself, on the border (so to speak) between the personal unconscious and external reality, is the center of consciousness, although important portions of the ego are also unconscious.

4. *The ego mediates between the unconscious and the outside world.*

The ego represents the vantage point of consciousness to which all conscious contents are related. Located conceptually between the unconscious inner world and the external world, the ego mediates, and copes with unknown stimuli from each of these areas. Jungian theory asserts that a strong, well-structured ego is the result of ideal normal development. A strong ego encounters the archetypes as they enter into the structural arrangement of complexes located in the personal unconscious.

A person with a healthy, strong sense of *ego identity* experiences himself as having continuity, sameness, individuality, and autonomy over time; likewise he experiences a sense of firm inner and outer ego boundaries flexible and relatively permeable when appropriate, and he has a feeling that he can contain and locate what is "inside" *as distinct from* what exists separately "outside." At birth the newborn perceives only sensations originating within his body. Only gradually does he turn from inner stimuli to outer perception, from fusion to dialogue.

The ego rests on both somatic and psychic beginnings. In the earliest non-differentiated stage of life, the ego is not separate from the self. The baby does not distinguish what is "I" from what is "not-I," the ego from the self, let alone any precise perceptions of his environment (Tate, 1961). In the first few weeks and months of life the infant remains in a state of what Jung has variously called "primitive identity" or "participation mystique" with the mother, or with parts of her body (i.e., the breast or nipple, a *"part-object"*). This part-object state is called *projective identification.* Gradually, projective identification states change to include gradual perception of the mother as a whole person (simultaneously good *and* bad), rather than as a split "all or nothing" person (idealized *or* persecuting). These "all or nothing" primitive affects of love and hate in relation to images of the inner and outer personal mother integrate substantially as development proceeds. As this occurs, the infant is said to have achieved what Melanie Klein (Segal, 1973) called the *depressive position* (M. Fordham, 1969a). The depressive position starts in the fourth or fifth month of life and reaches a peak at about seven months. The achievement of the depressive position implies that a baby has developed the capacity to tolerate intense ambivalence toward the mother with a sense of concern for her vitality and well-being. It also implies that schizoid mechanisms against infantile paranoid fears (e.g., of being devoured), such as primitive denial, splitting, idealization, and massive projective identification need not be pathologically and automatically employed to preserve the early ego. Separation of the ego out of the original state of unconscious identity with the self-mother-breast has taken place. Ego fragments then form a more coherent and organized island around which a vast sea of personal and collective unconscious material exists (cf. Plaut, 1959, 1966, 1974).

In connection with the earliest stages of life, Michael Fordham (1957, 1963, 1965, 1969a, 1971a, 1971b), building on Jung's foundation, has extended Jungian theory. Fordham's seminal work on the complicated processes involving "deintegration" of an innate "primary self" constitutes a major advance not only in Jungian theory but in psychoanalytic theories. Fordham's major contributions relate to the ego and its dynamic relationship to the self during infancy and childhood (1976). His focus on "defenses of the self" (1974a) is highly original. His concept of the *primary self,* however, must be cited, *since it is generally assumed in Jungian developmental theory that an integrated self system is primary. It exists in the very beginning. Consequently the infant or fetus is looked on as a unitary self or basic psychosomatic unity out of which the archetypes and the ego are derived. The self, in the sense of a basic undivided wholeness, is precursor of the ego.* Fordham (1961) explains:

> The theory of the original self grew first of all from the empirical observation. Self images could be observed in childhood and could be conjectured in infancy; the conjectures were supported, amongst other indirect evidence, by statistical studies made by Gesell on the appearance of the word "I" in childhood. The theoretical source derived from Jung's idea that the self lies behind ego development, a conception which, applied to infancy and childhood, led me to postulate an original state of the self prior to the appearance of the ego. This would explain the observed phenomena and made it possible to postulate an initial wholeness. The original state was assumed to be a simple integrate without other manifestations than its wholeness. It could be compared with the zygote before it begins to divide. (p. 78)

5. *The primary self represents an original state of psychobiological wholeness.*

Jung's views of the *self* embrace two fundamental ideas: (1) innate potential wholeness, and (2) an integrating and organizing archetype. The self system includes not only the ego but also the archetypes. Following Jung, analytical psychologists tended to conceive of the self as a stabilizing, centralizing, and even closed system (Redfearn, 1969). However, Fordham (1972) reflects neo-Jungian theoretical advances when he writes that "exclusive emphasis on stability and organization is not suitable when applied to developing periods of infancy and early childhood" (p. 463). Rather, it is assumed that a dynamic relationship between the self and the ego exists; this relationship, viewed in developmental perspective, involves fluctuating periods throughout the life cycle of integration-deintegration of the primary self. Life-crisis states of deintegration are characterized by the spontaneous release of archetypal activity and the activation of archetypal potential during important developmental phases (Fordham, 1967; Maduro, 1980).

Among Jungians there is some controversy about whether the self can be called a separate archetype, although in many places Jung calls it an archetype. However, today more attention is given to Jung's earliest and most important discovery of the primary self as an original state of psychobiological wholeness. The notion of a supraordinate self as the total psyche is in keeping with Jung's definition in *Psychological Types* (1921) as he revised it for the *Collected Works*.

6. *Archetypes function as organs of the collective unconscious psyche.*

Jung initially used a variety of words, such as *primordial image*, to describe an early and relatively undifferentiated formulation of the archetypal dimension of the psyche, but the word *archetype* first appeared in 1919. For the remainder of his life, the major focus of his theoretical work and clinical practice was devoted to the serious exploration and elucidation of the role of the collective unconscious, or what he later came to call the *objective psyche*.

From the very beginning Jung widened and deepened Freud's position. Jung felt his colleague's views were correct but not comprehensive enough to adequately describe the complicated workings of the mind. He could not accept Freud's exclusive emphasis on sexuality and personal psychobiological determinism.

In the light of Jung's balanced approach to the psyche, a relevant remark made by the anthropologist Clyde Kluckhohn is paraphrased here: *Every man is in certain respects like all other men, like some other men, like no other man.* This statement is particularly helpful to put Jungian psychology and the concept of the archetype into proper perspective. Although Jung never denied the importance of culture and strictly personal life history variables in the development of an individual, he contributed most richly to psychoanalysis by addressing himself to the psyche's phylogenetic heritage and to the psychic unity of mankind. It was Jung's contention that the psyche and the unconscious cannot be understood without a consideration of the interpenetration of sociocultural, personal, and archetypal (transpersonal) forces. With Jung's approach in mind, Kettner (1967) refers to Kluckhohn and puts it well: "That, in a nutshell, is how an archetype works—a basic theme, recognizable patterns of variation, and the unique individual twist taken in a specific case" (p. 34-35).

Jungian theory holds that the mind is not a *tabula rasa* at birth but that there is an archetypal ground plan built into the structure of the human brain. It would take us too far afield here to discuss modern biology in relation to the theory of archetypes. Such a focus would have to include research on the limbic system and on right-left hemispheres of the brain, modern behavioral genetics, and how natural selection and the mutation of germ plasm are viewed by modern scientists (cf. M. Fordham, 1957; Osterman, 1968). These studies would clearly indicate, moreover, that there need be nothing "mystical" about archetypes, which are inherited predispositions to apperceive typical or nearly universal *situations and figures*. The archetype can further be described as a "system of readiness" to respond to environmental cues, a dynamic nucleus of concentrated psychic energy ready to be actualized, as an affect-image and as an *autonomous,* numinous structural element outside the comprehension of the ego. M. Fordham (1969a) sheds further light on the problem of defining archetypes.

Though most studied in their complex symbolic forms, i.e., in dreams, fantasies, mythology, folklore and religion, the essential core that emerges from Jung's work is that an archetype is a psychosomatic entity having two aspects: the one is linked closely with physical organs, the other with unconscious and potential psychic structures. The physical component is the source of libidinal and aggressive "drives"; the psychic one, the origin of those fantasy forms through which the archetype reaches incomplete representation in consciousness. (p. 96)

Although at first Jung considered mainly archetypal images, he later considered patterns of emotions and predispositions to species-specific behavior as well. Jung's concept of the archetype, as developed and refined (cf. Jacobi, 1959), provides for two essential distinctions: (1) *the archetype as such,* and (2) *the archetypal image.* It is important to keep these two distinctions in mind, since Jung's contributions have been greatly misunderstood and misrepresented by confusing these theoretical issues. Misinformed opinion would have it, for example, that actual ideational content is inherited. Although Jung never ruled out such a possibility, he could never accept Freud's strictly Lamarckian concept of a "racial memory."

The Archetype as Such. Archetypes are not inherited ideas or images but are a priori possibilities.

For Jung the "primordial image" or "archetype as such" belonging to the deepest unconscious is an a priori, phylogenetically transmitted predisposition or "readiness" to apperceive a universal, emotional core human experience, myth, or thought-image-fantasy. This "archetype as such" can never be exactly pinpointed or apprehended because it exists in such a primitive formal state. Jung (1947) summarizes his views:

> The archetypal representations (images and ideas) mediated to us by the unconscious should not be confused with the archetype as such. They are very varied structures which all point back to one essentially "irrepresentable" basic form. The latter is characterized by certain formal elements and by certain fundamental meanings, although these can be grasped only approximately. The archetype as such is a psychoid factor that belongs, as it were, to the invisible, ultraviolet end of the psychic spectrum. . . . It seems to me probable that the real nature of the archetype is not capable of being made conscious, that it is transcendent, on which account I call it psychoid (quasi-psychic). (p. 213)

The Archetypal Image. There is a dynamic relationship between environmental situations and archetypal response. Unlike the archetype as such, the image is a representation already perceived by at least a portion of ego-consciousness: "A primordial image is determined as to its contents only when it becomes conscious and is therefore filled out with the material of conscious experience" (Jung, 1938a, p. 79).

Jung's theory stresses the role of culture in activating and symbolically structuring ("clothing") archetypal activity arising from the deep unconscious. It follows that the same environmental experience may evoke different archetypal responses and that various environmental factors may evoke the same or similar archetypal responses. To turn again to Jung (1936a): "There are as many archetypes as there are typical situations in life. Endless repetition has engraved these experiences into our psychic constitution, not in the forms of images filled with content, but at first only as *forms without content,* representing merely the possibility of a certain type of perception and action" (p. 48).

The passage above indicates that Jung considers the archetypes to be innumerable. Yet certain archetypal images, situations, and experiences are more commonly encountered than others during a personal analysis, in the course of individual human development, or in everyday life. They are found in dreams, literature, religious mythologies, art forms, symptoms, and so on. Several examples are presented below.

Symbolic Death and Renewal. A common archetypal situation experienced cross-culturally relates to Jung's emphasis on potentiality in the human psyche for symbolic transformation involving reconstitutive experiences of death and rebirth, and on his extremely positive evaluation of therapeutic regression. For Jung it is clearly the birth of the ego, or part of the ego, which renews the sense of self (feeling centered and whole). Ego-consciousness is reborn, experiences growth, is expanded; it emerges dynamically from a state of projective identification or fusion with a primordial state of unconsciousness (non-ego). This healthy process in later life repeats the earliest separation of the ego from identification and containment in the primary self. The ego feels threatened by death and experiences (perceives) rebirth (Perry, 1961).

The concept of symbolic death and rebirth, as an archetypal/transpersonal motif, came to characterize Jung's overall theoretical approach to man's unconscious, psychological growth during analysis (Jung, 1911, 1940a), as well as patterns of initiation or *rites de passage* (Henderson, 1967). While there are no specific *contents* common to the death-rebirth motif in all cultures, the mythological *form* may be seen as an important archetypal given.

The Child. The symbol of an infant or child is an example of a common archetypal *figure.* It can foreshadow or accompany forward movement and progression through creative regression leading to symbolic death and renewal in the psyche (cf. Jung, 1940b; Maduro, 1976a; Maduro, 1980; Von Franz, 1970).

The meaning of the child symbol is highly overdetermined. In addition to all the personal (e.g., a sibling) and biological (e.g., child-penis-breast) associations, the archetypal dimension can at times assume great importance. The appearance of a child in dreams may signify a turning point in one's life or analysis; it may also indicate a good prognosis. The image of the "divine child" is found in many cultures and can stand for new life and direction, the free playful child in oneself, new awakenings, new beginnings, new symbolic identities, futurity, creativity, potential, and growth (the good internalized breast or fecundating phallus).

Children in fantasy life may stand for potentiality and creativity, because they are always on their way to developing into something else. Babies stand for wholly new ideas born out of the unconscious and therefore not yet known, as against the mere juggling of old ideas into forming what appear to be new ones.

It is easy to see that this particular archetypal figure, when analyzed, takes on an added future-oriented significance. Narrow causal-reductive (personal) explanations alone cannot account for its full symbolic meaning. Jungian theory posits the appearance of this particular symbol (the child) at different phases of human development and asserts that it is more a question of symbolic transformation requiring teleological explanation than one of simple causalities. The true symbol, according to Jung, looks not only backward in time but also forward. It may accompany positive or negative transformations.

Anima-Animus. Two part-personalities frequently encountered in dreams, visions, and literature are the contrasexual archetypes of the anima and animus: the inherited potential carried by a man to experience the image of woman (his anima), and in a woman the experience of man (her animus).

The unconscious of a man contains a complementary feminine component which takes the image of a woman: "An inherited collective image of woman exists in a man's unconscious, with the help of which he apprehends the nature of woman" (Jung, 1928e, p. 190). When a man has repressed his feminine nature, undervalued feminine qualities with contempt and neglect, or conversely has identified with his anima image, he is cut off from his own creativity and wholeness. The anima performs a mediating role to the creative unconscious and can stand for the whole unconscious in general (Jung, 1936a).

The anima is expressed in creative process involving fantasies. With regard to the anima and the mother who first carries this projection for a man, Frieda Fordham (1953) writes:

> The image only becomes conscious and tangible through the actual contacts with woman that a man makes during the course of his life. The first and most important experience of a woman comes to him through his mother, and is most powerful in shaping and influencing him: there are men who never succeed in freeing themselves from her fascinating power. But the child's experience has a marked subjective character and it is not only how the mother behaves, but how he *feels* she behaves that is significant. The image of his mother that occurs in each child is not an acccurate picture of her, but is formed and colored by the innate capacity to produce an image of woman—the anima. (p. 53)

Likewise, the personal father first embodies the animus image for a girl.

Thus, in addition to parental figures who first activate and symbolically structure the contra-sexual images in culturally patterned ways, anima and animus are derived from the inherited collective images of man and woman, as well as the latent masculine and feminine principles found in all individuals who are, according to psychoanalytic theories, assumed to be fundamentally bisexual.

7. *Unconscious psychic reality is as important as the external world.*

With the fundamental role of external (sociocultural) reality in mind, Jung (1945b) notes: "Try as we may to concentrate on the most personal of personal problems, our therapy nevertheless stands or falls with the question: 'What sort of world does our patient come from and to what sort of world has he to adapt himself?' " (p. 95).

At times Jung demonstrates an astute awareness of interpersonal processes and external influences on the development of personality. We have already noted that Jung's psychology stresses an inner realm, the deepest layers of the psyche, as being equally significant to outer reality. His major orientation gives *far greater attention to unconscious dynamic structures as motivating forces* than do other analytical models, with one exception: Melanie Klein's concept of an inner world which differs significantly from classical and neo-Freudian theories, comes close enough to original Jungian formulations to warrant the term "Klein-Jungian hybrid" (cf. Jackson, 1961b, 1963a, 1963b; Plaut, 1962).

Jung was personally most comfortable exploring the inner world. He opens his autobiography (1961) with a consideration of an inner dialogue between ego and self, stating that "outward events" are no more real to him than "inner experiences." He writes: "I can understand myself only in the light of inner happenings. It is these that make up the singularity of my life, and with these my autobiography deals" (p. 5). So also Jung's psychology—and that of Klein (Maduro, 1974b).

Jung's theory of personality development posits intrapsychic potential for altering the perception of external reality and its reintrojection. Fantasies are not purely escape and defense against internal and external realities, although they may serve these ends too; they are also natural mental expressions of "the instincts." In line with his assertion that the unconscious is not just a repressed unconscious and that there are creative unconscious contents which have never been conscious and subsequently have been repressed, Jung writes (1921): "The psyche creates reality everyday. The only expression I can use for this activity is *fantasy*. . . . Fantasy, therefore, seems to me the clearest expression of the specific activity of the psyche" (p. 52). Put differently, development and maturation of the individual take place through natural, spontaneous fantasy as the psyche "reaches out" for what it needs to grow and to further integrate inner and outer experiences. Innate developmental potential for individuation exists throughout the life cycle; Jung places great emphasis on phylogenetically determined autonomous forms, events, and broad developmental themes which are emergent entities in their own right. For example, Jung (1928a) asserts that, "From a consideration of the claims of the inner and outer worlds, or rather, from the conflict between them, the possible and the necessary follows" (p. 205). The life process or development is, to all intents and purposes, the result of energy freed from the counterplay of inner and outer world tensions. For this reason, Jung (1929a) adds: "We must be able to let things happen in the psyche" (p. 16).

Jung (1913) claimed that, "We must never forget that the world is, in the first place, a subjective phenomenon. The impressions we receive from these accidental happenings are also our own doing. It is not true that the impressions are forced on us unconditionally; our own predisposition [i.e., psychic reality] conditions the impression" (p. 177). Personal experiences, like a key, may be said to unlock developmental potential (Neumann, 1959). The following remarks made by Jung (1943b) in setting forth this basic viewpoint make his position on the primary importance of innate, endopsychic developmental potential clear: "Our consciousness does not create itself—it wells up from unknown depths. In childhood it awakens gradually, and all through life it wakes each morning out of the depths of sleep from an unconscious condition" (pp. 569-570). As the first psychoanalyst to revise Freud's classical libido theory, one of Jung's major theoretical contributions to a comprehensive object relations theory is the idea that the internal objects which furnish our inner world of psychic reality *may originate intrapsychically* (cf. Gordon, 1980).

8. *Jung's focus is on central preoedipal experiences, anxieties, and defenses.*

Although Jung never systematically developed a comprehensive and clear theoretical statement on the intricacies of child development, he thoroughly appreciated the importance of childhood and infancy. Where the analysis of infantile fixations and complexes in adults was indicated, he most often encouraged classical reductive methods and techniques, in addition to his own "constructive" or synthetic approach (cf. Adler, 1967; Whitmont, 1969; Whitmont & Kaufmann, 1973), which may be said to take into account both growth and repair.

Jung took no special interest in child analysis as such, although he supported his students who built on his theories to include a full appreciation of how conflicts in a child may be understood in terms of unconscious processes in parents (Wickes, 1927), as well as archetypal activity and individuation processes in childhood (M. Fordham, 1969a, 1971a). For an analyst more attuned to the developmental complexities of later life, Jung nevertheless made significant contributions to child psychology.

Maintenance

Personality is both developed and maintained by how the psyche handles conflict which arises from various sources. Opposition and conflict are basic to encounters between the ego and the archetypes via the complexes. As an overall "relatively closed" energy system (cf. Jung, 1928c, p. 7), the psyche includes all conscious and unconscious processes. Anything coming into association with the ego will partake of consciousness and its attributes to some extent (cf. Jung, 1926b. p. 323). Everything else outside the purview of ego-consciousness is unconscious.

With this hypothetical energy system in mind, Jung's model assumes systemic tendencies toward balance and homeostasis. Systems of personality interact and affect each other through the principles of (1) *compensation,* (2) *opposition,* and (3) *unification.* The following concepts in Jungian theory relate to or utilize these three principles and are, therefore, important to the maintenance of personality:

1. The self-regulating and compensatory nature of prospective unconscious processes.
2. Ego mechanisms of defense.
3. The spontaneous self-actualizing tendency within the psyche.
4. Symbolic processes of transformation in periods of deep therapeutic regression.
5. The nature of psychic energy.
6. Jung's notion of psychological types.

10. *A self-regulating psyche utilizes constructive unconscious compensation.*

Jung contended that consciousness and the unconscious exist in a reciprocal, complementary relationship. Dreamwork is a good example of the interaction of different systems of the personality. Although dreams at times disguise repressed negative or painful instinctual wishes and fears, Jung insisted that the dream's major function is not to conceal but to reveal (Maduro, 1978).

A dream arising from the unconscious part of the psyche complements or completes consciousness by presenting feelings, attitudes, identifications, and images outside conscious awareness. What is within the comprehension of the ego is only a tiny portion of the total psyche or self. Often healing symbols, synthesizing various aspects of a conflict and pointing toward potential resolution, arise where discrepancies between conscious and unconscious attitudes are severe, sharp, and growth-restricting. Limited one-sided consciousness is compensated for in dreams by what is felt and observed in the unconscious. In other words, the dream is richer and more complete than conscious awareness.

Regarding the nature of dreams and the principle of compensation, Jung (1934b) wrote: "The relation between conscious and unconscious is compensatory. This is one of the best proven rules of dream interpretation. When we set out to interpret a dream, it is always helpful to ask: What conscious attitude does it compensate?" (p. 153). And in 1916, Jung wrote:

> I should like to distinguish between the *prospective* function of dreams and their *compensatory* function. The latter means that the unconscious, considered as relative to consciousness, adds to the conscious situation all those elements from the previous day which remained subliminal because of repression or because they are simply too feeble to reach consciousness. This compensation, in the sense of being a self-regulation of the psychic organism, must be called purposive. (Jung, 1916a, p. 255)

Dreams have adaptive, healing, and synthesizing functions. The Jungian approach stresses the natural and spontaneous attributes of dream, myth, and artistic vision. Jungians see the unconscious not only as the repository of unacceptable garbage but also as a dynamic, creative unconscious: life giving as well as death-dealing. It is a natural creative function of the psyche to produce symbols—not fundamentally a disease process. Dreams are like an X ray of the human psyche, a view of one's psychic reality or inner world, at any given time. Jung (1934a) wrote: "The dream shows the inner truth and reality of the patient as it really is: not as I conjecture it to be, and not as he would like it to be, but *as it is*" (p. 142).

Dreams may also be looked at for unrecognized cultural stresses, sources of social support, and hidden creative potential, outside conscious awareness. Jung's teleological viewpoint frees the dream from being relegated automatically to classical causal-reductive analysis.

Art, myth, and dream all express the natural creative spontaneity of the psyche, available to all who will make the most of the lifelong process of individuation. In addition to the neurotic and negative, a person's dreams also reveal his positive side, the creative potentialities which lie dormant in his unconscious. Jungians assert that often the brightest, most creative side of a personality is repressed, undeveloped. Interpretations by an analyst seek to develop an awareness of these potential lines of development in the patient, as well as the causes of neurotic anxieties. Projections of positive and negative potential reflected in dreams also constitute extremely important elements in the transference.

Growth potential is commonly realized and maintained by an uncrippled capacity for ego participation in the *symbolic process*. If unimpaired, this process involves the containment and experiencing of symbolic opposites from which new life and direction eventually arise. Psychic energy made available to the human psyche for creative symbolic, expressive behavior comes through the union of opposites, or more precisely, from the tension caused by the polarization of psychic opposites contained *simultaneously* in the mind.

Throughout his life Jung was fascinated by symbolic process, as well as content, especially in relation to the growth and maintenance of personality (cf. Gordon, 1967). As early as 1916, he refers to the process as the "transcendent function" (Jung, 1916a). In later work he referred to the hidden third quality born out of the unconscious (i.e., a new awareness of greater importance than the two opposites from which it has sprung) as the uniting or reconciling function of the symbol, or "uniting symbols" (Jung, 1940b). The child symbol (discussed earlier) is one of the most common of these.

Symbols of polarity are well known in every art form and mythology the world over: male-female, light-dark, good-bad, right-left, thinking-feeling, father-mother, heaven-earth, and so on. In Jungian theory the contrasexual components (anima and animus archetypes) are never left out or discarded for a strictly patriarchal model of human consciousness and personality dynamics. Nor is the satanic (Jung's "shadow") dismissed as simply unwanted and valueless. The shadow is given some positive value, even nobility in terms of its ability to activate oppositional tensions that facilitate growth through the symbolic process which aims at achieving ultimate integration and wholeness: completeness, not perfection.

Ego Functions. If the ego matures, it is strengthened by contact with good educational experiences with parental figures who mirror parts of the child's self and its integrating functions. We may then speak appropriately of various *functions of the ego complex,* once they are acquired and take on significance for the maintenance of healthy personality during development. For Jungians many of these differ little, if at all, from current Freudian concepts (cf. A. Freud, 1936). Only those ego functions related to how Jungian theory differs from other schools in emphases, therefore, will be elaborated here.

Reality Testing. Adaptation to both external reality and a *sense of inner psychic reality* requires adjustment to things, persons, and situations. The well-functioning ego can accurately scan and assess the external world and its shared symbolic meanings, as well as encounter its internal resources.

Regulation and Control of Drives. The healthy ego tolerates strong affects such as *depressive anxiety,* postponement of satisfactions, and instinctual wishes, without inappropriately giving way to compulsive urges.

Capacity for Object Relations. The ego has a capacity to form and maintain intimate, close affectionate attachments to other people, without being overwhelmed by forces of hate, i.e., destructive feelings of hostility such as envy and greed which militate against experiences of interpersonal warmth, empathy, and sustained love. Unlike external reality where justice may not necessarily prevail, love and goodness must triumph over hate and bad parts of the self in psychic reality from where all capacity healthy joyful living and feelings of security derive (cf. Hubback, 1972; Klein, 1957).

Ego-Self Polarity.   Jungians may appear to place relatively little emphasis on the executive functions of the ego. The Jungian concern is not so much with ego capacity for control "from the top down," as a classical Freudian ego-id (instinctual antiego) dichotomy would imply, as with how, in what ways, and under which specific circumstances the ego complex assists in the self-actualization of the total psyche. Moreover, it is important in some situations, such as in creative process or in later life, for the ego to give way to a larger aim or sense of meaning associated with increased interiority, and in accord with the importance given to the self as the center of the personality, rather than the ego (Edinger, 1972; Maduro, 1974a).

Perceptive Processes.   The ability to think in terms of categories, classifications, the future, similarities, and differences is important for day-to-day living. This ego function includes good judgment, concentration, and a capacity to sort out what is important from a welter of internal and external stimuli, so that one can make sound conclusions.

Autonomous Functions.   These include intelligence, perception, motility, speech, thinking, and language. They develop relatively independently of instinctual demands.

Synthetic Functions.   Jungian theory places most emphasis on the integrating activities intrinsic to the ego. The ego organizes, assimilates, and integrates material arising from the unconscious. This activity is at times a response to external needs and situations, but the process is a natural, autonomous, healthy one which is assumed to arise intrapsychically as well. It is a striving toward wholeness and self-realization, an instinctual process *sui generis* of becoming, in which the ego assists. Dreams are a good example, according to Jungian theory, of the psyche's natural tendency toward growth—its push toward greater consciousness and awareness. Although he recognized the central role of resistance and the need to come to terms with it if growth is to occur at all, Jung's theory tends to stress the ego's synthesizing capacity and lines of future development more than any other psychoanalytic school. This difference makes Jung one of the major precursors of contemporary humanistic psychology.

11.   Normal and pathological ego defenses are basic oppositional forces to handle conflict in a self regulating psyche.

Defense Mechanisms.   The ego must defend itself against anxiety of a depressive and persecutory character, generated by impulses unacceptable or alien to it. These maneuvers are unconscious attempts to keep various wishes, thoughts, feelings, and unconscious fantasies from awareness, and therefore they feature prominently in any deep Jungian analysis. Defenses are oppositional forces which constitute an essential part of the psyche's self-regulating functions, without which there could be no balance (or imbalance). This is the case because ego development is closely linked to the formation of characteristic defensive organizations in the psyche and social masks—what Jung called the *persona* (cf. Jung, 1928a, 1928d: Whitmont, 1969).

Ego defenses are normal and help maintain personality. They have been investigated phylogenetically, and it is easy to see that without them a human being would be overwhelmed by inordinate and unmanageable amounts of guilt and anxiety. As with everything, however, there is a psychopathology of defenses too.

Jung clearly recognized defenses as being both necessary and pathological. In stressing that every encounter with an archetype involves a moral or ethical problem, Jung recognized that the avoidance of the moral or ethical dimension (superego) would be an avoidance of an encounter between ego and archetype. Athough necessary, typical defenses (e.g., denial, repression, projection, reaction formation, undoing, isolation, and others) can also be destructive. Therefore they need to be analyzed to facilitiate ego encounters with the archetypal psyche. Of the various defenses, projective identification (inflation), introjection, splitting, primitive idealization, denial, devaluation,and the manic defenses against depressive anxieties are perhaps most highlighted in Jungian personality theory, since they are acquired early and reflect Jungian psychology's preoedipal developmental bias.

12. The psyche spontaneously strives toward wholeness, integration, and self-realization

Jung's attention to the growth factor intrinsic to all psychopathological states appears in his earliest work. One of his finest contributions to the entire psychoanalytic movement is the point that symbols look not only backward in time but also forward. In 1902, Jung wrote:

> It is therefore, conceiveable that the phenomena of double consciousness are simply *new character formations, or attempts of the future personality to break through,* and that in consequence of special difficulties (unfavorable circumstances, psychopathic disposition of the nervous system, etc.) they get bound up with peculiar disturbances of consciousness. In view of the difficulties which oppose the *future character,* the somnambulisms *sometimes have an eminently teleological significance,* in that they give the individual who would otherwise inevitably succumb, the means of victory. (p. 79, emphasis added)

This early evidence for the prospective (forward-looking) function of unconscious mental contents provided an empirical foundation for much

of what Jung and his followers would formulate and study phenomenologically in the future. Jung's characteristic point of view that the psyche strives
towards self-realization is perhaps most lucidly reflected in another observation made later, in 1917, in *Two Essays on Analytical Psychology:*

> The symptoms of a neurosis are not simply the effects of long-past causes,
> whether "infantile sexuality" or the infantile urge to power; they are also
> attempts at a new synthesis of life—unsuccessful attempts, let it be added in the
> same breath, yet attempts nevertheless, with a core of value and meaning. They
> are seeds that fail to sprout owing to the inclement conditions of an inner and
> outer nature. (Jung, 1917a, p. 46)

Even before their association, Jung held views which were radically different from Freud in relation to the nature of unconscious processes and
symbolism. This is especially clear now that many of Jung's letters have
been published (cf. Adler, 1973; McGuire, 1974). In a letter dated April 2,
1909, Jung tells Freud: "I had the feeling that under it all there must be
some quite special complex, a universal one having to do with the prospective tendencies in man. If there is a 'psychoanalysis' there must also be a
'psychosynthesis' which creates future events according to the same law"
(Adler, 1973, p. 4). In addition to the many forms of resistance which exist,
there is also in the unconscious mind the wish to master the drives and to
self-actualize.

The classical Jungian position is clear: Neurotic phenomena are regarded
as positive events offering new life and direction under growth-fostering circumstances. Jung never lost sight of this theoretical perspective: the notion
that conflict, compensation, and unification are basic to future growth and
the maintenance of a healthy personality. Because Jung saw creative potential in the unconscious, he was the first psychoanalyst to stress the adaptive
significance of regression, a concept which remains central to his school in
both theory and clinical practice.

*13. Therapeutic regression takes place "in the service of the ego" and
"in the service of the self."*

In *Symbols of Transformation* (1911), Jung underlined the positive value of
regression of ego-consciousness, in contrast to then current Freudian
theory. Early in his career, Jung stressed the teleological function of symbolic interpretation *in addition* to causal-reductive analyses. He felt that
growth during analysis was possible only through regression of the ego
to the very deepest levels of the unconscious psyche. Here powerful
integrative forces urged not only compulsive repetition of previously
experienced personal conflicts but future-oriented self-actualization as well.
This was a major difference between the two greatest pioneers of
psychoanalysis. Jung (1911) writes:

As against this [i.e., the "one-sided 'biological' orientation of the Freudian school"], *therapy must support the regression,* and continue to do this until the "prenatal" stage is reached. It must be remembered that the "mother" is really an imago, a psychic image merely, which has in it a number of different but very important unconscious contents. The "mother," as the first incarnation of the anima archetype, personifies in fact the whole unconscious. Hence the regression leads back only apparently to the mother; in reality she is the gateway into the unconscious, into the "realm of the Mothers." Whoever sets foot in this realm submits his *conscious ego personality to the controlling influence of the unconscious,* or if he feels that he has got caught by mistake, or that somebody has tricked him into it, he will defend himself desperately, though his resistance will not turn out to his advantage. For regression, if let undisturbed, does not stop short at the "mother" but goes back beyond her to the prenatal realm of the "Eternal Feminine," to the immemorial world of archetypal possiblities where, "thronged round with images of all creation," slumbers the "divine child," patiently awaiting his conscious realization. This son is the germ of wholeness, and he is characterized as such by his specific symbols. (pp. 329-330)

Clearly, Jung's early stand in 1911 on the need for regression to archaic object relationships and to innate primordial modalities of the autonomous, unconscious psyche outside the comprehension of the ego relate directly to his emphasis on growth *and* repair (i.e., an analytic method which is both reductive-reconstructive and synthetic). The central issue raised above turns on Jung's general definition of libido or psychic energy—on his acceptance, in particular, of a separate creative instinct which is *sui generis.*

14. *Psychic energy is a general force that invests mental processes and structures.*

In contrast to Freud and Adler, it is an essential feature of Jungian theory that libido is not automatically committed to purely sexual, aggressive, or will-to-power ends. Jung insisted that psychic energy may take many forms which satisfy many different drives, all deeply rooted in the human psyche. Thus the goal of art can be power, sexual gratification, symbolic death and renewal, release of destructive-aggressive impulses, or creativity, as well as to fill social, "religious," or other aims. There are many different possibilities, paths, or "myths" libido can take. Only in the analytic theory of Jung do we find creativity (play) elevated to the status of a separate instinct in its own right, subject to the same vicissitudes and transformations as any other instinct. Creativity may not be reduced simply to something psychosexual.

Jung's concept of psychic energy is monistic. It is a pure, "sheer," or general force which charges all psychic contents or mental representations of the instincts (i.e., archetypal images) with intensity. Jung's concept is related to polarities, of which psychic and physical reality are one example and out of which the union of opposites, the symbol, is born. Jung (1917b) writes that, "It seems to me simpler to define libido as an inclusive term for psychic intensities, and consequently as sheer psychic energy" (p. 53). Thus he rejected a strictly dualistic model in which dynamic processes are conceived exclusively in terms of play between the life (*Eros*) and death (*Thanatos*) instincts.

At another level of abstraction and interpretation, however, Jung is strictly dualistic, or pluralistic. In referring to Freud's concept of the death instinct, Jung (1917a) states: "What Freud probably means is the essential fact that every process is a phenomenon of energy, and that all energy can only proceed from the tension of opposites" (p. 29). Jung's dualism stresses that there is no energy unless there is tension of opposites in the psyche. Gordon (1961) clarifies this issue:

> Ultimately eros and thanatos are only parts of the general life process, just as anabolism and catabolism are interdependent functions of the metabolic process. And though Jung may reject an over-riding dualism in terms of two principal and opposed instincts, he is in fact very much alive to the essential conflict which is at the root of all behavior and experience. (p. 131)

Jung accounts for destructive-aggressive impulses and negative violent phenomena in terms of *Eros-Phobos* (fear) opposites rather than *Eros-Thanatos* (death) (Jung, 1917b, p. 53). The love-hate, or *Eros-Phobos*, opposites exist *as a pair among pairs of opposites*. The *Phobos* aspect of the pair can be seen as fundamentally based on anxiety, fears of intimacy, instinctual excitement, and the wish to destroy.

Jung's concept of psychic energy also assumes purpose and forward-moving aims or roughly predetermined goals. In "On Psychic Energy" Jung (1928c) explains:

> The energic point of view . . . is in essence final; the event is traced back from effect or cause on the assumption that some kind of energy underlies the changes in phenomena, that it maintains itself as a constant throughout these changes and finally leads to entropy, a condition of general equilibrium. The flow of energy has a definite direction (goal) in that it follows the gradient of potential in a way that cannot be reversed. (p. 4)

Jung's concept of a "religious instinct"—for individuation and goal-oriented self-actualization—has been particularly controversial. Jungians differ from other analysts in their appreciation and understanding of this "spiritual" instinctual force as separate from sex or aggression. This powerful "drive" to individuate is thought to emanate from the self, not the ego. Perhaps more than most Jungian concepts, it has generated misunderstanding and acerbic criticism. If we assume the existence of psychic-physical polarities (opposites) and a transitional phase of development in which the infant separates out from primary identity with the mother, moving from part to whole object relations, as well as the essential bipolarity of archetypes, there need be no incompatibility between what Jung spoke of as a "religious instinct" and modern object relations theory. Religious forms and all other "higher" cultural achievements would arise from and take on form and meaning in the transitional period (M. Fordham, 1969a; Winnicott, 1951) when *the first true symbol—the transitional object—is formed through play*. Early self-representations are the transitional objects and the body image.

The concept of *value* is important in Jung's understanding of psychic energy. By this he means that "The amount of psychic energy in an element of the personality is called the value of that element. Value is a measure of intensity" (Hall & Lindzey, 1957, p. 91). It relates to how much power a particular idea or feeling may have as a motivating force in the psyche and can also be thought of in terms of degree of cathexis, or the extent to which a force with potential to instigate behavior is "invested" with available psychic energy. To the extent that energy is intensively deployed in one part of the psyche, it will be diminished in another, although the psyche is not strictly a closed system. Jung (1928a) explains his view of the principle of equivalence and the transformation of psychic energy:

> The disappearance of a given quantum of libido is followed by the appearance of an equivalent value in another form . . . for a given quantity of energy expended or consumed in bringing about a certain condition, an equal quantity of the same or another form of energy will appear elsewhere. (pp. 18-19)

15. *Individuation processes proceed throughout life in relation to one's "psychological type."*

The two basic ego attitudes toward life are *extraversion* and *introversion*. The extravert's libido (or psychic energy, or interest) flows outward to the object; objective facts or external happenings are the most important factors of life for him. People, things, and events are endlessly interesting to him, and he adapts himself easily as well to his environment. His interest is held and his mind stimulated by the external object; he reacts to it on a specific basis and does not tend to either generalize or introspect from it. He talks fluently, makes friends readily, and is in general a useful and appreciated member of society.

The libido of the introvert is directed predominantly inward, not outward. For the introverted person the significance of the internal object lies not in itself but in how it relates to his own psychology. It is not the situation objectively considered, but the situation as he reacts to it, that is the dominating factor. The introvert is never completely at home in the external world of men and things but prefers his own inner life, where he is quite at ease. He cannot only endure solitude to a degree which would break the extravert; he must have a considerable amount of it for his mental health.

Outer activities may be difficult for him, but he has a richly differentiated inner world where he feels at home. The normal introvert also cultivates friends but tends to limit them in number. It might be said that he forms vertical (depth) relationships as opposed to the horizontal (breadth) relationships of the extraverted person.

The two modes of perception are *sensation* and *intuition*. These two alternatives are nonrational functions, not because they are contrary to reason but because they are outside the province of reason and therefore not established by it.

The term *sensation* as used here refers to sense perception through the five senses. The sensation type individual perceives mostly through his senses; outer and inner spontaneously sensed convictions constitute reality for him. He perceives these realities as they exist now, in the present.

The intuitive's psychological function transmits perceptions via the unconscious of the other person. Intuition is an immediate awareness of the whole configuration, without a real comprehension of the details of the contents. It concerns itself with inner or outer phenomena. The focus is on possibilities.

Whereas the sensation-type person is interested in things as they are now, the intuitive-type person sees things as they may be. The solid inner or outer facts of the sensation type tend to be uninteresting to the intuitive, and the possibilities which are so full of life to him have little meaning for the sensation type. The intuitive tends to live in the future or the past, the sensation type in the present. The sensation type depends on concrete data for reaction; the intuitive finds himself hampered by such inflexible matters. The sensation type can't see the woods for the trees; the intuitive can't see the trees for the woods.

Thinking and *feeling* are the two functions used in assessing or judging capacity. They are termed *rational functions*.

Jung considered the thinking individual as one whose every important action proceeds from intellectually considered motives. He meets a situation with logical thought, shaping his actions by its conclusions. Thinking often takes into account the known rules of human experience. Thinking must always be concerned with content, whether inner or outer. It classifies, clarifies, and names; it can be impersonal.

Feeling involves an appreciation or depreciation of inner or outer realities. Feeling imparts to the content a definite value in the sense of acceptance or rejection. The feeling person judges by an evaluation of the time, the place, and the person. The feeling function represents the individual's acceptance or rejection of something based on his own values, but it is also related to its intrinsic worth. It is chiefly concerned with values and morality—although not necessarily related to conventional attitudes.

Every individual utilizes both ego attitudes—extraversion and introversion—and all four functions—sensation, intuition, thinking, and feeling.

One of these attitudes and several relatively more developed functions, however, generally predominate and characterize a person's typical way of relating to inner and outer life.

APPLICATIONS

Assessment

Jung's ideas have had a profound impact on techniques of personality assessment and research. MacKinnon's (1962, 1963, 1965) important work on creativity is one example. The so-called projective techniques rely heavily on the Jungian assumption that *everything* unconscious—psychic reality—tends to get projected into ambiguous external stimuli.

Carl Jung was the first psychiatrist to apply the scientific method in studying disturbed patients. In developing his Word Association test, he produced the first experimental data on unconscious processes. Jung thus constructed the very first projective test, which became a part of routine testing in mental hospitals and inspired others to construct tests and to conduct research. McCully (1971) notes that,

> As progenitor of the [projective test] movement, Jung's word association technique earns him the title of father of the indirect way of activating subjective processes, as a means to understanding individuals. Some of the major pioneers worked with Jung personally or knew him. Others were influenced by reading his works. Among these are Bruno Klopfer, Henry A. Murray, [Florence] Miale and [James] Holsopple, and Hermann Rorschach himself. He trained and influenced some of the major thinkers in this existential approach to symbol interpretation, including Ludwig Binswanger and Medard Boss. (p. 2)

Word Association Tests.   Jung's word association experiments at the turn of this century located feeling-toned complexes, thus corroborating the existence of an unconscious realm of the psyche which Freud and others had been exploring. These experiments laid the foundation for all later attempts to assess, by word association, free association, biofeedback techniques, or sentence completion, the structural and dynamic dimensions of personality, both qualitatively and quantitatively. These highly original scientific works (1904) now comprise over 600 pages of Volume 2 of Jung's *Collected Works.*

Rorschach Test.   Hermann Rorschach, a Swiss psychiatrist, closely followed Jung's work and relied heavily on basic Jungian concepts, such as introversion and extraversion, in the development of what is perhaps the most respected projective technique in clinical psychology, the Rorschach Psychodiagnostic Inkblot Test. Like Jung, Rorschach was a student of

Bleuler; he also attended two lecture courses given by Jung at the University of Zurich and, according to Ellenberger (1954), used Jung's techniques prior to learning about Freud's methods and psychoanalysis. In another work Ellenberger (1970) sheds historical light on the subject: "Hermann Rorschach. . . . followed the development of Jung's typology with keen interest, integrated the notions of introversion and extraversion into the framework of a psychological theory linked with the invention of a new and original projective test" (p. 840).

Bruno Klopfer, a Jungian analyst, made major advances in Rorschach technique (Klopfer, 1955; Klopfer & Kelley, 1942; Klopfer, Ainsworth, Klopfer, & Holt, 1954). Klopfer is well known for developing a widely used Rorschach scoring system, and he was also interested in Jung's psychological types, ego development, personality growth in later life, and complex symbolic interpretation. Moreover, Klopfer's sphere of influence outside clinical psychology was wide indeed, and many psychological anthropologists (e.g., I. Hallowell) and psychoanalysts of other schools (e.g., B. Boyer) learned Rorschach methods and techniques from him.

Other Jungians have made significant contributions to Rorschach theory and technique (Brawer & Spiegelman, 1964; McCully, 1971; Mindness, 1955). McCully has been particularly prolific and innovative. His book *Rorschach Theory and Symbolism: A Jungian Approach to Clinical Material* (1971) provides original and convincing data for archetypal analyses of Rorschach responses.

Thematic Apperception Test.   The TAT, a widely used projective technique, was designed by Henry Murray, who spent time with Jung in Zurich and helped found the first Jungian training institute. He was strongly influenced by Jungian analysis and psychology (cf. Murray, 1962).

Tests of Psychological Types.   A second major Jungian contribution to personality assessment and research stems from Jung's typology (cf. Hinkle, 1922; Meier, 1971). At present two tests are widely in use: the Gray-Wheelwright Questionnaire (Gray & Wheelright, 1946), and the Myers-Briggs Type Indicator (Myers, 1962). Bradway (1964), notes that:

> Despite the fact that Jung presented his theory of psychological types nearly half a century ago (Jung, 1921) American psychology has continued to classify individual differences in personality, almost exclusively, according to psychological theories based upon a normal distribution of personality traits from none to much. This is in contrast to Jung's concept of a pair of opposing attitudes: introversion and extraversion; a pair of opposing perception functions: sensation and intuition; and a pair of opposing judgment functions: thinking and feeling. (p. 129)

Bradway found the Gray-Wheelwright test more useful in discriminating between the thinking-feeling classification than the Myers-Briggs. The

Gray-Wheelwright has been applied to many areas of Jungian psychological interest (Gray, 1949b; Gray & Wheelwright, 1945), including marriage (Gray, 1949b; Gray & Wheelwright, 1944), the aging process (Gray & Wheelwright, 1946), and type differences between Freud and Jung (Gray, 1949a).

In experimental psychology, a wide range of studies by or based upon the work of Raymond Cattell, J. P. Guilford, and Hans Eysenck have all indicated strong evidence for the existence of an introversion-extraversion factor (cf. Dicks-Mireaux, 1964). These studies and others support Jung's original ideas and complement the results of the Gray-Wheelwright studies which assess dichotomous typologies.

In psychotherapy, a theoretical understanding of psychological types and ways to assess ego functions and attitudes may assume great practical significance. Wheelwright (Henderson & Wheelwright, 1974) notes that:

> It is enormously helpful to the therapist to be able to estimate the abilities and limitations of his patients, in terms of their possible behavior and adaptation. And it is essential that he speaks to them in a language that they understand. To talk intuitively to a factual man, or intellectually to a woman who lives through feelings, is a waste of breath. (p. 813)

Treatment

Theoretical models of personality development and maintenance lead inevitably to considerations and questions of appropriate treatment situations and techniques. Jungian psychotherapy or analysis, in many respects, does not differ at all from basic psychoanalytic practice. Several observations on treatment, nevertheless, are required, due to the uniqueness or distinctiveness of Jungian theory (M. Fordham, 1978).

Stages of Psychotherapy. Jung's equal theoretical attention to a variety of instincts and to a collective unconscious, in addition to personal and social demands, always presupposed the inclusion of other relevant techniques, notably those of Sigmund Freud and Alfred Adler. Gerhard Adler (1967), a Jungian analyst, summarized Jung's point of view on four overlapping phases of treatment, each requiring a special technical approach:

> . . . the first stage of "confession" (or the cathartic method); the second stage of "elucidation" or "interpretation" (in particular the interpretation of the transference, thus being very near to the "Freudian" approach); the third stage of "education" (the adaptation of social demands and needs, thus most nearly expressing the standpoint of Alfred Adler); and finally what he calls the stage of "transformation" (or "individuation"), in which the patient discovers and develops his unique individual pattern, the stage of "Jungian" analysis proper. . . .

These stages are not meant to represent either consecutive or mutually exclusive stages of treatment, but different aspects of it, which interpenetrate and vary according to the needs of the particular patient and the therapeutic situation. Thus, treatment has to be undogmatic, flexible, and adjusted to the needs of the individual patient, and this specification is one of the main tenets of analytical psychology. (p. 338)

Believing that theories are indispensable for sound, day-to-day analytical work, Jung remained skeptical of holding to any one general theory. His flexibility anticipated new developments in other psychoanalytic schools by many years (Zinkin, 1969). For example, Jung (1926a) wrote: "This means that the method of treatment is determined primarily by the nature of the case. . . . The real and effective treatment of neurosis is always individual, and for this reason the stubborn application of a particular theory or method must be characterized as basically wrong" (p. 113). Jung took a dim view of dogmatism but not of theoretical consistency and orientation toward any given individual patient.

Jung's great concern for enhanced individuation in later life and his fruitful researches into the phenomenology of this creative life process have always inspired many Jungians to treat older persons. The Jungian emphasis on growth throughout the life cycle stands in sharp distinction to analysts of most other schools. The Jungian approach to older patients who seek analytical treatment is, therefore, radically different in its optimism (Dunn, 1961; Wheelwright, 1980).

Creative Regression. Jung's early positive emphasis on the adaptive significance of regression has led to the use of at least the following treatment modalities among contemporary Jungians:

1. Greater frequency of interviews per week and use of the couch, chiefly in England, to facilitate active imagination (Jackson, 1961a, 1963a), the analysis of infancy and childhood, and creative regression within the transference situation, to activate "prenatal" archetypal potentialities.
2. The treatment of schizophrenics in residential settings. They are allowed to become deeply regressed, often without medication, in an effort to promote self-healing and natural reconstitutive processes which might otherwise remain dormant in the unconscious (Levene, 1978; Perry, 1961, 1974).
3. The use of sandtray therapy with both children and adults to activate archaic, waking fantasies, memories, and other playful states of awareness. This technique may accompany artistic efforts at painting, drawing, clay modeling, or dance.
4. The analytical treatment of severely damaged and regressed borderline and schizophrenic patients who are often considered by non-Jungian analysts to be unreachable by analytic techniques (F. Fordham, 1964).

Therapy as a Dialectical Process.   Because Jung viewed the psyche as self-regulating, Jungian analysis and psychotherapy both seek to establish dialogue between ego-consciousness and an activated, dynamic, integrating self. The compensatory or reciprocal relationship between conscious and unconscious is assumed, and the analyst is a participant-observer in this process. He brings his total personality (conscious and unconscious) to the treatment context, using the countertransference (his own thoughts, fantasies, and feelings) creatively, interactively, in ways that provide for a dialectical relationship in which his interpretations and confrontations compensate for what is unconscious in his patient. To work effectively, the analyst must be in touch with his own feelings and have developed access to his own unconscious processes. The idea that every psychoanalyst should undergo a personal-training analysis began with Jung.

Jung (1939) wrote: "Psychotherapy is at bottom a dialectical relationship between doctor and patient. It is an encounter, a discussion between two psychic wholes, in which knowledge is used only as a tool" (p. 554). Although Jung made a distinction between analysis and psychotherapy, seeing them as two psychotherapeutic modalities among many, the goal of treatment is in both cases self-realization. The inevitable entering into the process of the reality of an interacting therapist means growth for both analyst and analysand, and Jung's early attention to this working alliance (1913, 1921) constitutes yet another of his unique contributions to psychoanalysis (cf. M. Fordham, 1969b, 1974b). Gordon (1979) has explored the difference between "curing" and "healing" in Jungian psychoanalysis by relating these two concepts to activities of both the ego and the wider self.

The Jungian analyst is an *activator of potential,* since the unconscious is not thought of only in pathological terms. Because Jungian theory holds that attributes of the most creative and positive side of a personality may be repressed, including never-before-awakened archetypal activity, the task is to facilitate regression and to activate potential by providing a facilitating environment. Jung uses an alchemical term, *temenos,* to describe the analytical container in which transformations and integrations of personality take place and exist *in potentia.* Following current Jungian emphasis on early object relations (cf. Davidson, 1965; Edwards, 1972; Newton, 1965, 1975; Plaut, 1966, 1974), *the treatment situation may be described in terms of both structure (= containing, holding), and dynamics (= growth, repair, transformation).* Jung's object relations theory has implications for technique: intuition, empathy, great attention to helpful countertransference reactions, nonverbal communications, and therapeutic interaction have always characterized Jungian approaches to the analytic process. Frequent interpretations of unconscious fantasy situations going on in the here-and-now of the analytic encounter are given as much, if not more, attention than the interpretation of instinctual drives and defenses against them underlined by classical Freudian psychoanalysis. Jungians value interpersonal immediacy and liken the actuality of the analytical hour to a chemical interaction between two people in which both are to some extent transformed in the process. M. Fordham (1978, 1979) has described Jung's open systems model at length, and Klaif (1978) the role of empathy in analysis. Moreover, Jungian analysts today would tend to view the entire analytical process as a series of ever-recurring, guided experiences of symbolic death and rebirth.

The Archetypal Transference.   The extremely complicated and controversial concept of transference as the fulcrum of analysis is central to all psychoanalytic schools. Jung (1946) held that the success or failure of long-term analytical treatment depends on the successful resolution of the dependent transference neurosis (cf. M. Fordham, 1969b; Gordon, 1968; Henderson, 1955; Plaut, 1956). Jung differs from other schools in that he highlighted:

1. The reality-based personal therapeutic alliance between two collaborating people and the importance of the analyst's own personality in the work (Lambert, 1974).
2. The archetypal aspect of transference projections, which may be positive or negative and represent repressed positive potential as well as repressed "shadow" material unacceptable to the ego.
3. The cultural importance of transference in psychohistorical perspective.

Thus, in addition to the analysis of transference projections derived essentially from unconscious personal complexes (e.g. parental, sibling) or from culturally patterned unconscious fantasies, feelings, and thoughts related to racial and ethnic identity issues (Maduro, 1975, 1976b), the analyst also captures or is the inevitable recipient of transpersonal (archetypal) affects and images (cf. Adler, 1955, 1967; M. Fordham, 1974b; Plaut, 1966). In any deep analysis, the analyst also carries the archetypal images projected into him. M. Fordham (1978, p. 137) notes that, ". . . the analyst contains for the patient the bit of self that is becoming realized." This is a prospective view of the transference/countertransference situation, and it raises issues related to how and when reductive-reconstructive interpretations and what Jung has called "synthetic/constructive" (forward-looking) interpretations can be made—alone, or in combination.

Two further considerations on the archetypal nature of transference emerge from Jung's work. First, the real relation to the analyst occurs naturally, as all the stages of the individuation process are reflected in the transference, and as the personal projections are simultaneously dealt with analytically, reductively, and reconstructively (Lambert, 1970). Only then may the real relation to the analyst genuinely emerge, as self-realization increases and the possibility for what Henderson (1955) calls the "symbolic friendship'' ripens naturally—as the fruit of a process begun long ago in the unconscious.

Second, the archetypal elements of the transference are intensely evoked and may be dramatically observed and lived through in the deepest states of therapeutic regression and active imagination, where a "delusional transference" is contained and allowed to flower, in contrast to more personal and superficial "illusion" states (cf. Campbell, 1967; Cannon, 1968; Davidson, 1966; Jackson, 1963a). Jung's work contributes the concept that there is an inherent evolution in the transference in the direction of individuation, or a relative shift in emphasis away from strictly personal or culturally patterned contents and meanings to a living connection with the archetypal psyche.

Institutional

Many of Jung's ideas can be applied to institutional settings, although this research domain remains relatively undeveloped at this time.

Education. All institutions that highlight self-actualization and creative expression as primary goals of the educational process are, generally speaking, in basic agreement with Jung's humanistic perspective (Jung, 1926a, 1928b, 1928f, 1934a, 1943a). This may mean the accentuation of at least the following purposes:

1. To activate hidden potential, outside conscious awareness, in children.
2. To teach children to respect and value the inner promptings of the unconscious and its symbolic fantasy productions (e.g., dreams).
3. To provide a facilitating environment in which the idea of wholeness or completeness is presented as a viable alternative to rigid social adaptation, one-sided intellectual development, or strivings for perfection.
4. To insist on teacher attention to unconscious processes in themselves which may communicate messages just as strongly as conscious intents (i.e., transference-countertransference issues).
5. To encourage free play, so that innate natural growth processes are released.

In connection with the fifth point, Jung was always quick to insist that children should not be expected to act like adults at too early an age. He felt, in general, that they should not have their fantasy worlds destroyed by adult "rational" explanations before they have had enough time to "play through" normal developmental conflicts. Jung (1910) wrote:

As a result of this and similar observations, I have been left wondering whether the fantastic or mythological explanation preferred by the child might not, for that very reason, be more suitable than a "scientific" one, which, although factually correct, threatens to clamp down the latch on fantasy for good. . . The fact that the fantasy activity simply ignored the right explanation seems, in my view, to be an important indication that all freely developing thought has an irresistible need to emancipate itself from the realism of fact and to create a world of its own. (pp. 33-34)

Jung's attitudes toward children and therapeutic aspects of regression are reflected (although usually not acknowledged as Jungian ideas) in diverse settings, especially in progressive preschools, kindergartens, and other learning contexts such as mental hospitals, where art and play therapy techniques are encouraged and employed with both child and adult patients.

Group Psychology.   Although Jung placed great emphasis on individuality, he thought of it always in relationship to larger social groups. For example, in 1921 he wrote: "The psychology of the individual can never be exhaustively explained from him alone: a clear recognition is needed of the way it is also conditioned by historical and environmental circumstances. His individual psychology is not merely a physiological, biological, or personal problem; it is also a contemporary problem" (p. 431).

Jung's concept of the "shadow" is closely related to contemporary scapegoat theories. In group therapy, as well as in society at large, individuals and ethnic or racial minorities (e.g., blacks, Chicanos, Jews) are apt to capture the archetypal shadow projection. People in every culture must locate or identify feelings of "badness" somewhere. All too often these feelings are not consciously accepted or owned as a part of oneself or one's own society; thus badness gets disowned or projected into another individual or group singled out for this unconscious purpose. One may then disown destructive impulses, have the pleasure of attacking them somewhere "out there" in projection, and feel safe and self-righteous about it. In considering these sociopsychological mechanisms, Jung's ideas concerning the need for individuals and groups to come to terms with the nature of good and evil by wrestling with what he called the "shadow" have great social meaning (cf. Frey-Rohn, 1967; Progoff, 1953; Von Franz, 1974).

At times whole nations or social institutions may be seized by negative archetypal forces. For example, Jung anticipated and warned against the Nazi holocaust. He viewed Hitler as possessed by the mythological figure, Wotan, who, when in control of the ego complex, could produce what Jung called "the psychosis of the German nation." Moreover, more recent cold war conflicts as in Vietnam may be considered in terms of one nation's inability to come to terms with its own internal "shadow" problems. Adding conscious insight to the phenomenon of scapegoating decreases the likelihood that unconscious prejudicial attitudes and feelings will be blindly acted out.

Self

Jung's ideas touch on numerous aspects of everyday life, from "slips" of the tongue or pen to creative activities of all kinds, and thus may be of special interest to students who are psychologically minded.

Students willing to accept the living reality of the unconscious mind as central to all thought and behavior may wish to undertake Jungian analysis or psychotherapy. Such an undertaking would hold the possibility of greater consciousness, psychological wholeness, and self-understanding. Through self-understanding one also comes to perceive others more clearly: this occurs as a multitude of unconscious projections into others are recognized and withdrawn. Only then is one free to experience friends and family members more as they really are than what one internally needs them to be. The analytical process fosters more successful living, through a greater sense of reality (inner and outer) and less of a feeling of being crippled by anxieties related to infantile fixations and complexes.

Personae. To experience growth and a creative relationship to unconscious processes, courage and self-criticism are needed, since owning up to one's own darkest side is certainly never a pleasant or easy undertaking. Analytical therapy requires a willingness to suffer defects and to sacrifice identification with false personas. "The persona," wrote Jung (1928a), "is a complicated system of relations between individual consciousness and society, fittingly enough a kind of mask, designed on the one hand to make a definite impression upon others, and, on the other, to conceal the true nature of the individual" (p. 192).

Although personae may be as necessary to normal daily life as ego defenses, they too can become maladaptive. As artificial, superficial personalities, personae are those masks which in reality one is not—false selves. Nevertheless, confrontation with oneself offers hope of greater internal freedom, interpersonal warmth, and the activation of repressed positive potential. It also introduces the analysand to a lifelong process of working with the unconscious which can be carried on outside, or after the analysis has ended. One may, for example, continue to self-analyze dreams, using new skills and attitudes acquired in analysis.

Greater consciousness adds to the quality of the individual's life in many ways. He learns to accept greater responsibility for his own life and also for the unconscious choices he makes to repeat or not to repeat the painful past in the present. In short, consciousness favors dissolution of repetition compulsions. One may come also to accept oneself in a nonpunitive way, with enhanced awareness of both strengths and limitations. Finally, although Jungian analysis and psychotherapy do not provide any magical answers to the universal problems of life, they can promote growth and lead to the acquisition of new values, a fresh approach to life, a new gradient. Several examples clarify what is meant by insight into unconscious motivations.

Workaholism. Jungian theory asserts that life and health call for the rounding out of personality, that the notion of balance and harmony of the mind-body must be taken into consideration. Executives and academicians, to cite two examples, often lack a balance or integration of feeling and thinking. It is a self delusion to suppose that the mind is only rational and that irrational, unconscious, instinctual, and emotional factors may be neglected. Jung's psychology emphasizes the well-known fact that the tree of knowledge (thinking) may become the tree of spiritual or psychological death, without any connection to life (people and feelings). Jung (1938b) expresses this archetypal metaphor concisely: "The educated man tries to repress the inferior man in himself, not realizing that by so doing he forces the latter into revolt" (p. 79). This in turn produces emotion.

Jung's theories place high value on hidden emotional life, intuition, and openness to the irrational or spiritual dimension of human existence. The person who would employ a manic defense against underlying depressive anxiety, through becoming a work addict or workaholic, could by means of self-understanding come to accept unwanted destructive impulses as part of his wholeness. This in turn could release unrecognized feeling and lead to a balanced devotion to business or intellectual pursuits that would not be experienced as anxious, compulsive addiction to work.

Individuality. Jungian psychotherapists are likely to place greater emphasis on intrapsychic adjustment than on adaptation to external conventional morality. The goal of psychotherapeutic work is individuation or development—dialogue with constructive creative unconscious processes—and not, strictly speaking, "cure," mere rational understanding, or symptom removal. For these and other reasons, many creative artists and inner-directed (introverted) persons have often preferred Jungian psychotherapy and analysis to other systems of psychotherapy.

Jung took an extremely strong position in favor of individuality, even to the point of insisting that individuals have the creative prerogative to remain "abnormal." In support of the individual, Jung (1921) writes: "It is obvious that a social group consisting of stunted individuals can not be a healthy and viable institution; only a society that can preserve its internal cohesion and collective values, while at the same time granting the individual the greatest possible freedom, has any prospect of enduring vitality" (p. 448).

Although individuality involves arriving at a truly symbolic or "religious" attitude toward life (conscious and unconscious), Jungian theory refers more to the acquisition of a system of personal ethics than to religion in any conventional sense.

Changing Male-Female Roles. Jung's theory of the fundamental bisexuality of human beings—both physiologically and psychologically—frees men and women to experience both the masculine and feminine components of their personalities. The masculine or the feminine is each incomplete, relative, and one half of the same whole (cf. the Chinese Yin-Yang premise). Singer (1976) has explored the concept of androgeny as an inner psychological experience, and in the context of contemporary Jungian psychology and modern life. Jung's theory that the difference between man and woman is qualitative stands in sharp opposition to Freud (Whitehead, 1975), who took the natural inferiority of women for granted (e.g., an assumed intellectual inferiority because of stronger sexual repression in women, and a masochism and passivity Freud felt was natural to women). Jung held that the difference is not of inferiority and superiority, and that the sexes are psychologically complementary to each other (his theory of the anima in man and the animus in woman).

In this regard, Jung's theory has strong ties to views held by Alfred Adler, Karen Horney, and Erich Fromm. Contemporary interest in Jungian theory and the "women's movement" reflect, in part, yet another way in which Jung's genius was far ahead of his time. As we have seen, Jung never could accept Freud's overestimation of maleness, the phallus, and the phallic phase of psychosexual development characteristically marked by the activation of the Oedipus complex.

Marital Relationships. Many vexing marriage situations revolve around the business of psychological types. Research using the Gray-Wheelwright Questionnaire (Gray & Wheelwright, 1944) demonstrated that in a series of over a thousand subjects, the overwhelming majority have married their polar opposites, although for friends the same subjects tend to pick similar types. It is a little startling to think of most of us marrying people whom we would never pick as friends.

An understanding of Jung's theory of types encourages the development of tolerance toward others who differ from us. Type theory allows us to imagine standing in the other person's shoes and to appreciate the variety of equally valid responses to any given situation.

Jung's idea of individuation is closely related to types. As long as we are content, in a marriage, to let somebody else carry our introverted side or our feeling, we remain relatively unconscious and undeveloped. Growth involves a constant increase in consciousness—that is, the incorporation into our conscious personalities of aspects of our psyche that have hitherto lain in the unconscious. Marriage inhibits growth processes in individuals when it is not viewed as a psychological relationship (Jung, 1925), and when the willingness to accept a partner's inherent differentness or to develop one's own least developed psychological functions is absent.

VALIDATION

Evidence

The discovery of the dynamic unconscious gave rise to modern depth psychology (Ellenberger, 1970). Although at the turn of this century the new science of psychoanalysis contained much that was rooted in the intellectual tradition of the 19th century, it nevertheless constituted a threat and an expansion of the earlier psychology, which had been severely limited in scope to the study of conscious mental processes and observable behavior.

Jung sought to prove the existence of unconscious processes by examining hysterical symptoms, dreams, and free association. He studied hypnosis in France and was inspired by the work of Jean Charcot, Hippolyte Bernheim, and Pierre Janet in their attempts to show that the repression is a major factor in mental malfunctioning, and it could be removed by "talking cures" or hypnotic suggestion.

Jung's early experimental research on word association, somnambulism, and mediumistic trance states complemented and corroborated Freud's attempts to prove the existence of an unconscious realm. Jung's methodology and techniques continue to be used and empirically validated today by criminologists, biofeedback therapists, and others who use galvanic skin responses to monitor a wide variety of subjective processes occurring in the mind-body.

Archetypes of a Collective Unconscious. Nothing has caused more misunderstanding between Jungians and students of other schools of personality theories than Jung's concepts of the archetypes and a collective unconscious (i.e., the importance of heredity and constitutional factors in a broad sense). At such an early time in the history of depth psychology, it took courage for Jung to explore these areas of the mind and to report his findings (cf. Jung, 1919, 1929b). He often met with resistance, misinterpretation, rejection, and ridicule. He continued, nevertheless, to explore assiduously, to report on the analysis of dreams and other symbolic systems (e.g., alchemy), and to refute the impressions that he was a "mystic," something he denied throughout his long life.

Today, what Jung and his followers have said concerning archetypal activity in the psyche can be related to recent scientific findings in other fields, where controlled studies by eminent researchers postulate and provide very convincing evidence for the presence of basic, a priori structures in the mind. Personal experiences are necessary but not sufficient conditions for their actualization. These studies confirm much of what Jung had to say. We can note, for example:

1. Psychedelic drug experiences which, for better or worse, plunge individuals into transpersonal layers of the psyche.
2. Levi-Strauss's structural theories in modern anthropology ("binary oppositions").
3. The ethological work done by Konrad Lorenz and many others ("innate releaser mechanism").
4. Jean Piaget's innate "schemata."
5. Rene Spitz's "innate organizers."
6. Melanie Klein's "unconscious phantasy" or "unconscious knowledge."
7. Michael Balint's "pre-object" or "object-*Anlage*."
8. Noam Chomsky's rules for transformational grammar in linguistics.
9. Modern ego psychology, whereby archetypes in action are described as the unfolding of the genetically social character in response to an average, expectable environment.

Jung's original ideas have become the focus of serious study in many scientific quarters, without being labeled mystical. That Jung's contributions have so long been relatively unacknowledged is remarkable, to say the least; but the validity of his theoretical work is corroborated independently by scientists in other fields.

Innate Ego. The ego is one basic structure of the mind that has been the focus of much recent attention. It is important to note Jung's reference to the ego as a *complex.* This implies that such a psychic structure has an innate archetypal core or nucleus around which personal associations are formed as maturation proceeds.

Outside the limitations of classical drive theory, modern ego psychologists now recognize the importance of an "innate ego" or an ego present at birth, which to all intents and purposes is as far back as we can go, even though recent advances in embryology promise to shed light on these issues. Here, too, modern Jungian theory differs in emphasis and is corroborated by research and clinical inference (e.g., Call, 1964). Until recently the idea that ego exists with a *capacity to initiate* activity and to be object-related very early in infancy (i.e., part-object relatedness) has not been acknowledged widely or given much importance in models of development. Students of Jung, Klein, and Sullivan have given great attention to the ego's capacity for primitive albeit absolutely fundamental states of relatedness in earliest infancy.

Current Jungian theory, in other words, does not accept the concept of "primary narcissism" which remains basic to Freudian developmental theory and which implies that a baby must be coaxed out of a pool of narcissism by the mother (cf. M. Fordham, 1971a). Much more ego exists from the beginning than Freud or Jung recognized. *Neo-Jungians therefore place great emphasis on the normal development and management of part-objects.* Fordham (1971a) clarifies this as follows:

> Deintegration was conceived as the active contribution by the infant in bringing about states from which it was previously assumed he passively began. Thus the idea that mother, infant togetherness is created by the mother alone is done away with and attention is focussed on what the baby does to help bring this about. The idea that the self deintegrates, rather than splits or disintegrates, grew out of this line of thought. (p. 86)

Evidence suggests that object relations begin very early. Much more observation and experiment are needed to shed light on postulated unconscious (archetypal) processes working behind perceptual development. Fordham's concept of *deintegration* of the primary self implies alternating sequences of stable integrative and unstable deintegrative phases at critical periods of the life cycle when maturational potentials are activated and released (for example, the Oedipal drama, or the earlier depressive position).

Comparisons

A great deal of what has already been said about Jungian theory implies comparison with classical or orthodox Freudian psychoanalysis. A number of more specific issues concerning the work of Freudian, Jungian, and Kleinian analysts will now be highlighted.

Ego Psychology. Controversies among analysts of diverse schools involve a wide variety of mutual misunderstandings and the different use of language. Although words such as *ego, symbol,* or *self* are commonly used, they may carry different meanings. We are indebted both to the Freudian school for major advances in the field of ego psychology and to the Jungian school for its consistent, theoretical emphasis on a psychodynamic self. Although Jung's concept of a self (total psyche), as distinct from the ego, is implied in his earliest works (1902), he first used the term *self* in 1921. Providing an overview of contemporary Freudian psychotherapy, Fine (1973) remarks: "Since 1923 all of psychoanalysis has been ego psychology" (p. 4). In accord with this point of view, Fenichel (1945) refers to the Freudian model: "All neurotic phenomena are based on insufficiencies of the normal control apparatus" (p. 19). This position stands in sharp contrast to the Jungian emphasis on a psychodynamic self in a self-actualization relation to differentiating and synthesizing ego processes. Thus Jung (1925) writes:

> A dissociation is not healed by being split off, but by more complete disintegration [cf. therapeutic regression, the delusional transference, guided psychosis, etc.]. All the powers that strive for unity, all healthy desire for selfhood, will resist the disintegration, and in this way he will become conscious of the possibility of an inner integration, which before he has always sought outside himself. He will then find his reward in an undivided self. (pp. 196-197)

Jung's use of the word *self* differs from current Freudian usage, since his concept is not interchangeable with the term ego or thought of as a representation within the ego. In 1921, Jung wrote:

> Inasmuch as the ego is only the centrum of my field of consciousness, it is not identical with the totality of my psyche, being merely a complex among other complexes. Hence I discriminate between the ego and the self, since the ego is only the subject of my consciousness, while the self is the subject of my totality; hence it also includes the unconscious psyche. (p. 590)

Later, in 1939, he wrote: "For this reason I have elected to call it the 'self,' by which I understand a psychic totality and at the same time a centre, neither of which coincides with the ego but includes it, just as a larger circle encloses a smaller one" (p. 142). Jung gives special emphasis to the somatic pole of the archetypal self and to developmentally early experiences of the body ego/self when he writes: "The symbols of the self arise in the depths of the body and they express its materiality every bit as much as the structure of the perceiving consciousness" (Jung, 1921).

While both Jung and Freud were concerned with the central importance of ego strength, Freudian psychology stresses ego "control" and Jungian psychology creative "dialogue" between the ego and the dynamic unconscious. Moreover, the Jungian emphasis on the inner reality of the psyche may at times make modern Freudian egopsychology, with its exclusive emphasis on adaptation to the external world, seem inordinately mechanistic, limited, one-sided, and overly abstract for students of Jung. In this connection, it is telling that contemporary Freudians still find it necessary to refer to the inner world or psychic reality as metapsychology, when for Jungians it is simple plain psychology. Again, we are talking about a matter of emphasis, since Jung places great importance on the personal evocation of the transpersonal.

In contrast to Jung's fundamentally introverted position vis-a-vis the unconscious, Anna Freud (1926) sums up the Freudian orientation with this position statement: "In working with an adult we have to confine ourselves entirely to helping him to adapt himself to his environment" (p. 61). Her remark obviously posits quite a different intellectual slant on a "psychic apparatus" and on the relative weight given in therapy to intrapsychic dynamic structures as motivating forces in the unconscious, in comparison to outer interpersonal reality. "Although Freudian theory also relies on the concept of psychic reality in its own way, the emphasis with regard to maturational potentials and developmental factors differs radically from that of Jung. Jungians may accept the orthodox Freudian view as being true but extremely limited to the elucidation of psychopathology (e.g., the depreciation of primary process per se), rational ego control, and adaptation to the external world. In comparison, Jung's model stresses the *whole human personality in the process of growth and repair,* an ego-self polarity.''

Symbols or Signs. Freudian psychoanalytic interpretations and analyses seem too heavily weighted in favor of psychic determinism (causality). Lacking any appreciation of the creative functions of the psyche as a self-regulating teleological system, which Jung's model adds, the scope of Freudian theory appears to be narrow indeed. Any idea of a creative self which adds meaning to life is neglected for a systemic man-as-machine model. While such a model may seem to create tight and neatly packaged systems within the psyche, it ignores the positive attributes of a tolerance for ambiguity from which new syntheses, symbolic representations, and theoretical constructions flow.

The psychological point of view which Jungian theory contributes is ignored when Freudian analyses reduce everything to concrete, literal body parts—when they might equally well talk of *signs* or *substitutions* (known, conventional) rather than emerging dynamic living *symbols* (ambiguous, transforming, with no fixed meanings).

The tree, for example, may be an elongated phallic symbol, as Freudian theory rightly posits. To reduce it to this level of concrete biological reality alone, however, would be a grave error, from a Jungian perspective. The tree may also stand for the father as something old rooted in tradition; it may be a mother symbol par excellence, as something which bears fruit and is nurturing (lays down shade, protects and harbors birds). It may stand for psychological differentiation (the many branches) and wholeness. Because it loses its leaves, dies in the winter, and seemingly comes to life again in the spring, it may stand for the process of symbolic death and rebirth. Finally, the tree may stand for the connection between heaven and earth, the *axis mundi,* a link between the polarity of matter (mother earth) and spirit (father sky) which transcends each alone by combining or unifying both.

These are only some of the richer symbolic dimensions of the tree symbol; many more could be added. Which facet or combination of facets would be important to a particular dreamer and his unique life history and present circumstances would be the question. From a Jungian point of view it would be wrong to simplistically equate the tree *literally* with a phallus, simply because it is an elongated object. This illusion should help the student see that from a Jungian point of view Freudian analyses often appear to deal with signs rather than symbols (cf. Stein, 1957).

Freud's "Racial Memory." It is of interest to note that although Freud and his followers have almost completely neglected the archetypal nature of the psyche, Freud in this respect was not in basic disagreement with Jung. Sigmund Freud (1918) asserts: "I fully agree with Jung in recognizing the existence of this phylogenetic heritage" (p. 97). In contrast to what is generally acceptable in Jungian psychology, however, Freud held that actual ideational contents, "racial memories," are transmitted. Near the end of his life, for example, Freud (1918) wrote, in *Moses and Monotheism:* "The archaic heritage of mankind includes not only dispositions, but also ideational contents, memory traces, the experiences of former generations" (p. 98). Jung (1928e), on the other hand, stresses the innate capacities and potentials for all human beings sharing the same brain structure to be moved by the power of the archetypes and complexes associated with many of them: "The universal similarity of the brain yields the universal possibility of a similar mental functioning. This functioning is the collective psyche" (p. 147).

Eschewing a strictly Lamarckian stand, Jung underlines archetypal potentialities available to all members of the human species. Freud's notion that something could happen only once in the human race and be forever passed on phylogenetically in terms of specific ideational content (cf. S. Freud's highly speculative primal horde theory in *Totem and Taboo,* 1913) is equally untenable for Jungians, as well as for modern anthropologists concerned with the importance of culture. Jung is very clear on this point, and the following passage, written in 1938, should dispel the mistaken interpretation that archetypal analysis precludes the concept of culture and societal forces:

> *Again and again I encounter the mistaken notion that an archetype is determined in regard to its content,* in other words that it is a kind of unconscious idea (if such an expression be admissible). It is necessary to point out once more that archetypes are not determined as regards their content, but only as regards their form and then only to a very limited degree. A primordial image is determined as to its content only when it has become conscious and is therefore *filled out with the material of conscious experience.* Its form, however, as I have explained elsewhere, might perhaps be compared to the axial structure of a crystal, which, as it were, preforms the crystalline structure in the mother liquid, although it has no material existence of its own. This first appears according to the specific way in which the ions and molecules aggregate. *The archetype in itself is empty and purely formal, nothing but a facultas praeformandi, a possibility of representation which is given a priori. The representatives themselves are not inherited,* only the forms, and in that respect they correspond in every way to the instincts, which are also determined in form only. (Jung, 1938a, p. 79—emphasis added)

Phallocentrism. That Jung should have made the mother so central a figure in understanding the psychodynamics of normal personality development at a time when Freud emphasized the role of the father (i.e., castration anxiety in oedipal dynamics) is an important distinction between them, no less so as Freudian theory moves closer and closer toward acceptance of the original Jungian position. Jung's early insight is today axiomatic. Indeed this theoretical difference was a major cause of the split between Freud and Jung in 1914; when Jung wrote *Symbols of Transformation* (1911), he went his own way. In this landmark work he writes about the heroic ego's task of separating from the mother complex as if he were discussing adolescence; it is unclear whether Jung was completely aware of all the implications of his work for early object relations. Nevertheless he describes separation from symbiotic attachment to the mother, important features of splitting in part-object relations, and developmental hurdles related to working through what Klein later called the depressive position (cf. Segal, 1973; Winnicott, 1954).

Jung's emphasis on the mother imago, in contrast to Freud, takes the feminine principle and preoedipal dynamics seriously into account. Unlike Freudian patriarchal formulations, Jungian perspectives—at least in theory—are not as permeated by unconscious resistances to the analysis of early conflicts and anxieties associated with the mother, a developmental level deeper than the oedipal complex. Freud's theories treat both the feminine genitalia and vital feminine aspects of secure male identity (cf. Jung's anima in males) with severe patriarchal contempt. Such a hyper-masculine pose may well make male insecurities in relation to conflicted attributes of femininity, passivity, orality, and breast-womb envy.

Klein's emphasis modifies Jung's but also seems to represent a rather extreme position, inasmuch as masculine aspects of identity are often devalued in favor of an overemphasis on the female breast. Man is seen as merely the extension of the nipple (Whitehead, 1975). Moreover, Klein's conceptual formulation of an inner world, although very similar to Jung's, differs significantly in that Klein's is, according to Plaut (1962), "first and foremost a hostile murderous place where aggression and anxiety, greed and sadism abound" (p. 6). Jung's inner world does not overly stress anxiety and disease to the exclusion of healthy aspects of personality. It is a much less pathological place—a both friendly and hostile territory.

In reaction to the Victorian era, Jung's theoretical stance with regard to the masculine and feminine components of the personality is truly remarkable for its balanced and relatively unbiased assertions, in comparison to either Freud or Klein. Jungian theory provides a starting point that can synthesize the best of Freud and Klein to meet the feminist challenge of our time. Jung's work needs to be further extended and modified so that an even more objective and accurate psychology of women may evolve. There is a special need to elucidate developmental issues where personal experiences and archetypal patterns closely interrelate. It is particularly important to move on to the position that women can relate to life directly and not only through men.

REFERENCES

Adler, G. On the archetypal content of transference. In *Report of the International Congress of Psychotherapy, Zurich, 1954.* Basel/New York: Karger, 1955.

Adler, G. Methods of treatment in analytical psychology. In B. Wolman (Ed.), *Psychoanalytic techniques* (pp. 338-378). New York: Basic Books, 1967.

Adler, G. (Ed.). *C. G. Jung letters, I: 1906-1950.* Princeton, N. J.: Princeton University Press, 1973.

Adler, G. (Ed.). *C. G. Jung letters, II: 1951-1961.* Princeton, N. J.: Princeton University Press, 1975.

Bolen, J. *The tao of psychology, synchronicity and the self.* New York: Harper & Row, 1979.

Bradway, K. Jung's psychological types: Classification by test versus classification by self. *Journal of Analytical Psychology,* 1964, *9*(2), 129-136.

Brawer, F., & Spiegelman, J. M. Rorschach and Jung: A study of introversion-extraversion. *Journal of Analytical Psychology,* 1964, *9*(2), 137-150.

Call, J. D. Newborn approach behavior and early ego development. *International Journal of Psycho-Analysis,* 1964, *45*(2-3), 286-295.

Campbell, R. The management of the countertransference evoked by violence in the delusional transference. *Journal of Analytical Psychology,* 1967, *12*(2), 161-174.

Cannon, A. Transference as creative illusion. *Journal of Analytical Psychology,* 1968, *13*(2), 95-108.

Davidson, D. A problem of identity in relation to an image of a damaged mother. *Journal of Analytical Psychology,* 1965, *10*(1), 67-76.

Davidson, D. Transference as a form of active imagination. *Journal of Analytical Psychology,* 1966, *11*(2), 135-146.

Dicks-Mireaux, M.J. Extraversion-introversion in experimental psychology: Examples of experimental evidence and their theoretical implications. *Journal of Analytical Psychology,* 1964, *9*(2), 117-128.

Dunn, J. Analysis of patients who meet the problems of the first half of life in the second. *Journal of Analytical Psychology,* 1961, *6*(1), 55-67.

Edinger, E. *Ego and archetype.* New York: G. P. Putnam's Sons, 1972.

Edwards, A. Fantasy and early phases of self-representation, *Journal of Analytical Psychology,* 1972, *17*(1), 17-30.

Ellenberger, H. F. Hermann Rorschach, M.D., 1884-1922. *Bulletin of the Menninger Clinic,* 1954, *18*, 173-219.

Ellenberger, H. F. *The discovery of the unconscious.* New York: Basic Books, 1970.

Erikson, E. *Childhood and society.* New York: W. W. Norton, 1950.

Fenichel, O. *The psychoanalytic theory of neurosis.* New York: Norton, 1945.

Fine, R. Psychoanalysis. In R. J. Corsini (Ed.), *Current psychotherapies* (pp. 1-33). Itasca, Ill.: F. E. Peacock, 1973.

Fordham, F. *An introduction to Jung's psychology.* Baltimore: Penguin Books, 1953.

Fordham, F. The care of regressed patients and the child archetype. *Journal of Analytical Psychology,* 1964, *9*(1), 61-74.

Fordham, F. Some views on individuation, *Journal of Analytical Psychology,* 1969, *14*(1), 1-12.

Fordham, M. *New developments in analytical psychology.* London: Routledge & Kegan Paul, 1957.

Fordham, M. Comment on the theory of the original self. *Journal of Analytical Psychology,* 1961, *6*(1), 78-79.

Fordham, M. The empirical foundation and theories of the self in Jung's works. *Journal of Analytical Psychology,* 1963, *8*(1), 1-24.

Fordham, M. The importance of analysing childhood for assimilation of the shadow. *Journal of Analytical Psychology,* 1965, *10*(1), 33-48.

Fordham, M. Active imagination—deintegration or disintegration? *Journal of Analytical Psychology,* 1967, *12*(1), 51-66.

Fordham, M. *Children as individuals.* New York: G. P. Putnam's Sons, 1969. (a)

Fordham, M. Technique and counter-transference. *Journal of Analytical Psychology,* 1969, *14*(2), 95-118. (b)

Fordham, M. Maturation of ego and self in infancy. In *Analytical psychology: A modern science, Library of Analytical Psychology* (Vol. 1, pp. 83-94). London: William Heinemann Medical Books, 1973. (Originally published, 1971). (a)

Fordham, M. Primary self, primary narcissism and related concepts. *Journal of Analytical Psychology,* 1971, *16*(2), 168-187. (b)

Fordham, M. A theory of maturation. In B. Wolman (Ed.), *Handbook of child psychoanalysis* (pp. 461-500). New York: Van Nostrand Reinhold, 1972.

Fordham, M. Defences of the self. *Journal of Analytical Psychology,* 1974, *19*(2), 192-199. (a).

Fordham, M. Jung's conception of transference. *Journal of Analytical Psychology,* 1974 *19*(1), 1-21. (b).

Fordham, Michael. *The Self and Autism. Library of Analytical Psychology* (Vol. 3). London: William Heinemann Medical Books, 1976.

Fordham, M. *Jungian psychotherapy.* New York: Wiley, 1978.

Fordham, M. Analytical psychology and countertransference. *Contemporary Psychoanalysis,* 1979, *15*(4), 630-646.

Freud, A. *The psychoanalytical treatment of children.* New York: Schocken Books, 1964. (Originally published, 1926.)

Freud, A. The ego and the mechanisms of defense. *The writings of Anna Freud* (Vol. 2). New York: International Universities Press, 1966. (Originally published, 1936.)

Freud, S. *Totem and taboo.* In *Standard edition of the complete psychological works of Sigmund Freud* (Vol. 13, pp. 1-162). London: Hogarth Press, 1953. (Originally published, 1913.)

Freud, S. From the history of an infantile neurosis. In *Standard edition of the complete psychological works of Sigmund Freud* (Vol. 17, pp. 1-104). London: Hogarth Press, 1955. (Originally published, 1918.)

Freud S. Moses and monotheism. In *Standard edition of the complete psychological works of Sigmund Freud* (Vol. 13, pp. 1-132). London: Hogarth Press, 1964. (Originally published, 1918.)

Frey-Rohn, L. Evil from the psychological point of view. In *Evil* (pp. 151-200). Evanston, Ill.: Northwestern University Press, 1967.

Frey-Rohn, L. *From Freud to Jung: A comparative study of the psychology of the unconscious.* New York: G. P. Putnam's, 1975.

Giegerich, W. Ontogeny-Phylogeny? A fundamental critique of Erich Neumann's analytical psychology. *Spring: An Annual of Archetypal Psychology and Jungian Thought,* 1975, pp. 110-129.

Gordon, R. The death instinct and its relation to the self. *Journal of Analytical Psychology,* 1961, *6*(2), 119-136.

Gordon, R. The concept of projective identification: An evaluation. *Journal of Analytical Psychology,* 1965, *10*(2), 127-150.

Gordon, R. Symbols: Content and process. *Journal of Analytical Psychology,* 1967, *12*(1), 23-34.

Gordon, R. Transference as a fulcrum of analysis. *Journal of Analytical Psychology,* 1968, *13*(2), 109-117.

Gordon, R. Reflections on curing and healing. *Journal of Analytical Psychology,* 1979, *24*(3), 207-217.

Gordon, R. Narcissism and the self: who am I that I love? *Journal of Analytical Psychology,* 1980, *25*(3), 247-264.

Gray, H. Jung's psychological types and

changes with age. *Journal of Clinical Psychology,* 1947, *3*(3), 273-277.

Gray, H. Freud and Jung: Their contrasting psychological types. *Psychoanalytic Review,* 1949, *36*(1), 22-44. (a)

Gray, H. Psychological types in married people. *Journal of Social Psychology,* 1949, *29,* 189-200. (b)

Gray, H., & Wheelwright, J. Jung's psychological types and marriage. *Stanford Medical Bulletin,* 1944, *2*(1), 37-39.

Gray, H., & Wheelwright, J. Jung's psychological types, including the four functions. *Journal of Genetic Psychology,* 1945, *33,* 265-284.

Gray, H., & Wheelwright, J. Jung's psychological types, their frequency and occurrence. *Journal of General Psychology,* 1946, *34,* 3-17.

Hall, C., & Lindzey, G. *Theories of personality.* New York: Wiley, 1957.

Henderson, J. Resolution of the transference in the light of C. G. Jung's psychology. *Report of the International Congress of Psychotherapy, Zurich, 1954* (pp. 75-91). Basel/New York: Karger, 1955.

Henderson, J. *Thresholds of initiation.* Middletown, Conn.: Wesleyan University Press, 1967.

Henderson, J., & Wheelwright, J. Analytical Psychology. In *The American handbook of psychiatry* (Vol. 2; S. Arieti, Ed.). New York: Basic Books, 1974.

Hinkle, B. A study of psychological types. *Psychoanalytical Review,* 1922, *9,* 107-197.

Hinton, L. Jung's approach to therapy with mid-life patients. *Journal of the American Academy of Psychoanalysis,* 1979, *7*(4), 525-541.

Hubback, J. Envy and the shadow. *Journal of Analytical Psychology,* 1972, *17*(2), 152-165.

Hubback, J. Development and similarities, 1935-1980. *Journal of Analytical Psychology,* 1980, *25*(3), 219-236.

Jackson, M. Chair, couch, and counter-transference. *Journal of Analytical Psychology,* 1961, *6*(1), 35-43. (a)

Jackson, M. Jung's "archetype": Clarity or confusion? *British Journal of Medical Psychology,* 1961, *33,* 83-94. (b)

Jackson, M. Symbol formation and the delusional transference. *Journal of Analytical Psychology,* 1963, *8*(2), 145-164. (a)

Jackson, M. Technique and procedure in analytic practice with special reference to schizoid states. *Journal of Analytical Psychology,* 1963, *8*(1), 51-64. (b)

Jacobi, J. *Complex/archetype/symbol in the psychology of C. G. Jung.* Princeton, N. J.: Princeton University Press, 1959.

Jaques E. Death and the mid-life crisis. *International Journal of Psychoanalysis,* 1965, *46,* 502-514.

Jung, C. On the psychology and pathology of so-called occult phenomena. In *Psychiatric studies,* Collected works (Vol. 1, pp. 1-88). Princeton, N. J.: Princeton University Press, 1957. (Originally published, 1902.)

Jung, C. Studies in word association. In *Experimental researches,* Collected works (Vol. 2). Princeton, N. J.: Princeton University Press, 1973. (Orig. pub., 1904.)

Jung, C. The psychology of dementia praecox. In *The psychogenesis of mental disease,* Collected works (Vol. 3, pp. 1-152). Princeton, N. J.: Princeton University Press, 1960. (Originally published, 1907.)

Jung, C. Psychic conflicts in a child. In *The development of personality,* Collected works (Vol. 17, pp. 1-36). Princeton, N. J.: Princeton University Press, 1954. (Originally published, 1910.)

Jung, C. *Symbols of transformation.* Collected works (Vol. 5). Princeton, N. J.: Princeton University Press, 1956. (Originally published, 1911).

Jung, C. The theory of psychoanalysis. In *Freud and psychoanalysis,* Collected works (Vol. 4, pp. 83-226). Princeton, N. J.: Princeton University Press, 1961. (Originally published, 1913.)

Jung, C. General aspects of dream psychology. In *The structure and dynamics of the psyche,* Collected works (Vol. 8, pp. 235-280). Princeton, N. J.: Princeton University Press, 1960. (Originally published, 1916.) (a)

Jung, C. The transcendent function. In *The structure and dynamics of the psyche,* Collected works (Vol. 8, pp. 67-91). Princeton, N. J.: Princeton University Press, 1960. (Originally published, 1916.) (b)

Jung, C. The eros theory. In *Two essays on analytical psychology,* Collected works (Vol. 7, pp. 19-29). Princeton, N. J.: Princeton University Press, 1953. (Originally published, 1917.) (a)

Jung, C. The problem of the attitude-type. In *Two essays on analytical psychology,* Collected works (Vol. 7, pp. 41-63). Princeton, N. J.: Princeton University Press, 1953. (Originally published, 1917.) (b)

Jung, C. Instinct and the unconscious. In *The structure and dynamics of the psyche,* Collected works (Vol. 8, pp. 129-138). Princeton, N. J.: Princeton University Press, 1960. (Originally published, 1919.)

Jung, C. *Psychological types,* Collected works (Vol. 6). Princeton, N. J.: Princeton University Press, 1971. (Originally published, 1921.)

Jung, C. Marriage as a psychological relationship. In *The development of personality,* Collected works (Vol. 17, pp. 187-204). Princeton, N. J.: Princeton University Press, 1954. (Originally published, 1925.)

Jung, C. Analytical psychology and education. In *The development of personality,* Collected works (Vol. 17, p. 63-132). Princeton, N. J.: Princeton University Press, 1954. (Originally published, 1926.) (a)

Jung, C. Spirit and life. In *The structure and dynamics of the psyche,* Collected works (Vol. 8, pp. 319-337). Princeton, N. J.: Princeton University Press, 1960. (Originally published, 1926.) (b)

Jung, C. Anima and Animus. In *Two essays on analytical psychology,* Collected works (Vol. 7, pp. 188-211). Princeton, N. J.: Princeton University Press, 1953. (Originally published, 1928.) (a)

Jung, C. Child development and education. In *The development of personality,* Collected works (Vol. 17, pp. 47-62). Princeton, N. J.: Princeton University Press, 1954. (Originally published, 1928.) (b)

Jung, C. On psychic energy. In *The structure and dynamics of the psyche,* Collected works (Vol. 8, pp. 3-66). Princeton, N. J.: Princeton University Press, 1960. (Originally published, 1928.) (c)

Jung, C. The persona as a segment of the collective psyche. In *Two essays on analytical psychology,* Collected works (Vol. 7, pp. 156-162). Princeton, N. J.: Princeton University Press, 1953. (Originally published, 1928.) (d)

Jung, C. The relations between the ego and the unconscious. In *Two essays on analytical psychology,* Collected works (Vol. 7, pp. 123-244). Princeton, N. J.: Princeton University Press, 1953. (Originally published, 1928). (e)

Jung, C. The significance of the unconscious in individual education. In *The development of personality,* Collected works (Vol. 17, pp. 149-164). Princeton, N. J.: Princeton University Press, 1954. (Originally published, 1928.) (f)

Jung, C. Commentary on "The secret of the golden flower." In *Alchemical studies,* Collected works (Vol. 13, pp. 1-56). Princeton, N. J.: Princeton University Press, 1967. (Originally published, 1929.) (a)

Jung, C. The significance of constitution and heredity in psychology. In *The structure and dynamics of the psyche,* Collected works (Vol. 8, pp. 107-113). Princeton, N. J.: Princeton University Press, 1960. (Originally published, 1929.) (b)

Jung, C. The stages of life. In *The structure and dynamics of the psyche,* Collected works (Vol. 8, pp. 387-404). Princeton, N.

J.: Princeton University Press, 1960. (Originally published, 1930.)

Jung, C. The development of personality. In *The development of personality*, Collected works (Vol. 17, pp. 165-186). Princeton, N. J.: Princeton University Press, 1954. (Originally published, 1934.) (a)

Jung, C. The practical use of dream analysis. In *The practice of psychotherapy*, Collected works (Vol. 16, pp. 139-161). Princeton, N. J.: Princeton University Press, 1954. (Originally published, 1934.) (b)

Jung, C. Concerning the archetypes, with special reference to the anima concept. In *The archetypes and the collective unconscious*, Collected works (Vol. 9, part I, pp. 54-74). Princeton, N. J.: Princeton University Press, 1959. (Originally published, 1936.) (a)

Jung, C. The concept of the collective unconscious. In *The archetypes and the collective unconscious*, Collected works (Vol. 9, Part I, pp. 42-53). Princeton, N. J.: Princeton University Press, 1959. (Originally published, 1936.) (b)

Jung, C. Psychological aspects of the mother archetype. In *The archetypes and the collective unconscious*, Collected works (Vol. 9, Part 1, pp. 73-110). Princeton, N. J.: Princeton University Press, 1959. (Originally published, 1938.) (a)

Jung, C. Psychology and religion. In *Psychology and religion: West and east*, Collected works (Vol. 11, pp. 3-106). Princeton, N. J.: Princeton University Press, 1958. (Originally published, 1938.) (b)

Jung, C. Foreword to Suzuki's "Introduction to Zen Buddhism." In *Psychology and religion: West and east*, Collected works (Vol. 11, pp. 538-557). Princeton, N. J.: Princeton University Press, 1957. (Originally published, 1939.)

Jung, C. Concerning rebirth. In *The archetypes and the collective unconscious*, Collected works (Vol. 9, Part I, pp. 113-150). Princeton, N. J.: Princeton

University Press, 1959. (Originally published, 1940.) (a)

Jung, C. The psychology of the child archetype. In *The archetypes and the collective unconscious*, Collected works (Vol. 9, Part I, pp. 151-181). Princeton, N. J.: Princeton University Press, 1959. (Originally published, 1940.) (b)

Jung, C. The gifted child. In *The development of personality*, Collected works (Vol. 17, pp. 133-148). Princeton, N. J.: Princeton University Press, 1954. (Originally published, 1943.) (a)

Jung, C. The psychology of eastern meditation. In *Psychology and religion: West and east*, Collected works (Vol. 11, pp. 558-575). Princeton, N. J.: Princeton University Press, 1958. (Originally published, 1943.) (b)

Jung, C. Psychotherapy today. In *The practice of psychotherapy*, Collected works (Vol. 16, pp. 94-125). Princeton, N. J.: Princeton University Press, 1954. (Originally published, 1945.)

Jung, C. The psychology of the transference. In *The practice of psychotherapy*, Collected works (Vol. 16, pp. 163-322). Princeton, N. J.: Princeton University Press, 1954. (Originally published, 1946.)

Jung, C. On the nature of the psyche. In *The structure and dynamics of the psyche*, Collected works (Vol. 8, pp. 159-234). Princeton, N. J.: Princeton University Press, 1960. (Originally published, 1947.)

Jung, C. The ego. In *Aion, researches into the phenomenology of the self*, Collected works (Vol. 9, Part II, pp. 3-7). Princeton, N. J.: Princeton University Press, 1959. (Originally published, 1951.)

Jung, C. *Memories, dreams, reflections*. New York: Random House, 1961.

Kettner, M. Some archetypal themes in homosexuality. *Proceedings of the fifteenth annual joint meeting of the Northern and Southern California Societies of Jungian Analysts* (pp. 33-58). San Francisco: C. G. Jung Institute, 1967.

Klaif, C. Empathy in the analytic process. In *The Shaman from Elko*. San Francisco: C. G. Jung Institute, 1978.

Klein, M. *Envy and gratitude*. London: Tavistock, 1957.

Klopfer, B. Editorial dedication honoring Jung's eightieth birthday, *Journal of Projective Techniques*, 1955, *19* (3), 225

Klopfer, B., & Kelley, D. *The Rorschach technique*. New York: World Book Co., 1942.

Klopfer, B., Ainsworth, M. D., Klopfer, W. G., & Holt, R. R. (Eds.). *Developments in the Rorschach technique* (Vol. I, *Technique and theory)*. New York: Harcourt, Brace & World, 1954.

Lambert, K. Some notes on the process of reconstruction. *The Journal of Analytical Psychology,* 1970, *15*(1), 42-58.

Lambert, K. The personality of the analyst in interpretation and therapy. In *Technique in Jungian analysis*. Library of Analytical Psychology (Vol. 2, pp. 18-44). London: William Heinemann Medical Books, 1974.

Levene, H. An acute schizophrenic process treated by analytic therapy. In *Shaman from Elko*. San Francisco: C. G. Jung Institute, 1978.

McCully, R. *Rorschach theory and symbolism: A Jungian approach to clinical material*. Baltimore: Williams & Williams, 1971.

McGuire, W. (Ed.). *The Freud-Jung letters: The correspondence between Sigmund Freud and C. G. Jung*. Princeton, N. J.: Princeton University Press, 1974.

MacKinnon, D. The nature and nurture of creative talent. *American Psychologist,* 1962, *17*(7), 484-495.

MacKinnon, D. Creativity and images of the self. In R. W. White (Ed.), *The study of lives*. New York: Prentice-Hall, 1963.

MacKinnon, D. Personality and realization of creative potential. *American Psychologist,* 1965, *20*(4), 273-281.

Maduro, R. Artistic creativity and aging in India. *Internatinal Journal of Aging and Human Development,* 1974, *5*(4), 303-329. (a)

Maduro, R. Notes on the adaptive significance of regression in analytical psychology. In R. Davidson and R. Day (Eds.), *Symbol and realization: A contribution to the study of magic and healing* (pp. 116-131). Berkeley: University of California, Center for South and Southeast Asia Studies, 1974. (b)

Maduro, R. Hoodoo possession in San Francisco: Notes on therapeutic aspects of regression. *Ethos,* 1975, *3*(3), 426-447.

Maduro, R. *Artistic creativity in a Brahmin painter community*. Research Monograph No. 14. Berkeley: University of California Center for South and Southeast Asian Studies, 1976. (a)

Maduro, R. Journey dreams in Latino group psychotherapy. *Psychotherapy: Theory, Research and Practice,* 1976, *13(2)*, 148-177. (b)

Maduro, R. The clinical usefulness of an initial dream. In *Shaman from Elko*. San Francisco: C. G. Jung Institute, 1978.

Maduro, R. Symbolic equations in creative process: Reflections on Hindu India. *Journal of Analytical Psychology,* 1980, *25(1)*, 59-90.

Meier, C. A. Psychological types and individuation: A plea for a more scientific approach in Jungian psychology. In J. Wheelwright (Ed.), *The analytic process: Aims, analysis, training* (pp. 276-289). New York: G. P. Putnam's Sons, 1971.

Mindness, H. Analytical psychology and the Rorschach test. *Journal of Projective Techniques,* 1955, *19*, 243-252.

Murray, H. A. In *Carl Gustav Jung, 1875-1961: A Memorial Meeting* (pp. 17-22). New York: Analytical Psychology Club of New York, 1962.

Myers, I. *The Meyers-Briggs Type Indicator*. Princeton, N. J.: Educational Testing Service, 1962.

Neumann, E. *The origins and history of consciousness,* Princeton, N. J.: Princeton

University Press, 1954.

Neumann, E. The significance of the genetic aspect for analytical psychology. *The Journal of Analytical Psychology,* 1959, *4*(2), 125-138.

Neumann, E. Narcissism, normal self formation and the primary relationship to the mother. *Spring: Contributions to Jungian Thought.* (Analytical Psychology Club of New York), 1966, pp. 81-106.

Newton, K. Mediation of the image of infant-mother togetherness. *Journal of Analytical Psychology,* 1965, *10*(2), 151-162.

Newton, K. Separation and pre-oedipal guilt. *Journal of Analytical Psychology,* 1975, *20*(2), 183-193.

Osterman, E. The tendency toward patterning and order in matter and in the psyche. In J. Wheelwright (Ed.), *The reality of the psyche* (pp. 14-27). New York: G. P. Putnam's Sons, 1968.

Perry, J. Reconstitutive process in the psychopathology of the self. *Annals of the New York Academy of Sciences,* 1961, *96,* 853-876.

Perry, J. Emotions and object relations, *Journal of Analytical Psychology,* 1970, *15*(1), 1-12.

Perry, J. *The far side of madness.* Englewood Cliffs, N. J.: Prentice-Hall, 1974.

Plaut, A. Hungry patients, reflections on ego structure. *The Journal of Analytical Psychology,* 1959, *4*(2), 153-160.

Plaut, A. *Some reflections on the Klein-Jungian hybrid.* Paper presented to The Society of Analytical Psychology, London, May, 1962.

Plaut, A. Reflections about not being able to imagine. *Journal of Analytical Psychology,* 1966, *11*(2), 113-134.

Plaut, A. Part-object relations and Jung's "luminosities." *Journal of Analytical Psychology,* 1974, *19*(2), 165-181. (a)

Plaut, A. The transference in analytical psychology. In *The Library of Analytical Psychology, Technique in Jungian Analysis*

(Vol. 2). London: William Heinemann Medical Books, 1974, pp. 152-160. (b)

Progoff, I. *Jung's psychology and its social meaning.* New York: Julian Press, 1953.

Redfearn, J. Several views of the self. *Journal of Analytical Psychology,* 1969, *14*(1), pp. 13-25.

Sandner, D. *Navaho symbols of healing.* New York: Harcourt Brace Jovanovich, 1979.

Segal, H. *Introduction to the work of Melanie Klein* (Enlarged ed.). New York: Basic Books, 1973.

Singer, J. *Androgeny, toward a new theory of sexuality.* New York: Anchor Press-Doubleday, 1976.

Stein, L. What is a symbol supposed to be? *Journal of Analytical Psychology,* 1957, *2*(1), 73-84.

Stein, L. An entity named ego. *Journal of Analytical Psychology,* 1962, *7*(1), 41-54.

Tate, D. Invasion and separation. *Journal of Analytical Psychology,* 1961, *6*(1), 45-53.

Von Franz, M. L. *The problem of the Puer Aeternus,* New York: Spring Publications, 1970.

Von Franz, M. L. *The shadow and evil in fairytales.* New York: Spring Publications, 1974.

Wheelwright, Jane. *The death of a woman.* New York: St. Martin's Press, 1980.

Whitehead, C. Additional aspects of the Freudian-Kleinian controversy: Towards a "psychoanalysis" of psychoanalysis. *International Journal of Psycho-Analysis,* 1975, *56*(4), 383-396.

Whitmont, E. *The symbolic quest.* New York: G. P. Putnam's, 1969.

Whitmont, E. & Kaufmann, Y. Analytical psychotherapy. In R. J. Corsini (Ed.), *Current psychotherapies* (pp. 85-117). Itasca, Ill.: F. E. Peacock, 1973.

Wickes, F. G. *The inner world of childhood.* New York: Appleton-Century-Crofts, 1927.

Williams, M. The indivisibility of the personal

and collective unconscious. *Journal of Analytical Psychology,* 1963, *8*(1), 45-50.

Winnicott, D. Transitional objects and transitional phenomena. In *Through paediatrics to psycho-analysis* (pp. 229-242). London: Hogarth Press, 1975. (Originally published, 1951.)

Winnicott, D. The depressive position in normal emotional development. In *Through paediatrics to psycho-analysis* (pp. 262-277). London: Hogarth Press, 1975. (Originally published, 1954.)

Yandell, J. *The imitation of Jung, an exploration of the meaning of Jungian.* St. Louis, Mo.: The Centerpoint Foundation, 1977.

Zinkin, L. Flexibility in analytic technique. *Journal of Analytical Psychology,* 1969, *14*(2), 119-132.

CHAPTER V

CARL R. ROGERS

Person-Centered
Theory

**T.L. Holdstock and
Carl R. Rogers**

Person-centered personality theory, formerly known as *nondirective* (Rogers, 1942) and later as *client-centered* (Rogers, 1951), had its origin around 1940 in the growing dissatisfaction of Carl R. Rogers, a psychologist, with the theories and the methodologies then current in the treatment of emotional and behavioral "problems." His basic conception, held from the beginning to the present, is that the proper focus for any theory of personality or method of treatment is the person.

The latest name change accentuates this. The person is recognized as a Gestalt of thoughts, feelings, actions, perceptions, and complex biological processes, always in relation to time, as well as to the world of people, objects, and events around him. The present shift in emphasis to person-centered highlights the social outreach of the theory. Although Roger's theory has grown out of psychotherapy and is still developing as a means of growth and change, the principles underlying the theory are believed to be relevant to almost every aspect of man's behavior.

A distinctive feature of person-centered theory is and has been its continued stress on the self-actualizing and self-directing quality of people. This apparently simple notion of "empowering the person," trusting that he or she can know the proper direction of movement in his or her own actualizing process, is one of the most revolutionary aspects of the theory, cutting it loose from the materialistic determinism of some other systems.

Self-actualization occurs when one's own experience becomes more important than the values of others in maintaining one's self-concept.

Note: This chapter has essentially been written by Dr. Holdstock. He has enriched it with his special knowledge in neurophysiology and cognitive psychology. I have served as consultant, editor, and author of certain sections. I add my name as co-author to indicate that I have been involved and am fully in accord with the final product.—C.R.R.

Experiencing means to be aware how one attends, perceives, processes, and integrates information of one's internal, visceral world and one's external, interpersonal, and physical world. Openness to full organismic sensing comes when one experiences realness, caring, and sensitive, nonjudgmental understanding in relation with others.

These principles apply to all people, irrespective of age and adjustment, and they represent a total theory of humanness. In the special situation of therapy it is important that the therapist be real, caring, and trusting, and that he or she be seen as such. The person-centered therapist meets the client in a moment-to-moment encounter, continually focusing on the phenomenal world of the client.

The historical roots of person-centered theory reach across many cultures and many centuries, and it has considerable commonality with many present-day approaches within the perceptual-phenomenological and existential frameworks. In addition, person-centered theory has consistently attempted to validate its hypotheses through research.

INTRODUCTION

Our fascination with ourselves is seen by the varieties of myths about our creation and also by the very large number of theories and attitudes about human beings. Over the millennia a number of general positions have been taken about who we are, how we got to be what we are, and what to do about ourselves and others, especially those who do not act the way we want them to act.

Such personality theories are important, since they help organize people to cooperate, and, if the theories are valid, they help people to deal with one another in helpful ways. If it is possible to apply the advances of science to such theorizing, then it is possible for us to take a great step toward the age-long dream of a happy and peaceful world. We may also help accomplish the aim of alleviating human misery of the kind that to normal people seems so unnecessary, those states of misery called *delinquencies, neuroses*, and *psychoses*.

In philosophy, the direct ancestor of personality theories, a number of problems, still unsolved, were taken up. One has to do with the nature of the person. *Is the person exclusively body? Does something control that body?* These issues have not been settled. Some people take the monist position that there is only the body, while others implicitly or explicitly take the dualistic position that there are body and mind, or body and soul. Is the individual free or a slave? Is behavior determined, or does the person have a capacity for creative and independent judgment and decision? This issue of freedom versus determinism also is still with us. Are human beings rational, following the dictates of a kind of moral calculus, doing what is in their apparent best interests, or are they directed by feelings and emotions, conscious or unconscious? Here, too, modern personality theorists cannot come to agreement.

Many other positions have been taken in the attempt to understand human beings. Some come from religion, some from tradition, some from armchair theorizing, and some from experimentation. No fewer than 80 more or less scientifically oriented theories of personality are in existence at the present time, some wide and all embracing in nature, and some narrow and specialized. But all are in pursuit of truth, hoping to see us as we truly are.

In this chapter we will discuss a theory of personality formation and maintenance which, although started through clinical experience, has over 35 years developed and expanded while going through a variety of changes, as has also been true of other mature personality theories. Person-centered theory is validated through clinical experience, through research, through analogy, and through the latest knowledge about basic neurophysiology. It represents, in our judgment, not only a total and complete veridical picture of man and woman's nature, but also a philosophy of life which can help us realize the centuries-old dream of peace and harmony in this unstable world.

HISTORY

Precursors

To place person-centered theory in a historical perspective is easy, since the core aspects of the theory have been a central concern of humanity for many thousands of years. But it is also difficult, because it is not possible to determine specific occurrences as definite precursors of the theory.

The person-centered belief in the unique potential of each individual has religious overtones. It is conceivable that Rogers has given the concept of God new meaning, due to his unfailing belief in the worth of each person. The Hebrew word for God (*Yahweh asher Yahweh*) means *I am* or *I am what I am; I am who I am; I am as I am.* Further indications of the centrality accorded the person in biblical times are the commandments: Love thy neighbor as thyself, and love thy God as thyself.

Other central concepts of the person-centered approach have ancient ethical counterparts. Congruence, empathy, and unconditional positive regard have been key concepts in religion through the ages. Oden (1972) demonstrated that important antecedents of current encounter group processes can be found in the life and literature of Protestant and Jewish pietism. The universality of the concerns of the person-centered approach is evident in that its roots can be traced to Oriental philosophies. Zen holds that each person must find the answers to life within him/herself. The importance placed by Yoga on the physical and physiological aspects of the body closely resembles the importance attached to organismic experiencing by person-centered theory. Krishnamurti, for instance, said that the body has its own intelligence and that life is here and now, but if you are fearful you cannot live.

The philosophies which culminated in the existential movement (Patterson, 1973) have close ties to the person-centered approach. Edmund Husserl postulated that the real world can only be inferred on the basis of perceptions. Existential philosophy, originating in the work of Søren Kierkegaard and Karl Jaspers, is concerned with the nature of humans, their existence and involvement in the world, and with the meaning of existence for the individual. Aspects of existentialism are key concepts in person-centered theory: (1) being conscious of self and being able to choose at every moment; (2) the idea that man/woman is *being*, thus constantly becoming, evolving; (3) the notion that each person has the capacity to transcend the self and the physical world. The person-centered approach, like existentialism, is an attitude, an approach to life.

Since Alfred Adler has been considered to fall within the existential framework (Mosak & Dreikurs, 1973), it is not surprising to find close affinities between Individual Psychology and person-centered theory. Individual Psychology "views man holistically as a creative, responsible, 'becoming' individual moving toward fictional goals within his phenomenal field" (Mosak & Dreikurs, 1973, p. 35). The similarity between certain core concepts of the two approaches is striking. Even the titles bear close resemblance, with the emphasis being on the individual, or the person, in both cases. Rogers could have written: "We must be able to see with his eyes and hear with his ears" (Adler, 1958).

Thomas Hanna (1970) accords Sigmund Freud a special place in making us aware of the significance of our bodies. In this sense Freud can be regarded as a precursor to person-centered theory. Ever since Rogers (1959b) suggested that experiences are valued in terms of satisfactions organismically experienced, this concept of bodily felt sensing has become increasingly important, culminating in the Experiential Psychotherapy of Eugene Gendlin (Gendlin, 1973). We can move one step up the ladder of theory construction by conceptualizing the unconscious in terms of organismic processes.

Like Kierkegaard or Freud, Rogers must also be seen as reacting against the prevailing Zeitgeist of his time. The questions raised by wars, the materialism and competitiveness of American society, heavy reliance on modern technology, the rigid adherence of academic psychology to logical positivism as the only approach to scientific truth—all these served to sharpen Rogers's focus on the essence and dignity of human beings. Consequently, such global situations contributed to the development of the person-centered theory. The individualism of the American frontier, the belief in self-reliance, and the conviction that the individual could learn and do whatever was necessary probably also contributed to Roger's development of the person-centered approach, according to Meador (Meador & Rogers, 1973).

The widespread root system of person-centered theory seems to indicate that a collective unconsciousness is involved. It is conceivable that Rogers, in actually *being* the principles of person-centered theory, in tuning in and utilizing all of himself, made explicit some basic collective truths. He did so at a time when and in a language to which a great many people were receptive. Thus, there is yet another root to the person-centered plant, the root that grew from Jungian soil. However, the plant is vastly more than the sum of its roots. It is also much more than the sum of all its leaves, branches, and flowers. It is a growing, living thing, responsive to the conditions in which it grows.

Beginnings

In light of the centrality of religious concepts in person-centered theory, it is not surprising to find that Rogers grew up in a family "where hard work and a highly conservative (almost fundamentalist) Protestant Christianity were about equally revered" (Rogers, 1959b). His parents raised their children in a firm, gentle way; definite orders were seldom given, as with Rogers as a therapist. Although he rejected the family view of religion, he spent two years as a graduate student at the Union Theological Seminary. The freedom of philosophical thought and respect for honest attempts at resolving meaningful problems which Rogers encountered at the seminary gave him a taste of unconditional positive regard. He also experienced the same spirit of tolerance when he attended the World Federation of Christian Students in Peking during his third year at the university. His contact with Oriental philosophies was a moving and exciting experience.

As a child, Rogers loved solitude, preferring to work independently and alone on the farm. Luckily, from high school through graduate school he encountered several teachers who encouraged him to be original in his academic work. He spent two years studying medieval history and two years studying philosophy and religion before he began to study psychology. Besides Union Theological Seminary, he attended the University of Wisconsin and Teachers College at Columbia University and did his psychological internship at the Institute for Child Guidance in New York in 1927–28. After completing his doctorate in 1931, he was a clinician for 12 years at the Child Study Department of a Rochester social agency. In 1940, Rogers accepted a position as professor in the Department of Psychology at Ohio

State University, and in 1945 he moved to the University of Chicago, where he organized the Counseling Center. His next appointment, at the University of Wisconsin in 1957, was in the departments of psychology and psychiatry. In 1964 he moved to the Western Behavioral Sciences Institute and in 1968 was one of a group forming the Center for Studies of the Person.

Some of the main ideas, concepts, and people Rogers came in contact with at these places can be subsumed under general categories of history, scientific agriculture, philosophy and religion, education, and academic and applied psychology. In the educational field the emphasis John Dewey placed on the project method and on the importance of the phenomenal world of the student in the educational process was certainly meaningful to Rogers. At Teachers College, Rogers encountered not only Dewey's ideas but psychology as it was developing in the United States, with emphasis on the control and manipulation of operationally defined variables.

In the applied field, Rogers had extensive contact with major personality theory orientations. Only the approach of Otto Rank, however, directly affected the development of the person-centered concept. The relationship of person-centered theory with psychoanalysis during the early and later phases of its development was more congenial than during the middle phase. Rogers was at variance not only with psychoanalysis but also with many of the concepts held by nonmedical practitioners who believed in the medical-diagnostic model of counseling and therapy. His acquaintanceship with behavior modification, at least with its "theoretical underpinnings," is one of longstanding disagreement.

At Rochester, Rogers's ideas about therapy began to take shape. He "began to sense the orderliness inherent in the experience of therapy, an orderliness which emerged from the therapeutic relationship, not one which was imposed from the outside" (Meador & Rogers, 1973, p. 121). He also discovered the value of listening attentively to the client in therapy. A social worker with a background of Rankian therapy made him aware of the importance of listening for the feelings behind the client's words. "I believe she was the one who suggested that the best response was to 'reflect' these feelings back to the client" (Rogers, 1975c).

His contact with the ideas of Rank through social workers at Rochester and through the writings of Jessie Taft confirmed Rogers in the direction he was taking. It also encouraged him to continue exploring the orderliness which he sensed to be similar to what Rank regarded as the essence of psychotherapy. Rank believed that the individual client has within him the potential to grow. He believed that the therapist can best guide the client toward self-understanding and acceptance by relying on human qualities rather than on technical skills.

Although several stages characterize the development of person-centered theory throughout its development, the core idea of trust in the individual's capacity has remained unchanged.

The Precursor Stage.   The period before and during the full-time involvement of Rogers in counseling at Rochester can be considered as the precursor stage (Meador & Rogers, 1973). Through his experience in therapy, contact with the ideas of Rank and earlier contact with the ideas of Dewey, his view of the person as self-directing began to take shape (Rogers, 1973).

The Nondirective Stage.   Rogers pinpoints December 11, 1940, as the day on which person-centered theory was born. On that day he gave a talk at the University of Minnesota entitled ''Newer Concepts in Psychotherapy,'' and the reaction to this paper made him realize that he was saying something new which came from him (Rogers, 1974c). ''Reflection of feelings'' and ''nondirective techniques'' became the trademarks of this period. His main publication during this time was *Counseling and Psychotherapy* (1942).

The Client-Centered Stage.   The name change from *nondirective counseling* to *client-centered counseling* was introduced by the publication of *Client-Centered Therapy* in 1951. During this time Rogers developed his theory of personality and psychotherapy (see Rogers, 1959b). Client-centered theory stressed that the person seeking help was not to be treated as a dependent patient but rather as a responsible client.

The Experiential Stage.   During this stage the counselor became free. Organismic experience became as important a referent in guiding the therapist's behavior as it was for the client. Full humanization and mutuality of the professional relationship between psychotherapist and client paved the way for widespread applicability of the theory which began during this time.

Current Status

The Person-Centered Stage.   The current status of the theory is best portrayed by the change in emphasis from *client*-centered *therapy* to a *person*-centered *approach*. This indicates that the theory is conceived to have wider applicability than simply helping relationships. When the theory was extended to education, it was known as student-centered teaching. As it moved into a wide variety of fields, it seemed best to adopt as broad a term as possible. Rogers has helped to initiate and develop what might be called a person-centered approach, not only in counseling, psychotherapy, and education, but also in marriage and family relationships, in intensive groups, and, to a lesser extent, in administration, the problems of minority groups, and interracial, intercultural, and even international relationships. The principles underlying the theory are of relevance in every aspect of the behavior of human beings.

The shift in emphasis to person-centered emphasizes that it is as *person*, as *I am*, as *being*, and not just in some role identity as client, student, teacher, or therapist that the individual is the unit of all interactions. The name change conveys the full complexity of each person; it indicates that each individual is more than the sum of the parts that make the person.

It also focuses renewed attention on the importance of actualizing the full potential of each individual and on the meaning of concepts such as experiencing, organismic valuing, and organismic sensing. Experiencing had been regarded largely in terms of awareness of the richness of subjective feelings (Rogers, 1961). However, explaining experiencing in terms of inward references to feelings and bodily processes only represents at best a single aspect of the full human potential. Experiencing is more than just sensing visceral and feeling states. It involves being aware of the way one attends, perceives, processes, and integrates information of the internal visceral and external interpersonal and physical world.

Regarding experiencing in terms of the ability to perceive, process, and organize information is in line with the thinking of Wexler and several other person-centered theorists (Wexler & Rice, 1974). These theorists regard experiencing primarily as something created cognitively by the person. Since disappointment has been expressed about the lack of real understanding of the essence of person-centered theory (Farson, 1974; Gendlin, 1974), recasting the theory in terms of the language and concepts of cognitive psychology and information-processing theory may help to make the principles of the theory more readily understandable.

Rogers has consistently resisted continuing efforts to make him into a "guru, an idol, the leader of a movement." He is able "to let go of ideas, to share them, to prevent them from being dogmatized and identified solely with him" (Farson, 1974). These characteristics of Rogers are in keeping with person-centered theory. He demonstrates by his behavior his solid belief that each person has to discover experientially meaningful principles. Thus there are no exclusive societies, institutions, or journals devoted to the person-centered point of view. The theory as a way of life makes compartmentalization into exclusivity impossible and it is operative wherever and whenever people accept different realities of each other. Any approach to the theory which treats it in compartmentalized form fails to do justice to its potential. As in all aspects of living, however, the theory is only as good as it is implemented, and its implementation is not as easy as it would seem at first. In the final analysis it boils down to one's ability to live one's potential in terms of self and others; and such actualization is not restricted to any group of people, organization, or institution.

Person-centered theory continues to be vigorously researched. As the theory reached further afield, so did research related to the theory. For example, Reinhard Tausch, in a talk given at the University of California, San Diego, in February 1975, stated that at the University of Hamburg in West Germany, 120 masters' theses and nine doctoral dissertations exploring person-centered psychotherapy had been completed in the preceding six years. In addition to this spread of research in psychotherapy, the effectiveness of a person-centered approach has perhaps been most strikingly demonstrated by a decade of work by D. N. Aspy, F. N. Roebuck, and their colleagues in the field of education (Aspy & Roebuck, 1974).

ASSERTIONS

Development

Throughout the development of person-centered theory, the main concern has always been with dynamic aspects of the person, such as communication, relationships, and ability to change, rather than with the static structure of the person. Personality is not conceived of as something one has. It is "a living, holistic entity, with goals, purposes, needs and meanings" (Burton, 1974).

Person-centered theory has grown out of continuing experience in therapy, with a broadening range of clients, rather than out of armchair or laboratory formulation. It was not only the experiences of the clients as perceived by Rogers that was important in formulation of the theory, but also Rogers' awareness of his own experiences which provided the materials for building the theory.

Some of the tentative, though important, conclusions arrived at over the years have to do with the basic nature of the individual.

1. Each person has an inherent tendency to actualize unique potential.

Like all other living organisms, each person is born with "an inherent tendency to develop all his/her capacities in ways that serve to maintain or enhance the organism" (Rogers, 1975a). This growth force is part of the genetic makeup of all organisms. Human beings differ from other organisms only in that they are more complex. Thus, besides the fulfillment of basic biological potentials, human beings also have uniquely human and psychological potentials to be actualized. Each person, furthermore, is unique in the sense that the biological and psychological potentials of no two persons are the same. The physical, social, and cultural environment each one is born into can facilitate the actualization of our psychological and biological potentials to a greater or lesser extent. In both realms the tendency to growth is strong enough to overcome considerable hardships. One needs only to think of the many ways in which we behave irresponsibly toward our children, without destroying their ability to be accepting, understanding, and to love.

*2. Each person has an inherent bodily wisdom which enables
    differentiation between experiences that actualize and those that do
    not actualize potential.*

From the moment of birth the baby knows what feels good and what does
not. He or she knows this organismically and not consciously. The baby
trusts organismically. This trust in one's own body goes a long way to make
oneself known. Organismic valuing is not an elementary process. It is not
only continually differentiating unpleasantness from pleasant bodily states
but also monitoring varying degrees of pleasantness and unpleasantness
involving many different functions of the body. It is clearly directed from
within and based on a complex feedback system.

In the life span of the individual there are a number of critical
developmental periods. These are not only periods of genetically determined biological changes (completion of neuron development, maturation of
muscles), but also some periods which have been socially determined (such
as starting school).

3. It is crucially important to be fully open to all experiences.

The continuous use of bodily sensing is necessary for full development as a
human. Use of our senses after birth seems to be necessary in several
respects. First, receptor cells will atrophy if not stimulated. This is true for
those modalities receptive to external sources of stimulation, such as the
rods and cones in the retina of the eye. Investigators have shown that
depriving animals of the use of their visual modality from birth is as
deleterious as physically damaging the eye.

It is more difficult to demonstrate physical atrophy of cells responsive to
internal sources of stimulation. However, it is conceivable that the same
atrophying process will occur with disuse, since the receptor cells of the different sense modalities employ similar principles of operation. Continuous
use of sense modalities is necessary to ensure their development, not only at
peripheral levels (e.g., in the skin and muscles), but also at the level of the
central nervous system. If no neural impulses are forthcoming from the
receptor level, atrophy sets in at the different relay stations along the
pathways to the brain and in the areas of representation in the brain.

4. Significant others are important in helping us to experience fully.

As the infant grows older it becomes increasingly important that it differentiate between its various bodily sensings and learn to identify each appropriately. The mother is of greatest significance in helping the child differentiate between and identify each bodily sensing, such as being tired,
cold, and hungry, as well as the degree of tiredness, coldness, or hunger.

The process of bodily identification can be interfered with, not only by
the proverbial ''bad'' mother, but also by the too-careful mother. Such a

mother dresses the child too warmly in summer or not warmly enough in winter; forces the child to eat at mealtimes, whether hungry or not; punishes the child for wetting his pants, and so on. An overly careful mother may interfere with development of the organismic valuing process by not letting the child learn and by anticipating the child's needs to such an extent that the child never experiences a full range of organismic states, like never being cold or seldom being hungry.

Significant others, thus, can help a child focus attention on and symbolize his own organismic sensings appropriately. They can also be of help by not providing stimuli which interfere with the organismic sensings of the child; for example, spanking or scolding the child for wetting. In Assertion 7, under the topic of conditions of worth, this aspect is touched on again, while it is discussed in greater detail in the section on validation.

5. *Experiencing becomes more than bodily sensing as one grows older.*

The organismic valuing process is based on the organism's potential available for that purpose at any moment in time. It develops as the child develops. It starts out purely as a sensing of bodily states, but the child's potential to process information becomes more differentiated over time. When that happens integration of one's developing faculties is necessary for optimal organismic sensing. An example is the integration of cognitive abilities with bodily awareness. Integration can perhaps be described as awareness of the relative contribution of each of the components of an experience to that experience. As the individual grows older, his life space, especially his contact and interactions with other people, also becomes more differentiated. Full realization of the organismic valuing process requires these external experiences to be integrated with the information which the person obtains from his body.

6. *Through complex interactions with our body and with other persons, we develop a concept of self.*

The complex configuration of the self-concept begins when the individual experiences the physical self as separate from the environment. The infant at times bites its toys and at other times bites its fingers. The respective sensations are quite different, and on the basis of such experiences an awareness develops that the finger is "me" and the toy is "not me." At about the same time that the physical self differentiates from the environment, the social self emerges as part of the physical self. Thus, as the infant grows older he slowly builds up an increasingly differentiated field of experiences, called *self-experiences*, which become further elaborated through interactions with significant others into a *self-concept*. Once the self-concept is formed, a *need for positive regard* from others develops. Rogers believes this need is universal. We all need love—to be touched, literally and figuratively. In light of what happens to rhesus monkeys deprived of the companionship of others, it is clear that the need for contact, symbolic and physical, is of the utmost importance for the optimal development of a person's full potential (Harlow & Suomi, 1970). The need for positive regard, for love, influences perceptions, and perceptions in turn have a significant effect on self-concept. Since the individual's need for positive regard can only be satisfied by others, self-concept is increasingly differentiated in terms of others.

7. *One can sacrifice the wisdom of one's own experiencing to gain another's love.*

To the extent to which the individual perceives the need for positive regard from others to have been met, he or she develops self-regard. Both the need for positive regard from others and the need *for self-regard* are social manifestations of the actualizing tendency. It is important, first, to be liked by others, but eventually to like oneself, so that one's self-regard or self-worth is not always based on the regard of others.

Positive regard from others can be provided unconditionally (unconditional positive regard) or conditionally; that is, *conditions of worth* which are attached to others' positive regarding of a person. If an individual receives unconditional regard from another, he will regard himself positively and will continue to evaluate experiences in terms of the organismic valuing process. However, conditional regard from others is more or less consistently the rule in life. Early in life the child experiences that in some respects he is valued by significant others and in other respects he is not. However, many experiences satisfying to the individual may not receive positive regard from significant others. And since the regard of significant others is so important, the individual comes to disregard personal experiencing and adopts the view which significant others have of the experiences.

> This means that some behaviors are regarded positively which are not actually experienced organismically as satisfying. Other behaviors are regarded negatively which are not actually experienced as unsatisfying. It is when he behaves in accordance with these introjected values that he may be said to have acquired conditions of worth. He cannot regard himself positively, as having worth, unless he lives in terms of these conditions (Rogers, 1959b).

Such a sequence is not theoretically necessary. If the child is allowed to retain its own organismic evaluation of each experience, even though some behaviors have to be inhibited, life would become a balancing of these satisfactions. There is little chance this will occur in the lives of most children raised in Western cultures.

A common example of not allowing a child organismic experiences occurs when it has been hurt. Our first response to the crying child is usually something like, "Now, now, it is not so bad," if we are irritated with the crying and want it to stop. The child then is faced with two unpleasant stimuli, one in its own body and one from a significant other. Whichever stimulus is more important to the child will tend to inhibit awareness of the other. This is the way the nervous system operates. Due to the importance of significant others for the child's survival and the need for self-regard, the child is likely to pay more attention to stimuli emanating from significant others and so comes to ignore self-actualization in terms of organismic experiences. Thus the child may, for example, become an adult who denies the existence of pain or the painful symptoms of an illness.

Summary. Each person needs to actualize his or her own self. The fullest extent of actualization is to love and to be loved. Love provides the climate for optimal functioning of our organismic valuing process, which makes possible the full actualization of our unique potential. Unfortunately, the fulfillment of our potential is fraught with dangers, the greatest of which is sacrificing the self for another's love. The next section deals with this aspect.

Maintenance

Person-centered theory does not believe that development of personality is ever completed. The foregoing discussion can be regarded as developmental in the sense that it introduced the elements and interplay between elements of importance in shaping and reshaping that complex process we call personality. This section on maintenance, therefore, logically continues where the previous section left off.

8. *A rift can develop between what is actually experienced and the concept of self.*

When conditional regard takes the place of the organismic valuing process, the individual loses touch with organismic potential, and self-alienation begins. To maintain the existing self-concept, experiences inconsistent with conditions of worth, internalized into the self-concept, are perceived selectively and distortedly or denied to awareness completely or partly. Experiences in accord with the self, as defined in terms of others, are perceived and symbolized accurately in awareness. Thus the self-concept becomes increasingly inaccurate, unrealistic, and rigid over time. For the sake of positive regard from others, the individual comes to falsify some of the values experienced and to perceive them only in terms based upon their value to others. The person ceases to function as a unity as he or she did as an infant.

It is easy to lose contact with oneself, as demonstrated by the words of a well adjusted wife and mother of three.

> I have an overwhelming sense of sadness—that I am unable to let others be. The problems of each individual making me bury myself in the morass—my doing, not theirs! A negation of myself where I become a myriad tentacled meddler trying to be responsible for all but myself, because the me is not there. I am carried away by feelings that are not always my own. Have I lost the key to my own being? Did I ever have it?

A while later she says:

> Surely I should have learned that nonbeing can only be when I cease to exist in terms of my own consciousness. Why is it so hard for me to grow this way? I find I am repeatedly failing in trying to fight against this creature. To understand my own feelings and to recognize them is most important at present.

On another occasion this woman says: "I share with you this need for affirmation, and yet, if one has to lose oneself in the process, is it worth it? No and again NO!" She is experiencing the gap between her own experiencing, and the way of being she has taken on from others.

9. *When the rift between experiencing and self is too great, anxiety or disorganized behavior results.*

Experiencing new events enhances the likelihood of incongruence between the experiences of these events and the self-concept. If experiences highly discrepant with the self-concept are symbolized in awareness, the integrated balance of the self-concept would be broken, and anxiety or disorganized behavior may result.

Rogers (1974b) discussed the case of Ellen West as an illustration of self-estrangement. Ellen West was made to feel, in some of the most significant moments of her life, that her own experiencing was invalid, erroneous, and unsound, and that she should be feeling something quite different. She surrendered her capacity for valuing experience and substituted the opinions of her parents and later of her psychiatrists. Twice she fell in love with a man, and on both occasions she surrendered her love in favor of her father's wishes against it. Tragically, not only did she give up, but she came to mistrust her inner experiences. Rogers puts her feelings schematically. "I thought my feelings meant that I was in love. I felt I was doing the positive and meaningful thing to get engaged. But my experience cannot be trusted. I was not in love."

10. *Validating experiencing in terms of others can never be completed.*

Contemporary men and women are faced with an additional dilemma. They often ignore their own experiencing to be accepted, respected, and loved by others, but then they find that adopting the norm of significant others still does not guarantee them that acceptance. The person is faced with a bewildering array of beliefs and meanings, so that it is impossible to take on a generally approved self.

Incongruence, thus, exists not only between one's social experience and one's self-concept, but also between the self-concept based on the value of some groups and the values of other groups. It would therefore seem wise, if self-concept is defined in terms of the values of others, to maintain contact with a unified and strongly supportive set of beliefs and meanings. This is perhaps the life-saving "wisdom" behind many religious sects, various schools of psychology, and within subschools of various schools.

11. All maladjustments come about through denial of experiences discrepant with the self-concept.

Adjustment problems represent only part of a continuum of human behavior, ranging from disorganized behavior to self-actualizing behavior. Person-centered theory conceives behavior to differ not in kind but only in degree of incongruence between one's self-concept and one's experiences.

Incongruence between self and experience exists whenever an individual's perception of experience is distorted or denied, whenever he or she fails to integrate such experiences into the self-concept. Experiences not in accord with the concept a person has of himself are regarded as a threat in that, if such experiences were accurately symbolized in awareness, they would disturb the organization of the self-concept by being contrary to the conditions of worth which the individual has incorporated. Thus, such experiences create anxiety in the person and arouse defense mechanisms which either distort or deny such experiences, thereby maintaining the individual's consistent perception of self.

The continuing estrangement between self-concept and experience leads to increasingly rigid perceptions and behavior. If experiences are extremely incongruent with the self-concept, the defense system may be inadequate to prevent the experiences from intruding into and overwhelming the self-concept. When this happens the self-concept will break down, resulting in disorganization of behavior. This is conventionally classed as psychosis when the disorganization is considerable. During such a state of disorganization the person will at times behave in ways consistent with experiences which have hitherto been distorted or denied to awareness. At other times the person will behave in terms of the self-concept or will experience such conflict and anxiety that no action is possible.

Rogers's classification of behavior along a continuum denies the conception of neurosis and psychosis as discrete entities. Defensive behaviors include rationalization, fantasy, compensation, projection, and paranoid ideas. Incongruence between self ("I am intelligent") and experience ("I failed the exam") is handled by distorted perceptions of experience or behavior ("If I had only studied," or "The teacher dislikes me"). When defensive behaviors are unsuccessful, denied aspects of experience contradictory to the self-conception of the person come to the fore and over-whelm the individual. Acute psychotic and irrational behaviors fall into this category. After a period of disorganization, a process of defense sets in to protect the organism against the exceedingly painful awareness of in-congruence, but the self-concept now incorporates the idea of being sick and has even less trust in its own worth than before. However, considering the continuum of incongruence, diagnostic labels have little useful meaning, since Rogers does not have the slightest investment in diagnosis, symp-tomatology, and forms of treatment specifically designed for a particular dysfunction.

12. *Perhaps the most persistent denial of ourselves is by compensation.*

The incongruence between a self-concept of worthwhileness—others like me—and the experience of not really being liked, of not being worthwhile, is handled by defining the self in terms of some role definition. Instead of "I am," the core identity of the person now becomes "I am teacher," "I am student," "I am male," "I am female," "I am a Hell's Angel." By adopting an identity in terms of some clearly defined role, we are buying a ticket into a relationship with someone else. Although such a relationship most likely precludes meaningful communication, it at least allows contact with others. However, the core of all relationships must rest on that which we have in common with all other people, on being, on "I am."

Two members of an encounter group spoke eloquently and meaningfully on their decisions on who they wanted to be. One said: "After overhearing a conversation where I was referred to as a 'nice Jewish girl' I realized the absolute futility of trying to please all with whom I came in contact, for I became a no one. I would hate to be a somebody, but I do strive to be *a* someone (not someone)." It is difficult in our society to be *a* someone without being a somebody. Another member said: "To be somebody needs only willingness to barter—to be someone requires unconditional unvaluing interaction."

13. *To be accepted by others in terms of one's own reality rather than the realities of others facilitates acceptance of one's realities.*

So far in this section a great deal has been said about the conditions respon-sible for incongruence between self and experiencing. Perhaps the other side of the coin needs to be stated. We have a good idea about which conditions facilitate congruence between self and experiencing. One of the principal ingredients is interpersonal relationships in which a person experiences un-conditional regard and respect, and feels accepted in terms of his or her reality, and not another's. Such acceptance is a basic necessity for each per-son to accept his reality, all of his experiencing, the good as well as the bad.

APPLICATIONS

Assessment

It is a goal of scientific psychology to assess phenomena as reliably as possible, so that different measures of the same thing will agree. Also, of course, there is the aim to measure these phenomena accurately or validly. Psychologists have been very clever in devising all sorts of measurement methods. However, within person-centered theory, certain forms of assessment seem more meaningful than others. Since in this theory, life is seen as process rather than as content, static concepts such as *intelligence* or terms such as *insane* are of little merit; of much more concern is measuring movement, assessing dynamics or estimating strivings. It is not as important where one is as it is whether one is moving. In addition, person-centered theorists are interested in the here and now, attempting to be with the person in the moment of his being.

Accordingly, we will discuss two major assessment methods used by person-centered researchers:

1. The Q-sort, a technique refined by William Stephenson (1953), a colleague with Carl Rogers at the University of Chicago in the early 1950s, employed extensively in a number of research studies reported in Rogers and Dymond (1954).
2. A process scale (Rogers & Rablen, 1958) which offers a kind of measuring stick to determine the level of psychological functioning of any person at any time in terms of analysis of verbal productions.

The Q-Sort. Rogers used the Q-sort technique to give an operational definition to the self-concept as well as to evaluate the relationship of phenomenological changes occurring during psychotherapy to externally perceived diagnostic changes. The Q-sort consists of statements regarding the self, such as "I am an attractive person," which the individual sorts to present himself or herself as of the present. The Q-sort is a flexible approach; items can be constructed to serve a variety of purposes.

A popular use of the Q-sort is to obtain a measure, not only of the concept of self but also of a person's concept of his or her ideal self. The discrepancy between real and ideal self is believed to provide an index of a person's adjustment. Several researchers reported an increase in self-ideal self congruence as coinciding with successful psychotherapy. Individuals who know a person well can also be asked to complete a Q-sort of the same self-referent items to get a fairly "objective description" of another person. However, Hart (1970) questioned whether congruence of self and ideal represented congruence between self-structure and experience, which Rogers regards as the basis for adjustment.

The Process Continuum. In the late 1950s Rogers wanted to obtain a much more detailed view of the process of personality change. As he listened to a great many recorded interviews, he noted those points at which therapists agreed that change had taken place. He conceptualized a process continuum which gave both a microscopic view of the minute elements of change and a picture of the continuous flow inherent in change. Finally he evolved a process scale (Rogers & Rablen, 1958) in which seven stages were described. This scale involves recorded examples from therapy, rated as to their place on the scale. New samples of therapeutic interaction can be compared with these examples to indicate the state of process a client is in.

The low end of the scale describes rigid, static, unfeeling, undifferentiated, superficial functioning. The upper end of the scale is marked by personal fluidity, openness to change, richly differentiated reactions, personal feelings experienced in the immediate moment which are owned and accepted.

The scale can best be understood by some examples. Here is a client statement from Stage 2:

> Disorganization keeps cropping up in my life.

Note that the problem is not owned but is described as external. No responsibility is taken for it. The statement is impersonal, remote from subjective experiencing. Self resembles an object.

The following client statement is rated as Stage 3.

> I felt guilty for so much of my young life that I expect I felt I deserved to be punished most of the time anyway. If I didn't feel I deserved it for one thing I felt I deserved it for another.

This is typical of Stage 3 in that feelings are *described*, not expressed. They are in the past, not present. They are seen as bad. There is a freer flow of expression about self as an object. Personal constructs tend to be rigid, as the guilt is in this example. There is at times a beginning recognition that problems exist in the individual rather than externally.

An example from Stage 5, from a client in the middle of the change process, contrasts with the prior two examples:

> I'm still having a little trouble trying to figure out what this sadness—and the weepiness—means. I just know I feel it when I get close to a certain kind of feeling—and usually when I do get weepy, it helps me to kinda break through a wall I've set up because of things that have happened. I feel hurt about something and then automatically this kind of shields things up and then I feel like I really can't touch or feel anything very much....and if I'd be able to feel, or could let myself feel the instantaneous feeling when I'm hurt, I'd immediately start being weepy right then, but I can't.

Here we find a different relationship between the individual's feelings and personal meanings. Feelings are freely expressed in the moment of their occurrence. They are experienced in awareness and recognized as a contradiction existing in the self. The client is communicating his or her self in a highly differentiated way; personal constructs are fluid and open to question. The client's relationship to problems is one of self-responsibility.

An example from Stage 6 will give a sense of a high level on the process scale:

> I could even conceive of it as a possibility that I could have a kind of tender concern for me...how could *I* be tender, be concerned for *myself*, when they're one and the same thing? But yet I can *feel* it so clearly....You know, like taking care of a child. You want to give it this and give it that....I can kind of clearly see the purposes for somebody else...but I can never see them for...myself, that I could do this for me, you know. Is it possible that I can really want to take care of myself, and make that a major purpose of my life? That means I'd have to deal with the whole world as if I were guardian of the most cherished and most wanted possession, that this *I* was between this precious *me* that I wanted to take care of and the whole world....It's almost as if I *loved* myself—you know—that's strange—but it's true.

Here feelings previously denied to experience are felt, expressed, owned, and accepted. The experiencing is vivid and releasing for the individual. Incongruence is experienced and dissolved. Self, at any given moment, *is* the experiencing which is going on. Personal constructs are dissolved, and the individual feels "shaky." Problems are no longer objects. There is much more trust in relationships.

The process scale contributes to personality theory as well as well as to an understanding of therapy. It constitutes essentially a step-by-step description of the manner in which the fully functioning person evolves (Rogers, 1959a).

Treatment

"It began to occur to me that unless I had a need to demonstrate my own cleverness and learning, I would do better to rely upon the client for the direction of movement in the process" (Rogers, 1967). This statement, at the heart of person-centered therapy, is deceptively simple. Defining the activity of the therapist in terms of trust in the self-actualizing tendency of the individual, someone not functioning adequately, requires a great deal more from the therapist than would at first appear.

Therapist Attitudes. Attitudes most important for releasing the potential toward growth appear, on the basis of research findings, to be: (1) a sensitive and accurately empathic understanding of the client, (2) the therapist's complete acceptance of, or unconditional positive regard for, the client, and (3) the therapist's genuineness, or congruence.

The relative importance of these attitudes has been a matter of a good deal of research and discussion. Until recently Rogers and others considered genuineness to be most basic (Rogers, 1975a). J. K. Wood, however, regards unconditional regard as most basic (Rogers & Wood, 1974).

Rogers (1975c) now considers the three attitudes to be differentially important, depending on the life situation a person is in. Congruence seems to be most important in ordinary, everyday interactions. In certain other special situations, such as between parent and infant, or between therapist and "out of touch" psychotic, caring or prizing may turn out to be the most significant.

Several authors concur with Rogers in restoring empathic responding as the crucial ingredient in helping relationships (Raskin, 1974; Wexler, 1974). N. J. Raskin found that psychotherapists from many different orientations agreed that their ideal therapist would first of all be empathic. Therapy appears to be most effective when all three attitudes are present to a high degree.

Accurate Empathic Understanding. The most important aspect of the therapist's "work" is to try to understand what the other person (the client) is experiencing, thinking, and feeling. This requires more than merely understanding the client's words. It involves being sensitive, moment to moment, to the changing felt meanings which flow in this other person, to the fear or rage or tenderness or confusion or whatever the other is experiencing. It means temporarily living in the client's life, moving about in it delicately without making judgments, sensing meanings of which the client is scarcely aware but not trying to uncover feelings of which he or she is totally unaware, since this would be too threatening.

The therapist must also communicate his sensings of the client's world, frequently checking with the client as to accuracy and being guided by the responses. By pointing to the possible meanings in the flow of the client's experiencing, the therapist helps the client to experience meanings more fully, and to move forward in the experiencing.

To be with another in this way means that for the time being the therapist lays aside his own views and values to enter another's world without prejudice. Laying aside one's self in this way can only be done by those secure enough that they know they will not get lost in what may turn out to be the strange or bizarre world of others, and they can comfortably return to their own world when they wish (Rogers, 1975c).

Wexler (1974) considers empathy to be more than an attitude. He sees it as a consistent pattern of overt behaviors, an attempt by the therapist to organize the information presented by the client so that the *meaning* of the information stands out more clearly and accurately to the client.

Only if the client's *attention* is focused on important facets of meaning in the flow of experiencing can his nervous system process such information so that it stands out clearly in awareness. The more competing information is focused on by the client or introduced by the therapist, the less likely it is that experientially significant material will be processed.

Empathy is not sympathy. A person who is sympathetic negates himself and by an osmotic process is both absorbed and absorbing. With empathy there is an inner strength which can alienate the giver from the receiver, unless the person being confronted is prepared to stifle initial emotion and "feel" only after chewing the feedback, swallowing it, and then deciding whether to regurgitate it or not. Thus an intellectualizing process must be put into motion.

Caring or Unconditional Positive Regard. Understanding, or even just sincerely trying to understand, another person from the other's perspective contributes a great deal to fulfilling the second condition for psychotherapy, caring. Caring means that the psychotherapist accepts the client as he or she is—contrary, aggressive, or vulnerable, yet with potentialities for growth. It means valuing the client as a person, independent of the client's behavior or thoughts.

Acceptance of the client as a fallible but basically trustworthy human being is blended with an empathic understanding. These two therapeutic attitudes do not exist as separate entities. Respect without empathy is of little value, since the client may view such respect as indiscriminate. "If you knew the real me you wouldn't respect me," or "You like everybody, so there is nothing special about your liking me."

The person-centered approach to therapy has often been conceptualized as being purely a commitment in verbal terms. It should be pointed out that Roger's expressions of concern through behavioral acts is perhaps one of the least appreciated aspects of his work as therapist and of his theory.

Genuineness or Congruence. The third condition of therapy as described by Rogers in responding fully to another, interacting and accepting the person, can only be fulfilled if the therapist responds as a full human person and not just in terms of the role of therapist. Being real in a relationship is risky. However, it is precisely the fact that one is prepared to take the risk of being a fallible human being, of being a someone rather than a somebody, that indicates to the other person that he or she is cared for. Thus, in being transparent to the other person, in being open to the feelings and attitudes flowing at any moment, the therapist fulfills the essential prerequisite for empathic understanding of another.

Congruence can be considered as a precondition for being real in the fullest sense of the term. It requires that what one is feeling at an experiential or visceral level is clearly present in awareness and available for direct communication to another person when appropriate. *Genuineness* is not burdening the client or another person with one's own problems or feelings; it is not impulsive blurting out of feelings. For example, a therapist who is bored during the therapy hour does not express this to the client before considering his or her own responsibility in feeling bored. However, if such feelings persist in the relationship, genuineness means willingness to express such feelings.

In general terms, the process of change can be described as a sequence of experiences by which the client gradually comes to have the same regard for self as the therapist does. Someone really listening helps the client, little by little, to become sensitive and aware of communications and feelings from within. When the client can express feelings never before dared to be expressed and still experiences the unshaken regard of the therapist, it becomes easier to adopt that same attitude and to find self-acceptance just as one is.

When this happens the client is able to differentiate more accurately between the various components of experiencing: bodily state, perceptions, social situation, and the way the information from all these sources is integrated. In so doing the person is able to symbolize experiences more accurately in awareness.

In the process of growth, the self-concept the person has keeps changing, as previously denied experiences are assimilated. The individual also comes to realize personal responsibility for the meanings given to these experiences. Thus, the concept of self becomes more internally based, more congruent with immediate experiencing. And since experiencing is ever changing, the self-concept also becomes more fluid and changing. The increasing congruence between self and experience reflects the improved psychological adjustment.

Institutional

Richard Farson (1974), who regards Rogers as "one of the most important social revolutionaries of our time," considers the core of person-centered theory, empowering the person, to be the forerunner of such "political" developments as students' rights movements, the use of paraprofessionals, self-help groups in health and welfare, participative management in industry, and new concepts of children's rights. In the same sense the insistence of Rogers on the dignity and worth of the individual can be related to the dissent with American participation in the war in Southeast Asia of the 1960s and 1970s and large-scale draft evasion by American youth. Rogers (1977) in *On Personal Power* assesses the "political" effects of all that he and his colleagues have done and are doing.

The extent of the social outreach and subtle political implications of person-centered principles is nowhere more clear than in the encounter group movement. It has been estimated that an encounter experience has been part of the lives of perhaps as many as 10 million Americans. Not only in North America but in Europe and other countries, the encounter experience has had considerable influence. One encounter group (filmed) was used to endeavor to bring together the warring factions in Northern Ireland. A considerable number of interracial group sessions have been conducted in the United States. People from various racial groups in South Africa—black, white, and Indian—have also joined in basic encounter groups.

Education. At the present time, the spread of person-centered principles in education is of special significance and is evident in many respects. It is being realized that the basic concepts, theory, and even the methods of the person-centered approach have a clear relevance to education at all levels.

The publication of *Freedom to Learn* (Rogers, 1969) contributed to the widespread dissemination of person-centered principles in education. The teacher is regarded as a facilitator of cognitive learning and of emotional learning as well. The teacher is to provide a psychological climate conducive to self-directed learning and of resources necessary for full exploration by the student. Galileo said it long ago: "You cannot teach a man anything, you can only help him discover it within himself."

Person-centered education is committed to educating the total person, not just cognitive faculties. Rogers believes these goals can be achieved best if teachers trust and respect students as being able to, and indeed desirous of, actualizing their fullest potential. Teachers who accept students as "incomplete" at the moment and who care enough to involve themselves in an open, expressive, mutual relationship with students also learn.

Though the whole Winter 1974 issue of *Education* documented the influence of Rogers on education, it still did not cover the full range of his theoretical contributions to academic psychology and education, or his thinking on the nature of knowledge and the philosophy of science (Rogers & Coulson, 1968). The real challenge to education, institutional as well as general, is not blind commitment to a point of view but acceptance that there are as many realities as there are persons, and that open-minded exploration of these differing realities is the most promising resource for learning (Rogers, 1974a).

Social Responsibility. The emphasis Rogers places on separate realities does not mean social irresponsibility. It does not mean self-indulgence or self-centeredness; or that each one does his or her thing without regard for others.

Rogers considered that enhancement of the self in the long run "inevitably involves the enhancement of other selves as well....The self-actualization of the organism appears to be in the direction of socialization, broadly defined" (Rogers, 1951). Without social responsibility and social action, human life will atrophy (Gendlin, 1973). Maslow considered social interest as one of the characteristics of self-actualizing people, but even he failed to capture the very essence of social interest, which is the need to belong. Adler's concept of *Gemeinshaftsgefühl*, portrayed by this saying, comes close to describing this most basic of human motivations.

> I sought my soul, I sought my God; but neither could I see.
> But then I sought my brother, and then I found all three.

Community.   Although the emphasis of person-centered theory has shifted toward greater social awareness, the focus is still on individual personal growth. The time seems to be ripe for the application of person-centered principles to more fundamental changes in community and social structures, as has been the case in two school systems reported on by Foster and Back (1974) and Rogers (1974d).

The powerful advent of community psychology raises the distinct possibility that strategies of social change can have a far broader effect on optimal development of human lives and relationships than even encounter group procedures can have. William Rogers (1974) gives such an account of the South End Urban Renewal Project of Boston. The project started with an analysis of the identity and the decay of the South End community, noting, for example, the decreasing population and playground facilities and the increasing concentration of liquor stores. Various groups in the community were interested in reversing the trend. They coordinated their efforts and, in the best sense of the belief that the population with the problem has the greatest knowledge for solving that problem, they managed to contribute significantly to reversing the decay of the Boston South End. Their efforts ranged from the construction of housing units and new businesses to the development of improved educational facilities and the awakening of greater community awareness. The trust in and releasing of the capacities of the individuals in the community and of the community itself is a good example of person-centeredness in community development.

Other Applications.   Even more important than the contribution of person-centered theory to psychotherapy is the ethical base it provides for people to be with one another. This base has influenced some restructuring of almost every field of human endeavor. Areas other than those mentioned above in which the influence of the theory is acknowledged to a greater or lesser extent include religion, nursing, medicine, psychiatry, dentistry, law enforcement, race and cultural relations, social work, industry, and organizational development.

Of special significance is the impact of person-centeredness on marriage and family life (Rogers, 1972). These areas of interaction are so basic to the lives of all, and yet there is considerable floundering in this regard. It is safe to assume that being married and raising a family is much more complex than has been assumed heretofore.

A profound description of the complexity of marriage was given by a woman in an encounter group:

> Marriage is not voice and echo, but too often becomes two very definite and distinct voices wanting to be heard together, without harmony. It is to achieve the harmony that usually takes a lifetime of concentrated effort. But when the effort is too deliberate, conscious, the trying is more obvious than the result.

It is obvious that most people lack the skills to cope with such complexity. For these reasons Rogers urges that serious consideration be given to exploring the person's involvement with marriage and family life. Roger's views on marriage are that neither the success nor the failure of a relationship is to be sought in the format, the institution of marriage as a partnership. More likely the answer is to be found in the commitment of each person to the *process* of living together in harmony, in realizing what the woman quoted above said about her marriage: "In living with limitations there is a challenge and disciplined variety which builds resilience in adversity."

Self

Since most readers of this book are likely to be students, this section deals primarily with the student and the student's relation to the educational institution, and it addresses the student directly.

Person-centered theory believes wholeheartedly in something basically simple. *KNOW* yourself—*BE* yourself. By being yourself you can actualize the very best in you. You are like no one else in the world. Simply being ourselves is our greatest potential. We do not have to be great artists or scientists and contribute something worthwhile to *be* worthwhile. By tapping our individuality, each one of us can contribute as no one else can.

It sounds so easy. But, as it has been said so truly, "To be nobody but yourself in a world which is doing its best, night and day, to make you everybody else, means to fight the hardest battle which any human being can fight, and never stops fighting." Being yourself requires, first of all, *trust* in your own worthwhileness. And trust is not something that can be obtained from somewhere. Each of us has to experience our worthwhileness before we can know what it feels like. The opportunity for such an experience is all too rare in an educational and societal structure which consistently bombards you with the message that you are not worthwhile unless you behave in ways which others consider are important for you to follow. In the typical school situation, this means to learn facts. Others choose what you are to study and how you must study.

Person-centered theory maintains that you should have an integral part in deciding the content of your education and the manner in which you are to study that content. How many students have this opportunity? Person-centered theory also holds that the most meaningful way to learn about anything is to be actively, experientially involved with it. This means involvement not only with the theoretical nature of the subject matter but also with the practical aspects of the area you are interested in. In the case of studying personality, it is basic to be involved with people in a climate conducive to exploration of who you are, discovering slowly, through interaction with others, just who and what the forces are which go into the making of a person, into the making of you. How many students of personality theory have such an opportunity to learn about the person-centered theory in an affective-experiential way and not just theoretically?

Do you find it meaningful to do the course work required to learn about all the theories in this book? Do you want to go about it the way the teacher of the course does? This can be doubted. Yet your alienation from your studies is not over until you are evaluated. Will this be done in ways meaningful to you? External criteria are usually imposed on the already "foreign" evaluation. Your worthwhileness is dependent on achieving a certain level of performance on the examination of the subject matter, which may have some (but more likely than not will have little) significance to your real interests, to what your life is really about. Will the evaluation, like so many others, be only of your memory capacity? Yet will your whole person feel evaluated? Will you *allow* your whole person to feel evaluated?

To discover yourself you have to differentiate the components making up your experience. Recognize the demands of the institution, group, and society you are in for what they are, as having more or less meaning to what your life and the great gestalt of things are about. Listen to what you are saying to yourself, to the way you interpret these external pressures. What feelings are evoked by your interpretation of these pressures and your reaction to them?

Do you accept responsibility for the subjectivity of your interpretations? Do you accept that your eyes and ears and brain select, perceive, and process information differently from anyone else? This is your greatest strength, but it can also be your greatest weakness. While you are using your own emotional and cognitive experiencing as a referent for your behavior, you have to be sensitively in interaction with others and at the same time must allow them the opportunity to actualize their own unique potentials. You have to be responsibly independent, separately together. It is the belief of person-centered theory that in being yourself fully, you will come closer to, rather than more alienated from, others. In being yourself, you will discover your need of and kinship with other human beings.

In your interaction with the present institutional system, you have constantly to define and redefine who and what you are through your choices, perceptions, decisions, and commitments. In fact, you *are* your choices, perceptions, and interpretations. The better you are able to symbolize your experiences of internal and external processes in awareness, the clearer will be the various alternatives among which you can choose.

VALIDATION

Evidence

Most of this section will be devoted to work in other disciplines and areas of psychology which has a bearing on elements of the person-centered theory of personality, especially the concept of experiencing.

Experiencing. Experiencing emerged as a key concept in person-centered theory (Rogers, 1959b). It is variously referred to as organismic sensing, ongoing psychophysiological flow, or organismic experiencing. At the heart of Gendlin's Experiential Psychotherapy (Gendlin, 1973)—considered by Hart (1970) to represent the development of person-centered theory during the 1960s—it is the referent to which the individual can turn for guidance in understanding himself and in directing his behavior. Experiencing or organismic sensing has been defined above. Briefly, it represents utilization of all the person's faculties. It is an awareness by the person of the way he or she attends, perceives, processes, and integrates information of the environment internal and external to the body.

Each aspect of experiencing exists in relation to all other aspects. It is important to be aware of what is going on in the body—in touch with visceral activity—as well as to have knowledge of events occurring outside the body. It is also important to realize how the individual interprets the relationship between bodily and external events. Change in any aspect of experiencing influences the total experience. Work done in the areas of perception and sensory neurophysiology, brain research, cognitive psychology, and psychobiological approaches to social behavior have direct relevance to an understanding of the concept of organismic experiencing. A common thread which runs through all these disciplines is the importance of the information-processing capabilities of the organism.

Neurophysiology of Sensing Modalities and Perception. One aspect of experiencing or organismic sensing can be conceptualized as heightened sensory awareness. Or, stated differently, the average person is dead to the body and needs to be awakened to the world inside his or her skin. Paradoxically, to become more aware of bodily processes, the person has to pay less attention to stimulation emanating from the external world, for the nervous system processes sources of stimulation relative to one another (Rosenblith, 1961). This is true within each sensory system and also between different sensory systems (Von Békésy, 1969).

We constantly have to decide what we want to pay attention to. Thus, we really cannot be open to *all* of our experience at any one moment in time. However, there is a consolation prize. Although we have to focus our attention selectively for our perceptions to stand out clearly in awareness, the choice of what we want to focus on is very much ours. We restrict our attention to those physical cues that we find meaningful and relevant. We also choose the modality with which we respond. How, when, and where we look, listen, touch, taste, and smell are important factors in determining what we will perceive. For instance, such a simple act as turning our heads away from a sound diminishes the intensity of the sound just that much to allow further inhibition at neural level to occur. You are likely to close your eyes when you listen intently to what is being said.

The impulses controlling the activity of sensory neurons and pathways usually originate in the neocortex of the brain, which represents consciousness. However, it is not only in the brain that impulses controlling sensory activity originate. The body has a wisdom of its own by which it determines what is to be perceived. On many occasions the activity of the brain is "controlled" by visceral reflexes. A dramatic example of such control is provided by the way reflexes arising in the tendons of the muscle control messages sent to it from the brain, thereby preventing the muscle from reaching dangerous states of tension (Cranit, 1955).

Research in the controversial area of subliminal perception also has a bearing on organismic sensing. One of the most clear-cut examples of subception, or, in the present context, organismic experiencing, is Helson's (1964) demonstration that a subthreshold electrical stimulus to the skin influences the perceived intensity of subsequent shocks of differing intensities. The same phenomenon has been established on other modalities as well.

The tonic-sensory theory of perception of Werner and Wapner (Allport, 1955), and the research evidence related to their theory, demonstrates quite convincingly that organismic states are part and parcel of the perceptual process. Although we can seldom claim awareness of the activity of our proprioceptors and interoceptors, the effect of such activity on our perception is nevertheless marked.

Very few individuals are aware of the control they exert over their perceptions by attending with some and not other modalities. The extent of the sensory awareness we are capable of is just now being realized. It is possible to use our sense modalities in nontraditional ways.

The current wave of interest in biofeedback, yoga, and various forms of meditation has great promise in helping the person-centered dream of trust in one's ability come true. Indeed, it is irrelevant whether or not biofeedback control over physiological functions and other altered states of consciousness are achieved through mediation of such physiological mechanisms as respiration and muscular control. Large numbers of people in the Western world are beginning to realize some of their organismic potential by trusting the ability they have to control their own bodies.

Brain Research and Organismic Experiencing.   Organismic sensing can be considered not only in terms of receptor cell activity but also in terms of the activity of those areas of the brain, the so-called limbic system, which serve as the repository for phyletically significant instinctual behaviors. The limbic system organizes such behaviors as eating, drinking, renal activity, basal metabolism, digestion, temperature regulation, aggression, and sexual and maternal responses. In obesity, for instance, the ventromedial nucleus of the hypothalamus may be underactive due to the lack of attention being paid to the viscera. It is generally accepted that babies who are stuffed with food by their mothers have a good chance to become obese. They learn to ignore messages not only from the viscera but from the hypothalamic nuclei as well.

There is no disagreement that memories accumulated within the lifetime of an individual are stored in the brain. How it is done is still an open question. Although the genetic code has been broken, it is thought to be primarily a memory in terms of physical characteristics. Is it not conceivable, however, that the limbic system, for instance, also harbors archetypes along Jungian lines? Work on the transfer of memory from one animal to another and from one species to another indicates such a possibility. An uneducated flatworm or laboratory rat can apparently get an education by digesting educated flatworms or the brains of rats trained to do things. (Domagk, Laufenberg & Kuebler, 1976)

The integration of the functions of the left and right hemispheres of the brain has been of special interest during the past decade, with evidence emerging that the psychological natures of the functions of the two hemispheres differ. Psychological functions of the right hemisphere have been described as preverbal, prelogical, subjective, intuitive, global, synthetic, and diffuse, compared to the linear, logical, rational nature of the functions of the left hemisphere.

Thus, organismic sensing or experiencing is more than heightened sensory awareness of internal bodily states and of limbic system activity. It is the integration of this awareness with awareness of those functions represented by the neocortex. It is also the integration of the activities of the left and right cortices. Interpretation of organismic sensing along these lines is analogous to the way R. W. Sperry (1969) considers consciousness to be more than the activity of millions of neurons.

Psychobiological Approaches to Social Behavior, Cognition, and Organismic Sensing. The ingenious demonstrations of Stanley Schachter indicated the importance of physiological arousal and of awareness of such arousal in being emotionally alive during everyday living (Schachter, 1965). However, Schachter also demonstrated that although the pattern of physiological activation is necessary to experience feeling, it does not determine the nature of the emotion. Thus persons injected with adrenalin, if not told about its effects, experience anger or joy depending on the "behavior" of the stooge with whom they are placed.

Trying to find a one-to-one correlation between physiological activation and emotional experience has been one of the great wild-goose chases of psychophysiological research (see Sternbach, 1966). The specific nature of the emotion is dependent on the way we interpret the social situation in which we find ourselves. Thus, the perception of the social situation provides the label to the emotional experience. A woman cries when she is happy and when she is sad. She interprets the same physiological event quite differently, depending on circumstances.

Schachter's theory of emotion has been called a jukebox theory; although the electrical mechanism is all-important in the playing of a record, it does not determine which record is being played. That depends on which button is pressed. Social situations can be likened to the array of selector buttons.

In his cognitive theory of experiencing, self-actualization, and therapy, Wexler (1974) acknowledges but underplays the importance of physiological activation. Schachter (1965), however, has shown that physiological underarousal, such as that following chlorpromazine injections, causes flattening of the emotional response to situations with emotional-evoking potential. Schachter has also related psychopathic behavior and crimes committed against people to lowered levels or lowered awareness of physiological arousal. In his more recent work he has indicated how obese people are much more responsive to external stimuli than nonobese persons and, by inference, less responsive to stimuli originating within their own bodies (Schachter & Rodin, 1974). A major implication of much of his work is that greater awareness of internal bodily states can have far-reaching consequences for many, if not all, aspects of living.

Schachter's views are of direct relevance to the state of "being high" following the taking of drugs. It is clear from his work, and from many other studies, that the state of being high resides not in the drug but in the cognitive interpretation by the person of the change in the pattern of physiological activity caused by the drug. Thus, if drugs are to be used as a means to achieve altered states of consciousness, it must be done with full awareness of all the interactive elements involved in the experience.

Experiencing consists of many components, ranging from possible representation and utilization of Jungian-like archetypes in the molecules of the brain to human beings' most vivid cognitive abilities. What constitutes the differential proportions for optimal integration of these elements, however, is certain to remain a mystery for a long time to come.

Quantification of the concept of experiencing will have to assess the extent to which a person is aware of and utilizes the different facets of experience, especially perceptions pertaining to the body and to the prevailing situation. It will also assess the extent to which a person is able to integrate the different components making up the raw data of experience.

Research. This section will not attempt to present an overview of research in the area. Several such reviews are in existence (Cartwright, 1957; Seeman & Raskin, 1953; Shlien & Zimring, 1970; Truax & Mitchell, 1971).

It has repeatedly been shown that clients whose therapists offered high levels of positive regard, genuineness, and empathy evidenced significant positive personality and behavior change, while clients whose therapists offered low levels of these core conditions evidenced no change, or even exhibited deterioration in personality and behavioral functioning. These relationships held over a number of conditions, such as the theoretical or practical orientation of the therapist, the "type" of client, whether in an individual or group setting or in a therapeutic setting at all, and time of follow-up (as long as nine years).

In view of the importance of empathy as perhaps the most significant of the three basic therapist attitudes (see the section on treatment above), the following summary statements of the research reviewed in an article by Rogers (1975c) on empathy should be considered:

1. A large number of therapists of all persuasions agree that the ideal therapist is first of all empathic.
2. Empathy is correlated with self-exploration and process movement.
3. Empathy early in the relationship predicts later success.
4. The client comes to perceive more empathy in successful cases.
5. Empathy is provided by the therapist, not drawn from him or her.
6. The more experienced the therapist, the more likely he or she is to be empathic.
7. Empathy is a special quality in a relationship, and therapists offer more of it than helpful friends do.
8. The better integrated the therapist is within himself, the higher the degree of empathy he exhibits.
9. Even experienced therapists often fall far short of being empathic.
10. Clients are often better judges of the degree of empathy than are therapists.
11. Brillance and diagnostic perceptiveness are unrelated to empathy.
12. An empathic way of being can be learned from empathic persons.

Variables relating to the client have also been found to be of considerable importance to the outcome of therapy. The level of involvement of the client in the therapy process from the very beginning is an important predictor of improvement. If the client's level of functioning is too low initially, little improvement will result. The other variable which should be mentioned relates to the client's perception of the core conditions as being present in the relationship.

The research described in this section has been in the field of psychotherapy. But the effectiveness of a person-centered approach has perhaps been most strikingly demonstrated by a decade of work by Aspy, Roebuck, and their colleagues in the field of education (Aspy & Roebuck, 1974). They recorded over 3,500 hours of classroom interaction, involving 550 elementary and high school teachers in various parts of this country and abroad. They studied many variables of teacher behavior based on ratings of these classroom hours, and measured numerous achievement and behavioral outcomes in the students involved. They consistently found that the teacher's empathy—her or his attempt to understand the *meaning* of the school experience to the student—was the factor *most* conducive to constructive educational outcomes. When taken together with positive regard (respect for the student) and congruence or genuineness, the results were most confirming. These three facilitative conditions correlated clearly with academic achievement, more positive self-concepts in the students, decreased discipline problems and truancy, and higher morale. Students who had teachers with "high" levels of these conditions were more creative and more effective at problem solving.

The full implications of this series of studies has yet to be felt, for the findings are just now being disseminated. But the totality of the research adds up to the statement: It *pays*—in countless ways—to be person-centered in the classroom.

The recent trend to view person-centered principles from an information-processing and cognitive framework may add an additional impetus to research in the area. Attempts are made to translate the concepts of the theory into overt behavior (Wexler, 1974). Also, the language used may be more congruent with the Zeitgeist and thus may make it easier for people who trust their cognitive faculties to understand and utilize the theory.

Comparisons

This section compares the person-centered approach with other theories and therapies generally and then with two specific approaches to personality with which it has experienced the greatest degree of conflict. In contrast to the person-centered approach these two approaches believe that the basic nature of man is reactive.

Relation to Theories in General. It has already been stated that person-centered theory is an approach, a way of life, upon which can be superimposed various specific techniques or theories. In a sense, then, the manner in which a theory is presented is more distinctive than the specific theory.

Person-centered theory attempts to look at the person as completely as it can. On the one hand it recognizes the importance of the microscopically small biochemical structure of the body. It considers the possibility that the genetic structure encapsulates even greater "wisdom" than generally recognized, in the form of primordial images of behavior patterns serving mankind. On the other hand, it views man macroscopically, with each person being inseparably related to the others. Person-centered theory recognizes the unique individuality of each person as well as the relatedness of each person to the other—the necessity of community.

Traditionally, the theory has been regarded as stressing primarily the emotional-experiential component of being. Emphasizing the emotional aspect has been necessary to complement the imbalanced view of man which has emerged from the scientific views of this century. But perhaps that point has been made, and the interactive and gestalt nature of the theory can be stressed. Like its view of man as a being in the process of becoming, an integral aspect of person-centered theory is that it too is constantly in process, constantly becoming.

Viewed from such a perspective, person-centered theory is distinguishable from those theories that deal only with certain aspects of the person. But since the person is an infinitely complex organism, it is highly likely that each theory, emphasizing a particular aspect of behavior, has value. Intellectual, perceptual, experiential, and other limitations have made it necessary to split investigations of the person into various fields and perspectives, such as physiological, political, spiritual, sociological, verbal, nonverbal, or past, present, or future oriented. However, the artificial barriers erected between different approaches should not blind us to the basic unity of the processes underlying the organismic functions. The life processes continue inexorably on their course, whether they are approached from the viewpoint of a behaviorist, psychoanalyst, Rolfian, or Rogerian. The person does not have a separate set of phenomena for each theorist. But the same phenomenon looks quite different when its different aspects are viewed from different approaches, methods, and preconceptions.

Relation to Psychotherapy in General. It is clear, then, that person-centered theory acknowledges the value of multiple perspectives and reacts against any compartmentalized approach which claims to be more than it is. The same is true with regard to other psychotherapeutic procedures. In contrast to most other methods of psychotherapy, the person-centered approach does not rely primarily on the technical training or skills of the therapist for therapeutic success. A fact seldom appreciated, however, is that the person-centered approach does not exclude such expertise from therapy, as long as it is made available to and not forced on the client. The person-centered approach is not a technique but a philosophy of life, more specifically an *attitude* toward interpersonal relationships, which when lived allows for variation in the concrete transactions of a relationship, in the specific symbols used in communication. How therapy is done is more important than what therapy consists of—the medium is the message. The melody remains the same, irrespective of whether the tune is played on a piano or violin or is sung.

Making the contributions of various techniques, such as Gestalt, transactional analysis, and behavior modification, available to the client actually is very much in keeping with the rationale behind the person-centered approach. It acknowledges that people perceive and are differentially receptive to various symbols. Some individuals may be particularly receptive to therapies working with the body. Others may find techniques dealing with skills in interpersonal behavior useful or may prefer to deal with situational and behavioral aspects, or with the existential and spiritual dimensions of their existence.

It is not only the idiosyncratic needs of the individual client which are catered to by making a variety of procedures available for exploring him or her. Such a procedure also allows the facilitator to contribute that skill or technique most congruent with his or her own level of experiencing.

Behavior Theory.   Diehard behaviorism sees man as a biological organism at the mercy of stimuli from his environment. Rogers (1974c) describes this view as follows: "The universe was at some point wound up like a great clock and has been ticking off its inexorable way ever since. Thus, what we think are our decisions, choices, and values are all illusion." According to strict determinism you have been destined to read these very words which we have been destined to write ever since time immemorial.

However, behavior theory, or at least some learning theorists, are moving away from such a deterministic viewpoint. They seem to be realizing more and more that awareness and cognitive processes form part of behavior theory. In his presidential address to the American Psychological Association in 1974, Albert Bandura, for instance, stated that by representing foreseeable outcomes symbolically, future consequences can be converted into current motivators of behavior.

In yet another sense certain learning theorists have become more open to the full complexity of living in their thinking and practice of therapy. These individuals even allow feeling states and the actual expression of such feelings to enter into transactions with their clients. Reading Lazarus (1971) is a good example of the discovery by a learning theorist of the kinds of things Rogers has been talking about for decades.

Much can be said about the controversy surrounding the philosophical viewpoints of person-centered and behavior theory. However, only one last statement ought to be made. Person-centered theory has never disclaimed the importance of the principles of behavior theory in the lives of each and every one of us; neither does it disclaim the value of the methodological procedures of behaviorism in science. In fact, person-centered theory has all along acknowledged the importance of the environment to such an extent that it perhaps overemphasizes individualism—in the same way that it accentuates the emotional-experiential aspect—to counteract the increasingly pervasive and dominant role social situations and institutions play in alienating the person from himself.

Psychoanalytic Theory. Psychoanalysis also views the person as reactive. Rather than being a victim of the environment, each individual is seen as a victim of innate drives, motives, and needs, influenced by past frustrations and satisfactions. Person-centered theory, however, holds that the behavior of man and woman is exquisitely rational, even when the individual is not aware of that rationality.

In contrast to the view of the person as reacting solely to forces or stimuli, in the one case from without and in the other from within, person-centered theory regards the person as both reacting and acting, a being in the process of becoming, personal, conscious, and future oriented.

Many distinctions between person-centered and the two theories discussed above—behaviorism and psychoanalysis—as well as other theories have not even been touched upon. The main reason is that each theory probably has a great deal of merit and a great deal of meaningfulness for its adherents. In the person-centered framework the person is the theory; thus the other theories all contribute in the sense that they reflect what is meaningful for each person. Although what is meaningful for one theorist may not have the same significance for another, the theory of each represents a stage of conceptual-experiential development at that moment in time. It cannot be more, it cannot be less. Only in being that stage of theoretical and personal development as fully as possible in relation to others can there be movement and change. Only if the various theorists, learning theorists included, accept the different realities of one another, in a climate of trust, care, and respect, will there be optimal development in the area.

PROSPECT

In several recent papers Rogers has emerged as an outspoken prophet of the future.

In all candor I must say that I believe that the humanistic view will in the long run take precedence. I believe that we are, as a people, beginning to refuse to allow technology to dominate our lives. Our culture, increasingly based on the conquest of nature and the control of man, is in decline. Emerging through the ruins is the new person, highly aware, self-directing, an explorer of inner, perhaps more than outer space, scornful of the conformity of institutions and the dogma of authority. He does not believe in being behaviorally shaped, or in shaping the behavior of others. He is most assuredly humanistic rather than technological. In my judgment he has a high probability of survival. (Rogers, 1974c)

Rogers goes on to describe the emerging person as someone who hates phoniness, who is opposed to all rigidly structured institutions, who desires intimacy, closeness, and community. Such a person is willing to live by new and relative moral and ethical standards, is open to his own and other's feelings, is spontaneous, and is determined to translate his ideals into reality (Rogers, 1972).

Eventually this emerging person would foster a culture which would move toward nondefensive openness in all interpersonal relationships, toward exploration of the self as a unity of mind and body, toward prizing of the person as she or he *is*. This culture would seek greater respect and balance with the natural world, deemphasis on and the more equal distribution of material goods, a society more interested in human needs than rigid adherence to structure. It would value leadership based on competence for meeting specific needs, greater care for those who need help, a more human view of science, and creativity in all aspects of living (Rogers, 1975b).

ANNOTATED BIBLIOGRAPHY

Hart, J. T., and Tomlinson, T. M. (Eds.). *New Directions in Client-Centered Therapy*. Boston: Houghton Mifflin, 1970.

An easily digested book which presents a good account of person-centered theory as it developed up to and during the 1960s. The bulk of the book is devoted to principles in psychotherapy, process scales, client-therapist interaction variables, developmental theory, group experience, and phenomenological and experimental methodologies.

Rogers, C. R. *Client-Centered Therapy*. Boston: Houghton Mifflin, 1951.

This book introduced the name change from *non-directive counseling* to *client-centered*. The change was not merely semantic. It indicated a shift in emphasis from the negative, narrower statement, *nondirective*, to a positive focus on the growth-producing factors in the individual client.

Rogers, C. R. "A Theory of Therapy, Personality and Interpersonal Relationships as Developed in the Client-Centered Framework." In S. Koch (Ed.), *Psychology: A Study of a Science*. Vol. 3, *Formulations of the Person and the Social Context*. New York: McGraw-Hill, 1959.

Though written two decades ago, this article is still brand new. It is a classic, but the full extent of the experiential and cognitive wisdom portrayed in it remains to be discovered, even by adherents of the person-centered theory. Rogers presents his theory of personality, psychotherapy, and interpersonal relationships.

Rogers, C. R. *On Becoming a Person.* Boston: Houghton Mifflin, 1961.

This book has changed the lives of many individuals and may influence your life as well. Rogers shares his experiences as a person, a man, a husband, a father, and a professional in the terms of what he sees as their relevance for personal living in a perplexing world.

Rogers, C. R. *Freedom to Learn: A View of What Education Might Become.* Columbus, Ohio: Charles E. Merrill, 1969.

Rogers presents a design of what education might become, what its full potential involves. This is a book to help you maintain your sanity while you are receiving an "education" and also, like all Rogers's writing, to help you maintain faith in the great gestalt of things.

Wexler, D. A., and Rice, L. N. (Eds.). *Innovations in Client-Centered Therapy.* New York: Wiley, 1974.

A stimulating and scholarly work. Some of the chapters certainly represent a fresh and invigorating approach to person-centered theory.

Client-centered therapy. Film No. 1 in E. Shostrom (Ed.), *Three Approaches to Psychotherapy.* Sound film in color, 50 minutes (1965). Psychological Films, 105 West 20th Street, Santa Ana, California.

A therapeutic interview with explanatory comments.

REFERENCES

Adler, A. *What life should mean to you.* New York: Capricorn Books, 1958.

Allport, F. H. *Theories of perception and the concept of structure.* New York: Wiley, 1955.

Aspy, D. N., & Roebuck, F. N. From humane ideas to humane technology and back again many times. *Education,* 1974, *95,* 163–171.

Burton, A. The nature of personality theory. In A. Burton (Ed.), *Operational theories of personality.* New York: Brunner/Mazel, 1974.

Cartwright, D. Annotated bibliography of research and theory construction in client-centered therapy. *Journal of Counseling Psychology,* 1957, *4,* 82–100.

Cranit, R. *Receptors and sensory perception.* New Haven, Conn.: Yale University Press, 1955.

Domagk, G. F., Laufenberg, G. & Kuebler, G. Chemical transfer of acquired information in mice. *The Journal of Biological Psychology,* 1975, *13,* 13–17.

Farson, R. Carl Rogers, quiet revolutionary. *Education,* 1974, *95,* 197–203.

Foster, C. M., & Back, J. A neighborhood school board: Its infancy, its crises, its growth. *Education,* 1974, *95,* 145–162.

Gendlin, E. Experiential psychotherapy. In R. J. Corsini (Ed.), *Current psychotherapies.* Itasca, Ill.: F. E. Peacock, 1973.

Gendlin, E. Client-centered and experiential psychotherapy. In D. A. Wexler & L. N. Rice (Eds.), *Innovations in client-centered therapy.* New York: Wiley, 1974.

Hanna, T. *Bodies in revolt.* New York: Holt, Rinehart & Winston, 1970.

Harlow, H. F., & Suomi, S. I. Nature of love—simplified. *American Psychologist,* 1970, *25,* 161–168.

Hart, J. T. The development of client-centered therapy. In J. T. Hart & T. M. Tomlinson (Eds.), *New directions in client-centered therapy.* Boston: Houghton Mifflin, 1970.

Helson, H. Current trends and issues in adaptation level theory. *American Psychologist,* 1964, *19,* 16–38.

Lazarus, A. *Behavior therapy and beyond.* New York: McGraw-Hill, 1971.

Meador, B. D., & Rogers, C. R. Client-centered therapy. In R. J. Corsini (Ed.), *Current psychotherapies.* Itasca, Ill.: F. E. Peacock, 1973.

Mosak, H. H., & Dreikurs, R. Adlerian

psychotherapy. In R. J. Corsini (Ed.), *Current psychotherapies*. Itasca, Ill.: F. E. Peacock, 1973.

Oden, T. C. The new pietism. *Journal of Humanistic Psychology*, 1972, *12*, 24–41.

Patterson, C. H. *Theories of counseling and psychotherapy*. New York: Harper & Row, 1973.

Raskin, N. J. Studies of psychotherapeutic orientation: Ideology and practice. *American Academy of Psychotherapists Research Monograph*, 1974 (No. 1).

Rogers, C. R. *Counseling and psychotherapy*. Boston: Houghton Mifflin, 1942.

Rogers, C. R. *Client-centered therapy*. Boston: Houghton Mifflin, 1951.

Rogers, C. R. A tentative scale for the measurement of process in psychotherapy. In E. Rubinstein (Ed.), *Research in psychotherapy*. Washington, D.C.: American Psychological Association, 1959. (a)

Rogers, C. R. A theory of therapy, personality, and interpersonal relationships, as developed in the client-centered framework. In S. Koch (Ed.), *Psychology: A study of science* (Vol. 3, *Formulations of the person and the social context*). New York: McGraw-Hill, 1959. (b)

Rogers, C. R. *On becoming a person*. Boston: Houghton Mifflin, 1961.

Rogers, C. R. Autobiography. In E. G. Boring & G. Lindzey (Eds.), *A history of psychology in autobiography* (Vol. 5). New York: Naiburg Publishing, 1967.

Rogers, C. R. *Freedom to learn*. Columbus, Ohio: Charles E. Merrill, 1969.

Rogers, C. R. *Becoming partners: marriage and its alternatives*. New York: Delacorte Press, 1972.

Rogers, C. R. My philosophy of interpersonal relationships and how it grew. *Journal of Humanistic Psychology*, 1973, *13*, 3–15.

Rogers, C. R. *Do we need "a" reality?* Unpublished manuscript, 1974. (a)

Rogers, C. R. *Ellen West—and loneliness*. Unpublished manuscript, 1974. (b)

Rogers, C. R. In retrospect: Forty-six years. *American Psychologist*, 1974, *29*, 115–123. (c)

Rogers, C. R. The project at Immaculate Heart: An experiment in self-directed change. *Education*, 1974, *95*, 172–189. (d)

Rogers, C. R. Client-centered psychotherapy. In A. M. Freedman, H. I. Kaplan & B. J. Sadock (Eds.), *Comprehensive textbook of psychiatry II*. Baltimore: Williams & Wilkins, 1975. (a)

Rogers, C. R. The emerging person: A new revolution. In R. I. Evans, *Carl Rogers: The man and his ideas*. New York: E. P. Dutton, 1975. (b)

Rogers, C. R. Empathic: An unappreciated way of being. *The Counseling Psychologist*, 1975, *5*, 2–10. (c)

Rogers, C. R., & Coulson, W. R. (Eds.). *Man and the science of man*. Columbus, Ohio: Charles E. Merrill, 1968.

Rogers, C. R., & Dymond, R. F. (Eds.). *Psychotherapy and personality change*. Chicago: University of Chicago Press, 1954.

Rogers, C. R., & Rablen, R. A. *A scale of process in psychotherapy*. Unpublished manuscript, Center for Studies of the Person, La Jolla, Calif., 1958.

Rogers, C. R., & Wood, J. K. Client-centered theory: Carl R. Rogers. In A. Burton (Ed.), *Operational theories of personality*. New York: Brunner/Mazel, 1974.

Rogers, C. R. *On personal power*. New York: Delaconte Press, 1977.

Schachter, S. The interaction of cognitive and physiological determinants of emotional state. In P. H. Leiderman & D. Shapiro (Eds.), *Psychobiological approaches to social behavior*. London: Tavistock, 1965.

Schachter, S., & Rodin, J. *Obese humans and rats*. New York: Wiley, 1974.

Seeman, J., & Raskin, N. J. Research perspectives in client-centered therapy. In O. H. Mowrer (Ed.), *Psychotherapy: Theory and research*. New York: Ronald Press, 1953.

Shlien, J. M., & Zimring, F. M. Research directives and methods in client-centered therapy. In J. T. Hart & T. M. Tomlinson (Eds.), *New directions in client-centered therapy*. Boston: Houghton Mifflin, 1970.

Sperry, R. W. A modified concept of consciousness. *Psychological Review*, 1969, *76*, 532–536.

Stephenson, W. *The study of behavior: Q-technique and its methodology*. Chicago: University of Chicago Press, 1953.

Sternbach, R. *Principles of psychophysiology*. New York: Academic Press, 1966.

Truax, C. B., & Mitchell, K. M. Research on certain therapist interpersonal skills in rela-

tion to process and outcome. In A. E. Bergin & S. L. Garfield (Eds.), *Handbook of psychotherapy and behavior change*. New York: Wiley, 1971.

Von Békésy, G. Similarities of inhibition in the different sense organs. *American Psychologist*, 1969, *24*, 707–719.

Wexler, D. A. A cognitive theory of experiencing, self-actualization, and therapeutic process. In D. A. Wexler & L. N. Rice (Eds.), *Innovations in client-centered therapy*. New York: Wiley, 1974.

Wexler, D. A., & Rice, L. N. (Eds). *Innovations in client-centered therapy*. New York: Wiley, 1974.

CHAPTER VI

Personal-Constructs Theory

Lee Sechrest

GEORGE A. KELLY

George A. Kelly's theory of personal constructs is unique among personality theories, the most psychological of all theories in that it is "all in the head"—consisting entirely of a way of looking at how people construe life, meaning how they organize, perceive, evaluate, structure, and predict events. As such, it is almost entirely a cognitive theory and pays virtually no attention to learning, emotions, motivations, needs, or even behavior, but at the same time it encompasses all of them, subsuming them as aspects or elements of the total personality controlled by these constructs of the individual. On top of this, Kelly's theory offers difficulty for anyone who likes to make orderly arrangements of theories in that it simply rejects as invalid or unimportant usual ways of seeing life. Kelly had his own unique ways of seeing things, and he used language in an idiosyncratic manner.

The psychology of personal constructs differs considerably from other theoretical constructions of personality, because of its indigenous origins in the heartland of America, by a man who was a clinical psychologist and who did not write much, and because it is not supported by an infrastructure of enthusiastic devoted followers, as well as because of its unique point of view.

INTRODUCTION

Psychology is usually defined as the study of human behavior, and human behavior has two aspects: implicit and explicit. Implicit behavior ordinarily is known as phenomenology, the realm of the "mind," and often is divided into cognition and affection, that is, thinking and feeling processes. These also have been divided into awareness and unawareness, and so psychologists speak of consciousness and unconsciousness. It must be evident that there should be some relationship between behavior and phenomenology, and for the man in the street, the layman, how one behaves depends on one's thinking and feeling. But how one thinks or feels is a very great mystery, especially when people seem to act, as a result of their thinking processes, in unusual or peculiar ways. As a matter of fact, when we cannot understand a person's thinking, we call him insane.

Now one view toward understanding man is to see him as a scientist. The student of personality and his subject are both simultaneously trying to predict and control each other's behavior, establishing and testing hypotheses, maneuvering to attain desired results. How it came to pass that scientists studying other people should view their own activities as on a separate level from those of the people they are studying is an interesting question.

In an attempt to understand people, scientists have been seeking convergence, hoping to find a superordinate theory, that is, a final theory to explain all human behavior. An alternate point of view is that there is not necessarily one single correct theory but rather a multiplicity of correct theories, each having value for a variety of purposes. Theories are good if they help to attain desired ends, to make sense of a corner of the universe. No theory is likely to be correct for a wide range of purposes. A theory helpful in explaining man's aesthetic pleasures may not be helpful in understanding how to motivate people or explaining how investors behave in a declining market.

The preceding ideas may seem obvious, but they have profound implications (to be discussed later) which have not been grasped or even recognized by many theorists in the field. They are intended to set the stage for the personality theory of George A. Kelly, who asked and answered unusual questions in an unusual way. His theory is quite different from other theories in this book, since Kelly proposed entirely new ways of thinking about man[1]—what goes on in his head and about his behavior. He made little effort to deal with the traditional concerns of personality theory. Kelly explicitly stated the purpose of theory for him:

> A theory may be considered a way of binding together a multitude of facts so that one may comprehend them all at once. When the theory enables us to make

---

[1]George Kelly lived and wrote in a time preceding the increased consciousness of the many manifestations of sexism in our language and so used the literary masculine nouns and pronouns that were then thought adequate to represent statements pertinent to both sexes. The author of this chapter is confident that Kelly would have been quite sensitive to the nuances of sexism in language had it been any sort of issue in his time. However, because of the frequent quoting and paraphrasing of Kelly's work, he has adhered to the linguistic forms actually used by Kelly in the preparation of this chapter. *Man* and kindred terms should be taken to refer in the broadest sense to persons, with no disrespect intended.

reasonably precise predictions, one may call it scientific....our anticipations of daily events, while not scientifically precise, nevertheless surround our lives with an aura of meaning....A theory provides a basis for an active approach to life, not merely a comfortable armchair from which to contemplate its vicissitudes with detached complaisance. (1955, pp. 18–19)

Kelly made three fundamental assumptions about the world:

1. It is objectively real.
2. It has integrity with "all its imaginable parts having an exact relation to each other" (1955, p. 6).
3. The universe is an ongoing process which can only be understood in the perspective of time: time proves the ultimate bond in all relationships (1955, p. 6).

From this it may be evident that Kelly's theory covers cosmology as well as epistemology. It is, paradoxically, the narrowest and the broadest of all personality theories. It is an adventure into the mind of a great man to understand Kelly's thinking about man.

At this point we should define our major term *construct* and the combination term *personal construct*, as well as the verb form *to construe*, since this is what Kelly's theory is all about.

To construe means roughly to interpret, to understand, to deduce, or to explain. It may be seen as a process of coming to a comprehension about something, such as finding out the answer to a problem. Just as a detective, given clues, may finally come to a reconstruction of a crime and develop a hypothesis to explain how the crime occurred and who is guilty, so too are ordinary people constantly in the process of trying to make sense out of their lives and out of events and people.

A simple example will make this clear. An individual may report to a therapist that he feels inadequate and unloved. The therapist may conclude that his client is indeed very capable and is highly regarded by many. We now have two constructions: the client's that he is inadequate and unloved, and the therapist's that the client has no reason for these constructions.

Thus, personal constructs are an individual's conclusions or interpretations or deductions about life. And Kelly's psychology of personal constructs relates then to one's cognition or private logic.

HISTORY

Precursors

Though it is difficult to determine the precise origins of the philosophical views at which he finally arrived, George A. Kelly dealt directly with several of the great issues presented by the classical philosophers. His universe was real and not the shadows on the walls of Plato's cave. A philosophical monist, with an avowed similarity to Spinoza, Kelly stated that for given purposes it might be desirable to think of the plural attributes of the monistic substance. Kelly's views about the importance of time have an obvious relationship to Henri Bergson's ideas, and he notes ways in which he tried to avoid the criticisms of Aristotelian thought. Kelly also specifically notes that his ideas about the anticipatory nature of behavior bear a resemblance to the thinking of John Dewey, stating that Dewey's philosophy and psychology can be read between many of the lines of the psychology of personal constructs. Nevertheless, Kelly refers to Dewey in only three places, and then only fleetingly. There is also something of a similarity between Kelly's conception of man as gradually approximating but never, perhaps, achieving truth in his progression of thought and the dialectic of G. W. H. Hegel, a point which Kelly himself notes in one place. Kelly was known to have had a considerable collection of Hegel's works in his own library (Leon Levy, personal communication, 1975).

In the first, theoretical volume of his major work, *The Psychology of Personal Constructs* (1955), Kelly cites 14 philosophers ranging from Empedocles and Heraclitus to William James and Percy Bridgman. However, only Aristotle, Dewey, and Auguste Comte are cited on more than one page, and for none of them is there more than passing reference. It might also be noted that Kelly cites only 28 psychologists, other than his own students, and four of them are merely mentioned as his teachers. Only 11 of the 28 are cited on more than one page, and, again, rarely is the citation more than a passing reference. Carl Rogers is cited in seven places, and Sigmund Freud in six. To complete the inventory, Kelly cites 16 additional "persons" ranging from Hamlet (four times) and Solomon to Darwin, Dickens, Shelley, and Nabokov. Five of these additional citations are, however, former teachers mentioned in passing.

The point of this inventorial paragraph is to show, in part, the rather wide acquaintance Kelly had with classical philosophy and, to a certain extent, classical literature. It is also intended to show that his work is a very personal *integration* of all the influences which came to bear upon him, and his theory is not a mere collection of ideas from here and there or even some synthesis of his readings. Rather, the psychology of personal constructs is an *invention* of George Kelly, for which he borrowed bits and pieces here and there. But even his borrowing is only of a very general sort, and one can detect only similarities to the work of others, not direct influences.

Beginnings

George Alexander Kelly was born on April 28, 1905, and died in March 1967. He was the only child of devoutly religious parents. His father had been a Presbyterian minister and farmer but had given up the ministry for reasons of health. Both parents were active in the church, hard-working, and somewhat puritanical. Kelly never outgrew his early religious upbringing and remained an active churchman. He was the focus of a good bit of attention as an only child, but his parents had ambitions for him and sent him away to school when he was 13, and he lived away from home for most of the time after that. It can be supposed that his parents, though devoted to him, were wise enough in their religious perspective not to spoil young George, and he unquestionably profited intellectually and personally from his early independence. Out of these early experiences Kelly probably developed the view that life is not so much a matter of objective happenings as it is of what one makes of those happenings. It is difficult to describe Kelly's adult personality without lapsing into the jargon of some other theorist, but at least in this writer's view, in those early days Kelly learned to construe experiences in such terms as strong versus weak, moral versus immoral, clever versus dull, and calm and reliable versus excitable and undependable. Kelly's adult behavior was so unfailingly characterized by the left side of each pair of these terms that, by the application of his own theory, one can only suppose that to him to be otherwise was to be like the right side of the pairs.

It is also probably important that Kelly was born and grew up in Kansas, the heartland of the United States, in the wide open spaces and in an area in which to survive one had to be practical. Not for rural Kansas were debates about angels on heads of pins. Life there revolved around the question "Does it work?" Yet for all that the question is straightforward and practical, it is penetrating. It is, in fact, at the heart of *American* philosophy, pragmatism, which originated with Charles Peirce, William James, and John Dewey. Out of his midwestern rural beginnings Kelly came to construe experience in terms of the practical rather than the useless. He had little regard for the latter, however fancy or elegant.

After three years at Friends University in Wichita, a Quaker school, Kelly moved to Park College where, in 1926, he received a B.A. degree in physics and mathematics. At that point, uncertain about his future, Kelly considered briefly a career in aeronautical engineering, an experience that left him with a lifelong habit of carrying a small slide rule in his shirt pocket. At this point, for reasons that remain obscure, Kelly developed more of an interest in social problems and attended the University of Kansas, where he received an M.A. in 1928, with a major in educational sociology. Kelly's interests shifted in the direction of education, and after several brief teaching positions, including one at a junior college where he met his wife to be and helped coach dramatics, he was awarded an exchange scholarship in 1929 that enabled him to spend a year at the University of Edinburgh. At Edinburgh, Kelly studied under Sir Godfrey Thomson, an eminent statistician and educatior, with whose mathematizing of behavior Kelly never agreed but from whom he contracted his interest in psychology.

In 1930 Kelly returned from Scotland with some urbanity grafted into his Kansas background, although he later claimed never to have gotten all the Kansas mud off his shoes. He entered the State University of Iowa as a graduate student and in 1931 was awarded a Ph.D. with a dissertation on the common factors in speech and reading disabilities. He had also begun some work on physiological psychology while at Iowa. Kelly stated that Carl Seashore and Lee Travis were his intellectual mentors while he was in residence at Iowa, but there is very little indication in any of his later work how they influenced him. One noteworthy thing about Kelly's educational history is that he studied at five different schools, and after his first three years as an undergraduate, he never spent longer than two years in any school. One suspects that Kelly must have been highly flexible and adaptive, and that any influences on his intellectual progress were in terms of breadth rather than depth. He never studied long enough under one man to become "his student."

The beginnings of the depression of the late 1920s and 1930s found Kelly in 1931 back in western Kansas, at Fort Hays, Kansas State College. There, under a variety of pressures, including no doubt his own desire to do something useful and humanitarian, Kelly began to develop an interest in psychological services, and he soon established a program of traveling psychological clinics that served the entire state. These clinics were the forerunner of today's psychological consultants who do their work through other people, such as teachers. In his attempts to solve important practical problems Kelly came to see that it was not necessary, or even desirable, to make any distinction between scientific and applied psychology; they were one and the same.

Kelly was also an innovator, an inventor, even a tinkerer. (Kelly's home, automobile, and office provided many examples of his own little inventions to make life more efficient, practical, or even just interesting.) He began to apply his inventive nature to the understanding and solution of human problems and to experiment (again, tinker might be a better word) with new approaches to diagnosis and treatment, as well as new ways of looking at problems. During the 1930s, while at Fort Hays, Kelly produced a remarkable lot of students, several of whom went on to positions of eminence in psychology, although none ever became a "Kellian," perhaps because his theory and innovative practices at that time were inchoate. His influence on students arose out of his enthusiasm and dynamic personality.

When World War II began, Kelly entered the Navy along with so many other dustbowl midwesterners. He entered as an aviation psychologist. During his Navy experience Kelly worked closely with other psychologists and with members of other professions in developing an appropriate role in the service for psychology, and particularly for clinical psychology. When the war ended, he was reasonably well known to psychologists returning to their academic positions. He accepted a position at the University of Maryland, and a year later, in 1946, he became professor of psychology and director of clinical psychology at the Ohio State University. With the assistance of Julian B. Rotter, himself a social learning theorist of growing stature, Kelly built the clinical psychology program at Ohio State to a point of virtual preeminence in the nation. Not long ago, a survey showed that there were more graduates of Ohio State directing clinical training programs than graduates of any other university.

While at Ohio State, Kelly brought his theory to maturity, slowly at first, then with growing intensity. He held regular meetings with students at which he read drafts of his manuscripts, discussed ideas, argued, and thought through his position. He also encouraged and fostered thesis and dissertation work that became empirical support for his ideas, and his debt to his students was as apparent to him as to anyone. His efforts culminated in 1955 with the publication of his two-volume work, *The Psychology of Personal Constructs*. The publication in the previous year of J. B. Rotter's *Social Learning and Clinical Psychology* (Rotter, 1954) represented a remarkable circumstance in a program involving only four professors and was indicative of the general intellectual ferment with which Kelly was surrounded.

Almost equally remarkable is the fact that Kelly's two-volume work is very nearly the corpus of his writings. His publications prior to 1955 were limited to a few very practical pieces published in rather obscure places, and after 1955 he published very little. After his death in March 1967, Brendan Maher, one of his most distinguished students, edited a collection of some of Kelly's more important papers, most of them never previously published. (Maher, 1969) In 1965 Kelly had left Ohio State to take the Riklis Chair of Behavioral Science at Brandeis University. By that time he had traveled extensively and was well known in many foreign countries, particularly Great Britain. Kelly looked forward with great anticipation to a new role at Brandeis. Unfortunately, his career ended quite prematurely with his death in 1967, and we can only speculate as to what he might have produced in the 10 years or so longer that should have been his lot.

One last point to be made about Kelly's experiences and their impact on his thinking has to do with the fact that nearly all of Kelly's career was spent in work with relatively young and intact people. He had very little experience with the more severe forms of psychopathology, and more of his direct clinical experience was with people associated in one way or another with universities. To the extent that Kelly's theory may be regarded as cognitive, or rational, or intellective, it is perhaps understandable in terms of the events with which he was trying to deal.

Current Status

In the late 1950s and early 1960s some really exciting developments growing out of Kelly's theorizing were expected. Jerome Bruner (1956) referred to

Kelly's work as the greatest single contribution to the theory of personality functioning of the decade ending in 1955, and Kelly had produced a group of active and dedicated students. Yet, nothing much has happened in the decades since 1965, and the major developments have to do with the utility of the Role Constructs Repertory Test (Bannister & Mair, 1968)[2] rather than with the theory itself. The literature about Kelly's theory in any given year is sparse, and, in the opinion of this writer, not inspiring. It is not clear why. Few of Kelly's students are still associated with his theory, and, in fact, his most consistent disciples are now the English psychologists, Fay Fransella and Donald Bannister (Bannister, 1970; Bannister & Fransella, 1971). No doubt many individuals have been influenced indirectly by Kelly, and some of his ideas (e.g., constructive alternativism) find wide acceptance today, indeed are often widely accepted without any special acknowledgment to Kelly. Still, there are no institutes bearing his name, there are no departments or training programs identified with his theory, and one would be hard put to specify any particular impact that Kelly has had on contemporary thinking about personality.

On the other hand, as new textbooks in personality appear, Kelly continues to be included as a major theorist, so that his ideas are apparently surviving, to be presented to successive generations of students in psychology. However, it seems inevitable that the theory will fade and gradually fall into disuse if it is not taken on by at least a small group of dedicated and highly competent persons who can discern and test the many implications it has for personality and for the practice of clinical psychology. In fact, Kelly's theory is one of the most comprehensive and broad theories to be introduced since psychoanalysis, more clearly rooted in clinical experience than most others, so that it is fraught with implications. What the theory seems to lack at present is disciples who will spread the word.

ASSERTIONS

More for the psychology of personal constructs than for nearly any other theory of personality, it is easy to state what the theory asserts about personality. However, it is not always so easy to understand just what these assertions mean in other terms. Kelly set forth his theory in a rather formal way, beginning with a Fundamental Postulate and then proceeding to 11 corollary assumptions. Those 12 statements are the content of his theory. Then, since his theory has to do with the ways in which people make sense

---

[2]The author is indebted in no small measure for his current understanding of Kelly to the fine exegesis of Bannister and Mair. Their work will be cited only on specific points, but their influence is pervasive.

out of and anticipate experience, Kelly developed 12[3] formal characteristics of constructs, three ways in which constructs exert control over the elements with which they deal, 15 constructs diagnostic of the nature of an individual's construct system, and 8 constructs relating to transition or change in an individual and his construct system. Obviously, there are too many terms and too much material to cover Kelly's theory adequately in the space allocated here. Consequently, the presentation that follows will be directed toward achieving a more general understanding of the psychology of personal constructs rather than a technical cataloging of all terms.

To have a good grasp on Kelly's approach to personality, it is necessary to comprehend Kelly's philosophical position, the essence of which can be stated in the first assertion.

1. All our interpretations of the universe are subject to revision.

Kelly assumed from the beginning that there is *no* final truth, that there is *no* interpretation of *any* event not susceptible to some other interpretation of events as good as any other. Some views definitely have more usefulness for some purposes than others, but the position that Kelly called *constructive alternativism* meant that individuals with decidedly different views of things were not necessarily divisible into those who are right and those who are wrong.

A parent may view a disciplinary act as a corrective action taken for the good of the child; the child may view the same act as an unavoidable occurrence in a capricious world; and a social worker may view the discipline as cruel punishment. And all three viewers may be "right," and all three may need to recognize that their individual view is not the only tenable one. In terms of final truth, we achieve only successive approximations, each approximation a bit more satisfactory than previous ones, and it is unlikely in the extreme, if not actually impossible, that we would ever know if we had somehow arrived at the final truth. While Kelly stated his position in terms of the constructs of individuals coping with their lives and experience, the position of constructive alternativism is quite applicable to scientific constructs and systems. Those constructs and systems, too, are only gradually improved and, no matter how persuasive at any one time, are always subject to revision and replacement.

Development

As has been pointed out by others (e.g., Levy, 1970) Kelly's theory is essentially ahistorical, somewhat akin to the phenomenologists in this respect.

---

[3]Here and in other places we follow the excellent presentation by Bannister and Mair (1968), to whom, in general, a debt is owed for a concise and penetrating explication of Kellian theory.

Kelly did not concern himself with the origins of personal constructs (Sechrest, 1963) for the reason that, as he saw it, the construing of experience is a natural, ongoing process which begins at birth and continues for as long as we live. There is no possibility of an individual *not* construing experience. The only question of interest is in what terms experience will be construed. Kelly expressed no interest in the ways in which some individuals come to construe in different terms than others. He seems to have taken for granted that this would happen. In his theory, what is important is an individual's contemporary view, his construction of reality at a moment in time when a choice must be made. Consequently, the theory of personal constructs may be seen as a here-and-now theory. Kelly did suggest that understanding of a contemporary view might be facilitated by studying the historical processes by which an individual came to that view, that study of changes in the construct system over time could be enlightening, so he did not eschew the study of personal history altogether.

Kelly did not see the need for positing any special processes of development corresponding to developmental stages in children. He viewed the child and his psychological processes as continuous, with the infant preceding and the adolescent and adult following. Kelly did not discern any discontinuities in psychological development, or at least no discontinuities inherent in growth and maturing. He was not overly interested in the "facts" of people's lives, and that disinterest can probably be stated in the form of the single assertion relative to development which can easily be derived from the psychology of personal constructs (Assertion 2).

2. *No person needs to be a victim of his own biography.*

Kelly concluded that it is not objective experience that is important for constructions but rather what we tell ourselves about experience. There is no one necessarily correct way to look at things. Every individual may construe or reconstrue his experience differently to anticipate the future. A "difficult" childhood can be viewed as a "toughening" childhood; a physical "handicap" can be viewed by the individual as an opportunity to develop special sensitivities. Kelly never suggested that we are not victimized by experience, but to the extent that we are, we are somewhat willing participants in that victimization.

Do we really have freedom to interpret experience? Isn't our construct system determined to some degree by the nature of our experience? Kelly distinguishes two different problems relative to determinism and freedom. The first he considers relatively trivial. The universe flows smoothly without being divided up into discrete events, and no event ever occurs more than once. To say that an event was an invariant consequent of past events the only time it ever did or will occur is not very helpful. The more important issue has to do with whether events determine our views of them or whether, since our views can vary in infinite ways, those views, or constructs, produce control we have over events. If a man dies from eating a poison berry, Kelly would say that he dies not because of the objective characteristics of the berry, but because of his view of the berry as delicious-looking, hunger-assuaging, relief-producing, or perhaps because he viewed the berry as an object, the eating of which would impress his companions with his bravery.

To quote from Kelly:

> Ultimately a man sets the measure of his own freedom and his own bondage by the level at which he chooses to establish his convictions. The man who orders his life in terms of many special and inflexible convictions about temporary matters makes himself the victim of circumstances. Each little prior conviction that is not open to review is a hostage he gives to fortune; it determines whether the events of tomorrow will bring happiness or misery. The man whose prior convictions encompass a broad perspective, and are cast in terms of principles rather than rules, has a much better chance of discovering those alternatives which will lead eventually to his emancipation. (1955, pp. 21–22)

Kelly points out that culture is often taken to be an important source to explain similarities and differences between people and suggests that persons are often grouped according to similarities in upbringing and environment, a grouping that, to him, implies a stimulus-response theory. However, Kelly notes that culture is also often taken to mean similarity in what members of a group expect of each other, and that view is more compatible with the psychology of personal constructs. Thus, the impact of culture on the development of construct systems is that it provides expectancies about what other individuals may do and also what others expect of the individual whose construct system is being considered. There is, perhaps, a determinism provided by culture, but it is weak in contrast with the views of many other, more patently deterministic theorists.

Maintenance

Since Kelly's theory is essentially ahistorical and supposes that an individual's behavior develops out of his construction and anticipation of events at any given moment, it follows that most assertions made in the theory concern the maintenance or ongoing processes of personality.

3. *A person's processes are psychologically channelized by the ways in which he anticipates events (Fundamental Postulate).*

Kelly explained every word of substance in the Fundamental Postulate; he chose those words with care. It is not possible to present all his rationale for the postulate as stated (those desiring the complete rationale would do better to consult Kelly in the original), but we can summarize his views (1955, pp. 46–50). First, the focus of his theory is the individual person (*person's, he*) rather than any part of the person, any group of persons, any particular process within the person, or any nonperson set of phenomena. In choosing the word *processes* as the focus of the theory Kelly centers on a behaving organism, one not requiring any external source of energy. Kelly does not find the concept of motivation useful and thus dispenses with it. *All* living organisms are behaving, acting, moving, metabolizing, and to indicate that they are in a state of motivation or that they are energized is pointless and redundant.

By the third term, *psychologically*, Kelly designates the realm with which he intends to deal; his is a psychological theory. However, it is not the particular events in one's life that are important, but one's unique way of looking at them. Kelly admits his theory is limited and that some phenomena explained within physiological or sociological systems may lie outside personal construct theory, but he makes no apology for the limitation. A person's processes do not operate in a chaotic or random manner but rather within a system of flexible, modifiable, but restrictive pathways that constitute a network. These pathways channel the processes of an individual so that they go in one direction rather than another. According to Kelly a person's interpersonal processes work in reasonably consistent but modifiable ways. The various processes in interpersonal relations operate as an integral subsystem of the individual, much in the manner of a network.

The network of pathways or channels is purposive in nature. That is what is meant by *ways*; that there is an end, or aim in the system. That aim is the anticipation of real events. Consequently, personal constructs represent a teleological system to some degree. Kelly's conception of man is that he is engaged in an unending attempt to improve his ability to predict and to anticipate the real world. Herein lie the predictive and motivational features of Kelly's view of man: "Anticipation is both the push and the pull of the psychology of personal constructs" (1955, p. 49). Since, like the scientist, any man is constantly striving for better understanding and prediction, the consequence of anticipations that are fulfilled or disappointed is incorporated into the system, which then is modified in terms of outcomes. In short, constructions are constantly being reestablished by experiences.

The basic building block in Kelly's theory is the *personal construct*, the specific way in which a person anticipates certain events. Constructs are *personal*, specific to individuals, and are *constructed* in the sense that they are not "given" to an individual but are created by the person. The process of construing is active. As used by Kelly, *construct* refers to how things are seen as being alike and yet different from other things. For example, friendly is a way that some people may be seen as being alike, and at the same time being friendly differentiates them from people who are hostile, or mean, or not friendly, or whatever the person who uses the construct thinks is the difference. The characteristics of constructs, how used, how organized, as well as other aspects, are defined in the corollaries to the Fundamental Postulate.

4. *A person anticipates events by construing their replications (Construction Corollary).*

This assertion (first corollary) indicates that the interpretations man places on his experiences enable him to predict, and hence to control, those things that will happen to him in the future. The process of construing is active but also abstractive. The person develops constructs of similarity and contrast by abstracting from an ongoing flow of events those features that appear to provide meaning. Another person might abstract different features from these events and consequently arrive at a distinctly different meaning.

Although we have verbal labels for many constructs, the process of construing is not synonymous with verbal labeling. Kelly points out that if a person is asked how he proposes to digest his dinner, he will probably not be able to answer the question, because such matters seem outside his control. Yet, digestion is a structured process, and what the person anticipates has a good deal to do with the course that digestion takes. Constructs reside in the individual, not in events. Kelly was fond of pointing to the shoes of a member of an audience and alleging that the shoes were "neurotic" and then noting that everyone in the audience tried to get a look at the shoes as if they really might possess neurotic qualities, instead of looking at him, Kelly, to see what it might be about him that would cause him to think of shoes as neurotic.

Whatever a person construes is a process; it is unending and undifferentiated. A person's universe will begin to make sense to him only when he begins to look for recurrent themes, the *replications*. To use Kelly's example, time does not mark itself off into segments, and it does not double back on itself. Today is not yesterday, nor is tomorrow today; but the construct of *day* "is erected along the incessant stream of time—a day which is, in its own way, like other days and yet clearly distinguishable from the moments and years" (1955, p. 53). Only after events have been interpreted in terms of their beginnings and endings and in terms of their similarities and contrasts does it become possible to try to anticipate them. We do not predict that tomorrow will be a duplicate of today, but rather that there are certain ways, which can be predicted, in which tomorrow will replicate today.

5. *Persons differ from one another in their construction of events (Individuality Corollary).*

This second corollary is simply an expression of the universally accepted notion that people differ from one another. But here Kelly is saying that people can be seen as differing from one another not only in the events anticipated but in the approaches taken to anticipate the same events. One person with an invitation to dinner with a Vietnamese family may think of having to eat something strange and unpleasant, while another person may think of it as an opportunity to try something new and exciting. No two people play quite the same role in any event, no matter how similar they are, how closely related they may be, or how much they try. Each experiences himself as the central figure in the event, each experiences the other as an external figure, and inevitably each gets caught up in different aspects of the stream of events.

6. *Each person characteristically evolves, for his convenience in anticipating events, a construction system embracing ordinal relationships between constructs (Organization Corollary).*

This corollary states that construct systems are organized in such a way that some constructs may subsume others, that is, be more comprehensive. There are several ways in which constructs relate to one another. For example, the construct *extravert–introvert* may subsume the construct *likes parties–dislikes parties* in such a way that, among other things, being an extravert implies liking parties while being an introvert implies disliking parties. However, the construct *likes parties–dislikes parties* might also be subsumed by the construct *social characteristics–nonsocial characteristics*, so that liking or disliking parties would be viewed as a social characteristic and contrasted with other constructs (e.g., *musical–nonmusical*) not having to do with social behaviors. Moreover, at a still higher level, a person might distinguish between constructs *having to do with human behavior* and those *applicable to nonhumans only*. Each person will develop a construct organization pattern different from that of every other person; for example, liking parties might imply extraversion for some people rather than the other way around, *musical–nonmusical* might be thought a social characteristic for some persons, and another person might not make any distinction between constructs applicable to humans and others.

7. *A person's construction system is composed of a finite number of dichotomous constructs (Dichotomy Corollary).*

Of fundamental importance in understanding Kelly's theory, a view that sets him apart from classical philosophers, is the Dichotomy Corollary. The idea that any given person's construct system is finite poses no difficulties, for we would not suppose otherwise than that any given person would have a limited array of constructs. However, Kelly proposes that constructs are dichotomous, either–or in nature. There are, in fact, two facets of the dichotomy corollary of interest. First, do people actually think in dichotomies? When we hear a person say "John is intelligent," Kelly maintains that the word *intelligent* implies both a similarity and a contrast. The construer abstracts from the overall perception of the object of his attention, John, the characteristic of intelligence, which he must see as a replication of something seen before and hence, as a way in which John is similar to some other person (or "event," since, presumably, the characteristic of intelligence might have been seen previously in something other than a person). However, to construe John as intelligent also implies a *contrast*. The contrast to intelligence for one person might be "stupid," while for another the contrast might be "not intelligent," two rather different contrasts in terms of their implications. In Kelly's view, it is impossible to see a similarity without at the same time having in mind a contrast, a way in which *some* other events are seen as different.

But, when John is construed as intelligent, similarly, let us say, to Jim and Mary, and different from Joe and Bill, is it necessarily true that the construer can see no gradations in intelligence, that he sees people as either intelligent or not intelligent, without gradations? That goes against experience and common sense. According to Kelly, at any given moment, for any given construction, the choice must be dichotomous. However, across a series of choices, constructs may be modified slightly so as to produce a gradation of intelligence or any other characteristic in question. Consider, for example, the following set of individuals with their tentative scores: John, 135; Joe, 125; Mary, 115; Helen, 105; Bill, 95; and Sam, 85. The admissions officer for a college might construe John, Joe, and Mary as similar because they are *intelligent* (IQ 115 plus) and Helen, Bill, and Sam as different because they are *not intelligent*. Now suppose this same admissions officer has in mind a special honors program for unusually promising students. He could now construe John and Joe as "highly intelligent" and others, by contrast, as "not highly intelligent." He has a dichotomy still. Mary is now lumped with the others at the low end of the scale. If that same admissions officer were planning a special program for students at the lower end of the scale, he might see Sam as a "slow learner" in contrast to the others as "average or better." Across a series of choices, the admissions officer would have behaved as if he perceived a gradation of intelligence, but at any one moment, his construct would have been dichotomous.

That is how Kelly proposes to construe our thinking. The reader should keep in mind that whether this is *really* the way we think would not interest Kelly very much. He would say, "Well, suppose we *think* of constructs as dichotomous, rather than as continuous, and let's see where that gets us."

A second facet of Kelly's view of constructs as dichotomous that is of critical importance is that there are events which are irrelevant to any given construct and therefore do not need to be lumped together with the contrast.

8. *A construct is convenient for the anticipation of a finite range of events only (Range Corollary).*

Every construct has its focus and range of convenience, just as do theories. Personal constructs, by their nature, are relevant to everything. Constructs evolve around the resolution of certain issues, the anticipation of certain events, and they may be extended with experience to other more challenging events, but eventually one reaches limits beyond which the construct no longer applies. For example, the construct *intelligent–not intelligent* evolves for most people around the issue of anticipating academic success and success in related areas. It can be extended to a variety of problem-solving efforts. One might think of an intelligent sculptor, of an intelligent fish, perhaps of an unintelligent amoeba, or even, stretching considerably, of an "intelligent" plant that seeks out water with its roots and the light with its leaves so effectively. But pies can scarcely be either intelligent or unintelligent, nor can enzymes, or languages, or lights, or smells, or temperatures, or weather conditions. For all these things the construct is irrelevant. Classical logic lumps together the constrasts with the irrelevant; personal constructs theory does not. Things are black *or* white *or* neither. To understand a personal construct it is necessary to know the contrast as well as the construct. To know that a person construes some situations as "nice" is not very comprehensible until one knows that the contrast to the construct is "immoral," "dangerous," "lonely," "financially unrewarding," or some other notion.

9. *A person chooses for himself that alternative in a dichotomous construct through which he anticipates the greater possibility for extension and definition of his system (Elaborative Choice Corollary).*

This corollary is the only direct link in Kelly's theory between a person's construct system and his specific behaviors. As will be pointed out, even this link is not very dependable. As suggested elsewhere (Levy, 1970; Sechrest, 1963), transition from cognition to behavior is difficult in personal constructs theory. By this elaborative choice corollary Kelly posits a fundamental and continuing human motivation akin to other general, monolithic motives such as self-actualization, self-consistency, and cognitive congruity. In Kelly's view we strive to anticipate events correctly to improve our capacity to predict and control our future. This is the heart of the theory of personal constructs.

One way we improve our ability to anticipate events is (perhaps alternately) to extend and define our construct system. To *extend* means to be able to account for a wider variety of events, to be able to anticipate events in new settings or with new persons and to develop new constructs. To *define* our system means to eliminate uncertainties, to sharpen predictions, to make clearer the constructs we employ. Kelly believes that individuals build their lives upon one or the other of the alternatives represented in the dichotomies of each construct. People place relative values upon the ends of their dichotomies. Kelly means that people value a pole of the construct, not the specific elements or events subsumed under that pole. For example, a person may value intelligence as opposed to stupidity quite independently of the value he places on any intelligent or stupid thing, person, or idea. Kelly then proposes that a person will choose for himself behavioral alternatives that appear to present the greatest possibility for enhancing his ability to anticipate and control future events.

Let us consider an example. A salesman seemed to apply the construct *aggressive-failure* to a wide variety of events and possibilities having to do with his role as a salesman, and he "chose" for a period of about two years to comport himself as a fairly stereotypically aggressive salesman. He was never successful as a salesman, and, predictably enough, he became inactive, quit his job, began drinking fairly regularly, and regarded himself as a failure. Strangely, however, he did not seem uncomfortable in the role of a failure, and ultimately it seemed to the clinician he was glad to be a solid failure if he could not be a solid success. The clinician came to believe that being a failure rendered much of his life unambiguous and, in fact, even opened some new opportunities to him, such as a chance to try out the role of ne'er-do-well.

Presumably under most circumstances a person would rather be intelligent than stupid, would rather be friendly than hostile, would rather be sophisticated than naive. However, there may also be circumstances, even if only temporary, in which a person who usually thinks of himself as intelligent may, if placed in the company of a number of extraordinary persons, see that he may be better able to predict and control what is going to happen if he temporarily abandons his conception of himself as intelligent and thinks of himself as "stupid." What is important from the standpoint of the psychology of personal constructs is that he chooses one or the other of the two alternatives available to him from the construct he sees relevant to the situation at hand, in terms of his general purpose to make sense and fit into the stream of life.

10. *A person's construction system varies as he successively construes the replication of events (Experience Corollary).*

Systems of constructs are not static. Whenever a person makes a prediction, and what he anticipates does not happen, there is an opportunity to reconstrue. If a new construction is not devised, there is a risk that anticipations will become increasingly in error. The succession of events that a person faces represents a continuing test of the validity of the construct system. At any one time a person's construct system may be thought of as a set of working hypotheses, much like those of a scientist, to be revised in the light of experience, outcomes of predictions, and hence to be progressively revised.

A rather important implication of the Experience Corollary reveals Kelly's view of *learning* as a process. It is another given, and like motivation, learning is assumed to take place continuously, and it is assumed that learning is not a special class of psychological processes. Learning *is* psychological processes. It does not happen to a person on occasion; it is what makes that person in the first place.

11.   *The variation in a person's construction system is limited by the permeability of the constructs within whose range of convenience the variants lie (Modulation Corollary).*

Any variation in a construct system must itself take place within a system: "Even the changes which a person attempts within himself must be construed by him." (Kelly, 1955, pp. 78–79) It is necessary here to introduce the notion of *permeability* of constructs: a construct is permeable if it can be applied to new events not yet construed within its framework. For example, the construct *miraculous-natural* is permeable if applicable to ongoing events. It would be considered impermeable if the construer took the position that there was a time when miracles occurred, but that the age of miracles is over. The Modulation Corollary states that if a person is to change his construct system, there must be permeable constructs within which to fit, or make sense of, the changes. At the present time, to point to an instance, many people in our society are undergoing a change of construction with respect to homosexuality, which has for a long time been construed largely in terms of such evaluative constructs as *good–bad, moral–immoral, strong–weak*, and *healthy–sick*. Now, however, different constructions are being applied, and, while it is difficult to specify both poles of the constructs, homosexuality is being construed as tolerable, non-threatening, a matter of lifestyle, and as "normal" for certain people. For such changes in construction to occur, the Modulation Corollary states that there must be permeable constructs capable of making sense out of the change. One such construct might be something like *legitimate concerns of the public-legitimate private concerns*. If matters of morality or immorality are reconstrued from being public concerns to private concerns, then it may also be possible to reconstrue homosexuality as a private and tolerable lifestyle for some people and as not especially threatening to the lifestyles of other persons. Another superordinate construct within which change might be construed is *things people choose to be—things people become*. If evaluative constructs such as *good—bad* and *moral—immoral* make sense only when applied to people's chosen behaviors, and if homosexuality comes to be seen as a state of being rather than as a choice, the change from evaluative to non-evaluative constructions may be possible.

12.   *A person may successively employ a variety of construction subsystems which are inferentially incompatible with each other (Fragmentation Corollary).*

The Fragmentation Corollary simply says that people need not be consistent over time in employing their construction systems, although the inconsistencies should be comprehensible in light of the Modulation Corollary. All changes must take place within a larger system, but they need not be particularly consistent at an obvious level. Shifts may occur because construct systems are loose (e.g., a person's definition of a "friendly" gesture may not be very precise), but shifts may also occur because the *regnant* or currently applicable construct switches, as when a "cute" cuddly child comes to be seen as "bothersome."

> 13. *To the extent that one person employs a construction of experience which is similar to that employed by another, his processes are psychologically similar to those of the other person (Commonality Corollary).*[4]

The idea expressed in this corollary straightforwardly states that people will be psychologically similar in their processes to the extent that they construe experience in the same way. People need not be similar in actual experiences; they need only be similar in the way they have come to construe those experiences. Without regard to any realities, if two people have come to think of the world largely in terms of good as opposed to wicked events, their processes will tend to run in similar channels. They may not agree on what sorts of things are to be regarded as wicked, but they will be similar in their attempts to force events into that dichotomy and in trying to verify that the events do actually fit.

> 14. *To the extent that one person construes the construction processes of another, he may play a role in a social process involving the other person (Sociality Corollary).*

As Bannister and Mair (1968) so cogently note, in the Sociality Corollary Kelly produces a truly psychological definition of *role*. He states that a person plays a role with respect to another person when he tries to make sense out of what the other person is doing, when he arrives at an interpretation of what the other person has in mind or is intending. Behavior may be described and understood as behavior, and there need be no implication of role. For example, an announcer may describe all of the complex behavior of a professional athlete in a very insightful and accurate way, but he is not involved in a role with respect to that athlete until he attempts himself to construe the athlete's own experience of what is going on. When the announcer says something to the effect, "Well, he knows he's got to do it this time or else. He is undoubtedly taking a little extra time in order to get himself up psychologically and physically for this next try," the announcer is in a position to play a role in a social process involving the athlete. Similarly, the announcer can call the contest as he sees it, or he can call it in terms of his understanding of what the fans want to get from his description. Only in the latter case is he playing a role in social processes involving

---

[4]As Bannister and Mair (1968) point out, Kelly originally stated that it was the "psychological processes" that were similar, but in a later unpublished paper (Kelly, 1966) he realized that what he wished to say was that the processes would be "psychologically similar."

the fans. Note that the announcer need not be *correct* in his inferences about the fans or the athlete for him to be playing a role, and he *may* be playing a role even though seemingly totally objective and dispassionate in his description, for it may be his understanding of the athlete and/or the fans that that is the way they want the game called. What is critical to Kelly's notion of role is that the individual attempts to infer the view or outlook of another person.

The foregoing 12 statements—the fundamental postulate and 11 corollaries (in this book, Assertions 3–14)—constitute the basic structure of Kelly's theory. They do not, of course, exhaust the content of the theory. Several other assertions are needed to have a reasonably complete comprehension of what Kelly intended his theory to be and to do. A major criticism of Kelly's theory, made by this writer (Sechrest, 1963) and more recently by Levy (1970), is that nothing in it links an individual's construct system to his behavior. That is, there does not appear to be any provision in the theory for the prediction of specific behaviors. Levy refers to the missing link as the *operation function* and notes that it is absent in most cognitive-perceptual theories. In most other cognitive-perceptual theories *incongruity* results in initiation of action to reduce the tension produced by the incongruity. However, as Levy notes, incongruity plays no part in Kelly's theory. Kelly did not deal at all with the prediction of behavior in terms of his theory, but in a posthumously published work, he set forth his views about behavior as an element in his theory (Kelly, 1969). In that paper Kelly makes the following assertion:

15.   Behavior is man's way of posing a question.

How can behavior pose a question? At this point Kelly reverts to his notion of "every man a scientist" and reminds us that the behavior of scientists as scientists is not seen as the outcome of a sequence of unavoidable events. Rather, the scientist intervenes actively in some process, behaving in such a way to get an answer to a question. Why, then, should it be supposed that the behavior of more ordinary men, or that the behavior of scientists in their more ordinary moments, is somehow or other so very different? Our behaviors, Kelly insists, should be thought of as our own independent variables in the experiment of living. It would be virtually impossible to understand the behavior of a chemist testing a substance without taking into account the purpose of the chemist's behavior, the question he would like to answer. Similarly, Kelly suggests, we lack an adequate understanding of a person behaving in a hostile manner if we do not understand the question he is posing by that behavior. What question? The following are possible: Are these people strong enough to stand up to me when I am nasty, or can I brow beat them? Do these people love me enough that I can be bad when I need to? Are these people really as nice as they have always seemed or do they, too, have a mean streak?

Like the scientist, the man-as-scientist also has in mind some hypothesis about the outcomes expected from his behavior, and consequently his hypotheses may be confirmed or disconfirmed. However, Kelly points out that confirmation and disconfirmation, like other events, depend in part on the way the original question was asked and the way the outcome is construed. Thus, for example, there may be self-fulfilling prophecies for which disconfirmation is scarcely at issue, at least from an outsider's point of view. Other hypotheses (questions) may be phrased so loosely that the nature of the confirmation would appear inappropriate, although to the person putting the questions, they might seem reasonable and the answers satisfactory. The important point about confirmations as Kelly sees it is that they suggest that one has a construct system that permits some events to be more or less well anticipated; there always remains the good possibility that the construct system can and will be improved and will do a better job.

Perhaps Kelly never meant personal constructs theory to provide exact predictions of behavior. In his 1969 paper, much of which was devoted to the specific issue of understanding behavior, Kelly did not express any embarrassment concerning the failure of his theory to relate specifically to behavior. Kelly's view was that behavior is to be explained in terms of an ongoing, progressively moving sequence, rather than in terms of discrete units. Viewing behavior sequentially led Kelly to conclude that while it is perfectly possible to describe and perhaps to explain behavior in terms of "stimuli" leading to "responses," it is also possible, and Kelly thinks potentially even more profitable, to interrupt the sequence at a "response" and then observe what stimulus changes follow. For example, a young man may be invited by friends to a party, go with them to the party, find himself in exciting company, put forth some of his best social efforts, and make new friends. Surely it is possible to think of the invitation and the exciting company as stimuli and the attendance at the party and the putting forth of social efforts as responses to those stimuli. But suppose we begin one step further back and discover that the young man originally went to see his friends to ask what they were doing that evening. Then his behavior led to a particular set of stimuli that provided the occasion for another response that further affected his stimulus situation. The sequence of events that follows from a behavior contributes as much, Kelly believes, to our understanding of the behavior as do the antecedents of the behavior. Thus, perhaps behavior is not so much to be predicted as it is to be a focal point of study in order that one can understand the bets a person is placing in his life and the changes he seeks and produces.

Kelly also developed a system for thinking about the properties or characteristics of constructs. We will here follow the lead of Bannister and Mair (1968) in presenting Kelly's views first with respect to the more or less formal characteristics of constructs and then in terms of the ways in which constructs relate to their elements. However, as a general proposition, we might begin with an assertion that Kelly might have made.

16.   *Constructs possess formal properties that help to understand the processes of construing.*

The most obvious aspect of constructs is the *labels*, usually verbal, that attach to either side of the dichotomy. However, Kelly did not believe that labels were always necessary, nor that they especially needed to be verbal. He also did not believe that the fact that two persons had constructs with highly similar labels meant that the constructs were actually similar. A construct may be represented by a *symbol* that stands not only for itself but for the construct by which it is abstracted; for example, one of the writer's students employed a construct associated with feelings of near panic which she could only describe as "the blocked doorway situation." The things or events to which a construct applies or which it abstracts are called *elements*, and the *context* of a construct is the set of elements to which the construct usually applies.

Any construct has two *poles*, one on each side of the dichotomy. Whatever elements are abstracted by the construct are like each other at each pole and unlike the elements at the opposite pole. For example, the construct *good quality–poor quality* may abstract a wide variety of elements such as refrigerators, jewelry, beer, and novels. All the things that are abstracted as good quality become in that way alike and at the same time different from those things lumped together on the poor quality side of the dividing line. The term *likeness end*[5] is used to describe that side of a construct that is the focus of attention at any given time, and *contrast end* refers then to the opposite pole. If one describes several items as alike because they are of good quality, then good quality may be thought of as the likeness and poor quality as the contrast end of the construct. In another instance, however, those descriptors could be reversed. In any given usage or context in which a construct is employed, one side of the construct will often appear to account for the larger portion of the context. When that is so, that side is called the *emergent pole* of the construct. If a student is contemplating the purchase of a motorcycle and says, "The Japanese makes are of good quality," that would represent the emergent pole of his construct. The *implicit pole* of a construct refers to the contrast side of the emergent pole. The implicit pole may be or even need not be stated, and in some instances the person may have no ready way of symbolizing it; but its existence is implicit in the emergent term.

The *range of convenience* of a construct refers to the extent of breadth of things or events for which a user of a construct finds it useful, and the *focus of convenience* refers to those things for which the construct would be optimally useful. For example, the construct *threadbare*—one pole of the construct would probably have as its focus of convenience things made of

---

[5]The writer himself is a bit uncomfortable with the use of either *end* or *pole* to designate one side of a dichotomy, since either term seems semantically to imply a continuum. However, *end* and *pole* are the terms used by Kelly.

cloth, but still for many persons the notion of "threadbare ideas" or "threadbare plots" is acceptable, that is, ideas and plots lie within the range of convenience of the construct. However, automobiles, dogs, and hamburgers lie well outside the range of convenience of threadbareness, at least for most people.

Another assertion derivable from Kelly's theory is here labeled Assertion 17.

17. Constructs may be characterized by aspects that account for differences and similarities in the ways they function.

Not only do people's construct systems differ from one another, but even within the same construct system (i.e., one person's system), constructs function in widely different ways. The way constructs function is to be understood in terms of characteristics of the constructs, recognizing that what we are talking about here is constructs about constructs. These constructs about constructs are no more inherent in the constructs themselves than sincerity is inherent in behavior being construed. There are some ways of thinking about constructs that Kelly found useful in anticipating the application of constructs.

Constructs differ in terms of their *permeability*, the extent to which a construct can take newly perceived elements into its context. The construct *patriotic* is permeable if the user is willing to consider new elements as potentially patriotic. If the user believes that the age of patriotism is past, then the construct would be impermeable. A *comprehensive* construct is applicable to a wide range of events, while an *incidental* construct is applicable to only a narrow range. For most people the construct *good–bad* would be comprehensive, while a construct such as *neat–messy* would be relatively incidental. *Tight* constructs lead to unvarying predictions, while *loose* constructs result in predictions that vary from time to time and occasion to occasion. If the construct *moral–immoral* were a tight construct for a particular individual, it might result in the invariant prediction that any person construed as immoral would be unlikeable. Used loosely, it might result on some occasions in the prediction that a person construed as immoral would prove to be unlikeable and on others that an immoral person would be likeable. A *core* construct is fundamental to an individual's maintenance of himself as a person, and a *peripheral* construct is one with only limited implications for those processes. Core constructs can be changed only with difficulty and with far-reaching consequences, whereas peripheral constructs are more easily changed, and changes do not ramify throughout an individual's construct system. As was suggested earlier, one construct may include another construct as one of its elements, in which case it is a *superordinate* construct; if one is referring to the construct included as an element, the appropriate term is *subordinate* construct. Core constructs tend to be superordinate, and peripheral constructs tend to be subordinate, but the terms super- and subordinate are definitely relative.

Constructs also differ in terms of the obviousness and accessibility of distinguishing labels or symbols. Some constructs lack consistent verbal labels and are called *preverbal*. Such constructs may have been formed prior to the development of high-level language skills. Many constructs that relate to such feelings as security are preverbal or are inconsistently labeled. If one or the other pole of a construct is less available for use, it is termed *submerged*. For many people the term *hippie* represents one end of a construct used to construe people who seem to represent that type; the opposite side of the dichotomy is less consistently labeled and is not ordinarily invoked as a description. Sometimes a revision of a construct system will result in the omission from the context of a construct a particular element once subsumed by the construct. Such an omitted element is said to be *suspended*. An example might be a revision in a person's use of the construct *moral–immoral* in such a way that another person once judged immoral is excluded from the context and is simply no longer subsumed under the construct. It was Kelly's belief that some of the phenomena thought of by psychoanalytically inclined clinicians as "unconscious" could involve suspended elements. In general, Kelly believed that *level of cognitive awareness* differs from construct to construct, with some involving a high level of awareness, that is, with socially effective symbols, readily accessible construct poles, and not involving suspended elements, while others involve lower levels of cognitive awareness.

Another way constructs differ is in how they relate to, or control, their elements. If an element belongs exclusively to the realm of one construct, the construct is then a *preemptive* construct. There is a strong tendency during wartime, for example, for participants to apply the label "the enemy" in a preemptive way. That is: If he is the enemy, then he is nothing but the enemy. He need not be thought of as human, as a father, as a worker doing his job, or as a lover of good music. He is the enemy, and that is it. Somewhat in contrast to the preemptive construct, the *constellatory* construct determines other constructions of its elements. The commonly encountered "halo effect" in ratings of people is a good example of constellatory construction. If a person is construed as successful, then he is also likely to be construed as intelligent, handsome, friendly, and so on. Stereotypes involve constellatory constructs: To complete the set of contrasts here, the *propositional* construct involves no particular assumptions about the applicability of other constructs. The construct *enemy-friend*, used in a propositional way to construe someone as an enemy, does not have any particular implications for other characteristics such as intelligence and quality as a human being. Preemptiveness, constellatoriness, and propositionality are relative terms. Probably every construct is in some degree preemptive and at the same time also in some degree constellatory and propositional. It is a question of which characteristic is predominant.

There is a final general proposition to be considered, again a proposition not stated by Kelly but used here to introduce those ideas that relate Kelly's thinking to the more familiar terms of personality and clinical psychology.

18. *Many of the important processes of personality and behavior arise as a person attempts to change or is threatened with forced change in his construct system.*

Kelly supposed, probably out of theoretical necessity, that the most important phenomena of personality arise out of the prospects for change or actual changes in construct systems. After all, a perfectly static system, just chugging along in a satisfactory way, would not produce much material of interest. Kelly related the various possibilities for change in construct systems to some of the major constructs or issues that have concerned personality theorists over the years (e.g., 1955, pp. 486–533). However, Kelly related his own ideas to those of others only in limited ways, and while he came to use some of the same terms as other theorists, he used them in special ways, and no direct translations should be contemplated. The problem is something like that of false cognates between languages; there is some sort of a connection, but it is misleadingly indirect or incomplete. For example, the French word *ancien*, meaning *former*, and the English word *ancient* are obviously related but cannot be taken as cognates. Similarly, while it is probably true that Kelly's notion of anxiety is related to the ideas of anxiety held by other theorists, the constructs are clearly not intersubstitutable. It is important for the student of Kelly to understand familiar terms as Kelly uses them and not as they are commonly used.

In the Fragmentation Corollary, Kelly indicates that a person may successively employ construct subsystems incompatible with one another. The incompatibility may be tolerable, but it may also lead the person to try to change his construct system to reduce or eliminate the incompatibility. A typical example would be a person whose religious tenets are at variance with his everyday life. There are two opposite processes by which the incompatibility may be reduced. One is to broaden his perceptual field in order to reorganize it on a more comprehensive level, a process called *dilation*. A person might, for example, attempt to develop superordinate philosophical constructs to reconcile apparent contradictions between his everyday behavior and his professed religious principles. There was a time, as an instance, when American businessmen adopted a Calvinist view that wealth was a sign of God's favor and therefore a wide variety of sharp business practices was rationalized and made "right." On the other hand, a person might also try to reduce incompatibilities by narrowing his perceptual field so as to exclude parts of it, a process referred to as *constriction*. A person might give up religious practices, the reading of moral treatises, and so on as a way of eliminating incompatibilities between them and his everyday life.

At times a person may be faced with the necessity for change in his construct system. Depending upon the extent and nature of the change, the person might or might not be troubled. Presumably most changes in peripheral constructs will be easily tolerated. Invalidation of the prediction that "All Mexican foods are spicy" should not upset anyone, and even a revision of one's food construct system to distinguish "hot" from "heavily seasoned" foods should not present any special problems. However, the prospect of change in core structures, those governing the very maintenance of a sense of personal identity and integrity, is likely to prove troublesome.

Kelly distinguishes three types of reactions to change in core structures: fear, threat, and guilt. *Fear* is the awareness of imminent incidental change in one's core structures. A rider is likely to experience fear when his horse bolts, bringing about thoughts of being thrown and bodily damage. Still the fundamental identity and integrity of the rider would probably not be jeopardized. Even the risk of death might represent a relatively incidental change if it promised only the end of life and not devastating damage to a person's reputation. *Threat* is defined by Kelly as awareness of an imminent comprehensive change in one's core structures. Death would be relatively more threatening if it carried with it the likely degradation and insult to dignity of the person. If a person had spent his whole life building up a reputation as an expert in some field and if crucial aspects of his identity were involved in that reputation, then what might appear otherwise to be a fairly incidental and ever peripheral change resulting from being wrong about something could be a source of threat.

Guilt is also related to changes in core structure, specifically to changes in core role structures. Those aspects of the core structure that enable the individual to predict and control essential interactions of himself with other persons and groups constitute his *core role*. The experience of guilt lies in one's apparent dislodgement from one's core role structure. For example, a young man may construe himself in relation to his girl friend as a responsible, dependable, and caring lover, and he will enact this role in the light of his understanding or interpretation of his girl friend's behavior. If an important part of his being, of his identity as a person is involved in this role, then it is a part of his core role structure. Suppose one day he can only construe his recent behavior as irresponsible, undependable, and uncaring. Then he will feel guilt.

Another very similar young man may construe women as exploitable objects for the gratification of men, as placed on earth to nurture men, and the same behavior of irresponsibility, undependability, and uncaringness will produce no guilt at all. Kelly states that guilt need not be thought of as awareness of evil, but that notion is not incompatible with guilt as dislodgement from core role structure. Kelly does not insist that dislodgement from core role structure needs to be voluntary. Some Moslems would feel equally bad upon learning that they had accidentally eaten pork as they would if they had eaten it deliberately (an act they could scarcely comprehend, however). As defined by Kelly, guilt may as well involve awareness of inadequacy, weakness, or physical limitations as of evil. A person who fails to save a drowning child for want of knowing how to swim may feel as guilty as a person who fails for cowardice. Guilt would depend upon the degree to which being protective in relation to the child (or children) was a part of the core role structure.

Upon occasion we may become aware that perceived events lie mostly outside the range of convenience of our construct systems, in which case we will experience *anxiety*. "Things that go bump in the night," for example, produce anxiety only when they seem to be unconstruable. Once one figures out that a raccoon has knocked over the garbage can, anxiety disappears. On the other hand, if the noise is clearly construable as an intruder, the experience is fear, not anxiety. Anxiety is not produced merely by being wrong; anxiety is the result of a wrong prediction with no alternative to take its place. Anxiety may be experienced over trivial matters or over critical ones. A chess player bewildered at the unfamiliar and impenetrable strategy of an opponent may be said to be anxious, although probably not to the same degree, as a physician whose patient begins to go into a state of complete physiological collapse for unknown reasons. One defense against anxiety, says Kelly, is a loosening of the construct system so that it can encompass more events by permitting greater variability in construction of them from time to time or by relaxing the requirements by which they are fit into categories. If a chess player's construction system for different strategies can be loosened somewhat, he may see something familiar in his opponent's style that will reduce his own anxiety. Or if the physician faced with a rapidly deteriorating patient can loosen his system a bit, the patient may be construed as simply an anomalous case not fitting textbook patterns and expectations.

When a person is faced with an enforced change in his core structure, he will be threatened if the change is relatively comprehensive and will experience fear if the change is likely to be only incidental. Any awareness of events confronting him which lie outside the range of convenience of his construct system will make the person anxious. Presumably if the person is in the process of actively seeking to change his construct system, he will not feel afraid or threatened, although anxiety may be the stimulus to change. One type of change in the construct system that may make it at least temporarily more effective is a conceptual reorganization based on either broadening or narrowing the perceptual field so as to change perspectives and take account of a wider or narrower range of events. Broadening the perceptual field is called *dilation*, and narrowing it is called *constriction*.

Two additional maneuvers a person may perform when his construct system proves inadequate or otherwise unsatisfactory are aggressiveness and hostility. When a person actively attempts to elaborate his perceptual

field, Kelly calls this *aggressiveness*. Aggressiveness involves action and initiative rather than attack. The aggressive person takes matters into his own
hands, presses issues rather than just letting them lie. Kelly's view of aggressiveness is closer to the usage implicit in speaking of aggressive salesmen
or aggressive tennis players rather than of criminal behavior and fighting.
Kelly thinks of aggressiveness as the active extending and elaboration of the
perceptual field so that one can incorporate more and more events into
one's construct system. From Kelly's viewpoint an aggressive salesman actively pushes to extend his ability to anticipate, and hence to control, the
events with which he must deal, whether they involve other people or more
impersonal processes of the marketplace.

Hostility, according to Kelly's theory, is the continued effort to extort
validating evidence in favor of a social prediction that is failing or which has
already failed. The myth of Procrustes' bed is the archetype for hostility.
Procrustes had a bed which he insisted all of his visitors must fit. If his
guests were too short, he stretched them some, and if they were too long, he
cut off their legs. Procrustes always validated his prediction that anyone
could fit his bed. Similarly, says Kelly, forcing people or events to fit our
construct system, rather than the other way around, is hostility. A mother
who keeps trying to validate her predictions about her "darling little girl,"
long after it is amply clear that the girl is neither darling nor little, is showing hostility. Bribery is another nonobvious display of hostility, for it
amounts to an attempt to extort a confirmation of a prediction that is not
working out. Probably most of the things that we would ordinarily think of
as hostility would also be called hostile by Kelly, but the commonality of his
view of hostility is an attempt to force someone else or some other things to
fit one's private view of the world.

Two other processes of change in Kelly's system have no clear counterparts in other personality theories. The *C-P-C Cycle* (circumspection-
preemption-control) has to do with how we make construction choices,
since there are a variety of ways in which any set of events may be construed. When faced with the necessity for choice, the usual sequence is to
apply a series of constructs propositionally, a process termed *circumspec-
tion*. For example, a student with a Friday evening facing him may construe
the evening successively or simultaneously as an opportunity to rest and
relax, or as an opportunity to fulfill obligations by writing letters. Sooner or
later, however, if he is not to lose control of the situation altogether, the
student must construe the evening *preemptively*, in terms of one or the other
of the available constructs. "O.K. To study or not to study, that's it. That is
the real issue and nothing else." Then having decided what the crucial
choice is, the student will choose that alternative through which he
anticipates greater extension or elaboration of his system. If he chooses not
to study, then he will have to go through another C-P-C Cycle in order to
arrive at another preemptive construct. But the student may also get stuck

ple and the technique quite straightforward, the final directions arrived at by Kelly were the result of many trials and revisions. A verbatim quotation of the directions gives an indication of what is involved. Kelly states that the clinician may say:

> I want you to write a character sketch of Harry Brown (i.e., client's name), just as if he were the principal character in a play. Write it as it might be written by a friend who knew him very *intimately* and very *sympathetically*, perhaps better than anyone ever really could know him. Be sure to write it in the third person. For example, start out by saying, 'Harry Brown is. . . .' (1955, p. 323)

According to Kelly, "The object of this kind of inquiry is to see how the client structures a world in relation to which he must maintain himself in some kind of role." (1955, p. 324)

Analysis of the Self-Characterization is clinical rather than quantitative and is based on several different types of cues to important material, including the sequence of and transition between topics, the organization of the material, terms that are repeated and linked, shifts of emphasis, and different contexts provided for interpretation. The personal constructs clinician is looking, of course, for the dimensions, or constructs, through which the client attempts to make sense of his life and experience. Topical areas covered and themes presented are also important in the analysis.

Neither the Self-Characterization nor the RCRT (REP test) has been standardized or provided with norms to make objective interpretation possible. However, Fransella and Bannister (1977) have provided a highly useful manual on how to quantify and analyze the RCRT. Aside from research uses that permit rather arbitrary, if quantitative, analyses, both instruments are dependent upon clinical acumen.

Treatment

Applicability is the raison d'etre of Kelly's theory. The major emphasis in Volume 2 of Kelly's work is treatment, and even a fairly cursory reading reveals that Kelly was a flexible, imaginative, "mainstream" therapist. He proposes no tricks, the transcripts that he presents produce no great surprises, and he appears to have thought and worked as a therapist about the same as most other therapists think and work. He attempted to produce changes in patients' cognitions, to get them to explore new forms of behavior and to explore and express their innermost feelings. Neimeyer (1981) has acquired a set of therapy tapes representing Kelly's work. The transcripts are quite interesting and bear out the views expressed here of Kelly as a therapist.

In many discussions of Kelly's views about therapy, there has been an almost total concern with *fixed-role therapy*. Kelly devoted a whole chapter to fixed-role therapy in the first, more theoretical volume of his book. Fixed-role therapy represented a considerable departure from standard practice at the time Kelly proposed it, and the prominence he gave it probably led many of his readers to suppose that it constituted Kelly's major therapeutic intervention and, perhaps, his treatment of choice. Yet, fixed-role therapy was never even attempted on more than a handful of cases, was not a major feature of Kelly's teaching about therapy, and was never a focus of any lasting research effort. Because it is so consistent with Kelly's theory, however, it is worthwhile to take a brief look at fixed-role therapy.

Kelly believed that we all are unnecessarily constrained by our view of things, how we construe things. Our health-related behavior, for example, is determined by what we believe about our health rather than by the "objective" facts. People who seek help with their personal problems are likely to be victims of their particular (and not especially useful) ways of looking at things. Their views and resulting choices are what get people into trouble. If people could be led to view things differently and to try new choices or behaviors, their lot in life might improve, along with their views. A shy, timid soul validates his predictions about other people; for example, if he slinks around and keeps out of their way, people leave him alone, and if he asserts himself occasionally, he meets with rebuffs. The problem faced by the therapist is how to get a person to try new behaviors, to "lay some new bets" on the outcome of which the construct system may be changed, for example, so as to view people in terms other than say *tolerant* versus *intimidating*.

Fixed-role therapy was developed as a way of helping therapy clients try out new behaviors. Kelly perceived that people have difficulty in simply "trying out" new behaviors because the therapist tells them to. The suggestion that the client should change himself in fundamental ways is often quite threatening. Kelly wanted a procedure that would permit people to "try on new behaviors for size." He believed trying new behaviors temporarily might facilitate change in the client's construct system. To help the client explore new behaviors and new ways of thinking, the therapist employing fixed-role therapy prepares for the client a role sketch, a prescription for behavior, which the client is to play out in various situations, beginning with roleplaying. The behaviors are not necessarily behaviors the therapist thinks the client ought to adopt permanently. Rather, they are behaviors devised to open new possibilities for the client to consider, new ways of looking at things as well as new behaviors. While roles are written with the aim of providing sharp contrasts to a client's usual ways of behaving, the client is afforded the protection of a "make believe" activity that does not require any commitment and hence is thought not to arouse much initial resistance or sense of hopelessness about bring about lasting change.

In employing fixed-role therapy, extensive use is made of Self-Characterization as a guide to developing the role, with an emphasis placed upon providing interesting and potentially useful contrasts. Therapy sessions are devoted to exploring the implications of the role and actually practicing the playing of the role vis-à-vis the therapist. Later sessions are devoted to discussions of experiences in playing the role and in the changes the role brings about in behavior and outlook.

The emphasis placed on fixed-role therapy by reviewers of Kelly's work is understandable, but it is largely misplaced in terms of the more usual ways in which Kelly went about therapy and helped his students learn it. It is clear from the material presented in Volume 2 of *The Psychology of Personal Constructs* that Kelly's therapeutic techniques usually involved heavy reliance on face-to-face interviews, such as might be employed by most other "talk" therapies. Naturally, Kelly's aims in therapy, as well as some of his specific therapeutic tactics, reflected his concerns with the construct systems of his clients and his attempts to understand those systems, to bring his clients to an understanding of them, and to bring about change in them. However, even though it might seem that Kelly's therapy is heavily cognitive—perhaps even intellectualization to some—he was much attuned to the need for *behavior* change, and clients were encouraged strongly and helped in definite ways to try out new behaviors outside the therapy setting. Kelly expressed over and over his conviction that the proof of any theory, including any theory held by a client, is in the accuracy of predictions to be made from it. Consequently, he quite carefully led clients to test the implications of their views of things by altering their behaviors to see whether the anticipated results in fact did occur. He also believed that therapists needed constantly to check their understanding of their clients by making verifiable predictions about them. If a therapist really understood a client, the therapist could predict what the client would talk about in the next therapy session, what happened at home between sessions, and how the client would react to a specific suggestion for new behavior.

Probably the best statement of Kelly's view of the psychotherapy situation is that he thought of it as a laboratory where the client could carry out experiments that might be impossible or hazardous in real life. The client in therapy can test alternative views, can try out different behaviors, in actuality or symbolically, and so on, without fear of dire consequences. The therapist's task is to facilitate such experimentation. Kelly did not, however, think of the therapist as some sort of a passive matrix within which the client's experiments could be carried to conclusion. Rather, he conceived the therapist to be an active facilitator and in some cases even an instigator of the client's experimentation. Kelly described therapy as a carefully planned enterprise and not a spontaneous, "let's see what happens today" activity. It was incumbent on the therapist to know just what was going on at all times, to anticipate what would occur in every session, and to plan the kind of activities that would bring about desired client behavior. In particular, Kelly made heavy use of *enactment* procedures, quite similar to roleplaying but perhaps more flexible in conception and practice. It was in enacting various problems and possibilities that the client could carry out his within-session experiments and explore new ways of seeing his world.

A good indication of the nature of therapy as Kelly proposed it can be had from suggestions he made concerning ways of encouraging psychotherapeutic experimentation (1955, pp. 1127–1135). The first technique is *permissiveness*. Kelly viewed it as a technique rather than, as for Rogers, a pervasive outlook. He believed that by taking a permissive attitude the therapist provided the patient with a setting in which experimentation could safely be carried on, without fear of recrimination or embarrassment. The second technique is reaction on the part of the therapist. When the client experiments, something must happen, and that happening is the task of the therapist, whether it be a facial expression, a gesture, a comment, or an invitation to further experimentation. The third technique is the therapist's *creativity* in providing some novel situation in which old, familiar modes of responses are not appropriate. While it may at times be advantageous for a client to be in a novel life situation (e.g., a vacation in a new place), the therapist can also provide novelty within the therapy situation itself by such tactics as changing his manner on occasion or changing the rules by which sessions are conducted. A fourth technique which may at times be required is to provide *equipment* which gives the client the "tools" necessary to carry out experimentation. A client may not be able to explore new types of employment or social interactions without proper clothing, and an adolescent may need financial assistance to plan a date. The fifth technique is to get the client to *hypothesize*, preferably in the form of reasonably specific predictions. The client who has stated a fairly specific prediction based on his own behavior will find it difficult to resist carrying out the experiment. *Interpretation* is still another technique for promoting experimentation. In Kellian therapy, this refers to the interpretations made by the client. If the client can be led to interpret the behavior of others, he or she will experience strong pressures to find out more about the views of those people, to fill in gaps of knowledge and understanding. The seventh and eighth techniques involve getting the client to try to portray how another person views himself and how another person *views* the client.

These techniques, along with interpretations, involve role constructs, the client's understanding of another person's construct system in relation to himself, and valuable clues for the client as to what behaviors may be expected from others and what effects his own behavior may have on other people. Still another technique, *biographical hypotheses*, is designed to get the client to elaborate the biographical conditions under which he would behave differently. For example, if the client claims that his behavior is the result of inadequate behavior on the part of parental figures, the client can be asked to describe the sorts of conditions that would have to have existed in order for different behavior to be possible. The therapist can then utilize the hypothesized links between the client's revised biography and the behavior expected to promote experimentation. Finally, Kelly notes that experimentation may be facilitated by the direct approaches of *encouraging* a client directly to experiment, to try something out, and by *manipulation*—putting a client into situations in which there are good social examples of the kind of behavior desired. If a client has difficulty in "letting go," in behaving spontaneously and expressively, exploration with such behavior in some situations is clearly easier than in others.

Mention needs to be made of the "axis" of "tightening" and "loosening" as applied to therapeutic activities. The axis refers to the exactness and variability with which predictions can be made from constructs (Kelly, 1955, pp. 39–40), and creativity requires an initial loosening of constructs followed by tightening. Given this, it is clear why the loosening and tightening of constructs becomes a major focus of activity for a Kellian therapist. Loosening of thought is characteristic of fantasy, including dreams, and Kelly notes the usefulness of dreams as material for exploration in therapy. However, loosening is also produced by relaxation, by chain association, and by the therapist's uncritical acceptance of the client. When tightening becomes desirable, it is produced by encouraging the client to take a judgmental attitude, by asking the client to "step aside" and take a look at his or her own behavior, to summarize what he or she has been saying and to take a historical approach to his or her thoughts. The therapist encourages tightening by determining whether the client can relate his or her thinking, by asking the client directly to be more explicit, asking for validating evidence, attempting time-binding of constructs, and other similar techniques.

All of Kelly's therapeutic maneuvers, however similar they may seem to those of some other therapists, have as their aim the altering of a client's construct system in such a way as to make likely more useful and accurate predictions and ultimately more extensive control over the client's fate.

Institutional

Kelly had no questions about the implications of his views for various social institutions. Perhaps the most important implication was that it is necessary for institutions to recognize that the problems they see in their clientele reside in the views of the institutions themselves, rather than being inherent in the clients. When a school regards a portion of its pupils as lazy or as unteachable, that does not change the pupils in any way, and it does not necessarily tell us much about the pupils. What it tells us is something about the school and the way it chooses to see reality. When a school comes to regard its failures as having origins in characteristics of the pupils, that view then determines much of the subsequent response of the school to those failures, a phenomenon Caplan and Nelson (1973) called "blaming the victim." As Kelly was fond of noting, the very child labeled "lazy" by a teacher might very well seem extraordinarily active to another observer. The important question is, what kind of a school or teacher views pupils as lazy?

And once pupils are viewed as lazy (versus industrious), who can doubt that the same laziness will be found again and again? The very label leads to the prediction that if the student is given a new challenge, laziness will be the response, and the prediction works just about every time. What is needed in such a situation is a new way of looking at children, of construing them and their behavior, which will lead to more useful and productive institutional behavior. Note that in Kelly's view, to the extent that a school insists on viewing some of its pupils as lazy and continues to try to produce evidence for the accuracy of its predictions, the school is coming close to what Kelly would call hostility.

It may not be obvious that institutions have construct systems just as individuals do, but it can be useful to think of institutions in such a way. Consider, for example, a prison system. It is likely to be primarily characterized by the superordinate construct of *prisoner–nonprisoner*. The construct ramifies throughout the prison system and affects almost everything that goes on in it. Then, too, the prisoner construct is quite likely to be applied preemptively; that is, an inmate of the prison is a prisoner and nothing but a prisoner. He is, perhaps, scarcely regarded as human, let alone as a husband or lover, a father, a friend, a worker, a fisherman, or a philosophical thinker. The preemptive construct of prisoner is likely, then, also to imply a constellation of other characteristics—such as dangerous, stupid, immoral, prone to escape, potential troublemaker, and animalistic—which leads inexorably to methods of management that all but ensure that the constellation will be validated. Such a construct system (only a part of it has been pointed to here) can be as characteristic of an institution as of an individual and just as surely can determine choices and institutional treatment.

What is needed in institutions are more useful construct systems that could make greater use of propositional constructs (e.g., this man is a prisoner and he may also be a father, a fisherman, and a nice guy—or he may not be) and permeable constructs which can take account of new events (e.g., he is a youthful drug offender and may not have all the characteristics so often found in other prisoners). Institutions should provide more opportunities for people to change, elaborate, and test their construct systems, occasions on which people can grow. If, for example, some children do not have a chance to change their conception of themselves as "dumb," their behavior is likely to continue in the same old destructive grooves. That does not mean that such children necessarily have to come to think of themselves as "smart" or as standing in some other contrast to dumb. The change might involve tightening up the construct somewhat by delimiting it (e.g.,

"I'm dumb in math but not in social studies or in fishing"), or it might involve abandoning the *dumb-smart* construct as a major way of differentiating among people, including the self. Schools, prisons, hospitals, mental health clinics, welfare agencies, and probably most other social institutions all too often construe their clientele—and their own roles—in terms that tend to foster the very behaviors they are in existence to eliminate. These institutions do not often enough provide opportunities for change in construct systems through experimentation and creativity cycles. To the extent that institutions are meant to be therapeutic or to help people change, they need to provide for the same kinds of growth experiences as are provided by psychotherapists.

Self

Both the Self-Characterization and the Role Constructs Repertory Test are so simple in conception and (at least at some levels) in analysis that any reasonably intelligent person could complete them without professional assistance. A careful study of both could well be a fruitful enterprise, perhaps surprising in outcome for many persons. Most of us are too little aware of the nature of our construct systems and of the views and choices that they entail. Consider, for example, the construct *intelligent-stupid* often found on the RCRT protocols of college students. The very fact that people are dealt with in terms of this dimension is of interest when one thinks of the many alternatives that might have been employed. For example, would not *advantaged-disadvantaged* provide equally good predictions in many areas of human functioning, and would not such a construct have quite different implications for the ways in which one might relate to and try to help people? Would the construct *interested in the same things as I-interested in different things* overlap the *intelligent-stupid* construct and be more constructive in many instances? To what extent is the *intelligent-stupid* construct used propositionally as opposed to constellatorily? If it is a propositional construct, then we may say that an individual is, among many other things, stupid. He may or may not also be friendly, pleasant, unclean, good looking, and cruel. But, in fact, the construct more often than not carries with it a constellation of other traits so that the person construed as stupid is automatically assumed to be unworthy, dirty, cruel, unpleasant, ugly, guilty of poor manners, and a host of other things.

Constellatory constructs often lead to nonconstructive but stubbornly persistent ways of thought and action. When used preemptively, the *intelligent-stupid* construct suggests that an individual need not be regarded as anything *but* stupid (or intelligent). He is stupid, and that is all there is to it! He is not a fine fellow, a good athlete, or someone's sweetheart; he is stupid! It is worth asking ourselves just what kinds of constructs we have and how we ordinarily apply them. Note that the *intelligent–stupid* construct is couched in fairly extreme terms, especially at what we would take to be the unfavorable end. It is probably not without meaning that the construct is rarely, if ever, labeled *genius–stupid* or *brilliant–stupid*, for to do so would be to establish a very discomfiting dichotomy when applied to most of us. And yet, the construct is fairly demanding with respect to the behaviors of most people most of the time, for the alternative to doing something postively intelligent seems to be to do something positively stupid. That is a high standard to expect most people to meet much of the time or to expect anybody to meet all of the time. The range of convenience of the construct is also worth examining, because if it applies only to a very narrow range of behaviors, its implications may be limited; for example, if it applies only to academic behaviors, most of what most people do most of the time will escape the judgment implied. However, if the construct has a very wide range of convenience, it will result in many judgments about many people. The construct might be relatively impermeable with respect to behaviors that are to be accounted for; for example, the construct might be developed in a predominantly academic context and be impermeable to events met later in life outside that context. Thus a former student might be unable to admit such behaviors as throwing a pot, caring for a family, and welding a broken rod to the realm of the *intelligent–stupid* construct. And finally, the construct may be used in either a relatively tight or a loose way, as reflected in the definiteness of the predictions to which it leads. If the construct is a tight one, the person employing it will expect *intelligent* people to be quite consistent in their behavior and to conform fairly closely to expectations. A tight use of the construct might result in the statement, "She is an intelligent woman; therefore, she will not watch stupid daytime soap opera TV programs." A looser construct might lead to such a statement as "She is an intelligent woman; therefore, she will not be overly fond of some of the less intellectual TV programs."

From Kelly's viewpoint, we are constantly evolving our construct systems. However, not all of our construct creation attempts need be accidental or unplanned. Just as the scientist plans deliberate experiments to test his hypotheses, so may we experiment deliberately with our construct systems, trying new ways of looking at things, extending our predictions into previously unexplored areas, and observing carefully the consequences of successive tightening and loosening of our constructs. We may ask ourselves the question "What would happen if...?" and try to get an answer to it. We will ordinarily find it easiest to experiment and try to elaborate our construct systems at times or in areas in which we feel most comfortable and sure of ourselves; we will, correspondingly, find it difficult to experiment elaboratively when we are insecure and will attempt then to achieve greater definiton of our systems. For example, the time for a young man to invite a new date is in a situation that he has well under control; the first formal reception he attends, or a dance being given in honor of the mayor's daughter, is a good time to stick with a partner who is predictable and dependable.

The result of our planned experimentation with new constructs should be an elaborated and more useful system, making it possible for us to function effectively in new areas, with new people, and with new problems not previously manageable. Many students, for example, have a great deal of difficulty relating to their college professors, viewing them as aloof rather than friendly, as intellectuals rather than interested in ordinary things, as busy rather than as having spare time, and as uninterested rather than interested in students. However, professors are often lonely, bored, aware of one or two generation gaps, and convinced that nearly all students care nothing for their respective fields. Both students and professors could probably profit from more experimentation with their views of each others. Since this book is addressed to students, however, the point can be made here that suitable elaboration of and change in the construct systems that students apply to their professors and to academic work might very well lead to a more useful and satisfactory system that would promote rather than impede desired interactions and the students' ultimate intellectual and personal development. Similar changes could probably be explored in almost all areas of functioning (e.g., relationships with parents, vocational plans and social interactions). The key to improvement is recognition of the fundamental sense in which the person is a scientist, striving by experimentation to improve his understanding, prediction, and control of the events with which he must deal or chooses to deal.

VALIDATION

Kelly, at least as much as any other theorist, insisted that the proof of any theory lies in the accuracy of the predictions it permits. However, Kelly also recognized that a theory does not make predictions; *people* make predictions, based on a theory, and the accuracy of the predictions depends on the understanding and intelligence of the predictors as well as on the adequacy of the theory. Moreover, the outcome of any prediction will depend on the characteristics of the prediction. Obviously the tighter and more exact a prediction becomes, the greater the probability is that it will be proven wrong. On the other hand, predictions can be made that are so general that they are all but impossible to disprove. There is another problem with a theory as broad and general as Kelly's—no really direct test of the theory is possible. Only after years of research and application might it become possible to state in a general sort of way whether or not the theory seems tenable and useful. It is early, perhaps, to be evaluating Kelly's theory. It has taken 70 years or so for evidence relevant to the adequacy of psychoanalytic theory to accumulate to any interpretable bulk. Kelly's theory, not yet 30 years of age, is young.

Evidence

No special honesty is required to admit that the evidence bearing in any direct way on the adequacy of personal construct theory is disappointingly thin. For anyone having any sense of identification with Kelly or with his theory, the research product of the past 25 years is disheartening. Kelly's students never produced much work of central and critical relevance to the theory even when they were graduate students, and few of them, Alvin Landfield being the principal exception, are currently identifiable as Kellian theorists. A search of *Psychological Abstracts* will turn up only a small number of articles related to personal construct theory in any given year, and few of those will be research reports. The recent book entitled *Personal Construct Psychology: Psychotherapy and Personality* (Landfield & Leitner, 1980) presents no new findings and most of the research discussed lies outside the theory.

Most of the chapters in the book are discussions of the theory and its applications that, while interesting, are not in the nature of evidence. Other recent publications (Bannister, 1977; Fransella, 1975) are of the same nature.

Why the research base for Kelly's theory is so scant is difficult to say. Perhaps part of the problem is that Kelly was not himself an active research partisan of his own theory. He is not the author of a single piece of research on the theory, and it may be that he did not do a good job of engendering research enthusiasm in his students, at least not enthusiasm for the theory itself. Perhaps also the theory is so novel and so large that it is difficult for single investigators to get a good grasp on it. It may not be evident to a lot of potential researchers just what the important and testable propositions are. And perhaps Kelly was simply not approachable enough as a person to be able to instill in the students close to him a dedication and sense of identification that would keep them working once they had left his direct supervision. Kelly was a formal man, and he could be formidable, too.

The research that has been stimulated by Kelly's theory does not, for the most part, test propositions derived from the theory but provides elaboration of certain points in the theory. There is not space here to do a complete review of the research on psychology of personal constructs, but interested readers may want to consult Bonnarius (1965) for a review of early research and Bannister and Mair (1968) for a slight updating. The material to be presented here is more illustrative of what has been done rather than probative with respect to the theory.

One might begin with the issue whether personal constructs as elicited from individuals are of any particular value in understanding the person, it being possible, often with less effort, to get other comparable information, such as ratings on standard lists of traits or constructs. Kelly's theory proposes that an individual's processes are psychologically channelized by the way *he* anticipates events, not by the way in which events are usually anticipated or ought to be anticipated, or whatever. The issue can be put in concrete terms by asking whether the construct *intelligence* is generally useful, or whether it is more useful for people who spontaneously use it themselves in construing the behavior of other people. In the earliest study bearing on this point, Payne (1956) determined that better predictions about individuals are made from knowledge of those individuals' personal constructs than from rating of those individuals by other persons; that is, knowing the constructs an individual uses in describing others is more useful than knowing the constructs that others apply to him. That finding is of definite interest for the personal construct theorist, but it is in no way critical. However, other findings generally support the notion that the individual's own personal constructs are of particular value in understanding and predicting reactions.

In a series of studies, Landfield and his associates (Landfield & Nawas, 1964; Nawas & Landfield, 1963; Ourth & Landfield, 1965) have found that it is important for therapists to understand the language systems of clients as reflected in personal constructs and, most interestingly, that clients who improve in therapy tend to become more strongly committed to their own construct systems rather than coming to adopt the construct system of their therapists. Carr (1980) developed a simplified version of the RCRT, which he calls the *Interpersonal Discrimination Task*, to measure the complexity of personal construct systems. He found that patients improved more in psychotherapy if the complexity of their systems matched that of the therapists to whom they were assigned. Messick and Kogan (1966) found that certain aspects of individuals' personalities could be predicted from knowledge of their personal constructs, a finding consistent with data provided by Sechrest (1968) for three different traits. Levy (1954) found that constructs determined to be constellatory by reason of their extensive relationship with other constructs had more information value than did more propositional constructs, and, similarly, Williams and Sechrest (1963) found that persons tended more often to invoke more general constructs and described such constructs as more useful in making interpersonal predictions.

Such findings as the above contribute in general ways to the credibility of Kelly's theory, and they rather clearly suggest that the theory has distinct practical implications in understanding what a person is like, in predicting what a person may do in important interpersonal realtionships, and in indicating something about the way in which the most important personal constructs may be determined.

The findings are also of some specific relevance to the Sociality Corollary, which states that an individual can play a role in relationship to another person to the degree that he can construe the construction processes of that other. Apparently to know something of another's construct system is helpful in relating to that person, perhaps more helpful than knowing how that person is viewed by others. One type of role that one may play in relation to the social processes of another person is by *identification* with that person. Jones (1954, 1961) found the RCRT to be of some value in assessing identification, as did Sechrest (1962). Moreover, Jones found that psychiatric patients tend toward either over- or underidentification with others; that is, they see themselves as either too similar or too dissimilar from others, suggesting an inability to play appropriate roles in relation to other people. Shoemaker (1955) found that when people construe others similarly, they predict that they will behave similarly, indicating that the idea that a person's processes are psychologically channelized by the way he anticipates events is tenable. Shoemaker also found evidence consistent with the Sociality Corollary in that his subjects were better able to predict the behavior of people with whom they feel "comfortable" than with whom they feel "uncomfortable," and they are better able to predict the behavior of people to whom they see themselves as being similar (Carr, 1980).

In many ways a critical issue is what happens when a person makes a prediction that is subsequently invalidated. Unfortunately, perhaps, the theory is not precise on that point; different things could happen. Still, from Kelly's theory it would seem a frequent occurrence that there should be a polar shift in construction. For example, based on my construction of a person as *kind*, I expect that he will affect not to notice when I drop my chicken in my lap; when he does, in fact, note my faux pas and laughs, I might well decide that instead of being *kind*, he is *cruel*. Another possibility, of course, is that I might change constructs, and decide that he is *crude* as opposed to *refined*, however *kind* he might be. In effect, such a switch in constructs suggests that laughing at a faux pas is outside the range of convenience of the *kind-cruel* construct. Another possibility, of course, is that the whole business could seem quite confusing, for example, if the *kind-cruel* construct seemed not to apply and no other construction of the events readily offered itself. In that case, I would experience anxiety stemming from the overall loss of structure, the phenomenal experience being something like "What the hell is going on here?"

Which of the above, or perhaps other, consequences of invalidation of a prediction should obtain is not easy to say. In the earliest study on the topic of invalidation of predictions, Poch (1952) asked students to make sets of predictions based on their personal constructs about acquaintances and then gave them back information designed to make them believe that their predictions about one person were generally correct, while those about the other person were generally incorrect. Poch found that "validated" constructs changed almost not at all during an interim period prior to retesting, but invalidated constructs did tend to change somewhat, although less than had been expected. However, the more important finding was that constructs that were invalidated were less likely than those validated to be invoked for the second set of predictions; that is, the invalidated constructs intended to be dropped. Levy (1954), employing similar methodology involving invalidated predictions, found that strong invalidation led to more changes in construction than weak invalidation, but he also found that invalidation of *constellatory constructs* (i.e., constructs having many implications for, or connections with, other constructs) produced especially widespread changes in the construct system.

In an intensive study of construct systems, Hinkle (1965) extended the work of Poch and Levy, but he was especially interested in differential effects of changes in superordinate as opposed to subordinate constructs. Essentially Hinkle hypothesized that superordinate constructs would be more resistant to change than would subordinate constructs, but changes in superordinate constructs would have more ramifications when they occurred. In his study, Hinkle limited his attention to what he called "slot change"—the type of change that occurs when an individual is reconstrued as being *cruel* rather than *kind*, for example.

Hinkle first elicited what he assumed to be subordinate constructs from his subjects by having them construe successive triads of people in the ordinary way. He then had his subjects indicate for each construct which pole of the construct was more nearly descriptive of the kind of person the subject would like to be. The technique for eliciting superordinate constructs which followed was to ask subjects *why* they would prefer to be like the pole they indicated. For example, if initially a subject produced the construct *friendly-unfriendly* and indicated a preference for being friendly because if one is friendly, one is likely to be happy, therefore *happy-unhappy* was taken to be superordinate to *friendly-unfriendly*, the subject was then asked whether he would prefer to be *happy* or *unhappy* and why. The response then was taken to be suggestive of an even more superordinate construct, as with a person's response that it is better to be happy because that implies a *satisfying life*.

By repeating the procedure described, Hinkle obtained for each subject a set of superordinate constructs. He then presented constructs to subjects two at a time and required them to indicate for which construct a slot change would be more tolerable if they had to change on one construct but could remain the same on the other. Thus he could determine which constructs were most resistant to change, and he found, as expected, that superordinate constructs were most resistant; that is, a person would rather give up being happy than give up having a generally satisfying life and would rather give up being friendly than give up being happy. Finally, by asking subjects to imagine they had changed on one construct and then indicate on which other constructs they supposed they would also have changed, Hinkle determined that superordinate constructs have more implications, in the sense that change on them leads to changes on more other constructs.

At least in a general way the work of Poch, Levy, and Hinkle indicates that some of the general propositions of Kelly's theory lead to testable hypotheses, and the findings are more or less in accord with expectations. However, none of the tests was very stringent, and probably in every case failure to obtain expected results would have been quite inconclusive. Their findings do show quite clearly that methodologically good research can be done on Kelly's theory and that RCRT measurement provides a useful tool in exploring the theory. On the other hand, the research is obviously "artificial" in important senses, and whether people behave in accordance with expectations from personal constructs theory in everyday life situations remains to be explored by some inventive and determined researcher.

The RCRT itself has been the subject of a fair amount of research, mostly designed to show that it is a reliable and otherwise acceptable measuring instrument. Pedersen (1958) deserves credit for doing the first work on what he called the "consistency" of the RCRT. By administering the measure two times over a period of one week, he found that subjects are fairly consistent in the figures they give for role titles, in the constructs they produce, and in the relationships among their constructs. Kieferle and Sechrest (1961) obtained RCRT protocols from subjects and then showed that efforts to get additional constructs did not produce many that were discriminable from those already produced. Further, giving subjects new construct labels gave results highly similar to those elicited by their own constructs. These findings indicate that the RCRT probably does elicit a good sample of an individual's constructs, maybe in many cases a fairly complete sample.

Much additional work on the RCRT as a measuring instrument has been done by Bannister and Mair and their students and colleagues and is reported in their book (Bannister & Mair, 1968). They point out that the RCRT is a complex measurement technique, and consequently it is difficult to specify *a* reliability or validity value for it. There are many different aspects which have to be studied separately. For example, the verbal labels attached to constructs might be quite dependable over time and might be indicative of important aspects of an individual's functioning. However, the relationships among those labels, as indicated by the system of checks for the applicability to role figures, might not be especially reliable and might not be a valid index of anything important even if reliable. Fransella and Bannister (1977) have developed a useful manual for analysis of the RCRT.

Clearly the body of research on personal constructs theory is not large, although we would hasten to point out that we have not surveyed all of it here, by any means. The really important research from a theoretical standpoint has been limited mostly to dissertations and theses; the published research has tended to focus more on the RCRT as a measurement tool. This is unfortunate, for Kelly's theory is not unreasonable. However, it needs to be reiterated that the Fundamental Postulate and the 10 corollaries are the *assumptive* structure of Kelly's theory and are, hence, not directly testable. As far as testing the validity of Kelly's theory, all that can be done is to test propositions *derived* from the basic assumptions. It may be a long time before enough evidence accumulates to make it possible to say one way or another whether or not Kelly's theory is generally useful.

Of course, Kelly's ideas are not utterly lacking in precedent. Writers from Epictetus on have noted that what a person *thinks* is real is usually more important than what is real, which is just another way of saying that a person's construction of events will psychologically channelize his processes. The eminent sociologist W. I. Thomas put it rather neatly by saying, "If men define situations as real, they are real in their consequences" (Thomas & Thomas, 1928, p. 512). Such views do not necessarily *prove* anything, but they do suggest a degree of consensual validation for portions of Kelly's theory. Still other parts of the theory are consistent with currently accepted views and research in personality and social psychology. For example, Kelly believed that if his therapy patients could be induced, without any particular pressure, to act in a particular way, their outlook and behavior might very likely be altered in a reasonably congruent manner. That is an expectation very similar to that stated by Festinger in his presentation of dissonance theory (Festinger, 1957) and verified in at least a general way by a 15-year history of research (Wicklund & Brehm, 1976). There are, of course, many other points of correspondence between Kelly's theory and both past and contemporary thinking about human thought and behavior; his theory is in various ways supported by both common sense and consensus.

Actually, however, in the opinion of this writer one of the main reasons for the dearth of research supporting Kelly's theory is the relative disinterest of Kelly himself in such research. It cannot escape the attention of a reviewer of Kelly's work that he rarely in his own writings or speeches, subsequent to publication of his book in 1955, referred to any research of any kind. In the posthumously published volume of Kelly's papers (Maher, 1969), 15 of the 17 papers have no bibliographic citations at all, and the other two have only six apiece, only two of which are research papers. Most of the other citations are to Kelly's own work. Two of the 17 papers set forth Kelly's own view of the proper way to do research, but few trained researchers in psychology would be able to identify a coherent strategy and methodology. A good bit of the substance of each paper is, in fact, an attack on the usual methods of psychological research, but no clear alternative is posed.

It is very likely that Kelly saw the eventual verification of his ideas as lying in clinical practice, in the applications of his theory in clinical setting with real-life cases. Thus he states:

Translated into the more familiar terms of the psychological laboratory, what I have been saying suggests that the researcher is more likely to mobilize his ingenuities in devising important hypotheses if he goes to where the psychological problems are. In my own case I interpret this to mean going to where persons are disturbed enough to try to make something new out of their lives as, for example, where children are, for they are continually trying to make something new out of themselves—counting each year as they grow up and making plans for what they will do when they escape the restraints of size, age, vocabulary, and parental control. Or it may mean going to where adults have taken a critical look at themselves as, for example, to the clinic or the psychotherapy room. Wherever man is struggling mightily to make something of himself there is a fertile place for the researcher to be. (Maher, 1969, p. 131)

While one can agree in general with Kelly's prescription for identifying fertile sites for research, the methods that he espouses appear to be more nearly like those of Freud than of contemporary researchers in personality. And like other theorists of a clinical bent, Kelly would have had more pleasure in discovering that his theory had important and constructive implications for bringing about changes in people's lives than any amount of experimental, laboratory evidence could have provided him.

Comparisons

Leon Levy (1970), one of Kelly's students, makes a strong case against thinking in terms of *theories* of personality, on the grounds that what are currently called theories of personality are too loosely structured to qualify as theories and that theories of *personality* are unlikely ever to be achieved, because of the extraordinarily wide range of phenomena encompassed by the term. Levy believes that it is possible to develop theories about different aspects of personality, but an overall, integrative, coherent theory is beyond the realm of probability, if not possibility. What so-called personality theorists since Freud have provided is a set of *conceptions* of personality, "ways of thinking about human behavior that are bases for the development of a variety of methods of scientific research into these phenomena and theories about them" (Levy, 1970, p. 89). Levy also believes that little of either the research or the clinical techniques fostered by the various theories that have been proposed derives in any rigorous way from the propositions of the theories. Rather, the work is more or less consistent with the theories in the same way that a painting of unknown or disputed origin can be said to be "in the style of" some known artist.

In the estimation of this writer, Levy is quite correct in his assessment of both the theories presented to date and the possibilities for theories in the future. Interestingly, Levy notes that it has been rare for any of the major personality theorists to label their own work as a theory of personality; in most instances it was someone else, often a disciple, who attached the label to the work. Kelly, however, did subtitle his book *A Theory of Personality*, so it is clear what he intended. The same is true of Rogers, who entitled a major presentation of his ideas *A Theory of Therapy, Personality, and Interpersonal Relationships* (1959). Kelly and Rogers have been among the few theorists—Rotter (1954) is another—to present their ideas in the form of basic postulates and corollaries (i.e., as formal systems), and for that they are to be commended. In so doing they have made clear much of what it is they assume, and their propositions can readily be examined for logical consistency, heuristic value, points of agreement with other theorists, and so on. However, in neither case do the propositions form a logically interrelated, coherent system. The corollaries do not follow from one another, do not obviously combine to form tight networks and provide no basis for judging whether the system is complete—that is, whether all the corollaries that are needed within the system are stated.

On the other hand, when one compares Kelly's presentation of his theory with those of other major theorists, it is at least reasonably impressive in the precision with which it is stated, in the care and completeness with which terms are defined or elaborated, and in the internal logic with which each proposition is developed. Kelly was a precise man, perhaps understandably so, in view of his early interests in mathematics and engineering. Moreover, Kelly was not tender-minded about science and the place of his theory in science. He thoroughly intended for his theory to be constructed, and ultimately judged, in terms of the strongest tenets of the philosophy of science. Where some may think he failed, it was not for want of trying. For that reason his theory stands well above others in the explicitness with which it is presented and developed.

Still, one must recognize that if Kelly places well in the science competition, it is in part because some of the other possible competitors never really entered the game. Freud and other theorists of his era were thinking, working, and writing at a time when most of what we now take to be the philosophy of science and scientific methodology had scarcely been imagined, let alone thought through and systematized. Other theorists (e.g., Kurt Lewin, Gordon Allport) never set out to formulate a comprehensive and coherent theory of personality that would meet rigorous tests that might be imposed by critics. Still other theorists have tried rather less to develop a theory of personality than simply to develop a system of description of personality traits which might well be incorporated into any one of several actual theories.

Kelly's theory, perhaps alone among theories developed in the past 50 years, strives for real breadth and scope of the kind that Freud achieved. Even Rogers, for all his pretensions to a theory of "therapy, personality, and interpersonal relationships," did not try for the scope sought by Kelly. To begin with, Kelly, in presenting his theory of personality, presents also the outlines at least of a theory of human thought and reasoning. It is clear that he did not believe that constructs would be coterminous with the domain of personality. *All* processes are psychologically channelized by the ways in which people anticipate and construe events, including the processes of medical diagnosis, decision making about the purchase of a new automobile, and the development of a theory called the psychology of personal constructs. Kelly's theory was reflexive in a way not even conceived by most theorists; for example, there is nothing in Rogerian theory, in Cattell's theory, or in Rotter's theory that gives a clue as to how the theory itself might have come about. This writer does remember a talk once given by B. F. Skinner in which he attempted to explain the origins of his own theory in terms of that theory; that is, how schedules of reinforcement and so on converged in such a way as to bring about the thoughts and habits that led to the production of his theory.

Beyond its reflexivity, however, Kelly's theory is extraordinary in the range of phenomena with which it aims to deal. Psychotherapy, dreams, moods, psychopathology, creativity, and suicide are indicative of the range of his thought and theorizing. And while not reaching quite the scope of Freud in his *Totem and Taboo* (1952) and *Civilization and Its Discontents* (1930), Kelly even had some thoughts about the cultural and societal phenomena that stemmed from his theory. Such breadth is rare and stands in stark contrast to most other modern theorists and to current trends toward more and more theorizing about narrower and narrower things. Perhaps Kelly pays the price of some degree of precision, but it is often helpful and comforting to be able to see the relationships between separate phenomena with which one is dealing.

Kelly's theory is richest in its clinical origins and implications, perhaps being considerably like Rogers in that respect. His theory is an attempt to deal with whole persons in life settings; it is explicitly opposed to approaches that attempt to represent persons by a set of dimensions that add up to considerably less than the whole person. Kelly might not reject out of hand the value of typical personality tests and the measurement of traits, but they would be regarded as of distinctly peripheral and limited interest, perhaps for what they might show about how a person would choose to present himself when forced to do so in someone else's terms. It is, in fact, difficult to see what the implications are of some approaches to personality. To describe a person in terms of a set of traits tells nothing about whether he ought to change, let alone the ways in which that change might be brought about. Kelly's views of personality come close to those of Allport in terms of the often-made distinction between the *idiographic* and *nomothetic* approach. Kelly's theory is oriented toward the understanding of the individual and his views of things and the choices he might make. That understanding is best achieved by study of the individual in his own terms rather than by comparisons with others on terms of presumed standards, but actually dubious meaning.

Most people who think about personality would probably agree that *self* is the central issue and the focus of personality. It is an individual's sense of identity, of being himself and no one else, that is the starting point from which the study of personality begins. Many personality theories deal not at all with the sense of identity, trait theories being especially notable instances but some social learning approaches being especially limited. The individual, his self and his identity, is the focus of Kelly's theory, but his theory has the additional advantage, one not much shared, of providing for the inner view, the view of the world as seen by the person, as well as for the outer view of the person as he is seen by others. While a good portion of Kelly's work is consumed with considerations of the individual's view of the world, Kelly was by no means oblivious to the outer view. Fixed-role therapy, for example, is designed in part with the deliberate aim of changing the impression the client makes on others, and the Sociality Corollary states that one must be able to construe another person's point of view in order to relate in a role way to that person. Unlike most phenomenological theorists (e.g., Rogers), personal constructs theory is not at all limited to comprehension of the individual's own view of the world.

Kelly's theory has been attacked by Bruner (1956) on the grounds that it ignores affect as an aspect of experience and behavior. Bruner alleges, in fact, that the theory is limited by reason of having been formulated largely out of Kelly's experiences with intelligent, articulate, and cognitively facile persons, mainly college students and faculty members. A perusal of the indices of several personality textbooks and sourcebooks on this writer's shelves reveals that neither *affect* nor *emotion* is often indexed as a topic covered in the books. Most writers on personality deal, as does Kelly, with such topics as anger and hostility, anxiety, and guilt, and to a lesser extent with some positive affective states, but little attention is paid in any of them to the phenomenology of affect or its origins. This writer would hazard the guess that most personologists take affect as an aspect of experience pretty much for granted, as not requiring any special consideration. Affect in personality is treated as a byproduct much as ideation is considered by Skinnerian psychologists.

Kelly himself is not neglectful of affect and clearly thinks it to be inherent in the choices individuals make and in many nonverbal and preverbal constructs. The emphasis on cognition in personal constructs theory is somewhat illusory, since there is more than ample provision for constructs at low levels of awareness, those lacking in labels, and those with implicit poles, or whatever. Constructs may be symbolized in nonverbal terms or in vague and imprecise ways. However, Kelly admittedly wished to push the model of man as an active, construing intellect to see how far it may take us, much as the model of "economic man" is pushed by economists, not as a literal image of the way people behave but as a model, a conception, to use Levy's terminology. Can we get along without the explicit formulation of strong affect that Bruner seems to press for? "Try it and see!" might well be Kelly's response.

A final critical point on which Kelly's theory differs from others is that it is ahistorical; the theory makes no provision for the development of construct systems. In that respect Kelly is clearly in the camp of Lewin and much like most phenomenologists, who argue that a person's behavior at any given moment is determined by his view of things at that moment; how he came to that view is irrelevant. Kelly explicitly states, and makes it a central point in his therapy, that we need not be victims of our own biographies. Our prior experiences may explain how we have gotten ourselves where we are today, but those experiences do not account for where we will be tomorrow. To many psychologists it is something of a disappointment that personal constructs theory does not account for the origins of constructs and for differences between individuals in their construct systems. To Kelly the question was not of much interest, a position he affirmed strongly to this writer, who is among those disappointed at the lack of ontological perspective. To Kelly the preoccupation of psychoanalytic theorists with history and the insistent reversion to historical explanations was unfortunate and unproductive. From Kelly's perspective, every individual's development begins today!

PROSPECT

As stated earlier in this chapter, Kelly's theory seems to be being kept alive by fairly regular inclusion in textbooks devoted to personality theory. However, it scarcely seems likely that any theory can survive indefinitely without the infusion of new ideas and the thrust provided by new energies from converts. The psychology of personal constructs is not currently being elaborated and tested by empirical research or clinical practice, and there are no new names associated with Kelly's in the promulgation of the theory. It is not unimaginable that the theory will simply die out, to be remembered chiefly by historians of the field as an anomaly in the days of narrow theories based largely on laboratory phenomena of limited scope.

But what if the theory does survive by attracting the interest of a hard-working, brilliant young psychologist; what will it come to be? This writer expects that a way will be found to link an individual's personal constructs more directly to the choices he makes and, ultimately, to his behavior and the impact he has on others. By taking into account the dimensions along which the individual's choices are construed to lie, considerably more accurate predictions should be possible than can be made by other approaches. Additional improvement in understanding, and in the theory itself, can come about through taking into account the constructs an individual applies to aspects of himself and his environment other than persons. For example, knowing what choices an individual sees in a set of situations may add considerably to the knowledge involved in choices about persons. It is not immediately apparent just how constructs may be linked to behavior (if it were, someone would have done it), but one line of investigation of seeming promise is a more careful study of the views that people have of the choices, of the behavioral alternatives that face them at any given time. Most efforts at studying behavior have concentrated, perhaps overly much, on the more or less objective characteristics of behavior, without consideration of its meaning to the actor. Knowing that a person sees his alternatives at a given moment as behaving in either a hostile or a friendly manner is not enough; it is also important to know what behaviors are seen as being hostile and what are regarded as friendly.

Probably the most interesting research stemming from Kelly's theory has been the work on *sociality*, the ability of people to play roles with respect to one another (1955, pp. 32–34). There is, in this writer's view, an excellent chance that more intensive investigation of the relationships between people and the ways those relationships relate to personal construct systems would have a good payoff. Here is an area in which Kelly's ideas might be elaborated into spheres of group relationships and perhaps even international understanding. For example, it appears that Americans tend to apply the construct *freedom-slavery* to a great many governmental actions, while Russians may view the same actions in terms of *order-chaos* (cf. Smith, 1975). Perhaps it should not be surprising that the two countries disagree so strongly on so many issues.

Another promising area of research, and one which would have distinct theoretical implications, is study of the conditions under which people are likely to decide to elaborate rather than to seek further definition of their construct systems. The two responses would seem to be mutually incompatible, and both are likely to be important over the long run. However, in order to comprehend a person over a briefer time span, it would seem necessary to know whether that person was at the point of seeking to elaborate his system so as to take into account new phenomena or so as to reorganize a group of constructs by a higher, superordinate construct, or whether he was about to seek further and tighter definition of his system. Theoretically, anxiety, being a loss or lack of structure, would seem to call for tighter definition, while boredom should lead to elaboration, but those are only hypotheses remaining to be tested, along with many others.

Finally, a substantial extension and elaboration of Kelly's ideas about clinical practice would seem to be a virtual certainty if active interest in this theory emerges. The theory was firmly based in ideas about the practice of clinical psychology, and it was directed specifically to clinical applications.

Fixed-role therapy is an especially salient and unique contribution to psychotherapy practice, even though it has as yet been little explored. There are many reasons for thinking that fixed-role therapy *ought* to work, at least to some extent, and it deserves experimental testing. However, as we suggested earlier, fixed-role therapy has received disproportionate attention; many of Kelly's other ideas about diagnosis and therapy are likely to have greater importance in the long run, and many of them are just as novel. A good example is Kelly's discussion of the use that can be made by an accomplished therapist of alternative loosening and tightening of parts of the construct system, to enable a client to explore effectively the alternatives open to him.

Whether any of the above developments will ever come to pass is difficult to say at this point. Recent publications (Adams-Weber, 1979; Bannister, 1977; Fransella, 1975; Landfield & Leitner, 1980; Mancuso & Adams-Weber, 1982) certainly help in understanding how the theory may be elaborated and applied. More complete realizations of the potential of Kelly's theory will require insightful commitment from a careful thinker and researcher and a devoted clinician. The combination is rare.

ANNOTATED BIBLIOGRAPHY

Primary Sources

Kelly, G. A. *The Psychology of Personal Constructs: A Theory of Personality* (2 vols.). New York: W. W. Norton, 1955.

This is the first and basic presentation of Kelly's theory and its applications. Volume 1 sets forth the basic assumptions and propositions constituting the theory; gives Kelly's views of the clinical setting in which the theory must prove itself; describes the major assessment procedures, the Role Construct Repertory Test and the Self Characterization; and presents fixed-role therapy as a fundamental clinical derivative of personal constructs theory. The final two chapters of the first volume discuss the basic diagnostic and clinical dimensions employed in the theory. The second volume of the set goes into considerable detail concerning Kelly's views about various clinical problems and ways of dealing with them. Several chapters deal with assessment for psychotherapeutic intervention; others deal

with types of problems and psychopathology; and five chapters are devoted to various aspects of psychotherapy. The first three chapters of Volume 1, which present the basic theory, are available as a separate publication.

Kelly, G. A. *A Theory of Personality*. New York: W. W. Norton, 1963.

Maher, B. (Ed.). *Clinical Psychology and Personality: The Selected Papers of George Kelly*. New York: John Wiley, 1969.

This is a posthumously published group of Kelly's papers, most previously unpublished. The book includes a brief biography. One of Kelly's best papers in terms of its contribution to a further understanding of his position is the initial one, "Ontological Acceleration." The book also includes some papers of a rather personal sort which can give the discerning, careful reader some grounds for understanding Kelly as a person and how he came to his views, and some papers indicative of Kelly's views about science and research methodology. Additional papers elaborate on Kelly's views about his theory and clinical practice, and the volume also includes his paper presenting the results of a nonparametric factor analysis of his and several other theorists' views of the same clinical case.

Secondary Sources

Bannister, D. *Perspectives in Personal Construct Theory*. New York: Academic Press, 1970.

This book consists of a series of 12 essays, two being previously unpublished papers by Kelly, and 10 written for this volume by a diverse lot of English, Canadian, and American psychologists and philosophers. The essays are cogent, and several are quite helpful in furthering understanding of George Kelly and his theory.

Bannister, D., & Fransella, F. *Inquiring Man: The Psychology of Personal Constructs*. Baltimore: Penguin Books, 1971.

A brief, readable introduction to Kelly's theory, with consideration of Kelly's views and the implications of the theory for such fields as social psychology, behavior therapy, and schizophrenic thought disorder.

Bannister, D., & Mair, J. M. M. *The Evaluation of Personal Constructs*. New York: Academic Press, 1968.

These authors do an unusually good job of summarizing personal constructs theory and of clarifying and elaborating some of the more obscure points. The remainder of the book is devoted to reviews of research on Kelly's theory and on the RCRT in particular. The book will be especially helpful to those who wish to employ the RCRT for clinical purposes or for research.

Levy, L. *Conceptions of Personality*. New York: Random House, 1970.

This book, by one of Kelly's students, is one of the most thoughtful and insightful books on personality. Levy presents the reasons why he believes it incorrect to think in terms of "theories" of personality, preferring "conceptions" as better representing what he thinks are merely different approaches to the problems of personality. Levy places personal constructs theory among the "cognitive-perceptual approaches" to personality, but he shows that there are numerous other connections between Kelly's ideas and those of other persons who have written about personality, including many who are not usually accorded the status of theorist but who are, nonetheless, important.

Rychlak, J. "The Psychology of Personal Constructs: George A. Kelly." In J. Rychlak (Ed.)., *Introduction to Personality and Psychotherapy* (pp. 471–499). Boston: Houghton Mifflin, 1973.

Another unusually thoughtful writer about personality who studied under Kelly. Rychlak presents one of the better summaries of Kelly's theory and manages at the same time to present some insights and clarifications. Unlike many other presentations of Kelly's theory, Rychlak's delves into its implications for clinical matters, including both psychopathology and therapy.

REFERENCES

Adams-Weber, J. *Personal construct theory: Concepts and applications*. New York: Wiley, 1979.

Bannister, D. *Perspectives in personal construct theory*. New York: Academic Press, 1970.

Bannister, D. *New perspectives in personal construct theory*. New York: Academic Press, 1977.

Bannister, D., & Fransella, F. *Inquiring man: The theory of personal constructs.*

Baltimore: Penguin Books, 1971.

Bannister, D., & Mair, J. *The evaluation of personal constructs.* New York: Academic Press, 1968.

Bonarius, J. Research in the personal construct theory of George A. Kelly. In B. Maher (Ed.), *Progress in experimental personality research* (Vol. 2). New York: Academic Press, 1965.

Bruner, J. You are your constructs. *Contemporary Psychology*, 1956, *1*, 355–357.

Caplan, N., & Nelson, S. On being useful: The uses of psychological research on social problems. *American Psychologist*, 1973, *28*, 199–211.

Carr, J. E. Personal construct theory and psychotherapy research. In A. W. Landfield and L. M. Leitner (Eds.), *Personal construct psychology: Psychotherapy and personality.* New York: Wiley, 1980, pp. 233–270.

Festinger, L. *A theory of cognitive dissonance.* Evanston, Ill.: Row, Peterson, 1957.

Fransella, F. *Personal construct psychology.* New York: Academic Press, 1975.

Fransella, F., & Bannister, D. *A manual for repertory grid technique.* London: Academic Press, 1977.

Freud, S. *Civilization and its discontents.* New York: W. W. Norton, 1930.

Freud, S. *Totem and taboo.* New York: W. W. Norton, 1952.

Hinkle, D. *The change of personal constructs from the viewpoint of a theory of implications.* Unpublished doctoral dissertation, Ohio State University, 1965.

Jones, R. *Identification in terms of personal constructs.* Unpublished doctoral dissertation, Ohio State University, 1954.

Jones, R. E. Identification in terms of personal constructs. *Journal of Consulting Psychology*, 1961, *25*, 276.

Kelly, G. A. *The psychology of personal constructs: A theory of personality* (2 vols.). New York: W. W. Norton, 1955.

Kelly, G. A. Ontological acceleration. In B. Maher (Ed.), *Clinical psychology and personality: The selected papers of George Kelly* (pp. 7–45). New York: Wiley, 1969.

Kelly, G. A. *A brief introduction to personal construct theory.* Unpublished manuscript, Brandeis University, 1966.

Kieferle, D., & Sechrest, L. Effects of alterations in personal constructs. *Journal of Psychological Studies*, 1961, *12*, 173–178.

Landfield, A. W., & Leitner, L. M. *Personal construct psychology: Psychotherapy and personality.* New York: Wiley, 1980.

Landfield, A., & Nawas, M. Psychotherapeutic improvement as a function of communication and adoption of therapists' values. *Journal of Counseling Psychology*, 1964, *11*, 336–341.

Levy, L. *A study of relative information value in personal construct theory.* Unpublished doctoral dissertation, Ohio State University, 1954.

Levy, L. *Conceptions of personality: Theories and research.* New York: Random House, 1970.

Mancuso, J. C., & Adams-Weber, J. (Eds.). *The construing person.* New York: Praeger, 1982.

Maher, B. (Ed.). *Clinical psychology and personality: The selected papers of George Kelly.* New York: Wiley, 1969.

Messick, S. M., & Kogan, N. Personality consistencies in judgment: Dimensions of role constructs. *Multivariate Behavioral Research*, 1966, *1*, 165–175.

Nawas, M., & Landfield A. Improvement in psychotherapy and adoption of therapist's meaning system. *Psychological Reports*, 1963, *13*, 97–98.

Neimeyer, R. A. George Kelly as therapist: A review of his tapes. In A. W. Landfield and L. M. Leitner (Eds.), *Personal construct psychology: Psychotherapy and personality.* New York: Wiley, 1980, pp. 74–101.

Ourth, L., & Landfield, A. Interpersonal meaningfulness and nature of termination in psychotherapy. *Journal of Counseling Psychology*, 1965, *12*, 336–371.

Payne, D. E. *Role constructs versus part constructs and interpersonal understanding.* Unpublished doctoral dissertation, Ohio State University, 1956.

Pedersen, F. *A consistency study of the RCRT.* Unpublished MA thesis, Ohio State University, 1958.

Poch, S. *Study of changes in personal constructs as related to interpersonal prediction and its outcomes.* Unpublished doctoral dissertation, Ohio State University, 1952.

Rogers, C. A theory of therapy, personality, and interpersonal relationships, as developed in the client-centered framework. In S. Koch (Ed.), *Psychology: A study of a science* (Vol. 3, pp. 184–256). New York: McGraw-Hill, 1959.

Rotter, J. *Social learning and clinical psychology.* New York: Prentice-Hall, 1954.

Sechrest, L. Stimulus equivalents of the psychotherapist. *Journal of Individual Psychology*, 1962, *18*, 172–176.

Sechrest, L. The psychology of personal constructs: George Kelly. In J. Wepman & R. Heine (Eds.), *Concepts of personality* (pp. 206–233). Chicago: Aldine Press, 1963.

Sechrest, L. Personal constructs and personal characteristics. *Journal of Individual Psychology*, 1968, *24*, 162–166.

Shoemaker, D. *Personal constructs and interpersonal predictions.* Unpublished doctoral dissertation, Ohio State University, 1955.

Smith, H. *The Russians.* New York: Quadrangle Books, 1975.

Thomas, W. I., & Thomas, D. S. *The child in America.* New York: Alfred Knopf, 1928.

Wicklund, R., & Brehm, J. *Explorations in cognitive dissonance* (2nd ed.). Hillsdale, N. J.: Erlbaum & Associates, 1976.

Williams, T. G., & Sechrest, L. The ascribed usability of personal constructs as a function of their generality. *Journal of Psychological Studies*, 1963, *14*, 75–81.

CHAPTER VII

Learning Theories: Operant Reinforcement and Social Learning Theories of B. F. Skinner and Albert Bandura

Robert W. Lundin

This chapter will concentrate mainly on the works of two men, B. F. Skinner (1904-   ) and Albert Bandura (1925-   ). Skinner's theory is commonly referred to as *operant-reinforcement* and Bandura's as *social-learning*. Both men share many principles of behavior in common, but their differences are great enough that they might best be handled in two separate sections of this chapter. The similarities and differences in the thinking of these two men will eventually become evident.

At the outset, it can be noted that both stress the importance of learning in personality development and so most of the assertions of both, in one way or another, relate to the learning process.

Both are concerned with behavior modification in which learning principles are applied to alter maladaptive behavior.

INTRODUCTION

The behavioristic approach to personality is the strongest departure from other theories in this book. Experimentation plays a major role in the development of behavioristic principles as they are applied to the study of personality. Skinner started his experimental analysis of behavior using animals as subjects. Later, Skinnerians dealt with human subjects. Bandura, on the other hand, has worked entirely with human subjects.

A second major departure is the behaviorist's avoidance of mentalistic constructs. Concepts such as mind, mental apparatus, consciousness and the like frequently used by many personality theorists, are rejected on the grounds that they are not objectively verifiable and do not have direct reference to natural events. On the matter of the rejection of mentalism, Skinner is much harder and firmer than Bandura. Both reject the idea of inner forces or inner conflicts as used by Freud, but Bandura allows for cognitions and inner feelings as a necessary part of his explanations of human personality. These, Skinner rejects completely.

Traditionally the behavioristic approach has been considered a form of S-R (stimulus-response) theory, in which the main events of study are responses an organism makes to stimuli in the external environment. These are not the only S-R theories of personality current, today, however. On this matter, Skinner is very specific that the stimuli which control our behavior must come from the external environment. Bandura tends to take a softer approach, allowing that our own cognitions, for example, can act as causes of our behavior.

Behavior is considered lawful and as such is subject to the prediction and control. The task of the psychologist is to discover the laws of behavior, especially through experimentation. Some behaviorists think that the simple discovery of laws as they apply to any species or cross-species is a sufficient task for psychology. Both Skinner and Bandura express this thought, particularly Bandura who has devoted virtually all his career to developing a social-learning approach to personality. Thus, Bandura more than Skinner stresses the social aspect of personality development (interaction with people).

Both men take a deterministic view toward personality. For Skinner, determinism comes strictly from the external environment. Bandura introduces the concept of *reciprocal determinism*: the causes can come from the environment, the person or one's own behavior.

HISTORY

Precursors

A reinforcement theory of personality should begin with Ivan P. Pavlov and his work on the conditioned reflex. Initially, Pavlov, a Russian physiologist, discovered that a dog would salivate to an originally neutral stimulus if it were paired with a naturally eliciting stimulus such as food. It was Pavlov who first used the word *reinforcement* in referring to the food (Pavlov, 1927). The new reflex of salivation could be elicited when the conditioned stimulus (CS) alone was presented.

Of particular interest to the student of personality were Pavlov's investigations into what he called the experimental neuroses which could be produced when animals were forced beyond their discriminative capacity or subjected to excessively powerful stimulation. Dogs, for example, were taught to make appropriate discriminations by salivating at sight of a circle and not salivating when an oval was shown. As the figures were made increasingly similar, the dogs' ability to make discriminations broke down and they became extremely disorganized, wrestled in their harnesses, barked, urinated, defecated, and became generally agitated. Pavlov suggested personality types among dogs to account for such individual differences in their behavior. He explained the neurotic conditions basically in physiological terms, as an excessive strain on the nervous system due to traumatic conflict.

Like Pavlov, Edward Lee Thorndike began his initial studies with animals (Thorndike, 1898). He constructed a series of puzzle boxes in which his subjects—cats—had to perform some kind of operation to escape to get food. In one type of experiment the cat was placed in the box, and the problem was to press a pedal. When the desired response was made, the door of the box flew open, the cat got out, and it was given a piece of fish. On successive trials, the time taken to escape gradually decreased, although from one trial to the next time varied considerably. Eventually, however, the cat improved its performance so that when placed in the box it quickly performed the desired response. Thorndike called this trial-and-error learning, because initially it seemed so haphazard.

Thorndike, like Pavlov, explained learning on the basis of association. For Pavlov, the association was between the conditioned and the unconditioned stimuli paired together. For Thorndike, the cat associated the appropriate response with escaping and getting food; that the cat got food for making the desired response was important.

Out of these initial experiments, Thorndike formulated what he called the *law of effect*, stated as follows: "Of several responses made in the same situation, those which are accompanied or closely followed by satisfaction to the animal will, other things being equal, be more firmly connected with the situation" (Thorndike, 1911, p. 244). Skinner later incorporated Thorndike's formulation into his *principle of reinforcement*, the learning tenet of his theory. Without reinforcement, learning does not occur.

In 1913 John B. Watson published an article in the *Psychological Review* entitled "Psychology as the Behaviorist Views It" (Watson, 1913). This article had considerable impact on the way psychology was to move in the future. Watson is generally credited as the founder of *behaviorism*, a movement to which Skinner and his followers adhere. Two points in Watson's article are worth noting. First, psychology, it was stated, is the study of behavior and not of mental events (consciousness, mind, and so forth). Watson declared introspection, then popular among other psychologists, to be an unreliable method of getting information. Another relevant point in this article was that the aims of psychology should be the prediction and control of behavior.

From a historical perspective, much of Watson's psychology was rather naive. However, what the modern behaviorist shares with Watson today is the concept that psychology should deal with the behavior of living organisms, not with mental phenomena. Watson, a determinist, stressed the extreme importance of the environmental position and more or less denied the importance of heredity, a position which Skinner had declared to be foolish (Skinner, 1974).

In his system Watson incorporated his conception of personality, which he considered to be a complex reaction system developed by training, including habits, abilities, emotions, remembering, and so forth. He also suggested that the way to change habits is by altering the environment in such a way that new habits could be learned (Watson, 1925). Impressed by Pavlov's work on the conditioned reflex, Watson used Pavlov's paradigm to experiment, with Rosalie Raynor (Watson & Raynor, 1920), on an 11-month-old boy, Albert. They paired a white laboratory rat (CS) and the striking of a steel bar (US) behind the child's head. The loud sound evoked a "fear" reaction, the boy exhibiting violent movements and crying. Eventually the mere sight of the rat caused the boy to exhibit the "fear" response (CR). Generalization was also demonstrated; without any further conditioning, Albert exhibited "fear" to a dog, a fur coat, wool, and even a Santa Claus mask. Watson and Raynor had planned to extinguish the "fear" by later presenting the rat on successive trials without the loud noise. However, Albert's mother, who had been working at the hospital, left and took Albert with her.

Mary Cover Jones (Jones, 1924), a student of Watson's, found a boy, Peter, who already had strong fears of furry animals. She presented a rabbit in a room where the boy was eating, each day moving the animal a little closer to the boy. Several repetitions of this procedure resulted in the elimination of the child's fear. After this extinction was completed, Peter's fear of other furry animals was also eliminated. Jones's experiment is significant, for it was the first practical demonstration of behavior therapy, a method of treatment widely used by behavior modifiers today.

B. F. SKINNER

Beginnings

Burrhus Frederick Skinner has had a long and distinguished career; his contributions to American psychology have been varied, and he has done much to alter its course. Born March 20, 1904 in Susquehanna, a small Pennsylvania town, he received his B.A. in 1926 from Hamilton College, Clinton, N.Y.; earned his M.A. in 1930, and was awarded his Ph.D. in 1931 by Harvard. After several years of postdoctoral study he went to the University of Minnesota, where he remained from 1936 to 1945. He became chairman of the Department of Psychology at Indiana University in 1945 and in 1948 returned to Harvard, where he remained.

During the 1930s Skinner's efforts were devoted to research in the development of principles of learning, using white rats as subjects. He devised an apparatus, often called a Skinner Box—a term Skinner deplores, preferring that the apparatus be called an *operant conditioning chamber* (Skinner, 1932). In its original form the chamber consisted of a small box with a lever mounted on one side which the rat could press to receive a pellet of food as reinforcement. In the 1940s he adapted his apparatus for use with pigeons, for which the designated response was pecking a small disk mounted on the side of the cage to receive grain.

Skinner was appalled by the antiquated methods used in teaching and pioneered in the development of programmed learning. He devised a teaching machine which employed the principle of small steps each followed by positive reinforcements in the learning process. Through the use of programmed learning (Holland & Skinner, 1961), a child could proceed in small steps to master the material he was studying. (See the Applications section for a further discussion.)

Skinner's first major book was *The Behavior of Organisms* (1938), in which he described some of his early experiments. As early as 1948, Skinner had become interested in the application of his principles to human behavior. *Walden Two* (Skinner, 1948), a utopian novel, was the result. *Science and Human Behavior* (1953) furthered Skinner's studies and applied his principles to human behavior. In this book he applied his psychology to social issues, education, government, law, religion, and psychotherapy.

Skinner's interest in the study of language was demonstrated in *Verbal Behavior* (1957), in which language is seen as an aspect of human behavior for which the same kinds of analyses are appropriate as for other forms of behavior. This book has never met with much favor among traditional linguists. In the same year Skinner published, with Charles B. Ferster, *Schedules of Reinforcement* (Ferster & Skinner, 1957), a large volume of research explaining many different schedules or ways in which reinforcements may be delivered. (See Maintenance.)

Current Status

Skinner has devoted himself to social issues and to his own reinterpretation of such concepts as value, freedom, dignity, and personal control. *Beyond Freedom and Dignity* (1971) was for many months on the best seller list of nonfiction books, but by and large it received poor reviews from psychologists and others. His book, *About Behaviorism* (1974), tackles certain problems which have plagued behaviorists—concepts which other psychologists refer to as inner experience, self, knowledge, and so forth—and reinterprets them in behavioristic terms.

Skinner has been a controversial figure in psychology, but his efforts have not gone unappreciated or unrecognized. In 1951 an honorary doctor of science degree was conferred on him by his alma mater, Hamilton College. He received the American Psychological Association's Distinguished Contribution Award in 1958 and its Gold Medal Award in 1971. In 1968 he was given the National Medal of Science Award, the federal government's highest award for distinguished achievement in science, mathematics, or engineering. Only one other psychologist has received this award.

Skinner's followers are so numerous that it is difficult to single out the most important ones. Teodoro Ayllon, Nathan Azrin, Sidney Bijou, Leonard Krasner, and Arthur Staats are important in the field of behavior modification and therapy. Charles B. Ferster, Richard Hernstein, Israel Goldiamond, and Donald S. Blough have dealt with rigorous experiments in psychology but have been concerned with applying behavior modification principles to human behavior. Robert W. Lundin has applied Skinner's principles to the field of personality.

ASSERTIONS

Development

1.   The basic aim of psychology is the prediction and control of behavior.

Like Watson (1913), Skinner (1953, 1971) has maintained that the two basic aims of psychology are the prediction and control of behavior. To achieve these aims, a functional relationship between antecedent conditions in the environment and the resulting behavior must be established. In this manner a science of psychology can be developed, and appropriate principles can be discovered.

The most desirable method whereby the principles can be discovered is through experimentation with proper experimental controls so that the antecedent condition (independent variable) can be varied, and resulting changes in behavior (dependent variables) can be observed and measured. Thus, a functional relationship is established. This is also possible outside the laboratory. The adage, "You can lead a horse to water but you can't make him drink," assumes *no* knowledge of the antecedent conditions. If we know, for example, that a horse has been deprived of water (antecedent condition), we can predict with considerable certainty that when brought to the watering trough he *will drink* (resulting behavior). Therefore, we can control an animal's drinking behavior by either depriving it of, or satiating it with, water.

If prediction and control are possible, then we can presume that behavior is lawfully determined. Skinner (1953, 1971) believes strongly that behavior is neither capricious nor the result of whim. When we make a choice which seems to be other than the result of antecedent conditions and only of our own free will, the presumption is wrong. The choice is determined because of antecedent conditions.

> When all relevant variables have been arranged, an organism will or will not respond. If it does not, it cannot. It it can, it will. To ask whether someone can turn a handspring, is merely to ask whether there are circumstances under which he will do so. A man who can avoid flinching at gun fire is a man who will not flinch under certain circumstances....when all relevant variables have been taken into account it is not difficult to guarantee the result. (Skinner, 1953, p. 122)

What may appear to some to be evidence of the nondeterministic nature of behavior is the result of errors of prediction. However, an alternate and superior conclusion is that we do not know all relevant variables, or they are not under our control. In other circumstances our predictions would improve.

Skinner believes that both genetic endowment and environmental conditions must be taken into account (Skinner, 1971). This does not mean he believes in hereditary causes as such but rather that our genetic endowment limits the kinds of responses an organism can make or might eventually be able to make. We can compare two examples mentioned above. Skinner trained rats to press a lever to get food and later trained pigeons to peck a disk for food. In these two species the responses were quite different. It would be quite awkward for pigeons to press levers and for rats to peck at disks, since their genetic endowments are quite different. As mentioned earlier, the crucial events from which we predict and control behavior are environmental stimuli. These are what control our behavior and the source from which predictions are made. For example, if we know a person is greatly in need of money (antecedent condition) we can then predict that he is likely to accept a bribe (behavior).

2.   *Behavior can be divided into two classes, operant and respondent.*

Skinner allows that some simple kinds of learning can take place according to the paradigm first developed by Pavlov. This simple kind of conditioning Skinner calls *respondent*: two stimuli, unconditioned and conditioned, are paired together, and eventually the organism will respond solely in the presence of the conditioned stimulus. The section on "History" mentioned Pavlov's work in which dogs were conditioned to salivate to the sound of a tone, as well as Watson and Raynor's (1920) experiment in conditioning "fear" in Albert. A practical example of respondent, or classical Pavlovian, conditioning can be found in the treatment of alcoholism. If a person is given a substance which produces nausea or vomiting, and if the sight or taste of alcohol is then paired with this substance, vomiting should eventually occur merely at the sight or taste of the drink. In humans, a number of unconditioned reflexes, such as coughing, sneezing, elimination, pupillary contraction, eye blink, and knee jerk, as well as internal reactions such as blood pressure and heart rate, can be conditioned to new stimuli.

Respondent behavior is so designated to indicate that the environment does something to the organism, which then responds. A piece of dirt in the eye causes blinking or tearing, or bright light causes pupils of eyes to contract. Respondent behavior, whether unconditioned or conditioned, constitutes only a small amount of total behavior.

For the most part, Skinner and his colleagues have emphasized *operant behavior*, so designated to indicate that the individual *operates on* the environment. We talk, walk to class, sit down at the dinner table, take a bath, play cards, read a book, and so on. In older psychologies, the distinction between operant and respondent was called voluntary and involuntary. However, since there is no behavior not under the control of environmental stimuli, the term *voluntary* is improper.

For the most part the rest of this chapter will be devoted to principles, examples, and experiments involving the acquisition, maintenance, or elimination of operant behavior. This distinction between operant and respondent behavior bears some resemblance to Mowrer's (1950) two-factor learning theory, since *respondent* roughly equates to *sign learning* and *operant* to *solution learning*. However, they are not exactly the same; Mowrer considers more kinds of behavior under sign learning and does not make as explicit a distinction between the two terms as does Skinner.

3. *Personality is acquired and maintained through the use of positive and negative reinforcers.*

Skinner was much impressed with Thorndike's statement (1911) of the *Law of Effect* and has found it to be the most important principle in behavioral development. However, he took exception to Thorndike's use of the term *satisfying consequences* (Skinner, 1953). How can we know objectively that cats are "satisfied"? Since this is a subjective experience about which cats cannot tell us, a restatement is necessary for an objective psychology. Skinner substitutes the *principle of reinforcement* for *satisfying consequences*. To reinforce means to *strengthen*, as a package is reinforced with tape and twine or a wall is reinforced with concrete. Applied to behavior, reinforcement means that a behavior is strengthened or the probability of its occurrence is increased when reinforcement is applied.

In his early studies, Skinner (1932) found that when a rat was placed in an operant conditioning chamber it would press the lever occasionally "by accident," but if food were presented following the response (positive reinforcement), the level pressing increased to a steady rate of responding in which the animal continually pressed, taking time out only to eat the food pellets. For this reinforcement to operate, of course, the rat had to be food deprived. The presentation of food following a response is designated as a *primary* positive reinforcement. Other primary reinforcers include water and other drinks, sex, or other stimuli which might meet some biological need. They are designated as primary because their function to reinforce does not have to be learned.

Azrin and Lindsley (1956) have applied positive reinforcement to the training of cooperative behavior among young children. Twenty children aged 7 to 12 were matched into 10 pairs. The two children in each pair were seated on opposite sides of a table, and in front of each child were three holes in the table and a stylus to be inserted in one of them. If the children happened to place their styli in the holes opposite each other (cooperative behavior), a red light flashed on and a single jelly bean was delivered, available to either child. Other arrangements were considered as uncooperative responses and yielded no reinforcement. All teams learned the cooperative response very quickly in the absence of specific instructions.

Almost immediately, eight of the teams divided the candy in some manner acceptable to both members.

In addition to the primary positive reinforcement discussed so far, there are also *conditioned* positive reinforcers which keep us going or help us acquire other behaviors which are not of direct biological significance. Such reinforcers as money (itself only paper or metal), diplomas, prizes, or the behavior of other people in granting praise, attention, or approval are conditioned reinforcers. They can serve as a powerful means of maintaining behavior.

Negative reinforcers can also strengthen behavior. A *negative reinforcer* is designated as a stimulus which *strengthens behavior when it is removed*, just as a positive reinforcer strengthens behavior when it is presented. Negative reinforcers can also be primary or conditioned. Some examples of primary negative reinforcement include putting on dark glasses to escape the glare of the sun, opening umbrellas to avoid getting wet, turning up the heat when it is cold, or turning on the air conditioning when the opposite holds. The removal of the aversive stimulus strengthens the behavior. With regard to conditioned negative reinforcers, we walk away from people who annoy us or slow down our car speed if we see police. Unfortunately, far too much of our behavior is controlled by negative reinforcement. Insurance companies ordinarily do not reward us for safe driving, but they do raise our rates when we have an accident. We pay heavy taxes only to avoid other penalties or be put in jail.

4.   *Behavior may be altered or weakened by the withholding of reinforcements.*

In Pavlov's early experiments, after he had conditioned dogs to salivate to the sound of a tone he found that if there were continuous sounding of the tones but no further food, the salivary response became weaker, until it died out completely. This process is called *extinction*. Likewise, operant behavior can be weakened by withholding the reinforcement following the response (Skinner, 1933). Gradually the rate of response slows down until it reaches a point of either no responding or the point where it was before reinforcements were applied. In many forms of personality development, both positive reinforcement and extinction must be applied. (See later Assertions below.)

Extinction is an effective means of getting rid of undesirable previously conditioned behavior. If a child throws a temper tantrum to get what he wants and we give in to his demands, we strengthen the temper tantrum behavior, but if we ignore the tantrums, they should eventually die out. If going to the movies has been positively reinforcing in the past and then later films are dull, movie-going behavior will occur less frequently. We can extinguish dull conversations by not paying attention or by failing to reply.

behavior punished was of a moral or ethical sort. We may be punished for many things, some of which are described as "bad." The problem is that punishment generates anxiety (guilt is a form of anxiety) which accomplishes nothing except to upset the person. (An objective interpretation of anxiety is given below.)

A second unfortunate consequence of punishment is that it may lead to anger and aggression. Although aggression may be used in warding off one's enemies, there are problems in that unnecessary aggression may impede social relationships, destroy or immobilize the punisher, or be directed against persons who were not responsible for the punishment (displaced aggression) (Azrin, 1966).

Another form of punishment not directly making use of aversive stimuli is called *time-out*, which involves removing a person from a situation which has been positively reinforcing into one which is not. Simple examples are sending a child to his room, the use of the penalty box for removing a player from a game such as ice hockey, or sending a man to prison.

Brown and Tyler (1969) report the use of time-out in treating an extremely aggressive delinquent boy of 16. It seemed that the boy was being strongly reinforced by bullying others, and he was informed that his aggressive behavior would result in social isolation from his peers. In being dethroned as the "duke" of the group, the reinforcement provided by the submission of those he bullied could be eliminated. The application of time-out, or being put in the "pokey," as he put it, had a marked effect not only in reducing his aggressive behavior but in improving his relations with his peers and the staff.

Anxiety is the fourth of the basic aversive conditions. Skinnerians interpret anxiety as behavior resulting from being placed in a situation in which escape or avoidance of the aversive stimuli are impossible. A warning signal is given, followed by some aversive stimulus. A child who has been naughty may be told that he will be punished when his father comes home; the waiting period constitutes the situation of anxiety.

In humans, anxiety has many manifestations, both in operant and respondent reactions. Among respondent reactions are changes in physiological functions (increased heart rate and blood pressure, perspiration, inclination to eliminate, shaking, and so on). On the operant side are feelings of nervousness, being upset, and fear, as well as increased inappropriate motor activity such as restlessness or heightened muscular rigidity.

Many personality theories, especially the psychoanalytic, find anxiety to be a condition which may lead to behavior disorders. Although the interpretations are different for behaviorists, both schools of thought tend to agree on the importance of anxiety. Too much early conditioning in anxiety can lead to later maladaptive behavior. Since neither escape nor avoidance is possible, there is no reinforcement. There is only the anticipation of punishment, and this anticipation may be more disruptive than the punishment. Excessive conditioning can lead to neurotic anxiety, in which the person feels chronically anxious and may have anxiety attacks in which he is overwhelmed with fear or panic.

Maintenance

8.   *Personality is maintained by a series of conditioned reinforcers.*

In the Development section, we distinguished primary from conditioned reinforcers. Primary reinforcement is natural or unlearned; conditioned reinforcers are acquired. Such reinforcers start out as neutral stimuli, but by being paired with primary reinforcement they later strengthen behavior in their own right. However, just any pairing will not work. For a conditioned reinforcer to acquire its power, it must first become a discriminative stimulus. The better the discrimination, the more powerful it will be as a conditioned reinforcer. However, unlike primary reinforcers, conditioned reinforcers can lose their power unless occasionally paired with primary ones.

A demonstration from the animal laboratory illustrates this. A rat is conditioned to press a lever, and as a consequence of this behavior it receives food. But it only gets fed if light is present and this condition becomes the discriminative stimulus. Eventually, a discrimination is formed; the animal presses in the presence of the light but not in its absence. Now a chain is placed in the cage. When the animal pulls it with his teeth it receives the light as the conditioned reinforcer. The rate of chain pulling will increase for a while, indicating that the conditioned reinforcer is working even if the animal is not otherwise rewarded by the primary reinforcer—the food.

Some of these conditioned reinforcers are specific to individuals, such as listening to music, or watching a football game. However, some classes of reinforcers are shared by many people. Skinner calls these *generalized reinforcers*; they include attention, approval, affection, submission of others, and tokens. (Skinner, 1953)

Attention can amount to a simple glance, a wave of the hand, a snap of a finger, or a verbal "hello." *Approval* is generally a powerful reinforcer; it includes verbal responses of praise ("Thank you very much," "You did a fine job"), applause, cheering, nodding, smiling, and so on. *Affection* is even more powerful. Signs of affection include hugging, cuddling, shaking hands, and verbal endearments such as "darling" or "sweetheart."

An example of the *submission of others* as a reinforcer is illustrated in the previously cited study by Brown and Tyler (1969), in which the "duke," who had been powerfully reinforced by the submission of those he bullied, was dethroned. Superiors are reinforced by acquiescence. Giving in to a child's demands puts him in a superior position by strengthening his demanding behavior.

What we have considered so far as generalized reinforcers are specific behaviors on the part of other people. *Tokens* are even more specific, since they involve inanimate objects which have a constant stimulus value. Money is probably the most powerful and most common token reinforcer. The acquisition of its function can be easily understood in a child. In the beginning, money for the child may be nothing more than paper or "shiny stuff." As the child learns that money can be exchanged for such primary reinforcers as candy or ice cream cones, however, it begins to acquire its reinforcement function. Eventually, it is generalized to reinforce countless behaviors. Other tokens for children include trinkets and toys. Education employs many tokens, such as prizes, diplomas, Phi Beta Kappa keys or being named to the dean's list.

9. *Behavior can be maintained by reinforcers delivered regularly or intermittently.*

Regular or continuous reinforcement means every response is followed by a reinforcement. This is not the usual case in everyday affairs, except possibly in the case of the spoiled child who gets everything he asks for or in some cases of verbal behavior in which a remark always receives some reply from another.

Ordinarily, behavior is reinforced on what are called schedules; that is, reinforcement is given intermittently. To reinforce on intermittent schedules develops stronger or more persistent behavior than if the reinforcement constantly follows the desired behavior (Ferster & Skinner, 1957).

There are four basic schedules: fixed interval, variable interval, fixed ratio and variable ratio. Others are variations of these.

In *fixed-interval schedules*, reinforcement is delivered on a regular time basis. In a laboratory it could be once every 30 seconds, or every minute or two. The reinforcement is delivered by some outside agency according to a designated schedule, regardless of how many responses an organism makes in between, just so long as it makes the response at the time designated for the reinforcement or soon thereafter. In human affairs, being paid by the hour or week illustrates this kind of schedule. When we eat or sleep at regular hours or get mail at a designated time, we are working on a fixed-interval schedule.

In a *variable-interval schedule*, reinforcement is based on a time schedule which varies but averages out to a specified time. For example, if one responds on a variable-interval schedule of two minutes, reinforcements would be delivered on the average of once every two minutes, although at times a particular reinforcement might come after 45 seconds or three minutes. Frequently, our social life operates on some kind of variable-interval schedule. Some weeks we may be invited out several times, or we may go for weeks without being entertained.

In *fixed-ratio schedules*, the reinforcements are delivered on a basis of how many responses an individual makes, regardless of time. In a fixed-ratio schedule of 10, one would be reinforced after every 10th response. If one works fast, one receives more reinforcements than if one works more slowly. Being paid on a piece-work or commission basis illustrates this schedule. The more cars a salesperson sells, the more money he will make, providing he is working on commission.

The fourth basic schedule is the *variable-ratio schedule*. This is like the variable-interval one in that the reinforcements are delivered irregularly but average out to a given figure. A variable ratio of 10 would mean that on the average of every 10th response, one will be reinforced. Many gambling devices, such as slot machines or roulette tables, work on this kind of schedule. When one is having a winning streak the reinforcements are close together, whereas in a losing streak they are few and far between.

10. *Motivation consists of depriving or satiating the organism.*

For behavior to be maintained, motivation must be present. In animal studies in which primary reinforcements are used, the reinforcement will not function if the organism is satiated with food—if food is being used as the reinforcing stimulus. The animal must, therefore, be food deprived for this primary reinforcement to function.

Some personality theories make use of complicated motivational principles such as instincts, drives, needs, and hypothetical or internal states. In the Skinnerian approach these are not necessary. The most acceptable motivational operations are the observable events of either depriving or satiating an organism with appropriate reinforcers.

Both operations can be applied to the practical control of behavior. We deprive a child of between-meal snacks so that he will eat enough at mealtime. When a child fails to eat his dinner, instead of coaxing or applying threats or other aversive stimuli, a better way to get him to eat, providing he is in good health, is to excuse him from the table. This increases his deprivation and also the probability he will eat properly at the next meal. Setting the time for a dinner party later than the guests' accustomed eating hour will ordinarily guarantee they will eat a hearty meal. If the goal is a short meeting, it should be scheduled just prior to normal eating time. Skinner (1953) has suggested if we want to make a man amenable to bribes, he should be encouraged to live beyond his means. The manipulation of deprivation of both primary and secondary reinforcers has been known as long as man has had a recorded history. Cutting off the lines of supply to opponents, for example, has been a basic military tactic.

Some advertisements aim at degrees of deprivation. They set up reinforcers, usually conditioned, as appeals for goods a person does not have.

Owning a fancy sports car will bring on the conditioned reinforcements of attention and approval for some. Sales or bargains help to relieve financial deprivation by reducing normal prices. Small compact cars which provide fuel economy also reduce financial deprivation by saving on gas purchases and making more money available for other purposes.

Deprivation and satiation can be effective methods in altering undesirable behavior in psychiatric patients. Ayllon (1963) describes a patient who weighed 250 pounds. She not only ate the food given her but would steal food from other patients or pick up unauthorized food from the counter. To change her behavior, first she was assigned a table by herself in the dining room. Whenever she approached the tables of other patients or the counter, she was discharged from the dining room. This procedure eliminated the food stealing in two weeks. After she was limited to eating merely her own food, her weight was reduced from 250 to 180 pounds in the 14 months she was in the hospital. In being removed from the dining room when she took unauthorized food she experienced deprivation and learned that she could only eat the food allowed for her consumption.

These, then, are some of the basic assertions of an operant reinforcement approach to personality. They are concerned with the development, maintenance, or alteration of many aspects of man's behavior. As principles which attempt to explain the basic nature of man as he behaves in a natural world, they are based on observable events and not hypothetical assumptions.

APPLICATIONS

Assessment

Skinner's first attempt to apply the behavioral principles established in the laboratory to human life was in his Utopian novel *Walden Two* (Skinner, 1948). He describes a self-sustaining community with its own farm, dairy, livestock, medical care, symphony orchestra, and so on. The community is run by planners and managers. Work is appropriately shared through a system of "labor credits." Each member spends only about four hours a day in work, so there is ample time for recreation and creative activity. *Behavioral engineering* is the key term as to how the system works.

Skinner believes that other communes have failed because their members sought immediate ecstasy. The design of Walden Two provides alternatives for men of "goodwill," and it could act as a model for larger social systems.

Positive reinforcement is the principle on which Walden Two is based. Punishment does not exist. Fraser, one of the planners, explains how positive reinforcement works:

"Now that we know how positive reinforcement works and negative doesn't", he [Fraser] said, at last, "We can be more deliberate and hence more successful in our cultural design. We can achieve a sort of control under which the controlled, though they are following a code more scrupulously than was the case under the old system, nevertheless feel free. They are doing what they want to do and not what they are forced to do. That's the source of the tremendous power of positive reinforcement. There's no restraint and no revolt. By a careful cultural design, we control not the final behavior, but the inclination to behavior—the motives, the desires and the wishes." (Skinner, 1948, p. 219)

A real community modeled after Walden Two exists in Virginia. Called Twin Oaks, at its inception in 1968 it contained only 23 people, but by 1973 the number had grown to 40. The community, located on a tobacco farm, consists of several farm structures. The money to run the community comes from its industry: hammock making and the fattening of calves. Unlike Walden Two, which was ideally self-sustaining, the members of Twin Oaks frequently have to go to neighboring communities to get temporary jobs. Although Twin Oaks farms its land, it has to go outside to buy products. The community does use the labor-credit system and a planner-manager system. All members must subscribe to a behavioral code which includes the sanctity of privacy, not talking behind another's back, abstinence from drugs, and giving up personal property.

Entertainment at Twin Oaks is much less elaborate than that described in Walden Two, consisting mainly of singing, guitar playing, and square dancing. One of the difficulties Twin Oaks has encountered is in turnover; members leave and new ones come in too frequently. Everyone who arrives does not have knowledge of Skinnerian principles, but those who stay are helped to learn the basic principles by classes in what is called behavioral psychology. In a book, *A Walden II Experiment: The First Five Years of Twin Oaks* (Kinkade, 1973), some of the problems and developments are described. Finding new members is no problem, but finding the right type of person is; there is no place for people who are irresponsible or lazy. The membership is subject to the typical human failings, however; there are encounter sessions (hardly a Skinnerian concept) in which they try to understand one another and improve their personal relations. Whether or not the experiment will succeed only time will tell.

In *Beyond Freedom and Dignity*, Skinner (1971) expanded some of his basic concepts. He has reinterpreted what he considers to be a number of outmoded notions on the nature of man, in the light of behavioristic psychology. Believing that man is a product of both his genetic endowment and the stimuli in his environment, he asserts that *man is not autonomous* but is always under the control of variables outside himself. He reiterates the strong determinism stated in his earlier works, which allows man to make decisions, but determined ones. To those who believe in man's free will to choose from his inner self or psyche, Skinner's assertions are considered inhuman. However, he interprets *freedom* to mean that man is no longer under the control of aversive stimuli which lead to escape, avoidance or punishment. In freedom, the control is positive reinforcement.

Concerning the design of a culture, Skinner writes:

> If the designer is an individualist, he will design a world in which he will be under minimal aversive control and will accept his own goods as the ultimate value. If he has been exposed to an appropriate environment, he will design for the good of others, possibly with a loss of personal goods. If he is concerned primarily with survival values, he will design a culture with an eye to whether it will work. (Skinner, 1971, p. 151)

Treatment

In operant reinforcement theory, the basic methods of treating personality disorders are classed under the general heading of *behavior therapy*, to distinguish them from the more conventional therapies. What is significant in behavior therapy is the application of principles of respondent and operant conditioning in altering or eliminating inappropriate or undesirable behavior. This section will describe briefly some of the most popular methods used by behavior therapists.

Behavior therapy, in its various versions, differs markedly from methods used in psychoanalysis or nondirective therapy. First, a specific problem is identified. If the problem is complex, each aspect must be treated separately. Thus the target behavior—that is, what the change or outcome should be—is identified. The behavior therapist is not concerned with how the condition came about or what were its causes, but only with the treatment of the specific problems that will alter behavior for the better.

Reinforcement Therapy. A number of examples of reinforcement therapy have already been given in the "Assertions" section to show how positive reinforcement can modify undesirable behavior in a more adaptive direction. The basic principle involves the conditioning of new behavior through the process of differentiation (shaping) or reconditioning of more adaptive behavior in lieu of the persistent maladaptive responding. With ingenuity on the part of the therapist, reinforcement therapy can be applied to a wide variety of behavior problems in children as well as to neurotic and psychotic adults. The illustrations which follow are only a few of the hundreds of examples reported on the effectiveness of reinforcement therapy.

Isaacs, Thomas, and Goldiamond (1960) describe the differentiation or shaping of vocal responses in a catatonic schizophrenic who had been mute for 19 years. Shaping involved the following procedure. A piece of chewing gum was placed in front of the patient. If the patient noticed the gum it was given to him at first, but then the therapist waited until the patient made lip-moving responses before giving him the gum. As the gum was held up, the subject was instructed to say "gum," and obtaining the gum was contingent upon his making vocal responses which successfully approximated the word. Thereafter, other vocal responses in the presence of other persons were requested. Eventually, the patient was trained in this manner to speak in group therapy sessions.

Wolf, Risley, and Mees (1964) used differentiation (shaping) to get an autistic boy three and one-half years old to wear glasses. Initially, when glasses were placed on his head he would tear them off and throw them to the ground. In the beginning of their treatment, they used a conditioned reinforcer by pairing the clicks of a toy noisemaker with a small bit of candy or fruit. The child was first reinforced for wearing merely the frames. Then a "roll bar" which would go over the top of the boy's head was added. Finally, lenses were added to the frame. The boy was required to wear the glasses during meals and snacks, on automobile rides and going out to play, all of which were positively reinforcing stimuli. At the time of his dismissal from the hospital, he had worn the glasses for a total of 600 hours.

Reinforcement therapy can be applied to more complex activities. Schwitzgebel (1967) gained therapeutic cooperation in a group of juvenile delinquents for a series of 20 interviews. The experimental group received positive reinforcement for statements of concern about other people and for prompt arrival at the sessions. Reinforcements included candy, cigarettes, money (25 cents to $1) for statements like "Joe is a good guy." The control group received no reinforcements. In a natural setting (a restaurant), the experimental group showed significant increase in such positive statements.

Sometimes *contracts* can improve behavior. The assumption in setting up a contract is that there will be a reciprocal exchange of reinforcement which depends upon specific behavior on the part of each party to the contract. Tooley and Pratt (1967) report a case where a husband agreed to cut down on his smoking in exchange for better housekeeping on the part of his wife. Thus the husband agreed to cut his smoking down to 10 cigarettes a day in return for the living room being tidy when he came home from work. The technique was mutual cooperation.

Aversion Therapy.   In aversion therapy, based primarily on the principles of respondent conditioning, the conditioned stimulus (CS) is paired with an unconditioned stimulus (US) which is naturally aversive to the individual. It might be a nausea-producing substance or an electric shock. Prior to the conditioning the CS has had some positively reinforcing function, like alcohol for the alcoholic. When paired with the primary aversive stimulus (US), however, it takes on the function of being aversive.

The idea of treating alcoholics by associating a noxious stimulus with alcohol goes back to the ancient Roman practice of placing an eel in the wine jug and making the individual drink from it. Voegtlin (1940) and

Voegtlin and Lemere (1942) used injections of an emetic, a substance which causes vomiting. The subjects were poured an ounce of whiskey and instructed to look, smell, and then taste and swallow it. Additional amounts of alcohol were given until the emetic took effect and the subject vomited. Ordinarily, the procedure was repeated at from four to seven sessions. Using a total of 4,096 subjects, they reported an average overall abstinence rate of 51 percent over a 1-10 year follow-up period.

Aversion therapy has frequently been used in the treatment of sexual disorders. Raymond (1956) reports the case of a man who had a fetish for ladies' handbags and perambulators which brought him into frequent difficulties with the law. The treatment consisted of showing him a collection of handbags and perambulators, along with colored slides of the subjects, just before the onset of nausea produced by an injection of apomorphine. Not only was the fetish successfully eliminated, but the man showed improvement in his social and legal relationships. He was promoted in his job and no longer used fetish fantasies to have sexual intercourse.

Although the above examples made use of nausea-producing substances as the US, it should be noted that electric shock is also frequently so used. For examples, see Rachman and Teasdale, *Aversion Therapy and Behavior Disorders* (1969).

Institutional

One of the most effective applications of operant conditioning principles in institutions has been the use of what is called *the token economy*. Ayllon and Azrin (1968) outlined a plan currently in use in mental hospitals as well as in schools. Basically, the idea is that the persons involved are given tokens for performing a variety of desired behaviors.

In mental institutions, tokens can be given for work done in the laundry, kitchen, waiting on tables, and so on. These tokens can be exchanged to buy privacy (a private room instead of the ward), sitting at more attractive tables in the dining room, or candy or cigarettes at the commissary. Through such a program, patients can be led to engage in more desirable activities and to acquire better social behavior, instead of just sitting around in the ward or being troublesome. As a necessary part of the system, ward assistants are trained to observe the behavior of the patients and are given direct responsibility for handing out the tokens. Generally, each attendant works with a small group.

In the use of the token economy in school or classroom situations, the teacher or an aide dispenses the tokens. The following two examples illustrate the use of the token economy, the first in a classroom and the second in a mental institution.

Chadwick and Day (1971) applied token economy to a group of

underachieving elementary school children. The behaviors measured were percentage of time spent at work, work output per minute, and accuracy. The study was divided into three phases: (1) a base-line or prereinforcement period; (2) the treatment period, in which tokens and social reinforcements were given; and (3) a period in which only social reinforcements were used. The combination of tokens and social reinforcement increased all aspects of the behavior studied over that of the prereinforcement period. When only social reinforcements were used, the average time at work decreased as compared to when tokens were applied, but the same degree of accuracy of work was maintained.

Schaefer and Martin (1966) used jobs for patients in a mental hospital as a basis for token reinforcement. The behavior of a dormitory cleaner was shaped out in specific steps until an entire chain was completed. To receive the tokens the sequence included: (1) pick up cleaning equipment, (2) dust partitions and sills, (3) mop entire floor except under beds, (4) shake out rag and dust mop outside the ward, (5) empty and clean water pail, (6) wash windows on Saturdays, and (7) turn in equipment. It should be noted that these behaviors were shaped separately with tokens before the entire sequence was accomplished.

Another application of operant conditioning principles in education has been the use of programmed learning (Skinner, 1968), a basic principle of which is that immediate reinforcement is given when the learner makes a correct response. As the first step in learning, the student makes a response to a given question, usually in writing. He or she then is given immediate knowledge of the result and moves to the next question (or frame, as it is frequently called). Skinner first thought that a machine was needed so the learner could not cheat by looking at the answer before he made his response, but it was later discovered that it was not necessary. Programs are now usually printed in book form, and a card can be used to cover answers while questions are being answered.

A course of carefully ordered small steps is followed in programmed learning, with each step (question) small enough that it can be easily accomplished. In this way the student works at his own rate and gradually gets closer to the target behavior, that is, the whole course of what is to be ultimately learned. If the steps are too large, the student may miss too many questions and become discouraged. Programs are designed for all educational levels, from children acquiring simple discriminations, to early school skills, to learning mathematics or how to do a simple task like making a bed properly, to the operation of complicated machinery.

Self

One who understands the basic principles of operant conditioning can control not only his own behavior but that of others. If it is known what positive reinforcements strengthen a particular person's behavior, they can be applied to the particular behavior to be shaped or strengthened. Undesirable behavior may be ignored, provided the intention is maintaining that behavior. Sometimes children engage in what is called *negative attention getting*, exhibiting obnoxious behavior just to get any kind of attention, even criticism or a spanking.

Children will be happier and more productive in school if the teacher uses positive reinforcement instead of punishment. This will facilitate learning and will lessen hostility in the classroom. However, time-out can be effective. While Skinnerians consider time-out a form of punishment, the behavior punished is not followed by an aversive stimulus.

A good coach applies shaping principles whether he realizes it or not. In learning an athletic skill, the novice needs some reinforcement even though his early efforts are clumsy. More effective responses will occur as selective reinforcement is applied until the skill has been mastered. The coach who never praises his team but only criticizes them will encourage poor morale and team spirit.

If certain discriminative stimuli are eliminated from the environment, it will be impossible to respond to them. One way to give up smoking is not to buy, borrow, or have cigarettes around. However, the problem is not that simple, because smoking is tied up with a variety of other stimuli besides cigarettes. We smoke when others around us do or while we are having a cup of coffee or a drink or after a meal. It is because smoking is involved in so many other contingencies that many people find it hard to quit. Of course, there are other stimuli, some aversive, which can help reduce smoking, such as the threat of lung cancer or heart disease or the high price of cigarettes.

Dieting is another exercise in self-control. A variety of positive reinforcements can help in losing weight: Our clothes are no longer tight, we look better in the mirror, and people tell us how our appearance has improved. We can weigh ourselves regularly to keep track of weight loss, count calories, and eliminate discriminative stimuli which quickly add pounds, such as candy and pasta.

Since we are all continually behaving organisms, correct behavioral principles are useful in all aspects of human existence, such as rearing a happy child or maintaining compatible marital relationships. We have gone a long way in understanding ourselves and others. The basic principles of operant reinforcement presented in the Assertions section suggest the great advantage of this personality theory: it is a practical system, easily understood. Any individual can try it for himself. Because the principles are not merely hypothetical constructs but have been derived from careful observations, we know we are on solid ground. This is one great advantage over other personality theories. Operant conditioning can be applied not only therapeutically but also to everyday living.

VALIDATION

Evidence

Skinner's primary method of validation has been laboratory experimentation, although recent studies in what is referred to as *applied behavior analysis* have made use of studies in real-life situations such as classrooms, homes, and institutions for retarded and disturbed people.

In departing from traditional experimentation, Skinner and his followers have stressed the use of individual subjects, for it is believed that when proper controls are exercised, large numbers of subjects are not necessary. When large groups are used, whether animals or humans, the effects of environmental variables may be masked if appropriate controls are not applied. The traditional experimenter then uses sophisticated statistical procedures to get significant results. When proper controls are exercised, only a single subject or at most only a few are required, and complicated statistics are not necessary.

In many experiments in operant conditioning a baseline rate is established, the independent variable is imposed, and subsequent changes in behavior are observed and measured. This method, referred to as *using the subject as his own control*, eliminates the many possible uncontrolled variables involved when experimental and control groups are used, since under many circumstances the two groups cannot be properly matched.

Throughout this chapter reference has been made to experimental studies which have supported Skinner's assertions. These experiments, which have used animals and normal and disturbed children and adults in a variety of settings, have validated the system with a great deal of supporting evidence. Other examples can be cited from areas not discussed above.

One such area is *psychopharmacology*, the study of the effects of drugs on behavior. Many ethical drug companies are employing psychologists trained in Skinnerian methodology to test the effects of new drugs before placing them on the market. An example is a study by Boren (1960) in which rats were trained in an operant conditioning chamber to press a lever to receive food pellets as reinforcement. Once the baseline rate of lever pressing had been established, a drug, chlorpromazine, was administered, and results indicated that the rate was depressed. It is now known that this drug is an effective means of suppressing aggressive and extremely active behavior in severely disturbed psychiatric patients.

Perhaps one of the most unique examples of the operant conditioning procedures was reported by Skinner (1960). This study, which involved an attempt to devise a method for controlling the flight of missiles, was carried on during World War II under the auspices of the U.S. government. The aim was to demonstrate whether pigeons placed in missiles could guide them to their targets. Pigeons were trained to respond by pecking at a stimulus which resembled the missile target. Since these birds have excellent visual discrimination, the stimuli could resemble any target—a ship, a part of a city, or a particular landscape. When the missile was on target the pigeon would peck in the center of the stimulus panel, directly at the pattern of the target. When the missile changed direction, deviating from the target, it would move to another display area, and an activity system which would change the course of the missile in the proper direction could be activated. If the target moved to the right, for example, the pigeon would peck an area to the right of center, and the missile would adjust accordingly. It was found that by using variable-interval schedules of reinforcement the pigeons would continue at their designated tasks for long periods, and satiation was no problem as it would have been if the birds were continuously reinforced. While this study was never put to practical use, pigeons could have been put in missiles for actual guidance.

We have already discussed the applications of behavior principles in the practical control of behavior. General principles can be applied outside the laboratory to everyday living conditions. Skinnerians do not typically rely on case histories, but some studies have reported the modification of behavior in more formal situations. Examples already mentioned are Williams (1959), in the control of temper tantrums, and Tooley and Pratt (1967), in the development of contracts to reduce cigarette smoking by the husband in return for improved housekeeping by the wife.

Comparisons

Skinner's primary objection to most other personality theories is that they are dualistic, making use of mental events as distinct from purely physical ones. In the behavioristic tradition, Skinner has abandoned mental events, regardless of their sophistication. Other theories depend on hypothetical constructs and intervening variables such as "inner states" as causative explanations, instead of the clear data of the behaving organism operating in a natural environment. The methodology of self theories or existential theories depends almost entirely on introspection. Because it is phenomenological, it is unreliable and not subject to objective validation.

With regard to psychoanalysis, Skinner (1954) has leveled some specific criticisms. First, the nature of the act is never clarified. Such concepts as "libido," "cathexis," "instinctive tendencies," or psychic energy can hardly be quantified as objective events, because they lack any specific physical dimensions.

Second, Freud and the psychoanalysts have imposed a complicated mental structure (ego, superego, id) as an explanation for the causes of behavior. Instead of going back to the original environmental events, they accept the construct of these hypothecated mental events as an operating principle, which, in Skinner's thinking, is little more than fiction. In accepting such a hypothetical construct, little is left for behavior itself.

Third, in psychoanalysis there is a shift or transference from the physical to the mental event and vice versa, but how this happens is never explained. The psychic energy which runs one's personality is said to be derived from some kind of instinctual energy, presumably physical, but Freud never told us exactly how this transference occurs. Furthermore, the mental apparatus supposedly has some topological dimensions, as described in *The Ego and the Id* (Freud, 1923), but they are not exactly real.

Describing the evolution of psychoanalysis, Skinner says:

> One may take the line that metaphorical devices are inevitable in the early stages of any science and that although we may look with amusement upon "essences", "phlogistons" and "ethers" of the science of yesterday, these were necessary to the historical process....However, if we have learned anything about the nature of scientific thinking...it is possible to avoid some of the mistakes of adolescence. Whether Freud could have done so is past demonstrating, but whether we need similar constructs in the future prosecution of a science of behavior is a question worth considering. (Skinner, 1954, p. 301)

Skinner's objections to psychoanalysis would apply equally well to Individual and Analytical psychology, as well as to other neo-Freudian systems.

With regard to trait and type theories of personality, Skinner (1953) has further objections. He has suggested that prediction is more reliable on the basis of a single response than on the basis of a trait configuration. A trait is at best a measure of a variety of behaviors which appear to have some common descriptive characteristic, whereas a single response can be readily identified and measured. In traits, many behaviors originate in a variety of situations. It might be said that a person has a trait of *dominance*, but the situations in which such a person may or may not dominate are never specified. Traits, therefore, are not the causes of behavior but are mere verbal descriptions. The fewer traits are defined, the more generalized is the analysis and the less accurate are the predictions. Thus, a prediction will have to be made within a wide range of probability, and the chances of being right may often be only as good as the possibilities of being wrong.

Most personality theories depend too much on theory and too little on supporting data. When data are presented, they are frequently unreliable. For example, psychoanalysis, as well as Individual and Analytical psychology, relies on casual observations, things told the psychotherapist by clients, such as reports of dreams. This may lead to some interesting conjectures, but it can hardly be called science.

PROSPECT

In terms of the development of personality theorizing, the Skinnerian approach has arrived rather late on the scene. This was not the first personality theory based on S-R learning principles; other psychologists such as Dollard, Miller, and Mowrer, besides directing their efforts to many areas of psychology, have applied learning principles to the field of personality. Although Skinner began his work with animal experimentation, he and his followers have increasingly devoted their experiments and theorizing to problems of human behavior and to applications in the modification of deviant behavior. As early as the 1930s Skinner was recognized as an important learning theorist, and though he was not the first to recognize the importance of reinforcement, he did put it on operational grounds. It was Skinner's followers who applied operant conditioning principles more specifically to the field of personality.

If the course of development of thinking along the lines of operant conditioning is considered in a general way, the future looks bright. There is a division of the American Psychological Association devoted to this train of thought (Division 25, The Experimental Analysis of Behavior) and two journals reporting research using Skinnerian methodology: *The Journal of the Experimental Analysis of Behavior* and *The Journal of Applied Behavioral Analysis*. Other journals devoted to experimental psychology as well as behavior therapy also publish articles in which operant conditioning principles are applied, the *Psychological Record* and *Behavior Research and Therapy*, to name two.

The number of psychologists devoted to Skinner's ideas is rapidly increasing. Of course, they are not all concerned with problems of human behavior or personality. Skinner also has opponents who feel that his rigorous experimental and operational approach has dehumanized not only psychology but in particular the human personality.

Considering the varieties of personality theories mentioned in this book, it is unlikely that the Skinnerian approach is going to dominate the field. However, because of its many adherents and the vast amount of research being generated, even its most ardent opponents can hardly deny its impact on psychology.

Operant conditioning does not appear to be an approach that is on the wane or about to die out. The general scheme is attracting young, vigorous people who are devoted to the basic ideas Skinner has laid out. Certainly the movement Skinner represents is one of the dominant forces in psychology today.

ANNOTATED BIBLIOGRAPHY

Ferster, C. B., and Parrott, M. C. *Behavior Principles*. New York: Appleton-Century-Crofts, 1968.

A basic text for undergraduates on principles of Skinnerian psychology. Examples and experiments are cited which deal with both human and animal behavior.

Lundin, R. W. *Personality: A Behavioral Analysis*. 2d ed. New York: Macmillan, 1974.

The latest attempt to apply operant conditioning techniques, using animal and human experimentation, to the area of human personality.

O'Leary, K. D., and Wilson, G. T. *Behavior Therapy: Applications and Outcomes.* Englewood Cliffs, N. J.: Prentice-Hall, 1975.

This book is outlined according to various behavior disorders: fear, autism, mental retardation, delinquent and sexual disorders, and so on. In each section various studies are cited showing how principles of behavior modification have been applied in treating the various disorders.

Rimm, D. C., and Masters, J. C. *Behavior Therapy: Techniques and Empirical Findings.* New York: Academic Press, 1974.

The organization of this book is by behavioral techniques, such as desensitization, aversion therapy, operant reinforcement, and extinction. Examples are given in each section of how these techniques can be applied to the treatment of behavior disorders.

Skinner, B. F. *The Behavior of Organisms: An Experimental Approach.* New York: Appleton-Century-Crofts, 1938.

Skinner's first major work presents his principles, based on experimentation with rats in an operant conditioning chamber.

Skinner, B. F. *Science and Human Behavior.* New York: Macmillan, 1953.

An application of behavioral principles to human conduct. Examples of control are treated as they apply to economics, government and law, education, religion, and psychotherapy.

Skinner, B. F. *Beyond Freedom and Dignity.* New York: Knopf, 1971.

This is an attempt to reinterpret in behavioral terms such concepts as freedom, dignity, value, and cultural design.

Ullmann, L. P., and Krasner, L. *Case Studies in Behavior Modification.* New York: Holt, Rinehart & Winston, 1965.

This is a collection of various studies using principles of behavior modification to alter neurotic and more severe disorders in children and adults. Some of the studies are reprinted from journal articles, others are presented for the first time in this book.

REFERENCES

Ayllon, T. Intensive treatment of psychotic behavior by stimulus satiation and food reinforcement. *Behavior Research and Therapy*, 1963, *3*, 53–61.

Ayllon, T., & Azrin, N. H. *The token economy.* New York: Appleton-Century-Crofts, 1968.

Ayllon, T., & Michael, J. The psychiatric nurse as a behavioral engineer. *Journal of the Experimental Analysis of Behavior*, 1959, *2*, 232–334.

Azrin, N. H. Suggested effects of punishment. In T. Verhave (Ed.), *The experimental analysis of behavior.* New York: Appleton-Century-Crofts, 1966.

Azrin, N. H., & Lindsley, O. R. The reinforcement of cooperative behavior in children. *Journal of Abnormal and Social Psychology*, 1956, *52*, 100–102.

Boren, J. J. Some effects of chlorpromazine on several operant behaviors. *Psychopharmacologia*, 1960, *2*, 416–424.

Brown, C. D., & Tyler, V. O. Time out from reinforcement: A technique for dethroning the "duke" of an institutionalized delinquent group. *Journal of Child Psychology and Psychiatry*, 1969, *9*, 203–211.

Chadwick, B. A., & Day, R. C. Systematic reinforcement: Academic performance of underachieving students. *Journal of Applied Behavior Analysis*, 1971, *4*, 311–319.

Ferster, C. B., & Skinner, B. F. *Schedules of reinforcement.* New York: Appleton-Century-Crofts, 1957.

Freud, S. *The ego and the id.* London: Hogarth Press, 1947. (First German edition, 1923.)

Holland, J. G., & Skinner, B. F. *The analysis*

of behavior: A program of self instruction. New York: McGraw-Hill, 1961.

Isaacs, W., Thomas, J., & Goldiamond, I. Shaping vocal responses in mute catatonic schizophrenics. *Journal of Speech and Hearing Disorders*, 1960, *25*, 6–12.

Jones, M. C. A behavior study of fear: The case of Peter. *Journal of Genetic Psychology*, 1924, *31*, 508–515.

Kinkade, K. *A Walden II experiment: The first five years of Twin Oaks.* New York: William Morrow, 1973.

Mowrer, O. H. *Learning theory and personality dynamics.* New York: Ronald Press, 1950.

Pavlov, I. P. *Conditioned reflexes* (G. V. Anrep, trans.). London: Oxford University Press, 1927.

Rachman, S., & Teasdale, J. *Aversion therapy and behavior disorders.* Coral Gables, Fla.: University of Miami Press, 1969.

Raymond, M. S. Case of fetishism treated by aversion therapy. *British Medical Journal*, 1956, *2*, 854–857.

Schaefer, H. H., & Martin, P. L. Behavior therapy for "apathy" in hospitalized schizophrenics. *Psychological Reports*, 1966, *19*, 1147–1158.

Schwitzgebel, R. Short term operant conditioning of adolescent offenders on socially relevant variables. *Journal of Abnormal Psychology*, 1967, *72*, 134–138.

Skinner, B. F. On the rate of formation of a conditioned reflex. *Journal of General Psychology*, 1932, *7*, 274–285.

Skinner, B. F. On the rate of extinction of a conditioned reflex. *Journal of General Psychology*, 1933, *8*, 51–60.

Skinner, B. F. *The behavior of organisms: An experimental analysis.* New York: Appleton-Century-Crofts, 1938.

Skinner, B. F. *Walden Two.* New York: Macmillan, 1948.

Skinner, B. F. *Science and human behavior.* New York: Macmillan, 1953.

Skinner, B. F. Critique of psychoanalytical concepts and theories. *Scientific Monthly*, 1954, *79*, 300–305.

Skinner, B. F. *Verbal behavior.* New York: Appleton-Century-Crofts, 1957.

Skinner, B. F. Pigeons in a pelican. *American Psychologist*, 1960, *15*, 28–37.

Skinner, B. F. *The technology of teaching.* New York: Appleton-Century-Crofts, 1968.

Skinner, B. F. *Beyond freedom and dignity.* New York: Knopf, 1971.

Skinner, B. F. *About behaviorism.* New York: Knopf, 1974.

Thorndike, E. L. Animal intelligence: An experimental study of the associative process in animals. *Psychological Review: Monograph Supplement*, 1898 (No. 8).

Thorndike, E. L. *Animal intelligence: Experimental studies.* New York: Macmillan, 1911.

Tooley, J. T., & Pratt, S. An experimental procedure for the extinction of smoking behavior. *Psychological Record*, 1967, *17*, 209–218.

Voegtlin, W. L. The treatment of alcoholism by establishing a conditioned reflex. *American Journal of Medical Science*, 1940, *199*, 802–910.

Voegtlin, W. L., & Lemere, F. The treatment of alcoholic addiction. *Quarterly Journal of Studies in Alcohol*, 1942, *2*, 717–802.

Watson, J. B. Psychology as the behaviorist views it. *Psychological Review*, 1913, *20*, 158–177.

Watson, J. B. *Behaviorism.* New York: Norton, 1925.

Watson, J. B. & Raynor, R. Conditioned emotional reactions. *Journal of Experimental Psychology*, 1920, *3*, 1–14.

Williams, C. D. The elimination of tantrum behavior by extinction procedures. *Journal of Abnormal and Social Psychology*, 1959, *59*, 260.

Wolf, M. M., Risley, T., & Mees, H. L. Application of operant conditioning procedures to the behavior problems of an autistic child. *Behavior Research and Therapy*, 1964, *1*, 305–312.

ALBERT BANDURA

Beginnings

Albert Bandura was born in a small town of Mundar in the Province of
Alberta, Canada, on December 4, 1925. His high school had only 20
students and two teachers. Thus, to a considerable extent, he was self-
educated in his early years. He received his B.A. degree from the University
of British Columbia at Vancouver in 1949. He then went on to graduate
school in psychology at the University of Iowa receiving his M.A. in 1951,
and the Ph.D. in 1952. Following a year's internship at the Wichita Kansas
Guidance Clinic, he accepted a position in the psychology department at
Stanford University where he has remained up to the present time.

Since his early years as a psychologist, Bandura has been concerned with
the development of a social-learning theory emphasizing modeling to
understand human personality. His earliest books *Adolescent Aggression*
(1959) and *Social Learning and Personality Development* (1963) were written in collaboration with the late Richard Walters. His book *Principles of
Behavior Modification* (1969) was one of the first to summarize research in
this area. As one might expect, the book is heavily loaded with experimental
reports of modeling.

Current Status

Bandura's book, *Social-Learning Theory* (1977), is considered by many to be
the most complete statement of his current position. He continues to be actively engaged in research supporting his theory. He received the Distinguished Scientist Award from the American Psychological Association in 1972 and
the Distinguished Scientific Achievement Award of the California
Psychological Association in 1973. In the same year he was elected president

of the American Psychological Association. He has served as a Fellow of the Center for Advanced Study in the Behavioral Sciences at Stanford University.

Albert Bandura is currently considered the leading figure in social-learning theory. He has not only been a pioneer in this approach to personality theory, but he is also one of the leading theorists and experimenters in the field of behavior modification. His earlier studies on aggression along with a later work in that area (*Aggression: A Social-Learning Analysis* ([1973])) make him one of the leading authorities in that field.

ASSERTIONS

Development

1. *The causes of human behavior are the reciprocal interaction of behavioral, cognitive, and environmental influences.*

This assertion has been labeled *reciprocal determinism*. Bandura claims he has abandoned the Freudian concept of inner causes. However, the same event can be a stimulus, a response, or an environmental condition depending on where the analysis begins. For example, although our behavior is influenced by environmental factors, that same environment can be of our own making. Thus, we have the power to exercise some control over our own environment which in turn can affect our behavior. Unlike Skinner's contention that we are solely the result of genetic factors and external environmental conditions, Bandura contends that we have the capacity for cognition through our use of symbols. He believes certain internal cognitions can act as causes of behavior. For example, people can feel sick by imagining revolting situations or will express external anger by thinking about people we despise, or can become sexually excited by engaging in sexual fantasies. Bandura (1977) states that "...any theory which denies that thoughts can regulate action does not lend itself readily to the explanation of complex human behavior" (p. 10).

Bandura rejects Skinner's emphasis on a totally controlling external environment. He believes that internal personal factors such as thoughts, preferences, expectations and perception of self operate as interrelated regulators of each other.

"In a social-learning view, people are neither entirely determined by internal causes nor environmental stimuli, but psychological functioning is accounted for by a reciprocal interaction of personal and environmental determinants." (Bandura, 1977, pp. 11–12)

2. *The primary factor in personality development is observational learning.*

This most distinctive feature of Bandura's theory is the premise that the vast majority of our behavior is acquired through the copying of others; that is, modeling our behavior after theirs. This contention is in contrast to Skinner's view that learning occurs only by actually performing certain responses which will be maintained or strengthened by their consequences. In contrast to Skinner, Bandura believes that behavior need not have to actually occur and be overtly reinforced for learning to take place. A vast amount of our human learning occurs vicariously through observation. Simply by observing others' behavior and the consequences, we can acquire that behavior presuming the consequences are evidently attached to the behavior. Thus, Bandura rejects, at least in part, Skinner's principle of shaping or differentiation through selective reinforcement. Through watching and instruction we can learn to perform a task correctly.

"Observational learning is vital for both development and survival. Because mistakes can produce costly or even fatal consequences, the prospects for survival would be slim indeed if one could learn only by suffering the consequences of trial and error" (Bandura, 1977, p. 12).

A child learns by watching, whether it be how to tie a knot, play a game or turn a somersault. Likewise, he or she learns by observation how to be aggressive or afraid, how to cooperate or to compete. Later on we learn how to swing a tennis racquet by observing our coach or how to bow a violin string by watching our teacher.

Furthermore, the observer can extract common features from different situations which will enable him to generalize what he has observed.

"By synthesizing features of different models into new analgrams, observers can achieve through modeling novel styles of thought and conduct. Once imitated, experiences with new forms create further evolutionary changes. A partial departure from tradition eventually becomes a new tradition" (Bandura, 1974, p. 864).

3. *Individuals may be influenced by symbols which act as models.*

Pictorial presentation such as those in movies and television are highly influential sources for modeling. Bandura, Ross, and Ross (1963) found that children who watched the aggressive behavior of live adult models were as aggressive as children shown a movie of the same behavior. Bandura has been concerned with the effects of viewing violence on television and in the movies on an individual's own behavior. It seems clear that seeing violence symbolically is not much different from seeing it *in vivo*. The same would hold true for other behaviors such as love making, generation of fear as in terror movies, or instilling desirable cooperative behavior.

4. *Modeling is governed by four interrelated processes: Attention, retention, motor reproduction, and motivation.*

A person does learn much by observation when attending to the important cues and characteristics of the model's behavior. One must note the important information and select the essential features. Bandura notes that among important attentional determinants are associational patterns. It is evident that people with whom we most often associate, either by our own preference or who are forced upon us, serve as important models for better or for worse.

Some people gain greater attention because of their status or assigned roles. Likewise, we will more often model those who have similar lifestyles and goals (Rosenkraus, 1967). Furthermore, models who are alleged to be experts, considered to be celebrities, or important people tend to have greater attentional vlaue (Rosenbaum & Tucker, 1962).

Second, the retention process is necessary for successful modeling. One cannot be influenced by a model's behavior if he or she does not remember the modeling act. For memory to work it must be coded in some symbolic form (words or images) that can be recalled.

Third, the symbolic coded memories must be translated into motor action, thus, mere observation may not be enough. Practice in performing the motor movements as well as self-correction is essential to perfect the modeled results. In more complicated modeling such as diving, playing a difficult piece on the piano, or painting a landscape, much practice is needed.

Fourth, an important component in modeling is reinforcement which Bandura more or less equates with motivation. Although Bandura believes that modeling can take place in the absence of reinforcement, he does not deny its importance. The advantage of incentives is that the modeling can be more quickly translated into action. The observation that another's behavior is seen to lead to positive reinforcements or tends to avoid aversive consequences is a compelling factor for the first three components to work. Reinforcement may be experienced vicariously (see below). We have the power to anticipate consequences and can look forward to similar consequences as we observe following the model's behavior.

Maintenance

5. *To a large extent behavior is maintained by anticipated consequences.*

We do not wait until our automobile is stolen to take out insurance on it, nor do we wait for our house to burn down before we take necessary precautions to prevent fire. In each instance we imagine the consequences symbolically. As human beings we have an unique capacity for foresight. Bandura does not deny Skinner's contention that behavior is strengthened or weakened by immediate consequences (reinforcement or extinction), but he goes beyond this notion. Whereas Skinner defines reinforcement as those stimuli which strengthen or maintain behavior (regardless of our awareness of the stimuli), Bandura contends that reinforcement must be informational to work, related to our conscious anticipations. We act in ways we believe will achieve positive consequences or which will avoid aversive conditions. Through knowledge and foresight we can anticipate consequences rather than merely waiting for them to happen.

"Skinner's concept of 'response strengthening' is merely a metaphor. Thus, if responses have been positively reinforced in the past, the reinforcement may not necessarily function in the future if the person believes from other information that this will not necessarily occur again" (Bandura, 1977).

Likewise, Skinner's notion of "resistance to extinction" may only exist in part because of a person's expectation that he will succeed. The important point here is that we cognitively interpret the consequences of our acts.

6.   *Behavior can be maintained by vicarious reinforcement.*

A novice bellhop in a hotel observes another bellhop being generously tipped for efficient, friendly service. This observation should increase the probability of an observant bellhop doing likewise. Observing the vicarious consequences of the other's behavior should play an influential role in regulating the behavior of the observer.

Generally, vicarious reinforcement works whenever we observe the actions of a model who has received some external reinforcement which we think has been contingent upon the model's actions. If the observation inclines us to imitate the model, we say that the vicarious reinforcement has been effective. Obviously, the same can hold for vicarious punishment when we observe the negative consequences of another's act.

Bandura (1977) has been concerned with how this kind of learning takes place. He suggests six regulatory functions as follows:

1. *Information function.* This involves the learner's observation of what happens to the model. For example, a child who observes another child's aggression being punished is less likely to exhibit his own aggression.

2. *Motivational function.* This involves seeing another person being reinforced. A person who observes another being reinforced by laughter may try the same. "She's a crashing bore." That's a funny expression! I'll try it.

3. *Emotional-learning function.* This function involves general heightening of emotional responses. The old saying, "Anxious mothers rear anxious children," or "An aggressive father will breed an aggressive son" illustrate this function.

4. *Influence-credibility function.* This is illustrated by a student who exhibits joy upon receiving a scholarship. Others who observe this event may share that joy. One might say in return, "I'm so happy for you."

5. *Modification of model status function.* This states that a model's social status can increase or decrease as a result of being reinforced or punished. A child praised by a teacher for excellent work achieves greater status in the eyes of fellow students. They might try to imitate that performance.

6. *Validation function.* This refers to the fact that reinforcement applied to a model has an effect on the observer's perceived validation of both the agent who applies the reinforcement as well as the model. A student (observer) who sees another student (model) unjustly chastised for speaking out in class is less inclined to speak out in a similar manner.

7. *Reinforcements (and punishments) can operate in a vicarious manner.*

Both social and antisocial behavior is increased or decreased by watching others perform particular actions and observing their consequences. Thus, the dictum "When in Rome do as the Romans do" holds. Observational learning (modeling) occurs primarily through our cognitions. We imagine ourselves in the same situation that we observe, and we are able to think about the consequences.

Another important factor in observational learning involves relational characteristics of the learner and the model. For instance, learning is more effective if the model is high in status and attractiveness or is similar to the subject in age and sex. Jakubczak and Walters (1959) found dependent children to be more influenced by the behavior of the model than less dependent children.

8. *Behavior can be self-governed by means of self-produced consequences (self-reinforcement).*

Although we may be affected by external reinforcers, it is also possible to reinforce ourselves, that is, exert control over our own behavior. This can be illustrated by the feeling of satisfaction one experiences for a job well done. As human beings we have the capacity to develop standards for our conduct. When we meet these standards, we can reinforce ourselves without the need of any external reinforcing agent. Likewise, when we do a poor job and we perceive that it is substandard, we can punish ourselves, perhaps by a feeling of guilt. This notion bears some relationship to the Freudian concept of the superego rewarding and punishing the ego for its acts.

When I complete a crossword puzzle without error I will be extremely pleased with myself and will be more inclined to try again even though there were no other people around to tell me how well I did. This is self-reinforcement.

Self-reinforcing systems employ the same learning principles responsible for the acquisition of other types of behavior. What individuals come to reinforce or punish in themselves reflects the reactions that their behavior has elicited from others: parents, peers, teachers, and other socializing agents. They set the behavior standards and reinforce the individual for living up to them. These externally imposed norms are "taken over" by the person and form the basis for later self-reinforcement systems.

In writing this text, I do not need some external person standing over me to reinforce each properly placed sentence with praise. I am guided by certain inner standards which relate to good or bad work. When the work is revised and completed to my satisfaction, I may experience a feeling of pride.

The notion of self-reinforcement is also related to the idea of a self-concept. This is a tendency to judge ourselves favorably or unfavorably. This bears some similarity to Carl Rogers' concept of the self. However, Bandura does not accept the belief that a single self-image is sufficient to account for vastly different behaviors. Instead, Bandura believes that one's self-concept varies in different situations as when studying, playing sports, or behaving at a social gathering.

9. *Human beings are capable of self-regulation of behavior.*

Bandura proposes three components of the self-regulation process. These are: *self-observation, judgment,* and *self-response.* In *self-observation* we note the quality or proficiency of our performance. The criteria we set up for ourselves depends on the kinds of action performed. A good golfer notes the accuracy of the shot while a writer observes the correctness of grammatical constructions.

In the *judgmental* process we value our own performances according to internal standards as being excellent, good, average, or poor. Of course, our judgments are relative in learning a particular task. In the beginning we do not expect as much of ourselves as we do when greater proficiency is achieved. A beginning piano student does not expect as much of himself as when he becomes more proficient. At first he may judge himself well if he merely hits the right notes. Later, the judgment of a performance becomes more demanding as to how rapidly one is able to play a particular selection. All of this involves self-assessment. We can judge ourselves either by comparing with previous performances or by comparing with that of some other person. A tennis player can note her own improvement or compare her performance with other players. The third component involves the *self-response process.* This typically involves self-evaluation. In a sense we are criticizing ourselves. If we do well, we feel good. Doing poorly involves self-punishment. "I did a rotten job."

"Self-evaluative reactions acquire and retain the rewarding and punishing value through correlations with tangible consequences. That is, people usually engage in self-gratification after achieving a sense of self-pride, whereas they treat themselves badly when they judge themselves self-critically." (Bandura 1977, p. 133)

10. Delay of gratification may be influenced by modeling.

Delay of gratification is defined as the postponement of an immediate smaller reinforcement for a larger and more valuable one in the future. Instead of spending our money immediately for a cheap secondhand car, we may save it up to buy a new and more expensive model in the future.

An experiment by Bandura and Michael (1965) illustrates the principle. Children were first given a choice between receiving a small candy bar which they could have immediately or wait a week for a larger one. As a result of this first condition, the children were divided into two extreme groups, those who typically chose immediate rewards and those who usually preferred to wait. The children then observed a live adult model who displayed behavior opposite to their original choices. Thus, those who chose immediate gratification were subjected to a model who preferred the delay of gratification and vice-versa. On later tests it was clearly evident that the children's choices were strongly influenced by the behaviors of the model. Thus, the children who had originally chosen the delayed reward, when subjected to the model who chose immediate reward, tended to follow the model. The reverse was equally true. The children, who had chosen immediate rewards and were exposed to the model who chose delayed rewards, tended to prefer the delayed rewards.

VALIDATION

Evidence

The amount of research available in validating Bandura's theory is extensive, much of it involving the modeling concept. Here we will mention only a few studies spanning several decades of research.

An early experimental study on modeling is representative of many others which were to follow. Bandura, Ross, and Ross (1961) chose nursery school children who watched a variety of aggressive responses, both verbal and physical, displayed by an adult model toward a large Bobo doll. Another group of children watched a nonaggressive adult who sat quietly in the room and paid no attention to the doll. Later, the children were mildly frustrated and placed in the presence of the doll. Those who observed the aggressive model gave many more aggressive responses toward the doll than those who had watched the nonaggressive adult. This experiment illustrates several main aspects of Bandura's theory. First, children can learn new responses merely by observing. Second, the experiment demonstrates that learning can take place without the subject making actual responses, and finally, learning can take place in the absence of external reinforcement.

Another experiment (Bandura, Ross & Ross, 1963) illustrates the role of vicarious reinforcement in modeling. Children were shown televised films in which models displayed both verbal and physical aggression. In one group the children saw the model's aggressive behavior being positively reinforced. In a second group the model's aggressive behavior was punished. In a third group no particular consequences were observed. Following the films, the children were placed in a play situation where the degree of their aggression was noted (i.e., kicks Bobo doll, strikes it with a ball, shoots darts at toy animals). Those children who have seen the model positively reinforced (rewarded) gave many more aggressive responses than those who had seen it punished.

Bandura believes this study and many others like it indicate serious implications of the effects of viewing violence on television and at the movies. Most Americans are avid television viewers. A study by Baker and Bell (1969) found some form of violence in 8 out of 10 programs (9 out of 10 in children's weekend shows with an average of five violent episodes per hour).

Another study, this one by Bandura and Perloff (1967), compared the relative effectiveness of self-reinforcement and externally applied reinforcement. Children worked at a manual task of cranking a wheel in which they earned scores (points) depending on the number of cranking responses they made. The more effort the children expended, the higher scores they would get. In the self-reinforcement condition children selected how many responses they would strive for in order to attain a given number of points. They then reinforced themselves with tokens which could be exchanged for prizes whenever they achieved their desired goal.

In the external reinforced condition a matched group of children were given the same standards as the self-reinforced group had set for themselves. They were then given the tokens whenever they achieved the standards set for them by the experimenters. A third group was given the tokens in advance of their performance, and a fourth group received no tokens at all for their work. In the groups, each child worked alone and was allowed to discontinue the task whenever he or she desired.

Results indicated that the children in the self-reinforcement and externally reinforced groups were more than twice as productive as those who got the reinforcements in advance or those who received no reinforcements at all. Furthermore, the self-reinforced group set extremely high standards for their performance. Although they worked alone and were allowed to set whatever standards they desired, all the children chose standards above the minimal allowed. Many in this group selected the highest standards of achievement allowed by the experimenters.

Comparisons

In the first part of this chapter, we compared Skinnerian theory with psychoanalytic and trait theories. In this section we will compare some of Bandura's concepts with some of Skinner's, pointing out similarities and differences.

Both claim to be behaviorists, which involves taking an objective approach and relying on empirical experimental findings. Bandura has depended entirely on studies with human subjects, while Skinner has drawn frequently from experimentation with animals.

Skinner had been described as a "radical behaviorist" stressing that we are the product of our native endowment and external environmental influences. Bandura has often been called a "soft" or "moderate behaviorist." A critical part of Bandura's theory relies on the importance of cognitive or internal thinking processes.

Skinner is a complete determinist, relying entirely on external environment as the causes of behavior once genetic forces are set. Bandura takes a more middle-of-the-road approach in his reciprocal determinism discussed earlier. This involves the reciprocal interplay of behavior, the person and the environment.

Both acknowledge the role of reinforcement in learning. For Skinner, the emphasis is on external stimuli which strengthens and maintains behavior. Bandura does not deny that in some instances external reinforcements operate, but he places a strong emphasis on vicarious learning and self-reinforcement.

While Skinnerians have not completely ignored the possibility of modeling or imitation, it plays a minor role in their theory. For Bandura most of human learning is the result of modeling. Thus, observational learning is the cornerstone of the theory.

Although not ignoring the importance of an objective approach to the study of human behavior, Bandura is more subjective than Skinner. In his concept of self-evaluation, subjectivity stands out. There are times when the hard-line Skinnerians would consider a number of Bandura's concepts outright mentalistic. Sometimes Bandura's ideas seem close to those of Rogers although each may use different words. In a sense, Bandura would like the "best of all worlds." He talks of self-generated influences on behavior but also allows for external influences.

APPLICATIONS

Treatment

People with psychological problems are unable to discover and emit behaviors that lead to appropriate consequences. Thus, the job of the therapist is to help restore the client's sense of self-efficiency, a belief that the person can master a situation and bring about desirable consequences through one's own efforts. When anxiety is present, that would be a sign that self-efficiency is lacking.

Bandura (1977) stated;

> The strength of people's convictions in their own effectiveness determines whether they will even try to cope with difficult situations...the stronger the efficiency or mastery expectations, the more active the efforts. Those who persist in performing activities that are subjectively threatening but relatively safe objectively will gain corrective experiences that further reinforce the sense of efficiency, thereby eventually eliminating the fears and defensive behavior" (pp. 79–80).

In the light of these goals, Bandura allows for a wide range of techniques of behavior modification similar to those used by other behaviorists (systematic desensitization, reinforcement therapy, extinction therapy, shaping and so on). In particular, however, modeling is of special importance. Furthermore, cognitive restructuring is useful in eliminating fears and expectations of failure. Like Skinner, Bandura takes a dim view of the "talk" therapies as represented in psychodynamic methods or the nondirective method of Rogers.

Self

Like Skinner, Bandura favors techniques of self-control. Self-control involves self-observation. One must be very systematic about developing this in noting the time, place, and rate at which a particular behavior occurs. Suppose one wished to give up eating jelly beans. He would note where the jelly beans are purchased, where they are kept in the office or at home, when one is most likely to eat them, and how many are eaten each day. One would also note the particular cues which incite eating them as well as the possible weight gain involved. One should keep charts and a behavioral diary.

The second step in self-control is much the same as suggested by Skinner; namely, the rearranging of the environment. In the case of the jelly bean eater, all jelly beans would be eliminated so there would be no temptation. Cues such as jelly bean jars or containers would be removed from the environment. If jelly beans contributed to a weight problem one might substitute chewing sugarless gum or some other nonfattening substance.

PROSPECT

Today, there are predominantly two behavioristic personality theories both of which stress the role of learning. Although Bandura has accepted many of Skinner's principles he has gone beyond them in stressing the role of modeling in his social-learning theory. His principles have been drawn typically from experimentation with human subjects from preschool children to adults. Besides emphasizing the importance of modeling, he has introduced concepts of *cognition, vicarious reinforcement, self-reinforcement, self-regulation* and *delay of gratification.*

Bandura's theories are becoming increasingly popular as evidenced in their appearance in books on personality theories, such as this one. Many of his ideas are extremely attractive as variants or corrections of the orthodox Skinnerian position. The experimental evidence is extremely impressive in demonstrating that a great deal of our behavior is acquired through observational learning. For many who have behavioristic inclinations, Bandura's position offers an attractive alternative to the Skinnerian position.

ANNOTATED BIBLIOGRAPHY

Bandura, A. *Principles of Behavior Modification.* New York: Holt, Rinehart & Winston, 1969.

One of the first books to survey various methods of behavior modification. The review of the literature on modeling is quite complete up to the date of the book. For other references on books on behavior modification see the section on "Skinner's Operant Reinforcement Theory."

Bandura, A. *Social-learning Theory.* Englewood Cliffs, N. J. Prentice-Hall, 1977.

The most complete statement of Bandura's entire theory to date. This represents the best organized expression with illustrative examples and experiments.

Bandura, A., & Walters, R. *Social Learning Theory and Personality Development.* New York: Holt, Rinehart & Winston, 1963.

An earlier statement of the development of a new theory of personality. An interesting place to begin and then compare with the later statement in 1977.

REFERENCES

Baker, R., & Bell, S. *Violence and the media: A staff report to the national commission on the causes and prevention of violence.* Washington, D.C.: U.S. Government Printing Office, 1969.

Bandura, A. *Principles of behavior modification.* New York: Holt, Rinehart & Winston, 1969.

Bandura, A. *Aggression: A social-learning analysis.* Englewood Cliffs, N.J.: Prentice-Hall, 1973.

Bandura, A. Behavior theory and the models of man. *American Psychologist,* 1974, *29,* 859–869.

Bandura, A. *Social-learning theory.* Englewood Cliffs, N.J.: Prentice-Hall, 1977.

Bandura, A., & Michael, W. Modification of self-imposed delay of reward through exposure to live and symbolic models. *Journal of Personality and Social Psychology,* 1965, *2,* 698–705.

Bandura, A., & Perloff, B. Relative efficiency of self-monitored and externally imposed reinforcement systems. *Journal of Personality and Social Psychology,* 1967, *7,* 111–116.

Bandura, A., Ross, D., & Ross, S. Transmission of aggression behavior through imitation of aggressive models. *Journal of Abnormal and Social Psychology,* 1961, *63,* 375–382.

Bandura, A., Ross, D., & Ross, S. Imitation of film mediated aggressive models. *Journal of Abnormal and Social Psychology*, 1963, *66*, 3–11.

Bandura, A., & Walters, R. *Adolescent aggression*. New York: Ronald Press, 1959.

Bandura, A., & Walters, R. *Social learning and personality development*. New York: Holt, Rinehart & Winston, 1963.

Jakubczak, L. F., & Walters, R. Suggestability in dependent behavior. *Journal of Abnormal and Social Psychology*, 1959, *59*, 102–107.

Rosenbaum, M., & Tucker, I. Competence of a model and the learning of imitation and nonimitation. *Journal of Experimental Psychology*, 1962, *63*, 108–190.

Rosenkraus, M. Imitation in children as a function of perceived similarity and vicarious reinforcement. *Journal of Personality and Social Psychology*, 1967, *7*, 307–315.

CHAPTER VIII

A Selection of Personality Theories

Anthony J. Marsella and
Raymond J. Corsini

INTRODUCTION

The purpose of this chapter is to provide the reader with condensed presentations of some of the major personality theories not included in the previous chapters. Now, there are as many as 100 personality theories. It would be impossible for any single volume to discuss all of these theories. However, it would also be unfortunate to exclude theories which have gained prominence. Thus, our purpose in preparing this chapter is to offer discussions of other major personality theories and theorists in an abbreviated format. Although the depth of coverage is more limited, we have not sacrificed accuracy and the reader will find a meaningful introduction to the theories in the following pages.

The chapter is divided into four sections. Each section represents a major personality theory orientation and contains examples of some of the major figures in that particular orientation. Section 1 covers *psychosocial theories* and includes discussions of the work of Karen Horney, Erich Fromm, Harry Stack Sullivan, and Erik Erikson. Section 2 concerns *personalistic theories* and includes the works of Gordon W. Allport and Henry A. Murray. Section 3 contains discussions of *holistic and humanistic theories* through the works of Kurt Goldstein, Fritz Perls, and Abraham Maslow. Lastly, Section 4 offers discussions of the work of *trait/type personality theories*; it includes the works of Hans J. Eysenck and Raymond B. Cattell. Each of the theories in the various sections is presented according to a common outline to facilitate the acquisition of the material.

331

PSYCHOSOCIAL THEORIES

As the personality theories of Freud, Adler, and Jung gained increased popularity, a number of people began to advance alternative views to those of the "big three." Many of the new theorists were students of these pioneers. In contrast to Freud and Jung, however, they perceived the need for theories which gave greater attention to the social forces which shape and influence human behavior. Although still *psychodynamic* in their orientation, the psychosocial theorists emphasized the role of the sociocultural milieu in both normal and abnormal behavior. Among the most prominent members of the new group of psychosocial theorists to emerge from the psychodynamic tradition were Karen Horney, Erich Fromm, Harry Stack Sullivan, and Erik Erikson who, according to many scholars, were really neo-Adlerians, since Adler, of the big three, most strongly stressed the importance of understanding the individual in a social context or milieu. (See Chapter 3.)

KAREN HORNEY (1885-1952)

Biographical

Karen Horney was born in Hamburg, Germany, on September 16, 1885, the daughter of a Norwegian father and a Dutch mother. She attended medical school at the University of Berlin, and subsequently studied psychoanalysis in Berlin under the guidance of Karl Abrahams, one of Sigmund Freud's earliest followers. She emerged as one of psychoanalysis' foremost leaders quite early in her career, and was certainly its most eminent female practitioner for many decades.

In 1932, she was invited to become associate director of the Chicago Psychoanalytic Institute. She accepted this invitation and left Europe behind for a new beginning in the United States. In 1934, she moved to New York where she assumed a position as a training analyst with the New York Psychoanalytic Institute. During this period she began to write extensively about her views of human behavior, especially neurotic behavior. She authored many papers and a number of books, several of which gained popularity with lay audiences. Her books are: *The Neurotic Personality of Our Time* (1937), *Our Inner Conflicts* (1945), *Neurosis and Human Growth* (1950), and *Feminine Psychology* (1967). The last book consists of a number of her early papers written in Germany and was compiled by Herbert Kelman following her death.

As Karen Horney continued her practice and teaching in New York, she gradually evolved a theory which focused on the role of sociocultural factors in neurosis. By the end of her life, she emerged as a major theorist whose conclusions only faintly resembled those of her psychoanalytic teachers. At the time of her death on December 4, 1952, Karen Horney was dean of the American Institute of Psychoanalysis, an institution devoted to furthering her seminal thoughts about the causes and nature of neurotic behavior.

In many respects, Karen Horney developed a theory of neurosis rather than a theory of personality, since she was primarily concerned with the causes and cure of neurosis. Yet, as one progresses through her books, her assumptions can be extended with little effort to the entire spectrum of human behavior, including child development, thinking styles, personality needs, and characterological orientations. She was a perceptive viewer of the human condition and a courageous thinker who extended the frontiers of psychodynamic thought to the regions of social functioning in spite of the many pressures of the time to adhere to orthodox psychoanalytic thinking. Her strength of character is also illuminated by the fact that she was a woman functioning in a world dominated by males. Her legacy is rich in insight and sensitivity to the world of her generations and the generation of today.

Assertions

1. *Mankind has a desire to strive for perfection.*

Horney was an optimist! This is puzzling, since most of her life was lived in a time in which the world was shattered by continual war and economic deprivation. On many occasions, she asserted that Mankind has the potential and the desire to rise above the conflicts and turmoil of life, and to move toward a more perfect world. In this respect, her thinking is similar to that of Alfred Adler and Erich Fromm, rather than the traditional Freudian conceptions of Mankind as a species doomed to neurosis and hostility.

In *Our Inner Conflicts*, 1945, Horney stated:

> My own belief is that man has the capacity as well as the desire to develop his potentialities and become a decent human being....I believe that Man can change and go on changing as long as he lives. And this belief has grown with deeper understanding (p. 19).

These words run counter to the deterministic orientation of Freudian thinking in which our childhood experiences force us to restricted paths of existence. For Horney, positive change is possible and likely, especially if the larger sociocultural milieu of the person provides opportunities rather than repression.

2. *Societal forces are the dominant influences on personality development.*

Although she came from a training tradition which stressed Mankind's biological nature, Karen Horney came to view society as the major influence on human personality. Society exercised its influence via societal orientations, themes, customs, values, roles, and conflicts. In this regard, she was allied with the *culture and personality movement* in anthropology which emerged in the 1930s under the leadership of Ruth Benedict, Margaret Mead, Abraham Kardiner, and others. For Horney, the world in which we live, with all of its difficulties and pressures, is the source of our troubles as well as the hope for their amelioration. She was not a cultural determinist, but she viewed the social world of our experience as the locus of many of our problems.

In contrast to Freud, she wrote, "My conviction, expressed in a nutshell, is that psychoanalysis should outgrow the limitations set by its being an instinctivistic and genetic psychology" (Horney, 1937, p. 8). People, she believed, mirror the conflicts and frustrations of their society. One of the reasons for this is that society often forces people to alienate themselves from their true nature and to become products of the expectations, rewards, and perceptions of others. They become a facade of their real selves!

3.   *There are two realities: inner (real) and outer (ideal).*

There is a tendency among human beings to strive for an illusory goal of the "ideal self" or perfect person as posited by the society in which we live. This ideal self is never attainable; it reflects unreasonable values and beliefs. In the course of striving for this goal, we may become alienated from our "true self" or inner self. This results in conflict and confusion. Normality consists of maintaining the inner reality and the outer reality in perspective. Adjustment calls for keeping the views of what one is, what one thinks he/she is, and what others perceive one to be in focus. This is done through self-knowledge and awareness such as the kind that can occur through psychoanalysis.

Karen Horney wrote *Self-Analysis* (1942), one of the first self-help books in the field of psychiatry and psychology. It created quite a controversy in its day, since many hours with a highly trained psychoanalyst were generally thought necessary for effective cures to occur. It is clear that America's heritage of self-sufficiency and individual effort, as well as its penchant for the new and innovative, captured Horney's European spirit and infused it with an egalitarian orientation.

The inner and the outer selves were for Horney the reflections of natural versus imposed forces which shape behavior. For Americans, perhaps because of their brief history, there has always been an optimistic view of Mankind's nature and perfectibility. In contrast, European views have been more static, with strong views of fixed roles determined by social class, status, and custom. The inner self (real self) is spontaneous and oriented toward change and growth while the outer self (idealized self) is oriented toward control and rigidity much like the Freudian superego's "ego ideal."

4. *Basic anxiety is the fundamental source of human problems.*

Childhood experiences characterized by great insecurity, rejection, parental domination and indifference can lead to the development of "basic anxiety," which is defined by Horney (1945) as "...the feeling a child has of being isolated and helpless in a potentially hostile world" (p. 41). It is an omnipresent state which governs a person's behavior. One outcome of basic anxiety is the development of a number of strategies or tactics for coping with anxiety. For example, the person might become highly dependent and submissive to gain psychological security; or, the person might become angry, hostile, and belligerent as an outgrowth of the anxiety. Or, possibly, a person may develop an unrealistic view of self as a perfect being who doesn't need people and who doesn't need to fulfill obligations.

According to Horney, these tactics can become relatively permanent styles of coping which assume the properties of needs and motives. In *Self-Analysis* (1942), she suggested that there were 10 needs that characterized neurotic human behavior.

5. *Basic anxiety leads to neurotic needs.*

Motivated by basic anxiety (the fear of being helpless in a potentially hostile world), the individual develops a number of faulty coping methods which ultimately become stylized ways of behaving. Initially, Horney suggested there were 10 neurotic styles which took the form of needs. They include: (1) power, (2) prestige, (3) self-sufficiency, (4) subjugation, (5) exploitation, (6) ambition, (7) affection, (8) withdrawal, (9) perfection, and (10) personal admiration. In her later book, *Our Inner Conflicts* (1945), Horney indicated that the 10 neurotic needs could be reduced to three basic personal styles, (1) *moving toward people*, (2) *moving against people*, (3) *moving away from people*.

These three styles become the Horneyian *character typology*, much like a psychiatric diagnostic system. Each of the 10 needs was associated with one of the three neurotic styles. *Moving toward people* is characterized by trying to please others and being deferential. It is a style of passivity and dependency, sometimes to the extent of being totally compliant and fawning. *Moving against people* is characterized by excessive competitiveness, hostility, power, domination, and a concern for self-aggrandizement at the expense of others. Lastly, *moving away from people* is characterized by indifference, insensitivity to others, withdrawal, psychological detachment, and isolation.

According to Horney, all people share each of these styles or orientation to some degree. However, *the neurotic person comes to be characterized by one of the three to the exclusion of the others.* Thus, the neurotic person is really an extremist with regard to one of the styles. Dependency, aggression, and withdrawal are not inborn, but emerge as reactions to childhood difficulties which stimulate feelings of basic anxiety.

Applications

Karen Horney's theory of neurosis offers a rich account of human experience. Her views indict society in the etiology and course of neurotic behavior. Because of this, her theory is a meaningful source of data and insight for social reformers and social analysts.

Her suggestions for therapy fit within the mold of neo-Freudian traditions, and her book, *Self-Analysis*, was a harbinger of the many self-help books published in the last decade as part of the "pop" psychology movement. Her character typology never gained widespread use, although Leslie Phillips adopted it in his work on social competence and role orientations (e.g., Phillips, Broverman, & Zigler, 1966, 1968). Horney's early work on feminine psychology anticipated the current interest in sex-role differences as well as the current studies on biological bases of sex-role performance. In questioning Freudian assumptions regarding penis envy and the Elektra complex, she opened the door for others to pursue new avenues of thought about sex-role development and pathology.

Assessment

Karen Horney is generally held in high esteem by many groups of neo-Freudian theorists and practitioners. Her work has a special appeal to the growing number of social theorists who choose to focus on the role of society in the etiology of Mankind's problems. Her observations of the human condition are considered particularly astute, and her insights into the psychological processes associated with different life orientations and styles are highly regarded.

As is the case with many clinicians, much of her work has never been subjected to careful empirical study or validation. Thus, there is a tendency among scientifically oriented researchers to ignore her contributions. Although she does not have a broad following, when contrasted to theorists like Freud, Sullivan, or Rogers, her work continues at the American Institute of Psychoanalysis in New York. In many respects, she was a social philosopher whose thoughts must be evaulated from the logic and reasonableness of her efforts rather than from their experimental validation.

History will probably judge the value of Horney's work within the context of her sensitive portrayals of the conflicts and frustrations of everyday life, and their cumulative effect upon the individual's efforts to strive for a life filled with happiness and hope rather than fear and despair. She will probably never be considered a major contributor to intellectual thought, but rather will continue to be cited as a compassionate human being who chose to live within the passions of her time and to work toward the improvement of the human condition.

Summary

Karen Horney presents a complex but compact view of human behavior which emphasizes the contributions of society to psychological adjustment. She persuasively argues against many of the assumptions and conclusions of Sigmund Freud and in their place offers alternatives which greatly appeal to common sense and to the experience of everyday life. She was a forceful commentator on the pernicious effects of society in producing individuals who were alienated from their own experience and nature. Her central concept of *basic anxiety* offers a new way to understand the lives of people who are troubled in the absence of traumatic childhood histories. Karen Horney's tridimensional character typology represents a clinically useful way for examining the lifestyles of maladjusted people. Her work, though unremarkable from the point of scientific inquiry, represents an appealing commentary on the sources and amelioration of human conflicts.

Horney affirms the dignity of persons and provides a sympathetic view of the person striving for growth and development in a world filled with conflict and frustration. Her concepts of perfection, inner-outer self, basic anxiety, neurotic styles, and self-analysis rightfully deserve recognition and acceptance in our efforts to understand human personality.

ERICH FROMM (1900–1979)

Biographical

Erich Fromm was born in Frankfurt, Germany, on March 23, 1900. He received a Ph.D. degree in social psychology from Heidelberg University in 1922 and then studied at the University of Munich and the Berlin Psychoanalytic Institute. In 1934, he left Germany and traveled to the United States where he assumed a number of different positions with various universities. In 1951, he became a professor at the National University of Mexico in Mexico City, and also director of the Mexican Psychoanalytic Institute. He subsequently divided his life between Mexico and Geneva, Switzerland. He died in 1979 in Switzerland. Fromm wrote more than a dozen books and published numerous articles over the course of his professional career. In addition, he was in great demand as a public lecturer, especially on university campuses.

In many respects, Fromm's work is quite similar to Karen Horney's by virtue of its emphasis on the role of society in determining behavior. In addition, Fromm, like Horney, offered broad and far-ranging commentaries on society and the world condition. Among his more popular books are: *Escape from Freedom* (1941), *Man for Himself* (1947), *The Sane Society* (1955), *The Art of Loving* (1956), and *The Revolution of Hope* (1968).

Fromm was influenced by Karl Marx. A number of Fromm's publications were efforts to synthesize Marx and Freud. In this regard, some critics have called him a sociopsychoanalyst. His erudition in a broad number of fields including psychology, sociology, history, philosophy, literature, and religion is immediately evident in virtually all of his books. He ranges widely over a large number of topics, drawing freely from these disciplines in building arguments which are both emotionally appealing and intellectually stimulating, albeit seldom yielding to formal scientific inquiry and discourse.

The essence of his theory is that human beings are alienated from nature and from one another because the societies in which they live make it impossible for them to fulfill their essential human needs. He points out that no society, neither capitalistic nor communistic, has been able to help Man work toward realizing his natural potential.

Assertions

1. Human beings are social beings.

Although Fromm's early training was influenced by traditional Freudian concepts which argued that Mankind's primary nature was biological, Fromm rejected this perspective and instead concluded that Mankind was primarily social. In this regard, society emerged as the most important influence in shaping personality. In his book *Escape from Freedom*, Fromm (1941) wrote:

> The most beautiful as well as the most ugly inclinations of Man are not a part of a fixed and biologically given human nature, but result from the social process which creates Man. In other words, society has not only a suppressing function...but it also has a creative function. Man's nature, his passions, and anxieties are a cultural product (pp. 12–13).

2. There are five human needs.

Human beings have both biological needs (i.e., hunger, thirst, rest) and human needs. Human needs are not created by society but rather have tended to evolve over time as a result of Mankind's social nature. They can be met in different ways, depending upon the type of society in which a person lives. The needs are always the same, but different societies can fulfill them in different ways. The ways which a society uses to meet the human needs of its members determine its social character.

According to Fromm, the basic human needs are the following:

1. *Rootedness.* The need to feel that one belongs and is a part of the world in which one lives. It involves an attachment to nature as well as to a particular social group.
2. *Identity.* The need to feel one is unique with a distinct identity, and to feel one knows oneself.
3. *Relatedness.* The need to relate to others and to nature, to derive a sense of oneness with Mankind and the world.
4. *Transcendence.* The need to create and, in the process, to change and to grow. Transcendence also involves a need to rise above one's nature and to pursue new directions and experiences. Love is one of the means by which humans can transcend and grow beyond their present condition.
5. *Frame of orientation.* The need to have a stable system of beliefs and values which one can use to mediate and make sense of the world. A frame of orientation involves a set of guidelines for dealing with the world, a set of acceptable rules which can provide a resource for action and uncertainty.

3. *Different societies produce different social character types.*

Although the five human needs are universal, different societies have alternative ways for meeting these needs. As a result, different social character types may appear. Humans adjust by reconciling human needs with societal demands. Child rearing is generally oriented toward socializing a child to live in a particular type of society. Thus, from a very early age, an individual may be forced to meet these human needs in ways which generate great conflict and frustration. This is because virtually all societies force the individual to sacrifice true nature for socially valued needs.

An example of this type of problem cited in Fromm's writing was Nazi Germany, where peoples' need for identity, relatedness, transcendence, and so forth were met by acquiescing to an authoritarian regime which offered a sense of belonging and relating, promoted at the expense of others through scapegoating, prejudice, catharsis, group identification, and blind acceptance of any belief handed down from above by the ruling Nazi party.

Fromm suggested that five basic social character types could emerge from an individual's interaction with a given societal pattern. (Most of the time, all of these character types are present in each individual, though one usually dominates the others.) In his book, *Man for Himself* (1947), Fromm provides an excellent analysis of the social character types which emerge from capitalistic society as a result of its materialistic and individualistic orientation.

The five social character types advanced by Fromm are: (1) receptive, (2) hoarding, (3) marketing, (4) exploitative, and (5) productive. In Fromm's opinion, only the productive character is truly healthy and adjusted. The productive character is motivated by love and reason, and works for the betterment of society while simultaneously promoting personal growth and development through a democratic and humanistic character orientation.

4.   *Love is essential to be a normal human being.*

In his book, *The Art of Loving* (1956), Fromm vigorously argued for the role of love in solving Mankind's many problems. For Fromm, love involves a number of elements including knowledge, respect, responsibility, and caring. All of these are interdependent in true love, and all are required for true love to exist.

Fromm wrote that there are five types of love: (1) brotherly, (2) motherly, (3) erotic, (4) self-love, and (5) love of God. True love is something like Art; it must be practiced to develop fully. Love, for Fromm, is Mankind's most hopeful way for producing a better world, in which human needs are not sacrificed for the sake of society.

5.   *Humanistic communitarian socialism is the best society.*

From Fromm's point of view, it is possible for societies to be abnormal, since a society may distort the pursuit of human needs, or fail to satisfy them at all. Fromm suggested that humans should work toward the development of a perfect society. He termed this type of society, *Humanistic Communitarian Socialism*. In this type of society, humans transcend but do not destroy; love provides the basis for solidarity without conformity, for transcendence without destruction, and for belief without distortion.

Such a society is a utopian ideal, but Fromm has written little about how such a society should be developed. In his *The Revolution of Hope* (1968), however, Fromm suggests some steps for transforming our technological society into a humanistic society.

The steps include the following:

> (1) A change in the pattern of production and consumption so that economic activity will become a means for the unfolding and growth of Man, in contrast to the present alienating system in which Man is forced to best serve the principles of maximal production and technical effectiveness. (2) The transformation of Man, the citizen and participant in the social process, from a passive bureaucratically manipulated object, into an active, responsible and critical person....(3) a

cultural revolution that attempts to transform the spirit of alienation and passivity characteristic of technological society; the aim of this transformation is a new man whose goal in life is *being*, not *having* and *using* (Fromm, 1968, p. 156).

Applications

Fromm was a practicing psychoanalyst even though his methods and assumption differed considerably from orthodox Freudian concepts. In many respects, Fromm's therapy approach is similar to existential therapists such as Rollo May and Victor Frankl in that he places the emphasis on his patient's acquiring awareness of their existential conflicts, especially with regard to the betrayal of their human dimensions in favor of social conformity.

As true of many other clinicians, Fromm's ideas never were the subject of objective scientific inquiry. No effort was made to build an organization sustaining Fromm's philosophy. Fromm's theories and thoughts are more likely to be applied in the late night discussions of students in their dormitories, when idealism and hope runs high, when the realities of the world are hidden by the darkenss of night and there is a common spirit of unbridled optimism.

Assessment

It is impossible to evaluate Fromm's theory against empirical research and validation, since neither he nor his followers ever conducted systematic studies of his concepts. But, it would be wrong to use this criterion for judging Fromm's theory, since he was a social philosopher rather than a behavioral scientist. He wrote in the tradition of Marx, Durkheim, and Rousseau, concerned with the "big picture" rather than with specific details; his target was all of society, not the psyche of an individual!

His appeal to all who encountered his writing is undeniable, although a few have been critical of both his logic and his assumptions (e.g., Scharr, 1961). He was an example of an idealist who provides us with the hope and the vision necessary to keep us going amid the everyday trials and tribulations of life.

Fromm chose to look at the impossible and asked, "Why not?" His ultimate contribution will probably reside in his intention to set standards for a better world. For this reason, he will probably continue to occupy a major position among personality theorists, political theorists, and social philosophers. His standards for society and human behavior will continue to be major measuring rods that are used by individuals and societies alike.

With regard to his specific concepts, it would appear that his five basic human needs will continue to be cited in any discussion of human nature, since they seem to capture those aspects of our existence which extend beyond hunger, thirst, and physical comfort. It is also likely that Fromm's book, *The Art of Loving* (1956), will remain on the best seller lists and will remain as his most enduring contribution, if only for the simple reason that love, be it brotherly or erotic, ultimately endures.

Summary

Erich Fromm's theory can best be described as a social psychoanalytic commentary on Mankind's current condition. He believes that human beings have evolved as social beings and have basic human needs. These needs are universal; they are satisfied in different ways, however, by different types of societies. The interaction between these needs and society results in the formation of different social character types. Of the latter, only the productive character type is considered by Fromm to be healthy. The society which can best reconcile Mankind's human needs with a political and economic system is *Humanistic Communitarian Socialism*. This type of system is based on love and its attainment, and requires a major cultural revolution, a revolution he describes in detail in his book, *The Revolution of Hope*.

HARRY STACK SULLIVAN (1892–1949)

Biographical

Harry Stack Sullivan was born on February 21, 1892, on a farm in Norwich, New York. He received his medical degree from the Chicago College of Medicine and Surgery in 1917, and then joined the United States Army. In 1922, Sullivan joined the staff of one of the largest mental hospitals in the United States, St. Elizabeth's Hospital in Washington, D.C. While there, Sullivan was influenced by William Alanson White, one of the foremost psychiatrists of the era. Sullivan was also influenced by the psychiatrist, Adolph Meyer, who advanced the psychobiological orientation in psychiatry, by the anthropologist Edward Sapir, and the sociologist, George Herbert Mead.

Sullivan spent most of his professional career in the Washington, D.C., area, where he directed the Washington School of Psychiatry and he served on the staff of several area hospitals including Shepard and Enoch Pratt Hospital in Maryland. He was especially interested in schizophrenia and most of his concepts are directed toward understanding the etiology and course/outcome of this disorder.

Sullivan published only one book, *Conceptions of Modern Psychiatry* (1953); his students, however, collected his lectures and papers and published them in five different volumes: *The Interpersonal Theory of Psychiatry* (1953), *The Psychiatric Interview* (1954, 1956), *Clinical Studies in Psychiatry* (1956), *Schizophrenia as a Human Process* (1962), and *The Fusion of Psychiatry and Social Science* (1964). Patrick Mullahy's book, *The Contributions of Harry Stack Sullivan* (1952) provides a complete listing of all of Sullivan's work.

Harry Stack Sullivan died on January 14, 1949 in Paris, France. He was in Europe at the time, attending a meeting of the World Federation for Mental Health. He had become extremely active in efforts to apply psychiatry to the amelioration of international tensions and the promotion of world peace. For Sullivan, psychiatry was essentially social psychology, and he believed that social psychological principles could be used to facilitate group understanding and relations. Sullivan (1950) wrote:

> The general science of psychiatry seems to me to cover much the same field as that which is studied by social psychology, because scientific psychiatry has to be defined as the study of interpersonal relations, and this in the end calls for the kind of conceptual framework that we now call field theory (p. 92).

Perhaps more than any other psychiatrist of the era, Sullivan recognized the need to approach both personality theory and mental disorder from a multidisciplinary perspective. He recognized that human beings function at many different levels (biological, psychological, and sociological) and that these levels were interrelated. In 1938, he founded a journal, *Psychiatry*, based on an interdisciplinary view of personality and mental disorder. This journal continues to be one of the foremost journals for the integration of psychiatry and the behavioral sciences.

For Sullivan, interpersonal relations were the most important aspect of human behavior. He believed human beings were social beings, and that it was impossible ever to consider an individual's life apart from its interpersonal relations. From the moment of birth to the moment of death, a human being is a social organism. Many people consider Sullivan to be America's foremost psychiatrist and personality theorist. His thoughts are promulgated by the William Alanson White Foundation in Washington, D.C. The recent advances in biological aspects of behavior have shifted some of the focus from the role of interpersonal processes in personality development. But Sullivan's theory will be likely to remain a source of stimulation and insight about personality and mental disorder well into the future.

Assertions

1. Personality is a function of interpersonal relations.

According to Sullivan (1953), an individual's interpersonal relations are the source of personal development. He defined personality as "the relatively enduring pattern of recurrent interpersonal situations which characterize a human life" (p. 111). No person can exist apart from other people and all behavior reflects a person's historical and interpersonal relations.

2. *Personality is organized according to personifications.*

Sullivan believed that in the course of life we develop certain psychological images of ourselves and of other people. These images or perceptions emerge from the context of our interpersonal relations, and serve to guide our relations with people. Sullivan acknowledged that these images were not accurate, but rather reflected our own particular needs and experiences. But he pointed out that they are one of the primary determinants of our relationship with ourselves and with others.

Personifications are perceptions derived from social experience. If a number of people hold them, they are termed *stereotypes*. Individuals form personifications of significant others in their lives and also of themselves. The latter personification is often called the "self-concept." But the important thing to remember about personifications is that we act upon them. They are our reality! We respond to people not as they really are, but as we think they are. We assume that our personifications are accurate and respond accordingly. We do this because personifications arise from our unique experiences with a person and our unique experience with ourselves.

3. *Personality is organized according to dynamics.*

Dynamisms are complex organizations of thoughts, feelings, and behaviors which characterize the individual. They are behavior patterns which emerge from the context of our interpersonal relations designed to meet our needs. Basically, all individuals have the same dynamisms because of our common nature; they are individual differences, however, in the dominance or pattern of certain dynamisms. Sullivan (1953) defined dynamisms as "the relatively enduring pattern of energy transformations which recurrently characterize the organism in its life" (p. 103).

A person can have a self-dynamism, a dependency dynamism, a hostility dynamism, a lust dynamism, a fear dynamism, and so forth. Dynamisms can change over time. But generally, the longer a dynamism has been in existence, the more pervasive it becomes and the more difficult it will be to change. Essentially, a dynamism is the smallest unit of analysis to which organized behavior can be reduced.

For Sullivan, all behavior involved not only overt aspects but also the covert feelings and thoughts associated with the behavior. Therapy is directed toward making people aware of their dynamisms and aware of the complex of feelings, thoughts, and behaviors integrated in a particular dynamism. For example, a person in therapy might report she had an "argument" with her employer. Sullivan would then work to help the person understand how her particular personifications of the employer were derived and how the "argument" is related to an entire complex of thoughts, feelings, and behaviors surrounding anger and authority.

According to Sullivan, one of the most important dynamisms is the self-dynamism, which refers to the person's behaviors regarding his/herself. The dynamism involves the self-personification of the *good me* and *bad me*, and is derived from the person's coping with anxieties and other threats to security. It is important to recognize that sometimes a certain dynamism may become so pervasive that an individual's entire life centers around it. For example, a dependency dynamism may become so extended that virtually all of the person's behavior involves concern for dependency. The broader a dynamism is, the less we may recognize its presence and influence.

4. Personality is organized according to tensions.

Sullivan believed two basic types of tensions impelled the organism to action: (1) physiological tensions, and (2) anxiety. Physiological tensions such as hunger and thirst are obviously important sources of behavioral activity. We must eat, drink, and sleep to survive. But for Sullivan, the most interesting tensions related to anxiety.

Anxiety occupies a major position in Sullivan's theory. The organism experiences a tension state when there is a perceived threat to one's security. Human beings are capable of experiencing anxiety from birth. This can occur through the process of *empathy* with the mother. If the mother is tense, the infant can sense this through proprioceptive mechanisms. The infant can also experience anxiety through exposure to noise such as yelling and screaming. It is possible that the mother can transmit anxiety during the course of breast-feeding by the way she holds and touches the infant.

Anxiety varies in terms of intensity. At low levels, anxiety may not become a severe problem. When there is a great deal of anxiety present in a person's life, however, it may become a debilitating force. Eventually, the infant may develop a dynamism of apathy or withdrawal as a method of avoiding anxiety. This can produce that flat, detached style of experience that we associate with chronic schizophrenic disorders.

5. Personality is organized according to three modes of cognitive experience.

According to Sullivan, human beings experience reality according to three modes of cognitive experience: *prototaxic, parataxic, syntaxic*. The prototaxic is the earliest and most primitive way for experiencing reality. It lasts from birth to the beginnings of speech. The infant experiences reality as a "stream of consciousness," with no differentiation among events. Undifferentiated feelings and images exist with no meaning or organization. The infant is a part of this undifferentiated mass of experiences, and there is no sense of observer-event separation. The infant is not individuated from the experience and there is no sense of self. But, Sullivan pointed out that even at this level, the quality of the prototaxic experience is critical. The undifferentiated flow of experiences can be filled with anxiety tensions. These can influence the future personality of the infant because even at this early age, the infant can learn to cope with anxiety through withdrawal and apathy.

As the infant begins to develop articulate speech, it enters the next cognitive level for experiencing reality, the *parataxic* mode characterized by a switch to experiencing causality according to *contiguity*. In this mode, relationships between phenomena are considered to exist by virtue of their occurring close together in time. This principle is active in the formation of superstitious thought. For example, the child at this point might fall down when a black cat was nearby. Thus, the child might associate falling down with the black cat and think that the cat caused the fall.

At this stage, there is no formal causal logic beyond proximity in time and space. It is, according to Sullivan, a primitive type of logic which obviously produces an incorrect representation of reality. But the parataxic mode is important in forming our experience of reality. The parataxic mode is heightened under anxiety; thus, anxiety can distort the accuracy of our perceptions of reality.

The last cognitive mode of experience is the *syntaxic* mode which emerges about the second year of life as the child begins to use speech to label objects and events. By the time the child is about five-years-old, the syntaxic mode is the dominant mode of experience. The syntaxic mode continues to develop well into adulthood as the use of symbols and words comes to be increased.

It is possible for an adult to regress to a parataxic mode or even a prototaxic mode. This occurs during the course of schizophrenic disorder. Or, it may occur during certain creative moments. As normal human beings, we have the ability to go back and forth across different modes of experience, although the highest level, according to Sullivan, is always the *syntaxic*. The syntaxic mode has the greatest linear logic and enables us to communicate accurately with one another through symbols.

6. *Personality develops in seven stages.*

Sullivan, like Freud, Erikson, and Maslow, concluded that personality develops according to certain stages. Sullivan's stages tended to blend with adjoining stages and were termed: *infancy, childhood, juvenile, preadolescence, early adolescence, late adolescence, adulthood.* Each stage will be briefly described to highlight its major characteristics.

Infancy. This stage occurs from birth to articulate speech. Generally this is from birth to about 18 months of age. During this period, the infant experiences reality in the prototaxic mode. Toward the end of the stage, the child comes to form a personification of the mother and of the self. Through *empathy* with the mother's tensions, the infant may experience anxiety of varying proportions. Coping with this anxiety may give rise to dynamisms of *apathy* or *somnolent detachment.* In the latter, the infant may spend too much time sleeping and may appear listless and apathetic as part of its effort to withdraw from tension.

Childhood. This stage occurs between 18 months and five years of age, or from the beginnings of articulate speech to the desire to play with playmates. The experiential mode is largely parataxic with movement toward syntaxic modes with increasing word use. Personifications continue to form, and there is a blending of personifications of the same person (e.g., good mother and bad mother).

During this stage, the child may experience the *malevolent transformation.* This is when the child learns that it lives in a dangerous world, a world with enemies who can do harm. This understanding can grow out of interpersonal relations with both family members and playmates. If the malevolent transformation is strong enough, it can immobilize a child and send him or her back to early levels of functioning. This is what occurs in many schizophrenic disorders, according to Sullivan, as a defense mechanism.

Juvenile. The juvenile stage occurs between 5 to 11 years of age. During this period of time the young child is in grammar school and must learn to deal with the world outside the home. Subordination to authority and getting along with peers are among the important interpersonal behaviors learned. In addition, the child learns about competition and cooperation and the devastating effects of social ostracism and rejection by playmates. Cruel and mean playmates can do much to influence the child's personifications of self as well as the personifications of other people.

Preadolescence. This stage occurs between 11 and 13 years of age as the child is developing into a teenager. This child is faced with a number of tensions during this stage, including the emergence of sexual impulses and the desire for close interpersonal relations. Sullivan termed this the "chumship" stage because during this period young people seek out a close friend of the same sex, a "chum."

During this relationship, the chum is the closest human relationship. They share secrets, dress alike, and spend extensive amounts of time together. In many respects, it is a time for the correction of personifications and perceptions of life which have to this point developed solely within the context of the family experience. It is a time for equality, reciprocity, independence. The absence of a close friend can result in faulty socialization and loneliness.

Early Adolescence.   This is the high school period between 14 and 17 years of age. This is a confusing and stressful period for the teenager, because sexual impulses are now quite strong in spite of societal sanctions against heterosexual activity. There is a switch in attachment toward an individual of the opposite sex, not only for sexual relations but for intimacy. Sometimes, however, conflicts and difficulties in this period can result in sexual identification problems, especially *homosexuality*.

Late Adolescence.   This stage lasts from about 18 years to the early 20s. During this period, the final stages of socialization are occurring, and the person is beginning to assume adult roles in his/her family and in society. There is some stabilization of dynamisms and behavior becomes more predictable. The sense of personal identity becomes firmer, and there are more mechanisms for coping with tensions. But, if personality development has been characterized by recurrent difficulties, it may be a time of great conflict and confusion. This is true for each of the ascending stages, since maladjustment in previous stages can prevent effective functioning.

Adulthood.   This is the stage of parenthood, and runs from about 20 to 30 years of age. The person is now a fully socialized being, capable of assuming a full role in society. The person is independent and, if development has proceeded well, can function as a "normal human being."

Applications

Much of Sullivan's work has a quality of timelessness about it. Many of his insights about schizophrenia are still accepted in spite of the many biochemical developments which have occurred since he first advanced his thinking. His work captures the intimate details of human development well, especially linkages between interpersonal experiences and thought processes. His work on the psychiatric interview is still popular, and his therapeutic methods, which emphasize warmth and sensitive communication, are still taught.

Although he has not achieved wide popularity in psychology, his thinking has influenced a number of scholars including Gregory Bateson, Jurgen Ruesch, Donald Jackson, Jay Haley, and Frieda Fromm-Reichman. Sullivan was at his best discussing the complexities of schizophrenic disorders and it is likely that his work in this area will remain his most enduring legacy.

Assessment

Harry Stack Sullivan's work continues to influence American psychiatric thought. He was one of the first to recognize the need for multidisciplinary approaches to human behavior, and his ability to integrate anthropological, psychological, and developmental concepts ensures his continued popularity.

His clinical insights on the causes of schizophrenic disorders are often brilliant in their penetrating analysis of the many factors which act upon one another to produce a mental disorder. Many of his thoughts regarding cognitive modes of experience are now being re-discussed as interest in altered states of consciousness increases.

It would probably be safe to conclude that Sullivan's theory will remain a wellspring of ideas for insights about the interpersonal process, and especially how the interpersonal process facilitates or limits our potential to grow and develop as human beings.

Summary

Harry Stack Sullivan believed that interpersonal relations were the most critical factor in shaping personality development and adjustment. He pointed out that during the course of development, we form personifications or social perceptions of others and ourselves. These personifications guide our behavior. For Sullivan, our behavior represents complex patterns of thoughts, feelings, and behavioral responses which are organized into units called *dynamisms*. Our dynamisms grow from our interpersonal experience and come to be the major methods by which we cope with the tensions produced by physiological needs and anxiety. One of the primary tasks of therapy is the analysis of a person's dynamisms. Another major aspect of our personality, according to Sullivan, is concerned with cognitive modes of experience including prototaxic, parataxic, and syntaxic levels of functioning. These levels are found at different stages of personality development. The seven major stages of personality development include the following: infancy, childhood, juvenile, preadolescent, early adolescent, late adolescent, and adulthood.

ERIK ERIKSON (1902-   )

Biographical

Erik Homburger Erikson was born on June 15, 1902 in Frankfurt, Germany. Holding no formal university degrees, he was trained as a lay analyst (nonmedical degree holder) at the Vienna Psychoanalytic Institute under the supervision of Anna Freud and August Aichorn. He migrated from Germany in 1932 to join Henry Murray's project on the in-depth assessment to personality.

Over the course of the next 25 years, Erikson has been affiliated with a number of American universities including Yale, the University of California, and the University of Pittsburgh. In 1960, he moved to Harvard University as a professor of human development. Over the course of his career, Erikson was influenced by a number of well-known scholars including Anna Freud, Margaret Mead, and Gregory Bateson. He sought to blend concepts from psychoanalysis with those from cultural anthropology. In this respect, he falls within the sphere of activity of Fromm, Sullivan, Horney, Alfred Kroeber, Margaret Mead, and others. In one of his earlier books, *Childhood and Society* (1950), he wrote, "This is a psychoanalytic book on the relation of ego to society." Among his best known books are: *Young Man Luther* (1962), *Identity: Youth and Crisis* (1968), and *Gandhi's Truth* (1969). His books on Luther and Gandhi represent efforts to bring together methodologies from history and from psychoanalysis in a new specialty area, *psychohistory.*

Erikson has emerged as one of the most popular figures in the fields of psychoanalysis, developmental psychology, and personality theory. He is revered as an original thinker who has done much to switch the focus of psychoanalysis to the role of the ego in personality growth and dynamics. In this sense, he can be considered an *"ego analyst."* But, his most enduring contribution will probably be his recognition that human development extends throughout the entire life span and does not stop in early adulthood as many other theorists have suggested (e.g., Freud, Sullivan).

Assertions

1.   The ego is shaped by society.

The Freudian notion of the ego was that it is between the forces of the id and the superego. Erikson more or less disregards these two forces and sees the ego as an autonomous function within the society in which the individual finds himself. This provides a simpler conceptualization of how personality functions: the self against society. Instead of considering personality as primarily affected by instincts or by parents, Erikson focuses on all of society, which includes parents, siblings, and other individuals. Instead of believing that personality is essentially shaped by age four or five, Erikson views personality as constantly emerging and developing in relation to society.

2.   The individual is in a constant process of challenge and growth.

Instead of seeing the individual as the plaything of social forces, Erikson posits the emerging individual, challenged by the crises of life, from which he/she can emerge victorious and strengthened. The person is in charge, the captain of his fate rather than a crew member who has to do another's biddings. Erikson has an optimistic-creative view of personality.

> 3. *The individual is preprogrammed to go through various developmental stages.*

Erikson is best known for his eight stages of development, part of his epigenetic principle. Before examining these stages it is important to understand the concept of *epigenesis*, which means that the individual, under normal conditions, will develop inevitably from stage to stage. The fully matured and realized individual goes through these stages successfully, meeting the various crises inherent in each stage in a successful manner. To move through these stages means that the individual has to struggle, since there always is some sort of conflict in the transition from stage to stage.

Figure 8–1, which illustrates Erikson's eight stages of ego development, should be studied carefully, with the following comments:

I. *Trust v. distrust.* During the first year of life the baby has a crisis problem of learning whether to trust or mistrust life. Naturally, his solution depends a great deal on his parents, especially the mother. If mothering is inadequate, he may develop basic mistrust that may never leave him. Not only should a child develop a trust in the outside world, he should also develop trust in his own ability to meet some of life's demands himself. The consequences of success or failure are either *hope* or *fear*.

II. *Autonomy v. shame and doubt.* At ages one to three, the child has a problem with self-control and ability to move around and to be self-sufficient. As the exploration drive shows itself, the child has to learn to move away from the protection of the parent. He or she learns to be more independent and to make decisions. He is no longer a baby and develops confidence as he expresses his ability to decide. He develops *self-control* or *self-doubt*.

III. *Initiative v. guilt.* In this third stage, ages four to five, the "play age," the child increases his degree of initiative and self-responsibility. He gives up complete dependency on mother and develops a sense of right and wrong. He moves on to creative play, and life begins to have purpose. He develops a sense of *responsibility* or *unworthiness*.

IV. *Industry v. inferiority.* This is the early school-age period, running from about 6 to 11, when the child begins to prepare himself for society and occupation. He has broken away from his home, at least for part of the day,

Ages	Stages ———➤	Consequences
I. Early infancy (birth–1)	Trust v. Mistrust	Hope Fear
II. Infancy (1–3)	Autonomy v. Shame and doubt	Self-control Self-doubt
III. Early childhood (4–5)	Initiative v. Guilt	Responsibility Unworthiness
IV. Middle childhood	Industry v. Inferiority	Competency Incompetency
V. Puberty and adolescence (12–20)	Identity v. Confusion	Loyalty Uncertainty
VI. Early adulthood (20–24)	Intimacy v. Isolation	Mutuality Promiscuity
VII. Middle adulthood	Generativity v. Stagnation	Caring Selfishness
VIII. Late adulthood (65 plus)	Integrity v. Despair	Acceptance Meaninglessness

FIGURE 8–1.   THE EIGHT STAGES OF EGO DEVELOPMENT ACCORDING TO ERIKSON

Source: E. Erikson, *Childhood and Society*. New York: W. W. Norton, 1950.

and competes with peers without the protection or domination of his parents. He now learns to "work" and gains recognition by his achievement, not just for being himself. During this period the child becomes vulnerable to feelings of incompetency, since no longer does he get credit or praise for inconsequential things. Success leads to *competency*, failure to *incompetency*.

V. *Identity v. confusion.*   For this period, ages about 12 to 20, Erikson has made the greatest contribution. The youth begins to separate from his family and at the end of the period should be an adult, having established his own values, associates, and way of life. Changes in the body, development of sexuality, and demands of peers lead to crucial problems of deciding his identity. Successfully meeting this crisis leads to the development of *loyalty*, the ability to remain faithfully in love; failure leads to *uncertainty*.

VI. *Intimacy v. isolation.* This is the period of adulthood, moving past adolescence. The individual now has the ability not only for love but for commitment and can achieve mutuality with one other person at a genital level of relationship. The inadequate or immature reaction is to remain apart from others, unable to sustain a deep or abiding relationship. The consequence of success in this stage is *mutuality*; failure leads to *promiscuity*.

VII. *Generativity v. stagnation.* An interesting period of later life is middle adulthood, characterized by generativity or stagnation. Generativity relates to feelings for others, concern with the younger generation. Usually it refers to proper parenting. Stagnation refers to inability to care for others, selfish self-concern. Such people, with excessive self-love, have no ability to give to others and are stale. Success here leads to *caring*, but failure leads to *selfishness*.

VIII. *Integrity v. despair.* To achieve total adult personal integrity, the various prior stages must have been successfully handled. At this stage the individual has wisdom, self-acceptance, a feeling of the rightness and fitness of life, and the ability to face death with dignity and fortitude. The end result is either *acceptance* or *meaninglessness*.

Applications

Erikson's theory has found applications at all levels of development. Perhaps because he is one of the few who have taken up adolescence and later maturity, it has been specifically favored by those working in these areas. Based on psychosocial rather than psychosexual concepts his theory is therefore useful to eclectic counselors. Erikson's (1968) concern for the "identity crises" of adolescence have seemed particularly appropriate in recent years as the problems of teenagers have increased. In recent years, too, this issue of identity seems to have become a concern for adults. The women's liberation movement, for example, has taken up the issue of who-ness and what-ness, as adults are rethinking their aims and ambitions, goals and values. Erikson's concepts relative to these eight stages of life relate to these problems, and Erikson is much quoted in popular periodical literature in terms relative to adult stages of development.

Evaluation

In evaluating Erikson's work, a prime issue is whether it really is an extension of psychoanalysis. Despite Erikson's assertions, it seems that he is his own person, a seminal thinker, who has not really accepted much of Freud's basic concepts. A good example has to do with determinism. Erikson makes an interesting contradictory point: while these stages are more or less determined biologically, nevertheless they are not inevitably decided either by biology or by the environment. True, both have a factor in the emergence of the stages, but the solution of the crises belongs essentially to the individual. Erikson's position is a variety of soft determinism. Also, Erikson does not depend much on the unconscious. As an ego-theorist, he concerns himself with rational aspects of individuals.

There has not been much research on Erikson's theories. Bronson (1959) demonstrated that Erikson's concept of ego identity has meaning with reference to college students. Waterman, Beubel, and Waterman (1970) provided further evidence that successful identity crisis solutions are related to normal personality.

Summary

Erikson started, as did so many others in psychotherapy and personality theory, as a Freudian psychoanalyst but then went on to develop his own theory. In Erikson's case, unlike such other theorists as Burrow or Sullivan, he does not call his views his own creation but states, in effect, that they are a natural outgrowth (not a contradiction) of psychoanalysis. Erikson's thesis is the effect of society on the maturing individual, how the person goes from role crisis to role crisis trying to find successively the answer to the questions: "Who am I? What should I be doing?"

Overall, the greatest impact of Erikson's thoughts seem to be on those counselors who deal with the problems of adolescence and early maturity.

PERSONALISM: GORDON W. ALLPORT AND HENRY A. MURRAY

INTRODUCTION

The personalistic view has been strongly advocated by Gordon W. Allport and Henry A. Murray. Pioneers, they helped shape the current field of personality theory and research. They share a common commitment to understanding the unique individual and both advanced research methods to study individual experience. Allport even suggested that personality theory alter its name to *personology*.

Personalism can be traced to the 19th-century German psychologists Wilhelm Windelband and Heinrich Rickert who distinguished between two different types of empirical sciences: the natural sciences (*naturwissenschaften*) and the cultural or humanistic sciences (*kulturwissenschaften*). Windelband believed the natural sciences are mostly concerned with *nomothetic* laws which can be generalized across large samples or even the universe. The cultural sciences are usually concerned with *idiographic* laws which apply to unique experiences and events. This distinction raised the issue of studying laws related to the unique individual versus studying laws related to large numbers of individuals. Do psychologists seek to understand the relationships among variables within a given individual or do they try to establish regularities in behavior across many individuals?

One individual who entered the debate regarding nomothetic versus idiographic laws of behavior was William Stern (1871–1938), a German psychologist who moved to the United States during the latter part of his life. An important figure in psychology's history, he deserves far more recognition than he has received. Two of his books, *General Psychology from the Personalistic Standpoint* (1938) and *Person and Thing* (three volumes, 1906, 1918, 1924) are particularly important for personality theory and research because they advocate the study of the person as a unified whole. Indeed, Stern used the term *unitas multiplex*, a unity composed of elements, to describe personality.

Stern (1938) stated that the person is "...a living whole, individual, unique, striving toward goals, self-contained and yet open to the world around him" (p. 70). Stern saw personality as the outgrowth of heredity and environment and he refused to separate mind and body. In these respects, Stern was a primary influence on the personalistic approach to personality theory.

Stern was one of the first psychologists to discuss traits as relatively constant components of personality. In addition, he suggested there were four different human motives: (1) self-preservation, (2) self-development, (3) social behavior, and (4) human activity such as intellectual curiosity. Stern's concepts of personality, traits, and needs and motives are crucial parts of the personality theories of Gordon Allport and Henry Murray. Both of these theorists sought to understand personality as a totality unique in form and pattern with the "person" at the center.

GORDON W. ALLPORT (1897–1967)

Biographical

Gordon Willard Allport was born in Montezuma, Indiana, on November 11, 1897. He grew up in Cleveland, Ohio, and received his B.S. degree in philosophy from Harvard University in 1919. Following a year's teaching experience in Istanbul, Turkey, he returned to Harvard and was awarded a Ph.D. degree in psychology in 1922 at the age of 24. After a number of years of additional study and teaching he returned to Harvard in 1930 where he remained until his death on October 11, 1967. Gordon Allport was truly a pioneer in the study of personality theory and research. He was the first American to offer a course in personality theory in the United States, having taught in 1924 a course at Harvard entitled, "Personality: Its Psychological and Social Aspects" (Sahakian, 1977).

Allport had a profound influence via his many famous students and his numerous publications. Among his most well-known students are Jerome Bruner, Gardner Lindzey, Hadley Cantril, Leo Postman, M. Brewster Smith, and Leonard Doob. From his very first publication, "Personality Traits: Their Classification and Measurement," which he published in 1921 with his brother Floyd, Allport's writings were to exert tremendous influence on personality theory and research. Some of his most popular books are: *Personality: A Psychological Interpretation* (1937), *The Nature of Prejudice* (1954), and *Becoming: Basic Considerations for a Psychology of Personality* (1955). In addition, Allport published more than 100 scientific papers in various journals.

No single thematic idea characterizes Allport's personality theory except his insistence that behavior is a complex phenomena which emerges from dynamic interaction of many forces. Allport has been considered a "trait," a "humanistic," a "motivational," and a "self" psychologist, because his theory contains elements of each of these perspectives. Yet, he is also none of these. His integration of concepts from different perspectives is unique. For Allport, challenge resided in developing a theory which could account for relatively enduring tendencies to behave in unique ways with a nondeterministic, rational, and future-oriented framework.

Assertions

1.   A definition of personality must include hierarchical, integrative, adjustive, and uniqueness components.

In his classic textbook, *Personality: A Psychological Interpretation* (1937), Allport reviewed scores of definitions of personality and grouped them into categories. He then developed a definition of personality which included the basic theme of each category into an all-inclusive standard definition. Personality was:

> The dynamic organization within the individual of those psychophysical systems that determine his unique adjustments to his environments (Allport, 1937, p. 47).

A number of terms in this definition reflect Allport's basic position. (1) The term *organization* states that personality is a stable and cohesive organized system. Yet, the organization is *dynamic*, subject to change and evolution. This occurs via growth and maturation. Thus, personality is a *dynamic organization*. (2) Personality consists of *psychophysical* systems rather than psychological *and* physiological systems. For Allport, there was continual interaction between mind and body and these did not function separately. (3) Allport believed personality is *determined* by an organized system within the individual that lies behind specific acts. In this respect, personality is both an object and a process. It is both an organized system and the results of an organized system in action. (4) Personality refers to those aspects of our lives that make us *unique* from one another. Clearly, although we human beings share similar characteristics, we are all very different from one another. The value of personality as a concept is partially a function of its ability to account for behavioral differences and similarities. (5) Allport believed that personality emerged as a system which had functional survival value because it determined an individual's unique *adjustment* to the environment. The adjustive component is both *reactive* to the environment and *proactive* since the person is both responsive to stimuli in its environment and also acts in a creative and spontaneous way upon its environment. Allport stated that the person's adjustment involves both "mastery" as well as "passive adaptation." In 1961, Allport changed his view about the adjustive function of personality and noted that personality was characteristic thought and behavior.

> 2. *Personality develops according to stages which involve the development of different dimensions of selfhood.*

This means that psychological development proceeds through a series of stages in which different aspects of selfhood emerge. The stages include the following:

1. Early Infancy (birth–three months)
   a. No conscious awareness of self; no differentiation of "me" from the rest of the world.
2. Early Self (three months–three years)
   a. Conscious awareness of bodily self.
   b. Emergence of self-identity as a sense of continuity of self.
   c. Emergence of sense of self-esteem and pride.
3. Extended Self (four–six years)
   a. Extension of self into the world in terms of possessions and ownership (i.e., "My dog, my daddy, this is mine").
   b. Development of self-image: "Who am I? What do other people think of me?"

4. Coping Self (6–12 years)
   a. Awareness of self as a problem solver and coper (similar to Freud's "ego" concept).
5. Striving Self (adolescence)
   a. Emergence of self as a striving, goal setting, intentional agent.

For Allport, the stages of selfhood development constitute the basis of personality growth and development. Selfhood represents that private or subjective aspect of our experience most intimately related to our sense of who we are as a total experiencing being.

3. *The proprium is the basic structural unit of personality.*

Allport applied the word *proprium* to refer to the different aspects of selfhood. But, the proprium was more than selfhood functions. For Allport, proprium is the central organizing force in personality and different from the "self" or "ego" because these are mere agents which we separate from the entirety of the person while the proprium is the force which makes for unity and consistency of behavior over time. It is the person's sense of "me."

4. *Traits, dispositions, and attitudes are the basic building blocks of personality.*

The proprium is the organizing force within personality giving it consistency and coherence, but the specific building blocks of personality can be divided into traits, dispositions, and attitudes.

Traits are actual "neuropsychic" structures with the capacity to "initiate and guide" behavior. Their presence in an individual can only be inferred. The basis for inferring traits is the similarity in response patterns to different stimuli in a given individual. Traits are common structural aspects of personality. Allport used the word *dispositions* to refer to neuropsychic structures peculiar to a given individual. Dispositions can "initiate and guide" behavior. Thus, traits can be studied across individuals while dispositions can be studied within a given individual. We can derive nomothetic laws through the study of traits and idiographic laws through the study of dispositional patterns.

Attitudes, like traits and dispositions, can "initiate and guide" behavior but they differ with respect to the specificity of their goals. Attitudes have to do with an individual's orientation toward specific aspects of the environment. Thus, we may have an attitude towards politicians, teachers, and so forth. Allport (1961) stated:

> Ordinarily, attitude should be employed when the disposition is bound to an object or value, that is to say, when it is aroused by a well-defined class of stimuli

and when the individual feels toward these stimuli a definite attraction or repulsion....The more generalized an attitude (the more difficult it is to specify its object or its polarity of affect), the more does it resemble a trait (p. 294).

Allport states that a man may have a "kindly" attitude toward his dog. But if he has a kindly attitude toward many things, he has a trait of kindliness. If he is predisposed toward kissing to express his kindliness we have a dispositional trait.

5.   Traits are hierarchically organized.

Allport believes that some traits are more important than others and are organized into hierarchies involving superordinate and peripheral traits. The major ones are termed *cardinal traits*. In general, individuals have only a few master or cardinal traits. They are powerful organizers and guides for human behavior and "there are few activities that cannot be traced directly or indirectly to [their] influence" (Allport, 1937, p. 337).

Cardinal traits are pivotal in human behavior. However, there are also *central* traits, more specific personality orientations, as well as *secondary* traits, less generalized and less conspicuous. Traits are common across people, according to Allport. But, different people may have different arrangements of traits. What is a cardinal trait for one individual is often a secondary trait for another.

6.   Temperament is the constitutional basis of personality.

Many of Allport's beliefs about the biological aspects of personality can be traced to his views about temperament. Allport (1937) defined temperament as:

> ...the characteristic phenomena of an individual's emotional nature, including his susceptibility to emotional stimulation, his customary strength and speed of response, the quality of his prevailing mood, and all the peculiarities of fluctuation and intensity in mood; these phenomena being regarded as dependent upon constitutional make-up and therefore largely hereditary in origin (p. 34).

For Allport, the more a disposition is linked to temperament, the more likely it is biological. Allport actively acknowledged the role of biology in behavior.

7.   Motives can become "functionally autonomous" from their origins.

A major element in Allport's theory is his concept of functional autonomy, his most highly regarded and best known concept. Functional autonomy refers to the fact that motives are not tied to the conditions of their origin. That is to say, an individual's motive for engaging in a particular behavior may have originated when he/she was a little child; but, over the course of time, the motive loses its linkage to the past and comes to be rooted to a totally different aspect. It then becomes "functionally autonomous" from its origins. For example, an individual may have originally hunted deer for food; but, he now may hunt deer strictly for fun. This view is in direct conflict with psychoanalytic concepts of motivation which view all actions as emanating from infantile sources. Allport (1937) stated, "The theory declines to believe that the energies of adult personality are infantile or archaic in nature. Motivation is always contemporary" (p. 194).

Allport believed that early reasons for behaving in a particular way are important; however, they need not account for present behavior. Present behavior reflects the forces present in the immediate situation. In this respect, functional autonomy provides Allport with the basis for continuing personal growth and development. The individual is not tied to the past. There is continuity with the past but there is also opportunity for new directions. Allport (1961) defined functional autonomy as:

> "...any acquired system of motivation in which the tensions involved are not of the same kind as the antecedent tensions from which the acquired system developed" (p. 291).

Applications

Gordon Allport did not advance any specific theory of therapy or behavior change; nor did he suggest any educational philosophy, nor any specific approach to measurement or assessment. As a result, it is difficult to consider applications of his work. For Allport, the emphasis was on the construction of a theory which could successfully describe the personality of a given individual. Most of his writing occurred in an era when theorists were involved in debates over such issues as *determinism*, the *role of the unconscious*, *teleogy*, and *situational versus person-centered influences* on behavior. Allport tried to address many of these issues in his theory; but, in the process, he did not attend to the implications of his conceptualizations for such problems as changing behavior, learning, and prediction. These topics were and are of primary interest to clinicians and Allport never was involved in clinical cases. He was an academician—a theoretician and researcher.

Evaluation

Gordon Allport was a pioneer in the area of personality theory and research; the first American professor to offer a course in personality theory. He was often the first researcher to address many of the content areas and issues which the emerging field encountered. More than anyone else Allport defined and clarified the concept of trait, and more than anyone else he defined and clarified the concept of personality as an object of study. A holistic thinker, he insisted that the person functioned as a whole or unity and was not a group of unrelated parts. Allport called attention to morphogenic research methods in which a small number of individuals were studied in depth across a large number of different variables. He pioneered social psychological studies on rumor and prejudice. For these reasons, and many more, Allport deserves a position of respect and eminence in the field of personality theory and research.

The validity of his concepts is difficult to establish since so many of them seem unamenable to experimental inquiry. For the most part, one accepts or rejects Allport's notions on the basis of common sense. For example, how does an investigator examine a concept like *functional autonomy of motives*? It seems impossible to prove that motives behind a given behavior do not possess elements which were present in their development and genesis. But, it is appealing and seems to make good sense to believe that "Motivation is always contemporary."

Another difficulty in validating Allport's theory is that he clearly favored the in-depth study of an individual person rather than the pursuit of nomothetic strategies in research. Allport encouraged the study of many different variables within a given individual with subsequent efforts to tie them together into a holistic portrayal of the person. This approach does not make for easy validation because each person is so unique.

Allport's legacy to personality theory and research may ultimately reside in the fact that he established the foundations on which others could build. He was the pioneer who provided direction for others to follow.

Summary

Gordon W. Allport advanced a personalistic theory of personality rooted in the belief that human beings are organized and unified wholes that must be studied in their entirety if an accurate understanding of behavior is to occur. Allport pioneered the field of personality theory and research in the United States. He worked tirelessly to clarify the meaning of the term *personality* and also developed the concept of trait. He suggested that personality develops across stages involving the successive emergence of various aspects of the self ranging from self as a bodily process to self as a goal-setting intentional agent.

For Allport, personality was structured across traits, dispositions, and attitudes, which are given order and cohesion by the proprium. Traits are relatively enduring neuropsychic structures which have the capacity to guide and initiate behavior. Traits are organized into a hierarchy ranging from cardinal traits through central traits to secondary traits. Allport's most famous concept, and perhaps his most controversial one, was *functional autonomy* of motives. This concept challenged the primacy of childhood experience in determining behavior and placed much more emphasis on contemporary factors. Because of his many contributions in personality theory and research, he is assured an important place in the history of the topic. His failure to extend his theory into the realm of application may limit his popularity but will not harm his stature as an innovative and intrepid theorist.

HENRY A. MURRAY (1893–   )

Biographical

Henry Alexander Murray was born on May 13, 1893 in New York City. He received his B.A. degree from Harvard University in 1915 and then attended Columbia College of Physicians and Surgeons where he received an M.D. in 1919. Following graduation, Murray received training in surgery and medical research. He was especially interested in biochemical aspects of embryological development. In 1927, he received a Ph.D. in biochemistry from Cambridge University in England. At the very same time that he was pursuing studies in medicine and chemistry, he was already beginning to experience some discontent with these fields and developed an interest in psychology. In 1923 he read Jung's book, *Psychological Types*, and he noted that it was "a gratuitous answer to an unspoken prayer" for him. In 1927, during Easter vacation from his studies at Cambridge, Murray traveled to Zurich, Switzerland, where he met Carl Jung. Jung helped him understand the basis of two problems which had troubled him all his life: stuttering and strabismus. By the end of his meetings with Jung, Murray was spiritually a psychologist regardless of his professional training as a surgeon and chemist.

In 1927 Murray returned to Harvard where he assisted Morton Prince in the development of the psychological clinic. He remained at Harvard for the rest of his professional career. At the clinic Murray began a number of studies of normal personality using psychoanalytic theory. He became quite involved with psychoanalysis and, following training in the area, he founded the Boston Psychoanalytic Society. This soon brought him into conflict with Karl Lashley, then one of most powerful individuals in Harvard's department of psychology. But Murray, an equally strong individual, did not bend before criticism of his work. In 1938, he published *Explorations in Personality*, a book based on an in-depth study of 50 Harvard students.

Some personality psychologists believe that there has not been anything new in personality since Murray published this book because of its innovative and comprehensive approach. An instrument used in the study was the famous *Thematic Apperception Test*, which Murray had published several years earlier. During the years of the study, Murray taught a number of Harvard graduate students who were to emerge as later leaders in the field of psychology, including Donald MacKinnon, Saul Rosenzweig, Nevitt Sanford, and Robert White.

In 1943, Murray set up an assessment office for the new Office of Strategic Services (OSS), the forerunner of the Central Intelligence Agency (CIA). With many of his co-workers from Harvard, he evaluated individuals for special espionage assignments. Following the war, he returned to Harvard. In 1948, at 55 years of age, he was finally granted tenure by Harvard. His controversial stands on psychoanalysis had for years prevented him from receiving tenure but this now was past. In 1962 he retired. He was still an active writer in the 1970s.

Murray is a productive author. Among his most noteworthy publications are: *Explorations in Personality* (1938), *Assessment of Men* (1948), *Personality in Nature, Society, and Culture* (1950, with Clyde Kluckhohn), and *The Thematic Apperception Test* (1943). In addition, he published more than a hundred articles in scientific journals on a variety of different topics.

Murray's theory of personality, like Gordon Allport's, is difficult to categorize because it contains elements of several different perspectives including psychoanalytic, humanistic, and trait psychology. But across all the diversity of his work, it is clear that he is committed to the personological tradition. Some of the influence in this regard was from Gordon Allport, his close friend at Harvard for many years. Murray was dedicated to the study of the unique individual and he believed in the value and worth of each individual. He sought to study each person as a distinct and unified whole in which each of the parts was inextricably linked to one another. For these reasons he is probably best described as a personological theorist.

Assertions

1. Personality is the basic subject matter of psychology.

The most common definition of psychology is the "scientific study of human behavior." For Murray, this definition fails to convey the importance of studying the total person at a given moment in time and across time. According to Murray, those concerned with human behavior should understand that behavior is a result of many forces both within and external to an organism acting simultaneously at a particular point in time. The unity or totality of these forces over time represents personality and personality is the most important unit for psychology. Personology is that branch of psychology concerned with the "study of human lives and the factors that influence their course" (Murray, 1938, p. 3). Murray preferred the term *personology* over the term *psychology of personality* because he felt the latter was a tautology. For Murray, psychology is personality—we cannot have a psychology of personality. We can, for convenience, study and analyze the component parts of personality but in the end, unless we recognize that each part belongs to a larger whole, we run the risk of reaching erroneous conclusions. Personology is concerned with the entire person because it is the person functioning as an entirety which is responsible for behavior.

2.   The brain is the foundation of personality.

In one of his expositions, Murray (1951) stated quite simply, "No brain, no personality..." (p. 267). Murray never forgot his training in the biological sciences. He always acknowledged the important role that the nervous system played in personality. Murray (1938) stated:

> Since in the higher forms of life the impressions from the external world and from the body that are responsible for conditioning and memory are received, integrated and conserved in the brain, and since all complex adaptive behavior is evidently co-ordinated by excitations in the brain, the unity of the organism's development and behavior can be explained only by referring to organizations occurring in this region. It is brain processes, rather than those in the rest of the body, which are of special interest to the psychologist (p. 47).

3.   Human beings strive for tension reduction.

A basic element of Murray's theory is the recognition that tension reduction is a primary motive. However, Murray does not believe that humans seek only *homeostasis* or a state of tension balance. Rather, Murray views human beings as also being driven by urges for growth and progress. The major sources of tension generation can be found both within and external to the person. These include *needs* and *presses*. These two terms are so synonymous with Murray's theory that his theory has come to be known as the need-press theory of personality.

4.   Behavior is a function of needs.

According to Murray, *a need is a hypothetical construct* we employ to understand relationships between conditions which provoke an action. A hypothetical construct is not a tangible quality but rather is a concept that refers to processes that we cannot understand or identify at this point in our scientific progress. For example, if a person gets up from sitting in a comfortable chair and begins to look around the kitchen and then subsequently eats food and returns to the chair, we can posit that the person was "hungry." We cannot see hunger in the body although we can examine its various correlates. Thus, we employ the word "hunger" as a hypothetical construct to help us link a stimulus and a response in some meaningful way.

Murray (1938) stated:

> Strictly speaking, a need is the immediate outcome of certain internal and external occurrences. It comes into being, endures for a moment and perishes. It is not a static entity. It is a resultant of forces. One need succeeds another. Though each is unique, observation teaches that there are similarities among them, and on the basis of this, needs may be grouped together into classes; each class being, as it were, a single major need (p. 60).

A need represents an organismic potential to respond in a particular way in the face of certain types of situations or conditions. Murray believes that needs can be separated into *viscerogenic* (body related) and *psychogenic* (no body referent). Viscerogenic needs require physiological satisfaction while psychogenic needs require mental or emotional satisfaction.

Murray developed a list of 13 viscerogenic needs and 28 psychogenic needs. All needs can be divided into three phases which constitute a need cycle: (1) *refractory* phase in which no incentive will arouse the need, (2) *inducible* phase in which the need is inactive but is capable of being aroused by an appropriate stimuli, and (3) *active* phase in which the need determines the behavior of the total organism (Murray, 1938). Sometimes a given behavior pattern can satisfy several needs at the same time: this is called *fusion* of needs. In addition, sometimes certain needs may become active in the service of satisfying still other needs in some sort of dominance hierarchy. In this case, the dominant need is called *determiner* and the other needs are called *subsidiaries*. Lastly, needs can come into conflict with one another and this can produce difficult problems for the person since it may pull one in mutually incompatible directions. Needs and their sources of satisfaction can eventually become organized into complicated structures involving bodily states, emotions, perceptions, images, and objects. This was termed a *need integrate* or *complex* by Murray. This concept resembles Sullivan's notion of *dynamism*.

Following a lengthy discussion of needs in his *Explorations in Personality* (1938), Murray reaches the following definition:

> A need is a construct...which stands for a force (the physico-chemical nature of which is unknown) in the brain region, a force which organizes perception, apperception, intellection, conation, and action in such a way as to transform in a certain direction an existing unsatisfying situation.

5. *Behavior is a function of press.*

In addition to need, Murray advances the concept of *press* to account for motivation and behavior. Press is a "directional tendency in an object or situation," and it is his concept for describing the external world of the person in psychological terms. He stated,

> The press of an object is what it can *do to the subject* or *for the subject*—the power that it has to affect the well-being of the subject in one way or another. The cathexis of an object...is what it can *make the subject do* (Murray, 1938, p. 121).

Murray's use of the concept of press establishes him as an interactional theorist. By introducing the concept, Murray expressed his view that human behavior was a function of the simultaneous interaction of factors both within and external to the organism. Murray's views on this matter were partially influenced by the work of Kurt Lewin. Murray distinguished between an *alpha* press and a *beta* press. An alpha press is the actual or "objective" press from the environment, while a beta press is the "perceived" press from the environment. By this distinction, Murray established the importance of the person's subjective impressions of what is occurring as opposed to what others may say is happening in the environment. Thus, Murray can also be defined as a *phenomenological* theorist like Carl Rogers and George Kelly.

Murray listed a large number of press forces including the following: danger, loss, rejection, aggression, birth of sibling, and so on. It should be remembered that *press* comes from the external environment while *need* comes from the internal environment. To bring them together in a new unit of analysis, Murray created the concept of *thema*.

6. *Behavior is a function of thema.*

The concept of *thema* constitutes the last major component of Murray's system of motivation and behavior. Thema represents a combination of a particular press and a particular need. Thema is the molar unit which must be studied to understand behavior. Sometimes, certain major themas develop out of the course of infant experience and these may become pervasive patterns which continue throughout a person's life. They can emerge from either excessive gratification or excessive trauma. But, whatever may cause their development and subsequent growth, they come to exercise a profound influence on the person by virtue of their continual dominance. Murray called major themes, *unity thema.* Sometimes the unity thema are difficult to recognize. But, if they can be discovered, they can provide important insights into an individual's unique patterns of behavior.

7. *Behavior is a function of vector-value forces.*

In 1951, Murray added additional concepts to extend his theory's capacity to understand behavior from a motivational perspective. An important concept was *vector-value*. According to Murray, it is important to understand that needs function to serve some value or intent and do not exist solely by themselves. These values co-exist with certain directions for activity which he called *vectors*. Vectors are behavioral tendencies which serve values. They are either physical or psychological directions in activities. Murray listed a number of vectors including rejection, reception, expression, transmission, avoidance, and so forth. These are forces going in a given direction. In addition, Murray stated that there exist various values in people including knowledge, property, authority, affiliation, ideology, and so forth. Values are reasons why we do things. Murray created a matrix with values on one dimension and vectors on another. The resulting cells are products of vector-value interactions, related to needs and presses and themas and the final theory is a comprehensive conceptualization of human motivation.

Within the context of Murray's theory, all behavior is considered to be a function of vector-values, need, press, and thema. At any given moment, a total organism within a given situation is responding. The forces are both within and external to the person but in all instances the person functions as a unified cohesive organism.

Applications

Henry Murray's theory has never been associated with a distinct therapy procedure except in those instances where he himself conducted therapy using his concepts as explanatory principles. Further, Murray's efforts have never found themselves applied in a school or educational system as a philosophy or technique for teaching. In many respects, Murray is the Linnaeus of psychology because of his classifying and categorizing many different aspects of human behavior, especially within the area of human motivation. In this respect, his previous training in the biological sciences appears to have played a strong role on his work in psychology.

Much of his theory has found its way into the psychometric field via such tests as the *Edwards' Personal Preference Schedule* (EPPS), an objective personality test which yields a profile of an individual's needs across 15 categories, and the *Thematic Apperception Test* (TAT). David McClelland has conducted extensive work on one of Murray's primary psychogenic needs, *n*-achievement (need for achievement). Many other researchers have used Murray's exhaustive list of needs and presses to study numerous aspects of motivation and behavior.

Evaluation

It is difficult to evaluate Henry Murray's theory because while it has clearly influenced the thinking of many others it has not been subjected to careful objective scrutiny. Much of its validation is simply derived from common sense rather than empirical test. One has the impression on reading Murray that his theory is in process of becoming rather than being finished. Many of his concepts were original ideas which influenced other theorists but yet his own theory never quite seems to hang together as a cohesive whole. It is almost as if his philosophical premises are more valuable than his actual theoretical and pragmatic components.

Summary

Henry Murray developed a personological theory of personality which emphasizes the individual as a total unified being which contains elements of many different perspectives including humanistic, phenomenological, holistic, interactional, and also trait psychology. Murray sought to establish an all-encompassing theory which will integrate biological and psychological aspects of human functioning. He focuses on motivation and suggests a framework for understanding human motivation via the complex interaction of needs, press, thema, and vector-value forces. He approaches his concepts with analytical precision and creates a perspective which has become a major resource for personality theorists and researchers.

Murray gained his greatest recognition from the development of the Thematic Apperception Test (TAT), an outgrowth of his classic study, *Explorations in Personality* (1938). This study represents one of the major theoretical and methodological advances in the field of personality theory and research. Murray advocates the in-depth study of individuals as a method of understanding the true complexities of human behavior. He is a talented taxonomist whose detailed analysis of the needs, press, and other major determinants of human behavior offers a rich legacy for the future. Murray also was one of the pioneers in the field of interactional psychology. Although his theory seems to lack a sense of cohesion, each of his concepts is a valuable advance in understanding complex human behavior.

HOLISTIC/HUMANISTIC THEORIES OF PERSONALITY: KURT GOLDSTEIN, FRITZ PERLS, AND ABRAHAM MASLOW

INTRODUCTION

The term *holism*, derived from the Greek word *holos*, means "complete, entire, whole, total." It was first applied to social scientific theory by Jan

Smuts, a South African philosopher, in his book, *Holism and Evolution* (1926) which advocated an organismic approach to government and political theory.

Holistic thought gradually found its way into personality theory and research via a number of theorists who believe that human behavior emanates from an organism which functions as a unified whole rather than a collection of parts. Among the foremost proponents of this approach to personality are Alfred Adler, Kurt Goldstein, J. R. Kantor, Gardner Murphy, Carl Rogers, Prescott Lecky, and Fritz Perls, who see human beings as organized, coherent entities motivated by internal drives toward growth and actualization. Within this context, efforts to understand behavior as isolated acts are considered artifactual because they fail to consider the total organism. This holistic perspective has gained many adherents in the field of health under the rubric of *holistic medicine* and *psychosomatic* or *behavioral medicine* (Hall & Lindzey, 1970).

Humanistic personality theory is closely related to holistic theory in that it shares a common assumption that behavior represents a response from a unified and integrated organism seeking to maximize its adjustment to the world. Like the holistic approach, it rejects reductionistic explanations. In addition, humanistic personality theory focuses on the complex aspects of human behavior including creativity and mystical experiences. It views the individual as being capable of choice and of personal decision making and it pursues an understanding of these processes through various research methods including case studies of subjective or private experience. Among the foremost proponents of the humanistic perspective in personality theory and research are Abraham Maslow, Charlotte Buhler, James Bugenthal, and Carl Rogers. In many respects, holistic, humanistic, and existential theorists share common beliefs and thus it is probably artificial to distinguish among them. But, for the sake of introducing the reader to these orientations, we have assigned specific names to the different approaches.

In the present section, the views of three theorists who exemplify the holistic and humanistic positions will be presented. These theorists include Kurt Goldstein and Fritz Perls, two pioneers in holistic theory, and Abraham Maslow, the founder of humanistic personality theory. Their positions will be discussed in order.

KURT GOLDSTEIN (1878–1965)

Biographical

Kurt Goldstein was born on November 6, 1878 in Germany. He received his medical degree in 1903 and then entered a series of training programs in psychiatry. By age 36 he had published numerous studies and had been appointed as the director of the Neurological Institute at the University of

Frankfurt. The onset of World War I brought Goldstein in contact with many brain-injured soldiers. His examination of these soldiers formed the background for much of his later theorizing about human personality. By 1930, his reputation as a clinician and theorist had become widespread, and he was appointed as professor of psychiatry and neurology at the University of Berlin, one of Germany's most eminent institutions. He became a target of Nazi persecution, however, and was soon forced to flee Germany.

In 1935, he entered the United States and he became associated with Andreas Angyal and Abraham Maslow at Brandeis University. These three scholars made Brandeis University a center for humanistic/holistic theory and research.

Kurt Goldstein died on September 19, 1965 in New York City. His death marked the passing of one of the most influential personality theorists of the 20th century. More than any other theorist, Goldstein was the formative influence and major resource for the many others who accepted the principles of holistic models of human behavior, including Carl Rogers, Fritz Perls, Gardner Murphy, Heinz Werner, Gordon Allport, and Henry Murray.

A complete listing of Goldstein's writings is presented in Marianne Simmel's volume of essays published in Goldstein's honor (see Simmel, 1968). Among his most notable books are: *The Organism* (1939), *Human Nature in the Light of Psychopathology* (1940), and *Language and Language Disturbances* (1948). His research on brain damage made him the major figure in this area for many decades, and his test for organicity (The Goldstein-Scheerer Blocks) remains a primary assessment resource. It is important to recognize that Goldstein used brain damage and psychopathology as a means for studying total human personality. Through his studies of disorder he came to see the supreme importance of organization, unity, coherence, and growth in human personality.

Assertions

1. Human beings function as organized wholes.

Kurt Goldstein believed that human beings function as integrated organisms. Organization is a natural part of the person, and reflects the innate tendency of the person to function as a holistic system of interdependent parts. For Goldstein, studies of human behavior which examine small aspects of functioning, independent of the total organism, were artifactual. The organism always functions as an organized and coherent whole. A response is a response of all aspects of the organism.

Goldstein was influenced by some of the early Gestalt theorists (e.g., Köhler) who believed that the whole is greater than the sum of the parts, because the whole equals all of the parts plus an emergent quality. Thus, we have this equation:

$$Whole = Sum\ of\ parts + An\ emergent\ quality$$

2. *Human beings have one basic motive: self-actualization.*

For Goldstein, human beings possess one basic motive which subsumes all other motives: *self-actualization.* This term refers to a drive to fulfill one's total potential, to utilize all possible opportunities for growth and development of one's abilities and talents. This drive is continuous, and never ceases. It represents the inherent tendency of the organism to master and transcend the influences of its external environment in an effort to grow and develop fully. Self-actualization is an inborn tendency of the organism, but the actualization potential interacts with forces in the environment. In this respect, Goldstein is a pioneer of the current interactionalism movement.

3. *The normal personality seeks to equalize organismic tension.*

When the organism experiences tension, it seeks to reduce this tension and return to a state of balance or homeostasis. When this state of equalization is achieved, the organism is said to be *centered.* The organism never achieves perfect centering, because at any given moment external and internal forces impinge on the organism and disrupt the centering. Nevertheless, the organism seeks the best methods to reconcile tensions so it may return to a centered position. Most of the sources of tension are external; in disease, however, they may be internal. The organism works as an organized and coherent whole to achieve equalization.

4. *The organism must cope with stressful environments.*

If the environment in which the organism exists is supportive, the organism will grow and develop in a healthy, coherent way. Its potential will be fulfilled. Sometimes, however, the environment may be harmful to the organism's thrust for self-actualization and can distort the organism's inherent nature by "shaping" a number of behavior patterns incongruent with the organism's veridical nature. Catastrophic experiences or long-term disruptions may prevent the organism from achieving some degree of centering.

Given continuously disruptive influences in the environment, the organism may find itself unable to "come to terms" with pressures. Thus, it cannot achieve equalization or centering. In this instance, the organism may no longer be able to function well; it would be in a state of disquiet which interferes with its sense of identity and predictability. Goldstein (1939) wrote:

The possibility of asserting itself in the world, while preserving its character, hinges upon a specific kind of coming-to-terms of the organism with its environment. This has come to take place in such a fashion that each change of the organism, caused by environmental stimuli, is equalized after a definite time, so that the organism regains that "average" state which corresponds to its nature, which is "adequate" to it (p. 111).

When the environment continues to elicit changes in the organism, the organism loses its constancy and behavior becomes disordered. There is no longer any sense of unity or continuity. Symptoms represent efforts by the organism to adjust to internal or external pressures which exceed typical equalization capabilities. Sometimes organisms have diseases or imperfections in their physiological systems, and sometimes they are confronted with extraordinary environmental demands. Both of these can become sources of maladjustment and can produce psychopathology.

Applications

Kurt Goldstein did not suggest a system of psychotherapy or a system of education which would apply his assumptions about human behavior. His work on brain damage, however, yielded a number of psychometric and medical procedures which remain in use. His study of "abstract versus concrete" thinking in brain-damaged patients is a classic psychometric study of measurement methods for organic patients (Goldstein & Scheerer, 1941, 1953; Hanfmann, Rickers-Ovasiankina, & Goldstein, 1944). The field of neuropsychology owes a considerable amount to Goldstein's pioneering efforts. His research has been applied in studies of language, intelligence, perception, motor coordination, and general psychopathology.

Evaluation

Kurt Goldstein's influence is so pervasive that it defies commentary in the limited space available. His writings represent the most systematic and detailed portrayal of the organismic position on human nature. His thinking is reflected in the work of numerous personality theorists in the areas of humanistic, organismic, self, and existential psychology. Further, many of his concepts and assumptions are still in use in tests of brain damage and psychopathology.

More than anyone else, he outlined a perspective that considers human beings as organized, integrated, and coherent organisms who function as unified systems striving for full growth and development. His concepts are responsive to the biological, psychological, and sociological aspects of human nature. They offer insights which can be applied to brain damage and psychopathology.

Many of Goldstein's concepts do not permit experimental study, and this tends to make him unpopular with some empirically oriented psychologists. Yet, his assumptions have a strong intuitive appeal. Goldstein provides a theory for understanding everything from the specifics of brain damage to the basics of human nature. Clearly, many of his assumptions are speculative; but this should not deny the validity of his thoughts. The growing popularity of interactional and general systems theories of behavior indicate that Goldstein's acceptance will grow in the future. His thinking captures what many psychologists recognize to be a logical and meaningful view of human nature.

Summary

Kurt Goldstein's theory emphasizes the unity, organization, and coherence of human personality. He believes organisms function as holistic units responding to the inherent drive for self-actualization and the imposed constraints of the physical environment. Organisms seek a state of equalization which balances internal and external forces, called *centering*. Sometimes, forces within or external to the organism interfere with the process of equalization, and this produces psychopathology. Goldstein was a pioneer in holistic psychology; he influenced a number of major figures in personality theory, including Carl Rogers, Abraham Maslow, Fritz Perls, and Gardner Murphy, to mention only a few. His work on brain-damaged soldiers is the foundation for the current field of neuropsychology, and his numerous tests and procedures for assessing brain damage and psychopathology are still in use.

FRITZ PERLS (1893–1970)

Biography

Fritz Perls was born in Berlin on August 8, 1893. He received his medical degree in 1916 from the University of Berlin, and then served as a medical officer in the German army throughout World War I. In 1929, following a period of training in psychotherapy, he became Kurt Goldstein's assistant at the Frankfurt Neurological Institute. He subsequently left Frankfurt for training in psychoanalysis in Vienna and Berlin. In the early 1930s, he migrated to Johannesburg, South Africa, and started a practice in psychoanalysis. During the course of World War II, he remained in South Africa and began to alter his thinking regarding psychoanalysis.

In 1947, he published his first book: *Ego, Hunger, and Aggression: A Revision of Freud's Theory and Method.* This book articulated the basic principles of a new form of therapy which was called *Gestalt*

Psychotherapy. Another major book by Perls was *Gestalt Therapy: Excite-ment and Growth in the Human Personality* (1951), co-authored with Ralph Hefferline and Paul Goodman. In 1946, Perls migrated to the United States and set up practice in New York City. He later moved to California where he resided until his death in March, 1970.

During the last decade of his life, Perls, Carl Rogers, and Abraham Maslow were considered the major figures in humanistic psychology. Toward the end of his life, Perls emerged as a guru for many therapists and lay people alike. His techniques of encountering patients by forcing them to deal with the contradictions in their psychological and physical behavior gained both fame and notoriety. Perls had become the "in" therapist of the 1960s and early 1970s, and the Gestalt aphorism, "You do your thing, and I'll do mine" came to reflect the very nature of American popular culture in the 60s and early 70s. By this time, Gestalt therapy had become a loosely organized group of methods which shared a commitment to pursuing per-sonal freedom through encounters that stressed awareness of one's total being. Perls became the embodiment of this commitment which was iden-tified with the "laid-back" Southern California lifestyle and personal growth movement.

Assertions

1.   The healthy personality functions as a whole Gestalt.

Perls believed the healthy personality is a Gestalt or whole which functions with unity and integration. He was against any dualisms which separate mind and body, self and external world, unconscious and conscious and so forth. Perls felt dichotomies are essentially neurotic in nature and confront human beings with a continual source of problems. The "neurotic dichotomies" can best be resolved by a Gestalt analysis which examines their existence in terms of the total context of a problem (Perls, Hefferline, & Goodman, 1958).

2.   All human behavior derives from organism/environment interaction.

All behavior involves the simultaneous interaction of the organism and its environment. Organism/environment interaction creates a field which is the basis for behavior. There are social, physical, and biological interactions in all fields. Perls believed the unique role of psychology was to study the point of *contact* between the organism and the environment. This point of *contact* is essentially the basis of experience. All contact is considered to be creative and dynamic and to fulfill the process of growth and development. The experience of *contact* produces an awareness of the moment. This awareness involves the achievement of a continuous series of Gestalts which are creative integrations of the experiences derived from organism/environmental *contacts*.

3. *The organism involved in experiencing and unifying organism/environmental contact is the self.*

Amid the needs and pressures of all organism/environment interactions, the self is the system which experiences all contacts and synthesizes them with previous experiences into a new moment of awareness. Perls, Hefferline, and Goodman (1958) wrote:

> Let us call the "self" the system of contacts at any moment. As such, the self is flexibly various, for it varies with the dominant organic needs and the pressing environmental stimuli; it is the system of responses.... The self is the contact boundary at work; its activity is forming figures and grounds.... But, the self is the integrator; it is the synthetic unity, as Kant said. It is the artist of life. It is only a small factor in the total organism/environment interaction, but, it plays the crucial role of finding and making the meanings that we grow by (pp. 234–235).

4. *Gestalt therapy promotes the integration of dissociated aspects of experience through awareness.*

The Gestalt psychotherapist attempts to enhance the patient's awareness of the unity which exists in one's essential nature. This is accomplished through various therapeutic mechanisms which focus on the immediacy of the moment. Thus, the therapist fosters an awareness of the "here and now" by calling attention to postures, gestures, facial grimaces, and tones of voice. For example, the therapist might say, "Do you notice how you jiggle your legs and breathe quickly whenever you speak of being evaluated?" There is no pursuit of developmental reasons for problems. Rather, the emphasis is placed on becoming alert to the totality of one's experience at any given moment. In many respects there is a continual encounter with oneself as a psychological, biological, and social being. Ultimately the patient must synthesize the disparate aspects of his experience. This involves the risk of encountering oneself in a totally new way. Perls, Hefferline & Goodman (1958) wrote,

> ...it is the sensory motor integration, the acceptance of the impulse, and the attentive contact with the new environmental material that results in valuable work.... We believe that the free interplay of the faculties, concentrating on some present matter, comes not to chaos or mad fantasy but to a gestalt that solves a real problem (pp. 246–247).

Applications

Gestalt personality theory has its primary application in Gestalt psychotherapy. It should be noted, however, that there are many variants of

Gestalt therapy, and some practitioners do not hold a strong allegiance to the thoughts advanced by Perls. Many of the techniques suggested by Perls, Hefferline, and Goodman (1958) have found their way into group dynamics exercises and self-help practices. For example, various fantasy and projection exercises are often part of executive development and management-training programs as well as personal growth groups. Thus far, there has been no effort to form an educational system according to Gestalt principles.

Evaluation

Gestalt personality theory, as proposed by Perls, has not been tested by any experimental study, possibly because many Gestalt concepts and assumptions do not lend themselves to measurement and appraisal. Like most practitioner/theorists, Perls evaluated his thoughts against their clinical utility. The proof of his thinking was his perception of the improvement in his patients. Throughout Perls' writing, there is a frequent appeal to the reader to examine his/her own personal life for validation of Gestalt therapy propositions.

Perls' theory is absent from most textbooks on personality theory. One reason is that Perls never articulated his theory in an organized way with references to personality development, organization, dynamics, and change. His writing is extremely difficult to follow, and makes frequent use of phrases unique to Perls' thinking (e.g., "the assimilating of novelty occurs in the present moment as it passes into the future"; "we exist in a chronic emergency and most of our forces...are repressed or dulled"; "excitement is the feeling of forming of the figure-background in contact situations, as the unfinished situation tends to completion").

Clearly, Perls addresses aspects of highly complex human experience. His writing, when followed closely, leads the reader on a valuable journey of insights about the commonplace and the sublime. But his thinking is often difficult to follow, and virtually impossible to validate in an experimental setting. This does not diminish its value; it simply makes it difficult to attract the attention of scientists who must eventually pass judgment on it.

Summary

Fritz Perls did not advance a formal theory of personality. Rather, he suggested a general orientation for psychotherapy which was built around the Gestalt notions of "wholeness" and "unity." During the decade of the 60s, Perls became the most visible person associated with the Gestalt psychotherapy movement although he did not promote himself as the founder or leader of this position.

The central feature of Perls' thinking regarding personality was his notion that the person functions as a whole in continual *contact* with the surrounding environment. The experience of contact is associated with an awareness of the moment which involves, in well-adjusted people, a sense of integration with all previous experience of the organism. His major theoretical construct was the concept of *self*, which Perls considered to be an organized system of responses which serve to integrate and provide interpretive meanings for our ongoing experiences.

Perls' efforts have found their greatest application in the field of psychotherapy. In many respects, his writing is often difficult to understand because of the complex issues which he addressed and his tendency to form new concepts that are often difficult to grasp without a total familiarity with his perspective. Nonetheless, Perls achieved considerable popularity and is the principal resource for the Gestalt position.

ABRAHAM MASLOW (1908–1970)

Biographical

Abraham Maslow was born in Brooklyn, New York. Much of his early life was unhappy, and he reported frequent feelings of loneliness and isolation. He received his Ph.D. in comparative psychology in 1934 at the University of Wisconsin where he studied with Harry Harlow. As he began to read the works of Sigmund Freud, Ruth Benedict, Alfred Adler, and various social psychological theorists, he switched his orientation to *humanistic psychology*. He taught psychology at Brooklyn College between 1938–51, and then assumed a position as chair of the Department of Psychology at Brandeis University, a position he held until his death in 1970. In 1968, he was elected president of the American Psychological Assoication.

Maslow wrote numerous books and journal articles. In many respects, he literally developed the field of humanistic psychology. Among his books are: *Motivation and Personality* (1954), *Toward a Psychology of Being* (1962), *Religions, Values and Peak Experiences* (1964), and *The Farther Reaches of Human Nature* (1971). Although he did not coin the terms *self-actualization* or *humanistic psychology*, he did a great deal to popularize them. For Maslow, human beings have a unique nature characterized by a tendency to develop to their fullest potential. He wrote:

> First of all and most important of all is the strong belief that man has an essential nature of his own...Second, there is involved the conception that fully healthy and normal and desirable development consists of actualizing this nature, in fulfilling these potentialities, and in developing into maturity along the lines that this hidden, covert, dimly seen essential nature dictates, growing from within rather than being shaped from without (Maslow, 1954, pp. 340–341).

In contrast to other personality theorists who came to conclusions about human nature through the study of disordered personalities, Maslow arrived at his conclusions through study of normal and "super" normal personalities. Motivated by the horrors of World War II, Maslow sought to develop a personality theory which emphasized an optimistic view of human nature, focusing on the positive aspects of human experience. He helped establish the American Association for Humanistic Psychology. Its tenets provide a good summary of his orientation. These tenets can be described as the following:

1. Meaningfulness is more important than method in choosing topics for study in psychology.
2. Private, subjective experience is more important than simple overt behavior.
3. Human psychology cannot be reduced to findings derived from animal psychology research.
4. Unique aspects of human experience should be given equal attention in research to the more regular and predictable aspects of human experience.

Throughout Maslow's work, there was a commitment to topics which most of psychology has chosen to ignore, because they do not lend themselves to ordinary research methods. He was concerned with "peak experiences," "actualization," and "love." In the end, his theory came to represent a somewhat idealized view of human potential. When reading Maslow, one is reminded of Oscar Wilde's comment, "We are all born in the gutter, but some of us choose to look at the stars."

Assertions

1. Human needs are arranged in a hierarchy.

According to Maslow, psychology is overly concerned with basic human needs like hunger and thirst, while ignoring higher human needs such as love, self-esteem, and self-actualization. He suggested that all needs must be considered to understand motivation adequately. He proposed that needs exist in a prepotent hierarchy in which basic needs must be met before other needs can emerge as forces for motivation. He believed there are five basic human needs. In ascending order, these needs include: (1) *physiological needs* (e.g., hunger, thirst, air); (2) *safety needs* (e.g., physical security, economic security); (3) *love, affection, and belonging needs* (e.g., acceptance, sexual love, psychological love); (4) *esteem needs* (e.g., self-respect, self-confidence, trust, recognition); (5) *self-actualization needs* (e.g., the

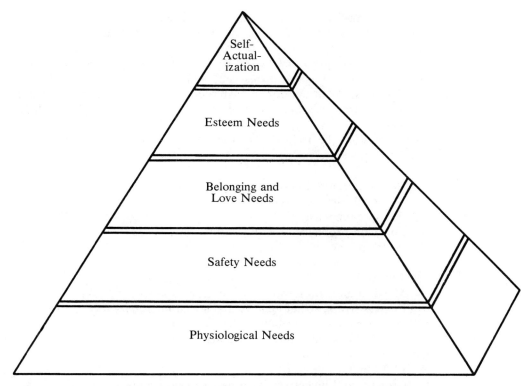

FIGURE 8–2. PYRAMIDAL CONCEPTUALIZATION OF MASLOW'S HIERARCHY OF NEEDS

thrust to develop our full potential; when inhibited we feel bored, unfulfilled, unable to move or grow).

Maslow also wrote of *metaneeds*, like beauty, order, unity, and morality. Metaneeds are growth needs, whereas basic needs are deficiency needs. Metaneeds, unlike basic needs, are not *prepotent*. A human being can readily substitute one for the other. This is not the case for the basic needs. One cannot go to a higher need without first satisfying the previous need.

In *Motivation and Personality* (1954), Maslow speculates that the continual frustration of certain basic needs leads to the development of a behavior syndrome thematically organized around the particular need. Thus, a "safety" syndrome or a "self-esteem" syndrome may develop in which practically everything the person does comes to be associated with meeting the need. In many respects, the person is "fixated."

2.   *Self-actualized people possess certain desirable attributes.*

According to Maslow, self-actualized human beings are characterized by 17 attributes, which were identified through interviews, historical study, biographical analyses and so forth. Among the famous historical figures Maslow found to be self-actualized were the following: Albert Einstein, Thomas Jefferson, Eleanor Roosevelt, Ludwig von Beethoven, Henry David Thoreau, Walt Whitman, Abraham Lincoln, Franklin Delano Roosevelt, George Washington Carver, Albert Schweitzer, and Jane Addams.

Maslow posited the following characteristics of self-actualized people. They are/do/have:

1. Perceive reality accurately.
2. Accept themselves and others.
3. Act spontaneously and naturally.
4. Focus on problems.
5. Prefer privacy and have air of detachment.
6. Independent and autonomous.
7. Appreciate and enjoy new experiences and life.
8. Mystical and transcendent; have peak experiences.
9. Possess strong social identity and social interest.
10. Have strong relationships with a few friends.
11. Oriented toward democratic values.
12. Strong sense of moral values.
13. Philosophical sense of humor.
14. Creative and inventive; fresh perspectives on ideas.
15. Resist conformity and acculturation.
16. Well integrated, total, whole coherent.
17. Transcend dichotomies, bring opposites in harmony.

3. *Self-actualized people are motivated by values of being (B-values).*

In his last book, *The Farther Reaches of Human Nature* (1971), Maslow expanded his thoughts regarding the motives which characterize self-actualized people. He suggested that self-actualized people are not motivated by deficit motives (i.e., physiological, safety, belonging, esteem, self-actualization needs); rather, they are motivated by *metamotives.* Metamotives are the enduring values of human history; they include truth, beauty, wisdom, peace, unity, freedom, and so forth. Maslow called these *metamotives* values of being, or simply, *B-values.*

For Maslow, metamotives are the source of human progress and direction. Clearly, most human beings are not driven by metamotives. Rather, they are concerned with meeting basic or deficit needs. But the important thing for Maslow is that everyone is capable of being motivated by *metamotives.* In his last book, he offers plans for maximizing self-actualization through the education of youth. He suggests youth be taught a number of things about life, including the following:

1. Control is necessary; disorganization leads to confusion.
2. Life is precious and should be appreciated.
3. The serious problems of life should be pursued; these include justice and peace.
4. Decision making is an important skill which is necessary for growth and development. Decision making must be learned.
5. We are children of the entire world and not solely members of a given culture.

Applications

Maslow did not advance a system of education or a technique for psychotherapy. In many respects, however, he was an applied theorist because he offered criteria we can use to appraise people, institutions, societies, and the progress of humanity. For example, teachers can evaluate students with regard to Maslow's deficit needs to determine why the former's progress may be impaired. Students who are trying to meet basic physiological, safety, belonging, and esteem needs have little desire or opportunity to be concerned with literature, poetry, philosophy, and the higher cultivations of the human spirit. Life, for them, is essentially a matter of survival at basic levels of existence. The theory offers a valuable philosophy for human relations in any institutional setting.

His concern for aspects of human experience which traditional psychology ignores, stimulated research on transpersonal human experiences. For example, Maslow studied *peak experiences*, those moments in our lives when we transcend normal concepts of time, space, and causality. They are moments when we are at one with the world about us; when we are in harmony with nature and with ourselves. In this regard, Maslow launched psychology into studies of the mystical experience.

Evaluation

It is difficult to evaluate Maslow according to the criteria of traditional scientific methods. He investigated aspects of human experience that other psychologists avoided. But, as was noted in his biographical summary, Maslow wanted psychology to pursue meaningful areas of human experience.

More than any other theorist, Maslow is responsible for the growth of humanistic psychology. This approach to psychology represents a "third force" which can be contrasted to *psychoanalysis* and *behavioral psychology*. He focused on "normal" behavior rather than psychopathology, and in the process, he forced us to look beyond our immediate lives to our full potentials. His research methods are not scientific in the classic sense of the word. He appealed to our intuition. His arguments are logical in the face of his premises.

Maslow was a pioneer who launched psychology into axiological areas of study generally ignored by psychologists in spite of their importance. His theory of motivation extends the biological theories of motivation that fill our current textbooks.

Summary

Maslow proposed that human beings are motivated by a prepotent hierarchy of needs which included physiological, safety, belonging, esteem and self-actualization needs, termed deficit needs. When deficit needs are met, human beings can then become motivated by "being" needs like justice, peace, harmony, beauty, and unity. He suggested a number of attributes which characterize self-actualized people. Maslow was concerned with normal people and for studying aspects of human behavior which go beyond reflexes and conditioning. His theory dealt with "peak experiences" and the more complex aspects of human experience. He was a visionary theorist whose thoughts will continue to open many new areas of inquiry.

TRAIT/TYPE THEORIES: HANS J. EYSENCK AND RAYMOND B. CATTELL

The trait/type approach to personality research is a unique perspective. It is different from many other approaches because it relies on scientific research rather than clinical intuition for the validation of its assumptions. The trait/type approach grew out of laboratory investigations of intelligence by Charles Spearman in England during the 1920s. Two of Spearman's students, Hans Eysenck and Raymond Cattell, applied Spearman's methods in correlational analysis to the study of personality. Of special value was the statistical method of factor analysis which Spearman created in 1902 as a method for identifying the common components of a number of different variables.

Trait/type theorists seek understanding about the organization and functions of personality through investigations of the structural components of personalitylike traits. Traits are organized into various patterns or types which constitute characterological orientations. In addition to Eysenck and Cattell, other major trait/type personality theorists include J. P. Guilford, Jack Wiggins, Warren Norman, William Stephenson, and Lewis Goldberg. On different occasions, trait/type theories of personality have been called factor theories, statistical theories, quantitative theories, and scientific theories of personality. The present chapter discusses the work of the two major researchers in the area: Hans J. Eysenck and Raymond B. Cattell.

HANS J. EYSENCK (1916–   )

Biographical

Hans Jurgen Eysenck was born on March 4, 1916 in Berlin, Germany. He attended school in Germany but left in 1934 when the Nazi regime came into power. After traveling about Europe, he settled in London, England. In 1940, he was awarded a Ph.D. degree in psychology by the University of London. During the course of the war, he worked as a medical psychologist treating stress victims. During this time he began his research on basic personality characteristics of neurotic patients. Following the war, Eysenck remained on the staff of the University of London as director of the Psychology Laboratory at the Maudsley Hospital. He conducted and published a number of studies on personality during this period. In 1955, the University of London awarded him a chair in psychology.

Eysenck expects psychologists to maintain high standards of research excellence. He seems to enjoy assuming the role of the devil's advocate in defending unpopular positions while causing his opponents to wince in pain and embarrassment before his sharp-tongued retorts. Yet, despite the controversy that surrounds him, Eysenck has managed to compile one of the most productive records in the history of psychology. By anyone's standards, Eysenck must be considered one of the leading psychologists in the world today. He has studied numerous topics including psychopathology, personality classification, political attitudes, humor, crime, smoking, behavior therapy, and test construction. He has published more than 300 scientific articles and 15 books. Some of his more widely known books are: *The Scientific Study of Personality* (1952), *Uses and Abuses of Psychology* (1953), *The Dynamics of Anxiety and Hysteria* (1957), *Behavior Therapy and the Neuroses* (1960), *Crime and Personality* (1964), *Fact and Fiction in Psychology* (1965), *The Biological Basis of Personality* (1967), *The Structure and Measurement of Personality* (1969), *Handbook of Abnormal Pyschology* (1979).

On various occasions, Eysenck has attacked the value of psychotherapy claiming that there is no evidence that it provides cures for mental disorders; attacked claims by scientists that smoking causes cancer, claiming there is no substantive proof of a relationship; and attacked psychoanalysis as a foolish philosophy with no scientific credibility. The basis for all of his stands is scientific data. Quite simply, Eysenck believes that if you don't have facts, you should not be making pronouncements! He is a persuasive speaker who supports his conclusions with research.

In general, Eysenck's research focuses on the nature of personality structure. Through the use of multivariate data analysis methods, he has identified relationships among a wide number of variables. Through hundreds of investigations, he has attempted to relate personality dimensions to personality traits to habits to specific responses. He has studied both biological and psychological variables using many different assessment methods. In many respects, Eysenck's writings are difficult to grasp because of his reliance on complex mathematical procedures like factor analysis and his penchant for integrating biological, psychological, and behavioral data in arriving at his conclusions.

Many psychologists have been critical of both his methods and his results. Indeed, some of his critics have suggested that the very foundations of his theory (i.e., conditioning and personality functions) have no substantive basis; e.g., Biggs, 1962; Brewer, 1975; Spence & Spence, 1964; Yates & Lazslo, 1965). But through all of the din and roar, Eysenck has provided psychology with a stimulating viewpoint with many applications to personality theory and psychopathology.

Assertions

1. *Heredity and environment determine the complex interactions that comprise personality.*

In one of his earliest books, Eysenck (1947) defined personality as the sum total of:

> . . . behavior patterns of the organism, as determined by heredity and environment; it originates and develops through the functional interaction of the four main sectors into which these behavior patterns are organized: the cognitive sector (intelligence), the conative sector (character), the affective sector (temperament), and the somatic sector (constitution) (p. 25).

Though this definition is quite old, Eysenck has never strayed far from it in his research and theorizing. His goal has been to demonstrate the interdependencies among these different sectors of the personality and to establish their roots through the interactions of heredity and learning.

2. *The basis of personality is the balance between cortical excitation and inhibition.*

Eysenck (1957) believes that the balance between cortical excitation and inhibition determines various patterns of conditioning; the patterns of conditioning subsequently result in basic personality dimensions. Thus, there is interdependency among biology, learning, and personality.

According to Eysenck, personality is ultimately a function of the balance between excitatory versus inhibitory potentials in the brain's cortex. As a result of genetics, some people have a cortex which is underaroused. Thus, impulses from the lower areas of the brain (i.e., the reticular activating system) can readily flow through the cortex producing higher arousal and emotionality. This type of situation occurs with *extraverts*. For extraverts, therefore, there is a strong inhibitory potential in the cortex and a weak excitatory potential. In contrast, some people have a cortex which is very easily aroused. This tendency for easy arousal or excitation produces greater inhibition of the impulses coming from lower brain areas. Thus, the cortex is not flooded by emotional stimuli. This situation occurs in *in-*

troverts. In brief, according to Eysenck, extraverts have weak and slowly generated excitatory potentials in the cortex resulting in greater stimulation of the cortex by lower brain areas associated with emotionality. But, introverts have strong excitatory potentials in the cortex resulting in greater inhibition of impulses from lower brain areas and subsequently less emotionality.

>   3.   *Cortical excitation-inhibition balances determine conditioning patterns.*

Among individuals with weak cortical excitatory potentials (extraverts), conditioning of a response is quite difficult and extinction of a response is quite easy. This is related to the nervous system's tendency to develop *reactive inhibition*, a state in which there is opposition or resistance to the continuation of an ongoing activity. Because of reactive inhibition, conditioned associations can never be established; the result is extraversion.

In contrast, among individuals with strong cortical excitation potential, conditioning of a response is quite easy and extinction is quite difficult because reactive inhibition is low. The low reactive inhibition permits associations to be readily conditioned and this increases their resistance to extinction; this is introversion.

In brief, weak cortical excitation results in less inhibition of impulses from lower brain areas resulting in greater arousal; the greater arousal produces more reactive inhibition which makes it difficult to condition a response and easy to extinguish it. In contrast, strong cortical excitation results in greater inhibition of impulses from lower brain areas resulting in less arousal and less reactive inhibition. This makes it easier for an association to be established and more difficult for it to be extinguished.

Through this complicated bit of theorizing, Eysenck establishes an intimate link between personality and biology. In doing so, he adheres to his definition of personality as something which arises from heredity and environment. But, what is most important in his theorizing is the connection between biology and those complex aspects of human functioning that we call personality.

>   4.   *Personality consists of different levels of functioning.*

Different patterns of conditioning which emerge from the excitation-inhibition balance of the nervous system result in the development of specific responses. These specific responses become organized into different habits. The habits, in turn, come to form enduring and predictable tendencies to respond; these are called traits. Organizations of the traits result in a given personality type. A personality type is a function of three dimensions. These dimensions are the fundamental orientations of human activity. All human beings can be ordered across the three basic dimensions.

>   5.   *There are three basic dimensions of personality, extraversion-introversion, neuroticism, and psychoticism.*

Through the use of factor analysis, a complex mathematical procedure for reducing large amounts of data to smaller amounts through manipulations of correlations, Eysenck arrived at a primary dimension of personality: *Extraversion-introversion*—the tendency to be impulsive, friendly, outgoing, talkative, and sociable versus restrained, shy, reserved, and quiet. As we have seen, this dimension is related to excitation-inhibition balances in the brain's cortex.

A pathological extension of these tendencies can be found in the inclination to respond with excessively high levels of emotionality. This inclination was termed *neuroticism* by Eysenck. Neuroticism does not have an opposing pole like extraversion-introversion. Rather, it is simply a continuum which runs from high to low levels.

These two dimensions were arrived at following considerable research by Eysenck and his co-workers. He believes every individual possesses a certain amount of these two dimensions. In subsequent research on abnormal personalities, Eysenck identified a third dimension of personality, which he believes is fundamentally distinct from the other two dimensions. He termed this dimension, *psychoticism*. Psychoticism refers to a tendency to develop confused and disoriented styles of thinking and feeling. This tendency is low in normal populations; but Eysenck believes that it does constitute another major dimension of personality along with neuroticism and extraversion-introversion. Eysenck also believes that *intelligence* is a major dimension of personality. However, he has not done much research on this dimension himself, but rather relies on the classical studies of Charles Spearman (1927) at the University of London.

According to Eysenck, every human being can be placed at different points on these dimensions. The resultant plot of these points in space offers the best predictability of the individual's personality across situations. This can be seen in the following diagram:

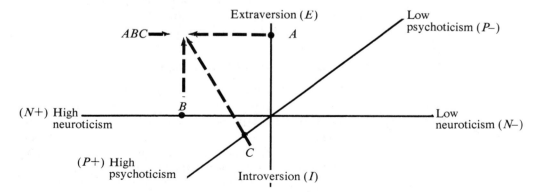

An individual at point *A* on *E-I*, and point *B* on *N*, and point *C* on *P* would probably be a highly agitated and emotional schizoaffective mental patient.

This three-dimensional plot is Eysenck's basic contribution to personality classification and typology. He arrived at these three orthogonal dimensions after extensive research and he is confident that the dimensions represent fundamental aspects of human behavior. He has developed a questionnaire to measure an individual's levels along each of these three dimensions. It is called the *Eysenck Personality Inventory* (1964).

> 6. *Theories of personality must be based on scientific facts generated through experimental and correlational methods.*

As noted previously, Eysenck prides himself on being a tough-minded scientist firmly committed to research. He has openly heaped scorn on those individuals who arrive at conclusions through clinical speculation or intuition. In one of his books in which he attacked the scientific foundations of psychiatry, Eysenck (1955) wrote:

> Scientific theories are generalizations from firmly established empirical facts which make possible the prediction of new and hitherto unknown facts; where there are few, if any, firmly established facts we cannot in the nature of the case, have (scientific) theories... (p. 5).

Eysenck uses a wide variety of research methods which include both experimental and correlational strategies. He frequently uses correlational techniques to examine the relationships among variables across a certain level (e.g., traits or specific habits) while using experimental methods to examine relationships between different levels (e.g., what traits are related to particular types). Factor analysis and multiple discriminant function analysis have been among his favorite methods of data analysis. He uses these multivariate methods to investigate intercorrelations between large numbers of variables which he administers to sizable samples. He uses questionnaires, objective, physiological, and motor tests, and scores of other measures to obtain personality information.

Eysenck's favorite research strategy is to separate two groups of people on a variable through the use of valid measurement instruments (e.g., separate individuals into polar introverts and polar extraverts on the EPI), and then examine differences between these two groups across scores of other tests. If large differences appear, he is able to assess the predictive value of the variable and also gain a good understanding of its nature. This method is called *criterion group* design.

Applications

Eysenck's theory has resulted in the development of several psychological tests designed to measure his views on personality dimensions. In addition, some of his thinking has been applied to the classification of psychopathology. For example, based on his research, it is possible to view neuroses and psychoses as totally different dimensions of functioning. This view stands in contrast to the traditional view that there is a continuum from normality to neurotic behavior to psychotic behavior. Eysenck has developed no system of therapy which reflects his assumptions; however, he is a strong supporter of the behavior therapies and founded the journals, *Behavior Research and Therapy* and *Multivariate Clinical and Personality Research*.

Evaluation

Hans Eysenck is a behavioral scientist who has probably done more than any other person to establish connections between complex personality variables and neurophysiological levels of functioning. His research activities span a very broad spectrum of topics and he has managed to integrate his findings creatively. His theories and researches stimulated much controversy, especially in regard to his assumptions about the number of basic dimensions in personality structure.

There have been numerous criticisms of both his research methods and findings but these criticisms have not prevented Eysenck from proceeding on his course, tarnished but undaunted. He and Cattell have engaged in a series of arguments over such issues as the number of basic factors which comprise personality and the issue of reliability of these factors (Cattell, 1972; Eysenck, 1972, for examples). His reliance on factor analysis as a method of data analysis has led to numerous complaints because of the limitations inherent in this method. Essentially, the results yielded by a factor analysis are a function of what goes into it. If the variables entered into a factor analysis have questionable validity and reliability, then the results of the factor analysis are highly questionable.

Though Eysenck is to be credited for his efforts to link personality to biology, he has sometimes been too quick to reach a conclusion about the nature of the nervous system. For example, his concept of excitation-inhibition balance in the cortex ignores the fact that most people are not polarized in the various extremes but rather share both excitation and inhibition tendencies at different times. Further, the new research on hemispheric specialization may have great implications for his notions but he has not integrated these new findings into his theory. Lastly, he has not attended to situational-organismic interactions in behavior.

Summary

Hans Eysenck proposes that personality is an outgrowth of heredity and environment acting upon four major sectors of human functioning including cognition, character, emotion, and somatic behavior. He believes genetics leads to differences in the balance of cortical excitation/inhibition. This balance is related to the amount of reactive inhibition in the cortex which subsequently influences conditionability. These processes ultimately produce certain personality dimensions like extraversion-introversion, neuroticism, and psychoticism. Eysenck is extremely productive and relies heavily upon scientific experiments for the validation of his findings. He is heavily critical of assertions made by other theorists because of their failure to use scientific methods in arriving at their conclusions. Much of his research is based upon the use of factor analysis and other multivariate data analysis methods.

RAYMOND B. CATTELL (1905–   )

Biographical

Raymond Bernard Cattell was born on March 20, 1905 in Staffordshire, England. He received a B.S. degree in chemistry from the University of London in 1924 and was awarded a Ph.D. degree in psychology under the supervision of Professor Charles Spearman from the same university in 1929. Spearman was a pioneer in the use of quantitative methods of data analysis and the rigor of his methods appealed to Cattell. Cattell has continued to pursue the development and application of quantitative methods of data analysis, especially factor analysis.

Upon graduation from the University of London, Cattell worked as a professor at the University of Exeter and as director of the Psychological Clinic in Leicester, England. In 1938, E. L. Thorndike invited Cattell to join the staff at Columbia University. Cattell accepted the position and worked for a short period with Thorndike and C. Stanley Hall, one of the founders of psychology in the United States. In 1944, Cattell accepted a position at the University of Illinois in Champaign-Urbana, Illinois. He remained at the latter institution as a research professor of psychology until his retirement in 1976. He then moved to the University of Hawaii in Honolulu. He maintains an active role in the Institute for Personality and Ability Testing in Illinois, which he founded.

Raymond Cattell has published more than 35 books and over 400 scientific articles, and a score of psychological tests including the well-known 16 PF Test. He is an unusually energetic scientist whose mind has been a continual source of new ideas and research methods. He has attracted a small, loyal group of followers, largely in experimental and psychometric psychology, who continue to work with him on new aspects of his theories and methods. His interests include personality theory and measurement, intellectual functioning, behavior genetics, cross-cultural psychology, and multivariate statistical methods. He continually introduces new material into his personality theory, thus making many of his previous writings outdated. Among his books are the following: *Personality: A Systematic, Theoretical, and Factual Study* (1950), *The Scientific Analysis of Personality* (1965), *Handbook of Multivariate Experimental Psychology* (1966), *Handbook for the Sixteen Factor Personality Questionnaire* (1970, with co-authors H. Eber and M. Tatsuoka), *Personality and Mood by Questionnaire* (1973), and *Personality and Learning Theory* (1979 & 1980). A journal paper which provides a recent update of his thinking and reflects his movement toward an interactional model of personality was published in *Multivariate Behavioral Research*, 1980, *15*, 371–402.

Assertions

1.   Personality is the total behavior of the individual.

In one of his early books, Cattell (1950) defined personality as "...that which permits a prediction of what a person will do in a given situation." He went on to say that it is concerned with "...all the behavior of the individual, both overt and under the skin" (pp. 2–3). This definition is admittedly broad, but it does make sense within the context of Cattell's research efforts since he seeks to identify the basic structural components that will ultimately enable one to predict behavior through an equation combining person, environment, and situational variables. He terms his fundamental behavioral equation a *"specification equation."* It takes the following form:

$$\text{Behavior} = \text{Function of situational} \times \text{Person variables}$$

Each of these variables has a number of different dimensions.

Thus, a person's behavior in a given situation is ultimately a function of a "...multidimensional person (coming) into contact with a multidimensional situation, and the result is a response of magnitude particular to that individual" (Cattell, 1965, p. 81). Cattell's entire career has been devoted to specifying the variables that enter into this equation.

2.   There are three sources of information about a person's personality.

As Cattell launched his quest to identify the major dimensions of the behavioral equation, he recognized different sources of information could be used to obtain scientifically valid information. The first source of information comes from a person's school records, legal records, and so forth. He terms this source life record data, or *L-data*. The second major source of personality is *Q-data*. This is generated by self-report measures. It provides the researchers with the subject's own view of feeling, moods, and behavior. Q-data measures are generally multiple answer questionnaires. The last type of data is called *T-data*. This is objectively scored information gathered from paper-pencil, psychomotor, or other instrument-based sources.

Cattell uses these three sources of information to generate data on different aspects of personality. He thus samples a variety of information sources and escapes the problem of coming to conclusions from a single data source. This approach is a major strength of his theory and enables him to declare that his research findings are representative of a wide spectrum of human functioning. Through factor analysis, he determines the various clusters of data from these three sources and thus can identify basic structural dimensions of personality.

> 3.   *The basic unit of personality structure is the trait.*

According to Cattell, the basic unit for understanding personality is the personality trait. A trait is a relatively enduring disposition to respond in a given manner across a wide variety of situations. It is a characteristic which gives predictability to an individual's behavior. For Cattell, there are three basic kinds of personality traits: (1) *Source Traits*: Pure and independent sources of behavior which have both hereditary (*constitutional source traits*) and environmental (*environmental-mold traits*) bases. Source traits are limited in number and are essentially the building blocks of human personality. Source traits exist in a number of different modes including motivation (*dynamic traits*), goal attainment effectiveness (*ability traits*), and affective and constitutional styles (*temperament traits*). There are also (2) *common traits*, shared by a broad number of individuals, and (3) *unique traits*, specific to a given individual.

Source traits are the basic unit of personality. Through the use of *factor analysis*, a mathematical procedure for reducing large amounts of data to smaller amounts through correlational methods, Cattell has identified a limited number of source traits. In recent years, he has introduced a number of other determinants of behavior like moods, roles, and situations.

> 4.   *A finite number of source traits characterize human personality.*

Through the use of L-data, Q-data, and T-data, Cattell has gathered extensive information about the three different types of source traits: dynamic traits, ability traits, and temperament traits. It is important to recognize that the different types of data measures (e.g., L-data) yield different personality traits. This is because each type taps into a different source of functioning. By creating a matrix of data sources for each of the three basic types of sources traits, it is possible, according to Cattell, to arrive at the basic traits which comprise motivation, temperament, and ability components of personality.

5.   There are a finite number of dynamic (motivational) source traits.

Cattell employed more than 68 objective personality tests (i.e., T-data) to identify basic dynamic or motivational traits. Cattell called some of these motivational traits, *ergs*, in agreement with the unit of energy used in physics. According to Cattell, there are 10 *ergs* or motivational source traits: sex, gregariousness, curiosity, escape, self-assertion, aggression, dependency, constructiveness, parental protectiveness, and narcissistic sex or self-indulgence. *Ergs* are inherited or innate sources of motivation. There are also a number of acquired motivational source traits called *sentiments* by Cattell. Some of the sentiments found by Cattell include those for self, religion, sweetheart, interests, parents, and career. In other words, sentiments are acquired targets for motivational or drive states. Cattell (1950) defined sentiments as "...major acquired dynamic (motivational) trait structure which cause their possessors to pay attention to certain objects or classes of objects, and to feel and react in a certain way with regard to them" (p. 161). Both *ergs* and *sentiments* manifest themselves through attitudinal expression. Cattell measures both the ergic and sentiment motivational source traits through the Motivational Analysis Test (Cattell, Horn, Sweeney, & Radcliffe, 1964).

The ultimate structure of motivational or dynamic source traits is based on the assumption that ergs are primary. They influence the acquired source traits, sentiments, and these in turn, result in attitudinal expressions. These arrangements are discussed by Cattell in his concept of the *dynamic lattice*. The lattice represents the analysis of the interrelationships among ergs, sentiments, and attitudes for a given individual.

The *self-sentiment* is particularly important for Cattell because virtually all of the ergs and the other sentiments are related to it. In many respects it is a master sentiment. Cattell (1966) wrote, "It contributes to all sentiment and ergic satisfactions, and this accounts also for its dynamic strength in controlling, as the 'master sentiment' all other structures" (p. 272).

6.   There are a finite number of temperament (constitutional) source traits.

Based on studies using more than 120 different personality measures spanning L-, T-, and Q-data sources, Cattell believes there are 35 primary temperament source traits. These primary source temperament traits can be reduced to 15 second-order traits through factor analysis and these second-order traits can be reduced still further to 5 third-order traits. Cattell's well-known personality test, The Sixteen Factor Personality Questionnaire (16 PF) enables researchers to assess individuals for the second-order traits. For Cattell, third-order traits are very far removed from the specifics of behavior; thus, he favors doing most personality description with the second-order level of temperament traits.

TABLE 8-1. MAJOR PERSONALITY SOURCE TRAITS ACCORDING TO CATTELL (ADAPTED FROM CATTELL, 1965)

Second-order factor: *Exvia v. Invia* (Extraversion v. Introversion)
1. Factor A: *Affectia v. Sizia* (Warm, outgoing, sociable v. Cold, detached, reserved)
2. Factor H: *Parmia v. Threctia* (Venturesome, bold v. Inhibited, shy, restrained)
3. Factor F: *Surgency v. Desurgency* (Carefree, enthusiastic v. Glum, serious, sober)
4. Factor Q2: *Self-sufficient v. Group-oriented* (Independent v. Group adherence)

Second-Order Factor: *Corteria v. Pathemia* (Alert, controlled v. Dreamy, emotional, sensitive)
1. Factor I: *Harria v. Premsia* (Tough minded v. Tender minded)
2. Factor M: *Praxernia v. Autia* (Careful, practical v. Imaginative, nonconforming)

Second-Order Factor: *Inner controlled v. Uncontrolled*
1. Factor G: *High super ego v. Low super ego* (Conscientious v. Expedient)
2. Factor Q3: *Strong self-concept v. Low integration* (Controlled, disciplined v. Careless, casual)

Second-Order Factor: *Neurotic v. Stable* (Nervous, anxious v. Stable, relaxed, calm)
1. Factor C: *Low ego strength v. High ego strength* (Unstable, emotional v. Stable, mature)
2. Factor L: *Protensia v. Alaxia* (Suspicious, guarded v. Trusting, open)
3. Factor O: *Guilt prone v. Assurance* (Apprehensive, tense v. Confident, placid)
4. Factor Q4: *Ergic tension v. Low ergic tension* (Tense, aroused v. Relaxed, peaceful, calm)

Note: Other second-order primary source factors exist but are not clustered in higher factors at the present time. These include Factor B: High intelligence v. Low intelligence; Factor N: Shrewd v. Artlessness; Factor Q1: Radicalism v. Conservatism.

The primary source temperament traits include 12 traits associated with maladjustment (e.g., depression, paranoia, nervousness) and 23 traits associated with normal behavior. These traits exist as polar dimensions. Cattell has assigned various letters to each of the second-order primaries. Table 8-1 provides a description of the various second-order temperament factors as developed through L-data and Q-data. Cattell (1965, 1973) provides a more in-depth discussion of these topics.

7. Personality temperament, motivation, and ability are interrelated.

According to Cattell, human behavior is a complex phenomena which involves the interdependency of different aspects of functioning. Our temperament, motivations, and abilities are related to one another. Through the use of various personality assessment measures, it is possible to determine what ergs, sentiments, and attitudes are related to specific personality temperament dimensions (e.g., Factors A, C, Q, and so on) and how these, in turn, are related to various ability factors. Personality ultimately involves the traits in all of these areas interacting with particular situations.

8. *The person-centered environmental representation (PCER) model of personality provides the most comprehensive view of behavior.*

Cattell continually adds to his theory in an effort to expand its utility and applicability. In 1980, Cattell published several additions to his theory calling for the integration of personality and situational variables in the behavioral equation. Quite early in his career, Cattell acknowledged the value of Kurt Lewin's notion that behavior is a function of person-environment interaction (see p. 628 of present text).

In his specification equation, he includes the situation as an important variable. However, for many years, he did not make any major efforts to sample situations or to include them in his data analysis except as they might be represented in various trait dimensions. For example, he separates the situation into *focal* aspects and *background* aspects. These aspects are akin to figure-ground conditions in which we attend to one task (focal stimulation) while we are present in a larger situation (background stimulation) (Cattell, 1970).

However, Cattell has now increased his interest in situational contributions to behavior. This is a function of his new interest in interactional models of human behavior which he calls the *PCER* that examines both person and situational dimensions (Cattell, 1980).

Applications

Raymond Cattell's theory has had its greatest application in the field of psychometrics where he and others have produced many personality and intelligence tests. These tests are used in medicine, personnel selection, and so forth. His work has not resulted in any theory of behavior change or therapy, nor has it achieved as much popularity among the public as the theories of Freud, Adler, Jung, and a host of others. The reason for this is that Cattell's assumptions and methods are highly complex and are not readily grasped. Cattell's efforts to popularize his theory in his book, *The Scientific Analysis of Personality* (1965), largely failed because of his reliance on quantitative methods (e.g., factor analysis), the complexity of which even exceeded the understanding of many psychology professors.

Evaluation

A complex theory opens itself to many questions and criticisms. Cattell's theory is no exception to this rule. For the most part, Cattell's theory has not gained much popularity among personality researchers, probably because of its complex technical foundations. However, it has been the topic of considerable research by a small number of investigators who worked in Cattell's laboratory. These investigators include John Nesselroade, John Hundleby, John Horn, John Scheier, John Digman, and Samuel Krug, to mention only a few.

Cattell's theory has come under criticism from researchers like Hans Eysenck, who has questioned Cattell's techniques of factor analysis. Eysenck (1972) contends that if Cattell would use orthogonal rotations in his factor analysis, he would not find many personality source traits. Eysenck thinks that Cattell's findings may be artifactual because of Cattell's research methods. Guilford (1975) and Digman and Takemoto-Chock joined this debate on the side of Eysenck. Digman and Takemoto-Chock (1981) argued that many of Cattell's factors or source traits have not been found by other researchers. Cattell has replied by pointing out his unique statistical methods (e.g., oblique angle rotation) are appropriate for personality research because no personality variables are truly independent from others and should not be separated by orthogonal factor analysis. His argument has not been generally accepted by other theorists.

The strength of Cattell's theory resides in the very aspects which have been most subject to criticism. It is based on massive amounts of research impressive for both their creativity and their rigor. For example, Cattell's use of many different sources of data is truly admirable. In addition, Cattell has pursued complex problems which others have ignored. He has examined genetic as well as acquired influences on human behavior and along the way he has developed many new methods of multivariate statistical analysis. Further, Cattell has shown flexibility in altering his theory as a result of new research and trends. His most recent *PCER* model places him in the midstream of contemporary interactionist theories of personality. Regardless of the controversy surrounding his assumptions and research methods, it is clear that Raymond Cattell has made impressive contributions to personality theory and research. His energy, dedication, and imagination have produced a challenging perspective on human behavior that will endure long into the future.

Summary

Raymond Cattell is an immensely productive scientist. A pioneer in the area of quantitative psychology, he brought high standards of scientific rigor to the area of personality theory and research. Cattell uses three different sources of data in his investigations (L-, Q-, T-data) to determine basic personality structure and dynamics. He is concerned with identifying source traits, common traits, and unique traits in his research. He believes there are three basic types of source traits: motivational, temperament, and ability.

Motivational traits can be divided into *ergs* (inherited) and *sentiments* (acquired). Both of these combine to form various attitudinal orientations in a given individual. There are many temperament source traits. However, factor analysis permits their reduction to second-order and third-order clusters. The second-order factors include extraversion-introversion, alertness-emotionality, inner control-casualness, neurotic-stable, and high intelligence-low intelligence. Recently, Cattell has proposed a new model called the *PCER* which emphasizes person-environment interactions.

REFERENCES

Allport, G. *Personality: A psychological interpretation.* New York: Holt, Rinehart, & Winston, 1937.

Allport, G. *The nature of prejudice.* Reading, Mass.: Addison-Wesley, 1954.

Allport, G. *Becoming: Basic considerations for a psychology of personality.* New Haven, Conn.: Yale University Press, 1955.

Allport, G. *Pattern and growth in personality.* New York: Holt, Rinehart, & Winston, 1961.

Biggs, J. The relation of neuroticism and extraversion to intelligence and educational attainment. *British Journal of Educational Psychology*, 1962, *32*, 188–195.

Brewer, W. There is no convincing evidence for operant or classical conditioning in humans. *Cognition and the symbolic processes*, eds. W. Weimer and D. Palermo. New York: Wiley-Interscience, 1975.

Bronson, G. Identity diffusion in late adolescence. *Journal of Abnormal and Social Psychology*, 1959, *59*, 414–417.

Cattell, R. *Personality: A systematic, theoretical, and factual study.* New York: McGraw-Hill, 1950.

Cattell, R. *The scientific analysis of personality.* Hawthorne, N.Y.: Aldine Press, 1965.

Cattell, R. (Ed.) *Handbook of multivariate experimental psychology.* Chicago: Rand-McNally, 1966.

Cattell, R. The 16PF and basic personality structure: A reply to Eysenck. *Journal of Behavioral Sceince*, 1972, *1*, 169–187.

Cattell, R. *Personality and mood by questionnaire.* San Francisco: Jossey-Bass, 1973.

Cattell, R. *Personality and learning theory* (2 vol.). New York: Springer Publishing Co., 1979-1980.

Cattell, R. The separation and evaluation of personal and environmental contributions to behavior in the person-centered model (PCER). *Multivariate Behavioral Research*, 1980, *15*, 371–402.

Cattell, R., Eber, H., & Tatsuoka, M. *Handbook for the Sixteen Factor Personality Questionnaire.* Champaign, Ill.: Institute for Personality and Ability Testing, 1970.

Cattell, R., Horn, J., Sweeney, A., & Radcliffe, R. *Handbook for the Motivation Analysis Test.* Champaign, Ill.: Institute for Personality and Ability Testing, 1964.

Digman, J., & Takemoto-Chock, N. Factors in the natural language of personality: Reanalysis, comparison and interpretation of six major studies. *Multivariate Behavioral Research*, 1981, *16*, 149–170.

Erikson, E. *Young man Luther.* New York: W. W. Norton, 1962.

Erikson, E. *Childhood and society.* New York: W. W. Norton, 1950.

Erikson, E. *Identity: Youth and crisis.* New York: W. W. Norton, 1968.

Erikson, E. *Gandhi's truth.* New York: W. W. Norton, 1969.

Eysenck, H. *Dimensions of personality.* London: Routledge & Kegan Paul, 1947.

Eysenck, H. *The scientific study of personality*. London: Routledge & Kegan Paul, 1952.

Eysenck, H. *Uses and abuses of psychology*. New York: Penguin Books, 1953.

Eysenck, H. *The dynamics of anxiety and hysteria*. New York: Praeger Publishers, 1957.

Eysenck, H. *Behavior therapy and the neuroses*. Elmsford, N.Y.: Pergamon Press, 1960.

Eysenck, H. *Crime and personality*. Boston: Houghton Mifflin, 1964.

Eysenck, H. *Fact and fiction in psychology*. New York: Penguin Books, 1965.

Eysenck, H. *The biological basis of personality*. Springfield, Ill.: Charles C Thomas, 1967.

Eysenck, H. *The structure and measurement of personality*. London: Routledge & Kegan Paul, 1969.

Eysenck, H. Primaries or second-order factors: A critical consideration of Cattell's 16PF battery. *British Journal of Social and Clinical Psychology*, 1972, *11*, 265–269.

Eysenck, H. (Ed.). *Handbook of abnormal psychology*. New York: Basic Books, 1979.

Fromm, E. *Escape from freedom*. New York: Holt, Rinehart, & Winston, 1941.

Fromm, E. *Man for himself: An inquiry into the psychology of ethics*. New York: Holt, Rinehart, & Winston, 1947.

Fromm, E. *The sane society*. New York: Holt, Rinehart, & Winston, 1955.

Fromm, E. *The art of loving*. New York: Harper & Row, 1956.

Fromm, E. *The revolution of hope*. New York: Harper & Row, 1968.

Goldstein, K. *The organism*. New York: American Book Co., 1939.

Goldstein, K. *Human nature in the light of psychopathology*. Cambridge, Mass.: Harvard University Press, 1940.

Goldstein, K. *Language and language disturbances*. New York: Grune & Stratton, 1948.

Goldstein, K., & Scheerer, M. Abstract and concrete behavior: An experimental study with special tests. *Psychological Monographs*, 1941, *53*.

Goldstein, K., & Sheerer, M. Tests of abstract and concrete thinking. In *Contributions toward medical psychology*, ed. A. Weider. New York: Ronald Press, 1953.

Guilford, J. P. Factors and factors of personality. *Psychological Bulletin*, 1975, *82*, 802–814.

Hall, C., & Lindzey, G. *Theories of personality*. New York: Wiley, 1970.

Hanfmann, E., Rickers-Ovasiankina, M., & Goldstein, K. Case Lanuti: Extreme concretization of behavior due to damage of the brain cortex. *Psychological Monographs*, 1944, *57*.

Horney, K. *The neurotic personality of our time*. New York: W. W. Norton, 1937.

Horney, K. *Self-analysis*. New York: W. W. Norton, 1942.

Horney, K. *Our inner conflicts*. New York: W. W. Norton, 1945.

Horney, K. *Neurosis and human growth*. New York: W. W. Norton, 1950.

Horney, K. *Feminine psychology*. New York: W. W. Norton, 1967.

Jung, C. G. Psychological types. Princeton, N.J.: Princeton University Press, 1971.

Maslow, A. *Motivation and personality*. New York: Harper & Row, 1970. (Originally published, 1954.)

Maslow, A. *Toward a psychology of being*. New York: Van Nostrand Rheinhold, 1968. (Originally published, 1962.)

Maslow, A. *Religions, values, and peak experiences*. Columbus, Ohio: Ohio State University Press, 1970. (Originally published, 1964.)

Maslow, A. *The farther reaches of human nature*. New York: Viking Press, 1971.

Mullahy, P. *The contributions of Harry Stack Sullivan*. New York: Hermitage Press, 1972. (Originally published, 1952.)

Murray, H. *Explorations in personality*. New York: Oxford University Press, 1938.

Murray, H. *The Thematic Apperception Test.* Cambridge, Mass.: Harvard University Press, 1943.

Murray, H. *Assessment of men.* New York: Holt, Rinehart, & Winston, 1948.

Murray, H., & Kluckhohn, C. (Eds.) *Personality in nature, society, and culture.* New York: Alfred A. Knopf, 1950.

Murray, H. Some basic psychological assumptions and conceptions. *Dialectica*, 1951, *5*, 266–292.

Perls, F. *Ego, hunger, and aggression: A revision of Freud's theory and method.* New York: Random House, 1947.

Perls, F., Hefferline, R., & Goodman, P. *Gestalt therapy: Excitement and growth in the human personality.* New York: Julian Press, 1958.

Phillips, L., Broverman, I., & Zigler, E. Social competence and psychiatric diagnosis. *Journal of Abnormal Psychology*, 1966, *71*, 209–214.

Phillips, L., Broverman, I., & Zigler, E. Social competence and psychiatric diagnosis. *Journal of Abnormal Psychology*, 1966, *71*, 209–214.

Sahakian, W. S. Personalism. In *Current Personality Theories*, ed. R. J. Corsini, Itasca, Ill.: F. E. Peacock, 1977.

Schaar, J. *Escape from authority: The perspectives of Erich Fromm.* New York: Basic Books, 1961.

Simmel, M. (Ed.). *The reach of mind: Essays in memory of Kurt Goldstein.* New York: Springer, 1968.

Smuts, J. *Holism and evolution.* New York: Macmillan, 1926.

Spence, K., & Spence, J. Relation of eyelid conditioning to manifest anxiety, extraversion, and rigidity. *Journal of Abnormal and Social Psychology*, 1964, *68*, 144–149.

Stern, W. *Person and thing (Person und sache).* Berlin: Barth, Vol. 1, 1906; Vol. 2, 1918; Vol. 3, 1924.

Stern, W. *General psychology from the personalistic standpoint.* New York: Macmillan, 1938.

Sullivan, H. S. *Conceptions of modern psychiatry.* New York: W. W. Norton, 1953.

Sullivan, H. S. *The interpersonal theory of psychiatry.* New York: W. W. Norton, 1953.

Sullivan, H. S. *The psychiatric interview: Vol. 1 & 2.* New York: W. W. Norton, 1954, 1956.

Sullivan, H. S. *Clinical studies in psychiatry.* New York: W. W. Norton, 1956.

Sullivan, H. S. Schizophrenia as a human process. In *Schizophrenia as a human process*, ed. H. Perry. New York: W. W. Norton, 1962.

Sullivan, H. *The fusion of psychiatry and social science.* New York: W. W. Norton, 1964.

Waterman, C., Beubel, M., & Waterman, A. Relationship between resolution of identity crisis and outcomes of previous psychosocial crisis. *Proceedings of American Psychological Association Convention*, Vol. 5, 1970.

Yates, A., & Lazslo, J. Learning and performance of extraverts on the pursuit rotor. *Journal of Personality and Social Psychology*, 1965, *1*, 79–84.

SECTION THREE
THEORETICAL ORIENTATIONS

CHAPTER IX

Existential Personality Theory

Suzanne C. Kobasa and
Salvatore R. Maddi

LUDWIG BINSWANGER

Existential psychology views the person as a biological, social, and psychological being whose primary task is the search for and establishment of meaning. This distinctively human endeavor goes on within a spatial / temporal context, with limitations such as past experiences, environmental conditions, and the exercise of freedom by others. According to existential psychology, man's consciousness and freedom, and the associated activities of decision making, value postulating, and goal setting, allow creative responsible manipulation of these limitations.

The specifically psychological adaptation of this view of human nature, originally found in the philosophies of Søren Kierkegaard, Martin Heidegger, Jean-Paul Sartre, William James, Karl Jaspers, and Paul Tillich, begins with the work of the Swiss psychiatrist Ludwig Binswanger (1881-1966), who reacted against the mechanistic psychology of Freud. Other figures who continue this extension of existential philosophical insights to psychological problems are Medard Boss, Viktor Frankl, Rollo May, R.D. Laing, Eugene Gendlin, and Salvatore Maddi.

Existential personality theory describes two basic personalities. The *authentic* person realizes fully the core existential assumptions about human nature. He exercises vigorously the psychological needs or functions of symbolization, imagination, and judgment and allows these to influence his biological and social experiences. He is well integrated and demonstrates originality and change. Having accepted the givens of his past and present, his basic orientation is toward the future and its associated uncertainty. Uncertainty leads him to experience anxiety, but he accepts this anxiety as a necessary concomitant of vigorous living. He is aided in this acceptance by courage.

The *inauthentic* person, in contrast, inhibits the expression of distinctively human psychological needs; he sees himself as a player of predetermined social roles and the embodiment of biological needs. His behavior is fragmentary and stereotyped and often includes exploitation of others, a rigidly materialistic attitude, and feelings of worthlessness and insecurity. He fears the uncertainty of the future; shrinking from it, he defines himself solely in terms of his past or present, in spite of resultant feelings of guilt and regret.

Existential psychologists discuss how one can get from the inauthentic to the authentic mode of being. For them, personality change is an issue across the entire life span and results from the interaction of psychological, social, and biological-physical factors.

INTRODUCTION

Existential thinking is at the same time popular and misunderstood. The bases for its popularity are clear. In the midst of the spiritual bankruptcy of modern times, it extends hope not only for psychological survival but even for dignity. It contends that a person can take hold of one's own life and shape it through active decision making. The existential approach encourages the deepening of consciousness and disentanglement from superficial conventions of society leading to growth in individuality. It counters prevailing views of the human as irrational and impotent and provides a rationale for attempting social change rather than passively adjusting to the status quo. Far from being empty theorizing, it offers psychotherapeutic help as well.

It is not surprising that there should be considerable misunderstanding of the existential approach. One reason for this is that several disciplines are independently involved in developing existential thought. Philosophy has made by far the most rigorous intellectual contributions. Perhaps because of this, psychology and psychiatry have overrestricted themselves to practical applications. Also involved in articulating existential views are writers, dramatists, and film makers; literary, drama, and art critics; sociologists and political scientists. Each profession has its own characteristic vocabulary, emphases, aims, methods, and standards of rigor. There have also been differences about existentialism within each of these profession. No single person or close-knit group has dominated existential thought to shape it into a unitary movement. This is true even in philosophy, though the major figures in existentialism have come from that discipline. Popular misconceptions of existentialism stem primarily from this heterogeneity. One person may have read only a bit of existential social criticism, another only the works of one philosopher, a third may have only undergone existential psychotherapy. Each person will have a one-sided view of existentialism but will imagine that he has understood all.

Because of the problem of heterogeneity, the main aim of this chapter will be integrative. The many diversified contributions to existential thought require combination and transposition into a set of coherent and systematic statements about personality. In this attempt the work of Ludwig Binswanger will be highlighted. Though not the founder or even the principal spokesman of this movement, he did concern himself primarily with the implications of existential thought for personality in his theoretical writings and in his application of an existential emphasis in psychotherapy.

Most existentialists employ a distinctive vocabulary and style of writing. Sections in Heidegger and Sartre, for example, are so highly idiosyncratic in choice of terminology that they seem to demand a special dictionary of existential terms. A deliberate attempt is made in this chapter to define terms straightforwardly, using simple language. However, like the original sources this chapter requires the reader to pay close attention to the context or theoretical network within which terms appear. Recognizing this, but also appreciating the reader's possible need for an easy reference guide, some frequently used existential terms are defined here:

Aesthetic. An inauthentic orientation to self and world characterized by: (1) an emphasis upon the pleasure to be derived from the present, and an attempt to deny the necessary integration of the present with past and future; and (2) a giving over of control of and responsibility for actions to accident or fate. This orientation is similar to the more familiar hedonism.

Authenticity. That form of human behavior which existentialists consider ideal, consisting of the individual's responsible exercise of his powers of awareness and decision making.

Being-for-itself (Sartre), *Dasein* (Heidegger). That mode of existence distinctive to the human being which is never static but is always in the process of revealing new things about itself and its world through decision making as a vehicle for creating meaning.

Daseinsanalysis (Binswanger, Boss). That form of psychotherapy committed to an understanding of the person as continuously involved in the creating and attributing of meaning to himself, others, and his environment.

Facticity. The given facts of a person's existence over which he cannot have total control; examples include physical stature, environmental resources, demands made by employers or teachers, and the inevitability of death.

Fundamental project. The primary choice or orientation about life and one's participation in it which underlies and informs all of the person's other decisions.

Idealistic. An inauthentic orientation to self and world which seeks to deny all of the necessary conflict and limitation in human living through allegiance to one immutable principle or goal.

Possibility. All that a person has not yet become but could be, through active use of his powers of awareness and decision making; that human ability to surpass or transcend limitations which mitigates or seeks alternatives to the specific facticity of each person's life.

HISTORY

Precursors

The roots of existential personality theory are found in existential philosophy, a movement which entails a reaction against emphases on the impersonal world of nature. Instead, existential philosophy takes the human being, with subjective perceptions, thoughts, feelings, decisions, and acts, as its starting point. In this emphasis on understanding existence concretely realized, existential philosophy adopts a subject matter similar to that of psychology.

The first and perhaps most complete existential philosophy was developed by Søren Kierkegaard (1813-1855). His work was a reaction against the kind of philosophy, best exemplified by Hegel, which attempted to construct a grand view of the universe supported by some external absolute in which the human was a passive participant. In throwing this view into doubt, Kierkegaard focused upon the subjective person. Regarding inner experience as the true reality, he provided an articulate portrayal of such human subjective phenomena as decision making, responsibility, guilt, anxiety, and alienation. He conceptualized the person's life as a series of decisions.

When a person contemplates making a decision in the direction of an unknown future, he experiences anxiety. Persisting in the face of anxiety regardless of circumstances is considered by existentialists as the way of growth and development, with individuality as its reward. Turning away from anxiety and holding on to the status quo is the way of stagnation, with a steady accumulation of guilt which finally constitutes despair (Kierkegaard, 1944, 1954).

Kierkegaard (1959, 1968) provided vivid descriptions of what amount to personality types, or modes of experiencing. The aesthetic, ethical, and religious lifestyles were presented as stages in the development toward maturity. Consistent with his whole approach, emphasizing change and subjectivity, Kierkegaard (1954, p. 173) defined personality as "a synthesis of possibility and necessity." However, common though these ideas may seem now, it should be remembered that Kierkegaard was thereby branded a heretic and ostracized by polite society.

Not many years later, William James (1842-1910), Karl Jaspers (1883-1969), and Paul Tillich (1886-1965) advocated a related view of life as struggle. James portrayed the world as a chaos that can only be given order by persons through interpretive actions. This view of life was echoed by

Jaspers in his discussion of "limit situations" which presented the person with conflicts unresolvable in familiar and well-exercised ways. Tillich emphasized how life of necessity was in the grips of anxiety over the human's frail ability to control events. All three philosophers conceptualized a generalized attitude or mode of functioning to help persons meet life challenges. For James, it was the "strenuous mood," for Jaspers, "transcendence," and for Tillich, "courage." The common element in these views is that as life is by its nature chaotic and threatening, the person lives it best if he recognizes the challenge and responds forthrightly.

Martin Heidegger (1889-1976) provided a philosophical analysis of human existence which contains much that can be interpreted psychologically. Heidegger (1962) described essential conditions of human nature, and, through his concept of *Jemeinigkeit,* or *each-to-his-ownness,* posited characteristics which differentiate individuals. Heidegger distinguished *Das man* (conventional or herd mentality) from *Dasein* (ability to reach high levels of consciousness and uniqueness through reflecting upon oneself, others, and the natural world).

The mode of experiencing known as *Dasein* is the special glory of the human being, though it brings with it such discomforting states as anxiety and confrontation with death. Such states are regarded as developmentally valuable, because they spur consciousness and activeness in constructing one's life. *Dasein* can also mediate positive states, such as caring. In this case, caring is not a passive comfort but rather an active, involving, and strenuous matter which takes into account the needs and resources of one's self, one's environment, and the other.

Very definitely a 20th-century figure, Jean-Paul Sartre (1905-1981) emphasized psychological as much as philosophical considerations. Sartre (1956) criticized Freudian psychology for viewing the person as the object of the therapist's manipulation, as a static collection of objectively defined inner drives, and as ruled by unconscious forces. In Sartre's sharply contrasting existential view, the person's behavior is determined by his subjective goals which define his "fundamental project" or overall purpose in life. Through the exercise of choice guided by this fundamental project, the person creates meaning and consciousness of what he is and is not. In this manner, the person is continually changing and developing. With this emphasis, it is understandable that Sartre was critical of the Freudian reliance on conceptualizing the person as unconscious of the biological and social forces that supposedly rule him.

For Sartre, a belief in the unconscious provides one with a ready excuse for failure to take responsiblity to create one's own meaning and directions. Failure to exercise choice amounts to irresponsibility, inauthenticity, or *bad faith*. Although Sartre is sometimes seen as a pessimistic existentialist, a good deal of his work involves evangelistic attempts to influence people to exercise choice and thereby achieve authenticity and individuality.

The philosophers mentioned have provided the primary sources for contemporary existential psychology. Among other less directly relevant philosophers are:

1. Friedrich Nietzsche (1844-1900), who emphasized subjective meaning but celebrated the irrational more than the others.
2. Martin Buber (1878-1965), who combined an existential with a Jewish Hasidic perspective, emphasizing interpersonal intimacy and commitment.
3. Gabriel Marcel (1889-1973), whose work was characterized by a strongly theistic conception of the universe.
4. Albert Camus (1913-1960), who pessimistically emphasized the absurdity of attempting to discern meaning in a meaningless world.
5. Edmund Husserl (1859-1938), who provided for existentialism the useful methodology of phenomenology.
6. Miguel de Unamuno (1864-1936) and Nikolai Berdyaev (1874-1948), who adapted existential doctrines to their own cultural contexts in Spain and Russia.

Beginnings

The first three quarters of the 20th century unfolded in ominous fashion. Ever larger and more destructive wars, the rise of technology concomitant with de-emphasis on humanistic enterprises, and corruption in social institutions once considered inviolable have shaken beliefs in traditional, familial, and religious values. Thoughtful persons, in ever-increasing numbers, have begun to question social institutions and look within themselves for grounding and understanding. This dilemma of existence has been fertile ground for the popularization of existential philosophy and its development into personality theory and psychotherapeutic practices.

Perhaps the most influential person in the rise of existential psychology was Ludwig Binswanger (1881-1966). He received a medical degree from the University of Zurich, studied with Carl Jung, and had a psychiatric internship under Eugene Bleuler. In 1911, Binswanger succeeded his father as medical director of the Sanitorium Bellevue in Kreuzlingen, Switzerland. There he specialized in the treatment of psychotics and continued in this work even after his retirement in 1956. Throughout his professional life, Binswanger strove to translate the philosophical concepts of existentialism into a theory of personality which would conceptualize individual differences and psychopathology. Basic to his work was the notion that existential concepts could be useful in identifying and curing mental illness. Showing clearly his debt to Heidegger, Binswanger called his technique of psychotherapy *Daseinsanalyse,* or analysis of the human capability of giving meaning to existence.

Just as Kierkegaard reacted against Hegel's assumption of an objective, impersonal order, Binswanger rejected Freud's belief in unchangeable biological (instincts) and social (protection of the common good) forces. Some of Binswanger's earliest existential formulations appear in a small book entitled *Freud: Reminiscences of a Friendship* (1957). This work questions many central contentions in psychoanalysis. Binswanger was particularly critical of Freud's biological emphasis, especially the slighting by psychoanalysis of spiritual elements in philosophy and religion. Freud was also attacked by Binswanger for his mechanistic approach, which left little room for recognizing a person's quest for meaning and construction of his own life through responsible decision making. Binswanger contended that Freud could never have created the theory and practice of psychoanalysis had his view of the person as ruled by the unconscious and driven by biological forces been true.

Binswanger's (1963) most important and best elaborated theoretical contribution is his discussion of the *existential a priori,* or *fundamental meaning structure.* This concept refers to the universal and unlearned human ability to perceive specific meanings in the world of events and to transcend any concrete situation on the basis of that attributed meaning. The existential a priori associated with a unique individual is a kind of recognizable meaning matrix which, when imposed on reality, allows the distinctive style and life direction of the person to emerge. Like Sartre's fundamental project, the individual's existential a priori underlies all of his choices and gives them their particular form.

Medard Boss (1903-   ), Binswanger's fellow Swiss, was involved in a similar personological enterprise. Boss served as director of the Institute of Daseinsanalytic Therapy and professor in the medical school at the University of Zurich. Like Binswanger, Boss derived his interpretations from the works of Heidegger and other existentialists, and criticized Freud for imposing invented abstractions (e.g., instincts) and categories (e.g., the Oedipal complex) upon human actions. For Boss, fantasies, emotions, thoughts, and body organs exist not as separate and static phenomena but rather as a complex and dynamic unity. According to Boss, "the essential structure of man is to be defined as none other than his possible modes of being" (Binswanger, 1963, pp. 20-21). His emphasis is on the construction of personality and individual life through the active investing of events with meaning and decision making which guides action.

Boss (1963) outlines attributes common to all persons, or *existentialia,* and emphasizes individual differences in content and effectiveness of various constructions of self and world which he encountered in clinical practice.

Binswanger and Boss are at their best when describing and illuminating case histories. Unfortunately, they were less gifted, or perhaps less interested, in the careful development of a theory of personality. Perhaps both were inhibited from theory development by the vehemence of their reaction to Freud's formalism. The intense concern with the practical activity of psychotherapy may also have distracted them from theoretical tasks. In any event, in neither Binswanger's nor Boss's writing is the interrelationship among their concepts really clear. Nor are relationships between the concepts and laboratory or natural observations always apparent. Consequently, it is difficult to discern how the concepts of these existential psychologists could be tested and further developed through empirical research.

Current Status

Although the work of both men gained some popularity in Europe during the 1930s, it was only in the late 1950s that their existential writings were translated and read in America. Interest in these writings continued through the early 1960s but now appears to be waning. This decline in interest does not signify a decrease in the influence of existential thinking; rather it indicates a transfer of attention to later existential psychologists more concerned with problems of broad sociopolitical importance and more willing to be systematic in theorizing about personality.

Contemporary existential thinkers have been influenced as much by Binswanger and Boss as by the earlier philosophers. From the philosophers, they learned the importance of considering the ultimate purpose of human life and have adopted the view that the person creates his own meaning through decision making and action in the pursuit of possibility. From Binswanger and Boss, they accepted the task of theorizing about psychotherapy. Inevitably, this has required them to consider how and why persons fail to realize ultimate existential fulfillment.

Rollo May is noteworthy not only for his psychological discussions of important existential experiences such as anxiety (May, 1953), love (May, 1967), and power (May, 1972), but also for his introduction of other existential works to the American audience (May, 1950; May, Angel, & Ellenberger, 1958). May has championed the interdisciplinary nature of existentialism. His books tend to be filled with philosophical and theological references as well as clinical experiences. In an early work, May (*The Meaning of Anxiety*, 1950) developed a lucid approach to personality showing the heavy influence of Tillich (who was his teacher), Binswanger, and Heidegger.

Viktor Frankl (1905-   ) has taught in the medical school and directed the Neurological Polyclinic at the University of Vienna. After being influenced early in his career by Freudian and Adlerian thought, Frankl shifted to existentialism in his attempt to come to grips with the shattering experience of being imprisoned in a World War II concentration camp (Frankl, 1963). He observed that those who did not survive had only conventional meaning to sustain them and had not sufficiently practiced creating their own individual meaning which existential psychology emphasizes. Out of these insights, he developed a technique of treatment called *Logotherapy,* in which the person is encouraged to ferret out what is meaningful for him in a seemingly indifferent and meaningless world.

Meaning, for Frankl (1965), is expressed through three types of values: *experiential values* (those realized through receptive being in the world); *creative values* (those realized through direct action in the world); and *attitudinal values* (those whose actualization is dependent only upon the person's consciousness and is possible even when the expression of experiential and creative values is blocked). This categorization of values provides an interesting way of distinguishing among persons. Unfortunately, Frankl offers little else to systematic and rigorous theorizing about personality.

The British psychiatrist R.D. Laing (1927-   ) began his formulation of existential psychology while at the Tavistock Clinic in London. His first book (Laing, 1960) is an attempt to apply the philosophy of Sartre in the description and treatment of psychosis. In this, Laing has been acclaimed for an appropriate psychological counterpart of Thomas Szasz's (1961) more sociological critique of psychiatric practice. Maintaining what he calls a strict phenomenological approach, Laing claims that schizophrenia can only be understood from the perspective of the person experiencing it. He accuses the families of patients, the psychiatric establishment, and society in general of failing to understand psychosis and of imposing their own categories and biases on the person diagnosed as schizophrenic. For Laing, misunderstandings and mismanagement lead to prolonging the patient's suffering. Although full of radical implications for psychotherapy, Laing's writings lack the psychological emphasis, precision, and clarity for further elaboration of existential theory.

With a background in both philosophy and psychology, Eugene Gendlin (1928-   ) combines clinical sensitivity with conceptual sophistication. A professor at the University of Chicago, Gendlin (1962) seeks to construct a new vocabulary to overcome the thought/feeling or mind/body distinction which existentialists have found objectionable. Important is the concept of *felt meaning*, or the intuitive sense of understanding, clarity, or directionality which arises when the person has put aside conventionalities and focuses upon his inner experience. He also attempts to provide a terminology within which personality change can be seen as the rule rather than the exception. Gendlin is also heavily influenced by Rogerian thought, which causes him to deviate from the main tradition of existentialism.

Also a professor at the University of Chicago, Salvatore R. Maddi (1933-   ) has made contributions to existential thought which reflect his concerns with the empirical testing of academic psychology, without losing the emphasis on usefulness and relevancy stemming from psychotherapeutic concerns. Maddi's writings (1967, 1970, 1975b) show clear influence of Kierkegaard, Tillich, Frankl and James, as well as his recognition of what existential psychology requires to become a viable theory of personality. Maddi's use of existential concepts in systematic research (e.g., Maddi, Kobasa, & Hoover, 1976); his formulation of existential personality types (e.g., Maddi, 1970); and his conceptualization of development across the life cycle, focusing on existential matters like the growth-facilitating effects of the acceptance of death (Maddi, 1975a), show his concern for practicality and theoretical rigor.

Existentialism as an approach to understanding personality can be assessed in several ways. It appears to have sustained a good reception among lay readers since the late 1950s. There seems no diminution in the works of fiction and art formulated from an existential perspective. Less impressive is the impact of existential thinking on psychology and psychiatry. The number of psychologists and psychiatrists claiming to be existential is small. There are virtually no full-fledged programs of graduate study in existential psychology in this country (though one can get some training in this approach at the University of Saskatchewan, the University of Chicago, Duquesne University, or the William Alanson White Foundation). Over the past three years, some empirical studies have attempted to operationalize the study of existential concepts. There also appears to be a growing personological interest in existentially relevant variables like decision making and planfulness (e.g., Mischel, 1973).

ASSERTIONS

Development

Most existential psychologists make assumptions about human nature (e.g., Binswanger, 1963, on *a priori conditions;* Boss, 1963, on *existentialia;* Maddi, 1976, on *core considerations*). The first nine assertions are a systematic categorization of what existentialists have said about universal, inherent aspects of humanness. Existential psychologists also consider how individuals come to differ from each other. The next seven assertions (10-16) depict developmental courses, emphasizing interactions that produce changes in personality across the life cycle.

1.   Personality is primarily constructed through attribution of meaning.

Human beings are distinctive in their ability to be consciously aware of themselves and the world around them. This involves more than simple perception. People tend, through the active use of their cognitive capabilities, to reflect on and to invest perceived events with meanings.

Binswanger (1963) defines the human as the *being-in-the-world* who constitutes the possibility of meaning. The same point is made by Boss (1963), who characterizes *Dasein* (the distinctively human form of existence) as having responsibility for disclosing all forms of reality; and by Frankl (1963) and Maddi (1970), who refer to the search for meaning as the fundamental tendency in all persons.

This process of attributing meaning to self, others, and the environment gives substance to another fundamental yet still more elusive characteristic of human nature—freedom. For existentialists, the terms *consciousness* and *freedom* are equivalent. In creating and recognizing meaning, the person is being free. For Sartre (1956) the human is constantly in the process of creating himself and his world. The person, a being conscious of what he is and what he is not, has a never-completed character. His nature is always changing and always disclosing something new about itself, its environment, and other persons (Being-for-itself). Sartre distinguishes this distinctively human sort of being from *being-in-itself,* which is complete and never changing. *Being-in-itself,* for example a rock, never has to face the task of creating meaning and freedom.

Although the human is essentially constituted as being-for-itself, some people deny this and aspire after the security of being-in-itself. Sartre calls this process man's attempt to become God. Simone de Beauvoir (1952) views the male in contemporary culture as more easily associated with being-for-itself, while the female is linked to being-in-itself. The degree to which particular persons actively engage in a search for meaning varies greatly. It should be kept in mind here that all persons have an inherent capacity for attributing meaning, and personality is an expression of this ability.

2. *Persons are characterized by symbolization, imagination, and judgment.*

This set of psychological functions directs the universal search for meaning. The explicit emphasis on these cognitive capabilities derives from Maddi's (1967, 1970) usage, but they are implied in the work of other existential psychologists. Symbolization involves the need for abstracting from concrete experience a representative category or idea. The more symbolization is exercised, the more categories with which events can be identified and classified. Imagination is the combining and recombining of ideas and categories in new ways, leading to conceptualization of change. Judgment involves assessing experiences with the result being values and preferences.

Much of this is implied in Binswanger's (1963) *Eigenwelt,* that form of being in which the person is primarily oriented to self. Looked at as a part of personality, *Eigenwelt* most directly reflects the personally or inwardly appreciated aspects of cognitive activities which create meaning. It would not be a misinterpretation to consider *Eigenwelt* a phenomenological sense of self, but it is a common misinterpretation to regard it as the only concern of existential psychology.

3. *Persons are characterized by their participation in society.*

The search for meaning goes on in what Binswanger (1963) calls the *Mitwelt,* the realm of interactions with others. This notion is found in Heidegger's (1962) *care,* Sartre's (1956) *being-for-others,* Boss's (1963) *trust,* and Maddi's (1967, 1970) *needs for contact and communication.* These writers grapple with the question of how a person can freely and responsibly establish meaning for self and world while necessarily interacting with the many others involved in the same task. The question of how one's meaning attribution can avoid interfering with that of another person is dealt with.

Existentialists discuss several possible ways a person interacts with others. For example, Binswanger (1963) and Boss (1963) provide the alternatives of *communion* and *distrust;* Maddi (1967, 1970), the distinction between *intimacy* and *exploitation;* and Sartre (1956) and Heidegger (1962), the alternatives of *individualism* and *conventionality.* These forms of social interaction differentiate the lifestyles of distinct individuals. By evaluating these lifestyles, existentialists arrive at an ethic.

4. *Persons participate in a physical and biological environment.*

Just as it is impossible to think of a human being in isolation from others, so is it impossible to think of him without a body or not occupying physical space. Conceptualizations of this fundamental characteristic appear in Binswanger's (1963) notion of *Umwelt* (the world around us), Heidegger's (1962, p. 133) discussion of the "aroundness of the environment and Dasein's spatiality," Sartre's (1956) and Boss's (1963) explication of the body as an essential structure of human existence, Gendlin's (1962) description of *felt meaning,* and Maddi's (1967, 1970) *biological needs.* In an existential scheme, one's biological or physical mode of being is evaluated in terms of how well the particular environment and its resources (examples include one's voice, sense of touch, and geographical location) serve as the vehicle for, as well as the expression of, one's symbolizing, imagining, and judging to other persons.

Assertions 3 and 4 do not imply that when considering an actual person's life, social, biological, and physical environments can be kept separate. Rather, all are regarded as occurring together. For example, intimacy between two persons is established through a combination of factors such as the exercise of judgment, the act of communication, and the expression of sexuality.

5.   Time is a necessary context for the construction of personality.

At any given moment, every person has a past, present, and future. Life also has a literal beginning and end. The person has the capacity for incorporating into his or her sense of meaning the notion that time is not a simple succession of isolated moments and the idea that he or she is not infinite (will die).

Of course, a time sense is not always exercised by people. A certain amount of strenuous effort is involved in the successful integration of past, present, and future. The person totally involved in the pleasure of the moment resists thinking about the past or the future and the constraints placed on him by the fact that time is limited. The person secure in a love relationship prefers to consider how well it is going now and to remember the good times of the past, rather than confronting the possibility of the end of the relationship which an undefined future holds.

The vigorous expression of symbolization, imagination, and judgment leads to the awareness of having a clear-cut past, present, and future, and to the integration of these three time periods in the development of personal meaning. By active symbolization, persons bring their past into their present; through imagination, from the present they grasp glimpses of the future; and through judgment, they apply remembrance of the past and contemplation of the future to their present situations.

6.   Life is best understood as a series of decisions.

The human activity which best epitomizes the interrelation of the psychological, social, and biological-physical environments and of time periods of existence is decision making. Whether the person realizes it or not, he or she is constantly making decisions which influence actions and have implications for the use of available time.

In understanding personality, the existential psychologist seeks not only the many concrete decisions a person makes, but also the underlying or generic decision that ties all of his decisions together. The universal search for meaning is characterized by some sort of generic or unifying decision. Binswanger (1963) calls it the *existential a priori,* and Sartre (1956), in a somewhat more psychologically accessible discussion, gives it the name *fundamental project.* According to Sartre, the fundamental project is the psychologist's veritable irreducible: the persons's ultimate choice about his participation and purpose in the world, which underlies all of his behaviors. To identify a person's fundamental project, the psychologist must consider as many of the person's choices, made in as many possible situations, as can be recaptured. As will be discussed in the section on maintenance, the specific form of the fundamental project—the kind of behaviors it encompasses, and the consistency among these—serves as an important indicator of individual differences.

The emphasis upon the person as decision maker shows existential dynamics in its clearest form. The next three propositions explicate the implications of decision making in the course of human life.

7. Personality is a synthesis of facticity and possibility.

Kierkegaard (1954, p. 173) points out that in the decision-making process the person takes into account both the hard facts of his existence (examples include his age and sex, job requirements, and the demands made upon him by a loved one), and his ability to surpass these through symbolizing, imagining, and judging. Personality involves both what one is, in a psychological, social, biological, and physical sense, and what one might become (Jaspers, 1963).

Through including facticity in decision making, existentialists indicate that the person does not have unlimited freedom. The human situation necessarily includes factors over which the person does not have total control. The best example is death. For the existentialists, however, death is not simply the termination of physical functioning or the end point of consciousness and social relations. Death symbolically penetrates all of the person's life and is represented in every limitation, disappointment, and failure of one's attempts to realize meaning.

These limitations and disappointments need not lead to resignation and passivity. When they occur in the life of a person vigorously oriented toward constructing his own life, they serve to establish the dialectic between what is unchangeable and what is possible. In this sense, acceptance of inevitabilities sharpens one's perception of and commitment to what can be influenced through personal effort.

8. A person is always faced with the choice of the future, which provokes anxiety, and the choice of the past, which provokes guilt.

Although the content of decision-making situations may vary widely, they have an invariant form, according to existentialists (Kierkegaard, 1954; Maddi, 1967, 1970; May, 1953). One alternative in the choice necessitates change and therefore precipitates the person into the future. The other alternative permits him to maintain the status quo; in that sense, he does not change but weds himself to the past. To choose the future brings *anxiety*—what Kierkegaard (1954) called "fear and trembling"—because one cannot predict or control what will happen. Choosing the past brings *guilt*, because in deciding not to change, one is left with a sense of missed opportunity. Emotionally speaking, these are the only two options available to the person who will emerge from every decision-making situation with either anxiety or guilt. Lest this sound overly pessimistic, a further clarification of the existential position is in order.

Existentialists consider anxiety and guilt to be *ontological,* rooted in the nature of being human. Thus, anxiety and guilt associated with decision making are not the result of unfortunate learning and development but are a necessary part of living. The guilt one feels at missed opportunity signifies that growth through changing and risking is ideal for humans. But when changing or the contemplation of it brings anxiety, this is because the person does not live in isolation and must contend with other persons and the force of circumstance. Thus he cannot be sure what consequences personal change will bring, and so he becomes anxious. But he also cannot be sure that change will be disastrous, whereas curtailing growth to avoid insecurity will surely lead to stagnation and feelings of guilt. The person's ability to create meaning for himself requires a continual increase in experience that can only come about through change. Thus, to choose the past, the status quo, is to court meaninglessness. Choosing the past characteristically will lead to an accumulation of guilt. There is a difference between realizing that you have missed one or two opportunities for growth and knowing that you have done so often enough to constitute a commitment to mere security, easy comfort, and personal stagnation. A buildup of guilt will amount to self-condemnation. Existentialists have referred to this as *dread* (Kierkegaard, 1944), *self-surrender* (Binswanger, 1963), and *meaninglessness* (Maddi, 1967).

9. Courage facilitates choosing one's future.

The ultimate implications of choosing to stand pat in the past are dire enough that everyone should want to choose the future. But that is not easy to do, because anxiety regarding the unknown is a significant obstacle. The buildup of guilt into despair and meaninglessness does not happen right away, requiring many choices of the past, whereas anxiety is vivid and uncomfortable whenever change takes place or is contemplated. Therefore, *courage* is necessary to choose the future (May, 1953; Tillich, 1952).

In existential psychology, courage has two components. First, courage amounts to faith in oneself as capable, through symbolization, imagination, and judgment, of exercising one's possibility and constructing a meaningful life (Maddi, 1970). This faith mitigates ontological anxiety by helping the person believe that the risk he takes through change is not foolhardy because he does have influence, though admittedly not complete control, over what change will bring. In addition, he believes that even if there should be dire outcomes (e.g., rejection, ridicule) to change, he can try again because failures do not damage his ability to symbolize, imagine, and judge. The second component of courage is a high consciousness that persons construct their lives through decision making and change, and that the buildup of guilt through choosing the past has worse consequences than tolerating anxiety in the process of choosing the future. In other words, the person must know and believe the existential view of life. If he does, he will reject mere security and easy comfort, though they will certainly have attraction for him. The emphasis shifts from concern over momentary discomfort to a fascination with what is to be achieved and learned through personal growth.

The following assertions in this section (10-16) concern the developmental process. Existential psychologists do not regard development to be automatic or simply maturational. Ideal development is difficult and must be stimulated and encouraged. But after the rudiments of courage and toleration of anxiety in decision making have been learned, development becomes much more self-determined and independent of others.

In considering development, existential psychologists scrutinize both facticity and possibility. With regard to facticity, the major question concerns the determining power of the biological, psychological, and social givens as the person moves through life. As to possibility, of concern is the person's ability to reinterpret and differentiate his given biological, environmental, and social situation, leading to new creative alternatives for action. This emphasis on the dialectic between facticity and possibility shows that existential psychologists regard development as difficult and strenuous. As mentioned previously, this emphasis differentiates existential psychology from self-actualization positions, which tend to assume that ideal development takes place automatically if adverse experiences are not encountered.

For all its emphasis upon development as shaping life, existential psychology is unfortunately vague as to precise propositions. It will therefore be necessary to elaborate what is rudimentary and render explicit what is implicit.

10. Development is the interaction of psychological, social and biological-physical components of existence.

In seeking to understand personality across the life cycle, existential psychologists investigate changes in the above three areas. Binswanger and Boss demonstrate this in case histories, showing how malfunctioning in one sphere of existence is accompanied by disruption in the other two spheres. For example, in the case of Lola Voss, Binswanger (1963) associates the emergence of schizophrenia with (1) her failure to exercise imagination in her persistent use of one narrow and distorting world-design (psychological sphere); (2) the predisposition for acute anxiety provided by a state of physiological weakness following typhoid fever (biological-physical sphere); and (3) the failure of her parents and teachers to provide adequate moral training (social sphere).

Maddi (1970, 1975a) views development as a series of confrontations between psychological, social, and biological needs and the environments which satisfy or frustrate these needs. All these needs are experienced through all portions of the life span. There is a sharp contrast here with

Maslow's (1954) developmental scheme, which organizes needs in a hierarchical form in which higher psychological needs depend upon the prior satisfaction of lower needs (e.g., before a person may exercise his need for creativity, he must satisfy basic physiological needs for food and shelter).

In Maddi's scheme, not only do the three different types of needs simultaneously characterize personality, but the satisfaction of one necessarily affects the others. In the ideal developmental course, the child is encouraged to exercise his psychological motivation for meaning. This not only leads to the maturation of the child's ability to symbolize, imagine, and judge, it also facilitates the child's growth in his biological and social realms of being. In ideal development, the child tends to perceive his body as allowing him potential accomplishment of certain goals. He realizes that, through careful exercise, he can become a good basketball player in spite of his small frame. The child who undergoes a nonideal form of development, on the other hand, sees his body as a source of good and bad feelings which he allows to take control—he decides to give up on basketball because he is too short. With regard to the effects of psychological needs on social needs in ideal development, the courageous child is more likely to approach intimate, rather than exploitative, relations with others. At dinner time, the child experienced in the exercise of symbolization, imagination, and judgment is more likely to engage in mutually interesting conversation with his parents and siblings, while the child not skilled in psychological functioning will see dinner as a time only to satisfy his hunger and may consider other persons as threats to his getting enough to eat.

11. Ideal development is facilitated by encouraging individuality.

Although existential psychologists agree that early development necessarily involves socialization (i.e., training of children in culturally shared norms and rules), their emphasis is upon how the child can become a unique individual. Binswanger (1963) utilizes Heidegger's (1962) notion of the inauthentic and authentic forms of caring to explain how adults hinder and facilitate individuality in a child. Individuality results from what Heidegger calls *leaping ahead* of the other person. When parents encourage the child by teaching him that he is really capable of doing more on his own than he has yet accomplished, they are exercising authentic care and promoting ideal development. Individuality in the child is thwarted when parents do what Heidegger calls *leaping in,* when they take over for the child what he is capable of doing for himself, thereby depriving him of a sense of competence and potentiality for greater control over himself and his environment. Joining Binswanger in the emphasis upon training for independence, Maddi (1970, 1975a) recommends to parents and educators the use of exercises in symbolization, imagination, and judgment to foster reliance on personal initiative and release from conventional constraints.

A lot is asked of parents and other developmentally relevant adults by existentialists. They must work hard to foster individuality (e.g., it often takes both patience and imagination to get a young child to see that he can really do an unfamiliar task on his own); and they must also be willing to accept a variety of positive and negative consequences associated with the child's exercise of independence (e.g., his experimentation in areas of life unfamiliar and worrisome to them). Parents must value self-reliance and growth, even though this may mean that their control over their children thereby diminishes.

Through exercising symbolization, imagination, and judgment, and by experiencing intrinsic and extrinsic rewards for acting as a distinct and assertive person, the child is on his way to learning to be courageous, to tolerate anxiety, and to choose his future.

12. Limits stimulate positive development.

An important part of learning that one can successfully influence one's environment is the recognition that one can try again if one fails in initial attempts to be effective. In this sense, it is better for parents to teach their children about facticity through the imposition of limits than to leave them with a false sense that everything is easily possible. Binswanger (1963) and Boss (1963) see the imposition of limits and discipline as necessary for this sort of instruction. They criticize "pseudo permissiveness," indicating that it is growth-inhibiting to allow the child to function without restraints. In Binswanger's view, the child's development of an "inner support" system and the abandonment of "external retreats" is dependent upon his early experience of struggling with something and of being self-reliant in the face of adversities. The imposition of limits leads to the child's recognition that his freedom is not absolute and that there are things beyond his control. His increasingly mature exercise of symbolization, imagination, and judgment in the attempt to carry through on his decisions in completing chosen projects helps his maturation as a self-responsible person. Limits actually facilitate individuality.

13. Richness of experience stimulates positive development.

In seeking to understand the developmental course of a patient, Binswanger (1963) and Boss (1963) ask the basic question: How much has he or she experienced in the psychological, social, and biological-physical spheres of existence? Binswanger evaluates the products of the interaction between the individual's fundamental meaning structure and the other persons, things, and events he encounters. Boss makes a crucial part of every diagnosis an assessment of what was missing from the person's early life; for example, a functional and structural psychosomatic disturbance is explained by Boss as due to lack of sexual experiences in adolescence and young adulthood.

Dealing with the same concern, Maddi (1975a) draws comparisons among developmental courses in terms of the breadth, variety, and intensity of the experiences. As noted in Assertion 12, growth-facilitating experiences need not always be positive. Maddi (1975b) discusses creativity as the result of a developmental course involving suffering, conflict, and frustration.

14. *Personality development ideally becomes increasingly self-determined.*

Simone de Beauvoir (1948) refers to childhood as a period of inauthenticity, when the person's exercise of freedom is blocked by others who have power over him. But once the child has practiced symbolizing, imagining, and judging and has developed self-reliance, sense of purpose, and courage, he becomes able to develop on his own. His decision making will bring him a continual flow of experience for further symbolization, imagination, and judgment. Existential psychologists do not associate chronological age estimates with the onset of this self-determined development, but it presumably does not occur vigorously until adolescence. Certainly, self-determined development continues throughout life. The emphasis in existential psychology is on continual change and growth.

To progress from early dependence upon parents and other adults for developmental stimulation, the child must receive the experiences referred to in Assertions 11 through 14. Should he not get independence training, richness of experience, respect for individuality, and imposed limits, his emergence into self-determined development will be jeopardized. He will not have learned to exercise symbolization, imagination, and judgment vigorously, nor will he have learned to rely on himself in making decisions, to accept facticity, and to take responsibility courageously for his own life. Instead, he will change little with the passage of years and will emerge into chronological adulthood without the individualized sense of meaning and purpose that is the special gift of human beings.

15. *Failure can stimulate self-determined development.*

During self-determined development, the limits to a person's exercise of individuality increasingly are recognized as being partially self-imposed. The person who has learned during early development to regard himself as worthy and capable of formulating his own goals and pursuing them successfully continues to learn through observing and evaluating his failures. Failures contain information which can be used to reevaluate goals, to reformulate plans, and to try again. Only for the person who did not get a sound developmental start in early interactions with parents should subsequent failure experiences be avoided or disguised, lest clear appreciation of these failures have an adverse effect on the individual.

16. *Self-determined development passes through three types of orientation: the aesthetic, the idealistic, and the authentic.*

As soon as a person emerges from the bosom of his family into the wider world with a freshly developed sense of freedom and self-reliance, he is likely to become self-indulgent. The excitement of being free of parental limits and of the mysteries beyond the home is great. The person may use his decision-making powers for pleasure, reveling in the moment and exploiting others and the environment. Kierkegaard (1959) refers to this period as *aesthetic orientation.* This orientation is not merely passivity and dependency but rather the first (and therefore perhaps understandably misguided) attempt at independent functioning made by someone whose early developmental experiences have been beneficial. The self-indulgence of aestheticism comes about because early child-rearing experiences, though beneficial, have nonetheless been strenuous. The child has had to strive and to assume responsibility, so he becomes hedonistic at the first opportunity.

Although the person derives pleasure through aestheticism for a while, sooner or later failure experiences will occur. All parties end at some point, and their enjoyment value does not outlive them. Relationships entered into without much commitment or discrimination also end quickly and are soon forgotten. What at first seemed like wonderful freedom becomes emptiness.

The inherent failure experiences deriving from an aesthetic orientation spur self-determined development. Though failures are painful, their import is usually perceived accurately by the person whose early development has given him a good start. Such a person begins to realize that the trouble with self-centered aestheticism is that it involves living in the present only, as if the future and past are unimportant. Making decisions only for the present results, paradoxically, in loneliness and emptiness. Such a person begins to recognize that aestheticism has led to surrendering control over his or her life to others—to whoever has the next party, to the next one to fall in love with, to the next political cause to be carried away by. The aesthetic lifestyle which seemed to promise such independence has only brought new forms of dependency.

Having learned this, the person in the grips of self-determined development proceeds to the next level—the *idealistic orientation.* The emphasis now is on incorporating the future and the past into the present by making decisions as if current commitments and values have always been and will always remain the same. When the person loves, he insists that it is forever. When he engages in pragmatic activities, such as politics, he does so out of undying beliefs. In his zeal to overcome his previous lack of commitment, he fails to recognize the real difficulty in determining the meaningful relationship between ideals and practical activities.

Because the person with an idealistic orientation acts as if he has complete control over events which in reality are complex, inevitably he encounters failure experiences. A love vowed eternally ends all the more painfully because its end was unexpected. Various practical enterprises force the recognition that shifting loyalties, vested interests, and even accidental factors play a large role in determining the outcome of complex social phenomena.

Failure experiences spur self-determined development. The person with an idealistic orientation learns that events are only partially under his control, regardless of his efforts and protestations. With the deepening and incorporation of this insight, the final and highest developmental orientation is entered upon: *authentic being*. At this level the person recognizes not only the importance of a time dimension, but also that he is not almighty. He accepts the facticity of his limited control and uses it to gain a clearer sense of what is possible. He commits himself to the possible, incorporating facticity by a vivid sense of urgency to accomplish and experience what is important to him.

Maintenance

This section concerns adult lifestyles which, according to existential psychology, have a number of component parts. Detailing will help clear what it means to live existentially. In presenting lifestyles, it is necessary to restate existential formulations in a way that might be objected to by some relevant writers. In the works of Laing primarily, but also of Binswanger and Boss, can be found an aversion to categorization and classification. This is clearly a reaction against those psychological approaches that have made rigid use of typologies, which to existentialists seem to do violence to the person's free ability to make decisions and to change. But the existentialists mentioned here have taken their reaction too far, ending in the inconsistent position of denying the utility of any classifications while at the same time themselves engaging in classifications congenial to them. For example, Laing's (1960) notions of *engulfment* and *depersonalization* seem to be classificatory diagnostic statements. Classification is a cognitive act which creates meaning and, as such, is a necessary tool for the mentally active human being. In personality theory, classification of adult functioning necessarily involves statements about lifestyles and their component parts.

17. Adults express lifestyles of authentic or inauthentic being.

It might fit the emphases of existential psychology more fully to consider a complex continuum stretching from authentic to inauthentic being. But for purposes of vividness and ease of communication, the continuum is here dichotomized into two general lifestyles.

Authentic being is the end result of facilitative early development and the self-determined development which follows. *Inauthentic being* is the result of inhibiting, destructive early development and a relative lack of self-determined development which is traceable to the earlier trouble. Although the inauthentic being is chronologically an adult, his psychological development is retarded. The sharp differences between inauthentic and authentic approaches to living are pinpointed in the assertions that follow.

> 18.   *The values, preferences, goals, and viewpoints of authentic being are distinct and individualistic, whereas those of inauthentic being are vague and stereotyped.*

Through a lifetime of exercising the cognitive capabilities of symbolization, imagination, and judgment, the authentic being develops values, preferences, goals, and viewpoints. In this sense, she or he will be a distinct person, with many ways of understanding experience, capable of fine distinctions, and with a richness of reflections upon what is taking place. The more one generates values, preferences, goals, and viewpoints, the more they will be original. In this sense, the authentic person will also be unusual.

By comparison, the inauthentic person does not strain, having been neither stimulated nor reinforced for doing so in early development. No one can exist without some values, preferences, goals, and viewpoints, but the inauthentic person has as few of these as is consistent with the conducting of human life. In that sense, he is a vague person. In addition, those opinions and goals he does possess will be adopted from other persons rather than developed through his own strenuous interaction with the world. In that sense, he will also be stereotyped and conventional.

The inauthentic being will not have clear impressions of what is taking place in his life, or why, and will certainly not be aware that he is able to exercise control over life problems through decision making. In contrast, the authentic being believes that through exercising mentality he can influence what happens to him. This will include recognizing clearly when and how he has been manipulated by circumstances and recognizing the steps that need to be taken for greater personal control. Because of this difference in level of consciousness, the authentic being possesses greater freedom than the inauthentic being.

> 19.   *In biological experiencing, the authentic being shows subtlety and taste, whereas the inauthentic being shows undifferentiation and crudeness.*

For the authentic being, the quality of food, drink, and sex is more important than their quantity, appreciating subtle, tasteful, and unusual biological experiencing. Small variations are recognized as important. The inauthentic being, on the other hand, remains relatively undifferentiated and crude, preferring quantity to quality.

The authentic being combines the expression of psychological, social, and biological functions, and in this manner achieves a conscious sense of self as someone who can understand and influence his biological experiences. In contrast, the inauthentic being does not have an elaborate consciousness and tends to perceive the biological side of his nature as isolated from the rest. Consequently, he assumes and acts as if he is ruled by creature needs, as are the lower animals. Physical survival and the swift satisfaction of biological wants are of paramount importance. Thus, he tends to develop materialistic values, investing importance not only in those things that directly satisfy biological needs (e.g., food) but those that are of indirect relevance as well (e.g., money). In comparison, the authentic being, while recognizing the importance of biological expression, regards the coordination of these needs with psychological and social expression as not only possible but more comprehensively satisfying. The emphasis shifts from survival and satiation at any cost to a less materialistic concern, directed at the priceless qualities of experiencing.

20. *In social interaction, the authentic being is oriented toward intimacy, whereas the inauthentic being is oriented toward superficial relationships.*

For the authentic being, the quality of social interaction is more important than the quantity, being appreciative of the challenge inherent in relating in depth with other humans. In contrast, the inauthentic person remains relatively undifferentiated in, passive toward, and fearful of social interactions, having little to contribute beyond conventionalities. Consequently, the inauthentic person prefers limited contractual relationships, because their purpose is clearly defined and will therefore not be surprising, threatening, or demanding.

In combining the expression of psychological, biological, and social functions, the authentic being understands and influences his social interactions. The inauthentic person, in contrast, does not have an elaborate consciousness and tends to perceive social interactions as externally determined. Consequently, he defines himself as a player of social roles, with little choice but to adjust. He tends to adopt values and habits stressing similarity to other persons and prefers smoothness of interaction more than individuality or uniqueness. Social interaction for the authentic person will emphasize a mutual fostering and enjoyment of unusualness and the exploration of individual differences as a basis for intimacy.

21. *Socially, the authentic being is active and influential whereas the inauthentic being is passive and acquiescent.*

The authentic person perceives society and its institutions as having been formed by persons and therefore as properly serving persons. His values regarding the social system tend to be egalitarian. He is able to implement his values through active attempts to convince others of his opinions and thereby have an influence in society.

In contrast, the inauthentic being has only rudimentary consciousness concerning the social system and regards it as an unchangeable entity which rules those living within it. He views himself as a passive player of roles assigned to him in this all-powerful social system. He is acquiescent, trying to play his "assigned" social roles well enough to avoid criticism or rejection. He will quickly go along with the majority and will have only conventional social opinions, if any at all.

22. *Thoughts, feelings, and actions of the authentic being are unified and planful, whereas those of the inauthentic being are fragmentary and aimless.*

The authentic being also demonstrates unified functioning and planfulness in orientation toward the future. Not only does he have many values, preferences, goals, and viewpoints, but he arranges these in order of importance. His priorities organize his actions. Since he is constantly engaged in the comparison, rejection, and ordering of the many components in his self-constructed hierarchy of meaningfulness, his priorities are generic rather than discrete and situationally specific. There is a true plan for an entire life in his behaviors, rather than a series of small plans easily reached or characterized by internal contradictions.

The lifestyle of the inauthentic person is fragmentary and disorganized. Because he is aided by neither vigorous symbolization, imagination, and judgment nor by an elaborate consciousness, he is unable to decide what are his values, preferences, goals, and viewpoints. Further, he is unable to recognize the givens in his experiment or to make decisions which incorporate them into his general life plan. The result often is fixation on one particular goal, with no appreciation of all there is to learn and do by more strenuous involvement in life. This difficulty is called *extravagance* by Binswanger to signify self-indulgence. For Binswanger (1963, p. 346), it is only by hierarchically organizing values, preferences, goals, and viewpoints that they can be "weighed against each other in life, art, philosophy, and science and . . . transplanted into words and deeds."

23. *The authentic being shows continual change, whereas the inauthentic being remains the same.*

The authentic person's manifestation of unity and planfulness should not be mistaken for monotonous and unidimensional activity. Integration features future orientation, originality, change, and creativity. In contrast, the inauthentic being is bogged down in repetitive, monotonous activity supporting the status quo. Whatever values, preferences, and goals she or he possesses are concrete and conventional, providing little basis for change. When change occurs it tends to be fragmentary and unintegrated, giving the appearance of an accidental occurrence.

24. *The authentic being tends to experience anxiety, whereas the inauthentic being experiences guilt.*

The authentic person experiences anxiety as the result of a vivid consciousness that he or she must decide and act without knowing what the outcome will be (Tillich, 1952). This anxiety simultaneously recognizes facticity and possibility. The authentic being faces anxiety because to avoid it would be to shrink from choosing the future and thereby relinquish growth, individuality, and the enactment of values, preferences, and goals.

The inauthentic person experiences anxiety less frequently and less intensely. He does not have the vivid awareness of lonely and unexpected death which Heidegger (1962) attributes to authenticity. He insulates himself from worry over outcomes of decisions and change-producing acts by choosing the status quo instead. He lives a superficial and routine life, never dwelling on the limited ability of persons to actually control occurrences. Having given up the possibility of growth, individuality, and fulfillment, the inauthentic person is inevitably beset by the guilt of missed opportunity and cowardice. As he gets older and guilt accumulates, a general condemnation of self sets in. He can no longer believe that at the next decision point he can make up for past missed opportunities. Rather, he begins to realize that his whole life has been wasted.

This is not to say that the authentic person escapes guilt entirely. It is, after all, impossible to act on every facet of one's possibilities. For example, being involved in one particular relationship, no matter how conducive to change and growth it may be, necessarily means that other possible relationships are ignored. Even choices of the future involve giving up some opportunity. With this in mind, Boss (1963) considers "the call of conscience" to be always present. Even the authentic being recognizes that he is "always in debt." He does not deny this guilt but tries to minimize it by choosing the future regularly and thereby maximizing opportunities. In this fashion, guilt is held to manageable quantities, and there is little risk of despair, meaninglessness, and comprehensive condemnation.

25. *The experience of failure precipitates psychopathology in the inauthentic being.*

For one whose early development was positive, the experience of failure has a special ability to stimulate self-determined development in the lifelong process of becoming an increasingly authentic being. But if early development has left the person in self-doubt and relatively unable to exercise symbolization, imagination, and judgment vigorously, her or his self-determined development will be stifled. In such a person, the experience of failure will not spur development but rather will have a further debilitating effect. The extent of debilitation produced by failure experiences will depend not only upon their magnitude and frequency but also upon the degree of the person's inauthenticity.

Maddi (1967, 1970) discusses three extreme experiences of failure: the threat of imminent death, social upheaval, and confrontation with one's own superficiality. For the inauthentic person, debilitation occurs with:

1. The threat of imminent death, because he has elevated physical survival to such importance that he has essentially (though implicitly) assumed that he will not die.
2. Social upheaval, because his emphasis upon adjustment and social role playing amounts to assuming that society is absolute and unchanging.
3. Confrontation with one's own superficiality (usually forced by another person who is suffering due to it), because the inauthentic being has spent much effort making himself acceptable and is not able to accept criticism for that very effort.

The three failure experiences mentioned have the effect of disconfirming the inauthentic person's values, preferences, and viewpoints concerning himself and the world (Maddi, 1967, 1970). The breakdown of personality which they produce is elaborated in the discussion of psychopathology in the following section.

APPLICATIONS

The development of existential psychology owes as much to attempts of practicing clinicians to assess and treat human problems as it does to existential philosophy. It is not surprising, therefore, to find a richness of concrete techniques for the application of existential psychotherapy, amidst some disarray concerning the niceties of formal theorizing.

Assessment

One important part of assessment involves determining a person's degree of authenticity or inauthenticity. This can be accomplished by measuring the various characteristics mentioned in the "maintenance" assertions discussed in the preceding section. To complete the task of assessment, however, attention must also be given to measurement of relevant psychopathological states.

Binswanger (1963) has been particularly articulate in identifying symptomatology. He provides four concepts for the analysis of schizophrenia. First, *inconsistency* (fragmentation) is in the various parts of existence. Because inconsistencies are bothersome, they are often masked by *extravagance,* or the overemphasis upon one idea or ideology which explains and orders everything, and thereby neutralizes all that one experiences. But extravagance is fruitless because it leads to *dichotomous thinking,* in which the person is totally involved in the struggle between realization of his extravagant ideal or its total denial. The schizophrenic must either actualize his idiosyncratic plan or fall into bottomless despair. Being trapped in dichotomous thinking, the person must then engage in *covering,* or the "Sisyphuslike effort to conceal that side of the [dichotomy] that is unbearable" (Binswanger, 1963, p. 258). The enormous effort involved in covering may finally lead to *being worn away,* a comprehensive resignation and retreat from life.

According to Binswanger, the schizophrenic process involves a progression from the experience of personal fragmentation, through adoption of a single rigid perspective on self and world and a denial of all that contradicts it, to a total surrender of selfhood. The case of Lola Voss stands out among the many Binswanger (1963) offers as examples. Through her inability to face inconsistencies like her anger at her parents for trying to break off her engagement and her simultaneous self-initiated rejection of her fiancé, Lola develops an extravagant belief in herself as ultimately alone, except for her relationship with a supernatural oracle which directs her activities. She attempts to stave off overwhelming despair and anxiety by slavishly following all of the decisions made for her by the oracle, even when this involves extreme behavior like cutting up her clothes. Her resignation is complete when she surrenders all of her decision-making powers to the "enemies" which populate her hallucinations and resigns herself to their persecution.

Maddi (1967, 1970) details forms of existential sickness falling in the neurotic range, all of which involve a breakdown of meaningfulness, as a result of psychological, social, and biological stresses. The most extreme form, *vegetativeness,* is characterized by inability to believe in the meaningfulness of anything one is doing or can imagine doing; by apathy and boredom, punctuated by periods of depression that become less frequent as the disorder is prolonged; and by low energy and general aimlessness. *Nihilism* is a less extreme form of existential sickness, because some sense of meaningfulness remains. The cognitive commitment is antimeaning or paradoxically finding meaning in the meaninglessness of everything. At the affective level, one finds anger and disgust; and at the action level, destructive competitiveness. The least extreme form of existential sickness is *adventurousness,* in which everyday life has lost all meaning. To experience meaningfulness, the adventurer must involve himself continually in extreme, dangerous activities. Maddi discusses these forms of illness in terms of not only their personal implications but their implications for the social system as well.

A word is in order concerning the techniques whereby the variables of authenticity, inauthenticity, and sickness are assessed. Existential psychologists agree that there is no real substitute for open-minded, comprehensive, depth interviewing. Binswanger (1963) advises that accurate assessment requires dropping one's preconceptions about the interviewee, in order to hear what he is saying. In addition, all available aspects of the interviewee's life must be examined, juxtaposed, compared, and integrated. Boss (1963) and Laing (1960) agree with this view. Sartre (1956) suggests a similar procedure for identifying a person's *fundamental project*. This method, which investigates the phenomenology of the patient, is employed with the assumption (agreed to by all mentioned above) that the interviewee cannot accurately assess himself. Assessment is in the hands of the interviewer as an external observer.

In a related assessment technique introduced by Gendlin (1969), the existential psychologist observes the subject's explication of his experience. Through rating this process the psychologist reaches conclusions concerning such relevant existential variables as *felt meaning* and decision making.

Failing more extensive information, questionnaire data are accepted by many existential psychologists. Maddi, Kobasa, and Hoover (1976) have developed a questionnaire measure (the *Alienation-Commitment Test*) of the various forms of existential sickness. Also, Crumbaugh and Maholick's *Purpose-in-Life Test* (1964) is intended to provide a quick paper-and-pencil assessment of several components of authentic being. These are discussed further in the Evidence section below.

Treatment

The general aim of existential psychotherapy is to help the person who seeks help to achieve authenticity. To move toward authentic being, the client must learn to begin to exercise symbolization, imagination, and judgment and thereby to achieve consciousness of his or her life as being partially under his or her control. He must begin to express these cognitive capabilities in his biological and social experiencing, moving thereby toward subtlety, taste, intimacy, love, and constructive social action. He must accept responsibility for the decisions he makes and attempt to tolerate anxiety so that he can choose to change and grow and thereby avoid accumulations of the guilt of missed opportunities. To learn to tolerate anxiety, he must begin to trust himself and to develop a generic set of goals which can lend direction to personal change. But he must also grow in ability to accept givens and inevitabilities, so that he is clear about what practical possibilities should be pursued.

In helping the client progress toward authentic personhood, the psychotherapist provides a facsimile of the presumably missing beneficial early development. But this does not mean that the past should be dwelled upon. The persistence of past conflicts in an unconscious mind is not an issue for existential psychology. Rather, the subject matter of present life should be dealt with in giving the client the bases for what here may be called *preliminary development* (analogous to early development, but occurring in an adult). Then, as self-determined development begins to occur in the client, the therapist's task is to support it until it has become vigorous enough to maintain itself as an authentic way of life. At that point, therapy is terminated.

More concretely, in this process of preliminary development, the therapist engages in independence training, shows respect for the client's individuality, encourages him to encounter a rich variety of experience, but also sets limits (see Assertions 11 through 13). As these procedures have their intended effects and self-determined development begins, the therapist helps in interpreting the significance of failures encountered by the client, thereby helping him to chart the life course best for him. Special attention is given to recognizing and formulating generic goals as well as appreciating facticity and possibility (see Assertions 6 and 7).

The discussion thus far has been both more concrete and more comprehensive than that found in the writings of many existential psychotherapists. Nonetheless, in the techniques and case studies reported, much is to be found which falls within this conceptual framework. This is true even though the early existential psychotherapists, Binswanger and Boss, employed many techniques reminiscent of Freudian psychoanalysis. Nonetheless, the general emphases of their Daseinsanalysis was clearly existential.

Although Binswanger and Boss explicate few specific techniques, they do say much about how to encourage clients to disclose subjective experience. Also, they offer suggestions on how to stimulate symbolization, imagination, and judgment. One technique involves asking the client, "Why not?" (Boss, 1963). The therapist raises considerations like: "If you are lonely, why not find some friends? If you are dissatisfied with your job, why don't you start preparing yourself for something more fulfilling?" Through questions of this sort, the client is confronted with his failure to search for meaning in various aspects of his existence. This technique is useful for exposing inauthenticity, stimulating self-reliance, and gaining in appreciation of facticity as well as possibility. Boss regards what he does as different from Freudian interpretation in that the latter tends to dismiss inappropriate behaviors by typing them as left over from childhood, thereby misunderstanding their importance in clarifying what the client is doing in the here and now.

Another technique for stimulating authentic modes of behaving is

Gendlin's (1969) *focusing*. He observed that clients do not tend to learn to use vigorously their cognitive capabilities for creating meaning simply as a result of just any psychotherapy. The exercises Gendlin employs involve the client in recalling a memory, or a sense impression. This continuous and dialectical sort of reflection necessarily changes the original mental event. In this fashion, experience is clarified and enriched.

A particularly striking technique for helping the client gain in control over his experiences is Frankl's (1965) *paradoxical intention.* A client troubled by a symptom he cannot control is encouraged by the therapist to exaggerate it rather than minimize it. Frankl has used this technique in cases of phobia, obsessive-compulsiveness, delusions, and even suicidal depression. In one case (Frankl, 1965), a young doctor discloses a phobia concerning perspiration from which he had suffered for years. Whenever the doctor feared he would sweat, the fear itself would precipitate the undesired state. Frankl advised him to try to sweat as much as he could whenever he feared that he would sweat. Whenever the doctor was in a situation with the potential of triggering the phobia, he was to say to himself: "I only sweated out a quart before, but now I'm going to pour at least 10 quarts!" After initially reacting to the instructions as absurd, the doctor began trying to sweat. In a matter of days, his fear of sweating and his sweating ceased.

By acting paradoxically in intending that which is feared, the client disengages himself from the overwhelming behavior. This involves what Frankl (1965) calls an exercise of humor. The result is perception of oneself as more than the unwanted behaviors. The attempt to exaggerate the symptom outmaneuvers it, and the client once again establishes control over his thoughts and actions. This reestablishment of control builds self-trust and self-reliance.

A common misconception of existential psychotherapy is that its applicability is restricted to the highly intelligent, relatively healthy and socially secure, those who have the leisure to speculate philosophically. Nothing could be further from the truth. Most existential psychotherapists, notably Binswanger, Boss, Laing, Frankl, and Gendlin, have treated psychotic clients to a greater degree than did Freud and his followers.

Institutional

There is no major systematic program currently operative whose primary aim is the utilization of existential psychology in prison reform, classroom revitalization, hospital care improvement, and such applications. Nonetheless, in many existential writings there is a call for social reforms and a consideration of how authentic being can be fostered through other than psychotherapeutic means. Of special relevance are the discussions of individualism and the debilitating effect of conformity.

The strongest argument for social reform in existentialism involves the writing and life of Sartre (1949), who not only advocated needed reforms but has actually worked for them, sometimes through such protests as declining the Nobel Prize. Laing (1967) has reformulated and celebrated Sartre's social criticism. Laing maintains that the cure of an individual's psychosis is dependent upon a radical alteration of the society in which he finds himself. Although one may not agree with all Laing says, he does speak for all existentialists when he contends that society will have to become more tolerant and supportive of deviant behavior if authentic being is to be possible for greater numbers of persons. He mounts many specific criticisms of modern industrialized societies.

Maddi (1970) agrees, but he highlights the necessity of persons helping themselves. Social reform cannot be done for the members of a society; they must do it themselves. The form of government most accessible to change instigated by its members is democracy. But just because a government is nominally democratic does not automatically ensure that the institutionalized channels whereby social change can be brought about are functioning properly. When a democracy becomes large and industrialized, the ensuing bureaucratization and technical complexity increase the likelihood that the public will lose touch with, and influence over, elected officials. If deviation from representational government has existed for some time, it may be difficult to effect social change through legitimized channels. In that case, extreme measures, such as nonviolent confrontation politics, may be necessary to reopen channels for effecting reform. In this, Maddi's viewpoint shows similarity to Sartre's. Maddi does not condone all confrontation politics, only those forms manifesting the clarity, responsibility, and commitment of authentic being. He cautions against endorsing confrontation politics engaged in by inauthentic beings and sufferers of existential sickness and provides an analysis of events in the late 1960s to bolster his points. In the peace, Black Power, and women's liberation movements there were authentic persons striving for social reforms, but also conformists, nihilists, and adventurers attempting desperately to find meaning in their lives rather than seeking constructive social change.

Paralleling the emphasis on participatory democracy should be an emphasis on creativity, for both are ways of producing social reform. Participating in the political process of representative governments—attempting to influence others, lobbying, electioneering—can alter institutions and officialdom. In a less political but nonetheless effective way, creativity can provide new ideas and approaches for dealing with human problems. Sartre (1949) regards creative writing as an example of public responsibility—that is, an identification of the ills of current society and suggestions for their remedy. While Maddi (1975b) contends that creativity provides an antidote for meaninglessness in the creative person, the creative product may well do something simple for others to whom it is communicated. Creative endeavor is a natural activity for authentic persons.

It may seem that the value of creativity is obvious. But most persons are inauthentic, and hence social institutions tend to reflect their commitment to the status quo. All too often, only lip service is paid to creativity. The creative person runs a sociopolitical risk, because the thrust of his endeavor is likely to alter the status quo and hence to be threatening to some people and some institutions (Maddi, 1975b). Creative persons have been persecuted and even killed (Christ, Socrates). Society should take special steps to protect those engaged in creative endeavors so that they can aid in the necessary but painful process of social reform.

A society can reward creative endeavor in many concrete ways. Parents and teachers can foster a view of life as strenuous, with change and anxiety regarded as signs of a maturing process, to help the young grow into adults who truly value creative endeavor and admire rather than condemn creativity in others. Employers can allow workers to utilize personal initiative and give them responsibility for what they produce. In this context, the recent emphasis upon mass production and the assembly line may be shortsighted because it fosters inauthenticity (e.g., irresponsibility) and meaninglessness. Seemingly less efficient procedures in which workers have greater freedom and responsibility may in the long run be best, not only for society but for production of quality work. Public officials should be chosen for their creativity, not their popularity or threatening demeanor.

Self

The special message of the existential approach is that each person can construct the unique life he chooses, but doing this is strenuous and involves risk. Giving in to pleasures and settling for comfort is suspect; true fulfillment requires development, and this is inherently a disciplined and stressful process. Although freedom and potency are the promise of humanness, this state is never reached by the timid or the idle.

An example of what the existential approach to life signifies is found in heterosexual relationships. The highest form of love occurs between two authentic beings, with emphasis on exploration in depth of intellectual, social and sexual experiences by persons who trust, admire, and desire each other. Because they know they are individuals and can accept the idea that their relationship may end, they can be intimate without losing the ability to go on alone. The implications of authenticity are violated if one of the persons makes all the decisions or is always dependent. To be fulfilling, an intimate heterosexual relationship calls for mutuality on the part of equal partners. Such relationships are best when integrated into the rest of the participants' lives. Being in love should facilitate being competent and imaginative at work, relating intimately with other persons, acting effectively in one's community, and contributing to one's wider culture.

As a young man, Kierkegaard made a decision to break his engagement for marriage to a young woman, Regina (Lowrie, 1938). It could be argued that the extolling of individuality in his work can be traced to a reaction formation due to the desperate loneliness he felt following this decision. From Kierkegaard's own writings (e.g., 1941), however, it becomes apparent that in Regina he had idolized a frivolous woman who would have interfered with his plans for a career of psychological, philosophical, and theological writing. It would have been difficult for Kierkegaard to compose those brilliantly scathing critiques of conventional Danish middle-class society while also keeping his wife happy by taking her to all the right parties in Copenhagen. Because he judged his own unconventionality and interest in social reform to be crucial to his existence, and he could not encourage Regina to develop out of her conventionality, he decided reluctantly to leave her. Kierkegaard might have considered Regina's conventionality as part of his facticity (something he could not change because of love) and stayed with her. But this would have been what Binswanger calls extravagance, assuming that Kierkegaard had carefully determined that his own individualistic trajectory could not be reversed. Kierkegaard suffered for his lost love but grew by choosing the future.

From an existential perspective, one might indeed be better off proclaiming a relationship—whether friendship, partnership, or marriage—broken if it is based on inauthenticity. The fact that a couple has been together over many years is not reason enough for them to continue if it becomes apparent to all involved that insurmountable inauthenticity exists. Care must be taken, of course, to determine whether the purported inauthenticity is indeed insurmountable. This judgment is based primarily on what each person recognizes as his or her unique set of priorities and crucial values, and on whether these two sets of priorities could possibly flourish in juxtaposition. If there is no way they could flourish together, then separation may be best. What happens as a result of separation is well understood by existential psychotherapists. The persons will feel remorseful and lonely but will also experience a lessening of the guilt of missed opportunity. Their loneliness will not distract them from engaging in activities which express the previously suppressed values and priorities. With the acceleration of this self-determined development, the loneliness will recede, and the relationship severed will be remembered with fondness but little regret.

Another example of the existential approach involves the life of students. The student-teacher relationship is rightly regarded as necessarily inauthentic; the student must be object and the professor subject. By becoming a student, one proclaims one's lack of knowledge, recognition of another as expert, and willingness (often financially sealed) to be taught, changed, manipulated. Of course, to many students, an educational relationship which allows the student to also act as subject would be most beneficial for both parties. Existentialists agree but add that this kind of encounter must be striven for. A school board's decision to "open up" the classroom or give only "pass-fail" grades is not sufficient. It is up to the individual student to demonstrate through creative activity, and through the exercise of imagination, symbolization, and judgment, that he is also capable of teaching his teacher.

The teacher should also heed the advice of existentialism. Recognizing the basically inauthentic structure of the educational relationship, the teacher must realize the responsibility of the task he has shouldered. He must have something worthwhile to teach and be able to communicate it effectively, so that it does indeed alter the life of his students. The teacher's role may be considered an exercise of what Heidegger (1962) calls *care*, mentioned in the section on development. In the inauthentic form of care, the teacher "leaps in" for the student—he does everything for the student, presenting the information in finished form and providing no opportunity for integration through use of one's own wits. In authentic care, the teacher "leaps ahead" of the student and stimulates him to produce his own integrations and directions. For example, the inauthentic teacher requires an objective summary of the literature, whereas the authentic teacher emphasizes the student's critique of it.

VALIDATION

Evaluation of existential psychology can be done in regard to its effectiveness in psychotherapeutic settings, as well as through systematic research. Also relevant to validation is a comparison of the existential approach with other personality theories, so that relative merits can be determined from logical inferences.

Evidence

It is a misconception that existential psychology involves no generalizations across persons, simply because it relies upon the phenomenological method. Binswanger (1963), as well as others, agrees that to perceive a client accurately it is necessary to drop preconceptions concerning human behavior. But this phenomenological approach, which stresses idiographic concepts, is not held so rigidly as to obviate arriving at generalizations and even universalizations, as long as they are the end result of an inductive process grounded in sensitive observation. Indeed, many concepts mentioned in this chapter came about in just this fashion. Laing's (1960) extreme (and unrepresentative) unwillingness to generalize, which misinterprets what Husserl (1931) meant in formulating phenomenology, would end in an unworkable solipsism. The fact is that it is not really adhered to even by Laing, who does indeed generalize across persons and thereby contributes to the scientific enterprise.

As a psychotherapy, the existential approach involves a body of concepts and techniques that can certainly claim successes. In the case studies reported by Binswanger (1963), Boss (1963), Frankl (1965), and others, there is convincing evidence that clients, whether neurotic or severely psychotic, can be helped by existential treatment. From all accounts, Binswanger (1963) and Boss (1963) struggle for detailed understanding of the client in his own terms and, in the process, aid him to develop new meaning in life. Often, clients they helped had previously been through one or more other forms of psychotherapy (usually psychoanalysis) unsuccessfully. Frankl (1963) gives example after example of how his technique of paradoxical intention led to swift and complete symptom remission, even when the symptoms were in the psychotic range. Although there is no evidence presently available with which to compare the relative effectiveness of existential and other psychotherapies systematically, the entire literature indicates that the existential approach helps people. In this practical sense, validity can be claimed.

Until recently, there was a paucity of systematic research on personality employing existential concepts. This can perhaps be traced to the relative disinterest of existential psychologists in performing personality research and to the general unfamiliarity of the existential approach to researchers. But some research of an existential nature is now being done, and many tests of existential personality variables are available.

Gendlin and Tomlinson (1967) have introduced the *Experiencing Scale,* a rating procedure applied by the researcher to verbalizations made by the subject. The ratings concern degree of experiencing, running from the lowest, in which the subject seems distinct and remote from his feelings, through the middle range, in which the subject gets his feelings into clear perspective as his own, to the highest, in which feelings have been scrutinized and explored so that they become a trusted and reliable source of self-awareness. Considering only a few of the findings concerning this test, it appears that the higher the level of experiencing, the better the outcome of psychotherapy and the greater the commitment to creative endeavor (Gendlin, Beebe, Cassens, Klein, & Oberlander, 1968).

Crumbaugh (1968) has developed a questionnaire, called the *Purpose-in Life Test,* aimed at measuring Frankl's concept of existential vacuum (meaninglessness). Subjects showing existential vacuum on the test had world views rated by judges to be negative, lacking in purpose, and devoid of transcendental goals. In addition, the test shows a positive correlation with the Depression Scale of the *Minnesota Multiphasic Personality Inventory,* as well as with a measure of anomie. Although more research clearly needs to be done, the *Purpose-in-Life Test* shows promise of validity.

Another related test, the *Existential Study,* is under development by Thorne & Pishkin (1973). This questionnaire has been developed factor-analytically to yield seven scales, on self-status, self-actualization, existential morale, existential vacuum, humanistic identification, existence and destiny, and suicidal tendency. Though Thorne has included along with these identifiably existential variables other factors from diverse personality theories, some of the results are of interest to existential theory. On existential morale, for example, followers of Ayn Rand's rational philosophy were highest, followed by students and felons, with alcoholics and unwed mothers appearing demoralized, and schizophrenics disintegrated. Much work remains to be done before the validity of this test can be considered established.

More recently, Maddi, Kobasa, and Hoover (1976) have devised a questionnaire, called the *Alienation-Commitment Test,* which assesses the powerlessness, adventurousness, nihilism, and vegetativeness aspects of meaninglessness which appear in Maddi's theorizing. Each of these dimensions can be measured across relationships to work, persons, social institutions, family members, and self. The test is uncorrelated to intelligence and sex and shows a small relationship to socioeconomic level and age. The scales of the test show negative correlations of varying degree with a measure of creative attitudes toward living. Persons scoring high on meaninglessness in interpersonal relationships describe themselves as enjoying time spent alone. For this test, also, additional research is needed before its value can be fully determined.

Although tests of various aspects of meaninglessness are just at the beginning of their development, there are two substantial bodies of personality research bearing on important aspects of authentic and inauthentic being. Despite the fact that neither body of research began with the special intent to validate existential theory, that is exactly what is emerging.

First is the burgeoning literature on whether a person believes that he has control over his own life or that his life is really under the control of someone or something external to him. A person is said to demonstrate *internal locus of control* when he locates the power for determining behavior within the individual. *External locus of control,* on the other hand, is attributed to the person who locates the control over behavior outside of the individual—that is, in fate or in society, understood in an abstract, nonpersonal sense. The findings are relevant insofar as the authentic person perceives himself as having a mental life through which he can understand and influence his experiences and treats life as a series of decisions he must make responsibly. This would clearly involve an *internal locus of control.* In contrast, an *external locus of control* would signal an inauthentic person, who perceives his life as manipulated by the forces of society or fate uninfluenceable by him.

After several refinements, an *Internal* versus *External Locus of Control (I-E) Scale* was made available for general use (Rotter, Seeman, & Liverant, 1962). One group of studies correlated this scale with primarily personal behavior (cf. Maddi, 1976). In general, it appears that internally controlled subjects obtain more information about matters in their world that could affect them, and they utilize this information to influence rather than to be influenced. For example, among hospitalized patients, as the degree of internal control increases, so does the amount of information they seek about their medical condition. In contrast, externally controlled subjects tended to remain ignorant of useful information, though no different in intelligence from their internally controlled counterparts. Internally controlled subjects also choose intermediate risks, banking on their skill to produce successful outcomes, whereas externally controlled subjects prefer large or small risks, wishing certainty or banking on chance. An intriguing study (Alegre & Murray, 1974) demonstrated that externally controlled persons are more susceptible to verbal conditioning, which, of course, uses extrinsic reinforcements. Other results (Cherulnik & Citrun, 1974) suggest that this resistance to external manipulation shown by internally controlled persons can be traced to their greater sense of possibility, compared to externally controlled persons.

Another group of studies using the I-E scale focuses upon social rather than personal behavior (cf. Maddi, 1976). In general, findings indicate that internally controlled persons are social activists, whereas externally controlled persons are acquiescent and conforming. For example, internally controlled subjects signed statements expressing the greatest amount of interest in social action concerning civil rights. That these were not empty statements was shown in another study, in which black social activists were shown to be more internally controlled than blacks who do not take part in civil rights activities.

In a series of studies (cf. Maddi, 1976) comparing scores on the I-E scale across ethnic groups, it was generally found that groups whose social position is low in power, either by class or by race, tend to score high in external control. To judge from the already reported attitudinal and action correlates of the belief in external control, it is easy to see why disadvantage due to class or race tends to perpetuate itself. This raises the possibility that social conditions determine whether one is internally or externally controlled. In contrast, the existential position interprets the belief in internal v. external control to be a causal influence on action. Fortunately, some experiments have been done by Rotter and his associates which favor the existential interpretation (cf. Maddi, 1976). For example, in one study, two groups of subjects performed the same task of predicting a sequence of events. One group was told that success on the task was due to skill in deciphering the ordering of events, whereas the other group was told that success was due to chance, there being no rational ordering. Despite the fact that both groups received the same number and sequence of reinforcements, subjects with skill instructions changed prediction expectancies more frequently and more in the direction of previous experience that did subjects with chance instructions. The differences in action between the two groups seemed understandable on the basis of whether subjects did or not did not believe that they could influence their own destiny. Similar findings have been obtained with other tasks. Apparently, persons who believe they can influence their own lives act accordingly.

Another large body of research bearing upon existential personality theory concerns the tendency to respond or present oneself in a socially desirable light. This tendency is clearly an aspect of the conformism of the inauthentic being. Among the several available measures of socially desirable responding, the *Social Desirability Scale (SDS)* of Crowne and Marlowe (1960) is especially noteworthy. Much correlational research has been done using this questionnaire.

The higher one's social desirability score, the greater is the tendency to give common word associations and fewer, more concrete responses on tests of fantasy. Subjects high in socially desirable responding are especially rejecting of people but tend to underestimate the extent to which their friends really reject them. Their tendency to perform better on simple, repetitive motor tasks may be due to heightened attentiveness produced by a wish to please the experimenter. Consistent with this interpretation is the finding that subjects high in socially desirable responding are less likely to rate a monotonous task as dull. In general, the picture emerges of a personality characterized by intense interest in appearing attentive, consistent, competent, and acceptable, in the context of conforming, and showing superficial interest in, but lack of deep commitment to, others—in other words, an inauthentic being. In addition, there is evidence of a general willingness to face these facts and to engage in defensiveness (Crowne & Marlowe, 1960).

Any information concerning the relationship between social desirable responding and degree of psychopathology should be of interest; Maddi (1967, 1970) has contended that an inauthentic being is predisposed to existential sickness. There is some evidence (Katkin, 1964) that the SDS correlates significantly with various scales of psychopathology as measured by the *Minnesota Multiphasic Personality Inventory*. That the highest correlation is with the Schizophrenia Scale is noteworthy, since Maddi (1967, 1970) assumes that many persons diagnosed as schizophrenic are actually suffering from existential sickness.

Before closing this section, it would be well to mention the gradually developing body of experimental studies relevant to, and for the most part inspired by, existential theorizing. For example, Houston and Holmes (cf. Maddi, 1976) subjected students to conditions of threat involving temporal uncertainty. Some of the subjects were induced to avoid thinking about the threat by immersing themselves in distracting activities, whereas the other subjects were left to their own devices. Physiological measurement showed that the subjects engaging in avoidance thinking actually experienced a greater stress reaction to the threat than the other subjects. Through interviews, it was determined that the subjects who did not engage in avoidance activities spent the time thinking about the threat and reappraising it as less serious than originally believed. Insofar as a temporal uncertainty is not very different from ontological anxiety, this study provides support for the existential belief that accepting such anxiety rather than avoiding it is consistent with personal growth. Liem (cf. Maddi, 1976) permitted some students in an undergraduate course to choose the type of recitation section they preferred and granted them considerable choice in the ongoing conduct of the section, but denied such choice to other students in the course. Subjects permitted choice performed better than others on a course examination and gave higher ratings of satisfaction with their sections than did subjects not permitted choice. This is another demonstration of the value, for personal comfort and growth, of control over one's own life.

Comparisons

Maslow (1962) stated that there are three major themes in contemporary American psychology—the psychoanalytic, behavioristic, and humanistic traditions. The existential approach is strongly opposed to psychoanalysis and behaviorism, and though similar to some other humanistic positions is nonetheless importantly different from them.

Freud (e.g., 1922, 1930) viewed the person as controlled by biological pressures from within and social pressures from without. The biologically determined instincts continually press for expression and are by their nature antisocial. To preserve some semblance of order, society must champion the common good through punishing unmitigated instinct expression. Although this psychosocial conflict cannot be abolished, it must be minimized if organized human life is to be possible. This conflict is invariably minimized if the person goes against his instinctual nature and only acts upon those socially acceptable aspects of his instincts. The compromise must always occur this way, because the individual is weaker than society, the child weaker than the parents.

This is a tragic view of life in which complete fulfillment is impossible and complete consciousness dangerous. Awareness of the real aims of the instincts would bring overwhelming guilt and the temptation to severely punishable action. Even the highest form of development, the genital character type, involves defensive sublimation in which one loves a spouse who unconsciously resembles the opposite-sexed parent, and works diligently to keep out of temptation's way. Although modern ego-psychology has taken some strides away from Freud's original position, pessimism about the individual and his world is still characteristic.

Existential psychology is diametrically opposed to the Freudian view. Freud's assumption of unchangeable biological instincts pitted against equally unchangeable social taboos, with the weak ego having to establish a compromise, actually represents inauthentic being, in the existential view.

For Freud, guilt expresses the internalization of social taboos and the perception of oneself as unsocialized. In the existential view, guilt shows a debt to oneself in the form of missed opportunity. Furthermore, the Freudian emphasis on adjustment to society and loss of consciousness concerning antisocial tendencies jars with the existential emphasis on the pursuit of individuality and possibility with heightened consciousness as a guide and a source of freedom. Finally, the Freudian belief in the importance of reducing tension and unpleasant emotions at almost any cost appears as complaisancy, in comparison to existentialism's emphasis upon courageous toleration of anxiety as that which facilitates growth.

Skinnerian behaviorism is equally antithetical to the existential view. According to Skinner (1971), the person is a "black box," about which nothing needs to be known. Behavior can be explained solely in terms of the effects of external stimuli impinging upon the organism. These external stimuli are the cues which precede the behavior and the reinforcements that follow it. When a change takes place in the rate of a particular response through the influence of a reinforcement, learning is said to have occurred, and the response is regarded as explained because controlled. In behavior modification therapy, the behaviorist increases the rate of desirable responses and decreases the rate of undesirable responses by employing various schedules of reinforcement. It is assumed by Skinnerians that what constitutes desirable and undesirable behavior patterns is more or less given by conventional values and role designations.

As was true for Freud, the behavioristic belief that social forces in the form of positive and negative reinforcements control responses, without any possibility of choice on the person's part, represents inauthentic being to existential psychologists. This elevation of inauthenticity to an ideal is also apparent in the behavioristic denial that consciousness and active decision making can have a constructive influence on living. Indeed, Skinner (1971) regards emphasis upon values such as freedom and dignity to be wasteful misunderstandings of the human condition. The existential position also cannot countenance the behavioristic emphasis upon conventionality in determining what are desirable and undesirable responses, and the associated discouragement of persons freeing themselves from control by external reinforcement through knowledge and decision making. It is becoming apparent that the success of behavioristic psychotherapy is based upon the client's exercise of self-control (see Maddi, 1976). That some behaviorists have blithely adopted the terminology of self-control should not dull our realization that such decision-making capability is neither stimulus nor response. Rather, it is a human capability (inside the "black box"), demonstrating the need for an existential formulation.

With its emphases, existential psychology clearly falls into the humanistic or third-force tradition. This does not mean, however, that existentialism agrees completely with all other positions classified as humanistic. In particular, there are distinct and important differences between existential psychology and self-actualization theory. According to Rogers (1959), individuals have a fairly automatic tendency to actualize their inherent potentialities. The inherent potentialities constitute a sort of genetic blueprint which is rendered actual in behavior through the action of the actualizing tendency. According to this self-actualizing view, this will happen without undue effort, socialization, guidance, or stimulation, if no inhibiting social forces are present. For example, a person does not have to grow in the ability to love. He can love from the very beginning and will retain this ability if uninfringed upon by destructive social pressures. Such undesirable social pressures take the form of conditional positive regard from significant others. Conditional positive regard occurs when some of the person's behavior is approved of and rewarded, whereas the rest is disapproved of and punished. This teaches the person conditions of worth which he will apply to his own behavior, and thereby he will lose the path to self-actualization. Most self-discipline, striving, and planfulness are regarded as maladjustment rather than self-actualization. The actualized person behaves effortlessly and has a generalized sense of well-being.

In contrast, the existential position regards authenticity as a difficult state to attain and one which must be striven for rather than being simply automatically realized. One way to understand authenticity is as an acquired taste, which yields satisfaction only after it has been developed. This requires stimulation and encouragement from significant others, at least early in life. For example, true loving is difficult, demanding, and ever fraught with insecurity, according to existentialists, and therefore it must be the outcome of much struggle and self-disciplined development. In this view, planfulness, courage, and an acceptance of the strenuousness of life are valuable aids, not expressions of maladjustment. The authentic person tolerates anxiety as the price he must pay for the freedom and potency to create his own life, a possibility available to only the human being. Actualization theory provides a view of life that is indeed pale by comparison.

The comparisions drawn have pinpointed the place of existential psychology among the major trends in contemporary personology, recognizing this viewpoint as a variant on humanism which emphasizes decision making, meaning creation, and life strenuousness. Several personality theories not yet mentioned are similar yet different enough to warrant comment. These theories are associated with Gordon W. Allport, Erik H. Erikson, Erich Fromm, George A. Kelly, and O. Hobart Mowrer.

Both Allport and Kelly assert that life is led through an active consciousness expressed in constructing and shaping experience through choice. But Kelly shows little appreciation of the strenuousness of such a commitment, carried on in anxiety about plunging into an unpredictable future through becoming unconventional. Kelly (1955) comes closest to recognizing such matters when he suggests that persons may make *adventurous* as opposed to *conservative* choices. But he neglects to offer any theoretical basis for understanding why anyone would choose adventurously, since, according to him, unexpected events bring anxiety and are avoided at virtually any cost. Oddly enough, although he extols the value of individuality, Kelly offers no formal theorizing with which to pinpoint its advantages and the disadvantages of conventionality. The apparent similarities between this approach and existential psychology are superficial at best.

Allport's approach may be somewhat closer to existential psychology than is Kelly's. After all, Allport (1955) does include among his *dimensions of maturity* such existentially relevant considerations as well-developed habits of rational coping with problems, and a philosophy of life which includes a generic sense of purpose. But it is far from clear just what role these dimensions are considered to play in decision making and the toleration of anxiety in order to minimize guilt. Even more important, Allport is not convincing on how these dimensions develop. He (Allport, 1955) assumes the importance of parental support and love in spurring psychological growth, and of *functional autonomy* in spurring the detachment of behaviors from their early beginnings as responses to externally imposed rewards and punishments. To existential psychologists, however, it seems doubtful that amorphous parental love and support, undirected toward specifically stimulating the child's creation of meaning through cognitive activity, and unmitigated by the imposition of limits whereby facticity can be appreciated, could lead to the aspects of maturity they agree with Allport in emphasizing. In addition, existential psychologists would regard "functional autonomy" as an inarticulate concept for elucidating the shouldering of risk, toleration of emotional upheaval, and belief in one's own capabilities which must be present if the struggle to transcend conventionality is to occur. For these reasons, his approach must be regarded as rudimentary, if attitudinally congenial.

Both Fromm and Erikson emphasize the importance of a subjective sense of meaningfulness about one's life, and this makes their positions of interest to existential psychologists. There is much in Fromm's (1941, 1947) discussion of the *marketing orientation* and *escape from freedom* which parallels emphasis in existential psychology on *conformism* and avoidance of *ontological anxiety* by shrinking from the future. Erikson's (1950) *ego integrity versus despair* is also reminiscent of the existentialist's emphasis upon *authenticity,* in contrast to *inauthenticity.* But it must be remembered that both Fromm and Erickson approach these concerns out of a basically psychoanalytic frame of reference in which importance is given to Freudian notions of psychosexual development, defensiveness, and a dynamic unconscious. For Fromm, the marketing orientation is traceable to a fixation in the period described rather like what Freud talked about as the latency stage. Further, Fromm's preceding three stages are quite reminiscent of the oral, anal, and phallic stages. Thus, when Fromm talks about his ideal, the productive orientation, as a combination of the valuable behaviors of the preceding stages, this needs to be understood in its implications as closer to Freud's genital character type than the words may signify. The same argument applies to Erikson, as his psychosocial stages lean heavily on Freud's insights. Thus, for existential psychologists, discussions of meaningfulness by Fromm and Erikson emphasize too much the vicissitudes of sex and aggression instincts filtered through libidinized parent-child interactions. Inevitably, Fromm and Erikson put less emphasis than do existentialists upon the creation of meaning through vigorous symbolization, imagination, and judgment as the basic fact of human life. A good example of this is Erikson's view that the crisis of meaning is the last developmental stage, engaged in when the person begins to look backward rather than forward. For existentialists, the earlier in life the person begins to construct his own meaning the better, because the commitment to self-determined development implied is crucial to reaching maturity and personal power.

Finally, Mowrer's (1961) recent emphasis upon guilt and meaninglessness as resultants of failure in accepting social responsibility may appear similar to the existentialist's emphasis. But Mowrer is concerned with something fairly close to conventionality, as the social responsibilities involved are consensually defined, and the guilt is toward others. It is for this reason that the concept of sin has explanatory value for him. In contrast, existentialists emphasize the guilt one feels toward oneself when possibility has been jeopardized. For Mowrer, guilt is best expiated by public disclosure of social selfishness and irresponsibility. For existentialism, guilt can only be reduced by dedicating oneself to choosing the future, and thereby changing and growing. The differences between these two seemingly similar positions are actually vast.

PROSPECT

For several reasons, existential personality theory has a bright future. First, personology appears to be entering into a new and vigorous phase, after a recent crisis (Bowers, 1973), in which the explanatory value of personality constructs was questioned and situational variables were offered as more powerful for scientific explanation. It is now clear that the person versus situation controversy was a pseudo issue (Carlson, 1975), and the evidence favors approaches that employ concepts concerning the interaction between person and situation variables. The emphasis now is shifting to theories of personality that highlight cognitive processes, consciousness, planfulness, decision making, and the like. Existential psychology is such a theory par excellence. In addition, its emphasis upon the dialectic between possibility and facticity is squarely in the interactionist camp. It can be expected that existential psychology will have a leading role in the coming personalistic renaissance, with other less cognitive and interactionist theories of personality, such as psychoanalysis, declining in importance. This prediction is quite in line with the conclusion reached by Maddi (1976), who found existential psychology to be among the fulfillment theories most supported by available personality research.

Also consistent with the new emphasis upon cognitive, interactionist positions is the recent rise of social learning theory. This approach should not be simply equated with behaviorism. It emphasizes learning that occurs without any responses or reinforcements. It is better understood as an emerging theory of personality in which are highlighted cognitive, interactionist, and strategy variables. In outlining this reconceptualization of personality, Mischel (1973) has not only emphasized such concepts as decision making and planfulness but even goes so far as to mention the similarity between his approach and existentialism. In the years to come, an accord between existential psychology and social learning theory is likely.

Also prompting the centrality of existential psychology are the recent commentaries on the psychological enterprise by prominent methodologists. Lee J. Cronbach (1975), for example, advocates aims for psychology that take into account the distinctiveness of its subject matter. Personality, he says, is no longer to be constricted by rigid models of causality imposed by the investigator. Instead, the subject is to indicate what about him is worth studying. This is certainly similar to the existential emphasis on beginning with the subjective experience of the person studied.

In this promising future, existential psychology could and should deepen ties with other areas in the field. For too long, existentialism has remained the concern of a few clinicians speaking a language too vague and insular for interaction with academic psychologists. Two fields where the value of cross-fertilization is obvious are cognition and aging. Existential psychology could gain from cognition a better understanding of decision making and symbolization, imagination, and judgment; and from aging, a context within which to specify further concepts such as temporality and the possibility/facticity dialectic. Existential psychology could give to both of these fields an emphasis upon organizing principles whereby research could be systematized and an overall picture of human life could be gained.

ANNOTATED BIBLIOGRAPHY

Binswanger, L. *Being-in-the-World: Selected Papers of Ludwig Binswanger*. New York: Basic Books, 1963.

This is the first translation of major writings by the existential psychiatrist-psychologist into English. It is a good collection of representative pieces, including Binswanger's critique of Freud, his description of his reliance upon the work of philosophers, his theoretical innovations in the field of psychopathology, and a case history with descriptive report and existential analysis.

The book includes a lengthy introduction by the translator, Jacob Needleman, which sets the philosophical stage for Binswanger's work, drawing comparisons with the writings of Kant, Heidegger, Husserl, and Sartre. Needleman also provides a systematic consideration of the important concepts which best distinguish *Daseinsanalyse* from traditional psychoanalysis.

Although an essential text for students of existential psychology, this book has its drawbacks. One wishes that Needleman had provided a more extensive consideration of the psychological context within which Binswanger's work should be evaluated. For the psychology reader, the philosophical discussion is insufficient. Also, reading Binswanger's writings is often a rather frustrating exercise. His choice of terms is awkward, and his style of writing is convoluted. Unfortunately, this complaint may be addressed to most existentialists, both psychologists and philosophers. There is clearly an existentialist "jargon" which, although emphasizing the uniqueness of the existentialist concepts, serves often to obscure their intended message.

Boss, M. *Psychoanalysis and Daseinsanalysis.* New York: Basic Books, 1963.

Boss begins this book with a case history of the "patient who taught" him the value of Daseinsanalysis and then cites many varied therapy cases throughout the text as illustrations of his theoretical points. Heidegger's psychological applicability is realized in terms of several diagnostic syndromes. Like Binswanger, Boss presents a systematic critique of Freud and extends it into the psychotherapeutic context. The differences between existential and Freudian analysis are discussed in terms of technique as well as theory. Especially distinctive in Boss's treatment of pathology in his consideration of psychosomatic illnesses from an existential perspective.

Gendlin, E.T. Experiential Explication and Truth. *Journal of Existentialism,* 1965-1966, *6,* 131-146.

Gendlin utilizes both his philosophical sophistication and his psychological skill in this article, which serves as a good introduction to the existentialist orientation. He provides effective discussions of issues like possibility and facticity, the integration of thoughts and feelings in experimental awareness, and existentialism's use of phenomenology. The deliberate intent of several of these discussions is the correction of erroneous assumptions about existential psychology. Among other clarifications, Gendlin convincingly argues that authentic freedom can never be solopsism.

Maddi, S. R. The Existential Neurosis. *Journal of Abnormal Psychology,* 1967, *72,* 311-325.

Maddi, S. R. The search for meaning. In M. Page (Ed.), *Nebraska symposium on motivation.* Lincoln, Neb.: University of Nebraska Press, 1970.

In these two articles, Maddi provides an elaboration of the psychological clarity of existential psychology and a systematic discussion of personality and psychopathology. An articulation between the existential orientation and other psychological systems is found here in the form of Maddi's use of concepts, such as needs, motivation, and personality types, in his existential theorizing, and in his reference to relevant personality research.

May, R., Angel, E., and Ellenberger, H. F. (Eds.). *Existence: A New Dimension in Psychiatry and Psychology.* New York: Basic Books, 1958.

This is a useful text for students. May provides a helpful opening section which introduces basic existential notions and sets the existential movement within the history of psychology. Selections from Binswanger's work are included: a discourse on the nature of *Daseinsanalyse,* and two case histories. The text also includes representative articles by phenomenological psychologists.

Although the authors recommend the reading of the philosophical texts from which existential psychologists draw many of their insights, they also recognize the excessiveness of this assignment in terms of time and energy required, and suggest that the reader might focus on the following selections from important philosophers. In M. Heidegger, *Being and Time* (New York: Harper & Row, 1962), one can focus on the discussions of death, care, and anxiety. In J. P. Sartre, *Being and Nothingness* (New York: Philosophical Library, 1956), the psychologist should read carefully Sartre's section on "Existential Psychoanalysis," in which he provides a critique of Freud, a comparison between Freud's and his own work, and an explication of his distinctive method of psychoanalysis. The introduction from S. Kierkegaard, *The Concept of Dread* (Princeton, N. J.: Princeton University Press, 1944) is also suggested. There Kierkegaard discusses how the psychological investigation of a phenomenon is essential for its understanding and also how this investigation differs from that of the philosopher and religious writer.

A second recommendation directs the reader to two books which present especially lucid summaries of the writings of existential philosophers:

Blackham, H. J. *Six Existentialist Thinkers* (2d ed.). New York: Harper & Row, 1959.

Grimsley, R. *Existentialist Thought.* Cardiff: University of Wales Press, 1955.

REFERENCES

Alegre, C., & Murray, E. Locus of control, behavioral intention, and verbal conditioning. *Journal of Personality,* 1974, *42,* 668-681.

Allport, G. W. *Becoming: Basic considerations for a psychology of personality.* New Haven: Yale University Press, 1955.

Beauvoir, S. de *The ethics of ambiguity* (B. Frechtman, trans.). New York: The Citadel Press, 1948.

Beauvoir, S. de. *The second sex* (H. M. Parshley, trans.). New York: Random House, 1952.

Binswanger, L. *Freud: Reminiscences of a friendship* (N. Guterman, trans.). New York: Grune & Stratton, 1957.

Binswanger, L. *Being-in-the-world: Selected papers of Ludwig Binswanger* (J. Needleman, trans.). New York: Basic Books, 1963.

Boss, M. *Psychoanalysis and daseinsanalysis* (L. B. Lefebre, trans.). New York: Basic Books, 1963.

Bowers, K. S. Situationism in psychology: An analysis and a critique. *Psychological Review,* 1973, *80,* 307-336.

Carlson, R. Personality. *Annual Review of Psychology,* 1975, *26,* 393-414.

Cherulnik, P. D., & Citrin, M. M. Individual differences in psychological reactance: The interaction between locus of control and mode of elimination of freedom. *Journal of Personality and Social Psychology,* 1974, *29,* 398-404.

Cronbach, L. J. Beyond the two disciplines of scientific psychology. *American Psychologist,* 1975, *30,* 116-127.

Crowne, O. P., & Marlowe, D. A new scale of social desirability independent of psychopathology. *Journal of Consulting Psychology,* 1960, *24,* 349-354.

Crumbaugh, J. C. Cross-validation of Purpose-in-Life Test based on Frankl's concept. *Journal of Individual Psychology,* 1968, *24,* 74-81.

Crumbaugh, J. C., & Maholick, L. T. An experimental study in existentialism: The psychometric approach to Frankl's concept of neogenic neurosis. *Journal of Clinical Psychology,* 1964, *20,* 200-207.

Erikson, E. H. *Childhood and society.* New York: Norton, 1950.

Frankl, V. E. *Man's search of meaning: An in-*

troduction to logotherapy (I. Lasch, trans.). New York: Washington Square Press, 1963.

Frankl, V. E. *The doctor and the soul* (2nd ed.; R. & C. Winston, trans.). New York: Knopf, 1965.

Freud, S. *Beyond the pleasure principle* (J. Strachey, trans.). London: International Psychoanalytic Press, 1922.

Freud, S. *Civilization and its discontents* (J. Strachey, trans.). New York: W. W. Norton, 1930.

Fromm, E. *Escape from freedom.* New York: Holt, Rinehart, & Winston, 1941.

Fromm, E. *Man for himself.* New York: Holt, Rinehart, & Winston, 1947.

Gendlin, E. T. *Experiencing and the creation of meaning.* New York: Free Press, 1962.

Gendlin, E. T. Focusing. *Psychotherapy: Theory, Research, Practice,* 1969, *6,* 4-15.

Gendlin, E. T., Beebe, J. III, Cassens, J., Klein, M., & Oberlander, M. Focusing ability in psychotherapy, personality, and creativity. In J. M. Shlien (Ed.), *Research in psychotherapy* (Vol. 3). Washington, D.C.: American Psychological Association, 1968.

Gendlin, E. T., & Tomlinson, T. M. The process conception and its measurement. In C. R. Rogers, E. T. Gendlin, D. J. Kiesler, & C. B. Truax (Eds.), *The psychotherapeutic relationship and its impact: A study of psychotherapy with schizophrenics.* Madison: University of Wisconsin Press, 1967.

Heidegger, M. *Being and time* (J. Macquarrie & E. S. Robinson, trans.). New York: Harper & Row, 1962.

Husserl, E. *Ideas: General introduction to pure phenomenology* (W. R. Boyce Gibson, trans.). New York: Macmillan, 1931.

Jaspers, K. *General psychopathology* (J. Hoenig & M. W. Hamilton, trans.). Chicago: University of Chicago Press, 1963.

Katkin, E. S. The Marlowe-Crowne social desirability scale: Independent of psycho-

pathology? *Psychological Reports,* 1964, *15,* 703-706.

Kelly, G. A. *The psychology of personal constructs* (Vol. 1). New York: W. W. Norton, 1955.

Kierkegaard, S. *Repetition: An essay in experimental psychology* (W. Lowrie, trans.). New York: Harper & Row, 1941.

Kierkegaard, S. *The concept of dread* (W. Lowrie, trans.). Princeton; N. J.: Princeton University Press, 1944.

Kierkegaard, S. *Fear and trembling and the sickness unto death* (W. Lowrie, trans.). Garden City, N. Y.: Doubleday, Anchor Books, 1954.

Kierkegaard, S. *Either / or* (D. Stevenson & L. Swenson, trans.). Garden City, N. Y.: Doubleday, Anchor Books, 1959.

Kierkegaard, S. *Concluding unscientific postscript* (D. Swenson, trans.). Princeton, N. J.: Princeton University Press, 1968.

Laing, R. D. *The divided self: An existential study in sanity and madness.* New York: Tavistock, 1960.

Laing, R. D. *The politics of experience.* New York: Ballantine Books, 1967.

Lowrie, W. *Kierkegaard.* New York: Oxford University Press, 1938.

Maddi, S. R. The existential neurosis. *Journal of Abnormal Psychology,* 1967, *72,* 311-325.

Maddi, S. R. The search for meaning. In M. Page (Ed.), *Nebraska Symposium on Motivation.* Lincoln: University of Nebraska Press, 1970.

Maddi, S. R. The development value of the fear of death. *Proceedings of the American Psychological Association Convention, 1975.* Washington, D. C., 1975. (a)

Maddi, S. R. The strenuousness of the creative life. In I. A. Taylor & J. W. Getzels (Eds.), *Perspectives in creativity.* Chicago: Aldine, 1975.(b)

Maddi, S. R. *Personality theories: A comparative analysis* (3d ed.). Homewood, Ill.: Dorsey Press, 1976.

Maddi, S. R., Kobasa, S. C., & Hoover, M. *The Alienation-Commitment Test: Reliability and validity.* Manuscript in preparation, 1976.

Maslow, A. *Motivation and personality.* New York: Harper, 1954.

Maslow, A. H. Some basic propositions of a growth and self-actualization psychology. In *Perceiving, behaving, becoming: A new focus for education.* Washington, D. C.: Yearbook of the Association for Supervision and Curriculum Development, 1962.

May, R. *The meaning of anxiety.* New York: Ronald Press, 1950.

May, R. *Man's search for himself.* New York: W. W. Norton, 1953.

May, R. *Love and will.* New York: W. W. Norton, 1967.

May, R. *Power and innocence: A search for the sources of violence.* New York: W. W. Norton, 1972.

May, R., Angel, E., & Ellenberger, H. F. (Eds.). *Existence: A new dimension in psychiatry and psychology.* New York: Basic Books, 1958.

Mischel, W. Toward a cognitive social learning reconceptualization of personality. *Psychological Review,* 1973, *80,* 252-283.

Mowrer, O. H. *The crisis in psychiatry and religion.* New York: Van Nostrand, 1961.

Rogers, C. R. A theory of therapy, personality, and interpersonal relationships, as developed in the client-centered framework. In S. Koch (Ed.), *Psychology: A study of a science* (Vol. 3). New York: McGraw-Hill, 1959.

Rotter, J. B., Seeman, M., & Liverant, S. Internal versus external control of reinforcements: A major variable in behavior theory. In N. F. Washburne (Ed.), *Decisions, values, and groups* (Vol. 2, pp. 473-516). London: Pergamon, 1962.

Sartre, J. P. *What is literature?* (B. Frechtman, trans.). New York: Philosophical Library, 1949.

Sartre, J. P. *Being and nothingness* (H. Barnes, trans.). New York: Philosophical Library, 1956.

Skinner, B. F. *Beyond freedom and dignity.* New York: Knopf, 1971.

Szasz, T. W. *The myth of mental illness: Foundations of a theory of personal conduct.* New York: Dell Delta Books, 1961.

Thorne, F. C., & Pishkin, V. The existential study. *Journal of Clinical Psychology,* 1973, *29,* 387-410.

Tillich, P. *The courage to be.* New Haven, Conn.: Yale University Press, 1952.

CHAPTER X

Constitutional Theories of Personality

Franklin C. Shontz

WILLIAM H. SHELDON

Three approaches taken by constitutional theories of personality are described in this chapter. The *structural* approach relates character to physical appearance. Its best known advocate was William Sheldon, who postulated that body build virtually determines personality. This theory maintains that somatotypes, or body structures, are unchangeable and that temperamental or personality types are associated with body types. The structural approach sees maladjustment as stemming either from poor heredity or from failure to accept the personality required by one's bodily form. It advocates social programs to improve heredity and to aid individuals in adjusting to their biological predispositions.

The *experiential* approach, developed by Paul Schilder and championed today primarily by Seymour Fisher, grew out of other theories, particularly psychoanalysis, but it has acquired its own unique features. It relates body processes to psychological development and emotional organization. Experiential theory is consistent with therapeutic techniques which rely on verbal uncovering and interpretation, but innovative methods, based on exercise and improvement in body awareness, are currently being developed.

The *holistic* approach, proposed initially by Kurt Goldstein, maintains that body and mind are inseparable. Holistic theory describes the person as a self-regulatory system capable of healthy development to maturity if provided with an environment containing an adequate variety of minimally threatening opportunities. The holistic approach sees disturbances of behavior not as symptoms but as efforts on the part of the organism to restore its natural and rightful integrity.

In general, the structural approach asserts that the body is primary, while personality is derivative and secondary. The experiential approach asserts the primacy of learning and points out that the body becomes psychologically important as it acquires meaning within the personality; this meaning comes from experience, not heredity. The *holistic approach* argues that neither body nor mind is primary but that basic principles (like self-actualization) apply to both and operate only when the organism is whole, intact, and unconfined. The three approaches complement one another and provide a comprehensive picture of relationships between body and personality.

INTRODUCTION

Although the term *constitutional psychology* is typically used to refer only to the structural theory of personality proposed by William Sheldon, it can be applied to all types of theories about body and behavior. Because it is necessary to set limits on what is covered in this chapter, it will be helpful to employ a distinction originally proposed by Robert W. White (1956) in a textbook on abnormal psychology and later used by Shontz (1975) in a book on the psychological aspects of physical illness and disability. It contrasts the somatogenic and psychogenic assumptions about behavior determination.

In its most extreme form, the somatogenic assumption asserts that all mental events are caused by physiological events. By contrast, the psychogenic assumption asserts not only that mental events have mental causes but also that psychological factors contribute to the production of at least some important physiological states, such as psychosomatic illnesses.

Sheldon's theory clearly belongs near the somatogenic pole of this distinction, because it leaves little room for subjective experience to alter character or for learning to change the basic pattern of personality, which is laid down in the properties of the body. The only role that experience is permitted to play in this theory is either to facilitate or interfere with the course of personality development that is inherent in the body as part of its physical makeup.

Sheldon's theory more directly concerns physique; that is, the outward form or appearance of the body, than its internal operations. It must be distinguished, in principle, from psychobiological theories (cf. Bakal, 1979) that relate aspects of personality to the functions of less obvious, internal processes, such as those taking place in the nervous and endocrine systems. Psychobiological, psychophysiological, and neuropsychological research is yielding valuable information about some body-behavior relations. However, it has not yet produced a theory of personality that is sufficiently comprehensive to justify consideration here.

A serious question arises as to the extent to which a structural theory, like Sheldon's, can be called psychological. Because it accepts the somatogenic

about + .23, indicating a slight tendency for body measures and intelligence test performances to be positively related. In 1927 William Sheldon repeated Naccarati's study and found correlations of only about + .13. Sheldon also attempted to correlate body measures with personality traits but had equally disappointing results (Sheldon, Stevens, & Tucker, 1940/1970, pp. 16-20).

In Germany, Ernst Kretschmer (1921) observed that patients diagnosed as manic-depressive, who have extremes or rapid shifts of elated and depressed moods, tended to be *pyknics* (Kretschmer's term for the macrosplanchnic type), while schizophrenic patients, whose problems mainly involve disordered thought processes, tended to be *asthenics* (microsplanchnics). Unfortunately, Kretschmer's data were confused and confusing (Paterson, 1930). As Sheldon put it: "With Kretschmer, insight and an observant eye came first, tools of quantification were to be applied later" (Sheldon, Stevens, & Tucker, 1940, p. 24).

Experiential Approach. One source of scientific interest in body experience was the study of unusual behavior which follows damage to the brain or the loss of body parts. Damage to the right hemisphere of the brain produces weakness or paralysis of the left side of the body (left hemiparesis or left hemiplegia). Sometimes associated with this condition is the behavioral disturbance known as *anosognosia,* in which the patient acts as though he or she has forgotten or denies having difficulties with the left side of the body. When questioned about his left arm or leg, the patient claims that nothing is wrong, even though the evidence of his incapacity is in plain view. Sudden denervation or amputation of body parts commonly produces phantom experiences. A phantom limb exists when the person seems to receive sensations from or believes that he can control an extremity that is no longer connected to the sensorimotor centers of the brain. Classic examples of the phantom limb are provided by the patient who tries to catch a ball with an amputated hand or attempts to stand on an absent leg.

The central component of personality, as Freud described it, is the ego, and Freud himself said that the "ego is first and foremost a body ego" (1927, p. 31), meaning that personality grows primarily from body experience. Fenichel (1945) and others applied this idea within the bounds of orthodox psychoanalytic theory.

Paul Schilder (1935), a psychoanalytic neuropsychiatrist, expanded psychoanalytic theory by describing in detail the concept of the body image. To Schilder, the body image is the core and essence of the whole personality. Furthermore, the body image is not confined to the physical body but is capable of expanding and contracting, or of merging with the body images of other persons in moments of personal intimacy. Later investigators, like Seymour Fisher, were stimulated by Schilder's thinking to develop ideas described in a subsequent section of this chapter.

Holistic Approach. Philosophically, holism may be traced to Benedict (Baruch) Spinoza (1632-1677), but it was espoused more explicitly in modern times by Jan Smuts (1926), a South African statesman and philosopher. The fundamental doctrine of holism is that mind and body are inseparable. The human organism cannot be analyzed without destroying it; it must be studied whole to be properly understood.

Late in the 19th and early in the 20th centuries, Adolf Meyer (1957) rejected mind-body dualism in the treatment of psychiatric patients and promulgated what has come to be known as the *psychobiological* approach. Other theorists adopted similar views. Notable among psychologists was Wilhelm Stern (1938), who developed an approach called *personalistic*. Additionally, but from a different observational base, Kurt Goldstein (1939, 1940, 1942) proposed *organismic* theory.

Some physicians concentrated on studying the effects of psychological events on bodily states, particularly when the events involve emotional conflicts and when the outcomes are physical diseases. Interest in this subject was first stimulated by H. F. Dunbar's book *Emotions and Bodily Changes,* which appeared in 1935, and by the founding of the *Journal of Psychosomatic Medicine* in 1939. Psychosomatic medicine has been advanced by the efforts of theorists like Franz Alexander (1950), who have applied psychoanalytic theory to the understanding of physical disease (see also Alexander, French, & Pollack, 1968). The fields of psychosomatics and psychobiology developed rapidly, particularly with the advent of psychoactive drugs and the growth of interest in stress and stress responses. However, these constitute areas of specialized clinical study that are not related to particular theories of personality and do not concern physique, as the term is used here.

Interest in psychosomatics was followed by the definition of its complement, *somatopsychology,* by Barker, Wright, and Gonick in 1946 (see also Meyerson, 1971; Shontz, 1975; and Wright, 1960). This field of study was identified primarily out of concern for the psychological aspects of physical disability, a subject long ignored in psychology and psychosomatic medicine. Recently, the topic of somatopsychology has tended to become subsumed under the more general heading of rehabilitation psychology (Shontz & Wright, 1980).

Current Status

Generally speaking, the structural approach has had little encouragement from American psychologists. Experimental psychology in the United States concentrates on the effects of environmental manipulations and emphasizes the plasticity and controllability of behavior. Clinical psychologists and counselors also fail to find constitutional psychology appealing. The "reality" to which they help clients adjust rarely takes into account clients' unique constitutional endowments.

By and large, American psychologists prefer to believe that all behavioral possibilities are open to everyone equally, if environmental conditions are properly arranged and controlled. American psychologists generally reject assertions that body structures affect behavioral potentialities. Occasionally research on constitutional theory appears, but no strong movement publicizes or applies constitutional psychology, particularly as developed by William Sheldon.

Suggestions that culturally valued characteristics, such as intelligence, may be linked to genetic factors arouse indignant responses. Jews remember all too well what happened in Nazi Germany when a distorted constitutional psychology was carried to such an absurd extreme that it resulted in the systematic extermination of six million persons. Nevertheless, theories relating body structure and function to personality have always been appealing. Sheldon observed that the early data of constitutional psychology were never fully convincing but were always suggestive enough to indicate that something important remained to be discovered (Sheldon, Stevens, & Tucker, 1940, pp. 17-20).

Experiential and holistic approaches have been given a more favorable reception. The concept of the body image is popular, especially in the psychiatric literature. Research interest in the body as a stimulus object remains high, particularly in social psychology and in studies of emotional expression and communication through gestures and movement (Argyle, 1975; Birdwhistell, 1970; Spiegel & Machotka, 1974).

Holistic theories have had an evident influence on clinical practices. Some therapists argue that mental disorders result from disturbances in the flow of energy within the body, while health, happiness, pleasure, and a better world for all come from proper body functioning (Lowen, 1958, 1965, 1972; Reich, 1944). These therapists propose exercises they alleged would restore proper somatic functioning and promote psychological maturity (Feldenkrais, 1949, 1972; Lowen, 1970; 1972; Masters & Houston, 1978; Rolf, 1972).

Lindzey (1967) pointed out that there are several reasons to expect physique and behavior to be correlated. First, there is the obvious fact that some life events affect both body and behavior; for example, prolonged stress not only increases anxiety but is also likely to reduce or increase appetite and thus to affect body weight. Second, physique places limits on what it is physically possible or impossible for an individual to do. Third, society pressures people into roles that suit their physiques (a person with an unusual physique may be solicited to work as a "freak" in a carnival) and expects certain behaviors or personality traits to be shown by persons with particular body builds. Fourth, biological factors sometimes determine *both* behavior and physique; obvious examples are cases involving inherited disabilities, like Huntington's Disease or Down's Syndrome.

ASSERTIONS

Development: Structural Approach (Sheldon)

1. The somatotype provides a universal frame of reference for growth and development that is independent of culture.

This assertion points to the *somatotype* as the key construct in William Sheldon's theory. A somatotype is not a static form or fixed structure. It is a theoretical term describing the course of bodily development through which an individual will pass, provided nutrition is adequate and grossly disturbing pathology does not occur. Thus, the somatotype is dynamic rather than static; a process, not a thing. The somatotype cannot change; it remains constant throughout life (Sheldon, 1971).

The hypothetical structure which assures constancy of the somatotype is the *morphogenotype*. However, the morphogenotype is not directly observable, and it is not the sole determinant of physical appearance. Nutrition and experience modify body structure, though nothing can alter the morphogenotype fundamentally. A person's physical appearance displays the *phenotype,* which expresses the influences of both heredity and environment. From careful observation and measurement of phenotypes, inferences are drawn about somatotypes and, hence, about the basic, but hidden, morphogenotypes.

2. Three polar extremes called endomorphy, mesomorphy and ectomorphy, identify the essential components of the somatotype.

Endomorphy develops from predominance of the internal (endodermal) embryonic layer, which matures into internal, visceral organs. Extreme endomorphs are round-bodied and blubbery in appearance. In his *Atlas of Men* (Sheldon, Dupertuis, & McDermott, 1954), Sheldon called such persons manatees, dugongs, whales, and ancient hippopotamuses.

Mesomorphy develops from the middle (mesodermal) embryonic layer. An extreme mesomorph shows overdevelopment of muscle, bone, and connective tissue; physique is rectangular and athletic. Sheldon identified mesomorphs with aggressive birds of prey, like owls and eagles.

Ectomorphy represents predominance of the external (ectodermal) embryonic layer. Extreme ectomorphs show the greatest development of skin surface and nervous system relative to over-all body size. The ectomorph is linear and fragile, exposing a relatively large proportion of the body surface to the weather. Sheldon identified such persons with insects like walking sticks and wasps.

Sheldon found that a good approximation to somatotype is obtained by height divided by the cube root of weight. When height is taken in inches and weight in pounds, endomorphs tend to score between 11.2 and 11.8; mesomorphs, about 12.5; and ectomorphs, about 14.0 or higher.

Sheldon's classificatory scheme is similar to those that preceded it. The endomorph is similar to the macrosplanchnic, pyknic, and apoplectic types described by others. The ectomorph is similar to the microsplanchnic, asthenic, and phthisic types. The mesomorph is like the athletic type described by Kretschmer. An important difference between Sheldon's approach and those of earlier workers is that they tended to see each individual as belonging exclusively to one body type. This is not true in Sheldon's theory, as is explained in the next assertion.

3. *Somatotypes are present to a greater or lesser degree in all individuals.*

The best way to represent the somatotypes is by an equilateral triangle, with sides curved slightly outward and with the extreme of one type at each apex (Figure 10-1). Each somatic component corresponds to a line from one extreme, at an apex, to the other extreme, at the midpoint of the opposite side of the triangle. Moderate levels of all components are represented by points near the center of the triangle, where all lines cross.

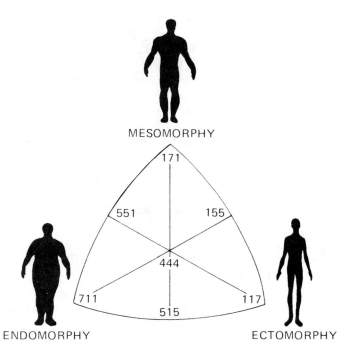

FIGURE 10-1.   THE SOMATOTYPES

By convention, the somatotype of a given person is specified by a combination of three numbers, one for each component. The first number represents the degree of endomorphy, the second the degree of mesomorphy, and the third the degree of ectomorphy. Each number may range from 1 to 7, in half-point intervals. Seven represents the extreme, at the apex of the triangle; 4 is at the center of the triangle; and 1 is at the intersection of the line from the apex at the opposite side. A person may be represented by a point anywhere within the triangular space. A 117 (read one-one-seven, not one hundred seventeen) is an extreme ectomorph and is located at one apex of the triangle. The commonest male somatotypes lie between 344 and 353. Women tend to be more endomorphic; their average appears to fall somewhere around 433.

Sheldon used a triangular diagram because it conveys the range of possible somatotypes more accurately than does the conventional system of rectangular coordinates. If *X, Y,* and *Z* axes were mutually perpendicular, intersecting at the value of 1 on each component, it would be possible to locate a point in space corresponding to a 777 somatotype, even though such a somatotype never appears in a real person and is barely conceivable theoretically. No such point can be plotted on the triangular coordinates. Generally the sum of the numbers in a description of a somatotype is not less than 9 nor more than 12.

In somatotyping, a set of *second-order* components of physique is also taken into account. These are:

1. *Dysplasia.* The extent of disharmony among somatotypes in different regions of the body.
2. *Gynandromorphy.* The prominence of characteristics of the other sex in the physique.
3. *Hirsutism.* Abundance of body hair.
4. *Texture.* An aesthetic quality, based on such considerations as physical harmony, symmetry, and beauty; it does not refer exclusively or even primarily to the quality of the skin.

Although second-order components are descriptively useful, their relevance to personality is not as clearly spelled out as is the relevance of the primary components—endomorphy, mesomorphy, and ectomorphy.

   4.   Each somatotype predisposes toward a particular temperament or personality.

Persons whose bodies are high in endomorphy possess a *viscerotonic* temperament. Viscerotonia is a positive, relaxed, amiable, tolerant, and extraverted orientation with a stable emotional flow. Also prominent is love of polite ceremony, of food, and physical comfort.

Persons whose bodies are high in mesomorphy possess a *somatotonic* temperament. Somatotonia is characterized by boldness, love of risk and chance, and Spartan tolerance of pain and discomfort. The somatotonic person is assertive, aggressive, dominant, combative, callous, and action-oriented.

Persons whose bodies are high in ectomorphy are *cerebrotonic* in temperament. Such persons are tense, restrained, apprehensive, secretive, idea-oriented, and introverted. Though sensitive to pain, cerebrotonic persons resist the actions of drugs, even anesthetics. Yet, when cerebrotonics do react, they tend to do so to excess. Therefore, the cerebrotonic is unpredictable as well as extreme, tending to be either underresponsive due to inhibition or overresponsive when nervous discharge predominates.

5. *Combinations of temperamental types are components of a whole person.*

An individual may be both viscerotonic and somatotonic, if his body build combines endomorphy and mesomorphy. An example might be a professional wrestler. Sheldon regarded as particularly dangerous for society the combination of ectomorphic ideation, which tends to be unrealistic, hyperactive, and theological, with somatotonic ruthlessness and drive for power, which can provide the means for carrying out insane dreams based on cerebrotonic doctrines of the world domination or destruction.

Fatalism. Structural approaches are often taken to task for being fatalistic (Sheldon & Stevens, 1942, p. 435); they seem not to allow for change. Sheldon argued that in the long run, constitutional psychology holds out optimistic possibilities. Knowledge of which constitutional components are associated with susceptibility to illness and suffering could stimulate social policies to control heredity and produce only healthy, happy, and productive people. Sheldon argued that the goal of the constitutional approach is "to develop every individual according to the best potentialities of his own nature" (Sheldon & Stevens, 1942, p. 438). This, he says, is not fatalism but naturalism.

Development: Experiential Approach (Schilder, Fisher, and others)

6. *Body sensations provide the primary basis for initial differentiation of self from environment.*

Most theorists assume that the human infant does not distinguish initially between self and environment. The distinction is learned through the psychological integration of sensory experience, which changes radically at birth. Sensations from within the body associated with arousal of physiological needs, like hunger, increase noticeably because of the discontinuous schedule of availability of the mother's attentions. Other sensations from within which were not prominent during intrauterine life also become more intense. Among these are sensations generated by the pull of gravity and the anxiety that seems to arise spontaneously as a result of sudden loss of physical support. Later, internal sensations associated with eliminative needs, and still later with genital sexual needs, become prominent.

Sensations from the surface of the body include active and passive touch; the reactions of sensory receptors such as the tongue, nose, eyes, and ears; and receptors sensitive to heat and cold. Because the surface of the body contains all internal sensations, like an envelope, and because it also responds to external events, the body surface becomes the locus of separation of self from environment. The child learns to distinguish the inner "me" from the outer world, and when this happens, personality begins to form.

7. *Differentiation between self and environment provides the basis for forming body image.*

Because the concept of the ego appears in psychoanalytic theory (described elsewhere in this book), this assertion need not be dealt with in detail. It is sufficient to note that Freud and the early psychoanalysts assumed that body processes, especially those related to sexuality, contributed heavily to personality development; detailed descriptions of how the ego forms out of early experience with the body, however, were provided only by later theorists. Freud was mainly concerned with psychological problems, but it was the observation of disorders of body experience resulting from actual somatic damage that stimulated theorists like Paul Schilder to elaborate the concept of the body image.

8. *The body image is a mental representation of the body.*

The body image is distinguishable from the *body ego*, for the latter has powers of decision and action which the former does not. When the ego acts it does so not in accordance with the actual physical properties of the body but in response to the image of the body. As long as image and actuality are in accord, no problems arise; when they differ, actions become unsuitable, ineffective, or unrealistic. Obviously, this proposition is especially important in states like schizophrenia, anosognosia, or phantom limb, where image and actual body fail to coincide. Even in normal experience, however, lack of agreement between image and body is common. Fisher and Cleveland (1958) concluded that the body image is not a picture of the real body and that their theory had almost "taken the 'body' out of 'body-image' " by recognizing the overwhelming importance of psychological rather than physical factors in its formation.

9. *The development of the body image proceeds through stages, each of which has a lasting effect upon the body image as a whole.*

T. S. Szasz (1957) identified three stages of body image development, though he indicated that his list is by no means exhaustive. The first stage produces a primary differentiation between ego (self) and nonego (nonself); this occurs very early in life and is prior even to recognition of the body as an object. In the second stage, separate objects (persons or bodies) are differentiated within both the ego and nonego spheres. In this stage, physical pain comes to be related to the infant's own body, while the mental counterpart of pain, anxiety, is related to the actions of the bodies of others as these threaten the personal ego. This stage occurs between the ages of four and nine months. The third stage (during which most psychosexual phases presumably take place) eventuates in the adult ego, in which the body and its associated feeling states become symbolically significant in the total personality.

There is no need to elaborate on Freudian theory or its derivatives, but it is important to note that the various erogenous zones associated with the phases of psychosexual development are usually regarded as having special significance. Thus, mouth, anus, and genital areas constitute nodal points in the body image and are thought to be especially strongly charged with symbolic meanings and emotional energy. Psychoanalytic theory also contains the notion of *displacement,* a mechanism by which psychosexual energy is channeled from one body region to another. The concept of displacement explains why regions of the body that are not obviously sexual may be reacted to as if they were, or why regions that are obviously sexual may lose their libidinous charge. For example, genital sexual energy may be displaced to the limbs and extremities, thus accounting for the symbolic equivalence between anxiety over the loss of an arm and the fear of castration. Similarly, the gathering-in quality of visual experience may lead to the displacement of oral energy to the eyes.

Development: Holistic Approach (Goldstein)

10. *The normal human organism is equipped to develop to maximum self-actualization, provided environmental forces do not interfere.*

If there is a single key assertion to all holistic theories, including those of Angyal, Maslow, and Carl Rogers, this is it. What distinguished Kurt Goldstein from others is that he drew his evidence primarily from study of the effects of damage to the body (more specifically to the brain) on adjustment and behavior. Goldstein observed that, despite difficulties in ability to think, speak, perceive, or move about effectively, persons with damage to the brain continue to exhibit strong tendencies to defend their integrity as internally consistent organisms. Actions that others described as symptoms of deficit or loss were explained by Goldstein as attempts to cope with a problem and retain wholeness in the face of the threat of disintegration.

For example, a common manifestation of brain damage is *perseveration,* the tendency to repeat the same action over and over again. Viewed negatively, as a symptom of incapacity, perseveration represents a patient's inability to inhibit action. Viewed positively, perseveration represents the person's tendency to maintain integrity in an uncertain and threatening world by continuing a performance that has been experienced as successful.

Although all behavior is undertaken to enhance or preserve self-actualization, not all behavior is equally effective. For example, a person may refuse medical care because he denies that he is ill, even though evidence of his condition is conclusive. Denial of illness may be thought of as "organic repression", i.e., as a form of psychological maladjustment. Or it may be viewed in the way Goldstein recommended: as an attempt to retain or restore personal integrity, to ward off the catastrophic collapse that threatens to follow recognition of the true situation.

11. *Self-actualization is manifested by maximum differentiation and by the highest possible level of complexity of an integrated system.*

This assertion applies to both bodily and mental aspects of the person. The human organism begins as a relatively undifferentiated union of sperm and egg. This union does not produce first a fully developed leg, to which is later added another leg, then a trunk, and so on. Rather, the organism starts as a whole and grows by differentiating parts and subparts within its overall system. For example, the embryo first differentiates into three layers. One of these layers further differentiates into visceral organs; another differentiates into bone, muscle, and connective tissue; the third differentiates into skin and nervous system. The healthy adult human body is a miracle of complexly interconnected structures and functions, each related to all the others throughout the entire course of its development.

The same is true of the person viewed psychologically. The earliest years of development begin a process of differentiation (recall, for example, the primary differentiations of self from nonself and of body from environment) which continues to increase organismic complexity to its maximum potential.

This assertion clearly reflects the influence on Goldstein of the Gestalt psychologists (Kurt Koffka, Wolfgang Köhler, and Max Wertheimer), and evidence of their influence is plain in other holistic theories as well.

12. *Evidence of psychological maturity is the ability to adopt an abstract attitude.*

In Goldstein's theory, an abstract attitude does not mean the ability to think like a philosopher; the abstract attitude is a quality of the behavior of the person as a whole. It means, among other things, taking several points of view into account when making a decision, shifting easily from one task or orientation to another when necessary, appreciating common properties among situations that superficially appear to be different, inferring relationships among things or events that are apparently dissimilar, and planning ahead effectively and realistically. Failure of the abstract attitude is the most prominent evidence of disruption of self-actualization.

Maintenance: Structural Approach

13. To the extent that personality is determined by physique alone, it is self-maintaining.

Just as the structural theorist maintains that no one can make an ectomorph out of an endomorph (all you would have is a skinny endomorph), so temperamental types are not interchangeable. Sheldon recognized that temperament exhibits greater flexibility than does somatotype. However, there are limits to this flexibility. When pressures become too great to produce behavior that runs counter to the pull of the somatotype, trouble follows. For society, the problem of education or rehabilitation is not to force misbehavers into a common mold or to change their basic temperaments. Rather, it is to alter situations so that people can express their biologically given temperaments in acceptable and unconflictual ways, thus making misbehavior unnecessary.

A good example of how Sheldon's theory emphasizes the self-maintaining character of the biological determinants of personality is afforded by his comment on a particular case—No. 80 in *Varieties of Delinquent Youth, Vol. 1, Constitutional Psychiatry of Delinquency* (Sheldon, Hartl, & McDermott, 1949a, pp. 335-357). The youth had been in serious trouble and had been institutionalized for his misbehaviors. Sheldon noted that a psychoanalyst had previously attempted to explain this case in terms of parent-child relationships, emotional snags, and disturbances of sexuality. Of this, Sheldon said:

> All that sort of thing is interesting, and sometimes useful, but in a case like this it is symptomatic of a profound social sickness. At best, it is cowardly evasion of reality. There is a biological reality in human life which in the end cannot be escaped. Sooner or later, this reality must return to human consciousness, perhaps in the chaos and uproar of a vital revolution (p. 357).

Sheldon recognized the value of self-knowledge in such cases. He described a nondelinquent, 17-year-old, extreme endomorph who was strongly gynandromorphic—Case No. 100 in *Varieties of Delinquent Youth, Vol. 2, Social Psychiatry of Delinquency* (Sheldon, Hartl, & McDermott, 1949b, pp. 416-418). The boy's parents brought pressure upon him to become a boxer, a baseball, football, or soccer player, or a track athlete. The boy felt humiliated because he could not succeed. However, he and his parents took a good look at his somatotype photographs, compared them with a few photographs of athletes—and remarkably, within a few minutes, everyone could see the problem and the solution. The parents removed the pressure for athletic success, and the boy's career took a dramatic turn for the better. Freed of the frustrations associated with attempts to become an athlete, he completed high school, performed military service satisfactorily, and prepared to go on to college.

14. *The task for the modern world is to create social institutions to ensure reproduction only by those constitutionally endowed with the best qualities of human temperament.*

Sheldon called for a program of *biological humanics* that would promote both science and human welfare by promulgating a moral philosophy based on somatic and temperamental moderation, allowing for full expression of all potentialities. The healthy 444 "is probably about as close as human flesh gets to God" (Sheldon, Hartl, & McDermott, 1949a, p. 93). Sheldon would prohibit hereditary transmission of wealth, thus depriving people of a major reason for money accumulation. His program would face up to the problem of war by establishing an effective, central world government. It would abolish the monogamous family and delegate reproduction (as opposed to individual sexuality) and child rearing to specialists. As early as the 1940s Sheldon recognized the dangers of overpopulation, but he wished to do more than limit numbers; he felt it necessary to control quality as well. His program also would rescue religion from the quagmire of fruitless theologizing and turn its attention to realistic plans for improving the human species. He saw religion's purpose as providing the moral basis for progress based on science (Sheldon, Hartl, & McDermott, 1949b, pp. 879-881).

He described modern society as delinquent in its failure to provide conditions under which individuals can develop fully to the limits of their potential without infringing on the rights of others. In modern society, the successful are delinquents who steal apples and get over the fence quickly enough to escape. Those who are caught and labeled delinquent are no different; they are merely slower runners. To change this situation Sheldon says, requires a change in the whole of society. The needed change can be accomplished through a merger of medicine and religion. The task of psychology is to catalyze the rapprochement between the two.

Maintenance: Experiential Approach

15. *The body image boundary supports and maintains the self-concept in the face of threat or stress.*

A firm body image boundary sharply delineates self from environment. Consequently, in modern Western society—which values, even demands, a strong sense of selfhood—a firm boundary facilitates good adjustment by maintaining self-integrity under conditions that would otherwise threaten effective functioning (Fisher, 1970).

A firm boundary provides innumerable benefits. Besides making the person resistant to mild stress, it promotes interest in achievement, desire for independence, greater self-confidence, sensitivity to and interest in others, and generalized receptivity to the environment. All in all, a firm boundary is a strong foundation for the personality as a whole.

16.   Body attention patterns link body experience to life situations by attaching learned meanings.

Because the body is the first object with which the person becomes familiar, it remains basic to all later contact with the environment. Body experience provides a background against which all other sensations and all later perceptions are related (Fisher, 1970, p. 595).

The field or background of internal sensations (body image) is articulated and patterned with symbolic meanings. Each meaning is located in a more or less specific body region, so that stimulation of that region arouses its assigned symbolic significance and associated reaction patterns. An obvious example, involving minimal indirect symbolism, is gentle stimulation of the genitals. The aroused sensations have obvious sexual meanings, and in most persons they also lead one to approach the stimulating person. Suppose, however, that a child were taught that genital arousal is bad and were punished for it. Genital stimulation would still have the meaning of sexuality (assuming that sublimation or displacement did not occur), but it would acquire the additional meaning of guilt or shame. In that case, feelings would be in conflict, and if the conflict were severe the result might be avoidance of sexuality or impotence.

A preceding assertion stated that body image growth proceeds through stages. Fisher's theory also proposes that, as each individual works out attitudes toward essential issues in life during such stages, these attitudes become coded in terms of differential awareness of specific body parts or regions. The pattern of differential awareness becomes self-sustaining and thus remains permanent within the personality. These parts or regions become nodes or "landmarks" in the overall organization of the body image.

With respect to the maintenance of personality, the body provides continuity for experience and action. Its patterns of sensory responsiveness and its propensities to activate behavioral responses constitute something roughly analogous to the program inserted into a computer. Having automatized behaviors that produced effective coping in the past, the individual may proceed through daily affairs, in a consistent and generally adequate way.

Just how far automatization of behavior stimulated by body sensation can go is illustrated in a psychoanalytic theory of pain (Szasz, 1957). In this view, pain is a psychological signal by which the ego registers the presence of danger to its own integrity. Although physical pain is a signal from the body, the "body" is not the physical organism but only whatever is recognized as body by the ego. Furthermore, the threat in the experience of pain is not damage to the body but damage to the *ego*. If the ego's program fails or ceases to regard a particular body part as essential, pain will not be experienced should that body part be damaged or lost.

Szasz is inclined to reject laboratory research on pain, because laboratory research cannot take into account complex unconscious determinants of behavior. Fisher's approach relies more heavily on research; however, the two theories are not incompatible. The main difference between them is that Szasz's theory relies upon the concept of the ego to provide an extra theoretical entity which holds the personality together. The term *ego* does not appear in the indexes of Fisher's major books.

Maintenance: Holistic Approach

17.   *The key to effective behavior is adequate functioning of part-whole relations.*

In Kurt Goldstein's theory, the model of all part-whole relationships is that between *figure* and *ground*. Gestalt psychology showed that every perception has at least two components: a *figure,* the object toward which attention is directed; and a *ground,* the setting or background with which the figure is contrasted. As you read a single word on this page, the word assumes figural properties: it stands out clearly and distinctly, provided your visual system is functioning well. The page and other words constitute the ground; they are less distinct or recognizable. If you shift your attention to the page as a whole, it becomes figure and the desk upon which the book rests becomes ground.

The distinction between figure and ground contains the fundamental principle that perception is always relational, and the ground against which an object is perceived, though usually ignored, is as important as the object itself.

So it is with behavior. No act is carried out in isolation. Each is influenced by (and in turn influences) the state of the whole organism. Every action, every thought is invariably a figure against the ground of the state of the organism as a whole. As long as figure-ground relations are adequate, behavior proceeds smoothly and effectively. When figure-ground relations break down, behavioral integrity collapses.

18.   *A major source of breakdown in organismic integrity is isolation or disruption of relationships between parts and wholes.*

Figure-ground relations imply tension between part (figure) and whole (ground). In the normal case, the organism tends to return to a state of equilibrium following stimulation. The process is called *equalization.* Should equalization fail, reorganization fails, and the result is disorder, a state equivalent to maladjustment.

A primary condition which interferes with equalization is *isolation,* or separation of a part process from the whole to which it belongs. For example, primitive reflexes ordinarily inhibited in the intact, healthy organism may reappear when there is interference or blockage of the pathways to the brain. Thoughts that we do not wish to acknowledge may take on an obsessive character; they bother us constantly, yet are not part of us. We may feel compelled to perform acts we know are irrational and unnecessary but are unable to control.

Any severe environmental, psychological, or physiological disturbance can threaten disorganization. Experience of threat is called anxiety, and although a certain amount of anxiety is necessary at all stages of growth, too much may bring about collapse. The ultimate end of a breakdown in equilibration is a disordered state, which Goldstein (1939) called the catastrophic reaction.

The need for certainty is especially strong in persons threatened with catastrophic reaction. This need is well illustrated by Goldstein's observation that, in physical disability, partial loss is often more distressing than total loss. One who is totally blind or deaf may regret or be angry about his condition, but he knows what he has to contend with because the condition is stable. The person who is partially blind or deaf is in an ambiguous (hence, partially disordered) state. Not knowing whether to regard himself as sighted or blind, as healthy or disabled, as normal or abnormal, the individual faces problems that are more distressing than those associated with the certain knowledge of even very serious loss.

Goldstein called the process of adapting to threats of disorganization *coming to terms*, and he recognized that the process of coming to terms usually involves adjusting the organism to the environment rather than the reverse. Everyone, normal or abnormal, experiences anxiety and must come to terms with the environment. The difference between normality and abnormality is essentially this: the abnormal person comes to terms in ways that block self-actualization, while the healthy person comes to terms in ways that promote it or at least do not prevent it.

From an entirely different standpoint, Bakan (1968) spelled out a somewhat similar conception of organismic functioning. Bakan was not stimulated by Goldstein but by the results of research in psychosomatics, by Selye's conception of disease as a response to stress, and Freud's concepts of personality defense and the wish for death.

Bakan's theory identifies two contrasting tendencies of organismic functioning. One is telic centralization; the other is telic decentralization. (The word *telic* means purposive.) Biologically and psychologically, *telic centralization* requires subordination of subsystems (parts) to an overriding determinant of form or function (the integrated operation of the whole). For example, centralization in an industrial firm assures that by submitting to a central authority, all departments, from design to sales, work together toward a common end.

Telic decentralization is the opposite tendency for parts or subsystems to pursue their own destinies. Decentralization is also essential to effective functioning, for subsystems cannot perform adequately unless they have a degree of autonomy. The brain is subservient to the needs of the total organism. Yet, the brain requires a physical setting in which it can develop as a unique and, to some extent, self-sufficient organ. It cannot be so subservient that its actions are totally governed by changes in other organs or systems, such as the stomach or the circulatory network.

The key to effective functioning is reconciliation of centralization and decentralization. When a decentralized process (an isolated part-process) begins to act too autonomously, it gets beyond the control of the centralizing agencies and threatens breakdown or disorganization of the total system. Breakdown is equivalent to sickness, and symptoms may be recognized as actions undertaken to restore integrated functioning.

19. *Maintenance of organismic integrity depends upon the availability of conditions under which the organism can maximize preferred ways of behaving.*

In general, holistic theories assume that each person has a kind of "natural wisdom" which will bring about the best possible adjustment if the environment does not interfere too strongly with the process. Therefore, what the individual prefers, when minimally coerced, may be assumed to be best for it.

An obvious example of interference with a preferred mode of performance occurs when one tries to teach a naturally left-handed person to become right-handed. It can be done, but the left-handed person may never become as efficient as possible, and is more likely to become ambidextrous than fully right-handed.

Goldstein realized that freedom has its limits. Social living requires that people exercise some restraint. No one should be allowed to actualize himself at the expense of another person. In social organization, as in all aspects of human behavior, part processes cannot operate in such a way as to damage the whole. In the final analysis, that society is best which provides for maximum self-actualization of the greatest number of individuals (Goldstein, 1940). Despite the differences between Sheldon's and Goldstein's theories, both would agree to this.

APPLICATIONS

Assessment

The structural and holistic views have perhaps made their greatest contributions by devising techniques of assessment. The appeal of the structural approach has always stemmed from the hope that it can provide a quick, easy way of diagnosing character from personal appearance. History and accumulated evidence show that this hope is vain. Nonetheless, the attempt to relate body build and personality brought about the development of valuable methods for the comprehensive study of individuals.

William Sheldon and Kurt Goldstein were superb methodologists and astute observers; both developed techniques which should serve as guides and models for anyone who studies individuals. A glance at the outline Sheldon, Hartl and McDermott (1949a, 1949b) used in presenting case studies of institutionalized delinquent adolescent males shows the thoroughness with which Sheldon prepared his material. Each study begins with a photograph of the unclothed subject, posed in three standardized standing positions against a plain background; all photographs were taken under uniform conditions of lighting, distance, exposure, type of film, and development. The photograph is followed by a verbal description of the somatotype, including both primary and secondary components. Next come a paragraph on temperament and separate paragraphs describing the behavior that got the person into trouble with society; his origins and family; his history of intellectual (i.e., academic and vocational) accomplishment; his medical background; a record of his behavior in the institution; quantitative indexes of delinquency, psychiatric classification, and IQ; and, finally, a paragraph of comment which allows the investigator to summarize, draw conclusions and, as Sheldon put it, to preach about the evils of the world and how to eliminate them.

Even more thorough were the methods of Kurt Goldstein, who could write a whole book about a single case. Goldstein stressed that close study of individuals is the only way to gain valid information about human behavior. Goldstein and Scheerer (1941) developed a set of materials for evaluating patients' abilities to adopt the abstract attitude. These materials are usually presented to subjects in such a way as to permit a variety of responses. For example, one set of materials, consisting of a plate, a lock, matches, nails, a pipe, and so on, is used to test capacities for abstract thinking. The subject might be given one article and asked to select others that belong with it. Or, the examiner might group the items in some way and ask the subject to explain why they are so grouped (knife, fork, spoon, and plate are all used for eating; key, nail, knife are all made of metal, etc.). The examiner might simply ask the subject to group the items in any way he wishes. Follow-up questions and instructions reveal the subject's bases for his or her groupings and determine whether the subject has the flexibility to revise classifications according to different sets of principles.

Tests like this do not yield scores; there are no uniform criteria for deciding whether a given response is right or wrong. Such tests are not designed to yield a score but to provide a set of standard materials which a well-trained examiner may use to observe and evaluate behavior in a variety of situations.

Variety is also the key to assessment in recent experiential studies of the influence of the body on personality. Fisher and Cleveland (1958) began by scoring responses to inkblots to obtain indexes of body-boundary definiteness (see the Validation section). In later work by Fisher measures of heart rate, galvanic skin response, and several questionnaires about body experience were added, as well as tests of response to distortions of perception induced by special optical lenses.

Fisher's approach to assessment is more classically psychometric, more laboratory oriented, and more analytical than is structural or holistic investigation. His research has tended to study subjects as groups rather than as individuals. This type of research produces volumes of quantitative data, but it deals with averages and may thus leave open the question of the applicability of the findings to individuals.

Structural and holistic assessments tend to be naturalistic and allow flexibility for the examiner. Laboratory and psychometric methods are more artificial, but they are also more objective and more precise. Because there is no uniform, standard way to assess personality, each investigator uses techniques with which he is most familiar.

Treatment

The theorists discussed in this chapter were not primarily oriented toward treatment. Only the experiential approach seems to justify treating personality by any method that resembles the traditional one-to-one, verbal approach to psychotherapy. Certainly, a psychoanalyst who feels that his patient's problems arise from a disturbance of the body image will focus on discovering the source of the disturbance so that the body image may be revised along more realistic lines. However, the psychoanalyst, like many other therapists, would regard the body image disturbance as the product of some more basic difficulty. Treatment would therefore be directed at the basic disturbance rather than toward body experience as such.

If the theory of body signals is correct, it follows that conventional psychotherapy is not the most efficient way to proceed. Body image theory suggests that controlled manipulation of the body should affect body experience and thereby alter psychological states in beneficial ways. The idea is not new: William James said that we do not run because we are afraid but are afraid because we run. Perhaps, then, we would no longer be afraid if we could only stop running and relax.

Since ancient times, sports and athletics have been thought of as vehicles for self-development and as devices of benefit to distressed people. Recent developments suggest that interest in sports and physical activity is growing, not always to promote competition or to channel aggression but to develop the self-concept and to promote psychological well-being (Harris, 1973; Kane, 1972).

Courses of exercise to develop the self-image have been outlined by Feldenkrais (1972; see also Masters & Houston, 1978). Lowen (1972) has integrated exercise into his recommended treatment for depression, a state recognized as the dominant malady of the 20th century. A form of deep massage known as Rolfing, based on the ideas of Ida Rolf (1972), is a method of repositioning the body structure. The concept is that the body tends to assume various typical postures, such as slouching, as a consequence of various attitudes toward life. The body gives the world a message relative to the person's attitude toward himself and others. As the person becomes aware of his own posture this affects, circularly, his self-concept. The massage-type Rolfing treatment is intended to break down tight muscle patterns so that the individual's body becomes free and relaxed. Not only does the body give the outside world a new message about the individual, but the person's attitudes toward himself change as the result of the proprioceptive messages his body gives him.

Sheldon rejected psychoanalysis as a form of psychotherapy. Indeed, he has not advocated any form of individual therapy but seems to share with Goldstein the conviction that the organism is competent to care for itself, provided that environmental conditions do not interfere and that the organism is not constitutionally incompetent.

Sheldon directed his attention to society and to long-term rather than short-term goals. This tendency appears also in the study of the psychological aspects of physical disability which began seriously just after World War II. Psychologists and psychiatrists were brought into the rehabilitation movement by medical personnel who found that rehabilitation often failed because patients lacked motivation to get well. They believed that psychology could resolve patients' mental problems and stimulate clients to desire and work for greater success. Naturally, the model psychologists applied was the one they knew best: talking with the patient about problems of adjustment to reality.

After 30 years of less than impressive success, authorities began to realize that they had been seeking in the wrong place for solutions to their problems. Some patients in rehabilitation or in medical settings do have low motivation for independence. But passivity and dependency are also rational responses to the dehumanizing, regressive, and often humiliating environments to which such patients are sometimes exposed.

In short, rehabilitation psychology is gradually accepting a view that would have been obvious to Goldstein and, probably, to Sheldon as well. The "cure" to problems of adjustment to physical illness and disability lies less in changing the internal dynamics of the patient than in altering the societies in which such people are required to live (Shontz, 1975, 1979; Wright, 1971, 1973, 1980).

Institutional

Constitutional psychology could have important and far-reaching implications for institutional practices. This is true even if one does not accept Sheldon's ideas for reorganizing the world.

Schools and other organizations for children would do well to recognize the special importance of body structure in development. If a physical education teacher gives high grades only to mesomorphs, who easily accomplish what is required, and ignores or downgrades the heroic struggles of endomorphs, who must work much harder to accomplish less, the teacher is not recognizing the importance of physique.

Throughout the school age, but especially from puberty on through the teen years and young adulthood, physical maturation plays a crucial role in social and personal adjustment (Clausen, 1975; Neisworth, 1978). As noted elsewhere in this chapter, stereotyped beliefs about relationships between physique and personality are almost universal, and certain forms of physique (the endomorphic, in particular) are uniformly regarded as being relatively unattractive in social stimulus value. The unattractive child may require special help and attention to achieve the self-esteem everyone needs; the too-attractive child may need guidance so that physique will assume a proper role in his or her life. Overattractiveness can be a burden to a child who does not desire to be the center of attention but is thrust into this position despite his wishes.

Information about somatotypes probably cannot predict a child's future precisely. However, in extreme cases, knowledge of the types of activities facilitated or blocked by different body structures can be most useful, as was shown in the case of the parents who were trying to create an athlete out of their endomorphic and gynandromorphic son (Sheldon, Hartl, & McDermott, 1949b, pp. 416-418).

In institutions like the military services, it would be helpful to measure, record, and take body type into account when assigning duties. Assigning a person who is constitutionally frail to a position requiring heavy labor or exposure to extreme temperatures or severe weather makes little sense. The principles of constitutional psychology require some loosening of the culturally popular belief that "anyone can do anything if he tries hard enough."

Another way in which constitutional psychology, especially in its experiential form, might improve social institutions, is through systematically applied programs of sport and recreation. The initial reaction to such a suggestion may conjure up scenes of masses of people in lines, dressed alike, and going through calisthenics in unison to the *Deutschland über Alles, The East Is Red,* or *God Bless America.* The proposal becomes more meaningful when one considers the almost infinite variety of meanings and experiences that can be created through sports, games, and physical activities. Some sports involve one-to-one personal relations and are highly competitive and physically dangerous (boxing, wrestling). Some require intense concentration all the time, but others leave the mind relatively free (jogging, long-distance running). Some require submission to a leader (football); others demand individual decisions as well as teamwork (basketball). Some are social; some are solitary. In some, one competes against another person; in others, one competes mainly against oneself or against some natural obstacle, such as a mountain or river. Some take more strength than skill; some more skill than strength. The number of variations is endless.

Many patients in institutions are unmotivated because they have nothing to do, therefore programs of individualized recreation and physical activity could change the situation dramatically. Granted that this possibility has been recognized for centuries, what has been lacking is a comprehensive theory to relate particular activities with particular needs and to show how to evaluate outcomes.

Self

The preceding section has shown that the three constitutional approaches do not agree in their recommendations for altering or improving social institutions. Sheldon's utopia sounds like something George Orwell or Aldous Huxley might have thought up, while Goldstein's ideas call for maximum self-determination. However, the three approaches are rather consistent in their general recommendations for personal application. All endorse self-knowledge as the key to the enrichment of individual life.

Few people have such extreme body builds that they feel compelled to develop a fitting kind of personality. Fortunately, the average body build is in the neighborhood of 444, a set of values which provides maximum flexibility. Nevertheless, nearly everyone has experienced private fantasies in which the body appears as extraordinarily handsome, strong, or virile. In mature adults, such fantasies are usually harmless, because experience has taught them not to require the impossible. But everyone can probably also remember the misery of times when heroic fantasies were dashed. Coming to terms with the body seems to be most difficult during periods of transition: at birth, puberty, during sickness, and at the approach of old age and death.

For many, the critical changes yet to be faced are those associated with aging. This is no small matter, and it poses problems poorly handled in American society. Young adulthood is none too soon to begin planning for later years: not only economic preparations for retirement, but concern for such matters as sexuality, health, diet, exercise, religion, and the unpleasant possibilities of physical disability as well as the certainty of death. No extensive formal educational opportunities are yet provided for this purpose, but interest is growing, and the day may come when society places as great importance on preparing citizens for aging as it now does on preparing them for young adulthood.

Of more immediate concern to most readers is the fact that anyone can avoid a great deal of grief by examining closely his or her standards of physical presentability. How much anxiety is justified that perspiration will show on clothing or that one may occasionally reveal one's organicity by way of odors? How necessary is it to be expensively dressed, and how much hard-earned money spent on deodorants, mouthwashes, foot powders, depilatory creams, colognes, special soaps, shampoos, rinses, sexy toothpastes, hair colorings, and other cosmetics is justified? Because modern life forces close personal contacts, it is well to be considerate of the impression we make. But it is not psychologically healthy to so completely reject biological reality that we heed every advertisement which sells body-care products as if they guaranteed escape from nature and assured success in a world of artificial people.

Within recent years, interest has developed in techniques to increase body awareness and control. One approach employs yogic practices—a systematically organized course of exercises designed to make the practitioner more sensitive to the body and more responsive to its urgings. Many such programs were originally designed to help achieve spirituality. However, it is not necessary to seek *nirvana* to derive psychological benefit from relaxation and increased personal sensitivity. In this regard, techniques of biofeedback appear to have considerable potential, particularly in making more efficient the teaching of relaxation and control over autonomic functions (Brown, 1974; Green, Green, & Walters, 1970).

On an interpersonal level, some psychotherapists have established encounter groups, which use body contacts to reduce defensiveness and raise levels of self-awareness. Problems with body experience are likely to manifest themselves in disturbances in sexuality. Some therapists specialize in treating this type of difficulty, a subject which can be handled quite matter-of-factly. Homosexuality, once identified as a symptom of underlying personality disturbance, is now accepted as a matter of personal preference rather than of internal, emotional compulsion. These developments have made it increasingly easy for people with problems related to body experience to find help and for people who are merely atypical to assert their right to social acceptance. Naturally, caution must be used before entering into a program of yoga, biofeedback, sensitivity training, encounter groups, or sex therapy. In these newly emerging fields, charlatans are likely to be abundant. Examination of the qualifications of persons offering such programs is essential and will, of course, be welcomed by any ethical professional.

People who wish to increase self-awareness may benefit from courses of exercises described in books by therapists like Alexander Lowen (1958,

1965, 1970, 1972) and Moshe Feldenkrais (1949, 1972; see also Masters & Houston, 1978). Some of their recommendations give an idea of what is involved. Lowen (1972) pointed out that most people are not well "grounded"; they struggle against gravity and are insufficiently aware of the lower regions of their bodies. One simple exercise that helps overcome this involves standing barefoot with knees slightly bent, arms hanging loosely at the sides, mouth slightly open, and belly, buttocks and pelvis relaxed. While in this position, the person is instructed to attend to sensations in the legs and feet and to try to keep the weight balanced between the heels and the balls of the feet. If tremors occur they are not to be fought or resisted but allowed to develop, so long as the subject does not feel uncomfortable.

Feldenkrais (1972) suggests a set of exercises in imagining, designed to increase awareness of parts of the body of which the person is not normally aware. In one, the subject, in a prone position on the floor, and with the head resting on crossed hands, imagines that a finger is pressing on the heel of the right foot and being drawn, under considerable pressure, up the calf to the knee. Then he imagines a heavy iron ball rolling along the same path, to the buttocks and back several times. As the exercise progresses, he imagines the ball rolling up to the shoulders, along the arms, and up and down the spine.

These exercises are not designed to develop strength or stamina but to increase self-awareness. They require full participation of the mind. One is asked to combine modest expenditures of both physical and psychological effort in a project involving the whole organism. The effect is intended to be pleasurable and stimulating, not painful and fatiguing.

VALIDATION

Evidence

Structural Approach. Sheldon's primary task was to observe physique in such a well-controlled and standardized way that he could identify the primary components of somatotypes. His strategy was to examine photographs of large numbers of persons and extract a set of conclusions about the nature of these components and a set of procedures which could be applied to produce standard assessments of body build. Examination of photographs showed to his satisfaction that only three extreme types stood out as distinctive.

Complete somatotyping involved gross visual inspection of a standard, three-view photograph. This yielded a preliminary estimate of the somatotype, which was checked against tabled values for the overall index: height divided by cube root of weight. Next, region-by-region determinations were made. Finally, region estimates were averaged to produce the final three somatotype values. A kind of primitive computer cranked out somatotype values for five body regions when 18 indexes were fed into the machine.

Somatotyping developed quite early into an objective, reliable procedure. By the time of the publication of the *Atlas of Men* (Sheldon, Dupertuis, & McDermott, 1954), data had been collected on 46,000 subjects; no one can argue that the sample Sheldon used was small.

Assessments of temperament were made on rating scales devised by Sheldon and used to evaluate individuals he interviewed and observed. The three well-known clusters of traits (viscertonic, somatotonic, cerebrotonic) emerged and were incorporated into a 60-item rating scale. Sheldon recommended that ratings of temperament with this scale be based on at least a year of observation of each subject, and 20 or more interviews.

When Sheldon compared somatotype with temperament ratings in a group of 200 persons, he found the relationship to be strong (Sheldon & Stevens, 1942, p. 400). Correlations ranged from 0.79 to 0.83, values far higher than those obtained in most psychological studies. His research has been criticized because Sheldon performed ratings of temperament and somatotypes himself. Sheldon replied that it would be unreasonable to expect a rater to get to know a subject well without ever seeing him.

This study alone is hardly responsible for the high level of interest Sheldon's theory aroused. Much more impressive are the 200 case studies presented in *Varieties of Delinquent Youth* and the comprehensive series of photographs and psychological sketches included in the *Atlas of Men*. Here Sheldon showed his skill as a naturalistic observer. His writings convey such assurance, such exceptional sensitivity and stylistic color, that he creates the impression of being a supreme authority. When the apparently universal appeal of the physiognomic hypothesis is combined with his superb expository skill, the result is nearly irresistible.

Other investigators have continued Sheldon's work, and some, though by no means all, have confirmed his findings. However, in no instances are correlation values obtained by others of the same magnitude as those reported by Sheldon (Bridges & Jones, 1973; Child, 1950; Cortes & Gatti, 1965, 1966; Deabler, Hartl, & Willis, 1973; Fiske, 1944; Lester, 1977; Slaughter, 1970; Walker, 1962; Watson, 1972).

Several studies confirm that somatotypes as social stimuli are significantly differentiated in many cultures. Stereotypes about personality correlates are almost universal, and data consistently indicate that the endomorph is least preferred, while ectomorphy is regarded most positively, (Devadasan, 1977; Felker, 1972; Iwawaki, Lerner, & Chihara, 1977; Johnson & Staffieri, 1971; Lerner, 1969, 1973; Lerner & Gellert, 1969; Lerner & Pool, 1972; Sleet, 1969; Stewart, Tutton, & Steele, 1973). Sheldon himself was not prolific, having produced only two major publications after 1954 (Sheldon, Lewis, & Tenney, 1969; Sheldon, 1971).

Sheldon's interest in delinquency was reflected in a classic study by Glueck and Glueck (1956), who found an extraordinarily high incidence of mesomorphy in a group of delinquent boys. This finding has been confirmed by at least two other independent investigations (Epps & Parnell, 1942; Gibbens, 1963).

Experiential Approach. Early evidence for the idea of the body image was largely clinical in origin. Mention has already been made of the disorders of body experience associated with anxiety, schizophrenia, brain damage, and denervation of body parts. Case studies provided early investigators like Schilder with ample illustrative material, and case studies are still prominent in many articles on the subject. Recent years have seen a tendency to rely more heavily upon systematically collected data and to employ some techniques of laboratory research in the study of body experience. For example, much of Fisher and Cleveland's early work (1958) was devoted to developing a measure of body image boundary properties based on subjects' responses to the Rorschach inkblot plates. Inkblots are presumed to be meaningless stimuli; consequently, all meaning perceived in them is regarded as coming from the perceiver.

Fisher and Cleveland reasoned that subjects would project their body images into their perceptions of inkblots. A firm body image boundary is represented in responses that stress the surface properties of the object. Examples are: man in armor; snail in a shell. The total of such responses constitutes the *barrier* score. Other responses represent the breakdown of barriers (e.g., bullet going through flesh); the total of these constitutes the *penetration* score. In general, the barrier score is believed to reflect more permanent psychological states; it is therefore more important to a theory about personality structure than is the penetration score, which is more sensitive to transient conditions. Barrier and penetration scores correlate modestly with measures of many other personal characteristics, from anxiety proneness to type and location of physical illnesses.

Other tests of body image have been developed, and some have achieved considerable popularity. Best known is the draw-a-person test (Machover, 1949), designed on the premise that people project their personalities into their drawings of human figures (see also Burns & Kaufman, 1972; DiLeo, 1973; Hammer, 1978). A related development required subjects also to draw pictures of a house and a tree, each of which was expected to represent the self, though in less direct and therefore more symbolic form (Buck, 1948).

Fisher and Cleveland's earlier research was criticized on two grounds. First, the validity of responses to inkblots as measures of the body image has been questioned; in fact, the validity of the theoretical concept of the body image itself has been doubted (Wylie, 1974). Second, although the results of most of the research performed on body image are statistically significant, their magnitude is not very great. Data often show small average differences between groups or low correlations between measures, but such findings are too weak to justify statements about individuals (Shontz, 1971).

Fisher replied by noting that the body of research evidence, all pointing in a consistent direction, is too large to be cast aside summarily. Inconsistent findings are few and can all be explained away. Also, it is unreasonable to expect powerful experimental outcomes in a field of research where the number of variables determining behavior is so great and the possibilities for controlling them are so low. Virtually no experiments in the field of personality have ever been able to account for more than 20 percent to 25 percent of variation in their data; body image research is no exception, and it should not be condemned on that basis (Fisher, 1971).

Fisher's research also concerns demonstrating the validity of the general hypothesis that body states are significantly related to psychological experience (Fisher, 1965, 1970). For example, one study showed that the number of stomach symptoms normal male subjects reported was associated with response bias in the up-down spatial dimension (Fisher & Greenberg, 1977). Another showed that body symptoms associated with body openings correlated with perceptual bias in the right-left dimension (Fisher & Greenberg, 1979). A final example of this line of investigation is a study in which subjects were exposed to taped themes (e.g., an oral theme, containing many references to food or eating) and were then tested for reports of tension in appropriate body regions; in the case of the oral theme, tension was expected in the eyes. (Surprised? Reread the last sentence under Assertion 9.) Tension in the region of the mouth was expected in response to a theme of hostility. Confirmatory results were strongest among these who reported previously experiencing symptoms in appropriate body regions. That is, "past somatization in a target landmark . . . better predicted tension in that landmark than past somatization in each of the nontarget landmarks predicted tension at their respective sites" (Fisher, 1980, p. 730). Studies like these are typical of the many that are being published in a steady stream to provide empirical support for experiential theory.

Holistic Approach. Some of the most important points Goldstein made had to do with methodology; he was highly critical of conventional modes of collecting scientific data. His criticisms strongly influenced the first chapters of Maslow's primary work, *Motivation and Personality* (1970).

Goldstein objected to the study of organs or behaviors in isolation from the total, living person. For example, in a classic experiment of the 17th century, William Harvey, often called the father of modern experimental biology, demonstrated that the blood circulates in a closed system. This finding generated the idea that the heart acts as a pump. A holist would claim that this conception is woefully incomplete. It is modeled on the assumption that the body is a machine, and it leaves no room for descriptions of the relationships between blood circulation and the rest of the organism. For instance, it does not recognize that, within limits which are greatly expanding now that biofeedback techniques are available (Green, Green, & Walters, 1970; Brown, 1974), the circulatory network can be controlled psychologically; given proper training, some persons can even control the expansion and contraction of surface blood vessels. It leaves no room for considering the interaction of blood and air in the lungs, or of blood and nutrients in the viscera. It can only explain these by proposing new mechanical analogies and by assembling its conception of the whole body piece by piece. The result is a view of the person as a gigantic, complex machine. Intact persons display characteristics that are not apparent in machines, certainly not in isolated parts separated out for observation. Examples of characteristics shown only by intact organisms are preference, intentionality, abstraction, and (above all) self-actualization.

Had Goldstein been entirely negative in his criticism, his views would have gained little ground. However, he used his own methods to obtain evidence to support his theory. Essentially, these methods involved close and systematic study of individuals. It is sometimes said that Goldstein advocated the use of case studies (Hall & Lindzey, 1970, pp. 311-314), but that is true only in a limited way. To Goldstein, there really was no such thing as a "case" of brain damage or schizophrenia. There were only people, some of whom had special problems induced by damage to the central nervous system or from functional sources. Goldstein studied persons, not diseases, and he studied each person systematically and completely, often for years.

While most scientists in psychology try to discover the particular by studying the universe, or as large a sample of it as possible, Goldstein sought to discover the universal by studying the particular. Unlike the scientist who relies on large samples to cancel out errors, Goldstein studied every attribute of a single individual, seeking to gain complete and error-free understanding of one subject at a time. Furthermore, he argued, certain phenomena can be studied only in this way.

Comparisons

Because constitutional psychology does not present a monolithic theory to which all advocates adhere, it cannot easily be compared to other, more unified, self-contained systems.

Unlike orthodox psychoanalytic theory, constitutional psychology does not sidestep the issue of the mind-body relationship. Not that simple answers have been forthcoming; but, as has been shown, the experiential approach does attempt to fill an important gap in psychoanalysis. It does not merely assume that body structures and processes influence personality, it attempts to describe how such influences operate. Even Freud did not undertake that task, though he was medically trained and qualified to do so.

A purely structural approach sees little need for psychoanalytic concepts. For, if personality is an expression of body structure, little is to be gained by penetrating to the depths of the psyche in search of hidden problems or unconscious conflicts. Sheldon would certainly have argued that time is better spent devising programs of social control to improve personality by improving heredity.

On the question of psychoanalysis, holism would agree, for Goldstein had little use for the idea of the unconscious. He recognized the importance of subjective experience; in fact, his own thinking became progressively more phenomenological. Goldstein also recognized that some contents of thought are more prominent, more in focus (figure) than others (ground), and that a person might attempt to isolate certain ideas so that they could never come clearly into the center of attention. Isolation is a source of disorganization but it in no way implies the operation of unconscious forces, as the psychoanalysts describe them.

For the holist, perhaps the least useful (and possibly actually harmful) theories are those that derive from the study of conditioned responses. Nothing exemplifies the type of science a holist opposes more clearly than do theories based on the conditioned response. Conditioning procedures violate nearly all the requirements that must be fulfilled if the organism is to function effectively. Conditioning requires such complete control over environmental conditions that the organism is not free to behave according to its own preferences. Small wonder that conditioning theorists do not recognize self-actualization as a legitimate motive; they never observe organisms under conditions that permit it.

Also deleterious is the specificity of conditioned learning. A child may learn multiplication tables by rote, but memorization does not teach the relation between multiplication and addition or why 6 times 2 equals 4 times 3. Similarly, a child may be conditioned to say *please* and *thank you* and still be anything but polite, for true politeness resides in the abstract capacity to appreciate the situations of other people, not in the automatic recitation of verbal formulas.

The holist rejects the dogma that observable acts alone comprise the subject matter of psychological science. To the holist a specific act has meaning only as it relates to the total organization of the person in his life situation. In this respect, holism and the structural approach tend to be similar; both are avowedly naturalistic.

The essence of naturalism is its unwillingness to simplify or manipulate the processes it studies and its appreciation of the complexity of events which occur outside the laboratory. Mention has been made of the tendency on the part of holistic theorists to drift away from studying biological determinants of behavior and toward the study of subjective experience. One might guess that the drift occurs as a way of escaping the complexity of the mind-body problem by leaving the body behind. More probably, it occurs because these theorists realized that the real complexities of human life do not stem from problems of satisfying biological needs; these are well taken care of in modern Western society. Rather, life is complex because today's human beings are more troubled by the problem of the meaning of human existence than ever before. This problem involves self-actualization in its most abstract form.

PROSPECT

Constitutional psychology has never been a dominant force in American theoretical thought, nor is it likely to become so. A computer-assisted search of the literature in psychology produced no reports of research between 1973 and 1980 under the headings *somatotypes* or *constitutional psychology*. The few that appeared between 1966 and 1979 showed no strong support for the contention that body type is correlated with personality, as it is usually measured in psychological research. The qualification is important because it is not at all certain that usual methods of measurement of personality are adequate to the task of revealing physique-behavior correlations if they do exist. No investigator of structural theory has been as careful about selection or development of measuring instruments as Fisher has been in his work on experiential theory. Nevertheless, the continued lack of impressive success in demonstrating correlations of any magnitude causes most investigators to regard this field of study as unpromising.

Even if American psychologists can be induced to take constitutional factors seriously, they would be more likely to regard them as challenges than as fixed conditions or limits. If Sheldon says that endomorphs cannot become track stars, someone will be stimulated to find a way to train endomorphs to break track records. At the very least, someone will insist that every endomorph has the right to be trained to run as fast as possible, even if he will never manage the four-minute mile.

The experiential approach has won a rather firm place for itself in modern versions of psychoanalytic theory. This chapter has examined the work of the most prolific investigator in the field, Seymour Fisher, but many others are investigating body image as well. It appears to be a topic of enduring theoretical and research interest. However, current body image theorists will probably not be regarded as initiators of new points of view but as contributors to the enhancement of the psychoanalytic tradition. In short, the future will not see the development of a body image theory of personality, though theorists will continue to use the term *body image* in their writings.

By contrast, the influence of holism will probably become broader and more pervasive. Practically no theorist today would deny that body influences mind or that mind affects body. The holistic position has become so convincing to anyone who works with people in clinical situations that denial of its validity is out of the question. Yet, part of the problem of holism is that it seems to present philosophical conclusions and value judgments rather than laws of behavior. Though the fundamental assertions of holism have been accepted, the problem of developing experimentally testable hypotheses remains unresolved.

There may always be a need for holism, or something like it, to remind psychological theorists that the subject of their inquiries is the human being. The mechanistic model is so attractive in its simplicity and promise of control over behavior that the temptation to return to it is always strong. A good example is provided by the fate of the concept of purpose in psychology. Until the middle of the 20th century, many psychologists regarded as unacceptable any purposive explanations which regard behavior as being influenced by a future goal or desired end. Scientists were firmly convinced that all causation is historical (i.e., represents the past operating on the present) or, at most, contemporaneous with its effects. Suddenly, however, scientific attitudes changed, because technologists had written programs which permitted computers to engage in what appears to be purposive activity. The concept of purpose became respectable because machines had been constructed that behaved purposively (Chein, 1972; see also Rychlak, 1968, 1977).

Whatever the ultimate resolution of the theoretical issues, constitutional psychology will probably never completely disappear from the scene. Though it will never develop into a major, unified theory, the problems it raises will persist in the treatment or rehabilitation of people in trouble. As long as people suffer psychosomatic disorders and physical disabilities, questions must be raised about the relationships between mind and body. Unless and until other answers come forward, some form of constititional psychology will be needed to deal with them.

ANNOTATED BIBLIOGRAPHY

Structural Approach

Sheldon, W., Dupertuis, C. W., and McDermott, E. *Atlas of Men: A Guide for Somatotyping the Adult Male at All Ages.* Originally published, Harper & Row, 1954.

Sheldon's basic writings, which originally appeared between 1940 and 1954, were republished in 1970 by Hafner Publishing Co., Darien, Conn., as a matched set of five volumes. Natually, anyone who wishes to learn about the structural approach in detail should read them all, but the best introduction and overall view of Sheldon's later ideas and of his inimitable style is the *Atlas of Men*. It begins with a survey of the philosophy and theory of the structural approach and then provides photographs and psychological descriptions of men who were selected because they display the widest possible variations in physique. This book presents Sheldon at his best.

Sheldon, W., Hartl, E. M., & McDermott, E. *Varieties of Delinquent Youth*. Vol. 1, *Constitutional Psychiatry of Delinquency;* Vol. 2, *Social Psychiatry of Delinquency*. Originally published, Harper & Row, 1949.

The two volumes called collectively *Varieties of Delinquent Youth* consist of case studies of young men, most of whom have been in some kind of trouble with society and have therefore been institutionalized. Both volumes display Sheldon's naturalistic methods and interest in whole persons.

Sheldon, W., Stevens, S. S., & Tucker, W. B. *The Varieties of Human Physique: An Introduction to Constitutional Psychology*. Originally published, Harper & Row, 1940.

The Varieties of Human Physique provides historical background and describes how Sheldon developed techniques for somatotyping.

Sheldon, W., & Stevens, S. S. *The Varieties of Temperament: A Psychology of Constitutional Differences*. Originally published, Harper & Row, 1942.

The Varieties of Temperament describes the three personality types and the results of Sheldon's attempts to relate each to its corresponding somatotype.

Experiential Approach

Fisher, S., and Cleveland, S. E. *Body Image and Personality* (2d ed.). New York: Dover Publications, 1968.

Fisher, S. *Body Experience in Fantasy and Behavior*. New York: Appleton-Century-Crofts, 1970.

Originally published in 1958, *Body Image and Personality* describes research conducted by Fisher and Cleveland which used measures of body image boundary *barrier* and *penetration* derived from subjects' interpretations of inkblots. It also provides a useful historical survey of body image theory and outlines the early version of experiential theory developed by the authors from their findings. By and large, the research is correlational: it relates scores on measures of body image to a variety of other indexes, from evaluations of subjects' behavior in groups to body sites of cancer and measures of physiological reactivity.

The second book, by Fisher alone, describes subsequent research which used a broader array of body experience indexes and measures of other personality and behavioral characteristics. In addition, it presents developments in Fisher's formal theoretical thought.

Holistic Approach

Goldstein, K. *The Organism: A Holistic Approach to Biology Derived from Pathological Data in Man*. New York: American Book, 1939.

Goldstein, K. *Human Nature in the Light of Psychopathology*. Cambridge, Mass.: Harvard University Press, 1940.

These are the two basic books describing Goldstein's holistic approach. *The Organism* is an English version of his original work, which was published in German in 1934. *Human Nature in the Light of Psychopathology* was drawn from lectures Goldstein presented at Harvard University.

Both books show clearly the two essential aspects of Goldstein's work: his critical attacks on analytic, atomistic, mechanistic, reflex-centered methods and theories of biological science, and his assertion and defense of holism as a more inclusive and satisfactory view of human nature. The influence of early Gestalt psychology on Goldstein's thinking, as well as the reasons for Goldstein's later profound influence on other more phenomenologically and existentially oriented holistic theorists such as Maslow and Angyal, is apparent in both volumes.

REFERENCES

Alexander, F. *Psychosomatic medicine.* New York: W. W. Norton, 1950.

Alexander, F., French, T. M., & Pollach, G. H. (Eds.). *Psychosomatic specificity.* Chicago: University of Chicago Press, 1968.

Ardrey, R. *The territorial imperative.* New York: Atheneum, 1966.

Argyle, M. *Bodily communication.* New York: Oxford University Press, 1975.

Bakal, D. A. *Psychology and medicine: Psychobiological dimensions of health and illness.* New York: Springer, 1979.

Bakan, D. *Disease, pain, and sacrifice: Toward a psychology of suffering.* Chicago: University of Chicago Press, 1968.

Barker, R. G., Wright, B. A., & Gonick, M. R. *Adjustment to physical handicap and illness: A survey of the social psychology of physique and disability.* (Rev. ed.). New York: Social Science Research Council, 1953 (Originally published, 1946.)

Birdwhistell, R. L. *Kinesics and context: Essays on body motion communication.* Philadelphia: University of Pennsylvania Press, 1970.

Bridges, P. K., & Jones, M. T. Relationships between some psychological assessments, body build and physiological stress responses. *Journal of Neurology, Neurosurgery & Psychiatry,* 1973, 36, 839-845.

Brown, B. B. *New mind, new body; biofeedback: New directions for the mind.* New York: Harper & Row, 1974.

Buck, J. N. The H-T-P technique: A qualitative and quantitative scoring manual. *Journal of Clinical Psychology,* 1948, *4,* 317-396.

Burns, R. C., & Kaufman, S. H. *Actions, styles and symbols in kinetic family drawings (K-F-D): An interpretive manual.* New York: Brunner/Mazel, 1972.

Caplan, A. L. (Ed.). *The sociobiology debate.* New York: Harper & Row, 1978.

Chein, I. *The science of behavior and the image of man.* New York: Basic Books, 1972.

Child, I. The relation of somatotype to self-ratings on Sheldon's temperamental traits. *Journal of Personality,* 1950, *18,* 440-453.

Clausen, J. A. The social meaning of differential physical and sexual maturation. In E. Dragastin & G. H. Elder (Eds.), *Adolescence in the life cycle: Psychological change and social context.* Washington, D. C.: Hemisphere, 1975.

Cortes, J. B., & Gatti, F. M. Physique and self description of temperament. *Journal of Consulting Psychology,* 1965, *29,* 432-439.

Cortes, J. B., & Gatti, F. M. Physique and motivation. *Journal of Consulting Psychology,* 1966, *30,* 408-414.

Deabler, H. L., Hartl, E. M., & Willis, C.A. Physique and personality: Somatotype and the 16 PF. *Perceptual and Motor Skills,* 1973, *36,* 927-933.

Devadasan, K. Personality evaluation as a function of personal appearance. *Asian Journal of Psychology and Education,* 1977, *2*(2), 5-8.

DiLeo, J. H. *Children's drawings as diagnostic aids.* New York: Brunner/Mazel, 1973.

Dunbar, H. F. *Emotions and bodily changes.* New York: Columbia University Press, 1935.

Epps, P., & Parnell, R. W. Physique and temperament of women delinquents compared with women undergraduates. *British Journal of Medical Psychology,* 1942, *25,* 249-255.

Eysenck, H. J. *Fact and fiction in psychology.*

Harmondsworth, England: Penguin Books, 1965.

Feldenkrais, M. *Body and mature behavior.* New York: International Universities Press, 1949.

Feldenkrais, M. *Awareness through movement: Health exercises for personal growth.* New York: Harper & Row, 1972.

Felker, D. W. Social stereotyping of male and female body types with differing facial expressions by elementary age boys and girls. *Journal of Psychology,* 1972, *82,* 151-154.

Fenichel, O. *The psychoanalytic theory of neurosis.* New York: W. W. Norton, 1945.

Fisher, S. The body image as a source of selective cognitive sets. *Journal of Personality,* 1965, *33,* 536-552.

Fisher, S. *Body experience in fantasy and behavior.* New York: Appleton-Century-Crofts, 1970.

Fisher, S. Complexity reflected. *Contemporary Psychology,* 1971, *16,* 744-745.

Fisher, S. Theme induction of localized somatic tension. *The Journal of Nervous and Mental Disease,* 1980, *168,* 721-731.

Fisher, S., & Cleveland, S. E. *Body image and personality* (2d ed.). New York: Dover Publications, 1968. (Originally published, Van Nostrand, 1958.)

Fisher, S., & Greenberg, R. P. Stomach symptoms and up-down metaphors and gradients. *Psychosomatic Medicine,* 1977, *39,* 93-101.

Fisher, S., & Greenberg, R. P. Body opening symptoms and right-left sets. *The Journal of Nervous and Mental Disease,* 1979, *167,* 422-427.

Fiske, D. W. A study of relationships to somatotype. *Journal of Applied Psychology,* 1944, *28,* 504-519.

Freud, S. *The ego and the id.* (J. Riviere, trans.) London: Hogarth Press, 1927.

Gall, F. J., & Spurzheim, J. G. *Récherches sur le système nerveux.* Paris: Schoell, 1809.

Gibbens, T. C. N. *Psychiatric studies of Borstal lads.* London: Oxford, 1963.

Glueck, S., & Glueck, E. *Physique and delinquency.* New York: Harper, 1956.

Goldstein, K. *The organism: A holistic approach to biology derived from pathological data in man.* New York: American Book, 1939.

Goldstein, K. *Human nature in the light of psychopathology.* Cambridge, Mass.: Harvard University Press, 1940.

Goldstein, K. *After-effects of brain injuries in war.* New York: Grune & Stratton, 1942.

Goldstein, K., & Scheerer, M. Abstract and concrete behavior: An experimental study with special tests. *Psychological Monographs,* 1941, *53* (2), 1-151.

Green, E. E., Green, A. M., & Walters, E. D. Voluntary control of internal states: Psychological and physiological. *Journal of Transpersonal Psychology,* 1970, *9,* 1-26.

Hall, C. S., & Lindzey, G. *Theories of personality* (2nd ed.). New York: Wiley, 1970.

Hammer, E. F. Projective drawings: Two areas of differential diagnostic challenge. In B. B. Wolman (Ed.), *Clinical diagnosis of mental disorders: A handbook.* New York: Plenum Press, 1978, pp. 281-310.

Harris, D. V. *Involvement in sport: A somatopsychic rationale for physical activity.* Philadelphia: Lea & Febiger, 1973.

Holden, C. Identical twins reared apart. *Science,* March 1980, *207,* 1323-1325, 1327-1328.

Iwawaki, S., Lerner, R. M., & Chihara, T. Development of personal space schemata among Japanese in late childhood. *Psychologia: An International Journal of Psychology in the Orient,* 1977, *20*(2), 89-97.

Jackson, D. D. Reunion of identical twins, raised apart, reveals some astonishing similarities. *Smithsonian,* 1980, *11*(7), 48-57.

Johnson, P. A., & Staffieri, J. R. Stereotypic affective properties of personal names and somatotypes in children. *Developmental Psychology,* 1971, *5,* 176.

Kane, J. E. (Ed.). *Psychological aspects of physical education and sport.* London: Routledge & Kegan Paul, 1972.

Kretschmer, E. *Physique and character.* (W. J. H. Spratt, trans.). New York: Harcourt, 1925. (Originally published, 1921.)

Lavater, J. C. *Essays on physiognomy* (H. Hunter, trans.). London: John Murray, 1789.

Lerner, R. M. The development of stereotyped expectancies of body build-behavior relations. *Child Development,* 1969, *40,* 137-141.

Lerner, R. M. The development of personal space schemata toward body build. *Journal of Psychology,* 1973, *84,* 229-235.

Lerner, W., & Gellert, E. Body build identification, preference, and aversion in children. *Developmental Psychology,* 1969, *1,* 456-462.

Lerner, R. M., & Pool, K. B. Body-build stereotypes: A cross-cultural comparison. *Psychological Reports,* 1972, *31,* 527-532.

Lester, D. Deviation in Sheldonian physique-temperament match and neuroticism. *Psychological Reports,* 1977, *41,* 942.

Lindzey, G. Behavior and morphological variation. In J. N. Spuhler (Ed.), *Genetic diversity and human behavior* (pp. 227-240). Chicago: Aldine, 1967.

Lombroso, C. *Crime, its causes and remedies.* (H. P. Horton, trans.). Boston: Little, Brown, 1911.

Lowen, A. *Physical dynamics of character structure.* New York: Grune & Stratton, 1958.

Lowen, A. *Love and orgasm.* New York: Macmillan, 1965.

Lowen, A. *Pleasure: A creative approach to life.* New York: Coward, McCann, 1970.

Lowen, A. *Depression and the body: The biological basis of faith and reality.* New York: Coward, McCann, 1972.

Marano, H. E. Biology is one key to the bonding of mothers and babies. *Smithsonian,* 1981, *11,* 60-69.

Maslow, A. H. *Motivation and personality* (2d ed.). New York: Harper & Row, 1970.

Masters, R., & Houston, J. *Listening to the body.* New York: Delacorte Press, 1978.

Meyer, A. *Psychobiology: A science of man.* Springfield, Ill.: Charles C Thomas, 1957.

Meyerson, L. Somatopsychology of physical disability. In W. M. Cruickshank (Ed.), *Psychology of exceptional children and youth* (3d ed.; pp. 1-74). Englewood Cliffs, N. J.: Prentice-Hall, 1971.

Morris, D. *The naked ape.* New York: McGraw-Hill, 1967.

Naccarati, S. The morphologic aspect of intelligence. In R. S. Woodworth (Ed.), *Archives of Psychology,* 1921, *6*(45), 1-44.

Neisworth, J. T., Jones, R. T., & Smith, R. M. Body behavior problems: A conceptualization. *Education and Training of the Mentally Retarded,* 1978, *13,* 265-271.

Paterson, D. G. *Physique and intellect.* New York: Appleton-Century, 1930.

Reich, W. *The function of the orgasm.* New York: Orgone Institute Press, 1944.

Rolf, I. *Structural integration.* New York: Viking Press, 1972.

Rychlak, J. F. *A philosophy of science for personality theory.* Boston: Houghton Mifflin, 1968.

Rychlak, J. F. *The psychology of rigorous humanism.* New York: Wiley, 1977.

Schilder, P. *The image and appearance of the human body.* New York: International Universities Press, 1950. (Originally published, 1935.)

Sheldon, W. The New York study of physical constitution and psychotic pattern. *Journal of the History of the Behavioral Sciences,* 1971, *7,* 115-126.

Sheldon, W., Dupertuis, C. W., & McDermott, E. *Atlas of men: A guide for somatotyping the adult male at all ages.* Darien, Conn.: Hafner, 1970. (Originally published, Harper & Row, 1954.)

Sheldon, W., Hartl, E. M., & McDermott, E. *Varieties of delinquent youth* (Vol. 1, *Constitutional psychiatry of delinquency*). Darien, Conn.: Hafner, 1970. (Originally published, Harper & Row, 1949).(a)

Sheldon, W., Hartl, E. M., & McDermott, E. *Varieties of delinquent youth* (Vol. 2, *Social psychiatry of delinquency*). Darien, Conn.: Hafner, 1980. (Originally published, Harper & Row, 1949.)(b)

Sheldon, W. H., Lewis, N. D. C., & Tenney, A. M. Psychotic patterns and physical constitution: A thirty-year follow-up of thirty-eight hundred psychiatric patients in New York State. In D. V. Siva Sankar (Ed.), *Schizophrenia: Current concepts and research* (pp. 838-912). New York: PJD Publications, 1969.

Sheldon, W., & Stevens, S. S. *The varieties of temperament: A psychology of constitutional differences.* Darien, Conn.: Hafner, 1970. (Originally published, Harper & Row, 1942).

Sheldon W., Stevens, S. S., & Tucker, W. B. *The varieties of human physique: An introduction to constitutional psychology.* Darien, Conn.: Hafner, 1970. (Originally published, Harper & Row, 1940.)

Shontz, F. C. Body image: Data galore. *Contemporary Psychology,* 1971, *16,* 362-364.

Shontz, F. C. *Psychological aspects of physical illness and disability.* New York: Macmillan, 1975.

Shontz, F. C. Theories about the adjustment to having a disability. In W. Cruickshank (Ed.), *Psychology of exceptional children and youth* (4th ed.). New York: Prentice-Hall, 1979, pp. 3-44.

Shontz, F. C., & Wright, B. A. The distinctiveness of rehabilitation psychology. *Professional Psychology,* 1980, *11,* 919-924.

Slaughter, M. An analysis of the relationship between somatotype and personality traits of college women. *Research Quarterly,* 1970, *41*(4), 569-575.

Sleet, D. A. Physique and social image.

Perceptual and Motor Skills, 1969, *28,* 295-299.

Smith, J. A., & Ross, W. D. (Eds.). *The works of Aristotle* (Vol. 4, *Historia animalium,* D. W. Thompson, trans.). London: Henry Frowde, 1910.

Smuts, J. *Holism and evolution.* New York: Macmillan, 1926.

Spiegel, J. P., & Machotka, P. *Messages of the body.* New York: Free Press, 1974.

Spurzheim, J. G. *Phrenology in connexion with the study of physiognomy.* Boston: March, Copen & Lyon, 1833.

Stern, W. *General psychology from the personalistic standpoint* (H. D. Spoerl, trans.). New York: Macmillan, 1938.

Stewart, R. A., Tutton, S. J., & Steele, R. E. Stereotyping and personality: I. Sex differences in perception of female physiques. *Perceptual and Motor Skills,* 1973, *36,* 811-814.

Szasz, T. S. *Pain and pleasure: A study of bodily feelings.* New York: Basic Books, 1957.

Walker, R. N. Body build and behavior in young children: I. Body build and nursery school teachers' ratings. *Monographs of the Society for Research on Child Development,* 1962, *27* (3, No. 84).

Watson, C. G. Psychopathological correlates of anthropometric types in male schizophrenics. *Journal of Clinical Psychology,* 1972, *28,* 474-478.

White, R. W. *The abnormal personality.* New York: Ronald Press, 1956.

Wilson, E. O. *Sociobiology: The new synthesis.* Cambridge, Mass.: Belknap/Harvard University Press, 1975.

Wilson, E. O. *On human nature.* Cambridge, Mass.: Harvard University Press, 1978.

Wright, B. A. *Physical disability—A psychological approach.* New York: Harper & Row, 1960.

Wright, B. A. Issues in overcoming emotional barriers to adjustment in the handicapped.

In C. H. Patterson & H. A. Moses (Eds.), *Readings in Rehabilitation Counseling.* Champaign, Ill.: Stipes Publishing Co., 1971, pp. 131-137.

Wright, B. A. Changes in attitudes toward people with handicaps. *Rehabilitation Literature,* 1973, *34*, 354-368.

Wright, B. A. Developing constructive views of life with a disability. *Rehabilitation Literature,* 1980, *41*, 274-279.

Wylie, R. C. *The self-concept* (Rev. ed.; Vol. 1). Lincoln: University of Nebraska Press, 1974.

CHAPTER XI

Soviet Personality Theory

Isidore Ziferstein

ANTON S. MAKARENKO

Soviet personality theory has its fundamental bases in the philosophical concepts of dialectical materialism of Georg Hegel, Karl Marx, Friedrich Engels, and Vladimir Ilich Lenin and in the neurophysiological findings of Ivan P. Pavlov. Its practical applications as well as its experimental research approaches have been largely guided by the work of A. S. Makarenko, an educator who in the 1920s had remarkable success in restructuring personalities and rehabilitating delinquent youth. As a result, the guiding principles of Soviet personality theory today are Makarenko's dicta:

1. Personality can most effectively be developed and maintained in, by, and for the collective.
2. The collective is *the* developer of personality.
3. Study the child while teaching him and teach the child while studying him.

The major research tool in Soviet Personality procedures is the "transforming experiment" which changes the phenomenon while studying it. Other specifically Soviet areas of research include human typology based on Pavlov's conditioned-reflex theories, the conceptualizations of A. R. Luria about brain functions, and the study of "set" by the Georgian school of psychology headed by D. N. Uznadze. Meticulous laboratory studies are also carried out on the development of speech, thought, perception, attention, and so on.

Soviet theorists have harsh criticisms of Western personality theory. They proclaim the superiority of their "unified" approach over the "babble of voices" (*raznoboi*) of the numerous Western personality theories, which they see as evidence of a "crisis" in Western psychology. However, in recent years this criticism has been moderating, and Soviet psychologists are becoming increasingly open to the rich store of data and concepts available from Western personality theories.

INTRODUCTION

Soviet personality theory employs a set of concepts and a terminology which appear strange to the uninitiated reader. However, the effort involved in familiarizing oneself with this terra incognita can prove to be stimulating and thought-provoking.

The Western reader of Soviet writings on personality theory is puzzled, and often put off, by the insistence of Soviet psychologists on proclaiming the correctness of the philosophical foundations of their Marxist theory, by the injection of political partisanship (*partiinost'*) into their formulations, and by the sometimes harsh polemics against "incorrect" philosophical foundations and what they consider the reactionary political applications of most, if not all, Western personality theories.

Soviet psychologists justify their emphasis on a "correct," dialectical materialist orientation, and their struggle against "bourgeois idealist," "vulgar materialist" personality theories, by maintaining that there cannot be valid practice without a proper philosophical base. Soviet personality theorists also maintain that the work of all scientists is based on a matrix of philosophical concepts, explicit or implicit, and that this matrix determines the direction that scientific research takes. For the Soviet personality theorist, one such basic philosophical question is the relationship of mind and matter.

The American psychologist Gardner Murphy (cited in Simon, 1957, p. 3) takes an analogous position:

> Perhaps the most prevalent attitude of contemporary psychologists is to regard the problem [of the relationship of mind and matter] as outside the scope of psychology as at present defined. This attitude, however, very naturally means in practice a refusal to admit that any such problem exists. This again turns out upon closer examination to mean among many psychologists that the answer to the problem is quite simple, and that philosophy has made itself much trouble over many unproductive and unreal problems. When we turn to ask what this simple and obvious answer is, we find persisting, without great alteration, a variety of answers prevalent in the nineteenth century, indeed, a number of them prevalent in the ancient world.

Similarly, Raymond A. Bauer (1952) writes,

> The theories of psychologists and prevailing political and social ideas act upon each other. The findings of psychological research carry political and social im-

plications and influence social and political ideas, just as social and political ideas influence the areas of interest of the psychologist and often condition his basic assumptions. . . . There can be no doubt, however, that the psychologists' theories of personality and the assumptions about human nature prevalent in society are related. (p. 3)

And he adds (p. 10), "The psychologist—usually unconsciously—adopts the assumptions of his culture as 'natural' or 'self-evident' truths."

Soviet personality theorists maintain that philosophical underpinnings must be made explicit. Otherwise, errors and biases creep in which vitiate theory and eventually lead to bad practice. Thus S. L. Rubinshtein writes, "One of the most important conditions for the successful development of psychology is a profound and penetrating analysis of theoretical questions" (Rubinshtein, 1957, p. 264).

Soviet personality theorists also insist that the basic philosophical problems of psychology must be solved before experimental work can get underway. "Experimental investigation is blind unless its course is illumined by theory. If theory is despised it always takes a cruel revenge; the abandonment of theory usually means the dominance of bad theory" (Rubinshtein, cited in Payne, 1968, p. 167).

Soviet personality theorists make certain to distinguish their materialist philosophic position from "vulgar" or "mechanistic" materialism, and they often discuss in detail the meaning of their philosophy, which includes dialectical and historical materialism. (See Assertion 1 below.)

HISTORY

Precursors

Historiographers of Soviet personality theory generally cite M. V. Lomonosov (1711-1765) as the earliest precursor of materialist personality theory. He interpreted sensations in a materialistic-mechanistic way, as a combination of physiological particles ordered according to mechanical laws. Lomonosov manifested "a profoundly progressive approach, in which he clearly recognized the enormous significance of speech and of verbal communication among people in the development and vicissitudes of human personality" (Boryagin, 1957, p. 163.)

The tradition of materialism in the study of human personality was continued by three professors at Moscow University. One was Ye. O. Mukhin (1766-1850), whose scientific *Weltanschauung* was that the material world is real and knowable:

Nature does not hide anything. She expresses everything significant by signals. We discover and determine these signals through the appropriate use of our developed sense organs. Of course, there are many things in nature which we cannot grasp because of the grossness of our perceptions: for example, gravity, the forces of centripetal and centrifugal force, magnetism, etc. But no one doubts that these natural forces indeed exist, because we all clearly see their effects. (Shumilin, 1957, p. 288)

A second member of this troika was I. Ye. Dyad'kovskii (1784-1841), who, along with Mukhin, formulated the concept of *nervism* (the central nervous system is *the* regulator and coordinator of all the other bodily systems). This concept later became a central theme of the work of Pavlov. Dyad'kovskii wrote:

> We know that the higher (i.e., central) nervous system has connections with all the other systems, and directly merges into the material of these systems, which are subordinated to it, such as the muscular, circulatory, reproductive, absorptive, and cellular. Hence we see that any change in the subordinate system can easily produce a change in the higher system. (1830, p. 194)

A third precursor of Soviet materialist thinking in psychology was A. M. Filomafitskii (1807-1849), who enunciated a principle which later became a fundamental tenet of Soviet materialist personality theory: the unbreakable connection of thought to speech. He wrote, "Animals cannot form words, not because they lack the necessary organs, but because they have nothing to say" (Filomafitskii, 1836, p. 90).

Related to these outstanding physicians-physiologists-psychologists were a number of Russian clinicians who were interested in the psychological treatment of somatic illnesses and are credited by Soviet historians as the founders of scientific psychotherapy. Thus, Lebedinskii (1971) writes:

> The most distinguished representatives of Russian medicine and physiology did extraordinarily much for the development of psychotherapeutic ideas. The tendency to take full account of the psychic aspect of any illness was characteristic of the foremost figures of Russian medicine. The scientific understanding of the role of the psyche in the causation, progression, and treatment of diseases was actively developed for almost two centuries. In Russia, as nowhere else, the most prominent figures in general medicine directly developed psychotherapy and advocated its use. In 1794, Skiadan, who was profoundly influenced by Lomonosov, refuted the pronouncements of many authorities of his day, and pointed to the cerebral cortex as "the abode of the soul." Skiadan noted that passions of the spirit may produce both a harmful and a beneficent effect on the organism, and he cited case histories of patients with various somatic illnesses who were cured by psychic influences. (p. 75)

I. M. Sechenov (1829-1905), known as "the father of Russian physiology" in his classical work *Reflexes of the Brain* (1863, p. 106), stated that "all acts of conscious and unconscious life are reflexes by origin."

However, he was not really a reductionist who attempted to explain all psychic phenomena as due solely to reflex activity. In subsequent writings he distinguished between two classes of reflex: one in which "conscious feeling" plays no part (as in decerebrate frogs and unconscious humans), and another class in which:

> ...conscious feeling is an indispensable factor, determining now the beginning, now the course, now the end of every act. Take, for instance, the evacuation of the bladder and of the rectum determined by the urge to urinate and defecate.... It is owing to the will that the actions of man are not machine-like, especially in the higher stages of psychical development. (Sechenov, 1904, pp. 344–345)

Another significant current in Russian philosophical and psychological thinking was contributed by a group of major 19th-century philosopher-writer-activists. Pavlov (1904) writes in his autobiography that he and his comrades were influenced by these thinkers to adopt an interest in the natural sciences.

One member of this group, V. G. Belinskii (1811-1848), stressed the special importance of social influences in the development of personality. A. I. Herzen (1812-1870) espoused materialist monism but maintained that the psychic processes, although derived from material physiological processes, were qualitatively distinct and were not reducible to physiology. Herzen viewed personality basically as the resultant of physiological and historical necessity and repudiated freedom of the will. N. G. Chernishevskii (1828-1889) contended that human sensations impart to the personality a knowledge of the real material world, which has objective existence. N. A. Dobroliubov (1836-1861) viewed psychic processes as reflections from material objects existing in the external world and regarded them as being produced by the activity of the cerebral hemispheres. He considered sociohistorical factors, rather than biological factors, to be primary in personality development. Character traits were acquired, he taught, as a result of sociocultural and historical influences, rather than by inherent, genetic or biological factors.

Another basic element in the development of Soviet personality theory consisted of the writings of the "Classics of Marxism," Karl Marx, Friedrich Engels, and V. I. Lenin. Soviet personality theorists would agree with the following formulation by V. N. Myasishchev (1958), a leading exponent of Soviet materialist personality theory:

> Without a scientific, materialist psychology, it is impossible to solve the problem of psychogenesis and psychotherapy. Modern Soviet psychology is developing on the foundation of the general theory of dialectical and historical materialism and on the foundation of the teachings of I. P. Pavlov. It takes as its point of departure the sociohistorical and natural historical understanding of

man....Man is not only an object, but a subject, whose consciousness reflects reality and at the same time transforms it. (pp. 7–8)

Beginnings

Present-day Soviet personality theory is the result of contributions by six individuals: Makarenko, Pavlov, Rubinshtein, Vygotskii, Myasishchev, and Uznadze.

Anton Semyonovich Makarenko (1888-1939) has had the greatest impact on Russian personality theory and practice. His major work, *The Road to Life—an Epic of Education* (1933-35), as well as his other publications are cited in practically all Soviet writings on personality development and in books on education and pedagogical manuals.

In 1920, at 32, Makarenko had the challenging assignment of rehabilitating children made homeless by the 1917 revolution and the civil war. In the course of his successful work in rehabilitating young delinquents, he developed a set of theories about personality development and character building which became keystones for Soviet personality research and educational practices. Makarenko stated the essence of his principle as follows: "To make the greatest possible demands of each person and to show the greatest possible respect for each person." He enunciated his system of the upbringing of the collective and of the individual personality as "the pedagogy of parallel influence."

In 1888, Ivan Petrovich Pavlov (1849-1936) began a study of the physiology of digestion in healthy, intact animals. He elucidated the neuromechanisms regulating digestive activity and the dependence of digestive activity on the nature of the ingested substances. In 1904, he received the Nobel Prize for this work.

In his experiments with the salivary response to foods, Pavlov observed a phenomenon which at first he considered a nuisance—the dog salivated not only in response to the introduction of food into its mouth, but also to a variety of neutral stimuli which coincided temporally with feeding. A systematic study of this learning process led to Pavlov's formulation of unconditioned and conditioned reflexes. Eventually, Pavlov formulated a conditioned-reflex theory, according to which all psychic activity of animals and man is due to the activity of the cerebral hemispheres and of the nearest underlying subcortical structures. The basic unit of this psychic activity is the neural reflex arc, involving three parts: (1) the receptors (or, as Soviet psychophysiologists call them, "the analyzers") and afferent nerves, (2) the central nervous system, and (3) the efferent nerves and effectors, such as the voluntary musculature.

In his experimental work with dogs, Pavlov arrived at the following hypotheses about human personality: Unconditioned, biologically fixed reflexes are mediated by subcortical structures and by the spinal cord. These structures can therefore be regarded as the seat of the instincts. The infant, having available a limited number of such inborn, "instinctual" responses in reaction to a few specific stimuli, has a limited capacity to adapt to its environment and is therefore dependent on others. As it grows and develops, the infant begins to elaborate an increasing number of conditioned reflexes which involve the cerebral cortex, resulting in a progressive enhancement of its ability to adapt to environmental changes.

A new element is decisive for personality development: the elaboration of the "second signal system"—human speech. Pavlov (1941) described two distinct systems of stimuli, or "signals" as effective in elaborating conditioned reflexes. The first is the direct sensing of objects and the second is speech.

Pavlov attributed maladaptive behavior to a breakdown in the responsiveness of reflex activity to changes in external reality. By manipulating the environment he was able to produce experimental neuroses in dogs. He later applied these laboratory findings to the study of human patients.

Another basic contribution by Pavlov to personality theory is his study of individual differences in dogs, which ultimately led to conjectures about individual differences in humans. He discovered that experimental animals differed in terms of the ease with which conditioned reflexes were established, the rapidity with which they could be extinguished, and also the ease with which experimental neuroses could be induced. He then classified "types of higher nervous activity." By "type," Pavlov meant a definite complex of fundamental properties of higher nervous activity, resulting from a blend of congenital and acquired characteristics. Experimental work in which puppies from the same litter were subjected to different methods of rearing convinced Pavlov that in this blend of the congenital and acquired, the latter characteristics were decisive.

Sergei Leonidevitch Rubinshtein (1889-1960) contributed more than any other psychologist toward a philosophical integration of dialectical materialism and Pavlovian psychophysiology. In 1935 he had published his first effort at a rounded, integrated formulation of the new Soviet psychology and personality theory, *Fundamentals of General Psychology*. This effort was refined with the publication of his most important work, *Foundations of General Psychology* (1940), in which he enunciated the basic principles of the application of dialectical materialism to the theory of personality. (These will be described in Assertion 1.)

Lev Semyonovich Vygotskii (1896-1934) had an extremely fruitful career as an original thinker and experimenter in personality theory, and his work has been continued by two distinguished pupils, A. R. Luria (1902-1978) and A. A. Leontiev (1903-   ). Vygotskii is credited with originating the sociohistorical origin theory of higher mental functions in man and being the first to demonstrate the Marxist thesis of the sociohistorical nature of human consciousness.

Vladimir Nikolayevich Myasishchev (1893-1973) made major contributions to the study of personality and to medical psychology. He was the founder of the "Leningrad School" of pathogenetic psychotherapy, which treats neuroses by elucidating those psychological causes of the illness of which the patient is unaware.

One major contribution of Myasishchev was his detailed study of the role of interpersonal relations in personality development. A second major contribution to personality theory was his study of the role of the patient's personality in the development of mental illness and an emphasis on restructuring the patient's personality in the course of psychotherapy.

Dmitrii Nikolayevich Uznadze (1886-1950) who contributed highly original work on *The Psychology of Set* (1949) found many followers in Georgia, and *Set* has become almost the exclusive preoccupation and domain of Georgian psychologists. For many years little was known abroad (or even in the Soviet Union) about the work of Uznadze and the Georgian school, because their research were published exclusively in the Georgian language.

Current Status

Present-day Soviet personality theory continues to draw heavily on "the heritage of Makarenko," the philosophical works of the "classics" of Marxism, and the conditioned-reflex theory of Pavlov. In practice, the emphasis is mainly on pedagogy. The majority of Soviet personality theorists have been associated with pedagogical institutes and the Academy of Pedagogical Sciences of the U.S.S.R. and of the Russian Soviet Federated Socialist Republic.

However, beginning in the late 1950s (apparently in connection with the "thaw" which followed the denunciation of the cult of Stalin), there has been a progressive expansion of personality studies into areas other than pedagogy and a broadening of theoretical and experimental bases. Concomitantly, there is an increasing willingness to acknowledge that the teachings of Makarenko, Marx, and Pavlov, while seminal, are not in themselves sufficient to cover so complex a phenomenon as human personality.

More and more voices are heard expressing dissatisfaction with the present state of Soviet personality theory:

> Although the term "personality" is frequently used, it is not adequately defined and is often used as a synonym for consciousness, or self-awareness, or "set," or for the psyche as a whole. (Bozhovich, 1968, p. 131)
>
> [This symposium] has demonstrated that in this problem [of personality theory] there are vaguenesses and slipshod definitions of personality; there remain discrepancies and contradictions. (Banshchikov, Rokhlin, & Shorokhova, 1971, p. 33)

The expanding interest in a many-sided study of personality has been demonstrated in recent years in the publication of a number of books and monographs devoted exclusively to problems of personality. (Bozhovich, 1968; Kon, 1967; Kovalev, 1965; Kovalev & Myasishchev, 1957; Myasishchev, 1960; Tugarinov, 1965.)

Indicative of the active interest in personality research was a three-day All-Union Symposium on Problems of Personality held in Moscow in 1970. Under the auspices of the Institute of Philosophy of the Academy of Sciences of the U.S.S.R. and the All-Union Society of Neuropathologists and Psychiatrists, 600 participants from all parts of the Soviet Union met to discuss: (1) personality as an interdisciplinary research problem, (2) philosophical and psychological aspects, (3) medicobiological aspects.

As a basis for discussion at this symposium, a two-volume work containing the latest researches on personality was published (Banshchikov, Rokhlin, & Shorokhova, 1969, 1970). The proceedings of the symposium were published in 1971 (Banshchikov et al., 1971). These three volumes give the most complete overview of the current status of personality theory in the Soviet Union. A survey of the views of the more than 70 discussants leads to the conclusion that they probably agree with Gardner Murphy's summing-up of the present status of personality theory, East *and* West: "Since the data-taking can never be complete, and since the perspectives constantly change with the advent of new methods, current personality theories cannot be regarded as anywhere near complete or exhaustive" (Murphy & Kovach, 1972, p. 429).

Similar Theories

Although Soviet historiographers emphasize philosophical materialism in Russian personality theory, dating back to Lomonosov in the early 18th century, there was also, at the time of the 1917 revolution, an influential current of philosophical idealism. The most influential idealist personality theorist was G. I. Chelpanov (1862-1939), who regarded the spirit as independent of matter. Chelpanov and fellow idealists developed experimental techniques for studying "spiritual" properties of personality. They maintained that the world was perceived by the soul, aided by the brain (Chelpanov, 1915). This school of thought included the distinguished personality theorists N. N. Lange (1858-1921), founder of one of the first psychology laboratories in Russia (Lange, 1893).

After the 1917 revolution, the majority of the younger personality theorists set themselves the task of developing a new Soviet psychology of personality. Since Marxism contends that all aspects of a society, including its science, are based upon economic relationships and that science serves the interests of the ruling class, these personality theorists had to free themselves of bourgeois influences to found a science of personality which would reflect the interests of the new "ruling class," the working people. Thus science was to serve the new society and the "new Soviet man": "From the beginning of the Soviet regime, it was recognized that the remaking of human personality was an integral part of the social, political, and economic revolution that Bolshevism represented" (Bauer, 1952, p. 80). The unlimited plasticity of the human personality, even at a mature and advanced age, was assumed, and there was heavy emphasis on those areas of personality theory applicable to child rearing and education, vocational guidance, motivation of workers, improvements in industrial productivity, and the mental health of the "toiling masses."

Soviet personality theorists had to concern themselves with the special psychological problems of revolutionary transition and with depicting the new Soviet man "so that the superiority of the socialist order can be made evident to all" (Wortis, 1950, p. 24). This was clearly a tall order, and in their enthusiasm, Soviet personality theorists welcomed all theories which gave promise of fulfilling these tasks.

From 1917 to 1929, numerous schools of personality theories, with wide-ranging experimentation and a search for new approaches to personality theory, emerged. Although suspicious of bourgeois psychology, Soviet personality theorists were open to all new "progressive" trends that were critical of the "European bourgeois psychology." Thus behaviorism was hailed as materialist, and John B. Watson (1927) was invited to write an article for the *Great Soviet Encyclopedia* (2nd ed., 1949). Gestalt psychology also was welcomed because its concept of holism was considered compatible with the philosophy of dialectical materialism. In the early 1920s, Soviet psychologists considered psychoanalysis "progressive"—a methodological application of historical materialism—and young personality theorists of the day wrote laudatory articles about it (Reisner, 1923, 1925; Bykhovskii, 1923; Petrovskii, 1967, p. 87).

Acrimonious Soviet polemics were carried on against the still influential idealist psychologists and Wundtians. When G. I. Chelpanov was deposed from his position as head of the Institute of Psychology and replaced by N. N. Kornilov (1879-1957), the event marked the demise of idealism in Soviet personality theory. The personality theories that survived in the 1920s were marked by an extreme mechanistic interpretation of Marxism, such as the *reactology*, elaborated by Kornilov, which became the dominant personality theory of the early 1920s. In 1926, Kornilov wrote a *Textbook of Psychology from the Standpoint of Dialectical Materialism*, in which he tried to synthesize the various concepts which then prevailed in personality theory throughout the world and to put them under the aegis of a Marxist materialist philosophy. His (1921) studies of the relationship between intensity of reactions and reaction time opened the way for the later Pavlovian investigations of the signaling functions of sensations.

Two other trends in the development and application of Soviet personality theory were psychotechnics and pedology. They flourished during the twenties and early thirties but were later rejected as being too mechanistic. Both resulted in theoretical and practical contributions to the later development of Soviet personality theory, however.

Psychotechnics is analogous to Western industrial psychology and was emphasized because work was looked upon as a central element in life. S. L. Rubinshtein (1940), for example, said: "For us man is defined primarily not by his relationship to his possessions, but by his relationship to his work." *Pedology*, the science of childhood, attempted to synthesize, through a study of "age syndromes," the anatomical, physiological, and psychological characteristics of the child. On the basis of his experimental work with school children, P. P. Blonskii (1935) concluded that thought comes about directly as a result of the child's activities: "Thought is not a priori activity, and cannot emerge from an empty intellect." Many of Blonskii's theoretical formulations and practical applications were later repudiated, but his work on the theory of behavior became the foundation for the cultural-historical concepts of personality later elaborated by Vygotskii.

In the middle 1930s, psychotechnics and pedology were severely criticized by the Communist Party as being "pseudo-scientific and anti-Marxist." The pedologists were accused by the Central Committee of carrying "pseudoscientific experiments, and numberless investigations on pupils and their parents in the form of senseless and harmful questionnaires, tests, etc., long since condemned by the Party" (Resolution of the Central Committee, 1936 (1950). The Central Committee also condemned the so-called two-factor theory, which holds that human personality is determined by heredity and environment, stating that this "law" was a heritage of bourgeois pedology. Instead, it enunciated a "three-factor theory" which stated that personality development is determined by inheritance, environment, and *vospitaniye*, a Russian word for which there is no exact English equivalent but which subsumes upbringing in the family, education and upbringing in the school, and training at work.

Later there was added the element of *samovospitaniye*, self-upbringing. In the struggle against the concept of the "all-powerful influence of the environment," it was maintained, the environment is changed by the child, who enters into active relationships with it and thereby alters its influence (Leontiev, cited in Bauer, 1952, p. 149). This concept became known as autogenetic movement (*samodvizheniye*). According to this concept, "a man takes part in the shaping of his own character, and he himself bears a responsibility for that character" (Rubinshtein, 1940, p. 475). In the process of development, new internal conditions for self-development are gradually created (Kostiuk, cited in Bauer, 1952, p. 149). Self-training comes about as the individual develops ideals and a definite image of the lifestyle he will adopt. For this reason, ideology and "communist morality" are intrinsic parts of education in the Soviet Union. The individual is taught to aid in molding himself to a "correct" lifestyle through self-encouragement and constantly practicing those traits of character he is trying to develop in himself (Selivanov, cited in Bauer, 1952, p. 149).

Soviet personality theorists contend that not only can the child be shaped from birth but that the human being remains plastic as an adult and can continue to shape his character even at a mature age, provided he is equipped with an adequate ideological picture of himself and the world. According to Rubinshtein:

> The early years of childhood play an essential role in the development of character. However, the Freudian notion that character is fixed in early childhood is erroneous. This error arises from the failure to understand the role of consciousness in character development. Man takes an active part in reshaping his own character to the extent that it is related to a Weltanschauung....(1940, p. 475)

Reflexology played a significant role in the development of personality theory in the 1920s. Initiated by V. M. Bekhterev (1857-1927), he tried to study objectively the effect of physical, biological, and social factors on psychic functioning by recording external reactions of the individual, such as facial expressions, gestures, and speech, and relating them to the provoking stimuli. He maintained that all psychic phenomena, conscious and unconscious, must be made manifest sooner or later by external behavior, and therefore it should be possible to investigate them by purely objective observations of behavior.

Bekhterev (1907, 1917, 1921) expressed an extreme reductionist, mechanistic view, positing that mental and physiological phenomena represent a single neural process and that consciousness and conscious activity are manifestations of neural energy or neural electricity, as also manifested in heavenly bodies and animate and inanimate organisms. He postulated that psychic processes resulted from tension which accumulated when the current of neural electricity encountered obstacles and was "detained."

Bekhterev investigated the reflex responses of voluntary musculature in humans. He noted that reflexes are elicited not only by adequate stimuli (for example, electric shock for retraction of the finger) but also by "associated stimuli." Bekhterev suggested that the complex behavior of human beings consisted of the compounding of these associated motor reflexes, and that thought processes depended on the inner activities of the musculature of speech, essentially a complex associated reflex: "Thought is an inhibited reflex...."

During the 1920s, Bekhterev's reflexology was more influential in Russia than the similar work of Pavlov. After Bekhterev's death in 1927, however, the influence of his work declined. The Second All-Union Conference of Marxist-Leninist Research Institutes concluded that reflexology was "a

revisionist trend which deviated from the true Marxist-Leninist position"
(Editorial, 1929).

ASSERTIONS

Soviet personality theorists attach great importance to explicit statements of
the philosophical basis on which personality theory is founded. Therefore,
in this chapter we begin with the relationship of mind and matter before
proceeding to specific personality theory assertions.

1. Psychic processes are a function of the brain.

This crucial statement of the philosophical-materialist point of view means
that mental phenomena derive from, and are subordinate to material processes. Matter is primary to, and exists independently of, any perceiving
mind. The external material world is real and would continue to exist even if
there were no mind to perceive it.

This philosophical-materialist concept opposes philosophical idealism,
which holds that mental processes are primary and that human beings can
be sure only of their own perceptions. In this concept, sensations, perceptions, thought, consciousness, and other mental processes derive from, and
are dependent on, material reality in two ways: (1) they are a product of
matter in motion, that is, of the various physical processes which take place
in the central nervous system, and (2) their contents are a reflection of the
external material reality.

To understand mental processes, according to the philosophical-
materialist view, the psychologist must study cerebral processes and must
take into account the objective reality these mental processes reflect: both
the material environment and the social environment—the history and
traditions of a given society, its economic organization, class structure, and
ideology. However, psychic processes and consciousness are *not* merely an
epiphenomenon. The psyche actively interacts with external reality, in the
process of which it is modified but also actively changes the environment. In
addition, human consciousness can voluntarily produce changes in itself,
thus promoting progressive development of its own personality (the principles of *samodvizheniye* and *samovospitaniye*—autogenetic movement and
self-upbringing—discussed above).

This leads to the principle of the unity and interaction of consciousness
and activity. Consciousness is formed in practical activity (most significantly, to the Soviets, in social labor). Since consciousness is revealed in the
course of activity, it can therefore best be studied in that course. Furthermore, changes in the form and content of practical activity produce changes
in the organization and development of mental processes. This leads to em-

phasis on upbringing and education as decisive influences on personality development and on collective living and work as decisive in the maintenance of desirable personality development in adults.

Development

2.   From the moment of birth, the child is a social being.

Because of the infant's helplessness, all its relationships to the environment have to be mediated by an adult. Every need of the infant is a need for another human being—that is, a social need. The adult becomes, for the infant, the psychological center of every situation, and consequently the child develops a need for communication as the most important factor in his psychic development.

3.   New stimuli are the infant's most important primal need.

N. M. Shchelovanov (1960) states that this need appears during the first month of life. The absence of stimuli, even if the infant is healthy, well-fed, and well-attended, will provoke crying which can only be stilled by presenting new stimuli. He explains that anatomical and functional development of the brain requires stimuli to provoke it into activity, for, as is true for all organs, it only develops properly through functioning.

4.   Psychic development is a genuine process of autogenous movement.

The need for stimulation emerges as the inner core of the process of psychic development, rather than being due to outside stimulating forces, as would be the case if other primal needs were to be considered the leading ones. This concept of the social nature of development, and those needs that stimulate the infant's psychic development (the need for stimuli and for communication and activity), depicts the psychological aspect of the infant differently from those theories that give primacy to the infant's biological needs and drives. If the primary need of the infant is stimulation, then the infant represents a being completely turned toward the outside world and constantly in need of its stimulation to bring him joy or satisfaction. Knowledge of the outside world is thus necessary for life in the infant and more required than the satisfaction of any other need.

In this view the needs for knowledge and for communication are also primary in all other stages of psychic development. In every stage these needs acquire a different content, a different structure, and a different embodiment in the behavior and activity of the individual. And at every age level, there is a specific functional complex of needs and strivings, which are genetically related to the primal needs of the child. This complex finds expression in forms of behavior and activity which are specific for individuals of that particular age.

5. *The second signal system has a basic significance in personality development.*

In animals, connection among stimuli occurs on the level of the first signal system, and for that reason it can lead, at most, to the formation of reflexes of only the second or third order. However, because man possesses the second signal system—speech—he is able to establish long series of associations. As a result of these he can be active in areas only remotely related to stimuli which have a direct, vital significance for the organism. This explains why unconditioned reflexes (i.e., the primitive, primal drives) rarely determine the behavior of man. Rather, it is determined by signals far removed from primal drives, because conditioned reflexes are produced in response to signals which are remote but still sufficiently significant to be effective. For animals, temporary associations are based on biologically significant stimuli; in man, influences of a social nature become "personally significant."

The presence of the second signal system brings a new principle into the higher nervous activity of man and determines the new character of man's interrelationships with the environment. It leads to another important function: because it permits generalization and systematization of experience, man can behave not only actively but also consciously, on the basis of his understanding of the social significance of his actions. This qualitatively distinguishes the conditional, temporary connections or associations of man from animal behavior. Speech enables man not only to adapt to the conditions of life but also to change them.

These concepts of the second signal system bring into personality theory consideration of the real needs, motivations, interests, and strivings of man as a determining factor in his psychic life. They elucidate the conscious activity of man, its sources, and its significance.

6. *Adults are the major factor in the child's early personality development.*

During early childhood, the support and approval of the adult is seen as essential for the child's "equilibrium" with its environment and for his emotional well-being. This powerful social need induces the child to behave in ways for which he does not feel a direct need but which are likely to gain desired adult-parental approval. Consequently, "sanctions" by adults are both important regulators of the child's behavior and stimuli for his moral development.

Cognitive activity progressively increases during early childhood. Walking extends the child's spatial and motor range; by mastering speech, his learning is no longer restricted to his own direct, personal experiences. The ever-increasing and complex cognitive activity which accompanies growth, even in the absence of systematic teaching or obligation to work, leads to a specific activity, roleplaying or creative play. This activity satisfies the basic requirements for the psychic development of the child: the needs for communication and for practical activity. Play gives the child an opportunity, in the "pretend" situation, to engage in those activities that, while attractive, are not yet accessible to him in reality. Thus play leads to learning and eventual mastery of more advanced forms of behavior. Play also gives the child the opportunity to maintain direct contact with adults, entering, on a level of pretending, into their world and considering their relationships, and interests. Since play embodies the age-appropriate development of needs, it is seen as the principal activity through which the preschool child masters the adult culture.

The direct connection of play with the satisfaction of the child's needs makes possible its use in education and upbringing. By converting the demands of adults and parents into the goal of the child's play, the need to fulfill these demands is evoked in the child. In this way, play can be employed as a specific technique for translating adult demands into the child's own need—a precondition for the child's fulfilling adult demands and making them his own.

7. *The peer group becomes increasingly crucial in personality development.*

Starting school at age seven marks a turning point in the social development of the child. He has new rights and obligations and for the first time begins to engage in socially significant activity. Soviet researchers find that toward the end of the preschool period, the child develops an insistent desire to go to school. The major needs of the child, cognition and social communication, take the form of a wish to fulfill important, socially significant activities which have value not only for the child but also for the adults around him. This results in a rapid formation of various personality traits essential for the successful fulfillment of school obligations.

In school, the teacher is an influential authority, while the child's association with his peers assumes ever-greater significance. Toward the end of the early school period, at about age 11, the child's need for approval of his peers becomes stronger than his need for adult approval. This new, overriding role of the peer collective creates significant changes in the child's social situation and prepares him for transition to adolescence.

In adolescence the demands and opinions of the peer collective become the most important factor in psychic development. Typically, the adolescent wishes to win acknowledgment and to gain and maintain a position of authority among his comrades. This creates a vividly expressed need to respond to peer demands as well as possible. In this situation, if the adult upbringer succeeds in becoming the senior member of the collective, the moral norms he presents will be adopted by the collective, thus ensuring that the development of the children's personality will accord with the norms of the adults. If, however, adult demands are imposed from without, by external pressure, the members of the collective will tend to resist them, and on this foundation there can develop wrong norms of behavior which have a negative effect on the formation of personality.

Association with peers and comparison of self with others result in the most important aspect of the psychic development of adolescence: the development of self-awareness. The adolescent manifests a great interest in his own personality and in demonstrating and evaluating his potentials. As a result, he develops a relatively stable self-appraisal and level of aspirations, and these give rise to a new need—the need to reach the level of the demands of those around him as well as of his own demands and self-appraisal. If the adolescent is unable to fulfill these aspirations, he experiences acute suffering, and his demands of himself become a new factor in his social personality development. Thus, a correct balance between the adolescent's aspirations, his self-assessment, and his potentials is decisive for his emotional well-being and his further development.

Another factor during adolescence is the gap between the adolescent's objective situation and inner position, between his psychic development and real-life opportunities. This gives rise to a striving to break out of the limitations of school and to be included in the life and activity of adults. Psychologists generally designate this trait as a striving for adulthood, for independence, and for self-affirmation. When these strivings are frustrated, suffering typical for this age group and conflicts within self or with others result. Research by T. Ye. Konnikova (cited in Bozhovich, 1968, p. 434) indicated that when there are opportunities for the adolescent to participate in the adult collective and to engage in socially valuable work, this not only eliminates sufferings and conflicts but produces an upsurge of vital activity, evokes positive life experiences, and stimulates creativity.

Assertions 6 and 7 are considered crucial by Soviet personality theorists because of their insistence on the preeminence of the social environment in determining the course of personality development and their repudiation of those personality theories (particularly psychoanalysis) that attribute primacy to instinctual, unconscious, irrational forces within the individual.

8. *Sexual maturation is an important factor in personality development in adolescence.*

Soviet personality theorist I. S. Kon (1967) states that in the process of sexual maturation, the adolescent begins to experience erotic needs. But this need and the need for emotional closeness with another person are not yet unified; eroticism is directed toward a member of the opposite sex and closeness to a peer of the same sex, because of common experiences.

The fantasies of the adolescent about love, Kon continues, are also contradictory. On the one hand, the adolescent fantasies a sublime, "pure" love in which there is nothing base or petty. On the other hand, conceptions of the physical side of love, which are largely drawn from vulgar anecdotes and are "reinforced" by masturbation experiences, seem appealing but also somewhat dirty. This dichotomy is further reinforced by lectures on moral themes by unqualified persons which are limited to the statement that sexual attraction is in contrast to romantic love: a variation on the theme of divine love versus carnal sin. The essence (and basic difficulty) of sexual maturation involves the psychological and practical overcoming of this false dichotomy.

The psychophysiological and the moral reality—the down-to-earth quality of individual love, with its intensity, vividness, and drama—is to be discovered not by moralizing phrases but by a rigorously scientific analysis of the physical aspect of love. Kon states that while there are unclear areas and theoretical difficulties in knowledge of sexual maturation, one thing is undeniable: the degree of gratification experienced in the process of sexual activity is in direct relationship to the depth of feelings. While social maturity presupposes sexual maturity, mature sexuality presupposes social-psychological maturity, which the individual achieves as the cumulative result of prolonged development and interaction with others. According to Kon (1967, p. 157, ff.):

> There is no full correspondence between these two aspects. The development of the human personality is contradictory. Not in vain does Erikson call his schema a utopia, emphasizing the difficulty of its realization. It is not only that the stages of sexual and social development may not coincide in time, but not infrequently a person who has been crippled by incorrect upbringing will prove incapable of deep and all-enveloping love; and this aspect of his life will perforce be limited to less perfected forms. However, this may not prevent him from being a useful member of society, nor from achieving outstanding successes in his chosen field. Likewise, the talent for loving may, in certain cases, be the only and exclusive gift possessed by an individual, subordinating to itself all his other qualities. We know nothing about the breadth of the socio-political horizons of Juliet, but this fourteen-year-old girl symbolizes for us all of the beauty of romantic love. People differ, and one must not try to include all under one category, and then blame them for a disharmony, of which they themselves, without knowing it, are victims. However, it is essential to strive for harmoniousness, and this striving the older generation hands on to the younger one. (p. 157 ff.)

The above assertion is as far as Soviet personality theorists are willing to go, at present, in acknowledging the role of sexuality and sexual conflicts in personality development.

9. *Personality traits of Soviet adolescents differ from non-Soviet adolescents.*

Soviet researchers maintain that the character traits traditionally attributed to the adolescent by Western observers—for example, that continuous sense of isolation attributed to the discovery by the adolescent of his own self and his experiencing of himself as a unique individual—are absent in Soviet youth. Instead, these young people report episodic but not continuous feelings of loneliness. The distinction between this kind of loneliness and the traditional descriptions of adolescent isolation is illustrated in the following statement by a Soviet adolescent girl:

> Nikolenka [the hero of L. N. Tolstoy's classic story, "Childhood, Adolescence, and Youth"] was lonely because he considered himself better than others, and could not include himself into any group of comrades. According to his viewpoint, some were beneath him, others he shunned because he felt inferior. I don't understand this. I sometimes feel lonely, when I quarrel with someone, or when I'm convinced that something is being hidden from me, which means that they don't like me. Everybody knows something, and I do not. It is so vexing! And sometimes you feel lonely because it seems that everybody has forgotten you. Then you feel sad and you want to cry. (Bozhovich, 1968, p. 357)

For Soviet personality theorists, such a statement illustrates the thesis that the experience of loneliness in Soviet adolescents is fundamentally different; these feelings are episodic and concretely based, rather than chronic, and are not the result of dissatisfaction with reality and a wish to retreat from it but instead stem from occasions in which the need for communication with the peer collective is not concretely gratified. Episodic loneliness occurs in adolescence because that is when one most intensely experiences the need to be (and to feel that one is) a member of a collective. At this age constant participation in the life of the collective, actual communication with comrades, and common, practical activity are needed. The adolescent may experience an acute feeling of loneliness in circumstances when, for reasons often connected with excessive sensitivity, he feels temporarily excluded from the collective.

10. *Formation of a scientific and moral world view is crucial for adjustment in postadolescence.*

The tasks the postadolescent sets for himself are joined into a unified system and embodied in a moral model. These tasks are stimuli for his behavior and also fulfill the function of organizing his other needs and aspirations. The resultant world view represents a significant qualitative change in the psychic development of the postadolescent.

Thus in postadolescence the motivational sphere becomes the decisive factor in personality development. In the course of the individual's development, needs increase in number, are enriched, and become sources for the development of new needs. As in all other psychic processes, primal needs change to mediated needs, which then acquire a conscious voluntary character. For the postadolescent, the moral world view organizes all motivations and resulting behavior.

The moral world view begins to be established long before postadolescence, however. It is determined in part by the development in the adolescent of ideal models whom the adolescent wishes to emulate. However, only in the postadolescent phase does the moral world view begin to represent a stable system of ideals and principles which becomes a continuously acting moral stimulus mediating her or his entire behavior.

11. *Socially desirable personality development is accomplished through social groups.*

Following the teaching of A. S. Makarenko and his thesis that the collective is the connecting link between the individual personality and society, Soviet personality theorists have conducted many researches investigating the influence of the collective on personality. They have given particular attention to those characteristics of the collective that have a desirable influence on personality development, the most important of which ensure for each person a definite place in the collective and an opportunity to demonstrate independence and self-reliance.

Many researchers have investigated the development of individual personality traits under the conditions of life and activity in the collective. The development of persistence was investigated by N. I. Sudakov (1950); of self-confidence, by F. I. Ivashchenko (1952); of setting high standards for the self, by A. A. Bodalev (1957). The researches of L. I. Bozhovich and her co-workers were concerned with how best to use the collective as a positive character builder. Special attention was directed to the impact of the collective on the structure of the personality, goal orientation, self-awareness, self-evaluation, and level of aspiration.

12. *Consciousness is formed and revealed through practical activity.*

Changes in practical activities can influence changes in the organization and development of mental processes: This is the principle of the unity of consciousness and behavior enunciated by Rubinshtein (1934). Soviet personality studies are aimed at organizing the life of the child so that his personality will develop in accordance with the aims of upbringing (*vospitaniye*). This task dictates a corresponding methodological principle: The laws of the formation of personality should be studied in the course of the actual conditions of upbringing. For this reason, the major research methods used are not nomothetic, but rather longitudinal observation, based on many-sided studies of individual children.

Another characteristic trait of Soviet research is that it is not limited to a passive observation of the developing child. Researchers strive actively to form desired character traits and qualities, to achieve certain desired goals based on specific psychological hypotheses. In accordance with this action-research conceptualization, one of the basic methods is the "transforming" experiment, which involves studying the personality of the child during the process of goal-directed upbringing. Research carried out in this way meets an important requirement of Soviet science—to guide those very processes whose laws of development are being investigated.

Kovalev (1949) describes how a classroom teacher who encounters undesirable behavior (shyness, impulsivity, rudeness), can achieve the reeducation of the child by employing appropriate pedagogical measures. The case histories cited demonstrate how negative character traits are produced by life situations and conditions of upbringing of the child, and also how a correctly structured pedagogical approach brings about positive results.

Maintenance

13. Personality means a certain level of psychic development.

In the process of achieving self-knowledge, the individual begins to perceive himself or herself as distinct from others. This level of psychic development is characterized by distinct outlooks and attitudes and particular moral values, as a result of which he becomes relatively stable and independent of influences alien to his own convictions. Having achieved this level of development, he has the ability to purposefully affect the surrounding reality, to change it to suit his purposes, and also to change himself.

The Soviet viewpoint holds that the person, as a completed personality, is capable of regulating his own behavior and actions, and to a certain extent, his own psychic development. When he has achieved that level of development where he can be called a personality, all psychic processes and functions, all qualities and properties have attained a specific structure. At the center of this structure are stable, dominant motivations which determine his hierarchical arrangement of needs. Such a level of development is achieved only in the adult personality.

14. The psyche is social in nature.

In Soviet psychology, personality is seen not as some kind of spiritual essence but as the product of sociohistorical development. The major determining condition for the maintenance of the personality is the place one occupies in the system of social relations and the activity one carries out within that system.

15. Man represents a product of historical development.

Only within the framework of a sociohistorical conception of personality is it possible to account for the distinctive features of personality in different historical epochs. Analyzing the development of the psyche in correlation with a particular epoch and its connection with the class struggle and the entire dynamic of the historical process make it clear not only that human personality depends upon the class to which an individual belongs but also that the psyches of the representatives of classes change as society changes.

Study of the development of personality (its interests, needs, tastes, aspirations and views) during the past century indicates how the representatives of different classes have undergone enormous personality changes. At the beginning of this century in Russia, the working man was still half peasant; later he became a proletarian, with an as-yet-dim social consciousness, and finally he became a revolutionary fighter. In the policy of the Communist Party, the working man in Soviet society is the conscious builder of a socialist society.

When personality is studied as a whole, changes in all interpersonal relationships can be noted. Although the abstractly studied functions seem unchangeable, the entire structure—the whole dynamic, the whole content of the personality—does change as a result of historicocultural change. In short, personality is a function of the society.

16.   Motivation assures maintenance of an integrated relationship to reality.

All a person's reactions, the entire structure of one's affective life, are determined by motivational properties of the personality which develop in the course of social experience. Vygotskii (1936) states, "Only pathology, only a personality disorder, can bring about a primitive reaction, which represents direct affective discharges which are not mediated by the complex structure of the personality" (p. 30).

This concept of personality characterizes the approach of Soviet psychologists to investigations of the formation and disintegration of personality. An important element is the study of the dependence of individual psychic processes on the needs and motivations which stimulate the individual to bring these processes about. The first to carry out such investigations were A. N. Leontiev (1948), A. V. Zaporozhetz (1948), and their collaborators (Zaporozhetz & El'konin, 1964). Later there emerged a significant number of facts demonstrating how individual psychic processes (for example, memory, or organization of behavior) are changed significantly by the motivations that stimulate them.

B. V. Zeigarnik (1965) writes, "In destroying the psychic activity of man, disease often changes precisely the personal component of man. For this reason, in analyzing psychopathological phenomena, we must take into consideration the disturbances in the personality of the patient, the changes in his orientation, his needs, his interests" (p. 9). Zeigarnik contrasts this point of view with another approach in which the psychopathological symptom is looked upon as a disturbance of individual psychic functions and this in turn is explained by the disturbance of physiological processes:

> And yet, the patient frequently has a memory-loss for certain material, precisely because of his changed attitude toward this material, and toward his activity with this material.... The pathological changes were in the motivational sphere, in the sphere of their attitude toward the activity to be carried out, and in their attitude toward others. These patients were profoundly indifferent to all that went on around them, to the consequences of their own activity, and this absence of a relationship produced their "forgetfulness." (1965, p. 10)

17. Distinctions must be made between meaning and significance.

This assertion derives directly from research about the role of motivation in maintaining an integrated relationship to reality. Motivation is determined by the significance to the individual of a given event or activity. Significance, then, is distinct from meaning.

Meaning denotes something *objective* in a phenomenon which can be observed in the system of its objective connections, relationships, and interaction. Significance, in contrast, denotes a *subjective* experience of the psyche. This concept derives directly from the Soviet formulation that the psyche is an adaptive instrument which is derivative from the material in two ways: its *processes* are a manifestation of the reflex activity of a material entity—the central nervous system—and its *content* is a reflection of material reality.

According to Pavlov, a conditioned reflex is formed only if reinforced by directly useful or directly harmful stimuli—that is, stimuli significant to the organism. Therefore, the mistake of associationism is its lack of understanding of the active principle in the formation of associative bonds. For the formation of a conditioned reflex, it is not sufficient that stimuli merely coincide in time. It is essential that one of them has significance; only then will other stimuli connected to it acquire significance.

18. Psychic activities are products of functional cortical systems.

Functional interacting systems of the cortex develop as a consequence of the organism's interactions with the environment. Damage to a localized area of the cortex need not produce permanent loss of a psychic function, because it is possible, by appropriate training, to organize a new functional cortical system which will successfully carry out the "lost" activity.

Over the years, A. R. Luria (1963, 1966, 1969, 1973) devised a series of tests of brain function, based on the hypothesis that "the brain, as the most complex, self-regulating system, consists of at least three basic organizations." The first, involving the reticular formation and brain stem, provides the tonus essential for the normal functioning of the higher areas of the cortex; the second involving the temporal, parietal, and occipital areas, ensures the reception, processing, and storage of information; the third, which occupies the frontal lobes, ensures the programming of movements and actions, the regulation of the appropriate succession of actions, and the comparison of the outcome of actions with the original intentions. The interaction of these three areas to produce a given behavior is a functional system. If there is impairment in a certain area, the disruption of a given behavior may or may not occur, depending on whether there is an alternative functional system which can take over. A program of rehabilitation may enable the impaired individual to learn to form alternative functional systems (Mironenko, 1977, p. 136).

Luria's test-battery enables the examiner to determine what functional system has been disrupted and to devise techniques for forming alternative functional systems. Soviet personality theorists believe that Luria's work confirms their optimistic assertion that the plasticity of the human brain makes it feasible to educate and reeducate people at all stages of their development and at all ages, including maturity and old age.

19.   *Work in, and for, the collective is essential for maintenance of a healthy personality.*

Soviet personality theorists maintain that love of work is essential for the emotional health of the "new Soviet man." It is understandable, they say, that under capitalism, where the worker is exploited, work cannot generally give the worker joy or pleasure. However, even in a society divided into antagonistic classes, there are individuals who find work a joyful need rather than merely an unhappy necessity, who see in work the meaning of their lives. Mainly, these people are involved in intellectual work and in the so-called free professions—artists, writers, musicians. People like Lomonosov, Darwin, and Tolstoy worked not for material gain but primarily under the pressure of filling a creative need. Tolstoy stated that he wrote because of an irresistible need to create and because of his awareness of the social significance of his work.

The emancipation of physical and intellectual work brought about by the October Revolution radically changed attitudes toward work, according to the Soviets, who maintain that the opportunity to work in accordance with one's abilities under conditions of comradely cooperation and mutual help gave birth to enthusiasm for work in the masses and the flowering of their creative abilities. They acknowledge that they have not yet achieved the ideal communist society, where the principle "from each according to his abilities, to each according to his needs" will become a reality and where work will be a primary life need. They quote Lenin (1963): "Communist work will be voluntary, without any consideration for reward; work as a habit for the common good, and as a conscious attitude (which becomes a habit), which recognizes the necessity to work for the common good; work as a basic need of the healthy organism'' (p. 199).

The psychological readiness to work in the Communist way has a complex structure which includes (1) consciousness of the social and personal meaningfulness of work; (2) the wish to work not only as a social duty, but also because of the love of work; and (3) the ability to work *po-kommunisticheski*, which means the ability to work in the collective, collectively, and in the interests of the whole collective. To satisfy these requirements, the mature, developed personality must possess the following qualities: (1) discipline, or the ability, consciously and responsibly, to relate to one's tasks; (2) collectivism, or the ability to give aid to one's comrades in the interests of achieving the goals and tasks of the collective; and (3) a creative attitude toward work, or not being content with what one has achieved but constantly striving to raise the productivity of labor by mastering greater skills.

20.   Human needs are of two kinds: immediate and mediated.

Human needs differ not only in content and dynamic properties (force, stability, mobility) but also in structure. Some needs have a direct, immediate character, and others are mediated by a long-range goal. The structure of needs determines how they stimulate action. For direct, immediate needs, the stimulus moves directly from the need to action and is related to the immediate desire to carry it out. This kind of stimulus is best represented by physiological needs. When there is a mediated structure of needs, the stimulus emanates from a consciously established purpose which may be in conflict with immediate desires. Mediated stimuli occur in cases where a powerful need cannot be directly satisfied but requires intermediate activities the individual may not have a direct ability to carry out immediately.

The presence of indirect needs (that is, of stimuli which originate from a consciously established purpose) characterizes that phase of development of the motivational sphere of the individual which makes it possible to consciously direct and regulate needs and strivings.

21.   The study of personality should not depend on tests and questionnaires.

The mechanistic approach to man, the subjective nature of the interpretation of the results, the attempt to ''study,'' by means of primitive and standardized techniques, an extremely complex object, quantifying personality traits and manifestations—all these factors, which are organically inherent in tests and questionnaires, have forced Soviet psychologists to reject once and for all this antiscientific method. (Krutetskii, 1962)

Soviet psychologists have established a number of principles for the scientific study of personality:

1. Character should be studied in an analytic-synthetic manner, with due regard for its wholeness.
2. Character can be studied only on the basis of objective data, that is, one should proceed from concrete reality, from man's behavior, and the motivations thus revealed.
3. Character can be studied only by taking into account the determining influences of external and internal conditions (conditions of life and upbringing, condition of the organism and its vital activity).
4. Character traits should be examined in their development and changes.
5. Individual personality can be studied only in the collective, through the collective, and against the background of the collective in which the personality is formed and developed.
6. Character should be studied on a plane involving plans for its development.

In addition, personality must be considered not only as an object of study but also as an object of upbringing; the study must have the practical purpose of controlling the processes of personality formation.

The basic method for studying character in Soviet psychology involves observation, under natural conditions, of the individual. The natural experiment usually assumes the form of an instructional or transforming experiment which combines a psychological study of the child with the bringing about of desired results. Laboratory experiments, biographical methods, talks, and an analysis of the products of activity are other research means. Usually several methods are combined, so that they supplement, correct, and control each other.

The late 1970s and the year 1980 have witnessed a significant broadening and deepening of the dialogue between Soviet and Western personality theorists, particularly on the subject of the unconscious. This culminated in the International Symposium on the Unconscious, held in Tbilisi under the auspices of the Georgian Academy of Sciences, in October 1979. The Symposium was attended by Soviet and Western personality theorists, including representatives of various school of psychoanalysis.

It is clear that there is disagreement among Soviet personality theorists. The views of the "anti-psychology" group were expressed in a paper by L. Kukuyev, in which he stated that "It is unscientific to consider the unconscious in dreams and psychopathology, and to do so is a manifestation of outmoded Freudian concepts." He also wrote that "the fact of wanting to elaborate a theory of the psychological unconscious amounts to an abstraction of neurology" (cited in Chertok, in press).

These assertions were responded to by an article by A. S. Prangishvill, A. Sheroziya, and F. V. Bassin, in *Voprisi Priskhologii, II* (1980), in which they stated that "an underestimation of the problem of the unconscious in Soviet psychology produces negative results. To ignore this problem is to hamper studies carried out in important areas of psychology. It is impossible to understand human behavior, creativity, psychosomatics, etc., without having studied the unconscious. The West has been studying the unconscious for a century, and it would be a grave mistake for Soviet psychology to turn its back on it" (cited in Chertok, in press).

The exchange of ideas on personality theory between East and West has by no means been a one-way street. Thus, a group of American neuropsychologists have found A. R. Luria's contributions on the investigation of cortical functions and restoration of function after brain injury to have great practical value (Luria, 1963, 1966, 1973). They have adapted Luria's test-battery and his rehabilitation techniques for use in the form of the Luria-Nebraska Test Battery (Golden, in press; Golden, Hammeke & Purisch, 1980).

It can be seen, then, that the exchange of information between East and West in the area of personality theory is mutually beneficial.

Summary

The above assertions have led Soviet personality theorists to optimistic conclusions about the individual's relationship to the physical and social environment and to self, and about the future:

1. An individual can know the true nature of the material and social environment, and the true nature of physical and psychic functioning.

2. This knowledge gives one the power to change the material and social environment and self for the better.

3. There is a continuous reciprocal ("dialectical") interaction between the person and the environment. By improving the environment, one makes possible self-improvement, and by improving self, one furthers the improvement of the environment.

4. The plasticity of the individual's brain and personality makes changes for the better possible at all ages.

5. The individual's "higher" social, ethical, and moral needs are more compelling than "lower" animal needs.

6. In the process of upbringing, "higher" needs can be used to inculcate socially desirable character traits in children.

7. This process of "correct" upbringing will be continued by the individual, by autogenetic movement (*samodvizheniye*) and self-upbringing (*samovospitaniye*). Thus, the individual who has been given a proper start by collective upbringing will continue to improve self, and society, thus

creating a self-perpetuating upward spiral.

8. A collective society provides optimum conditions for the improvement of mankind, by providing for collective upbringing of children and for a collective milieu throughout life.

APPLICATIONS

Assessment

Personality assessment is carried out in the Soviet Union in a number of ways. In the 1920s and early 1930s a proliferation of specially devised tests was widely applied in assessing the aptitudes of children to determine whether they should be assigned to regular schools, special schools for the emotionally or intellectually handicapped, or schools for the gifted. Tests were also widely used in industry to determine the aptitudes of workers for specific occupations. In the middle thirties, many of these tests fell into disrepute, and the Resolution of 1936 against pedology effectively curtailed their use.

Zeigarnik (1965; Zeigarnik & Rubinshtein, 1962), and her associates continued to employ various testing techniques in the diagnosis and treatment of patients with organic brain lesions, and defectology became an important area of research and practical application. Defectologists like Luria (1961, 1962, 1969) published extensively relative to diagnostic study and education of children with organic brain defects and the rehabilitation of patients with organic brain lesions.

In recent years there has been renewed interest in the use of tests in clinical diagnosis, including tests developed in the Soviet Union as well as adaptions of tests like the Rorschach, Thematic Apperception Test, and Minnesota Multiphasic Personality Inventory (Myasishchev, Bespal'ko, & Gilyasheva, 1969). Soviet clinicians have also made extensive use of conditioned-reflex techniques to determine the type of higher nervous activity in patients, in accordance with the meticulous experimental work on human typology by Pavlov, Teplov, and Nebylitsyn.

However, in keeping with their adherence to the principle of the unity of theory and practice, most Soviet personality theorists hold that the most valid techniques of personality assessment involve the use of the "natural experiment." They prefer this method to laboratory techniques, tests, or questionnaires, concluding that personalities can best be assessed by studying behavior and responses in the natural setting of the collective. There is an enormous literature about the transforming experiment (*preobrazuyuschchii eksperiment*), in which individual personalities are assessed in the process of efforts to change personality and behavior in a specified, desired direction. Similarly, Soviet personality theorists hold that assessment for purposes of vocational guidance is best accomplished by longitudinal observation of the child and young person in his natural setting, rather than by vocational aptitude testing. However, there has been a renewal of interest in recent years in the use of tests and questionnaires in assessing vocational aptitudes and motivation (Lomov, 1966).

Treatment

Psychiatric treatment in the Soviet Union leans heavily on Soviet personality theory. For example, Myasishchev, a leading Soviet psychotherapist, cites Makarenko's work as a paradigm for his conclusion that:

> ...the principle of treatment by the method of psychotherapy consists in the reconstruction of the personality through the process of social intercourse and working and living in common. The creative work of A. S. Makarenko exemplifies the feasibility and the realization of this approach. Psychotherapy represents a border zone which combines the treatment, rehabilitation and upbringing of man....The psychiatrist is the teacher of life to the patient. (1973, pp. 15–16)

Soviet psychiatric treatment rests on the same three theoretical pillars as Soviet personality theory:

1. The philosophical orientation of dialectical materialism.
2. The Pavlovian doctrine that mental disorders are caused by disturbances of the reflex activity of the central nervous system.
3. Myasishchev's interpersonal relations approach to the study of personality and the elucidation of intra-psychic conflicts.

In accordance with the principle of studying the personality while influencing it and influencing it while studying it, Soviet psychotherapists take an active role in treatment. They may intervene directly in the patient's life situation by manipulating his environment, occupation, or residence. They actively strive to maintain a positive therapeutic climate by giving the patient emotional support, warmth, and help. They try to reeducate the patient and guide him toward the development of such "socio-moral qualities as moral fibre, social consciousness, collectivism, and the ability to be guided by the collective and with its help to see and correct his mistakes" (Myasishchev, 1961, p. 44).

Work therapy is a major tool in treatment. Most psychiatric hospitals and clinics maintain well-equipped work shops where patients produce, for pay, articles to be sold to retail outlets. Soviet psychiatrists hold that work therapy is an important socializing factor; that it helps the patient retain contact with reality and prevents emotional isolation and retreat from the real world; that engaging in paid socially useful work helps restore and enhance the patient's self-esteem; and that the protected conditions of the therapeutic workshop prepare the patient for a return to life outside the hospital.

Because of the close interrelationship between psychology and neurophysiology, and between psychotherapy, psychiatry, and medicine, Soviet psychotherapists invariably combine psychotherapy with physiotherapy and medication. The psychiatrist carries out not only a psychiatric evaluation but also a thorough physical and neurological examination in a search for neurological and somatic causes of a mental illness—such as infection, trauma, malnutrition, or toxic manifestations in the central nervous system. The psychiatrist also becomes, in effect, the personal physician of the hospitalized patient, treating whatever somatic illness he may present or develop.

In keeping with the optimistic tone of Soviet personality theory, with its emphasis on the unlimited potential for change and rehabilitation, the psychiatrist demonstrates a great deal of therapeutic optimism and vigor in his approach and in the liberal use of various medications and physiotherapeutic modalities. Because of their Pavlovian orientation to the mental patient as someone suffering from a weakening of the cortical nerve cells, Soviet psychiatrists usually also prescribe various tonicizing and roborant ("generally strengthening") medications, therapeutic physical exercises, hydrotherapy, and acupuncture.

Basing themselves on Pavlov's formulation that mental illness is a manifestation of "protective inhibition," whereby the weakened cortical cells protect themselves "from the danger of being destroyed as a result of excessive stimulation" (cited in Andreev, 1960, p. 3), Soviet psychiatrists for many years made wide use of various techniques for inducing prolonged sleep to reinforce the already existing protective inhibition and give the weakened cortical cells rest and an opportunity to recover. In recent years, with the introduction of modern psychotropic drugs, the use of prolonged sleep has diminished.

Since the collective is considered to be a central factor in the security system of the individual, in the satisfaction of his material and emotional needs, and in the furthering of his growth and development, the Soviet psychiatrist calls upon the various collectives in the society to help. A psychiatric history of the patient is obtained not only from the patient and his family but also from members of his trade union collective, who are asked to maintain contact with the patient during hospitalization. The collectives of fellow patients and of the staff are consciously employed as an encouraging and supportive, but also a pressuring, corrective and reality-testing medium.

In accordance with the Pavlovian concept that speech (the second signal system) is a powerful stimulus in the formation of conditioned reflexes and of the "dynamic stereotype" of the personality, Soviet psychotherapists avoid giving patients interpretations which involve negative feelings. The rationale is that negative interpretations reinforce the already existing unhealthy "dynamic stereotype" of the patient and thus have an antitherapeutic effect. Instead, they give the patient countervailing suggestions to help extinguish the unhealthy stereotype (Ziferstein, 1965, 1966). In line with their emphasis on the crucial role of the collective, Soviet psychotherapists make extensive use of group psychotherapy. The combination of group psychotherapy and collective work therapy has become one of the hallmarks of Soviet psychotherapy (Ziferstein, 1972).

An important application of personality theory to the treatment and rehabilitation of patients with organic brain disease, and of the mentally retarded and the handicapped, is based on the research of A. R. Luria (see Assertion 18) which demonstrated that if a given function (e.g., reading) is lost because of damage to a localized area of the brain, a different cortical functional system can be trained to take over the "lost" function. In the case of mental retardation, the assumption is that certain functional cortical systems are not operative because of genetic or congenital damage, and appropriate training of new functional systems can enable the mentally retarded person to function more effectively in his environment.

Institutional

From the days immediately after the revolution, the major emphasis in the application of personality theory has been on rearing and educating the new Soviet man. Therefore, the large bulk of research and application has been in crèches (day nurseries), nursery schools, kindergartens, children's homes, and schools. Brackbill (1962) reported that "at present, a higher proportion of developmental behavioral research cannot be found in any other country."

The concerted, practical applications of personality theory to the task of rearing a physically, mentally, and morally healthy Soviet citizen begin almost from birth. In the crèches connected with factories, to which working mothers bring their infants at two months, one can observe nurses massaging, exercising, and verbally stimulating their charges. Every day the same nurse massages and exercises "her" child and talks to him. During a lengthy exercise period there is a great deal of nonverbal social stimulation and physical contact between nurse and child.

Several infants are usually placed in one playpen, to encourage early socialization. There they are exposed to new, stimulating, colorful toys, and when the *orienting reflex* is brought into play as one infant focuses on a toy, the object is moved to refocus his attention on his neighbors.

At the toddler stage, socialization and cooperation are encouraged by providing large blocks and toys which cannot be handled by only one child. Throughout the period of infancy a variety of techniques are employed to improve the children's visual, tactile, and other sensory discriminatory powers and to develop coordination, agility, motor and verbal skills. Toddlers are also taught to attend as much as possible to their own needs: to feed themselves, to pick up their toys at the end of playtime, to socialize with their table companions at meals, to prepare themselves for a nap.

Stress is laid early on social ownership: "Mine is ours, ours is mine." Children are taught to engage in criticism and self-criticism for the good of the collective, and to build a self-upbringing and self-disciplining collective.

Manuals for teachers describe in minute detail the daily class routine and the techniques to be employed by the teacher at each grade level, to achieve "the objectives of upbringing; namely: communist morality, a responsible attitude toward learning, cultured (*kul'turnoye*) behavior, aesthetic culture, and physical culture" (Boldyrev, 1960). For example, instructions for first-grade students are detailed in one official manual as follows:

> *In school.* All pupils are to arrive on time, wipe their feet before entering, greet the teacher and staff members by name, give a general greeting to classmates and greet seatmate by name....
>
> *At home.* On awaking, greet parents and thank them after breakfast...take care of your own things; sew on buttons, iron clothes, shine shoes, keep desk in order....
>
> *In public places.* Behave calmly. Obey all requests of adults...Dissuade friends from behaving badly....Learn about the work the adults in your family do for the common good.

Other manuals describe techniques to be employed by teachers and social administrators to develop "socialist competition"; for example, the rows in one classroom may compete with one another in areas such as orderliness, neatness, scholarship, and cooperation. Similar competition is developed among classrooms and eventually among a number of schools.

Another prevalent application of personality theories which stress the role of the collective is in trade-union organizations, housing committees, and so on, where the guiding principles are applied not by professionals but by the members of the collective themselves. One example is the "comradely court" (*tovarishcheskii sud*), which tries individuals for infractions of a collective's rules. It has no judicial powers but effectively uses the pressures of the collective to halt undesirable behavior. In recent years there has been a renewal of interest in the application of personality theory to problems of industrial psychology and to specific issues involving motivation, improvement of attitudes toward work, and development of work habits and skills.

Self

A Western reader might ask what value there is in learning about the personality theories and practices of a culture so different from his own. At first glance it may seem that the social conditions and ideology of the Soviet people, and their concepts and attitudes, are so different that they cannot possibly have any applicability to American life.

A major benefit of any cross-cultural study is that it may cause the reader to confront his own ethnocentrism. It can make explicit attitudes and values about others that have been accepted as a matter of course. Reexamination of these attitudes can result in a deeper, more objective self-exploration and self-understanding, not only as an individual but as a member of a particular culture. Uri Bronfenbrenner, after visiting Soviet schools and reading some of Makarenko's writings, concluded:

> ...the results of this inquiry indicate that the rather different Soviet approach to the upbringing of the young is not without significance for our own problems....perhaps we have reached the point of diminishing returns in allowing excessive autonomy and in failing to utilize the constructive potential of the peer group in developing social responsibility and consideration for others....What is called for [is]...Greater involvement of children in responsibility on behalf of their own family, community, and society at large. (1970, pp. 164–166)

And in an introduction to Makarenko's book *The Collective Family: A Handbook for Russian Parents* (1937), Bronfenbrenner writes:

> The question therefore arises whether we cannot profit by taking to heart Makarenko's injunction regarding the constructive influence of imposing communal responsibility within both family and peer groups....[These responsibilities] should involve the full range of human beings who make up the society, including those who most need and deserve the service of others—old people, young children, the handicapped, and the underprivileged....We too must teach morality through the imposition on children of concrete responsibilities and expectations consistent with the welfare of all and the dignity of each. (pp. xvii–xix)

This perhaps presents an overidealized picture of Soviet child-rearing and educational methods, and an equally overidealized prescription for us. Bronfenbrenner himself issues a caveat about not subscribing to Soviet insistence on the primacy of the collective over the individual or adopting their practice of shifting major responsibility for upbringing from the family to public institutions. Furthermore, one cannot simply transplant practices that may work for one society and expect them to work in an entirely different society, with different traditions and different values. However, this in no way invalidates the fructifying effects of cross-cultural exchanges of data and theoretical concepts.

VALIDATION

Evidence

Soviet personality theorists validate their theories in several ways. One is by citing the soundness of the philosophical concepts on which they base their hypotheses and which direct their research and its methodology.

A second type of validation is the large body of meticulous experimental work on conditioned reflexes initiated by Pavlov. This work, involving animal and human subjects, continues to be done in many psychophysiological laboratories. Soviet psychologists maintain that these carefully controlled laboratory studies demonstrate the correctness of the materialist approach to the study of personality. They cite the careful experimental studies in typology, initiated by Pavlov and continued by Teplov and Nebylitsyn, in which human subjects were studied for such properties of the nervous system as strength or weakness, mobility and speed of the appearance and cessation of the neural process, and the equilibrium of excitation and inhibition. They maintain that these studies lay the foundations for a truly scientific typology of human personality.

A third source of validation is the careful study of developmental psychology, under laboratory conditions, by specially devised experimental designs such as Vygotskii's "technique of dual stimulation," and in real-life settings. For example, the conclusion that the newborn has a primal "social" need for new stimuli and communication has been buttressed by observations of infants in the first month of life by Peiper (1962), Figurin and Denisova (1949), Shchelovanov (1960), Lechtreman-Abramovich (1949), Rosengart-Pupko (1948), and many others. Vygotskii's innovative studies of the development of thought and language (1934)—which were continued by his students Luria and Leontiev (El'konin, 1969) and by experimental studies like those of Smirnov and Zinchenko on the psychology of memory, Zaporozhetz on sensory training, and Kasatkin on the development of conditioned reflexes in early childhood (Cole & Maltzman, 1969)—are cited as evidence for Vygotskii's dictum that the child is a social being from the moment of birth.

Another type of validation is the contention that Soviet techniques of collective upbringing, combined with the influence of living in a collective society, produce healthier and "better" citizens. Some Soviet writings cite Western psychiatric sources on the high incidence of neurosis and juvenile delinquency in the West and maintain that the incidence is much lower in the Soviet Union. Myasishchev (1974) and other personality theorists state that the new Soviet man demonstrates such desirable qualities as: concern for the common welfare, pride in the achievements of the collective rather than in self-aggrandizement, cooperativeness, a new attitude of respect for work, and heroism on a mass scale.

Other evidence cited as validating Soviet personality theory is Makarenko's achievement in dramatically restructuring the personalities of several thousand delinquent youths through the influence of the peer collective. These successes led to the development of the type of experimentation and validation which Soviet personality theorists consider to be the most productive—the transforming experiment.

A typical experiment is described by N. F. Prokina (1961). The experiment was carried out in a class of 30 first-graders at a boarding school in Moscow, chosen because it was particularly disorganized and the teacher had had difficulty in getting the children to abide by the school rules. One bit of behavior was selected for investigation, having the children leave the classroom in an orderly fashion. This was chosen because it had practical importance: Much time was lost out of each school day due to the disorganized activities of the children. (This is one of the major characteristics of Soviet personality theory; the psychologist's work must not only have theoretical significance but must, even in the course of the investigation, make a direct, practical contribution.)

The experiment consisted of several stages. In the first, the desirability of leaving the room in an orderly fashion was presented to the children. The investigator outlined in detail what was required: standing up promptly when the bell rang, moving into the aisles and forming straight rows, and so on. Immediately after this explanation the children responded to the bell in the desired manner, although they had not previously done so.

In Stage 2, which involved motivating the children to use this ability consistently, audiovisual techniques were employed. The class was divided into six groups, and for each a chart was drawn on which a staircase was represented. The number of steps on the staircase equaled the number of lineups required each day. When a group lined up in the desired manner, the leader of the group had the honor of pinning a red flag to the step representing that lineup. This introduced the incentive of "socialist competition"—that is, competition on a group basis rather than by individuals vying for recognition. This motivation had the immediate effect of more orderly lineups, but it did not produce lasting results.

Stage 3 involved efforts to make the results more durable by adding more motivation, in this case by introducing the element of play. Each team was designated as aviators, sailors, and so on and then motivated to carry out the task in an orderly fashion, "the way pilots (for example) do." This additional motive helped to improve performance but did not achieve the desired durability. An additional element was introduced in the form of a three-minute hourglass to time the children as they lined up. Each step in the process of lining up was timed, and the teams were awarded points for being the first to complete each step, such as standing up, moving into the aisle, or walking out the door.

As a result of this combination of techniques, the average time for dismissal of the class was reduced from 10 minutes to 1½ minutes. Lasting results were achieved in that the improved performance was maintained for the remaining three months of the school year.

Prokina concludes that this was a successful experiment because it accomplished a desirable practical result, and it advanced the theoretical understanding that three basic conditions are needed to produce lasting improvements in behavior:

1. Strong motivation must be established in the form of "socialist competition" combined with pleasurable play activity, to evoke a strong desire to engage in the approved behavior and to continue it.
2. To facilitate learning of this behavior, it had to be analyzed into easily learned and timed components.
3. The child had to be taught how to carry out each of the behavioral elements in the time interval alloted.

Soviet personality theorists prefer this kind of practical, qualitative, holistic action-research approach to the quantitative statistical studies which characterize Western personality theory.

In a recent paper, Myasishchev (1974) states:

In personology, the investigation of the social ontogenesis of personality is especially essential. It seems to me that the socio-historical elucidation of the ontogenesis of personality will most likely be achieved by Soviet psychology....The socialist system is the system of Soviet humanism. Only on the foundation of this system is a genuinely scientific psychological understanding of personality possible.

...The historical-materialist concept is the only scientific concept of personality and its relationships....The relationships of man are studied as processes of genesis, formation, development and disintegration, in the course of his life, in the course of his social being. These relationships are the most dynamic products of his life and of his life experience. Therefore, the study of man in his relationships satisfies to the highest degree, the requirements of the genetic, dynamic, historical concept of personality. (pp. 5–25, passim)

Comparisons

Soviet psychologists severely criticize prevailing Western personality theories. For example, Myasishchev (1974) states:

Capitalist society stifles personality, and its science and philosophy cannot but distort the concepts of this most important problem of the history of social development and psychology.... In the polar tendencies on the one side of negation of the personality and of the mass depersonalization of the toilers in capitalist society, and on the other side, the cult of the individualistic "I," of the "unique superman," of the cult of the personality of the property owner, of the bourgeois, are shown most clearly the class tendencies and contradictions of the structure of capitalist society which is built upon the principle "everything for the few, nothing for the masses." (p. 21)

In these attacks on Western personality theory, the prime target most often is Freudian psychoanalysis. Myasishchev (1974) states:

Taking as our point of departure the definition of consciousness as the highest stage of the development of the personality, we perforce come to the conclusion that the psychology of the personality and of its relationships is essentially the psychology of consciousness. Therefore, the psychology of personality and its relationships is the exact opposite of the current reactionary bourgeois psychology of the unconscious, the typical expression of which is the psychology of Freud. (p. 8)

Until recently, the attacks on Freudian psychoanalytic personality theory were extremely harsh. One example is this statement by Ye. V. Shorokhova (1963): "The social function of Freudian depth psychology consists of an attempt to poison the minds of the intelligentsia and of the common people." Another example is Lebedinskii and Myasishchev (1966):

In the final phase of the development of his concepts, Freud arrived at the affirmation that the most powerful drive is that of the death instinct. Of significance here is not so much this assumption itself, which totally lacks any experiential validation, but its mystic pessimistic essence, which harmonizes with the decadent world view of the epoch of capitalism in decline. (p. 354)

And Svyadoshch (1959) says: "Freud and his students founded a pseudo-scientific school based upon neo-Kantian philosophical conceptions, which biologize the human personality" (p. 25).

In more recent Soviet writings on personality theory criticisms of Freudian psychoanalysis have been moderated, and they even speak positively about some aspects of psychoanalytic personality theory. A consensus of present-day Soviet criticism of psychoanalysis may be stated as follows: Psychoanalysis created an illusion that it had finally discovered an objective method for uncovering the deep, hidden roots of human experience. Since there was a need for a scientific conception of personality and for an adequate research methodology, the psychoanalysts unjustifiably broadened the conclusions at which they had arrived. And so, while the data obtained by the psychoanalytic method were true, the interpretation of these facts was invalid.

Soviet personality theorists generally applaud the efforts of Alfred Adler to move away from Freud's biologizing interpretation of human personality and to find a place in theory for the social factors in the development of the personality by limiting the role of the sexual drive and identifying other, nonsexual forces as motivating human behavior. During the Stalin era, official Soviet personality theory was critical of Adler, labeling his writings as "idealist" (*Great Soviet Encyclopedia*, 1949), but more recent Soviet evaluations of Adler are much more positive (e.g., Lyalikov, 1970). The Soviets now point out that there is a close parallelism between Adler's conclusion that personality is social in its formation and the Soviet formulations that the psyche is social in nature and that the major determining conditions for the maintenance of the personality are the place occupied in the system of social relations and the activity carried out within that system. (See Assertion 14.) They agree with Adler that the motive forces in man's behavior are social in nature and that there is in man a genuine need to find his place in life, in society.

According to Soviet personality theorists he correctly noted the enormous power of man's moral strivings, but he posited them as yet one more drive (along with the sex drive) which determines the psychic development of man. Jung convinced himself, from his clinical experience, of the importance of moral attitudes of which the person himself is often unaware and which often act not only independently of conscious intentions but even in opposition to them. In accordance with his philosophical world view, and because he did not have the materials necessary for a truly scientific analysis, he preferred to see them not as norms and rules of social morality, but rather as an innate category of divine origin (*bozhestvennoye proiskhozhdeniye*).

Soviet personality theorists are also critical of the neo-Freudians, such as Erich Fromm, Karen Horney, and H. S. Sullivan, although they acknowledge that their theories generally have a clearly defined social direction. Some Soviet psychologists see the attempts of contemporary neo-Freudians to introduce a social interpretation of human conflicts into psychoanalysis as a genuine response to the rapidly developing social sciences and particularly to social psychology. But others, including Soviet social psychologists like Ye. V. Shorokhova and N. S. Mansurov, look upon this change as merely a bow in the direction of what is in vogue and consider the propositions of the neo-Freudians about the social conditioning of the human psyche as mere lip service which adds nothing to the understanding of the social nature of human personality.

In spite of these steps in the right direction, the neo-Freudians have not succeeded in creating a new, original conception of personality; they did not employ their new-found facts to overcome Freudianism. Instead, Freudianism proved to have such a strong influence on them that they subordinated their data to theories which in essence were close to Freud's. According to Soviet personality theorists, Hall and Lindzey (1957) are quite right when they say that the neo-Freudians, Adler, and Jung all stand on the shoulders of Freud.

Soviet personality theorists generally view the personality theories of Carl Rogers and Kurt Lewin favorably because they pay greater attention to the effects of the social environment on the development of personality, and they study the personality from a holistic viewpoint. The Soviets credit Lewin with refuting the mechanistic concepts of associationism and demonstrating that the process of association takes place only when it is a necessary link in a series of activities directed toward the satisfaction of a person's needs. However, they criticize Lewin's general psychological conception of the personality as being far-fetched, artificial, and unproductive. They also feel that the "behaviorization" of Lewin after he emigrated to America caused him to lose a crucial direction, namely, the investigation of the internal psychological structure of the personality and of the role of the social environment in its formation. In Lewin's later work, both the personality and the environment were attenuated and replaced by the hypothetical reality embodied in his concept of the locomotion of the subject in his "life space," a concept which represents a mixing of the subject and the object, of the personality and the environment, in some kind of artificial conglomerate of quite abstract forces.

Soviet personality theorists also take favorable note of the work of Rudolph Dreikurs (1964) because of his practical interest in pedagogical work with children and his emphasis on the significance of the activity of the child himself in the process of child rearing. They applaud his view that the individual is not merely a reactive mechanism but an active participant in the resolution of the conflicts around and within him or her. However, they are critical of Dreikurs' concept that a basic motivation in the behavior of children, and a fundamental element of their experience, is the feeling of inferiority which inevitably arises in the child because he lives "in a world of giants" and therefore feels weak and helpless. According to Dreikurs, this incites the child to compete with others in a struggle for a definite position in the group, and the Soviets note that the development of a dog-eat-dog society is therefore inevitable. While they agree that the child "as a social being, invariably strives to find his place in the peer collective, that he wants his merits acknowledged and he wants the approval of those around him" (Bozhovich, 1968, p. 106), they counterpropose that "correct" child rearing in a cooperatively oriented society enables the child to find his proper place among his peers by cooperation rather than competition.

Despite this criticism, Soviet personality theorists are appreciative of the contribution made by Adlerians such as Dreikurs in their studies of the affective life of the child and its connection with the influences of the environment. They believe these studies "have contributed incomparably more toward the solution of problems of child rearing than the numerous experimental investigations carried out in the spirit of traditional empirical psychology" (Bozhovich, 1968, p. 107).

Soviet personality theorists are extremely critical of existential personality theory. They state that contemporary existentialism, as a philosophical basis for psychology and psychiatry, represents a trend of militant idealism which counterposes the doctrine of existence and essence to the Marxist-Leninist doctrine of being and consciousness. They argue that existentialism is an extremist reactionary-idealist doctrine which considers that awareness of essence is primarily introspective self-knowledge. "This doctrine is in the sharpest contradiction to dialectical and historical materialism and does not contribute anything new to the question of the relationship between the external (i.e., appearance) and the genuine essence of phenomena" (Myasishchev, 1960, pp. 410–411).

In conclusion, Soviet personality theorists maintain that "incorrect" Western theories have had a negative influence on the practice of child rearing. For example, American pedagogues claim that rearing children in institutions inevitably results in defective personality formation, because the child is deprived of satisfaction of its instinctual need for the mother. Soviet workers, on the contrary, find that children reared in well-run institutions are frequently more advanced, socially and intellectually, than peers brought up in their own families. They conclude, therefore, that the negative results observed by Western workers are due to inadequate institutional setups and *not* to frustration of the child's instinctual needs.

PROSPECT

Soviet psychology has undergone a number of vicissitudes, beginning with the acrimonious struggles for supremacy among the several schools of psychology in the 20s, continuing with the synthesizing contributions of Vygotskii and Rubinshtein in the thirties and forties, through the repressive era of Stalinism and to the relative "thaw" of the post-Stalin era. Throughout this period the development of Soviet personality theory has been hampered by two factors described by T. R. Payne (1968, pp. 168–169):

1. The construction of psychology on the basis of Marxism-Leninism has meant not merely adherence to its principles but even to the very words used by the Classics, when referring to psychological subjects.
2. The attempt to "Pavlovize" psychology, beginning in 1950, as a result of which Pavlov was raised "to the status of a 'Classic' whose ideas were quoted and never questioned."

Payne points out that these factors "acted as a brake on the normal development of psychological theory,...forced Soviet psychology into a theoretical strait-jacket, and produced a vast crop of purely exegetical problems."

There is increasing evidence that Soviet personality theorists are beginning to free themselves of rigid adherence to dogma. F. V. Bassin, a leading Soviet personality theorist, is openly critical of Soviet "dogmatism in the social and natural sciences, [the] uncritical attitude toward scientific authorities, and the resort to meaningless quotations as a substitute for independent research." He observes that "Instead of solving scientific problems in an atmosphere of free discussion among competent specialists, the declaration of theoretical postulates became more or less the rule" (Cited in Wortis, 1962).

Bassin criticizes the overemphasis on Pavlov's teaching and the neglect of other approaches, such as cybernetics, information theory, and factor analysis:

> The theory of the higher nervous activity should not be considered as the only possible method for the study of the functions of the higher regions of the nervous system. Other approaches to the problem must also be used....Both method and theory should be developed not only through a variety of disciplines, but also on the basis of diversified positions and from the point of view of diverse trends. (Cited in Wortis, 1962)

As part of this "thaw," there has been an increased interest in unconscious mental processes (Bassin, 1963, 1968, 1969) and in the affective aspects of personality. It is likely that the immediate future will see further development and refinement of the set theory of the Uznadze school, because it is seen by Soviet psychologists as a fruitful approach to the exploration of unconscious mental processes. In addition, it is likely that the studies of typology will be carried forward as part of the further development of personality theory based on precise laboratory observations and experimentation.

These specifically Soviet approaches to personality theory will probably be enriched by a willingness to incorporate the wealth of experimental, clinical, and testable data being made available by the numerous Western personality theory approaches. There is evidence that this is already happening, but this does not mean that Soviet personality theorists will abandon their fundamental materialist philosophical position that there is only one material reality. They will continue to adhere to the ideas that man's consciousness, including his scientific findings and theories, are a reflection of the single material reality; that these scientific theories can and must progressively become more accurate reflections of this reality; and that only a dialectical materialist philosophy, explicitly stated and employed, can assure such a "correct" scientific understanding of reality.

However, Soviet personality theorists can be expected to recognize that the material reality they are investigating is extremely complex and cannot be understood by a simplistic, one-dimensional approach. As they give up their fear that the purity of their dialectical materialist orientation will be "contaminated" or "subverted" by utilizing the vast store of data and formulations Western personality theory has to offer, they will acknowledge that it is in keeping with the tenets of dialectical materialist philosophy to employ in the study of a very complex reality a multiplicity of approaches and tools, including those available in the West.

ANNOTATED BIBLIOGRAPHY

Bozhovich, L. I. *Personality and Its Formation in Childhood*. Moscow: Izdatel'stvo Prosvesheheniye, 1968.

Although this book has not yet been translated into English, it is included here because it is the most well-rounded and most readable presentation of current trends in Soviet personality theory. In the preface, the author writes, "This book contains a resumé of the many years of research on the problems of personality development which were carried on in the Laboratory of Upbringing of the Academy of Pedagogical Sciences of the U.S.S.R. These researches reveal the conditions and the moving forces of personality development in children. The book also includes a critical analysis of various viewpoints on personality and its investigation in Western and Soviet psychological literature."

Cole, M. & Maltzman, I. (Eds.). *A Handbook of Contemporary Soviet Psychology*. New York/London: Basic Books, 1969.

Although this book covers the entire field of Soviet psychology, not limiting itself to personality theory, it contains contributions by leading Soviet psychologists which provide an excellent cross-section and convey the flavor of contemporary Soviet psychological thinking. The editors' introduction analyzes this thinking and discusses Soviet developmental psychology.

Makarenko, A. S. *The Road to Life: An Epic of Education* (I. & T. Litvinov, trans.; 3 vols.). Moscow: Foreign Languages Publishing House, 1951. (Originally published, 1933.)

Presents a detailed account and theoretical analysis of Makarenko's work in rehabilitating delinquent youth at the Gorky Colony in the early 1920s.

Myasishchev, V. N. *Personality and Neuroses* (J. Wortis, Ed. and trans.). Washington, D.C.: U.S. Department of Commerce, 1963.

To date this is the only Soviet book dealing specifically with the question of personality which has been translated into English. In this collection of articles published in various journals and books during the period 1935–60 are papers on the importance of personality in psychology and psychiatry, the problem of psychological type in the light of Pavlov's teaching, and the pathogenesis of the neuroses.

Pavlov, I. P. *Lectures on Conditioned Reflexes*. Vol. 2, *Conditioned Reflexes and Psychiatry* (W. H. Gantt, Ed. and trans.). New York: International Publishers, 1941.

A selection of Pavlov's works, during the period 1930–36, when Pavlov's interest turned to applying his conditioned-reflex theory to the study of neuroses and psychoses in humans. The individual chapters are republished from various journals and include a description of experimental neuroses in animals, with an introduction by the translator and editor, who worked for many years in Pavlov's laboratory.

Payne, T. R. *S. L. Rubinshtein and the Philosophical Foundation of Soviet Psychology*. Dordrecht, Holland: D. Reidel Publishing Co., 1968.

A penetrating analysis of Rubinshtein's attempt to reconcile the various schools of psychology in the Soviet Union which competed with one another during the 1920s and 1930s, and to produce a synthesis of dialectical materialist and Pavlovian doctrine. Payne's obvious admiration for Rubinshtein's genius does not prevent him from objectively and critically noting gaps in Rubinshtein's theoretical reasoning and unresolved philosophical problems facing Soviet psychology.

Uznadze, D. N. *The Psychology of Set*. (B. Haigh, trans.). New York: Consultants Bureau, 1966. (Originally published in the Georgian language in 1949.)

This book consists of two monographs which describe in detail the author's highly original experimental work, beginning in 1923. In the second monograph, considerable attention is devoted to the application of laboratory findings to personality theory and psychopathology.

Vygotskii, L. S. *Thought and Language* (E. Hanfmann & G. Vakar, Eds. and trans.). Cambridge, Mass.: M.I.T. Press, 1962.

Written by Vygotskii during his last illness, this book was published posthumously and represents an effort to sum up his life work. He describes his experimental work on the development of thought and its relationship to "internalized speech" and takes issue with many of Piaget's formulations in this area of child development.

REFERENCES

*Andreev, B. V. Sleep therapy in the neuroses (B. Haig, trans.). New York: Consultants Bureau, 1960.

Banshchikov, V. M., Rokhlin, L. L. & Shorokhova, Ye. V. *Problems of personality* (Vols. 1 and 2). Moscow, 1969 and 1970.

Banshchikov, V. M., Rokhlin, L. L., & Shorokhova, Ye. V. *Personality*. Moscow, 1971.

Bassin, F. V. Consciousness and "the unconscious." In P. N. Fedoseyev (Ed.), *Philosophical problems of the physiology of higher nervous activity and psychology* (pp. 425–474). Moscow: Izdatel'stvo Akademii Nauk SSSR, 1963.

Bassin, F. V. *The problem of the unconscious*. Moscow: Izdatel'stvo Meditzina, 1968.

*Bassin, F. V. Consciousness and the unconscious. In M. Cole & I. Maltzman (Eds.), *A handbook of contemporary Soviet psychology* (pp. 399–420). New York/London: Basic Books, 1969.

*Bauer, R. A. *The new man in Soviet psychology*. Cambridge, Mass.: Harvard University Press, 1952.

Bekhterev, V. M. *Objective psychology*. St. Petersburg, 1907.

*Bekhterev, V. M. *General principles of human reflexology*. New York: Arno Press, 1973. (Originally published, 1917.)

Bekhterev, V. M. *Collective reflexology*. Petrograd, 1921.

Blonskii, P. P. Memory and thinking. In *Selected psychological works*. Moscow: Izdatel'stvo Prosveshcheniye, 1964. (Originally published, 1935.)

Bodalev, A. A. On the development of self-exactingness in school-children. In *Papers of a conference on psychology*. Moscow: Izdatel'stvo APN RSFSR, 1957.

Boldyrev, N. I. *The program of upbringing in*

*Bibliographic references preceded by an asterisk are available in English.

the school. Moscow: Izdatel'stvo APN RSFSR, 1960.

Boryagin, G. I. The psychological views of M. V. Lomonosov. In M. V. Sokolov (Ed.)., *Essays on the history of Russian psychology* (pp. 102–164). Moscow: Moscow University Press, 1957.

Bozhovich, L. I. *Personality and its formation in childhood.* Moscow: Izdatel'stov Prosveshcheniye, 1968.

*Brackbill, Y. Research and clinical work with children. In R. A. Bauer (Ed.), *Some views on Soviet psychology* (pp. 99–164). Washington, D.C.: American Psychological Association, 1962.

*Bronfenbrenner, U. *Two worlds of childhood: U.S. and U.S.S.R.* New York: Russell Sage Foundation, 1970.

Bykhovskii, B. On the methodological foundations of Freud's theory. *Pod Znamenem Marksizma,* 11/12: 158–177, 1923.

Chelpanov, G. I. *Introduction to experimental psychology.* Moscow: Kushnerev, 1915.

*Chertok, L. The rehabilitation of the unconscious in the Soviet Union: *The Tbilisi International Symposium,* in press.

*Cole, M., & Maltzman, I. (Eds.). *A handbook of contemporary Soviet psychology.* New York/London: Basic Books, 1969.

Dreikurs, R. & Soltz, V. *Children: the challenge.* New York: Duell, Sloan & Pearce, 1964.

Editorial: A new phase: On the results of the Second All-Union Conference of Marxist-Leninist Research Institutes. *Pod Znamenem Marksizma,* 1929, 5, 1–5.

*El'konin, D. B. Some results of the study of the psychological development of preschool-age children. In M. Cole & I. Maltzman (Eds.), *A handbook of contemporary Soviet psychology* (pp. 163–208). New York/London: Basic Books, 1969.

Figurin, N. L., & Denisova, M. P. *Developmental stages of children from birth to one year.* Moscow: Medgiz, 1949.

Filomafitskii, A. M. *Physiology* (Vol. 1). Moscow, 1836. *Great Soviet encyclopedia* (2d ed.). Moscow: Aktsionernoye Obshchestvo "Sovietskaya entsiklopediya," 1949.

*Golden, C. J., Hammeke, T. A., & Purisch, A. D. Diagnostic validity of a standardized neuropsychological battery derived from Luria's neuropsychological tests. *Journal of Consulting and Clinical Psychology,* 1980.

*Horney, K. *New ways in psychoanalysis.* New York: W. W. Norton & Co., 1939.

Ivaschenko, F. I. *Development of self-confidence in poorly progressing schoolchildren.* Author's abstract of Kandidat dissertation. Moscow, 1952.

Kon, I. S. *Sociology of personality.* Moscow: Izdatel'stvo Politicheskoi Literaturi, 1967. (German translation, Berlin: Akademie Verlag, 1971).

Kornilov, K. N. *A theory of human reactions from the psychological point of view (reactology).* Moscow: Gosudarstvennoye Izd., 1921.

Kornilov, K. N. *Textbook of psychology from the standpoint of dialectical materialism.* Moscow: Gosudarstvennoye Izd., 1926.

Kovalev, A. G. *The role of the classroom teacher in the study of the child's personality.* Simferopol,' Crimea: Krimizdat, 1949.

Kovalev, A. G. *Psychology of personality* (2nd ed.). Moscow: Izdatel'stov Prosveshcheniye, 1965.

Kovalev, A. G. & Myasishchev, V. M. *Psychological features of man.* Vol. 1, *Character.* Leningrad: Izdatel'stvo Leningradskovo Universiteta, 1957.

*Krutetskii, V. A. Problem of character in Soviet psychology. In B. G. Ananiev (Ed.), *Psychological science in the U.S.S.R.* (Vol. 2, pp. 63–102). Washington, D.C.: U.S. Government Printing Office, 1962.

Lange, N. N. *Psychological investigations: The law of perception; The theory of voluntary attention.* Odessa, 1893.

Lebedinskii, M. S. *Essays on psychotherapy* (2nd ed.). Moscow: Meditzina Publishing House, 1971.

Lebedinskii, M. S., & Myasishchev, V. N. *Introduction to medical psychology.* Leningrad: Izdatel'stvo Meditzina, 1966.

Lechtreman-Abramovich, R. Ya. *Stages of development of play and activity with objects in early childhood.* Moscow: Medgiz, 1949.

Lenin, V. I. *On Communist morality* (2nd ed.). Moscow: Gospolitizdat, 1963.

Leontiev, A. N. Psychic development of the preschool child. In *Problems of the psychology of the preschool child.* Moscow/Leningrad: Izdatel'stvo APN RSFSR, 1948.

Lomov, B. F. *Man and technology. Studies in engineering psychology* (2nd ed.). Moscow: Izd. Sovietskoye Radio, 1966.

*Luria, A. R. An objective approach to the study of the abnormal child. *American Journal of Orthopsychiatry*, 1961, *1*, 1–16.

*Luria, A. R. Study of brain affections and the restoration of damaged functions. In B. G. Ananiev (Ed.), *Psychological science in the U.S.S.R.* (Vol. 2, pp. 611–656). Washington, D.C.: U.S. Government Printing Office, 1962.

*Luria, A. R. *Restoration of function after brain injury.* New York: Macmillan, 1963.

*Luria, A. R. *Cortical functions in man.* New York: Basic Books, 1966.

*Luria, A. R. The neuropsychological study of brain lesions and restoration of damaged brain functions. In M. Cole & I. Maltzman (Eds.), *A handbook of contemporary Soviet psychology* (pp. 277–301). New York/London: Basic Books, 1969.

*Luria, A. R. *The working brain.* New York: Basic Books, 1973.

Lyalikov, D. N. Alfred Adler. In the *Great Soviet encyclopedia* (3rd ed.). Moscow: Aktsionernoye Obshchestvo "Sovietskaya entsiklopediya," 1970.

*Makarenko, A. S. *The road to life—an epic of education* (I. & T. Litvinov, trans.; 3 vols.). Moscow: Foreign Languages Publishing House, 1951. (Originally published, 1933–1935)

*Makarenko, A. S. *The collective family: A handbook for Russian parents* (R. Daglish, trans.). Garden City, N.Y.: Doubleday, 1967. (Originally published, 1937.)

Mironenko, V. V. *Khrestomatiya po psikhologii* [*Psychological reader*]. Moscow: Prosveshcheniye, 1977.

*Murphy, G., & Kovach, J. K. *Historical introduction to modern psychology* (3rd ed.). New York: Harcourt Brace Jovanovich, 1972.

Myasishchev, V. N. Some problems of the theory of psychotherapy. In M. S. Lebedinskii (Ed.), *Problems of psychotherapy.* Moscow: Medgiz, 1958.

*Myasishchev, V. N. *Personality and neuroses* (J. Wortis, Ed. and trans.). Washington, D.C.: U. S. Department of Commerce, Joint Publications Research Service, 1963. (Originally published, 1960.)

Myasishchev, V. N. The nature of neuroses and the basic problems of combating them. In O. Janota & E. Wolf (Eds.), *Neuroses* (I Congressus psychiatricus bohemoslovenicus cum participatione internationali, 1959, pp. 41–45). Prague: Statni Zdravotnicke nakladatelstvi, 1961.

Myasishchev, V. N. Psychotherapy as a system of techniques for influencing the psyche of man for the purpose of restoring health. In B. D. Karvasarksii (Ed.), *Psychotherapy in nervous and mental illness* (pp. 7–20). Leningrad: Bekhterev Psychoneurological Research Institute, 1973.

Myasishchev, V. N. The problem of personality in psychology and medicine. In M. M. Kabanov and I. M. Tonkonogii (Eds.), *Current problems of medical psychology* (pp. 5–25). Leningrad: V. M. Bekhterev Psychoneurological Research Institute, 1974.

Myasishchev, V. N., Bespal'ko, I. G., & Gilyasheva, I. N. Methods of personality assessment abroad. In V. N. Myasishchev & B. D. Karvasarskii, (Eds.), *Assessment of personality in the clinic and in extreme conditions* (pp. 69–96). Leningrad: Bekhterev Psychoneurological Research Institute, 1969.

*Pavlov, I. P. *Lectures on conditioned reflexes, Vol. 2: Conditioned reflexes and psychiatry* (W. G. Gantt, Ed. and trans.). New York: International Publishers, 1941.

*Payne, T. R. *S. L. Rubinshtein and the philosophical foundations of Soviet psychology*. Dordrecht, Holland: D. Reidel Publishing Co., 1968.

Peiper, A. *Specificities of the activity of the child's brain*. Leningrad: Medgiz, 1962.

Petrovskii, A. V. *History of Soviet psychology: The development of foundations of the psychological science*. Moscow: Izd. Prosveshcheniye, 1967.

Prokina, N. F. Conditions of formation of organized behavior while implementing the regime of a boarding school. In *Problems of the psychology of personality of school children*. Moscow: Izdatel'stvo A.P.N., R.S.F.S.R., 1961.

Reisner, M. Freud and his school on religion. *Pechat'i Revolyutsiya*, 1924, *1*, 40–60 and 1924, *1*, 81–106.

Reisner, M. *Problems of social psychology*. Moscow: Burevestnik, 1925.

*Resolution of the Central Committee of the Communist Party on pedological distortions in the commissariats of education, July 4, 1936. In J. Wortis, *Soviet Psychiatry* (pp. 242–245). Baltimore: Williams & Wilkins, 1950.

Rosengart-Pupko, G. L. *Speech and development of perception in early childhood*. Moscow: Izdatel'stvo A.M.N.S.S.S.R., 1948.

Rubinshtein, S. L. Problems of psychology in the works of Karl Marx. *Psikhofiziologiya truda i psikhotekhnika*, 1934, *1*, 3–20.

Rubinshtein, S. L. *Fundamentals of general psychology*. Berlin: Volk & Wissen, 1959. (Originally published, 1935.)

Rubinshtein, S. L. *Foundations of general psychology* (2nd ed.). Moscow: Uchpedgiz, 1946. (Originally published, 1940.)

*Rubinshtein, S. L. Questions of psychological theory. In B. Simon (Ed.), *Psychology in the Soviet Union* (pp. 264–278). London: Routledge & Kegan Paul, 1957.

*Sechenov, I. M. *Reflexes of the brain*. Cambridge, Mass.: M.I.T. Press, 1965. (Originally published, 1863.)

*Sechenov, I. M. Biographical sketch and essays. New York: Arno Press, 1973. (Originally published, 1904.)

Shchelovanov, I. M. *Creches and children's homes: Problems of upbringing* (4th ed.). Moscow: Medgiz, 1960.

Shorokhova, Ye. V. *Contemporary psychology in the capitalist countries*. Moscow: Izdatel'stvo Akademii Nauk S.S.S.R., 1963.

Shumilin, Ye. A. Russian precursors of I. M. Sechenov. In M. V. Sokolov (Ed.), *Essays on the history of Russian psychology* (pp. 272–367). Moscow: Moscow University Press, 1957.

*Simon, B. (Ed.). *Psychology in the Soviet Union*. London: Routledge & Kegan Paul, 1957.

Sudakov, N. I. *Psychological characteristics of persistence displayed by senior students*. Author's abstract of Kandidat dissertation. Moscow, 1950.

Svyadoshch, A. M. *The neuroses and their treatment*. Moscow: Medgiz, 1959.

Tugarinov, V. P. *Personality and society*. Moscow: Izdatel'stov Mysl', 1965.

*Uznadze, D. N. *The psychology of set* (B. Haigh, trans.). New York: Consultants Bureau, 1966. (Originally published in the Georgian language in 1949.)

*Vygotskii, L. S. *Thought and language* (E.

Hanfmann & G. Vakar, Eds. and trans.). Cambridge, Mass.: M.I.T. Press, 1962. (Originally published, 1934.)

Vygotskii, L. S. *Diagnosis and pedological clinical considerations of emotional problems of childhood.* Moscow: Izd. Eksperimental'noi Defectologii In-ta im. M. S. Epshteina, 1936.

Watson, J. B. Behaviorism. In O. Ya. Schmidt et al. (Eds.), *Great Soviet Encyclopedia* (Vol. 6, pp. 434–443). Moscow: Aktsionernoye Obshchestvo "Sovietskaya Entsiklopediya," 1927.

*Wortis, J. *Soviet Psychiatry.* Baltimore: Williams & Wilkins, 1950.

*Wortis, J. A "thaw" in Soviet psychiatry? In *American Journal of Psychiatry*, 1962, *119*, 586.

Zaporozhetz, A. V. Development of logical thought in the preschool child. In *Problems of psychology of the preschool child.* Moscow/Leningrad: Izdatel'stvo APN RSFSR, 1948.

Zaporozhetz, A. V., & Ek'konin, D. B. (Eds.), *Psychology of preschool children: The development of cognitive processes.*

Moscow: Izdatel'stvo Prosveshcheniye, 1964.

Zeigarnik, B. V. The tasks of psychopathology. In *Problems of experimental pathopsychology.* Moscow: Gos. Nauch. Issled. In-t. Psikhiatrii, 1965.

*Zeigarnik, B. V., & Rubinshtein, S. Ya. Experimental-psychological laboratories in psychiatric clinics in the Soviet Union. In B. G. Ananiev (Ed.), *Psychological science in the U.S.S.R.* (Vol. 2, pp. 657–690). Washington, D.C.: U.S. Government Printing Office, 1962.

*Ziferstein, I. Direct observations of psychotherapy in the U.S.S.R. In *Sixth International Congress of Psychotherapy, London, 1964: Selected lectures* (pp. 150–160). Basel/New York: S. Karger, 1965.

*Ziferstein, I. The Soviet psychiatrist: His relationship to his patients and to his society. *American Journal of Psychiatry*, 1966, *123*, 440–446.

*Ziferstein, I. Group psychotherapy in the Soviet Union. *American Journal of Psychiatry*, 1972, *129*, 595–599.

YIN and YANG

CHAPTER XII

Asian Personality Theory

Paul B. Pedersen

Asian personality theory includes aspects of Asian religion, philosophy, and social theory which explain human behavior and provide systems that support or justify Asian styles or modes of behavior. Asian psychology borrows readily from Hinduism, Buddhism, Confucianism, Taoism, and Zen. While each region of Asia developed its own original variation, the spread of religious, philosophical, and psychological theory moved from India to China and from China to Japan. Asian psychology has succeeded in adapting outside influences in an eclectic mode combining both Asian and Western ideas. Western psychology, however, has largely ignored Asian theories of human behavior, although some aspects have recently attracted popular interest.

The assumptions underlying Asian psychological thought relate to the basic philosophical assumptions of human existence and the concept of self. There is much less emphasis on individualism and more on corporate identity in the various Asian psychologies, but there is also more emphasis on a positive interpretation of their interdependencies and dependence upon one another. The family plays a significant role in shaping personality in Asian cultures through defining roles that provide models of institutionalized social behavior in adult relationships.

Attempts to measure Asian personality have depended on using Western psychometric methods and assumptions in attempts to bend Asian data according to Western constructs. Extensive testing of Asian populations has produced few indigenous theories of personality. Indigenous modes of psychotherapy are being developed in Asian systems of mental health care. *Measured* validity, however, is unavailable for most Asian theories of psychology.

537

There are significant differences in the assumptions of Asian and Western psychologies. Western theories stress the individual, achievement motivation, rationally defined evidence, the scientific method, and direct self-disclosure. Asian theories, in contrast, emphasize corporate welfare, experiential evidence, intuitive logic, religiophilosophical methods, and subtle indirection in personal relationships. Extreme care should be used in comparing Asian and Western theories of psychology.

Increased interest in Asia is likely to influence Western psychological theory, incorporating concepts of Asian psychology in the interpretation of human behavior.

INTRODUCTION

It is impossible to give an adequate one-chapter representation of Asian thought relative to "personality" or to summarize adequately Asian ideas about how the organism becomes and remains human. Nevertheless, the world's Asian majority has its own explanation of human behavior, and all psychologists should have some acquaintance with Asian theories of personality. This chapter thus gives non-Asians a brief introduction to Asian alternatives in psychological thought about personality.

Research on Asian cultures has generally been of two different types: explanations of Asian phenomena using Western theoretical constructs, or "uniquely" Asian phenomena viewed in comparison to Western norms. In this chapter we will identify ways in which *individualistic* Western assumptions underlying the construct *personality* differ from Eastern assumptions. For example, in Asian cultures the basic structure of personality is *relational,* focused on the space *between* individuals, rather than *individualistic,* the implicit assumption in Western thought about personality.

Human fulfillment psychologies in Asia predate Western culture. Though largely philosophical, political, or religious, their function contains insights appropriate to psychological phenomena. The emphasis in Asian systems is mainly on the structure of family, clan, class, and state through which individuals relate to one another.

The task of making Asian psychology indigenous has been particularly difficult for Western-trained Asian psychologists who are writing about their own cultures and attempt to adapt, amend, or explain the categories and rationale of non-Western cultures in terms of Western theories of psychology. In this regard, psychology is perhaps the most culturebound of the traditional disciplines (Pedersen, 1979; Surya, 1969).

This does not mean that the interface of culture and personality has been neglected by social scientists. Kroeber and Kluckhohn (1952) listed 150 different definitions of culture, while Allport (1937) provided 50 definitions of personality, suggesting that there are at least 7,500 ways of considering the relationship of culture and personality. Price-Wiliams (1968) divided all personality theories into two groups: the individualistic, wherein the individual shapes culture; and the culturological, whereby the culture shapes individuals.

In reviewing the field of culture and personality, Singer (1961) identified three major problem areas: the relation of culture to (1) human nature, (2) the typical personality, and (3) individual personalities. While the study of culture and personality has typically been located in departments of anthropology rather than psychology, recent publications on cross-cultural psychology have broadened the cultural scope of psychology.

The separation of Asian and Western cultures, sometimes obscures more than it illuminates. Nakamura (1964) discounts various attempts to identify cultural traits that contrast East and West. He claims the common features of one hemisphere are either partly or imperfectly understood in the other hemisphere or were conspicuous in a particular country at a particular time and then generalized to include the whole hemisphere. Thus, he says, "we must acknowledge the fact that there exists no single Eastern feature but rather that there exist diverse ways of thinking in East Asia characteristic of certain people but not of the whole of East Asia" (p. 19). The whole idea of national character is in some disrepute among social scientists, as are research findings suggesting innate racial differences in personality. There is, however, empirical evidence of differences in suicide rate, character, mental illness, alcoholism, calorie intake, and other phenomena in different cultures (Lynn, 1971). There is indeed a unique, special emphasis, evolved for whatever reason, in particular cultures, such as India's emphasis on the spiritual, China's emphasis on the social, and Western emphasis on the rational aspects of human behavior. At the same time, we must realize that Asia includes a wide range of distinctive cultures, and this precludes accurate generalizations about the thinking of Asians.

This chapter can at best only hope to stimulate Western students toward greater interest in Asian ways of thinking. Examples of Asian thought are arbitrarily chosen and are in no way comprehensive enough to cover the many great traditions of India, China, and Japan, not to mention the abundance of less well-known systems in other parts of Asia.

HISTORY

It is difficult to untangle the concept of personality from the complicated histories of Asian cultures, religions, and philosophies without oversimplifying each unique tradition or artificially imposing non-Asian categories of thought. India, Japan, and China each perceive "history" quite differently within their own traditions—from emphasizing what happened in the past in Indian mythologies, to the detailed, factual chronologies of China. After surveying the separate traditions, the cultural systems of India, China, and Japan will be contrasted with one another and with Western notions of psychology, emphasizing similarities and differences.

Precursors

Psychological explanation is not a Western invention. Ancient India had developed a variety of personality theories, originally based on the *gunas* or attributes of the mind, dating back to Vedic literature of about 800-500 B.C. Each succeeding religiophilosophical system in India modified views of personality in its own way, generally emphasizing practical aspects of organizing, classifying, and understanding persons in relation to the family, society, and abstract values.

These Indian systems were developed into specific ways of thinking through the classical Hindu literature of the Rg-Veda, the Upanishads, Yoga, and the Bhagavad-Gita. The revolutionary teachings of Gotama Buddha, born in 563 B.C., spread throughout Asia to China and Japan, carrying, modifying, and adapting original ideas of the Aryans who invaded India between 1000 and 2000 B.C.

From Aryan philosophy there is the notion of mind, soul, or spirit rooted in the changeless reality of an inner self or *atman,* considered to be the core of reality both for individuals and for a Cosmic Unity. Murphy and Murphy (1968) observe: "From this philosophy of the *atman* develops a conception of purity, changeless nobility, freedom from deception, freedom from passion, deceit, and delusion which reappears in almost all the forms of Indian philosophy" (p. 6). The emphasis in Asian thought, however, is not on the *atman* as an individual entity or basic unit but rather on the principle of an Absolute which approximates the Western notion of God.

Beginnings

India. The development of psychological concepts in India went through the period of magic, in which people tried to control nature by recourse to mysticism; the period of gods, as in Hinduism, in which people tried to understand nature; and the period of man, as in Buddhism, in which inner harmony and psychic consciousness became the key to freedom (Govinda, 1961). Awareness of suffering is a constant theme of Indian psychology whereby the wise person escapes enslavement to selfishness by realizing the true nature of the universe.

Four basic concepts are needed to understand Indian psychology:

1. *Dharma.* Codes and rules which define goodness, maturity, and appropriateness of behavior.

2. *Karma.* The propulsion from previous incarnations, present deeds, and future destiny (which has been wrongly characterized as "fatalism").
3. *Maya.* The *illusion* of real knowledge and causes (which Westerners might describe as "reality").
4. *Atman.* The person, not as an individual and separate "self," but as part of an ultimate Cosmic Unity or Absolute.

These concepts were taught in the legends of the *Ramayana* and the *Mahabharata* and in the religious literature of the Upanishads and Bhagavad-Gita and are concerned with the struggle between good and evil.

The Upanishads ask the question "Who am I?" in a variety of contexts. The person is variously described as the one who sees, who speaks, who discriminates; the ear of the ear, mind of the mind, agency for memory and volition, austerity, and self-control. The Upanishads emphasize the *connection* between an individual and the Cosmic Absolute rather than taking any aspect separately.

Yoga likewise discriminated between self and the time-defined context in which self exists. The person was considered to exist outside the sphere represented by pure self. Undifferentiated consciousness separated self as "knower" from the object "known" which contaminated pure self. The separation of individual self—serene and changeless—from thought process is evident in disciplined self-training through the system of *Raja-yoga* (royal yoga) and the physiological discipline of *Hatha-yoga* (yoga of force), concerned with cultivating extraordinary bodily control (Murphy & Murphy, 1968).

The Bhagavad Gita presented three classifications of goal orientation and modes of existence (*gunas*) for persons: the *Tamas, Rajas,* and *Sattwa* systems. The *Tamas* and *Rajas* emphasized self-diminuation, while the *Sattwa* emphasized self-enhancement and self-realization. "Individuals abiding in *Tamas* prefer to lead an easy-going life. They are generally sluggish and lethargic and totally indifferent to any constructive action which calls for a rigorous discipline in life" (Beg, 1970, p. 13). The state of *Rajas* more clearly defined goals of power and the accumulation of wealth, perceiving others as objects for exploitation. Both *Tamas* and *Rajas* emphasize a closed system, depriving human relationships of harmony, happiness, and dignity. *Sattwa* stressed the goal of cosmic awareness, ecstasy, bliss, altruism, unitive consciousness, and spiritual enlightenment, emphasizing the value of knowledge, altruism, and nonattachment. The *Sattwa* emancipated human mind and body from bondage of passions, pride, anxiety, and the wasteful action of biological needs. There was an emphasis on human and transcendental values, ethical behavior, and "self-actualization" beyond the physical or psychological realities of life in a "transpersonal" psychology of personality.

Buddhism emphasized the four noble truths and the eightfold path. The four noble truths were: (1) all life is subject to suffering, (2) desire to live is the cause of repeated existences, (3) the annihilation of desire gives release from suffering, and (4) the way of escape is through the eightfold path. The eightfold path was: right belief, right thought, right speech, right action, right livelihood, right effort, right mindfulness, and right concentration to escape from desire. These ideas spread throughout Asia to influence the understanding of personality in a variety of settings (Sangsingkeo, 1969). Schweder (1982) provides a summary of how concepts of personality contrast between American and East Indian cultures. Since many of the Asian psychological perspectives we will discuss began in India, it is particularly important to understand the complexity of Indian psychology.

China.   When Buddhism was imported to China around the 1st century B.C., it was modified to emphasize the social responsibility of Buddha's ethical teaching. The Chinese have been fairly characterized as valuing common-sense and utilitarian ways of thinking. Even their philosophical teachings were based on practical subjects and included everyday examples of morality, politics, and a lifestyle that would result in successful living:

> Many of the teachings of Taoism dwell on the art of self-protection, on the method of attaining success, or on the right way of governing. Confucianism, which occupied the highest position in Chinese thought, is also largely a system of ethics for the governing class and a set of precepts for governing the people. (Nakamura, 1964, p. 234)

The indigenous Chinese view of personality developed from the teaching of Confucius (551-479 B.C.), emphasizing aspects of "characterological theory" (Hiniker, 1969). The basic aspects of this view emphasize the notions of face, filial piety, and proper conduct. The notion of *face* brings out an individual's felt moral worth, assessed according to his loyalty to his group rather than according to universal principles, with social deviance controlled more by public shaming than private guilt. Filial piety describes a compliant and submissive posture toward authority. Proper conduct (*Li*) defined the duty of persons and the necessity of observing proper forms of conduct for each social situation. These truths were described in four books: *Confucian Analects,* the *Book of Mencius,* the *Great Learning,* and the *Doctrine of the Mean.* The task of Chinese philosophy is to describe the "way" (*Tao*) to perfection of the personality along practical lines, synthesizing Confucian this-worldliness and Taoist other-worldliness to achieve sageness within and kingliness without. Chinese philosophy can be described according to five basic social relationships between (1) sovereign and subject, (2) father and son, (3) elder and younger brother, (4) husband and wife, and (5) friend with friend. Each contrasting layer of Chinese philosophy, from early Confucianism to contemporary Maoism, has emphasized variants of these basic themes.

More recent descriptions of Chinese perspectives in psychology are available through Kleinman et al. (1975) on comparative studies of health from a Chinese perspective. Brown (1981) traces the evolution of theories, principles, and developments in Chinese psychology since the Institute of Psychology was developed in China in 1956. Psychology in Contemporary China is the theme of the spring 1980 edition of the journal, *Chinese Sociology and Anthropology*.

Japan. The Japanese way of thought was strongly influenced by both India and China, particularly in the period before the Meiji Restoration in 1868. Evidence of these influences is apparent both in the language and philosophies of the Japanese culture. Chinese writings and thought were introduced in Japan in the sixth Century, with particular emphasis on Confucianism and Buddhism. The Japanese selectively adapted these viewpoints to develop their own unique way of thinking, emphasizing what Nakamura (1964) calls the limited social nexus of the Japanese people themselves.

Current Status

Most studies of culture and personality have been written by anthropologists who generally have taken a relativist position in classifying and categorizing psychological phenomena, identifying deviations as culturally unique, allowing multiple notions of acceptable behaviors to co-exist with one another, and examining each culture as a separate configuration (Caudill & Lin, 1969; Child, 1968; Hsu, 1961, 1971; LeVine, 1974; Singer, 1961). Schweder (1979) questions the validity of examining culture and personality from an anthropological perspective. Psychologists, on the other hand, tend to link social characteristics and psychological phenomena with a minimum of attention to intercultural "maps" and "mazeways" of differentiated cultural values.

Students of culture and personality have failed to develop a grounded theory based on empirical data because (1) they have emphasized abnormal rather than normal behavior, (2) research on a pancultural core has only emerged in the 1970s and then only for more serious psychoses, (3) the complexity of cross-cultural mental health variables discourages empirical research, (4) most research has neglected applied problems of practical concern, (5) there has been insufficient interdisciplinary cooperation, and (6) the research has emphasized symptoms as dependent variables rather than the cultural context (Pederson, 1982; Tapp, 1982).

The Nakamura (1964) and Murphy and Murphy (1968) books should be supplemented by more recent surveys of Asian mental health such as Caudill and Lin (1969), Lebra's (1972, 1974, 1977) series of edited volumes, or Marsella and White (1982). There is considerable recent interest in comparing Eastern and Western perspectives (Pedersen, 1979; Wohl, 1981) both with regard to exporting Western methods (Higginbotham, 1979; Marsella, 1980) and importing Eastern methods (DeVos, 1980; Prince, 1980; Reynolds, 1980). Kleinman et al. (1978) go beyond transferring the Asian "technologies" of healing to the relationship of culture and healing in a more holistic framework emphasizing interdisciplinary and cross-cultural comparative methods as they might apply to non-Asian cultures.

Transcendental meditation (TM) has developed psychological insights from Asian religions and has increased in popularity since the 1960s in the United States. While there is the quality of a fad in the rapid popularity of TM, nevertheless it conveys some basic viewpoints of Asian psychology. TM is quite distinct from schools of Yoga and Zen which maintain greater authenticity with their Asian roots and which are also increasing in popularity in Western cultures, as disciplines of meditation and exercise. Capra (1977) persuasively argues for similarities between the theories of quantam physics and the views of Eastern religious mysticism regarding the nature of reality and material seeing them as conceptual links between Asian and Western psychological thinking. Prince (1980) argues persuasively for non-Western "endogenous" mental health resources emphasizing inner resources within the group or within the person, as being more effective than typically Western reliance on "exogenous" experts, in the practical application of mental health services.

Zen Buddhism can be divided into *Bompu, Gedo, Soojo, Daijo,* and *Saijojo,* each offering a meditative technique aimed at a different level of consciousness. They are united in the Zen belief that if a person is "emancipated from the dualistic bondage of subjectivity and objectivity of mind and body . . . he can be . . . awakened to his . . . true self" (Mills & Campbell, 1974, p. 192). This condition is intended to lead to a condition of enlightenment or *Satori,* a state in which the person is completely tuned to the reality outside and inside of himself, in which he is fully aware of reality and fully grasps it. In his Zen mental health center in Los Angeles, Reynolds (1980) emphasizes "phenomenological operationalism" which means focusing and regulating the flow of consciousness in the person. The "uneasy" mind is misfocused and misplaced. Morita therapy applies the three principles of recognizing purpose, accepting feelings, and controlling behavior. In Naikan therapy, guided self-reflection on the past leads to realization of how much others have done for the client and how little has been done in return. Naikan therapy explicitly aims at producing existential guilt, and simultaneously, a sense of having been loved and cared for in spite of one's inadequacies (Reynolds, 1981a, 1981b).

Yoga has been divided into the subsystems of *Mantra, Laya, Bhakti, Raja,* and *Hata* yoga. Each system aims toward meditative techniques with eyes closed and employs a repeated sound (*mantra*) to help the person meditating achieve *Samadhi* or knowledge of the absolute, by becoming oblivious of external or internal sensory stimuli. More attention to *Ayurvedic* medicine based on Indian traditions such as Yoga has grown out of "holistic health" movements (Kleinman, 1978; Leslie, 1976; Waxler, 1977), which combine the influence of mind and body in definitions of health interactively. Yoga consists of meditation practices and physical techniques performed in a quiet environment, with the participant typically seated in the "lotus" position and concentrating on the repetition of a special mantra. Yoga emphasizes body control through muscle tension, blood flow and pressure, heart rate, body temperature, and brain waves (Stewart, 1974). These measurable changes have been most attractive to Western-based research.

Biofeedback techniques, currently employed with sophisticated electronic equipment, also have developed from Asian techniques of psychology and have been used to treat muscle tension problems, to control heart rate and blood pressure, and to solve sexual problems as well as a variety of other difficulties, such as control of epilepsy. In addition they are cited as aiding creativity, psychic integration, and improving learning and problem-solving abilities (Brown, 1974; Jacobson, 1974; Kanellakos, 1973). Research on a positive relationship between alpha rhythms and feeling states has been disappointing (Grossberg, 1972), although biofeedback techniques such as electromyographic, electrodermal, thermal, and cardiovascular feedback are being used widely today for diagnosis, feedback to the therapist on progress in therapy and for relaxation training (Forgione & Holmberg, 1981).

At a practical level the influx of Asian refugees and migrants has forced greater attention to Asian perspectives. The best discussion of Indochinese refugees is provided by Liu (1979) encompassing flight, camp placement, and resettlement influences on mental health. Penner and Tran (1977) discuss contrasting value systems of Indochinese as a result of such contact with Western societies.

The field of "transpersonal psychology" is represented by a journal and by books such as Tart's (1975) which attempt to integrate contributions of Asian and Western thought in psychology. The Asian emphasis on *balance* and the Western emphasis on *solutions* may lead to a new emergent, combining both positions. In the non-Western systems there is less emphasis on solving problems or curing illnesses or eliminating pain or avoiding sadness than in Western systems. The tendency is not to locate difficulties within an isolated individual but rather relating the difficulties to society.

ASSERTIONS

Some unique Asian points of view about personality emerge as we examine assertions which differ significantly from Western points of view. Many of these assertions challenge the basic assumptions of personality theory as we know it, substituting concepts we have normally relegated to the areas of philosophy or religion. The Asian psychologies do not fit easily into Western categories, sometimes providing answers to questions not being asked by Western psychologists. The first three assertions describe basic assumptions which define reality and the goals of personality development in Indian and Chinese society. The next three describe assumptions in parent-child relationships, and the final seven deal with maintenance strategies.

Western classroom psychology may be guilty of teaching relative facts as universal truth. Tart (1975) provides an extensive discussion (pp. 60-101) on contrasting assumptions and assertions of Western and Asian societies. The contrast has been pointed out elsewhere as well (Pedersen, 1979; Sampson, 1977) pointing out that Western biases in psychology are becoming more evident. Non-Western orientation toward interdependency in which all elements are part of a whole and where the priority is harmony among the parts contrasts with a reductionistic and analytical perspective in which parts exist in isolation from wholes and the biological, psychological, and spiritual levels of a person are treated separately (Marsella, 1981). While there is a danger in oversimplifying generalizations between Asian and Western perspectives there is also general agreement that such a difference exists.

Development

It is appropriate first to establish the nature of individuality itself. The very construct of *personality* assumes a particular view of the individual as a basic unit in the structure of psychology. Some examples from Indian, Chinese, and Japanese thought clearly contrast with that understanding by Western psychologists.

1. A newborn infant, as a result of its previous lives, has certain personality and character traits which, after his present life, are transmitted to its next existence.

We think of an individual starting his personality at birth and ending it at death. The Hindu concept is that the personality extends before the birth and after the death of a particular individual, a process of identity which extends over many generations. The Sanskrit equivalent of "individual" is *vyakti*. However, the concept is defined as a transitional state. To the extent that the individual is a self, it has independent reality. The ultimate end of spiritual freedom guides that individual's behavior in a particular way. To the extent that the self is embodied in the particular body as a product of nature, with a capacity to produce offspring, there is an indisolvable bond between the embodied individual and all other individuals. An individual caught in an otherwise hopeless web of misery can always hope for a better world after rebirth which gives him a degree of hope for the future. Contrariwise, there is the possibility that an individual will be reincarnated into a more painful existence. There is also the frustrating possibility that in spite of noble aspirations, one's unavoidable *karma* will shape one's destiny through a long series of rebirths before the basic "badness" within can be purged away. Thus, the individual is important because he or she has the metaphysical status of "permanent substance coeternal with God" (Nakamura, 1964, p. 46). This concept should not be familiar to the Westerner who believes the individual soul is created by God and is co-eternal with God.

The profoundly Asian implications of that doctrine are the rejection of the reality "mine," or one's own possessions up to and including one's own body. All these possessions are regarded as changeable, passed on to others after death and therefore impermanent or temporary. What, then, is left to transmigrate from one existence to the next? "Life is like fire: its very nature is to burn its fuel. When one body dies it is as if one piece of fuel were burned: the vital process passes on and recommences in another, and, so long as there is desire of life, the provision of fuel fails not" (Murphy & Murphy, 1968, p. 22)

> 2. *Self, the substance of individuality and the reality of belonging to an absolute cosmic self are intimately related.*

The self or *atman* is regarded as identical with the Absolute or ultimate Ego throughout Indian philosophy. While there is disagreement among the various Indian religions about the essence of the *atman* as a metaphysical principle, there is no disagreement regarding the *atman's* significance as the moral agent for individual action. The ultimate goal of the process of emancipation is the recovery or discovery of one's true self. "Hell" is continued bondage to others; "heaven" is mastery of one's self. Thus the true *Atman* is the ultimate or pure wisdom without internality or externality, indestructible and imperishable. The self therefore participates in this condition of unity with all things, with the changing manifestations of the phenomenal world being illusory and temporary.

In the contemporary emphasis of humanistic psychology on rediscovering the nature of "real self," some religiophilosophical teachings of Indian thought have demonstrated their attractiveness. The emphasis is less on individual or particular surface qualities of the self and more on the relational meaning of personality to all other realities. This provides an unchanging stability at the core of personality which is genuinely eternal, participating in ultimate reality and demonstrating the unity of all things. Consequently, the more an object is individualized, the less it participates in the essence of reality. This basic monist view was developed in the Rg-Veda and developed to the Upanishads as a major theme throughout most of Indian thought.

The Indian view of self takes an ontological rather than an epistemological view of truth, leaning in the direction of monistic idealism and contending that all reality is ultimately One and ultimately spiritual. The emphasis is on the underlying features or "essence" of the individual, rather than on surface qualities of the self. The individual or particular self is dependent on the universal which supports and defines reality, emphasizing the *relational* meaning of a person or thing rather than its fundamental uniqueness. By fixing limits between self and not-self, the person limits and defines a place in the universe that gives him an identity. There is thus a balance due to the harmonious tension between self-affirmation and self-negation.

> In terms of modern psychology: the tendency of self-affirmation is extravertive, directed toward the external world; the tendency of self-negation is introvertive, i.e., directed toward the inner world, within which the ego-illusion is dissolved (because an ego can only be experienced in contrast to an external world). The extravertive and introvertive movements are as necessary in the life of humanity as inhalation and exhalation in the life of an individual (Govinda, 1961, p. 29).

3.   Asian theories of personality generally deemphasize individualism and emphasize social relationships.

Western views of personality see it as a separate entity, distinct from society and culture (Hsu, 1971, p. 23). Individuals express and create society. The extreme Eastern view concentrates on relational cultural differences without specific reference to individuals. Traditional Western definitions of personality move from a central core of the unconscious, to the expressible conscious behavior. Hsu (1971), representing Asian thought, substitutes the term *psychosocial homeostasis* as the basic unit to be studied, instead of personality. These relationships are central in the Chinese concept of *jen,* which translates as "person" but emphasizes the person's transactions with fellow human beings. Western concepts of personality emphasize what happens within an individual's psyche, while external behavior is seen as the overt effects or expressions of these forces. *Jen* emphasizes interpersonal transactions and evaluates the central core of individualty according to how well it serves to enhance interpersonal adjustment.

This humanistic trend caused the Chinese to de-emphasize discrimination between the individual and human organization to which the individual belongs. *Jen* defined the core of morality and humanity itself. A person was considered a person only when he observed the right behavior, so that birds, animals, barbarians, and extremely immoral individuals were excluded from *jen,* or the definition of human. Hsu (1971) contends that the concept of *jen* is superior to the Western concept of personality, illustrating a more "Galilean" view than the "Ptolemiac" view of personality theory. The locus of cultural change or resistance is not in the individual personality but in the circle of humanity, ideas, and things that define goodness in interpersonal relationships. This notion is close to a field theory concept of personality in the Western world, most specifically like Kurt Lewin's Gestalt concept of personality as the summation of vectors of force.

While Indian psychology describes the world as impermanent and mortal, with very little difference between persons and other living things, Chinese thought attaches considerable importance to individual human beings as the highest form of existence. As a result, Chinese psychology emphasizes practical ethics, while Indian psychology makes individuals subject to discipline of a spiritually religious character. Chinese psychology is "situation centered" and socially controlled, with less "inward" introspection. In this connection Hsu (1963) provides an elaborate chart comparing Chinese, Hindu, and U.S. orientations on situational emphases.

4. *The Hindu ideal of maturity emphasizes continuous dependency relations.*

In the Hindu extended family the child and, to a lesser degree, the adolescent occupies special status, rarely being required to wait for anything or to tolerate prolonged frustration. The child is praised and compared favorably to other children. This permissive style of child rearing results in adults with a low tolerance for frustration and a consuming need for reassurance.

> If no one has the time or patience to say that he is a good lad, then he himself has to proclaim it. Friends, events, and the like exist and are valued only to the extent that they supply these narcissistic needs. Deep, durable friendships become difficult and threatening especially outside the family ingroup. (Surya, 1969, p. 388)

A therapist working with such a person would seek to reconcile independency strivings or to submerge the individual's complex interdependence. The concept of "mine—not mine" applied to material objects, time, thoughts, and emotions is branded as selfishness inside the extended family. A Western therapist working with a Western person would probably move in a nearly opposite direction.

In the Indian extended family, social relations are diffused among parents, aunts, uncles, grandparents, and siblings. Each stage of the person's development marks a new network of dependency relations, with never a final emergence into "adulthood" as implied in that concept in the Western sense. Each dependency relation is marked by a more or less rigid inherent status, perhaps most apparent in the caste system. Caste places strict limitations upon the liberty of the individual and constrains him to unalterable conformity with what is called *jatidharma,* the rule of the caste (Anant & Shanker, 1966). As a result, different personality patterns emerge for each of the different caste groups.

The *Kshatriyas* tend to be dominant, the *Brahmins* to be devoted to religious duties, the *Vaishyas* to be parsimonious, and the *Sudras* to be authoritarian. Rapid social change has diffused these caste distinctions, but the intricate network of dependency relations is continued in modern India.

The goals of maturity in India are satisfying and continuous dependency. Independency longings are considered to lead to neurosis, contrary to Western concepts of mental health and adjustment. The notion of *dependency* is viewed positively in the Indian notions of *bandha, sambandha,* or *bandhavya* (bond, bondship, kinship) and does not have the negative connotations of *immaturity.*

5.   *Interdependence in parent-child relationships is the Chinese ideal for personality development.*

Differences between Chinese and American cultural child-rearing practices are reviewed by Chiu (1972). Chinese elders employ more severe discipline than American parents; Chinese parents emphasize mutual dependence in the family rather than self-reliance and independence; Chinese children see the world in terms of relationships rather than with an individualistic self-orientation; Chinese are more strongly tradition oriented and more situation centered, as well as more sensitive to environmental factors—all of which results in a more passive than active attitude towards life. Consequently, Chinese children develop a cognitive style attuned to interdependence of relationships, while American children prefer to differentiate, analyze, and classify a stimulus complex in a more independent manner (Chiu, 1972). A key aspect to understanding these cultural differences lies in the parental role.

Chinese babies are normally breast fed whenever they cry, even in public, and are carried on their mother's back and sleep in their parents' bed. Breast feeding is prolonged, and the mother is typically extremely protective of the baby's bodily health, giving it herbs or medicines even when the baby is not sick. Continuous and immediate gratification is the ideal form of child rearing. Toilet training is very permissive. "It is the mother who 'trains' herself and sensitizes herself to the baby's rhythm. She does not train the infant to control himself. The Chinese mother assumes that she is responsible for her baby's function" (Tseng & Hsu, 1971, p. 7).

The Chinese child is taught to handle hostility without expressing anger. Aggressive behavior is severely punished. Sharing and collaterality is encouraged, thereby developing a "shame-oriented" conscience in the child. There is little sibling rivalry for parental favoritism, since both children would be punished for aggressive, competitive behavior toward one another. The handling of the child changes abruptly by about school age (six years old), at which time the teacher is expected to assume control over the child's discipline. The contrast between indulgence for young children and subsequent harshness to instill discipline in maturing youngsters indicates a way of handling aggressive impulses through the basic social rhythm of *ho-p'ing* (harmony) and *hun-luan* (the confusion of vented aggression). The earlier permissiveness instills a strong sense of self-esteem and feelings of self-worth in children, just as subsequent discipline teaches commitment to a family above self. "Thus the subsequent harsh disciplines of youth represent the parents' effort to arrest the development of that self-esteem which is the legacy of an indulged infancy. The child matures with a 'selfish' longing to recapture the oral pleasures and the sense of power known early in life" (Solomon, 1971, p. 80).

The system of filial piety resembles a mutual exchange. Parents devote themselves to children, who in turn are expected to support the parents in old age. Relationships among family members provided a model for moral virtue in all areas of society, with the ideals of family government becoming the basis of national statesmanship, sanctioned not merely by the family's emotional needs or political necessity but also by intellectual rationales with inherently religious meaning. Western parents send their maturing child into the world to gratify hostile or pleasure-seeking impulses outside the family. "The Confucian solution, however, rejects 'abandonment' as a solution to generational conflict in favor of the greater ends of parental security and the integrity of the family group. The son is to realize his social identity in a lifelong prolongation of his original state of dependency" (Solomon, 1971, p. 36). In this interdependent relationship, the child depends on parents and, later, the aged adult depends on his children, in a full cycle of reciprocity.

Currently, in the People's Republic of China, the breakdown of authority relations and equalization of the power of men over women or parents over children is expressed in new kinship terminology. The husband and wife now refer to each other as *ai jen,* or "loved one," suggesting equality. The wife now normally retains her maiden name, and children may assume either the mother's or father's name. While traditional concepts of filialism are still evident, particularly in overseas and Nationalist Chinese society, through respect and obedience of children to parents, the arbitrary authority of parents over children has diminished. The child is encouraged to become relatively independent at an early stage, and this lack of parental supervision is reinforced by the mainland regime's manuals on child rearing (Vogel, 1969).

A particularly valuable source for understanding differences between Asian and Western families is the book by Mace and Mace (1960) which draws clear contrasts with abundant anecdotal support between Asian and Western marriages.

6. *Japanese personality is molded by guilt sanctions through parental self-sacrifice.*

The principal controversy in the field of Japanese culture and personality has revolved around different interpretations of child-rearing practices on the formation of adult personalities. Recent explanations have shifted from emphasizing formal customs, such as use of the cradle or toilet training, to less formalized but more complicated factors. The current emphasis favors affective relations between parents and child, measured by the length of time a child sleeps with its parents, who bathes a child, and other means of gratifying or expressing affective impulses (Norbeck & DeVos, 1961).

In Japan, mothers view their babies as extensions of themselves, with the psychological boundaries between mother and child more blurred than in Western cultures. Compared with Western models, there is less emphasis placed on verbal communication and more on physical contact, with the expectation that the mother will be totally devoted to the child. For the first five years the Japanese child experiences unconditional love for what he or she is, rather than what he or she does. As the child approaches school age and must represent the family to the outside world, there is a shift to emphasizing the child's obligation. The duty to repay implies a duty to achieve in a cooperative framework, on behalf of the family and within the family, contrasted with a competitive stance toward outsiders. The Japanese mother contributes to this sense of obligation: "by exhibiting an uncomplaining striving and endurance on behalf of her family, and by taking upon herself responsibility for their failures, she demonstrates that there is really something which deserves repaying" (DeVos, 1973, p. 156).

These obligations continue through the adult Japanese person's life until retirement. When old age is reached, the individual is again free. As Benedict (1946) points out, this developmental curve allows most freedom at infancy and old age and most control during the middle range of years, and so it is the *opposite* of the developmental responsibility curve of Western society. The Japanese concept of *ie* or "family system" implies closely guarded family relationships as a model of total involvement and commitment to a group, with other social commitments approaching this final commitment. While modernization has eroded the *ie* tradition, it continues to serve as an ideal in Japanese society (Nakane, 1972).

At the present time there are coexisting traditional and modern family styles in Asia, as a consequence of rapid social change. Traditional values are less rigidly adhered to in nontraditional families, and self-direction displaces passive compliance to parental commands; differential role expectations are allowed for men and women; and role differences of age-graded siblings place less responsibility on the eldest son. At the same time, the traditional values are maintained to some extent as ideals and thereby continue to influence the development of personality.

Maintenance

The categories of development and maintenance assume a dichotomy that to some extent forces Asian psychologies along some artificial continua, and a uniformity that disguises the tremendous variation among Asian cultures is implied. Several of the assertions in this section consequently reflect the development of personality as well as its maintenance. The first three deal with maintenance of interpersonal relationships in Japan, the next two with authority relationships and consciousness in India, and the final two assertions emphasize the importance of balance in applied psychology for Chinese personality maintenance.

7. *Japanese social behavior patterns are maintained through modeling the unique relationshp between parents and children.*

In Japan, *amae* means to expect and depend upon another's benevolence. The term is generally used to describe a child's relationship toward parents, particularly the mother, but it can also describe a special relationship between two adults, such as husband and wife or master and subordinate. There is no such concept in English, which reflects a difference in psychological viewpoint between the two cultures.

The unique aspect of Japanese dependency is the fluidity of relationships without fixed roles of inferiority and superiority. There is rather a mutuality in the bond of *amaeru,* implying the tendency and necessity to presume upon another person. This dependency need is both accessible and acceptable to the consciousness of a Japanese adult, and in fact social sanctions encourage it. The positive value of dependency sharply contrasts with Western views which characterize dependency negatively (Doi, 1969, p. 339). This positive attitude toward dependency is greatly influenced by an emphasis on immediate personal relations as a basic principle of Japanese culture.

Doi (1969) reviews the importance of *amae* relationships for understanding Japanese culture. With the decline of loyalty to the emperor, and deemphasis on repaying one's *"on,"* or spiritual debts to emperor, parents, and ancestors which had regulated the psychology of *amae,* the delicate balance of powers maintaining Japanese personality are being disrupted. The result is present-day moral chaos, according to Doi (1974).

8. *Personality maintenance in Japan depends on role-playing socially approved interactional patterns.*

Relationships in Japanese culture stress groups rather than persons. While the basic social unit in the West is the individual, and groups of individuals compose the state, the Japanese society is more accurately understood as an aggregation of family units. Considerable importance is attached to esteem of the hierarchical order, with each person well defined in his role. Special attention is given to the family, clan, and nation as instrumental in defining loyalty through mutual exchange of obligation.

In abstract terms, human relations are divided into "vertical" categories, such as the parent-child and superior-inferior relationship, or "horizontal" ones, such as that between siblings or collegial associates. While the horizontal relationship has contributed to the formation of concepts of caste, as in India, or of class, as in America, the vertical relationship in Japan has taken the form of *oyabun-kobun,* as for example patron and pro-tege, landlord and tenant farmer, or master and disciple in the Japanese bureaucracy. Hierarchy in the group is usually determined by a seniority system, and this frustrates modern Japanese management systems, which emphasize individual competency. The sense of Japanese honor is closely tied to high esteem for a hierarchical order. Nakamura (1964) claims this hierarchy motivates the moral faculty of Japanese self-reflection and iden-tity: "It posits before man the ideal of the infinite good that he should strive for, it induces him to reflect, by contrast, upon the sorry fact that he himself is too weak and helpless to refrain from doing evil; and thus it awakens within him the consciousness of man's sinfulness" (p. 513). Nakane (1972) contrasts the notion of *attribute,* or any specific quality of an individual, with the notion of *frame,* or groups of individuals who share the same situation by living in the same neighborhood, working in the same company, or belonging to the same organization. The practical significance of a Japanese individual's identifying himself according to his frame reference rather than his individualized attributes is readily seen.

Role behavior, therefore, becomes the means of self-realization for even the modern Japanese. The individual is dedicated to and inseparable from his role, probably dating back to basic Confucian values embodied in the *samurai* elite of the 19th century. Carefully prescribed role relationships, beginning with the family, have significantly contributed to the stability of Japanese society in spite of rapid social change, at the cost of deemphasiz-ing a sense of personal self. Achievement is not considered an individual phenomenon but rather the result of cooperation, both collaterally and hierarchically, in the combined and the collective efforts of individuals. De Vos (1973) notes that "Internalized sanctions make it difficult to conceive of letting down one's family or one's social groups and occupational superiors. In turn, those in authority positions must take paternal care of those for whom they have responsibility" (p. 185).

The importance of human relations is further evidenced in elaborate rules of propriety. The exchange of greetings, for example, is elaborate rather than simple. There is an abundance of honorific words and phrases in the Japanese language. "It is said that if all such honorific words were taken out of Lady Murasaki's *Tale of Genji,* the book would be reduced to one half its length" (Nakamura, 1964, p. 407). At the same time, there is an acknowledgment and acceptance of natural desires or sentiments as they are. It is in the social realm that conduct is carefully regulated; within one's inner self one can think whatever one pleases. The strong collectivity orientation in Japanese culture stresses stability and security but can result in stagnation; while the American adjustment, through self-orientation and individual freedom, can result in anomie.

>   9.   *Internal contradictions in Japanese culture result in paradoxical*
>   *personalities from the non-Japanese point of view.*

Nakakuki (1973) discusses the psychodynamic mechanisms in Japanese culture which are reconciled in a balance of contrasting tendencies. In the title of her book on Japan, Benedict (1946) juxtaposed the symbolism of a "chrysanthemum" for the soft, tranquil delicacy of aesthetic character in tension with the militaristic, authoritative attitude of a "sword." There is a similar dynamic balance throughout Japanese culture which reconciles self-expression against conformity throughout the society. These contrasts are related to a basic tension between narcissism and masochism (Nakakuki, 1973).

The narcissistic element is indicated by achievement orientation, competitiveness, and ambitiousness in a self-centered, omnipotent, and grandiose manner. The Japanese self-consciously strive for higher goals to realize their ego-ideal and are further motivated in this direction by a family-related, shame-oriented drive to be successful. The masochistic lifestyle is demonstrated in attitudes towards work, illness, and death whereby the person is duty bound to repay obligations. The ideals of self-denial are prominent in Japanese culture. The traditional Japanese family provides models in a narcissistic father through his omnipotence in the household and a masochistic mother whose task it is to maintain harmony in the family. The narcissistic pattern is related to shame and the masochistic pattern to guilt, as these two tendencies coexist in Japanese culture. The individual reconciles this tension by living in accord with prescribed roles within family and society. The source of conflict most likely to occur is between individual ambition and role responsibility.

Mental health therefore depends on keeping these two opposing tendencies in balance, so that the individual can move freely from masochistic hard work in the daytime to narcissistic relaxation at home, without either tendency taking control of him. It is necessary for the individual to transcend these categories by balancing them without weakening either tendency. The notion of balance is familiar in other Asian cultures as well, as, for example, the harmonious tension between *Yin* and *Yang*, the female and male principles of Chinese philosophy. This emphasis on harmonious balance of forces once more underlines the basic theme of this chapter—human behavior in Asian countries requires an understanding of *relational* units instead of the individualistic assumptions of Western personality theory.

10. *Rigid authority relationships do not necessarily inhibit achievement-oriented individuality.*

While motivation patterns are greatly affected by family structure and ecology in any culture, the studies of families in non-Western countries have not confirmed predictive findings from Western research on the family (Chaubey, 1972). This may relate to the different role and function of the family in different societies. The Indian extended family usually includes husband, wife, children, husband's brothers, their wives, children, sisters, parents, and so on, living corporately. This system has been cited as an obstacle to economic development because it inhibits the growth of personalities motivated toward development (Sinha, 1968): "It is argued that the joint family reduces incentives for hard work, promotes idleness and irresponsibility among the members. It is associated with 'dependence proneness' rather than 'achievement' orientation."

However, there is evidence that extended families may lead to enhancement of family agricultural success (Chaubey, 1972), and large families also may contribute to the entrepreneurial spirit in a village. A spirit of cooperation is required to achieve harmony in the shared living accommodations of a joint family. This cooperation is assumed to be voluntary, since members of a joint family are always able to separate with honor. There is no clear evidence that the joint family is more favorable than the nuclear family in promoting achievement-oriented personality types. But the support provided in this joint family system and caste-based social organization maintains uniquely Indian personality traits of respect for authority and conformity. Sundberg, Rohila, and Tyler (1970) discovered that while Indian adolescents were higher than Americans on deference and conformity, Americans were not significantly more individualistic or autonomous.

In analyzing Indian school textbooks for orientations toward authority, Kakar (1971) discovered the "traditional-moral" source of authority to be the most popular. *Dharma* is the Hindu counterpart of traditional-moral, which prescribes duties through modes of conduct at different stages of the human life cycle. This traditional-moral base is supported by the "person" of the superior, as illustrated in the *Mahabharata* and other classical Hindu legends. The image of the superior in Kakar's findings was modeled after the paternal image of control or the maternal image of support, but rarely in the fraternal mode. The sanctions to maintain obedience included the arousal of guilt and the promise of emotional rewards. The "nurturant" mode appeared more effective than "assertive" styles of enforcement, resulting in an "actively submissive" mode of dependency in the core personality of Indian youth. Authority is often associated with the inhibition of freedom in Western psychology, while in India and elsewhere in Asia it can itself be a liberating element.

11. Experience rather than logic can serve as the basis for interpreting psychological phenomena.

While Western psychology seeks to integrate personality functions, the Indian ideal is toward dissociation and even detachment of higher from lower functions. The ego has a "witness function" in Indian thought—watching the body suffer, but essentially as a nonparticipant. This structure requires explicit acceptance of a higher consciousness beyond human control, with a capacity to influence behavior, as well as the individual's capacity to be in communication with power.

The more subjective method can be compared to a man looking out over the landscape from a high mountain watchtower, searching for the route he must travel to get where he wants to go. He does not study the total landscape only those aspects pertinent to his route, which is almost certainly not going to be a straight line. Thus while "reality" in the higher sense might be unobtainable within the confines of logical thought and reason, the alternative criteria, through experience, seek to go beyond the boundaries of logically abstract cognition. Even abstract ideas are expressed in concrete terms, endowed with substantiality in most schools of Indian philosophy. The idea of "being" is more important than the more abstract notion of "becoming." The universal tendency is more important than the individualistic attitude. By looking at psychological phenomena in terms of experience rather than logic, Buddhist psychology deals with criteria of reality that do not always differentiate between actual and ideal, or fact and fantasy.

Existence is compared to a river which has its source in birth and its mouth in death, winding through a continuous process of existence in which consciousness unites persons with one another and brings together the different moments or phases within one's life. All components are constantly changing in relationship to one another, giving the illusion of constancy, of "ego-identity," or of an unchangeable personality: "The relation between subject and object is that of two moving systems: if their movement is exactly of the same kind, it creates the impression of non-movement; if their movement is of different kinds, that system which is the object of perception appears to move, while the system of the perceiving subject seems to be stationary" (Govinda, 1961, p. 130).

The aim of spiritual training is to achieve higher stages of consciousness through experience and exploring inner potentials through meditation. Once the person understands the relativity of the objectively perceived world and the facility of consciousness to expand beyond this ordinary level of experience, he has moved toward the goal of liberation. Ultimately the goal is to participate in higher and higher levels of consciousness, approaching the final state of *Nirvana*.

12.   *Life is a dialectical, paradoxical process reconciling opposing forces.*

While authority provides security against conflict and material deprivation through reliance on a united, dominant, and personalized political leadership, there are limits to the manipulative or harsh qualities of that authority. The five moral or natural relationships of the Chinese (*wu-lun*) describe a pattern of deference and obligation between ruler and subject, father and son, husband and wife, brothers and friends. Solomon (1971) differentiates between this expectation and the notion of an individual's social role, because unlike a role, which is defined in terms of the action of the *individual,* the Chinese emphasis is on the *relationship* between individuals. The Confucian tradition defined an individual's social identity not so much by what he had achieved as by those to whom he was related through ties of kinship or personal loyalty.

There is a dependence on hierarchical authority rather than self-assertion, reflecting the authoritarianism of China's social tradition, wherein order is maintained through a structured, hierarchical series of relationships. The need for social harmony and peace is balanced with the need to express hostility and aggression. The child develops a fear of expressing hostility toward those in authority through his early experiences with harsh parental authority. He learns to "put into his stomach" the pain of parental discipline and to "eat bitterness" rather than to act out dangerous emotions when provoked by an older member of the family. At the same time, the child learns that hostile feelings can be appropriately released against those subordinate in status or power. In status-equal relationships, the intense expectations of friendship to embody the gratification of dependency needs, especially in times of difficulty, are so strong that even friendship takes on the flavor of a hierarchical obligation (Solomon, 1971, p. 133).

The irony is that the strength of authority, or dependent submission to it designed to create harmony, actually generates tensions by inspiring the holding in of resentments and hatred of oppressive authority. At some point the critical flash point will be reached, and the system will explode into unrestrained conflict, overthrowing the superior authority and allowing another power to reorganize the confusion in a new hierarchical ordering of social relationships. Thus in China early-life experiences and political orthodoxy are combined in tension to give cyclic and balanced coherence to otherwise contradictory forces.

13.   *Changes in political systems affect the interpretation of personality structures.*

The Chinese revolution grew out of a potential for unrestrained violence in the Chinese people. It stressed political education as a way of redirecting consciousness of the aggressive response to purposeful political action. The revolution combined emotional manipulation and political education as complementary dimensions of mass mobilization. By 1949 China's revolution on the mainland was providing an idealized, nonhierarchical brotherhood of friendship as a solution to problems of anger. However, the possibility of peer conflict, even in this idealized system, gives renewed meaning to the need for strong political authority, and the sense of ambivalence and tension remains unalleviated (Solomon, 1971, p. 122).

The Confucian order stressed emotional restraint and "eating bitterness" as the appropriate response of subordinates, but the revolution rejected this dependency orientation.

> Where Confucianism alluded to the virtues of tranquility and interpersonal harmony, Mao [Tse-Tung] has made activism the key to the behavior of the ideal Party cadre. Where fear and avoidance of conflict characterized the "cultivated" response to social tension in the traditional society, Mao has stressed the importance of criticism and controlled struggle in resolving those issues which block China's social advance. (Solomon, 1971, p. 513)

These assertions give evidence that the Western view of man as an independent person beginning with his life at birth and ending at death, as having freedom of will, being entirely responsible for his life, and moving upwards in the social scheme, is not the only possible way of seeing life and truth. Such views produce Western man. The Eastern person is surrounded by different traditions, different views of mind as right and wrong, different notions of proper relations, and is treated differently by his parents and relatives in childhood. Consequently, the Asian personality can be expected to develop a world view guided by relationship strategies rather than individualistic strivings, family and group identity rather than selfish ambitions, and submission to authority rather than rebelliousness.

APPLICATIONS

All Asian psychologies do not subscribe to the assumption that psychological theory is justified by its usefulness. However, usefulness need not be seen only in terms of material accomplishment. Some examples of how these Oriental psychologies are applied will show that Asian psychologies are useful and valuable by other than pragmatic criteria.

Assessment

The extensive literature on applying Western tests of personality measurement to Asian populations is readily available in standard journals of psychology. Excellent reviews of the cross-cultural psychometric literature generally are available in Brislin, Lonner, & Thorndike (1973), Spain (1972), Spiro (1972), and Triandis et al. (1973), who include personality measures in their broad review of cross-cultural psychological research. Brislin et al. (1973) discuss controversial issues in measuring personality factors from different cultures, such as the trend toward criterion-oriented (empirical) or construct-oriented (theoretical) measures. They cite numerous examples of both measurement styles and their strengths and weaknesses.

One of the problems of criterion-developed tests is that the criterion itself may be culture-bound. As an example, Kikuchi and Gordon (1970) point out that leadership in Korea is primarily defined in terms of one's relationships with one's *superiors* rather than with *subordinates*. There are other examples of how extraneous variables can affect test response. Klineberg (1949) gives an example from Chinese culture. Some years ago a group of Chinese psychologists applied a number of the standard inventories developed in the West to Chinese students and concluded that Chinese students were neurotic. From this evidence they appealed for more mental hygiene facilities in the universities. Klineberg (1949) reports this as follows:

> What had happened, of course, was that the specific items in the inventory were interpreted quite differently by the Chinese. One question went like this, "Do you allow others to push ahead of you in line?" Of course all the Chinese said "yes," which apparently is marked on the neurotic side. Well, there are no such lines in China: they all gather around together. So everybody turned out to be neurotic. (p. 103)

Perhaps the most promising application of Western psychological assessment technique to non-Western populations is Osgood, May, & Miron's (1975) measurement of affective meaning through extensive cross-cultural research which used a semantic differential to measure cultural universals of "affective cross-cultural meaning." A second example of the use of Western tests in Asia is the cross-cultural use of the Minnesota Multiphasic Inventory (MMPI), reviewed by Butcher and Clark (1980), who cite numerous examples of these tests being used appropriately as well as inappropriately. They state that profiles from normal populations in Japan and Pakistan (the only two Asian populations in their sample) were elevated one to two standard deviations above the normal mean profile, particularly for males and particularly on the scales measuring depression and schizophrenia. However, when appropriate new norm levels were determined for these Asian populations, the MMPI was highly predictive for clinical diagnosis.

There is a continuing controversy over whether Asian cultures are "guilt" or "shame" oriented. While the Chinese are more likely to direct their symptomatology outward, to act out against others and to perceive the outside world in unreal ways, the Japanese are more likely to turn against themselves and to see the major source of their problems within themselves. T. Lebra (1972) cites research in central Japan which indicates that guilt arises from a breakdown in social reciprocity, while shame occurs when a person finds himself in a situation incongruous with his status. There is no agreement whether Japanese culture should be regarded as a shame or a guilt culture. DeVos (1973) argues that the strong achievement drive noted among the Japanese is linked with a deep undercurrent of guilt, as well as a shame-oriented concern with community standards. Guilt is derived from a system of loyalties which cements the structure of traditional society, especially in complicated family relations. "The keystone toward understanding Japanese guilt is held to be the nature of interpersonal relationships within the Japanese family, particularly the relations of children with the mother. The Japanese mother, without conscious intent, has perfected techniques of inducing guilt in her children by such means as quiet suffering" (Norbeck & DeVos, 1961, p. 26). Culturebound aspects of Western personality theories are particularly evident in the attempts to assess non-Western personalities by Western criteria.

Treatment

In a study of "culturebound reactive syndromes," Yap (1969) describes a great variety of mental disorders unique to various cultures in Asia but largely undetected elsewhere. Just as the norms for personality are assessed differently for each culture, the nature of abnormality is likewise distinctive, requiring an adjustment of style for the therapist as well as the psychometrist. Pedersen (1981) surveys the literature on counseling "across" different cultures, while other chapters in the same book identify how counseling practice differs from one culture to another. Draguns (1981) discusses four questions related to the counseling process in different cultures:

1. Are psychological phenomena generally shared across cultures, or are they specifically unique to each separate cultural group?
2. Does effective counseling depend more on the relationship with a therapist or on sophisticated skills and techniques?
3. Should the counseling relationship be bilateral or hierarchical?
4. Should counseling attempt to change the individual to fit the environment or the environment to fit the individual?

Western treatment generally emphasizes teaching persons how to act appropriately in problem situations, while the emphasis in Asian therapy systems concentrates on how the client can become a better *person* who will then incidentally know how to act appropriately. There seems to be more of a partial, symptomatic emphasis in Western approaches, contrasted to a more total approach in Asia.

There are many forms of indigenous treatment for mental health throughout Asia, particularly in rural areas where the functions of mental health are closely related to spiritual well-being (Kiev, 1964). Literature on indigenous psychotherapy is readily available in journals such as *Transcultural Psychiatric Research Review*. As Torrey (1972) points out, indigenous healers in both Western and non-Western cultures use similar approaches in providing a "name" for the affliction, in depending on personal therapeutic qualities, in using credentials to gain a patient's confidence, and in applying well-defined techniques to change a patient's behavior. While the approach to treatment is similar, there are also differences. Several examples of indigenous therapy in Japan will illustrate different approaches to treatment.

In Japan, *Morita* psychotherapy is employed to treat the patient who worries obsessively about his mental ability or physical health. Iwai and Reynolds (1970) describe the treatment, which takes place in a removed hospital setting.

> Hospitalization customarily lasts four to five weeks and consists of four stages of treatment. The first is absolute bed rest (four to seven days). During this period the patient is not allowed to smoke, read, write, talk, work, or engage in any activity other than biological functions. He is instructed to sleep, suffer, and worry with complete acceptance of any experience that might occur. During the remaining three stages, the patient is permitted to take on increasingly difficult and tiring jobs; at the same time he is asked to keep a diary upon which his therapist comments. During these periods the patient receives advice from his doctor, learning that because man's meaning in life results from work, he must evaluate himself in terms of his work, not in terms of emotions or symptoms of illness. To work well and behave normally despite symptoms is the proper course to recovery and a satisfactory life. (p. 156)

The technique of *Morita* therapy is theoretically based on Zen Buddhism philosophy and emphasizes *arugamama* or "the accepting of phenomenological reality" as it is, rather than the more Western notion of rationalistic idealism, wherein objective reality must be brought in line with the patient's needs and desires (Reynolds, 1981a).

In another form of therapy called *Naikan,* patients are assigned to small individual rooms away from external stimuli and do not communicate with anyone but a *sensei,* or teacher, for about one week during treatment (Sato, 1968). Except for sleeping, meals, and bodily functions, they sit from about 5:00 A.M. until about 9:00 P.M., and devote themselves exclusively to self-observation. The *sensei* visits their rooms every hour or two and gives them instruction or advice. This concentrated self-observation is called *Shuchu Naikan,* but after the patients return home they are encouraged to practice

Bunsan Naikan, or distributed self-observation, for some hours every day. The instructions by a *sensei* are for the patient to examine one by one the past experiences with people who have molded her or his personality—mother, father, brother, and sister, grandparents, friends, teachers, or co-workers, with primary emphasis on the mother. The *sensei's* hourly visits encourage a patient to redirect his attention on self-examination through his relationship to these significant persons rather than on the persons themselves (Reynolds, 1981b).

The key to reevaluation of personality is through better understanding of the patient's relationships to these significant persons. The patient will normally at first concentrate on grievances, resentments, and hatreds toward these significant others, but in a later phase he acknowledges his deep indebtedness to parents and significant others and becomes more sympathetic to others' viewpoint toward him. A Japanese therapist, Nishimaru (1965), shows how this orientation is uniquely Japanese.

> A truly Japanese psychotherapy would have patients strive to accept life as it immediately is—good and bad, ugly and beautiful are false and tormenting dichotomies and there is no personality to get sick at all. In such terms the goal and problem of psychotherapy for the Japanese is how to live in the midst of this sad transitoriness of all things—one does not struggle against this, but becomes one with it. There is no need to look backward as in Western psychotherapy to seek for past causes which no one can prove to have really taken place. (p. 24)

Both of these techniques are indebted to Zen Buddhism for their origin and emphasize a point of view which tends to confuse our conceptual abstractions of the world with the real world itself. Zen opposes the notion of subject-object distinction. In the West we become aware of ourselves as subject and the rest of existence as object; Zen teaches that this dualism is not real, that both self and nonself are unified in the totality of existence so that the self is not an entity separate from experiencing but part of that experiencing itself (Sato, 1968). Instead, Zen recommends the condition of "No-thought" where the mind functions on its own, free of distractions and the illusions around us.

The developments of therapy in Asian psychologies apply to problems of mental health in our own Western culture as well.

Institutional

Rather than describing the social institutions—such as schools, military, or voluntary organizations—for each Asian society, this section will focus on basic assumptions which define institutional and social relationships in Asia as a whole. There is a wide range of styles by which the different Asian cultures relate to social institutions of their societies. Hsu (1963) characterizes the Hindu approach to the world as supernatural centered, or unilaterally dependent, while the Chinese emphasize individual centeredness, or self-reliance, and situation centeredness, or mutual dependence. As an extension of the family, the most important secondary interpersonal relationship in China is the clan, while for the Hindu the most important secondary group is the caste.

The Chinese situation-centered world is characterized by permanent ties which unite family and clan and allow the individual to experience and exchange mutual dependence with others in that group:

> The individual enmeshed in such a human network is likely to react to his world in a complacent and compartmentalized way; complacent because he has a secure and inalienable place in his human group, and compartmentalized because he is conditioned to perceive the external world in terms of what is within his group and what is outside it. (Hsu, 1963, p. 1)

Each individual clearly knows his role and place in society and is taught the skills of how to improve this position, with few incentives to change or attack that system. The individual is much more likely to accept his role, whatever it is, without complaint.

The Indian supernatural-centered world places less emphasis on family and kin and more on absolute ideals as a guideline. Each individual knows his place in society, and there is little chance of changing his status relative to the society. Individual behavior is of less importance, since temporal existence is, after all, transitory and illusory, and differences are reconciled in a future reincarnation. The Chinese and Hindu cultures differ: the Chinese allow for more reciprocity, while the Hindu tend to be more onesided in their interpersonal relationships. Dependence in Chinese society is limited to well-defined channels and limits, while in India there is an all-embracing and more widely diffuse dependence. The centripetal or cohesive tendencies of a Chinese family contrast with the centrifugal or divisive tendencies of the Hindu family and are further reflected in the contrast between cohesive Chinese clans on the one hand and amorphous caste groups on the other.

There is a tendency toward conformity in Chinese culture in the direction of a group norm. Meade and Barnard (1973) suggest that Chinese are more sensitive to group stress and thus, in conflict situations, tend to change their opinions, seeking harmony or balance, more frequently than would Americans. It is important to live in harmony and peace with one's surroundings, combining the powers of nature and the power of ideas or the role of the individual and the human organization as two aspects of the same universe. Consequently, they do not regard nature as opposed to humanity, but emphasize harmony with nature, an attitude which may have held China back in the development of natural sciences (Nakamura, 1964).

The basis of institutional relationships in Japan relates to a profound sense of duty or obligation described as *on* (Suzuki, 1962). While there is no corresponding English term, it approaches the notions of gratitude, favor, or obligation. Suzuki, as quoted by Sato (1960), thus explains the concept:

> We are living on earth with the support of the universe, and it is our awareness of this support and our appreciation for it shown to the universe (and its elements) which may be called the *shujo-no-on*. If ever those of non-Buddhist countries thought about the debt which we owe to the universe for our existence, it would not be difficult to arrive at this feeling of gratitude and appreciation. (p. 243)

This sense of obligation is applied to family, work, and other social relations. Less value is placed by the Japanese on individualistic self-realization and more on bringing pride to one's family. This is most evident in the use of honorific forms in the language.

This incredibly complicated social system emphasizes the code of behaviors which define interpersonal relationships. The well-adjusted person appropriately applies the honorific system in relationships. Inappropriate use of honorific terms, perhaps more than any other clue, reveals the person's level of maladjustment to a situation. However, the Japanese businessman, for example, behaves much differently with his colleagues and co-workers in the company office than he would with the same individuals late at night in a teahouse. Thus formal relationships are a function of the social situation and are not frozen. To the Western observer, it is a wonder to see a dignified executive operating with considerable formality during the day in relation to subordinates who know their place and are evidently subservient and these same individuals playing nursery-level games in a teahouse in the evening, evidently with complete familiarity. In Japan, this is how traditional relationships function for the same individuals in two different settings.

Wagatsuma (1973) discusses "instrumental" and "expressive" interpersonal dimensions, relative to the Japanese. Instrumental role behavior is motivated toward achieving a goal or meeting a standard of judgment, while expressive behavior operates in terms of immediate feeling. It is important to understand both aspects as implemented in the Japanese conception of appropriate "role" in the various institutions of society. It is very difficult for the Japanese to think of "self" as separate from a carefully defined and appropriate role.

The Japanese, Chinese, and Indian cultures differ considerably in their organized, institutional, interpersonal relationships. We may wonder why Japan so easily adapts the technological revolution with an achievement motivation which resembles, but is significantly different from, the Protestant ethic of capitalism. We may be puzzled at mainland China's seemingly deliberate and needless abortion of progress in a Cultural Revolution, wherein the institutional machinery valued so highly in Western society is deliberately brought to a halt. We may be offended by a society which allows starvation to exist alongside opulence, as in India. Only when we understand assumptions and goals of each society—both those similar to and different from our own—can we hope to accept each culture on its own terms.

Self

Some of the so-called "mysticism" in Asian psychology as experienced by Westerners is due to our lack of understanding of their values, goals, and aspirations. The same kind of misunderstanding applies to Asians who characterize Western culture as merely "materialistic." The specific differences between Asian and Western psychologies should be evident, and the simplistic and dehumanizing stereotypes of "strangeness" in Asian psychology can be rejected. The big difference between the psychologies of the East and the West, as Pande (1968) points out, is that for Asian psychologies the ultimate goal is consciousness or awareness, while for the West the ultimate goal is achievement. Western theories of cognition emphasize the resolution of emotional conflict, while Asian psychologies seek to transcend conflicts and restore a sense of relatedness between individuals and their environment. Asian psychology offers a new set of assumptions and, alternately, a new lifestyle.

These differences in lifestyle have practical implications for our own high pressure society as well. Matsumoto (1970) develops a hypothesis to explain the low rate of heart disease in Japan. He credits this to the Japanese being able to express a variety of feelings more freely than Americans. "Thus the Japanese man is free to relax with his co-workers and indeed is provided plenty of opportunity for recreation and informal relationships with them" (p. 9). There is a stronger sense of "personal community" in Japan than in countries like the United States, with its higher rates of heart disease.

Tseng and Hsu (1971, 1980) comment on the lower frequency of depression among Chinese patients. The Chinese are provided satisfaction and security in the early years of life: The strong tie between members of the extended family provides a feeling of belongingness, overt mourning is encouraged, and the Chinese are simply not used to expressing depressive affect verbally. On the other hand, they are especially likely to have somatic symptoms such as headaches, stomach aches, or other pains.

There is a new emphasis in the Occidental world relative to subjective as well as objective psychological phenomena. In some areas of the social sciences and certainly the humanities, the West is beginning to perceive itself as "underdeveloped" in contrast to Asian cultures. In the search for new solutions to our problems Asia offers new assumptions and conceptual frameworks. Gilbert (1973) discusses some of the potential contributions of Asian psychology in increasing our awareness of the world around us both through incorporating Asian content into the field of psychology and through better understanding the techniques applied in that context.

Asian psychology has typically been disregarded in Western texts on human behavior. However, as we come to understand the rich resources of alternative Asian psychologies we might well expect to find aspects of our own science of psychology overshadowed, even when those alternatives are tested by our own cultural criteria of truth.

Asian theories will help break down the cultural encapsulation by Western cultural values that has largely defined modern psychology. The constructs of *healthy* and *normal* are assumed to have a universal meaning, when in fact each culture defines them differently. By studying psychological theories radically different from our own we learn not only about cultural differences but about our own cultural bias as well.

Why should the individual play such an important role in the Western psychology of human behavior? Perhaps as we prepare for the future, a psychology of human interdependence will be more appropriate to our needs. We have valued freedom a great deal in our ideological thought, but it has been an externalized freedom from control by one another and not inner freedom, as defined in the religiopsychological thought of Asian philosophies. We have emphasized scientific and empirical evidence as the source of validation. If we can't measure it, it doesn't exist. These assumptions can function as blinders, limiting our sight to a narrow tunnel of existence. Asian psychology spends less time on the process of rushing around to accomplish things and more time teasing out of the original assumptions which motivated us in the first place and pointed us in one direction rather than another. Most of all, Asian psychology will put us in touch with the majority of the world's population outside the splendid isolation of Euro-American experiences.

VALIDATION

Systems of Asian psychology have been actively serving most of the world's population for several thousand years. The endurance of ideas must be considered as evidence of their vitality. Many aspects of Asian psychology, as they gain popularity in the West and among Western-trained Asian psychologists, have demonstrated their validity even when subjected to the judgment of non-Asian criteria.

Evidence

There is a profound difference in the assumptions relative to personality theory made in India, China, and Japan, compared to those of the West. Asian psychology emphasizes inner awareness as the ultimate goal, while Western theories concentrate on the reality of the outside world. Asians seek to transcend conflict, while Western psychology tries to resolve conflict. The individual Asian personality is absorbed into other primary relationships as the basic units of human behavior, rather than seeing others as hostile counterparts to one's self.

Evidence supporting self-induced altered states of consciousness as resulting in better mental or physical health and increased ability to deal with tension or stress has encouraged a growing interest in Zen, Yoga, transcendental meditation and biofeedback systems which have grown out of essentially Asian psychologies (Benson, Beary, & Carol, 1974). These techniques have emphasized greater dependence on inner resources rather than on external controls of behavior, resulting in the self-actualization of trained participants. Though they have been popular in Asia for centuries, they are being discovered by modern Western medicine as effective (Brown, 1974, Reynolds, 1980).

One of the most popular adapted techniques has been transcendental meditation, or TM. The measured response to this technique is described by Benson, Beary, and Carol (1974):

> During the practice of one well-investigated technique called Transcendental Meditation, the major elements of the relaxation response occur: decreases in oxygen consumption, carbon dioxide eliminations, heart rate, respiratory rate, minute ventilation, and arterial blood lactate . . . . The electroencephalogram demonstrates an increase in the intensity of slow alpha waves and occasional theta wave activity. (p. 38)

Benson, Beary, and Carol provide a comparative table describing the effect of TM, autogenic training, hypnosis, Zen, Yoga, and other relaxation techniques.

The very need to evaluate and demonstrate a personality theory's usefulness assumes a bias foreign to Asian psychology. Western psychologists as a rule both dislike and distrust a pessimistic view which questions the value of life.

> They [Europeans] can accord some sympathy to a dying man who sees in due perspective the unimportance of his past life or to a poet who under the starry heavens can make felt the smallness of man and his earth, but such thoughts are considered permissible only as retrospects, not as principles of life: you may say that your labor has amounted to nothing, but not that labor is vain. (Murphy & Murphy, 1968, p. 28)

Our belief in progress is so strong that asceticism and the contemplative life are immediately suspected or even offensive. As a result, when Western psychologists study Asian psychology, they tend to look for evidence of its usefulness measured objectively by external criteria (Wittkower & Termansen, 1969). They ask: "Does the Oriental way of life with its emphasis on social and emotional withdrawal, on meditation and contemplation, increase or reduce a tendency to develop mental disease?" or "To what extent is mental morbidity affected by prevailing Eastern value orientations—such as the traditional family structure, role and status of women—compared with prevailing Western value orientations?" To evaluate these points of view, they look at criterion factors affecting rates of mental disorder and the measured effects of rapid social change on behavior, social organization, and mental health.

Even from this achievement point of view, Asian psychology has gained importance in the West and promises to continue doing so. In part, this new popularity relates to a reorganization of our own values in Western societies and in part to the recognition of the need for alternatives. The increased international exchange of professional psychologists and international students has contributed to greater awareness, as has the increase of publications through cross-cultural writing and research. Increased political dependence by Western countries on Japan and China is likely to result in more attention to their social and cultural organization, as well as a better understanding of Asian behavior styles.

Sato (1968) documents a list of benefits as validating Zen training. They include promoting vitality; helping to cure chronic disease; adjusting nervous functions and helping to cure neurosis; changing temperaments; heightening self-control of the will; promoting work efficiency and preventing accidents; heightening intellectual functions; integrating the individual's personality into a "flexible and serene mind"; achievement of *Satori,* or realization of the interdependence between self and the universe; a deepened sense of compassion; and peace of mind. The emphasis in validating Zen within its own framework is on freedom from worries of life and death, in a variety of forms.

The ultimate task of validation is locating criteria sensitive to both the Asian and the Western criteria of importance. As the various systems exchange ideas with one another, such superordinate criteria may emerge. In the meantime it will be necessary to understand each system from its own assumptions and point of view to evaluate its importance adequately.

Comparisons

The notion of *personality* as described in Western theories is a direct product of preliterate concepts of Mediterranean, Greek, Hebrew, and finally

Judeo-Christian ideas, shaped and structured through the Roman and Holy Roman Empires and finally delivered to the world in the plastic package of "better-things-through-better living" consumerism. The assumptions which define this concept of personality are that the individual is not only free but somehow aloof from the rest of the universe. When this structure of reality is viewed in context—e.g., in perspective with the beliefs of non-Western societies—we can see that there are alternative ways to look at human behavior which emphasize not the individual but rather the lively space between individuals in relationship with one another. While we may meaningfully look at the outside world through direct observation, there are other cultural traditions that emphasize self-examination and subjective truth, beyond accepting apparent reality around us as the criterion of truth.

We may now ask the central question as to which tradition is more valuable, if indeed it is possible to compare them. Murphy and Murphy (1968) suggest that both viewpoints are valuable.

> So, after three centuries of observation of the outer world in a form which we know as science, we are coming around to a psychology which uses knowledge of the external world—physics and physiology—as a primary clue to the methods most suitable for the study of the world within . . . The basic human nature which is tapped, displayed, or distorted, or whatever you believe happens during such conditions, is apparently much the same in the East and in the West, but the East has made these special states so far from immediate, everyday, palpable reality, something to be sought; the West hands them to the aspirant or the casual inquirer as a gift from biological chemistry. (p. 231)

Pande (1968) further discusses how the categories of personality are different in the East and West. Western culture emphasizes rationality, an intellectual understanding of reality, the separation of work and play, and the perceiving intelligence as separate from the other parts of a person. This categorization is most clearly seen in our separation of stages in human development. Western psychology assumes a separation and even opposition of the individual and environment, building a system that assumes the ego to be the actively independent observer and controller of the environment. Watts (1961) describes the Indian alternative of intuitively assuming the unity of all life as central, substituting self-transcendence for self-assertion, and the Chinese assumption of nature's balanced harmony for the individual who follows Confucian rules of social responsibility. The task for Asian psychology is not to separate ego from environment but to relate these two elements meaningfully and harmoniously to one another. The emphasis is not on the autonomy of the ego, of distinctiveness of the individual, but rather, as in the Japanese culture, on individual ego and society becoming one interdependent unit.

Asian psychology provides an alternative series of assumptions for understanding, evaluating, and shaping human behavior. Pande (1968) mentions other contrasts such as the Western

. . . emphasis on work rather than relationships and love; self-direction and independence in life rather than interdependence and acceptance of guidance from others; a directional and linear attitude toward time rather than an ahistorical view of time; encapsulated individual consciousness rather than social if not cosmic consciousness; and a problem-solving, cerebral approach to life's conflicts rather than one emphasizing absorption and integration of experience. (p. 432)

Sometimes an apparent similarity between Western and Asian behavior leads Western psychology to assume similar motivation in the two cultures. Wagatsuma (1973) asserts that need achievement in Japanese society is as strong a work ethic as that guiding Northern European Protestants. While this may be true, DeVos (1973) cites the Japanese example of industrial productivity as an argument against McClelland's theory of motivation as depending on individualistic assumptions: "Principally, I attack the theoretical approach of David McClelland and his associates for the way it generalizes a relationship between need achievement and individualism that is recurrently apparent in West European culture" (p. 167). DeVos characterizes the economic and psychological understanding of Western countries as too dependent on individualistically motivated behavior.

To explain Zen to English-speaking readers, Sato (1968) attempts to identify parallels from Western systems of psychology. He compares some of the stages of Zen meditation with heightened awareness through psychedelic drugs and suggests that under controlled conditions drugs could contribute to a better understanding of Zen. He draws parallels with Rogerian emphasis on "an accepting and permissive attitude," suggesting that Rogerian theory could enhance its effectiveness through a better understanding of Zen.

Carl Rogers (Meador & Rogers, 1973) acknowledges his debt to Asian psychological thought. Sato compares the "true self" of Rogerian theory with the bottomless bottom of the "True Self" in Zen. He believes that in some other respects Zen provides much more direction than Rogerian theory would allow. Zen is described as more encompassing and broader, less restricted than Rogerianism.

A comparison of Zen and psychoanalysis is found in Fromm, Suzuki and DeMartino (1960). Erich Fromm (1959) describes Zen as a blending of Indian rationality and abstraction with Chinese concreteness and realism, which makes it uniquely Eastern, in contrast with the equally unique Western notion of psychoanalysis. While Zen is a more or less religious technique or way to achieve enlightenment and spiritual salvation, psychoanalysis is an emphatically nonreligious therapy for mental illness. Therefore, while the aim of "transforming the unconscious into consciousness" may approximate the Zen notion of enlightenment, the method of achieving that goal is entirely different. There is perhaps less flexibility in psychoanalytic theory than we find in Zen's ability to accommodate diverse approaches to the same goal. Many of the basic concepts of psychoanalysis, such as have been discussed in the Assertions section of this chapter, are closely tied to European cultural values.

Jungian analytical theory has borrowed some of its imagery and symbols directly from Asian cultures and would therefore seem to be most adapted to Asian cultures. The differences between Asian and Western interpretations of the unconscious, the self, sexuality, and paradoxical tensions such as Yin and Yang are sufficiently profound, however, that Carl Jung's interpretations often change or distort the Asian understanding of the same phenomena. Jung appears to apply Asian concepts to the non-Asian world, standing on the outside of Asia looking in. The Asian theorist, standing on the inside looking out, is not constrained by having to fit his experiences into non-Asian categories or explanations.

Rational-emotive therapy sees "irrational beliefs" as the source of emotional disturbance. But whose rules for rationality are applied? Even though the process of deduction may be eminently rational, it can begin from different basic assumptions about reality which lead two rational individuals in completely different and emotionally disturbing directions. In emphasizing the rational process of thinking, Albert Ellis neglects the diverse underlying cultural assumptions as well as the norms for cultures, deemphasizing rationality as the ultimate measure of reality. Rather, he requires us to accept *his* definition of rationality, reasonableness, and reality. Nonrational or irrational tendencies are viewed as destructive and evaluated as ineffective, so that "all serious emotional problems with which humans are beset directly stem from their magical, superstitious, empirically unvalidatable thinking" (Ellis, 1973, p. 172). Rational emotive therapy may not only be depending on Western assumptions; it appears to evangelize these assumptions to the less fortunate majority of the world's population.

Behavior therapy appears insensitive to the sociocultural context of behavior, attempting to isolate the individual from family, society, and significant relationships which Asian culture imposes and which deemphasize the individual self. Thus, while behavior therapy can successfully identify unadaptive behavior and learning processes, there is a mechanistically scientific assumption about factors motivating the individual (Goldstein, 1973, p. 245). The Asian is likely to be less concerned about factoring out behaviors in adaptive and maladaptive categories. From the Asian point of view, behavior therapy may be asking the wrong questions.

Behavior therapy needs to accommodate the sociocultural context of behavior, attempting to isolate the individual from family, society, and significant relationships which Asian culture imposes and which deemphasize the individual self. Higginbotham and Tanaka-Matsumi (1981) have identified an adaptation of behavior therapy approaches which is sensitive to non-Western cultural values and which emphasizes contextual variables.

Gestalt therapy is more all-inclusive in its emphasis, adapting to a wide range of personality styles and cultures to disclose the individual to himself and others. There is a directness and sometimes embarrassing openness implied in Gestalt which can easily become offensive and insensitive to the less direct stabilities of Asian relationships. Gestalt successfully captures the paradoxical and complex polarization of Asian motivation but then "demands the active expression of what one is and not a description of what one is" (Kempler, 1973, p. 260). Gestalt's emphasis on explicit awareness appears almost clumsy in its objectified analysis of human behavior. The Gestalt-oriented therapist working with Asians could easily violate the limits of self-disclosure and become more terrifying than the original problem for clients.

Reality therapy emphasizes personal responsibility for one's own behavior and is insensitive to family and social relationships which are more constraining in Asia than in Western culture. William Glasser "feels that blaming their failure upon their homes, their communities, their culture, their background, their race or their poverty is a dead end . . . " (Glasser & Zunin, 1973, p. 291). Such a view disregards the influence of *Karma* in Indian society, the situation-centeredness of Chinese culture, and the *amae* model of relationships discussed earlier. There is success-oriented optimistic emphasis on mankind's basic goodness and individual responsibility which must seem naive to many Asians. To this extent, reality therapy does indeed impose value judgments on non-Western clients.

Other experiential or existential theories of personality place more emphasis on the present, disregarding many traditions of critical importance to Asian culture. There is an emphasis on concrete experiencing that denies the mystic complexity of Asian psychology, as it includes both the past and the future through philosophy and religion. The emphasis on experience is authentic to Asian thought, making this view perhaps the most adaptable to Asian culture. At the same time, there is an analysis and explanation of human behavior in Asia which, while different from Western theories, nonetheless goes beyond experience. The existential or experiential explanation is not likely to satisfy the troubled Asian who would prefer to go beyond this immediate awareness to some external reality.

The Japanese are known for adopting ideas from India and China, as well as the West, to synthesize their own culture as an extension of tolerance and conciliation with their environment. Other aspects, such as the familistic custom, are deeply entrenched against change. Foreign ideas have been adopted in the context of a Japanese emphasis on an almost supernational ethnocentrism. The traditional Shinto worship of Japan places less emphasis on the moral distinction between good and evil and more on submission or nonsubmission to the authority of a corporate whole or the Emperor. The Japanese militaristic ultranationalsim of World War II emerged from this basic idea. Unlike the Indians and Chinese, the Japanese depended on a more concrete, tangible, and less abstract source of final authority. There is a "contempt for rational thinking and the worship of uncontrolled intuitionism and activism" (Nakamura, 1964, p. 400). The Japanese emphasis on loyalty and responsibility is limited to their own family, community, and ultimately country, but it tends to neglect the context of humanity as a whole and presents a serious weakness of traditional thought in dealing with the social confusion of contemporary international relations (Nakamura, 1964, p. 521).

Murphy and Murphy (1968) characterize European psychology as less pessimistic than Asian psychology, offering a belief in the possibility of realizing some modicum of happiness in this life. Asian psychologies have been more skeptical of this goal.

> Whether we take the disparagement of the body and of the world as we find it in the Upanishads, or the retreat into an inner discipline as expressed in the Bhagavad-Gita and in yoga, or the belief that a middle course, involving Buddha's noble eightfold way, must lead one into a loss of individuality, a state of *nirvana,* we seem to find very little faith that life is really good. (p. 226)

Since the actions of an individual are supervised and regulated by the ideas of *karma* and *Samsara,* there is a tendency toward submissiveness to whatever inequities exist in the present system and an escape to some future transmigration under better conditions. In this respect, Indian thought resembles Western romanticism's vague and undefined attraction to a distant Truth.

The subjective emphasis on infinite being offers both advantages and disadvantages. The disadvantages lead to tolerance for injustice and inequity, so that one may accept the ideas that one's efforts need not be commensurate with rewards. You may work more but eat less than your neighbor, but that is all right. This notion of acceptance of reality in a passive manner explains what is generally considered Oriental fatalism. It also demonstrates the nonimportance of suffering. As Surya (1969) points out, "if you work ten times harder than the next, it is no special virtue" (pp. 387-388). Some personal social benefits derive from viewing human relations as a fusion of self with others into a corporate identity. Nakamura (1964) quotes Albert Schweitzer in acknowledging the importance of acceptance, calmness or equanimity of mind. "The Indian people comprehend the essential weak point in the faith of modern Christianity. We Europeans believe that Christianity is only dynamic in its religious activity. There are too few occasions when we reflect on our deeper selves. We Europeans are usually devoid of equanimity of mind" (p. 79). In a context of activism the ideas of inner peace have become increasingly attractive to Western peoples.

PROSPECT

This chapter has introduced alternatives to Western psychology from Asian cultures and directed the reader to resources which adequately analyze them. In a sense, the whole chapter has been critical of the cultural bias in traditional Western psychology, attacking the culturally limited assumptions on which a construct such as *personality* is based. The examples cited have been more or less arbitrarily chosen, omitting other vitally important aspects of Asian culture and oversimplifying the wide diversity of thought within each of the major cultural traditions of Asia. The goal is to make readers aware of Western psychological theory as one—but not the *only*—way of understanding how personality contributes to human behavior.

In the cross-cultural understanding of personality, qualitative and not merely quantitative patterns differentiate one group from another. Although we all may share the same personality dimensions, we do not share them in the same context, which frustrates the accuracy of communication of culturally universally psychological statements. We are becoming more aware of the specific ways an individual's behavior is linked to the environment. Traditional societies tend to be more restrictive in patterning personalities toward sameness, while more open societies encourage individuation.

Because of this the discipline of psychology will eventually become enlarged to accommodate a variety of viewpoints and assumptions. We will invent new constructs to interpret human behavior. With the invention of new terminology, or perhaps rediscovery of parallel systems in non-Western cultures, psychology as a discipline will better interpret the varieties of human behavior in many cultures. Several changes are likely to occur.

1. Modernization and ''Westernization'' will contribute to cross-cultural similarity through the demands of industrialization, technological expansion, and military expediency. This does not mean that the traditional cultures will disappear. The phenomenon De Vos (1973) calls *psychological lag* continues despite changes. For example, the traditional notion of arranged marriages in Japan runs counter to popular opinion, but most marriages in Japan, even today, are arranged by the families. There is an underlying system of basic traditional and indigenous assumptions which in principle do not change but do in fact define change by their own stability. These basic cultural principles become disguised by the apparent similarity of modernization but will continue to influence behavior through their cultural entrenchment.

2. The need to establish an Asian identity for the Japanese, the Chinese, and Indian will result in the maintenance or perhaps even the deliberate

reinvention of cultural traditions to separate and distinguish Asians from non-Asians. These cultural differences will be more similar within nationality groups or linguistically defined dialect groups. Modernization is unlikely to destroy cultural uniqueness, beyond fairly superficial and subordinate goals of expedient necessity. If psychology is to be accurately applied to understanding behavior in a variety of cultures, we will need to develop expertise *both* in the cultural universals shared by all people *and* the unique circumstances of Asians on their own terms.

3. Western cultures will increasingly borrow ideas from Asian models of behavior that might apply to our own culture as well. We will learn about ourselves not just by comparison with other cultures in Asia but from within the assumptions of an Asian psychology. The popularity of Asian psychologies of meditation provides an immediate example of how Asian psychological insights might provide a more ''advanced'' and sophisticated alternative to our own traditional systems of mental health. The ''development'' assumption has otherwise too easily measured progress in underdeveloped countries by their approximation to the Western ideals of modernization. As non-Western countries increase in their political and economic influence, our increased dependence on them will no doubt extend to modeling aspects of their social organization in the future, as many of these countries have modeled themselves after ours in the past.

We need most of all to see history in a perspective of thousands rather than hundreds or tens of years. In that perspective our notions of psychology are relatively recent. Arnold Toynbee may have been right in predicting the rise of the East and the decline of Western civilization. Our survival and theirs will depend largely on our flexibility and evolutionary adaptability to the changing world around us. By increasing our awareness of the alternative cultures available to us, we might increase the likelihood of our survival in a future culture which is not known.

There is a tendency for modernization of non-Western cultures to include a considerable amount of Westernization. Higginbotham (1979) discusses the reasons for adopting Western models and Marsella (1980, 1981) describes some of the dangers for that adoption. It would appear that schizophrenia, for example, is of shorter duration and less serious in its effect in non-Western ''underdeveloped'' countries than in Western ''developed'' countries. We need to be careful that in the process of modernizing and consequently Westernizing other cultures that we are not teaching illness as well as health.

ANNOTATED BIBLIOGRAPHY

The resources cited in this chapter include materials in anthropology, philosophy, and religion as well as psychology, although each reference contributes to a uniquely ''psychological'' point of view on human behavior. While there is an abundance of material on separate and specific psychological aspects of Asian cultures, there are some books which provide an overall structure for comparing Asian psychological traditions with one another or with the West. The best books surveying Asian thought are Nakamura (1964), Caudill and Lin (1969), Hsu (1972), and Murphy and Murphy (1968). The best books for getting at each separate Asian tradition are De Vos (1973) for Japan, (Kleinman et al., 1975) for China, and Govinda (1961) for India.

Nakamura, Hajime. *Ways of Thinking of Eastern Peoples: India, China, Tibet, Japan.* (Philip P. Wiener, Ed.). Honolulu: University Press of Hawaii, 1964.

Professor Nakamura's book developed from conferences at the East-West Center in 1962-63 and was updated and revised by Philip Wiener. The book's theme is that there is no "Asia in the singular sense, but that there is a wide range of traditions which touch all extremes, just as there is in Western thought. The genius of Nakamura is to look at each culture's language as the key to a better understanding of their thought and psychology. The language provides a rich source of hard data for specific nuances of differences between cultures. While each cultural tradition is discussed comparatively with Western thought, each is approached from within its own assumptions and no attempt is made to enforce or impose evaluative criteria of Western traditions. The book is written from primary materials in Asian languages not otherwise readily available and is perhaps the best single resource on Asian psychology.

Caudill, William, and Lin, Tsung-Yi (Eds.). *Mental Health Research in Asia and the Pacific.* Honolulu: East-West Center Press, 1969.

The 30 articles in this book were written by leaders in the area of Asian psychology. The chapters review the issues in identifying mental illness cross-culturally and cultural

effects on human behavior. The chapters are largely self-contained, but there is some effort by authors to cross-reference with one another; Doi and Surya, for example, compare one another's comments on "dependence" as it is different and similar in Japan and India. The specialized focus of each chapter samples the diversity of Asian psychology. This book is part of a three-book series; the other two volumes were edited by William Lebra (1972, 1974). The more recent volumes continue the tradition of sampling a wide range of specialized topics in Asian psychology.

Hsu, Francis L. K. (Ed.). *Psychological Anthropology.* Cambridge, Mass.: Schenkman, 1972.

Francis Hsu is the anthropologist who is perhaps best known for his books in the area of Asian psychology. His publications are helpful for understanding the structure and systems of Asian psychology. This particular 14-chapter book is an updated revision of a popular 1961 edition. The chapter authors represent leading authorities from Western countries who have widely published articles interpreting psychological phenomena in Asia. The book surveys non-Asian cultures as well as cultures of Asia and the Pacific, reviewing psychological methods, techniques, processes, and assessment procedures in cross-cultural psychology. Asian psychology is seen, along with Western psychology, in the large world perspective.

Murphy, Gardner, and Murphy, Lois (Eds.). *Asian Psychology.* New York: Basic Books, 1968.

This book is part of a series exploring the possibility of some sort of "universal psychology" around the world's cultures. Whether or not such a phenomenon exists depends largely on how terms are defined. At times the book may oversimplify the complexity of Asian cultures, but generally it provides an interesting introduction to Asian psychology in a comparative framework. The authors enlisted help from well-known Asian authorities from the major areas in India, China, and Japan for the three sections of the book. Original translations of Asian traditional literature are widely quoted to illustrate psychological insights and to at least introduce the major psychological ideas in each culture.

De Vos, George A. (ed.). *Socialization for Achievement*. Berkeley: University of California Press, 1973.

With the help of Hiroshi Wagatsuma, William Caudill, and Keiichi Mizushima, De Vos has assembled essays that explore all aspects of Japanese cultural psychology. The book elaborates aspects of personality theory specific to human psychosexual and cognitive maturation, looking at the psychological structure of Japanese culture. While it admits to a psychoanalytic bias, and the influence of sociologists such as Max Weber and anthropologists such as Emil Durkheim, there is open criticism of these viewpoints as well. The authors provide valuable and unique insights into Japanese culture, although within the framework of fairly traditional personality theory.

Govinda, Lama Anagarika. *The Psychological Attitude of Early Buddhist Philosophy*. London: Rider, 1961.

Indian psychology is perhaps the most philosophically obscure of all Asian psychologies, though it contains the roots of ideas developed later throughout Asia. The book carefully sorts out the particularly psychological aspects of Indian thought to demonstrate the complex sophistication of a psychological system thousands of years old, predating many "modern" discoveries of contemporary psychology. The close connection between religion and psychology is particularly apparent and may be disconcerting to the traditional psychologist because it answers questions not being asked in modern Western psychology. The book provides a rich background for understanding popular psychologies of meditation and subjectivity

from within the Asian psychological system.

Kleinman, A., Kunstadter, P., Alexander, E. R., and Gale, J. L. *Medicine in Chinese Cultures: Comparative Studies of Health Care in Chinese and Other Societies*. DHEW (NIH 75-653). Washington, D.C.: U.S. Government Printing Office, 1975.

Chinese mental health includes both somatic and psychological symptoms combined in a holistic picture of personal "health." For that reason this extensive collection of chapters is a valuable perspective of health from within the Chinese perspective. While not all chapters relate to psychology directly, they all provide valuable information on understanding psychological processes in a Chinese context. The interdisciplinary background of the authors and the contrasting points of view emphasize the "strangeness" of a notion such as "psychology" in the Chinese context. Also the chapters attempt to go beyond the Asian technologies of health toward an understanding of the social and environmental assumptions which sponsor those methods. While other books would be preferred for specific aspects of Chinese psychology none is as easily accessible and inexpensive as this volume. For additional more specialized treatment other citations are provided in the references to this chapter.

None of the books annotated here presumes a profound acquaintance with Asian philosophy or religion. Any of these references will provide an easily read introduction to non-Western alternatives in psychology.

REFERENCES

Allport, G. *Personality: A psychological interpretation*. New York: Holt, Rinehart & Winston, 1937.

Anant, S. S., & Shanker, P. Intercaste difference in personality pattern. *Psychologia*, 1966, *9*, 225-231.

Beg, A. The theory of personality in the Bhagavad Gita: A study in transpersonal psychology. *Psychologia,* 1970, *15,* 12-17.

Benedict, R. *The chrysanthemum and the sword.* Boston: Houghton Mifflin, 1946.

Benson, H., Beary, J., & Carol, M. The relaxation response. *Psychiatry,* 1974, *37,* 37-46.

Brislin, R., Lonner, W., & Thorndike, R. *Cross-cultural research methods.* New York: Wiley, 1973.

Brown, B. B. *New mind, new body: Biofeedback: New directions for the mind.* New York: Harper & Row, 1974.

Brown L. B. *Psychology in contemporary China.* New York: Pergamon Press, 1981.

Butcher, J. & Clark, L. A. Recent trends in cross-cultural MMPI research and application. In J. Butcher (Ed.), *New developments in the use of the MMPI.* Minneapolis: University of Minnesota Press, 1980.

Capra, F. *The Tao of physics.* New York: Bantam Books, 1977.

Caudill, W., & Lin, T. Y. (Eds.). *Mental health research in Asia and the Pacific.* Honolulu: East-West Center Press, 1969.

Chaubey, N. Indian family structure and risk-taking behavior. *Indian Journal of Psychology,* 1972, *47,* 213-221.

Child, I. L. Personality in culture. In E. F. Borgatta & W. W. Lambert (Eds.), *Handbook of personality theory and research.* Chicago: Rand McNally, 1968.

Chiu, L. H. A cross-cultural comparison of cognitive styles in Chinese and American children. *International Journal of Psychology,* 1972, 235-242.

De Vos, G. (Ed.). *Socialization for achievement: Essays on the cultural psychology of the Japanese.* Berkeley, Calif.: University of California Press, 1973.

De Vos, George. Afterword. In D. K. Reynolds, *The quiet therapies.* Honolulu: The University Press of Hawaii, 1980, pp. 113-132.

Doi, L. Japanese psychology, dependency need and mental health. In W. Caudill and T. Lin (Eds.), *Mental health research in Asia and the Pacific.* Honolulu: East-West Center Press, 1969.

Doi, L. Amae: A key concept for understanding Japanese personality structure. In R. Le Vine (Ed.), *Culture and personality.* Chicago: Aldine, 1974.

Draguns, J. G. Counseling across cultures: Common themes and distinct approaches, in P. Pedersen, J. Draguns, W. Lonner & J. Trimble, *Counseling across cultures.* Honolulu: University Press of Hawaii, 1981, pp. 22-61.

Ellis, A. Rational-emotive therapy. In R. Corsini (Ed.), *Current psychotherapies.* Itasca, Ill.: F.E. Peacock, 1973, pp. 167-206.

Forgione, A. G., & Holmberg, R. Biofeedback therapy. In R. J. Corsini (Ed.), *Handbook of Innovative Psychotherapies.* New York: Wiley, 1981.

Fromm, E. Psychoanalysis and Zen Buddhism. *Psychologia,* 1959, *2,* 79-99.

Fromm, E., Suzuki, D. T., & De Martino, R. *Zen Buddhism and psychoanalysis.* New York: Harper & Bros., 1960.

Gilbert, A. Essay on the history of Asian psychology. *Proceedings, 81st Annual Convention,* American Psychological Associations (Vol. 8, Part 2). Washington, D.C., 1973.

Glasser, W. & Zunin, L. Reality therapy. In R. Corsini (Ed.), *Current psychotherapies.* Itasca, Ill.: F. E. Peacock, 1973.

Goldstein, A. Behavior therapy. In R. Corsini (Ed.), *Current psychotherapies.* Itasca, Ill.: F. E. Peacock, 1973.

Govinda, L. A. *The psychological attitude of early Buddhist philosophy.* London: Rider, 1961.

Grossberg, J. M. Brainwave feedback experiments and the concept of mental mechanisms. *Behavior Therapy and Experimental Psychiatry,* 1972, *3,* 245-251.

Higginbotham, H. Culture and the delivery of psychological services in developing nations. *Transcultural Psychiatric Research Review,* 1979, *16,* 7-27.

Higginbotham, H. N., & Tanaka-Matsumi, J. Behavioral approaches to counseling across cultures. In P. Pedersen, J. Draguns, W. Lonner, & J. Trimble (Eds.), *Counseling across cultures,* Honolulu: University Press of Hawaii, 1981.

Hiniker, P. Chinese reactions to forced compliance: Dissonance reduction or national character. *Journal of Social Psychology,* 1969, *77,* 157-176.

Hsu, F. L. K. (Ed.). *Psychological anthropology.* Homewood, Ill.: Dorsey Press, 1961.

Hsu, F. L. K. *Clan, caste, and club.* Princeton, N. J.: Van Nostrand, 1963.

Hsu, F. L. K. Psychosocial homeostasis and Jen: Conceptual tools for advancing psychological anthropology. *American Anthropologist,* 1971, *73,* 23-44.

Iwai, H., & Reynolds, D. Morita psychotherapy: The views from the West. *American Journal of Psychiatry,* 1970, *126,* 1031-1036.

Jacobson, L. Feedback on biofeedback. *Human Behavior,* 1974 *3*(7), 47-51.

Kakar, S. The theme of authority in social relations in India. *The Journal of Social Psychology,* 1971, *84,* 93-101.

Kanellakos, D. The psychobiology of transcendental meditation. Annotated bibliography by P. C. Ferguson, MIU International Center for Science Research (rev. 1973).

Kempler, W. Gestalt therapy. In R. Corsini (Ed.), *Current psychotherapies.* Itasca, Ill.: F. E. Peacock, 1973.

Kiev, A. *Magic, faith and healing.* New York: Free Press, 1964.

Kikuchi, A., & Gordon, L. Japanese and American personal values: Some cross-cultural findings. *International Journal of Psychology,* 1970, *5,* 183-187.

Kleinman, A., Kunstadter, P., Alexander, E. R., & Gale, J. L. *Culture and healing in Asian societies: Anthropological, psychiatric and public health studies.* Cambridge, Mass.: Schenkman, 1978.

Kleinman, A., Kunstadter, P., Alexander, E. R., & Gale, J. L. (Eds.). *Medicine in Chinese cultures.* HEW (NIH) 75-653. Washington, D.C.: U.S. Government Printing Office, 1975.

Kroeber, A. L., & Kluckhohn, C. Culture: a critical review of concepts and definitions. *Papers of the Peabody Museum of American Archeology and Ethnology,* 1952, *47,* 181.

Lebra, T. Intergenerational continuity and discontinuity in moral values among Japanese: A preliminary report. In W. Lebra (Ed.), *Transcultural research in mental health.* Honolulu: University Press of Hawaii, 1971, pp. 247-275.

Lebra, W. (Ed.). *Transcultural research in mental health.* Honolulu: University Press of Hawaii, 1971.

Lebra, W. (Ed.). *Culture-bound syndromes, ethnopsychiatry and alternative therapies.* Honolulu: University Press of Hawaii, 1977.

Lebra, W. (Ed.). *Youth, socialization and mental health.* Honolulu: University Press of Hawaii, 1974.

Leslie, C. *Asian medical systems: A comparative study.* Berkeley, Calif.: University of California Press, 1976.

LeVine, T. (Ed.). *Culture and personality.* Chicago: Aldine, 1974.

Liu, W. T. *Transition to nowhere: Vietnamese refugees in America.* Nashville: Charter House, 1979.

Lynn, R. (Ed.). *Personality and national character.* Oxford: Pergamon Press, 1971.

Mace, D. R., & Mace, V. *Marriage east and west.* Garden City, N.Y.: Doubleday, 1960.

Marsella, A. Depressive experience and disorder across cultures. In H. Triandis & J. Draguns (Eds.), *Handbook of cross-cultural psychology: Psychopathology.* Vol. 6. Boston: Allyn & Bacon, Inc., 1980.

Marsella, A. Culture, self and mental disorder. Paper presented at the Second Annual Department of Psychology Symposium on *Current Topics in Psychology.* Honolulu,

Hawaii, February 12-14, 1981.

Matsumoto, Y. Social stress and coronary heart disease in Japan: A hypothesis. *Millbank Memorial Fund Quarterly,* 1970, *48*(1), 9-36.

Meade, R., & Barnard, W. Conformity and anticonformity among Americans and Chinese. *Journal of Social Psychology,* 1973, *89,* 15-24.

Meador, B., & Rogers, C. Client-centered therapy. In R. Corsini (Ed.), *Current psychotherapies.* Itasca, Ill.: F. E. Peacock, 1973.

Murphy, G., & Murphy, L. *Asian psychology.* New York: Basic Books, 1968.

Nakakuki, M. *Japanese culture and mental health: Psychodynamic investigation.* Paper presented at the 9th International Congress of Anthropological and Ethnological Sciences, Chicago, September 1973.

Nakamura, H. *Ways of thinking of Eastern peoples: India-China-Tibet-Japan* (Philip P. Wiener, Ed.). Honolulu: University Press of Hawaii, 1964.

Nakane, C. *Human relations in Japan.* Tokyo: Ministry of Foreign Affairs, 1972.

Nishimaru, S. Mental climate and Eastern psychotherapy. *Transcultural Psychiatric Research Review,* 1965, *2,* 24.

Norbeck, E., & De Vos, G. Japan. In F. L. K. Hsu (Ed.), *Psychological anthropology.* Homewood, Ill.: Dorsey Press, 1961.

Osgood, C., May, W. H., & Miron, M. S. *Cross-cultural universals of affective meaning.* Urbana, Ill.: University of Illinois Press, 1975.

Pande, S. The mystique of "Western" psychotherapy: An Eastern interpretation. *Journal of Nervous and Mental Disease,* 1968, *146,* 425-432.

Pedersen, P. Non-western psychology: The search for alternatives. In A. Marsella, R. Tharp, & T. Cibrowski (Eds.), *Perspectives on cross-cultural psychology.* New York: Academic Press, 1979.

Pedersen, P. The inter-cultural context of

counseling and psychotherapy. In A. Marsella & G. White (Eds.) *Cultural Conceptions of Mental Health and Therapy.* Boston: D. Reidel, 1982.

Penner, L. & Tran, A. A comparison of American and Vietnamese value systems, *Journal of Social Psychology,* 1977, *101,* 187-204.

Price-Williams, D. The philosophy of science and the study of personality. In E. Norbeck, D. Price-Williams, & W. McCord (Eds.), *The study of personality: An interdisciplinary appraisal.* New York: Holt, Rinehart, & Winston, 1968.

Prince, R. Variations in psychotherapeutic procedures. In J. Triandis & J. Draguns, (Eds.), *Handbook of cross-cultural psychology: Psychopathology.* Vol. 6. Boston: Allyn & Bacon, Inc., 1980.

Reynolds, D. K. *The quiet therapies.* Honolulu: The University Press of Hawaii, 1980.

Reynolds, D. *Morita Psychotherapy.* Berkeley, Calif.: University of California Press, 1976.

Sampson, E. E. Psychology and the American ideal. *Journal of Personality and Social Psychology,* 1977, *35,* 767-782.

Sato, K. The concept of "on." Ruth Benedict and D. T. Suzuki. *Psychologia,* 1960, *2,* 243-245.

Sato, K. Zen from a personological viewpoint. *Psychologia,* 1968, *11,* 3-24.

Schweder, R. A. Rethinking culture and personality theory. *Ethos,* 1979, *9,* 60-90.

Schweder, R. A. Does the concept of the person vary cross-culturally? In A. Marsella & G. White, (Eds.), *Cultural conceptions of mental health and therapy.* Boston: D. Reidel Publishing Co., 1982.

Singer, M. A survey of culture and personality theory and research. In B. Kaplan (Ed.), *Studying personality cross-culturally.* Evanston, Ill.: Harper & Row, 1961.

Sinha, J. B. P. The construct of dependence proneness. *Journal of Social Psychology,* 1968, *76,* 129-131.

Solomon, R. *Mao's revolution and the Chinese political culture*. Berkeley, Calif.: University of California Press, 1971.

Spain, D. A supplementary bibliography on projective testing. In F. L. K. Hsu (Ed.), *Psychological anthropology*. Cambridge, Mass.: Schenkman, 1972.

Spiro, M. An overview and a suggested reorientation. In F. L. K. Hsu (Ed.), *Psychological anthropology*. Cambridge, Mass.: Schenkman, 1972.

Stewart, R. Self-realization as the basis of psychotherapy: A look at two eastern-based practices, Transcendental Meditation and Alpha Brain Wave Biofeedback. *Social Behavior and Personality*, 1974, *2*, 191-200.

Sundberg, N., Rohila, P., & Tyler, L. Values of Indian and American adolescents. *Journal of Personality and Social Psychology*, 1970, *16*, 374-397.

Surya, N. C. Ego structure in the Hindu joint family: Some considerations. In W. Caudill & T. Y. Lin (Eds.), *Mental health research in Asia and the Pacific*. Honolulu: East-West Center Press, 1969.

Suzuki, D. T. *The Essentials of Zen Buddhism*. (Selected from the edited writings of B. Phillips). New York: Dutton, 1962.

Tapp, J. Studying personality development. In H. Triandis and A. Heron (Eds.), *Handbook of cross-cultural psychology: Developmental psychology, Vol. 4*. Boston: Allyn & Bacon, 1982.

Tart, C. *Transpersonal psychologies*. New York: Harper & Row, 1975.

Torrey, E. *The mind game*. New York: Bantam Books, 1972.

Triandis, H. C., Malpass, R., & Davidson, A. Psychology and culture. *Annual Review of Psychology*, 1973, *24*, 355-378.

Tseng, W. S., & Hsu, J. Chinese culture, personality formation and mental illness. *International Journal of Social Psychiatry*, 1971, *16*, 5-14.

Tseng, W. S., & Hsu, J. Minor psychological disturbances of everyday life. In H. Triandis & J. Draguns (Eds.), *Handbook of cross-cultural psychology: Psychopathology*. Vol. 6, Boston: Allyn & Bacon, 1980.

Vogel, E. F. A preliminary view of family and mental health in urban Communist China. In W. Caudill & T. Y. Lin (Eds.), *Mental health research in Asia and the Pacific*. Honolulu: East-West Center Press, 1969.

Wagatsuma, H. Status and role behavior in changing Japan: Psychocultural continuities. In G. De Vos (Ed.), *Socialization for achievement: essays on the cultural psychology of the Japanese*. Berkeley, Calif.: University of California Press, 1973.

Watts, A. *Psychotherapy East and West*. New York: Pantheon Books, 1961.

Waxler, N. E. Is mental illness cured in traditional societies? A theoretical analysis. *Culture, Medicine and Psychiatry*, 1977, *1*, 233-253.

Wittkower, E. C., & Termansen, P. E. Cultural psychiatric research in Asia. In W. Caudill & T. Y. Lin (Eds.), *Mental health research in Asia and the Pacific*. Honolulu: East-West Center Press, 1969.

Wohl, J. Intercultural psychotherapy: Issues, questions and reflections. In P. Pedersen, J. Draguns, W. Lonner, & J. Trimble (Eds.), *Counseling across cultures*. Honolulu: University Press of Hawaii, 1981.

Yap, P. M. The culture-bound reactive syndromes. In W. Caudill & T. Y. Lin (Eds.), *Mental health research in Asia and the Pacific*. Honolulu: East-West Center Press, 1969.

SECTION FOUR
ASSESSMENT

CHAPTER XIII

Personality Assessment

Raymond J. Corsini
and Anthony J. Marsella

INTRODUCTION

The term *assessment* refers to the processes, methods, and tools used to measure or evaluate a given phenomenon. Professional psychologists are frequently called on to assess personality. This assessment may be used in hiring an individual or in determining an individual's sanity. In many cases, it is to help the individual understand more about him/herself as occurs quite often in personal and vocational guidance and counseling. Although there is considerable debate regarding the value of personality assessment (see the entire issue of the *American Psychologist*, 1981, *36*, no. 10), it is generally conceded that the merits outweigh the limitations. It would be difficult to imagine how schools, industry, the military, or health facilities could get along without the use of personality assessment since it constitutes the basis of judgments about an individual's abilities, aptitudes, achievements, interests, and general behavioral tendencies. The purpose of this chapter is to discuss the theoretical and methodological foundations of personality assessment and to acquaint the reader with some examples of different personality assessment techniques.

THEORETICAL FOUNDATIONS

The Nature of Assessment

All human beings are continually engaged in assessing the world about them. This assessment involves the perception and evaluation of various

585

aspects of their world and facilitates the individual's immediate adjustment and long-term adaptation. For example, every time we encounter another individual there is an instantaneous appraisal of the other person with regard to personal characteristics and expected behavior. This appraisal and expectancy for behavior provides us with the needed information to deal with the encounter effectively. In general, this process involves four elements:

1. Reality: Reality is what we want to measure, estimate, or appraise. It refers to what is *actually* there as the topic of our concern.
2. Mode: Mode refers to the way one assesses the topic of concern. It may involve measuring instruments or subjective impressions.
3. Conclusion: Conclusions are results we arrive at during the process of assessment. These conclusions can be in the form of quantitative data or highly impressionistic information which may be difficult to even put into words.
4. Evaluation: Evaluation represents the decisions which are reached from the conclusions. It reflects a complex consideration of all of the aspects of the assessment involving the nature of the topic, the accuracy of the assessment mode used, the validity of the conclusions, and the implications which the information has for the individual under study.

Problems can occur in all of these elements. For example, it is possible the "reality" we are measuring may not even exist. We may say we want to measure a person's *extrasensory perception*, but there may be no such thing as ESP. Thus, one of the questions we must ask in personality assessment is whether the topic we are assessing exists. In addition, we must also ask what is the nature of our evidence for believing that something exists. Although we can observe a phenomenon which has a tangible reality, we can make mistakes regarding its nature because of our inability to understand the object. If we examine a leaf, we might say, "This is a leaf," referring only to the small half-withered form we are holding in our hand. But, by failing to understand that a leaf is part of a total plant, rooted in a particular type of soil, within a certain type of climate, we can make serious errors about the leaf.

In the case of personality assessment, we frequently assess phenomena which have no tangible reality. For example, we might choose to assess "shyness," "love," "hope," "dependency," or "intelligence." All of these terms are *constructs* or terms we "create" to help summarize or make sense of the world around us. We see a given pattern of behavior and we say it is "hate" or "love," but we must remember that this is our interpretation and inference about the behavior we are observing. Under these circumstances, we can make many errors since the construct we invoke may have no substantive existence.

Errors can also occur as a result of the particular mode of assessment we use, since the mode may provide a limited or inaccurate portrayal of the topic under study. Sometimes the instruments we use are not *valid* and sometimes we may use the instruments incorrectly. For example, it would be difficult to assess an African villager's "dependency needs" by asking him questions developed for Western populations and plotting his scores against Western norms.

In some instances, we arrive at the wrong conclusions because we fail to interpret the data derived from our assessment properly. This is especially a problem when we use personality measures that require extensive subjective interpretation and clinical skill. In many of these instances, we can also reach decisions which are erroneous. Since our decisions are a result of the reality, the mode, and the conclusions, it represents a step which is subject to error at many previous points in the long process of assessment.

Thus, assessment is a complex process that begins with a set of assumptions about the nature of the phenomena to be measured and ends with a series of interpretations and decisions based on the information derived from the assessment process. Assessment is something we all do in an effort to describe, understand, predict, and control the world about us. For some people, assessment is a professional activity involving sophisticated instruments which measure a broad spectrum of human functioning including abilities, aptitudes, achievement levels, interests, personality traits and dynamics, interpersonal relations, psychomotor, and biological variables. In their endeavors, professional assessment specialists rely on many different assessment instruments including self-report tests, behavioral observation forms, psychomotor tests, biological indices (e.g., catecholamine excretion rates, blood sugar levels) and other assessment measures.

Some Issues in Personality Assessment

1. Terms of Reference. All of us rely on words to assess ourselves or others. Sometimes we do this with one word such as: "fool," "angel," "bastard," or "kind." However, most of the time, we combine a number of words in our assessment to increase our accuracy. Clearly, most of us would find it difficult to assess someone by using only one word. Personality is simply too complex to reduce it to a single term, although when we are angry at someone we tend to rely on single-word explicatives and profane terms to capture our emotion. This usually takes the form of something like "You are a __ __ __ __!" Obviously, under these circumstances, our appraisal may be less than accurate, although it certainly is highly descriptive and generally evokes a vivid image.

In the course of doing an extensive personality assessment of a person on behalf of a court or a business company, we may rely on many terms based on the use of several assessment instruments. We might conclude an individual is suggestible, mentally dull, kind, dependent, anxious, shy, passive, conforming, and cooperative. Based on these terms, we could begin to construct a profile of this person which would provide a good prediction of this person's behavior across a variety of situations.

Assessment is much easier in the physical sciences like chemistry or physics since the phenomena measured are often inanimate and easier to predict. If we want to measure a brick we can simply say it weighs 100 kilograms, has a width of 30 centimeters, a length of 50 centimeters, and takes the shape of a perfect rectangle. We could add the brick is made of clay of a particular density. All of this information provides us with a good understanding of the brick's characteristics and possible uses. Contrast the ease of measuring a brick with the difficulty of assessing the personality of someone as complex as Richard Nixon, the former president of the United States.

In many respects, good novelists are like specialists in personality assessment because they construct a cohesive and meaningful picture of a protagonist's personality by resorting to descriptive terms which provide cues about the person's behavior. They weave a story with their words, bringing to life a complex character. When we read *Hamlet*, we come to know him intimately, aware of his innermost hopes and fears and the roots of his subsequent behavior. All of this is done in terms of words which are carefully chosen and well placed. Sometimes, great novelists like Charles Dickens are able to build an entire character around a single personality trait. For example, Dickens developed Scrooge's personality in *A Christmas Carol* around the trait of "stinginess." He added a hunchedback, a long nose, squinting eyes, and shriveled skin, and what soon emerged was a caricature of the very image we conjure up when we use the term *miser*.

In personality assessment, we can sometimes use different measures such as reaction time, perceptual acuity, biochemical excretion rates, and so forth. But, most of the time we must rely on words. Allport and Odbert (1936) found 17,953 adjectives could be used to describe people. More than 4,000 of these words were considered personality traits, or relatively enduring behavioral tendencies which transcend different situations.

Both the number and the specificity of the terms we use to describe personality influences the accuracy of our personality assessment. As we have pointed out, one-word descriptions of personality are generally inaccurate in predicting future behavior. And, too, many descriptors can also lead to inaccuracy unless the latter are qualified by some attention to situations in which the different terms apply. But, it is the nature of the words themselves which are a greater strength and weakness in personality assessment. This is because of the denotative and the connotative meaning of various words. Reaching a conclusion that someone is "ordinary" is meaningless from the point of view of knowing something about the person, since it denotes nothing and connotes a great deal.

But, through all of this, it is words we must rely on, and in the hands of a skilled assessor, a personality assessment can bring a thorough and detailed understanding of a person. The key becomes our ability to tie our words to behavioral patterns and assessment techniques.

2. Dimensions of Human Personality. Given the many acknowledged traits of human personality, it is logical to ask whether personality can be reduced to a limited number of dimensions which capture the essence of human functioning. This research topic has been pursued with ardor by a number of investigators. For example, Hans Eysenck believes personality can be encompassed within three basic dimensions: extraversion-introversion, arousal, and psychoticism. The use of data analysis methods such as factor analysis permits researchers to reduce large amounts of data to a few basic dimensions. But, the exact number and the specific nature of the personality dimensions which have been derived by personality researchers differ greatly.

If we measure the physical dimensions of anything there are really only three units we can use: height, weight, and depth. But, the basic dimensions of personality are much harder to determine. Digman and Takemoto-Chock (1981) compared the basic dimensions in "the natural language of personality" through an analysis of the factor analytic studies of a number of prominent theorists. They acknowledged that the methods used to gather the personality data, the sources of the data, and the different populations are all important elements in understanding the various conclusions about the basic dimensions of personality. But, even within the context of these considerations, they found five dimensions appeared to be consistent across the theorists: (*a*) extraversion versus introversion; (*b*) anxiety (ego strength versus emotional disorganization); (*c*) will to achieve (conscientiousness, super-ego strength); (*d*) intellectual functioning; and (*e*) sociability.

Among studies not included in Digman and Takemoto-Chock's analysis, Borgatta (1964) suggested the basic dimensions of personality were assertiveness, likability, emotionality, intelligence, and task interests. Corsini (1956) concluded the basic personality dimensions were introversion-extraversion, social sensitivity, emotional stability, intelligence, activity level, dominance-submission, and mood. All of these studies suggest that there is some agreement across researchers in spite of differences in the samples studied, the techniques used to appraise personality, the methods of data analysis, and the source of the information.

3. *Sources of Information.* What is personality? Is personality what I say I am or what my close acquaintance says I am? Is personality my score on a measure which yields quantitative data (i.e., reaction time, visual acuity) or a measure which provides a qualitative score (i.e., tendency for conformity)? These questions are concerned with another major issue in

personality assessment; namely, the source of the information.

The researchers who have done the most to examine different sources of personality information are Raymond Cattell and Hans Eysenck. Both recognized the problems associated with using only one source of information about personality. It should be clear to the reader that I can report many things about myself which only I know and this is obviously important in obtaining an accurate picture of personality. But, I may not be capable of seeing myself as others see me because of perceptual biases. Thus, it is important to sample all sources of information including objective tests, record data, biological information, and family history.

The critical question in this issue is the purpose of the personality assessment. Certain sources of information may be more important than others in offering increased predictability. Yet another consideration is the amount of time available to gather information. George Kelly, the personality theorist discussed in Chapter 6, frequently said to his clinical supervisees, "If you want to know something about someone and you don't have much time, ask him!" Asking people about their personality is a good starting point but accuracy of prediction is increased by obtaining additional sources of information.

4. *Consistency versus Specificity of Personality.*   Another critical issue in personality assessment involves whether personality is *consistent across situations* or *specific to situations*. Obviously, if personality is specific to situations, then personality assessment must involve a sampling of personality in different situational contexts since personality would differ continually. But, if personality is consistent, then we can sample personality in a limited setting and generalize across situations. This issue came to a boiling point in 1968 when Walter Mischel published a book criticizing the "consistency" position (see Chapter 14). He claimed there was little evidence to support the idea of traits or relatively enduring tendencies in personality. His report elicited a number of criticisms of his conclusions and the issue became a hotbed of debate. In Chapter 14, we will discuss this issue in greater depth.

TECHNICAL CONSIDERATIONS IN PERSONALITY ASSESSMENT

In this section, we will discuss some of the technical considerations involved in personality assessment, including the topics of reliability and validity.

Reliability

Reliability refers to a test's consistency. If a test gives the same results on different occasions, it is considered to be reliable. This characteristic is very important since a test would not be very useful if it yielded different scores every time it was taken. For example, suppose you earned an IQ score of 118 on an intelligence test. Then, three months later you earned an IQ of 93 on the same test. Then, six months later, you earned an IQ of 136 on the same test. This test would be inconsistent or *unreliable* since it did not provide the examiner with similar scores across time. Thus, we would have no way of knowing your "true" IQ. Since IQ is considered to be relatively constant across one's lifetime, the use of this particular test would be questionable. Its reliability is too low.

Reliability is indicated by a correlation coefficient which can range from a perfect negative correlation (-1.00) to a perfect positive correlation (+1.00). A high positive correlation indicates that the test is consistent. Generally, the best tests of enduring personality characteristics have reliability coefficients which are in the 90s such as +0.94.

The idea of reliability can best be grasped by making an analogy to weight scales. Suppose that when you wake up in the morning you weigh yourself on your scales and you find that you weigh 186 pounds. To make sure the scale is consistent, you get off and then stand on them again. This time, you weigh 192 pounds. Perplexed at the change in reported weight, you step down from the scales and then stand on them once again. This time the scales indicate that you weigh 174 pounds. At this point, it should be obvious your scales are very *unreliable*. You cannot know what your weight is under such circumstances. This is the same problem we face in personality assessment. If the person's test results continually change in an area that is supposed to be constant, we have no way of knowing what the person is like.

There are three basic ways for measuring test reliability. The first is *test-retest*. This involves giving a test on one occasion and then re-giving the test on another occasion. We then compare the test scores for similarity. However, since there may be a practice effect, some researchers prefer to measure reliability a second way by using *alternative forms*. In this approach there may be two or three different forms of the test which are given. For example, if an examiner wishes to measure your general knowledge, he/she might ask you for the date of George Washington's birthday on Test A and the date of Abraham Lincoln's birthday on Test B. These should correlate quite highly since they are measuring the same general topic albeit with different items.

The third way to measure reliability is by using *split-half methods*. In this method, an examiner may compare the odd and even items on the same test to see if they correlate since an individual should not score in one direction on even items and in another direction on odd items. This method is a quick way to measure reliability since it involves only one test administration. In general, split-half methods should be used in conjunction with *test-retest* or *alternative forms* methods.

Not all tests require high reliability. For example, a test of moods does not need to show test-retest reliability since it is expected that moods will change across time. But, enduring personality characteristics such as intelligence, aggression traits, and dependency traits should evidence high test-retest reliability since they are not expected to change.

Validity

Validity refers to a test's capacity to measure what it claims to measure. If a test claims to measure intelligence, and we find it continually yields higher scores for mental retardates than it does for university professors, then we may say that the test has low validity (unless we accept the idea that university professors are really more dull than retardates). There are several forms of validity, but all forms of validity are based on the idea of "criterion." Let us first discuss this concept and then turn to a discussion of construct validity, face validity, content validity, and predictive validity.

1. *The Criterion for Validity.*   Let us take some examples to illustrate the concept of criteria.

> "He is very tall."
> "How tall?"
> "Four-foot two."

First there was a claim, then a question, than a statement of evidence.

Would you be convinced by what you just read that "he" is very tall? To evaluate the situation we need other information. If the person discussed is a pygmy or a six-year-old, the new data become the criterion. Let us try another statement with a counterargument. Remember we are looking for a criterion, something we can depend on.

> "Nancy is very smart."
> "I doubt it. She doesn't seem smart to me."
> "Well, she gets mostly As in school."
> "That doesn't mean anything. A lot of dumb kids get good grades."

We have in the above interchange, a claim (*Nancy is very smart*), a denial based on the other person's observations, and then evidence (As) and again a denial. So, the person who made the claim about Nancy's intelligence used school grades as a criterion but this criterion was denied by the objector.

A criterion is evidence of the validity of a statement or evidence of the accuracy of a test. In short, when we consider the criterion, we are saying: "What is the evidence of the accuracy of your assessment?"

Let us take another simple example.

"He is very tall."
"What makes you think so?"
"I took his height with a yardstick, and he is 6 foot, 7 inches."
"Wow. Is he tall!"

The yardstick is now the criterion. But now examine this situation.

She: I am cold. It's freezing in here.
He: You are crazy. It is comfortable.
She: I tell you it is cold.
He: (Examining a thermometer) See, the temperature is 78 degrees.
She: I don't care what it says. Maybe it is defective. In any case, no matter what it says, I feel cold.

We see two kinds of criteria here. The woman uses herself as the criterion: "I am cold," and she concludes it is "freezing" in here. The man uses a thermometer as a criterion.

In our subsequent discussions of various tests, instruments, and techniques, you should be alert to the evidence of the validity of the various measures; look for the criterion: *On what basis does this procedure assert its value*?

2. *Types of Validity.* There are many different types of validity. *Face validity* refers to whether a test looks like it measures what it is supposed to measure. For example, if I wanted to assess a person's tendency for aggression, I might create a rating scale which asks the person to reply true or false to a variety of statements like the following:

1. Do you enjoy watching boxing?   T   F
2. Do you frequently lose your temper?   T   F
3. Do you feel children should be strapped if they do not behave?   T   F
4. Do you enjoy shooting guns?   T   F
5. Do you get in verbal fights with people very often?   T   F
6. Do you feel capital punishment should be legalized?   T   F
7. Do you enjoy watching war movies?   T   F

Clearly, on the surface, these questions appear to deal with the topic of aggression. And, anyone answering "true" to all of the questions might be considered an aggressive person. But aggression is a very complex topic and it is possible an individual could answer many of these questions "false" and still be high in aggression because aggression takes many forms including being stubborn, uncooperative, resistant, excessively assertive, and so forth. In the absence of more detailed forms of validation, reliance on a test's face validity can lead to errors since it only *appears* to be valid.

Predictive validity involves the validation of a test against some future performance criterion. For example, suppose that I develop a personality scale which I claim will predict successful sales performance. I give the test to 100 people and 30 of them score quite high on my scale. Company ABC then hires all of these people because they believe that my test is valid. But, six months later only 5 of the 30 people are successful salespeople according to their criteria. In this instance, my test does not have good predictive validity because it did not predict future performance accurately.

But, if I develop a test which predicts future performance with some degree of accuracy, then the test does possess predictive validity. Quite simply, predictive validity means a measure enables an examiner to predict future performance on the basis of present performance. Predictive validity is a powerful way to validate any scale since businesses, governments, institutions, and clinicians need to predict future performance.

In selecting a test for use in personnel decisions, professional assessment specialists examine test specifications to see if a given test has good predictive validity. Since most personality tests do not have high predictive validity, assessors often turn to other types of validity like concurrent validity. *Concurrent validity* refers to a method of test validation which involves comparing test scores with another measure at the same point in time. Often, the other measure is another test. Thus, an examiner might give a test purporting to measure anxiety to an individual and then give the individual several other measures of anxiety including tests of arousal based on galvanic skin responses (GSR), muscle tension (EMG), hand steadiness, facial and armpit perspiration, and urine analyses. If the individual scores high on all these measures and also scores high on the paper-pencil test just administered, then the paper-pencil test can be said to have good concurrent validity.

It should be clear to the reader that test validity refers to a test's capacity to measure accurately what it claims to measure. If the test cannot predict future performance it does not have predictive validity. If the test does not correlate with other measures of the same characteristic given at the same time, it does not have concurrent validity. If both of these qualities are lacking, we must question the validity of the test.

There are still other types of validity. For example, suppose I develop a measure of psychological modernity or the degree to which a person holds modern versus traditional beliefs and attitudes. Let us suppose that I develop a series of 10 questions to measure this psychological construct. If a person obtains a score of 10, then he/she is quite modern, but if they obtain a score of zero, they are quite traditional. Now following the test, I ask them to simply state how modern they are on a scale of 1 to 5; and, in addition, I ask their friends to rate them on modernity accordingly on a scale of 1 to 5. In addition, I rate their behavior across a number of criteria such as food preferences, clothing, and sexual relations. All of these measures can be considered measures of psychological modernity and the extent to which they correlate can tell me the instrument's *convergent validity*.

If an individual rates him/herself as traditional and his/her friends rate the person as traditional and the evaluator rates the person's behavior as traditional but the test scores indicate the person has high psychological modernity, then there is no convergent validity across the measures. That is, they do not converge or correlate with one another in a high positive direction. In this latter example, it would be foolish for us to trust our paper-pencil test, since it does not show any agreement with the other measures we used as criteria.

At the same time that we use *convergent validation*, there is also an opportunity to use *discriminant validation*. Discriminant validation involves the administration of personality measures expected to correlate negatively with convergent measures. For example, although we would expect other measures of anxiety to correlate positively with our test of anxiety (convergent validity), we would expect measures of relaxation to correlate negatively. This provides us with a two-way validation approach. If our measure of anxiety is valid, it should correlate positively with other measures of anxiety (convergent validation), and it should correlate negatively with measures of relaxation and tranquility (discriminant validation).

Construct validity is yet another type of validity. In criterion measures of validity like we have just discussed (i.e., concurrent validity, convergent validity, predictive validity), the basis of our evaluations are tangible correlates as grades, performance success, and biological measures. However, sometimes we validate a test against personality constructs like drives or motives which have no real or tangible basis. In the latter case, these constructs have no absolute criterion but rather are defined in terms of references to theory.

In this regard, construct validity involves the use of variety of different methods that can confirm a theory. Cronbach and Meehl (1955) stated that construct validity "is not essentially different from the general scientific procedures for developing and confirming theories" (p. 300). This means anything we do (1) to confirm a hypothesis derived from a theory, (2) to demonstrate predictable correlations in either positive or negative directions, or (3) to conduct experiments based on criterion-based groups, are all capable of offering us construct validation. If a construct has good validity, a variety of research results should eventually emerge using different procedures that demonstrate the construct's utility for understanding behavior.

For example, consider the construct "locus of control." This construct was advanced as part of theory which suggested human behavior was a function of an individual's perception of whether reinforcing events were externally or internally determined (see Chapter 15). The construct was so appealing that it generated thousands of studies directed toward virtually every aspect of the construct including its correlates, its determinants, its predictive implications, and so forth. All of these efforts represent construct validity because they either supported or disconfirmed the construct's capacity to be useful and valuable in understanding personality.

TYPES OF ASSESSMENT PROCEDURES

According to Campbell (1963) there are seven ways to assess people. Sechrest (1968) elaborated on Campbell's suggestions and we will discuss the latter's conclusions.

Tailing

Tailing can also be called the "shadow technique." It is a detective method of following a person, with or without the person's knowledge, and observing the individual in action. This method, which has questionable ethical implications, is commonly employed through the use of a one-way mirror when the subject does not know that someone is observing him or her. It has, as is evident, some advantages, in that we see people as they really act rather than how they say they act or how others say they act. Imagine you wanted to know what a person was like and you could turn yourself into a fly and observe the person at his/her usual activities in a number of different situations for a week; how well would you get to know that person?

Episodic Recall

This method calls for person A to inform person B about A's past experiences. In psychotherapy, for example, it is common for the therapist to ask the client to reply to questions such as these: "Do you remember any incidents in your early life that involved your father?" or "Tell me how school was?" or "What was your first meeting with your wife?" In a very vague way, an episodic recall is a kind of tailing, in that A tells what he or she remembers of an incident. Evidently, B gets not only the true account of the incident, but also the distortions that inevitably occur. However, for some personality assessors whether the report is "true memory" or a "screen memory" (that is, false memory) is not important. In short, it doesn't matter whether the memory actually happened. Say that A reports getting beaten by his father many times, and say that A's mother and father both insist—and everyone who knows A's early life, including his brothers and sisters—also insist that the father never beat A; nevertheless from the point of view of the therapist this "screen" memory is very important. The facts may not be as important as the memory, whether it is true or not.

Situational Sampling

This represents a sampling of a person's behavior. Say you drop into a school to see how your child is doing. Suppose that you observed three or four times and each time you see your child by herself in a corner reading. At the same time you note that one of your neighbor's children is involved in action projects with other children. These occasional situational samplings would lead you to conclusions about the two children's personalities. However, it is evident that your samples, if too few in number, or if not properly spaced, might lead you to incorrect conclusions. When the supervisor of a section "drops in" to see how things are going, this is an example of situational sampling.

Contrived Situations

During World War II, the Office of Strategic Services (OSS), which eventually became the CIA, employed contrived situations, now known as role playing, to determine how a person would act in a real situation. To estimate a person's leadership ability, a candidate was asked to direct a crew of people to do a relatively simple job, such as put a very long ladder across a small ravine. The crew were actually people who had been predirected to act stupidly, to make mistakes, and to sabotage the project, meanwhile looking innocent. The candidate might or might not know that the situation was contrived to measure his abilities as a leader. Meanwhile, observers (and they could be the work crew) would estimate such qualities as ability to keep his temper and the clarity of his instructions.

In a sense, the ordinary interview is an example of a contrived situation. Most of us have had all kinds of job interviews or interviews for various purposes, such as being considered for acceptance in a school. At that time the interviewer is not only interested in the content of the replies, but also is alert to various signals in terms of tone of voice, appearance of distress, gestures, and so on.

In another sense, some situational observations occur during testing. For example, when we give a child an intelligence test, we note a considerable number of extraneous factors such as attention span, attitude toward the test, and towards the examiner. For example:

Examiner: I am going to give you a test to see how well you know
           things.
Subject C: Goodie. I like tests!
Subject D: Oh...I know I am going to fail...
Subject E: (Says nothing but looks sad.)

This kind of observation is especially important and is employed consciously in the Rorschach technique, which is a projective test procedure. Side comments, grimaces, and postures are all important.

Symbolic Stimulus Tests

This type of procedure is generally known as a "projective" test, in that the individual must project his/her needs, motives, and impulses into an ambiguous situation. Let us begin with a hypothetical set of six replies by two five-year-old children to a set of inkblots.

Child F	*Child G*
Rocks	A bat
Rocks	Two dogs
Rocks	Dancing men
Rocks	Bearskin
Rocks	Bird flying
Rocks	Bearskin

Even without knowing what the inkblots look like, it should be evident to the reader that these two five-year-old kids are probably different from one another with respect to various personality components. The writer would hypothesize that child F is probably fearful, because he or she will not take chances; possibly the child is not very bright, while Child G seems to be, even on this little bit of evidence, fairly bright with a good vocabulary for a five-year-old child. The child is also flexible in that he/she can see a wide variety of items.

The whole issue of the reliability of the various projective tests and their validity has been the subject of countless articles and many books, and it is enough to say that professional psychologists who are involved in the diagnosis and treatment of individuals fall into two broad categories of those who employ projective techniques routinely, and those who will have nothing to do with them. There is a small middle group that will employ them from time to time when they seem appropriate.

Respondents' Reports on Their Own Disposition

In doing therapy, we frequently say to a client: "Tell me as clearly as you can exactly what you think is wrong with you. . . ." We have found that very often people in trouble will evidence a lot of good sense. For example, this specific question brought the following reply (condensed) from a female client.

Client:	Well, you can see that I am obese. This is due to my simply eating too much and not exercising enough. What happens is that I go on eating binges at least once a week and sometimes three, four times weekly. I hate myself after I have done this, and have a lot of guilt. Nevertheless I can't seem to stop myself.
Counselor:	What makes you go on these binges?
Client:	My mother is in front of me. (Mother is actually dead.) I can see her looking at me, frowning. I know she always tried to get me to be slim. But I look at her and say to her, "I don't care!"
Counselor:	What do you think that means?
Client:	It means that I am still trying to fight her even though she is dead. I don't want to do what she wanted me to do and I am still in this stupid power-struggle with my mother, and I am the victim of this crazy situation.

This sample shows how a personality analyst can find information simply by asking the individual. This does not mean that a clever interviewer will either believe everything said or heard nor that the therapist will accept the client's perceptions or interpretations. But, self-report is a good start!

The usual way of assessing a person's individuality is to ask the individual specific questions, such as: "Do you dream much?" Often the answer is given in terms of *true* or *false*. Tests of personality such as the *MMPI* or *Edwards Personal Preference Inventory* depend on a person answering such questions.

In all of the examples given so far the types of methods for assessing personality, we have attempted to indicate some of the limitations of the various methods. Self-report has many problems including whether the person can understand the test items, whether the person is replying honestly, and so forth. Thus, if the question reads: "Do you frequently feel inadequate?" a person who is taking this test for a job and who has strong feelings of inadequcy may reply *false* since his/her perception may be that this question will, if answered honestly, hurt the chances of getting him the position. This tendency to respond with a "socially desirable" answer is called *social desirability*. It is an important variable in test-taking.

Respondent's Report on Views of the Stimulus

This is a somewhat complicated, but important point of view, and we have already alluded to it. Essentially, it has to do whether we take a naïve or a sophisticated view of replies or reports. If you accept things at face value, then you have the naïve view; and if you do not, you have a sophisticated view. Both can be right or wrong, depending on the situation, of course, and the importance of human intelligence, clinical sensitivity and judgment comes at this point.

We see this most clearly in ambiguous situations such as interviews, or replies to projective tests, where the personality assessor has to make a judgment. Say on a TAT card a person demonstrates a great deal of aggression, what can this mean? Does it mean that he is an aggressive person and is showing it on this test, or is it only the person's subjective view of the stimulus, or does it mean the person would like to be aggressive but is not, and so on.

In addition to the seven methods suggested by Campbell and by Sechrest, there are other possibilities. One of the most important and used frequently in real life is this:

Reports by Others.   We frequently judge people by what others say about them. We do this informally, as in a discussion between neighbors about someone in the neighborhood, or discussions about national figures, or husband/wife discussions about some friend. It is done quite extensively, as any teacher knows, by means of written letters of recommendation and by telephone interviews or other means by which person A finds out about person B from person C. This is probably the most common way that the FBI and the police learn about others. And, it can be quite valuable, depending on the judgment of the observer/reporter.

In the remainder of this chapter we will discuss two types of evaluating procedures: (*a*) symbolic stimulus tests ("projective techniques") and (*b*) respondents' reports of their own disposition ("self-report"), as occurs in paper-and-pencil questionnaires filled out by the subjects themselves.

PROJECTIVE TECHNIQUES

Rorschach Technique

1. Background. The Rorschach Test was developed by a Swiss psychiatrist, Hermann Rorschach, in 1921. He was seeking a method for understanding the person's unconscious motives, feelings, and conflicts. By accident, he came upon the method of asking someone to tell what they saw in an ambiguous inkblot. Since the inkblot itself had no "actual" meaning, he assumed the specific answer provided by the respondent reflected the respondent's needs and motives. The respondent "projected" his/her personality into the inkblot to provide meaning.

2. Procedures. The Rorschach technique consists of giving a subject 10 cards, each 8 by 10 inches, half of them black and white and half of them in various color combinations, and asking the person to hold the cards and tell the examiner what they see. The examiner notes how long it takes for the first reply to each card, how long the person held the card before putting it down, whether the person rotated the card, and whether the card was examined on the reverse side, and then in sequence all comments. This might be an example of how the notations might look:

Card I

1. (15 sec.)   V   V   (15) I don't know, . . . maybe a bat.

2. V   Could be just an inkblot, but it is too symmetrical.

3. V   Like a black swallow, just floating, you know what I mean, . . . gliding.

4. V   Could be a creature from outer space, a kind of a monster, . . . a pera - - you knowwhat I mean - - those birds that were prehistoric.

(I—40 sec.)

These notations show that for the first card, the individual turned the card upside down and then back again, and after 15 seconds called the picture a "bat," that the total time on Card I was 40 seconds, and so on.

After the subject finishes reporting on all 10 cards, the examiner goes over the cards to try to determine *how* the subject saw what he/she claimed. *Was there inherent motion? Did the black color influence the perception? Was the form of good quality? Was the level of verbalization such to indicate a person of good intelligence?* The protocol above might be the responses that a fairly normal adult of good intelligence might give to blot I of the Rorschach. Here is how an abnormal person might react:

Card I

1. (35 sec.)   V   I don't know what that is. Just an inkblot.

2. V   Maybe oil on water with the face of a dead man looking up through it.

3. V   Spaceship or a submarine filled with death.

4. >   The intestines of a frog crying because a fish bit him.

Here comes the judgment of the examiner! If the examiner can see a correspondence between the appearance of the blot and what the examinee saw, then this is a sign of normality. In the first case, say that 90 out of 100 normal subjects see bats and birds; this is an indication of normality in the statistical sense. And, if fewer than 1 out of 100 see frog intestines, then this is a sign of statistical abnormality. However, the examiner might also see frog intestines and then the examiner becomes the criterion and this unusual response is considered *creative* rather than *abnormal*.

The Rorschach is generally scored according to four components. The first is the *location* of the response. Does the subject use the "whole" (W) inkblot or does the subject respond to a "part" (D) or a very "small part" (Dd)? There are norms for determining the location and different types of locations have different diagnostic implications.

The second component examined is the *determinants*. This refers to the reasons the subject gives for perceiving a particular response. The reasons may include (1) form, (2) color, (3) movement, (4) tactile quality, and so forth. Each has different diagnostic implications. The third component is the *content* of the response. What does the subject see...animals, monsters, anatomical parts, people, sex organs, machines, inkblots? Each of these "contents" has different meanings to an examiner.

The fourth component examined is the "popularity" or "idiosyncracy" of the response. For example, most people see "bats" in one of the 10 cards. But, suppose a subject saw "the Vietnamese War and its implications for cosmic peace as seen through a glass darkly." The latter is a very unique response. It can reflect creativity or madness.

The Rorschach technique is a relatively unstructured situation to which the subject replies according to his or her perception. The examiner makes judgments based on either the experience of others (such as from manuals) or his or her own experience. Thus, if a young child sees "rocks" on all 10 cards, this is a normal example of "magical perseveration"; but, if an adult were to see only rocks, then this would most probably be diagnostic of something wrong in the person.

An understanding of cultural factors is called for in interpreting the Rorschach. For example, an examiner from one part of the country gave Rorschach to a number of people in another part of the country. A person saw one of the blots as a "quahog." The examiner put down that reply as an "original" and was doubtful about the form quality since she had never to her knowledge seen a "quahog." But, when more people in that community called that blot a "quahog," she realized that this reply for that population was a "popular" rather than an original reply.

As is the case with other techniques such as the interview, the value of the Rorschach lies in the judgment of the examiner and not in the instrument itself. The same situation as the use of a knife by a surgeon exists in the use of the Rorschach. If someone is really expert and has a good general knowledge, the Rorschach can be extremely valuable in many ways but in the hands of people who are inexpert, the Rorschach can have no value at all.

Thematic Apperception Test (TAT)

1. Background. The Thematic Apperception Test (TAT) was developed in 1935 by Henry Murray (see Chapter 8) as part of an effort to devise assessment methods for the in-depth study of human personality. In the years since the TAT was first introduced, it has emerged as one of the most popular projective tests in the field of clinical, personality, and social psychology. In addition, it has also found extensive use among anthropologists seeking to understand the personality of non-Western people.

The TAT consists of 20 pictures with ambiguous contents. For example, one picture consists of a young child sitting with his head in his hands before a violin which is casually placed on a table. Another consists of a younger woman staring at an older woman. In all instances, the pictures provide sufficient cues to relate a story; however, the cues are not specific enough to force a specific story. Rather, as was the case for the Rorschach test, the subject's own needs, motives, and impulses dictate the nature of the story which is told.

2. Procedures. The subject is told to "tell a story" about the picture. The story should have a beginning, a middle, and an end. As the subject relates the story for a given picture, the examiner will record the time the subject takes before beginning and then record the entire story told by the subject including pauses, changes in voice, and so forth. The examiner will score the story for a variety of factors including the needs or motives which are revealed by the story. For example, suppose that a subject tells the following story in response to a TAT card that contains two men talking before a kitchen table on which is a loaf of bread, a knife, and a tall, nondescript bottle. The man in front appears angry while the man in back is smiling.

Card 12B

(25 sec.)   The two men have just finished having an argument over a girl. The man in back is laughing because he has just made a fool of the other man. The man in front is filled with rage. He cannot think clearly any longer. He is looking at the knife on the table and wondering whether he should stab the other man . . . (30 sec.) Uhmmmm let me see . . . Uhmmmm. (15 sec.) He decides that he must revenge himself. In the next few moments he reaches for the knife and stabs the other man in the stomach. Then he laughs and says, "Guess who gets Sally now?" The other man coughs and asks for help but it is too late and he dies. The other man runs out the door but knows he will get caught eventually.

Clearly, the entire story has an aggression theme; it also reflects conflicted motives between aggression and control. Impulse control represents an area of concern for the subject. The inclusion of "the girl" as a source of the conflict may represent a sexual conflict. The time delays in the middle of the story also reflect the conflict of impulse control.

However, the same picture could evoke a totally different story. For example, another subject with different needs and motives may well relate the following story:

Card 12B

(5 sec.)   The two men are joking about who will clean up the dishes following a meal. They flip a coin and the man in front loses. He appears to be angry but is just acting. The men are good friends. In the end, the man who won the coin flip says, "Tell you what . . . if you clean up, I'll cook breakfast tomorrow morning."

In this story, the theme is friendship and obligation. The end shows a happy reconciliation of a minor conflict. An ability to emphasize and share feelings is also revealed. The same TAT picture yields totally different stories as a function of the needs, motives, and conflicts of different subjects. Because the pictures are unstructured, the structure must be provided by the subject and this offers an opportunity to understand the subject's personality.

Early Recollections

1. Background. According to Ruth Munroe (1955), the first projective test was Alfred Adler's use of *Early Recollections*. Of all the projective tests, this is the simplest, because it calls for no materials at all. The early recollection method is not well known in spite of the fact that it was the first of the projective techniques.

2. Procedures. The early recollection technique is easily administered: "Tell me your earliest memory," the examiner says; and then may explain: "I want specific, concrete, single memories." The memory is then written down exactly as reported. A second, and a third memory is then solicited. In the usual procedure, 10 memories are obtained, which may take up to a whole hour. Each memory is then analyzed to find in it the essential theme.

Below we shall give a memory exactly as reported with interpretative comments on the right side to illustrate how such a memory can be dealt with.

Reported Memory	*Interpretation*
I remember being on a train seated between my parents and I was bored and restless	He is a wanderer Likes to be close to people A wanderer, easily bored, need for change
I was looking through the window and all I saw was telephone poles and I wanted to get away but I was hemmed in and so I began to inch	An observer, but easily bored Wants his own way Resists control by others

my way down without my parents knowing and I finally got to the floor and began to look around	He is sneaky; wants his own way
and I noticed the legs of people and I remember the smell of the floor, and the dust there	He is a good reporter and has a good memory and is a story teller.
And I began to move forward being careful not to let anyone know I was there	He is aware of others
And I came upon an oilcan; it was brass and shiny	More evidence of novelistic tendencies; storyteller
And I picked it up and began to squirt oil on the shoes of a man	He is adventurous and a mischief maker
Suddenly, the man cried out and he reached down and pulled me out	A story teller, he gets caught in his misbehavior
And the conductor came and picked me up while I was screaming	An authority intervenes and he resists
and I was brought to my father who began to spank me	He gets punished. Life is dangerous for him.

Now, this single memory was for the person involved a complete summary of his personality, which was interpreted as follows:

> You are a wanderer, and you move not only from place to place but also from person to person, a kind of Don Juan. You are easily bored and always restless, and on the go, and you want excitement and will do things in a mischievous manner to get excitement. However, you know you won't succeed in getting away with your mischief and you expect to be caught and to be punished.

Here is an early recollection of another person. See if you, the reader, can make any sense of it—it should be easy to interpret.

Reported Memory	*Interpretation*
I was about 10 years of age and I wanted to build a wooden automobile using tires from an old baby carriage.	

And I announced this to everyone.

But most kids who made one of
  these used two strings to
  steer the wagon, but I wanted
  a steering wheel.

My father wanted to help me
  but I said I would do it
  alone.

However, when I came to making
  the steering wheel, I couldn't
  figure out how to do it.

So, I secretly got rid of the
  car, how much I had done and

I reported to everyone
  that someone had stolen
  my car, and that was the
  end of it.

However, I felt that my
  father had known what
  I had done.

Our interpretation of the above goes somewhat as follows:

> He is overambitious, trying to do better and bigger things than others, but he
> goes over his head and can't complete what he starts out doing; eventually he
> gives up but will not admit that he tried to do more than he could.

This person has made a number of business attempts; all very ambitious, and all eventual failures. He always operates alone and will not listen to the advice of others. He is a brilliant person, and thinks up extravagant schemes; he is able to get others to invest, and then—eventual failure.

We suggest the reader of this book ask some people to give their earliest memory and then attempt to make sense out of it. Early recollections, when interpreted by sensitive and perceptive people, can be most valuable. The primary source of information on this technique is a book called *Early Recollections* edited by Harry A. Olson (1979).

SELF-REPORT QUESTIONNAIRES

Introduction

One method of getting to understand a person is to ask the individual to assess himself by responding to a series of questions to which he or she can answer: True or False. Consider these items, for example, and assume that Person A would answer them all True and Person B would answer them all False. Assume both people are intelligent and are answering the questions as honestly as possible.

	A	B
Do you sometimes feel blue and miserable?	T	F
Are you often just plain lonely?	T	F
Do you think people dislike you?	T	F
Are you often discouraged?	T	F
Do you feel terribly inferior?	T	F

It would seem evident that the two college students who reply completely differently to these five questions, one all T and the other all F, are really quite different from each other.

Personality questionnaires ask individuals specific questions to which the person can readily reply in some objective manner such as:

ALWAYS   OFTEN   SOMETIMES   RARELY   NEVER

The instrument can then be scored to yield patterns in different areas. Thus, for example, say a person replies to 100 questions intended to measure certain dimensions or fields of traits, the examiner by scoring the test is able to "diagnose" the individual in terms of the dimensions or areas of the test.

Psychologists have developed probably thousands of such questionnaires, and we shall take up three based on different concepts of personality test construction: The Edwards Personal Preference Schedule (EPPS), the Minnesota Multiphasic Personality Inventory (MMPI), and the Cattell Sixteen Personality Factor Test (16PF).

The MMPI

The most often used personality inventory is the *Minnesota Multiphasic Personality Inventory*, and it is certainly the one with the greatest number of research studies. It consists of 550 items to which a subject is to reply either True, False, or Cannot Say. The test can be taken on cards or in a booklet; it can be taken as a group test or can be given individually. The test has four "validity" scales: (1) a *?* scale which indicates the number of Cannot Say items; and if one has more than 30 such items, this is considered evidence of avoidance; (2) a *Lie Scale* consisting of 15 items all derogatory but of which most honest people would admit some; if one answers too many of these in the wrong way, the assumption is that the person is attempting to deceive the examiner; (3) an *F*-scale, dealing with unusual items; a person who responds to too many of these probably did not understand the directions, or is upset, or is just shuffling cards or putting responses at random or is extremely maladjusted; (4) a *K* or correction scale, intended to make adjustments to the other scales for those who take a guarded position relative to self: it corrects for social desirability.

The 10 clinical scales are (1) hypochondria, (2) depression, (3) hysteria, (4) psychopathic personality, (5) masculinity/femininity, (6) paranoia, (7) psychastenia, (8) schizophrenia, (9) hypomania and (10) social introversion. Generally, only the numbers are listed for security purposes.

Essentially, the MMPI was constructed as follows: first, the list of items was prepared; second, they were then given to maladjusted individuals who in the judgment of experts fell into these various clinical groups; then, the responses of the groups were analyzed to see in which way they differed from normals, and the cards were then assigned to the various clinical entities. So, if 100 people diagnosed as schizophrenics took this test, their results were compared with normals, and only those items that discriminated them from the normals were used to make up the Schizophrenia scale.

The interpretation, as is the usual case with all these instruments, is something that can be done by a computer. However, many variables have to be considered, including the general sophistication of the person taking this test, his/her attitudes and intentions. The subject's profile across all these scales can be compared against an atlas which provides detailed descriptions of numerous profiles.

Edwards Personal Preference Schedule

The Edwards Personal Preference Schedule (EPPS) differs from the MMPI which was constructed from replies by individuals diagnosed as various clinical types, such as psychopaths and hysterics. The EPPS is based on the personality theory of Henry A. Murray, who developed the Thematic Apperception Test. A few words about the theory is appropriate. According to Murray, people are moved (motivated) by internal and external forces. The internal forces are called *needs*. Thus, if a person has a need to achieve, he has *n-achievement*. External forces operate to move the person into action, and these are called *press*. Alpha press refers to objective factors in the real environment and Beta press relates to perceptions of the outside forces.

Allan Edwards, in developing the EPPS, took 15 of Murray's needs and wrote statements intended to reflect these needs. The process forces a person taking the test to select between one of two needs on each question. In a sense, the assumption is that each person taking the test has all these needs to variable strengths. It is the intent of the schedule to find how much of each need is in the person. An analogy might be to assume that every piece of coal has so much carbon, so much petroleum and so much clay—and nothing else—and the analytical chemist's task is to discover the relative percentages of each.

To accept the Edwards' scale, it is necessary to accept the validity of Murray's conceptions of needs and press. All this makes validation of EPPS difficult since the criterion is of the construct type. Thus, if you accept Murray's theory, then the test is valid, but there is no objective way this can be determined. The EPPS measures the following needs: dominance, affiliation, deference, abasement, order, change, heterosexuality, dependency, succorance, aggression.

A strong point of the EPPS is that the forced-choice format provides some control over "social desirability." Social desirability refers to a person's tendency to present themselves in a way which is positive and socially acceptable. Obviously, this tendency can distort the "true" nature of the person and thus yield an inaccurate result. By forcing the individual to choose between equally desirable or equally undesirable choice, the EPPS controls social desirability.

Sixteen Personality Factor

Another personality questionnaire that is quite popular is the Sixteen Personality Factor Test (16PF) developed by Raymond B. Cattell. We shall attempt to go over the various steps taken in developing a test of this type.

1. We start by examining the 18,000 terms in the Allport and Odbert list (1936), every term an adjective describing various traits.

2. We now select from this enormous list a much smaller number of words which appear to have these qualities, among others: (a) the words are simple and generally used such as *sensitive* or *nervous* rather than difficult to understand words such as *loquacious* and *phlegmatic*; (b) we then make further eliminations by not having terms which appear to be essential duplicates, and so if we came across the words *bright, intelligent, clever, quick, smart,* we would use only one of these terms since the others appear to be synonymous.

3. We now will take about 100 to 200 terms (Cattell took 171) and make a preliminary test and administer them to a wide variety of individuals, normal and abnormal.

4. We then do an analysis of the intercorrelations of the items. In the case of 171 items, the formula becomes $N = 171 \times 170/2$ or 14,535 intercorrelations.

5. The next step is to take this enormous matrix of intercorrelations, and attempt to reduce them into more basic factors. So if items 1—37—53—89—117 intercorrelate highly with one another and if they also

do not correlate well with any others, they form a factor. Suppose, for example, these were the names of these items:

   1—Tense.
  37—Anxious.
  53—High-strung.
  89—Rigid.
117—Scary.

The examination would indicate that these five terms have logically something in common, and consequently that they measure a particular personality trait. We now have to give a name to what these five measure. Suppose you give a name? Would it be *Anger, Dominance, Social Sensitivity?* Probably not. The term *Anxiety* or *Tension* would most probably appear to be the proper name for this cluster of terms.

Cattell originally administered the test of 171 items to 100 subjects and after his factor analysis he came up originally with 12 factors. Further development of the test with more words and more subjects finally led to the 16 factors of the present form. One of the problems Cattell faced was what to call the various factors. Some did not appear to have any common names, and he was forced to use some of the factors with made-up names.

This particular questionnaire has been constantly researched, and like the others mentioned, has value when properly employed and intelligently interpreted. (See Chapter 8 for greater discussion of Cattell's work).

PSYCHOPHYSIOLOGICAL AND PSYCHOMOTOR TESTS

When professionals consider personality assessment, the tests which come to mind are the MMPI, the 16 PF, the Rorschach, the TAT, and one of the intelligence tests (e.g., Wechsler Adult Intelligence Scale, the Stanford-Binet). This particular battery of instruments, when used properly by an experienced professional, can yield a detailed analysis of personality. But, in recent years, there has been an increased interest in assessment approaches involving psychophysiological and psychomotor tests.

The basic value of psychophysiological and psychomotor tests is their objectivity in appraising particular functions and internal states. However, their use does require complicated technical skills and a familiarization with a new clinical and research literature.

Psychophysiological Assessment

Psychophysiological tests involve the use of measures which assess arousal states. Arousal states are characterized by a number of physiological changes in somatic and psychological functioning including increased blood pressure, heart beat, respiration, muscle tension, and perspiration. In addition, eye pupils dilate, salivation decreases, brain wave activity shifts, and digestion is slowed. At a psychological level, these changes are paralleled by increased rigidity in thinking, difficulty concentrating, and impaired memory.

Some of these changes can be assessed with simple equipment. For example, with a little training, an examiner can use a stethoscope and a sphygmomanometer to measure heart beat and blood pressure. With the use of a polygraph, an assessment specialist can measure galvanic skin response (GSR), which reflects arousal via electrical resistance on the skin caused by minute differences in skin moisture. In addition, the polygraph can measure muscle tension (electromylogram), and brain wave activity (electroencephalogram). The former is called an EMG and the latter is called an EEG.

All these measures provide the personality assessment specialist with access to another domain of human functioning which has considerable importance—internal arousal states. In the hands of trained professionals, this information can provide numerous insights about stress states, emotional patterns, coping skills, adaptational styles, and body-mind relationships.

Psychomotor Assessment

Psychomotor tests involve the assessments of relationships between cognitive and motor functioning; these include reaction time, information processing, weight discrimination, proprioceptive memory, visual tracking, and pursuit rotor tasks. These tests are particularly useful in providing detailed data about specific functions and skills. In the case of some tasks (e.g., weight discrimination, reaction time), the equipment needed is relatively simple; in addition, the time needed to administer the task is often brief. However, the fundamental question in their use involves the information value of the data. Frequently, personality assessment focuses on needs, motives, and conflicts and does not include an individual's ability to process information or the ability to use different sense modalities. However, new trends in personality assessment suggest future assessments will shift to a broader spectrum of topics since personality ultimately involves the whole individual and not a selected group of needs and motives.

In brief, in addition to standard personality test batteries, personality assessment can include appraisals of psychophysiological and psychomotor functioning. These two topics hold promise for broadening our information about the functioning of the total individual. In doing so, they may ultimately alter our entire conception of personality and human nature. The

Halstead-Reitan Battery is probably the most extensive and well-researched evaluation procedure of this particular mode. However, the recently developed Luria-Nebraska Battery has gained great popularity.

BEHAVIORAL ASSESSMENT

The application of behavioral principles to clinical problems in the early 1960s brought an emphasis on detailed descriptions of overt behavior. For many behaviorists, traditional methods of personality assessment are questionable because they explain behavior in terms of traits and personality dynamics which lack scientific rigor. In contrast to explaining *why*, behavior assessment specialists focus on describing specific behaviors in distinct settings. Today, the technology of behavior assessment has become quite sophisticated and many journals focus solely on evaluating behavioral assessment methods (e.g., *Journal of Behavior Assessment*).

Basically, behavior assessors record specific behaviors or behavior patterns through observational methodologies. These involve the use of recording forms which list specific behaviors, situations, and time dimensions. For example, if I wanted to know about a disruptive child, I might give the child a series of personality tests (e.g., Rorschach, Sentence Completion Tests, Wechsler Intelligence Scale for Children) and I may find he evidences a great deal of hostility toward authority figures, is very impulsive, lacks concentration, and possesses low average intelligence. The tests might also indicate the child has dependency needs but lacks the ability and skills to obtain social support. As a result, he has a great deal of ambivalence toward people. The child both needs adults to meet his needs but also feels angry toward them.

From the point of view of the behaviorist, these conclusions may or may not be accurate since they were derived in a single testing session lasting about two hours and involve tests of questionable validity. The behaviorist prefers to examine the problem in context (i.e., in the classroom) by observing behavior in the natural environment. Behaviorists believe the determinants of behavior problems reside in the socioenvironmental context and not in personality predispositions. Thus, the behaviorist proceeds to the classroom with his observational checklists and there he records the behavior of the "disruptive" child. To increase accuracy, the behaviorist samples a representative display of the child's behavior across the entire day and several different settings.

The results of the behavioral observation might reveal the child is not uniformly disruptive throughout the day. Rather, the disruptions consist of speaking with his neighbors in spite of continual reprimands from his "strict" teacher during two classes prior to the 11:00 recess. He does not evidence disruptive behaviors in his first class of the day nor in his afternoon classes when he has different teachers and different neighbors.

Thus, the behavioral assessment reveals the disruptive behavior occurs in limited settings and is not characterological. It may well be the child has conflicts with authority and also problems in impulse control; however, none of these are important for the behaviorist since the child's actual behavior is the key variable.

In recent years, behaviorists have broadened their perspectives to include appraisals of "internal" variables, but only as these related to observed behavior patterns. Radical behaviorists (i.e., those who are concerned only with overt behavior) still are actively involved in refining behavioral methodologies; however, the new emphasis in behavioral assessment is on linking overt and covert behavioral patterns. In this respect, there is a growing proximity to traditional personality assessment.

SOME CONCLUDING COMMENTS

Personality assessment represents an important professional and scientific activity. Since its development in the early 20th century, it has grown into a massive industry. Like many other areas of psychology, it is very controversial. The idea that some individuals can reach many conclusions about a person based on a very brief period of evaluation involving the use of few assessment instruments is rejected by most lay people. They contend human behavior is too complex to be captured by a few tests. In addition, the tests used (e.g., Rorschach, MMPI) are often puzzling to lay people, who find very little face validity in tests involving inkblots and questions such as "Do you stare into space?" Further, the tests which are used often seem inappropriate for assessing minorities and culture-deviant groups. The type of format, the questions asked, the skills required, and the norms available are often sources of problems. For example, as Olmedo (1981) and Garcia (1981) pointed out, most testing requires the use of language, and most minority groups do not speak standard English. This reduces the quality of test performance and keeps minorities tied to limited educational, economic, and social opportunities. Olmedo (1981) stated,

> I have argued that in addressing the topic of linguistic minorities, it is necessary to recognize the diverse social, political, and economic realities that these groups encounter in contemporary America. These realities are moderated by educational opportunities, which in turn are closely linked to various forms of standardized intelligence, aptitude, and ability testing. Significant segments of linguistic minority groups perceive that standardized testing has served to restrict rather than augment, their opportunities to participate fully in sharing the social, political, and economic benefits of our society (p. 1084).

Minority problems are only one of the many difficulties facing the testing enterprise. There is growing public distrust of testing both within the schools, businesses, and the courts. On the witness stand, personality assessment specialists are often subjected to considerable cross-examination about the validity of their conclusions. In the end, the assessment specialist must frequently rely on the following statement: "Based on my training and experience, it is my professional opinion that Mr. ABC is _____." In addition, many people are now requesting the results of their tests. This means they may challenge the examiner's conclusions.

But, ultimately the major problem confronting personality assessment as a profession and a scientific activity is the absence of new conceptual models for assessment which can provide different sources of data, different measurement formats, and different dimensions of human functioning. Green (1981) stated,

> Testing has been one of the most successful applied enterprises in psychology. Perhaps its weakest aspect is the relative lack of progress over the past decades. With few exceptions, we are testing the same old things in the same old way with moderate success (p. 1011).

In our opinion, assessment would be a more meaningful enterprise if it emerged from a model of human behavior which recognized that different sources of information, different measurement formats, and different domains of functioning must all be considered to understand human personality. Thus, we recommend examiners assess personality from the viewpoint of the person, the family, and the professional. We further recommend that different modalities be assessed including somatic, sensory, perceptual, cognitive, affective, motivational, self, and interpersonal domains of functioning. Lastly, we recommend assessment involve a variety of formats including interviews, life record data, questionnaires, objective tests, psychophysiological and psychomotor tests, behavioral observation, environmental appraisal, and so forth. This model will provide a spectrum of information and ultimately it will serve to validate constructs, methods, and the entire assessment process. It is reasonable to expect that the more you know about an individual from different perspectives the more you will be able to predict performance trajectories and establish the bases of past patterns of responding. These are the goals of personality assessment.

REFERENCES

Allport, G., & Odbert, H. Trait-names: A psycholexical study. *Psychological Monographs*, 1936, *47*, 211.

American Psychologist (R. Glaser & L. Bond, Eds.) Special Issue: *Testing: Concepts, Policy, Practice, and Research. American*

Psychologist, 1981, *36*, 10.

Borgatta, E. The structure of personality characteristics. *Behavioral Science*, 1964, *9*, 8–17.

Campbell, D. T. Social attitudes and other acquired dispositions. In S. Koch (Ed.). *Psychology: A Study of a Science*. Vol. 6. New York: McGraw-Hill, 1963.

Corsini, R. Multiple predictors of marital happiness. *Marriage and Family Living*, 1956, *17*, 240–242.

Cronbach, L., & Meehl, P. Construct validity in psychological tests. *Psychological Bulletin*, 1955, *52*, 281–302.

Garcia, J. The logic and limits of mental aptitude testing. *American Psychologist*, 1981, *36*, 1172–1180.

Green, B. A primer of testing. *American Psychologist*, 1981, *36*, 1001–1011.

Digman, J., & Takemoto-Chock, N. Factors in the natural language of personality: Re-analysis, comparison, and interpretation of six major studies. *Multivariate Behavioral Research*, 1981, *16*, 149–170.

Munroe, R. *Schools of psychoanalytic thought*. New York: Dryden, 1955.

Olmedo, E. Testing linguistic minorities. *American Psychologist*, 1981, *36*, 1078–1085.

Olson, H. *Early recollections*. Springfield, Ill.: C. C Thomas, 1979.

Sechrest, L. Testing, measuring, and assessing people. In E. Borgatta and W. Lambert (Eds.), *Handbook of personality theory and research*. Chicago: Rand McNally, 1968.

CHAPTER XIV

Personality Research: Methods and New Directions

Anthony J. Marsella

INTRODUCTION

Research on personality is an active area of inquiry in psychology. It involves the use of diverse research strategies to investigate topics such as anxiety, aggression, dependency, achievement, authoritarianism, locus of control, shyness, self-concept, extraversion-introversion, Machiavellianism, and consciousness. In this chapter we shall discuss the current research status of *anxiety, aggression,* and *locus of control.* Each topic will be discussed in terms of its meaning, measurement, theories, and exemplary research.

The Roots of Personality Research

Research begins with "doubt," the opposite of "certainty." As long as we are "certain," there is no need for research. Doubt and uncertainty provide the necessary impetus for sound research.

Doubt is an unsettling experience. Everyone wants to feel certain! If our beliefs are not shared by others or if we think our beliefs may not be "true," we experience discomfort; consequently, we actively seek to reinforce our beliefs. In doing so we achieve certainty but not truth. For example, we may avoid reading things which disagree with our beliefs and we may also avoid associating with people who hold radically different positions. Yet, doubt is the basis for change and growth for individuals, groups, and societies. Though we avoid doubt, it forces us to question ourselves and the world about us. Doubt is the impetus for change.

Research is any *careful, systematic,* and *organized inquiry to increase knowledge.* While there are many research methods, all begin with questions stemming from doubt.

Engaging in Personality Research

The questions asked by personality researchers are among the most profound asked in the course of human history involving basic human emotions, relationships, and purposes. The complexity of these questions prevents them from being resolved through simple research methods. For many personality researchers, the questions they pursue involve a lifelong search involving an entire gamut of research methods. Personality research is not easy. It involves commitment and dedication.

CONDUCTING PERSONALITY RESEARCH

Formulating the Problem

A researcher ordinarily selects a problem, which captures his imagination (The researcher must really want to know the answer!). Researchers must consider any biases with regard to the problem's solution. Motivated to find a particular answer, any bias may contaminate the research and its conclusions.

Formulating a research problem involves such practical questions as funds, equipment, and data analysis facilities. Sometimes, a major problem in conducting research is the absence of financial or organizational support.

Another step in research is locating and reading available literature on the problem. Researchers may become so involved with a question that they do not search for other studies on the topic, which results in duplicated efforts. Reading previous research reports is an important step before launching a new investigation. Prior reading may lead a researcher to *(a)* abandon a study, *(b)* to change methodologies, or *(c)* to replicate the original study to check the validity of the prior conclusions.

Formulating a Hypothesis

A useful step in the conduct of personality research is the formulation of a hypothesis, which is a speculation about the nature of relationships for a topic. For example, if we are interested in studying anxiety, we might advance the following hypothesis: "Subjects with high levels of trait anxiety on the *Manifest Anxiety Scale* will possess significantly higher levels of sodium lactate than subjects with lower levels of trait anxiety." This hypothesis can now serve to guide our thinking by sharpening what we are seeking to answer and by helping us plan our methods of data analysis. A good hypothesis in personality research focuses our efforts to obtain useful and relevant data. It prepares us to understand the results of the investigation. Of course, a researcher should always be prepared for findings which radically disagree with the hypothesis. T. H. Huxley (1825-1895), the famous biologist, once said, "The tragedies of science are the slaying of beautiful hypotheses by ugly facts."

Research Methods

Many research methods are used in personality research. One is the experiment, which exposes subjects to a "treatment" condition and then compares the results to other subjects not receiving the "treatment" condition. A good experiment in personality research is hard to conduct because it involves operationalizing the variables one wishes to study and making sure that all other variables that might influence results are controlled or systematically manipulated. It is often critical to control extraneous variables since many factors can affect findings including maturation, fatigue, sample selection biases, events occurring between first and second measurements, and so forth (see Campbell & Stanley, 1963).

Many questions on personality do not lend themselves to experimental study. As a result, researchers frequently use other methods including: (1) *library research*—historical documents and publications; (2) *descriptive research*—surveys, opinion polls, interviews, anecdotal summaries, all of which serve to describe in a systematic way a given topic or problems; (3) *developmental or longitudinal research*—subjects studied over long periods of time to determine the effects of maturation and development on a given behavior; (4) *case study research*—intensive investigations of an individual or group, focusing on historical development or current status; (5) *correlational research*—determining relationships that may exist across two or more variables.

All these methods have strengths and weaknesses. Efforts to understand complex phenomena like "love" may not lend themselves to experimental research; rather, it may be necessary to research love through historical, descriptive, or case study methods. Experimental or correlational methods may be the method of choice to examine variables with direct behavioral or objective referents.

Some research methods are more appropriate for certain topics than for others. The final decision to use one method over another is a function of the topic under study, the personal predilections of a given researcher, and factors such as the availability of equipment and personnel.

Personality Measurement and Assessment

For research methods which favor quantitative approaches the choice of instruments or techniques is important. Several types of measuring methods are popular: (1) *self-report* using data derived from personality question-naires and interview schedules; (2) *peer reports* in which an individual is rated or evaluated by peers or people familiar with his/her behavior; (3) *behavioral observation* in which ratings are made of a person's overt behavior by observers or judges; (4) *interpreted measures* including tests like the Rorschach or Thematic Apperception Test in which the conclusions reached about a person depend on a tester's ability to interpret the person's responses; (5) *life history data* involving facts about the person's life which may be found in life records such as school reports, hospital records, and work evaluation summaries; (6) *objective tests,* especially psychomotor tests, sensory tests, reaction time tests, and various biological or psychophysiological indices such as catecholamine excretion rates, blood pressure, galvanic skin responses, and electrocardiograms.

Important measurement instrument characteristics in personality assessment are *reliability* and *validity*. Reliability refers to a measure's *consistency*. If a personality researcher gives you a test purported to measure "trait anxiety" and you score high on the test one week but low on the test the following week, the instrument has questionable reliability.

The most important factor in personality assessment is *validity*. Validity refers to an instrument's ability to measure what it purports to measure. For example, if someone develops a questionnaire on "shyness," then it is logical to expect an individual scoring high on the scale would be "shy" in actual social situations. That is, the individual should be quiet, reserved, withdrawn, hesitant to speak to others, nervous in social encounters, and so forth. But, if the instrument is not valid, the individual scoring high in shyness might turn out to be socially poised, talkative, outgoing, confident and so forth. In this case, the instrument has little utility since it is not valid. It doesn't measure shyness.

Two important kinds of validity are *predictive* validity and *construct* validity. In predictive validity, scores on a given instrument "predict" how an individual will behave in future situations. A score on the "shyness" test should predict how an individual will act at a future dance or party. In construct validity, the concern is with the instrument's capacity to have a logical relationship to an associated "construct" which cannot be observed directly, such as "intelligence" or "creativity." For example, a shyness scale might show a close relationship to measures of extraversion, assertiveness, positive self-concept, and so forth. (Chapter 13 discusses these topics in greater depth.)

Statistics and Data Analysis

There are two types of statistical approaches in analyzing research data. The first is *descriptive* statistics used to summarize research findings in a clear, concise manner. Descriptive statistics include: (1) *measures of central tendency* such as the mean, mode, or median; (2) *measures of range* including the standard deviation or interquartile range; (3) *data display forms:* bar graphs, frequency plots, diagrams, and charts. Descriptive statistics enable researchers to present their data in summary form for easy understanding and display.

The second statistical approach involves *inferential* statistics which describe relationships between variables. They involve "statistical tests" based on certain premises like probability theory or the natural distribution of a given event. Inferential statistics often make use of extensive mathematical analyses. Some popular inferential statistics for the analysis of data from experiments and correlational studies include: (1) *t*-test, (2) *chi-square* test, (3) *Z*-test, (4) *F*-test (analysis of variance), and (5) various correlational analyses such as the product moment correlation, point biserial correlation, phi correlation coefficient, tetrachoric correlation, and rank-difference correlation. Because personality researchers are mostly concerned with the relationships among many interacting variables, there has been an increased emphasis in recent years in employing multivariate statistical methods. These include techniques such as factor analysis, path analysis, multiple regression equations, and multidimensional scaling. Some methods permit as many as 100 variables to be studied simultaneously.

Descriptive and inferential statistics offer an opportunity to quantify the phenomena under study. Quantitative methods provide clarity and precision. But, one should not sacrifice meaning for quantification. Many aspects of personality do not lend themselves to quantification without distortion of the phenomena. For example, it might be interesting to obtain ratings of the degree of "love" for various people in our lives. These ratings could then be compared across gender, age, or ethnocultural groups. Statistical differences might show that men feel more love than women for their parents. The ratings in this instance provide an interesting research finding, but it would be wrong to rely solely on ratings. We also could learn a great deal by evaluating a series of cases or longitudinal studies. The data from the latter may not lend itself to quantification but it would nevertheless be a valuable source of information about parental love.

Data Interpretation

The final step in research involves interpretation of the data. This step is difficult since the researcher must make sense of findings revealed by the data analysis. At this point, creativity is necessary to find linkages between sometimes seemingly disparate results. Theory offers a perspective for understanding a given finding. For example, if we are studying dreams, we might want to relate our findings to Freudian, Jungian, or Adlerian theories of dreaming. A good researcher separates the interpretations of findings from the actual findings. In reporting results, "evaluative"words should be avoided unless the researcher is clearly informing the reader that the results are an opinion and not a statement of fact.

Some Closing Thoughts on Personality Research

Our ability to transcend our need for *certainty* is the foundation of research. All good research begins and ends with *doubt*. Many readers may find this disquieting since they have been told the purpose of research is to answer questions. The particular perspective we favor is that we can never arrive at the "truth" since the universe is constantly changing and we are limited by the inadequacy of human linguistic and conceptual abilities.

The appeal of research, regardless of the methods used, is the excitement associated with bringing greater understanding, predictability, and control to our lives. Yet, even as we make sense of something, our understanding is at best tenuous and temporary and may some day yield to new insights brought on by new knowledge generated from new techniques and research strategies. This progression of knowledge has occurred from the earliest days of human history and we believe it will continue into the future.

Valuable unintended findings often emerge in research. Such results are called serendipitous because they are unexpected. An open mind which can live with doubt and uncertainty is more likely to find the unexpected.

CURRENT TRENDS IN PERSONALITY THEORY AND RESEARCH

Currently, many forces affect personality theory and research. Some stand out because of their capacity to redirect the field, including: (1) biological research, (2) cross-cultural studies, and (3) interactional theories.

Biological Aspects of Human Behavior

Interest in biological aspects of human behavior can be traced to the thinking of the early Greeks, like Hippocrates (460-377 B.C.) and the Roman physician, Galen (130-220 A.D.), who concluded that body humors (fluids such as blood, phlegm, black bile, and yellow bile) were related to different personality temperaments. In subsequent centuries, biological explanations of human behavior continued. For example, the philosopher, René Descartes, concluded that the mind was located in the pineal body, a small gland located in the middle of the brain.

It is abundantly clear that human behavior is correlated with biological functioning. Areas currently receiving considerable attention within the field of personality are genetics, neurochemistry, and physiology.

The following list details some of the biological areas in which advances are being made:

1. *Behavioral Genetics.* Mathematical and structural models of genetic functioning have led to a variety of discoveries regarding the biological basis of various personality variables such as food preferences, arousal patterns, and social behaviors such as dominance and sociability.

2. *Neurochemistry.* Advances in biochemistry have called attention to the role of neurotransmitters in moods, thinking, and other aspects of complex behavior. Much of the work has been related to severe mental disorders. Of special interest for personality theorists is the research on endogenous opiates produced in the central nervous system. More than 30 neurotransmitters are now known.

3. *Electrophysiology.* Interest in central nervous system arousal patterns has long been popular among experimental psychologists. Today, this interest has carried over into personality theory and research through research on stress, biofeedback, and cognition studies involving the orienting response. New methods for studying brain activity as well as new methods for analyzing electroencephalographic activity data via computers have provided new insights about brain activity.

4. *Neurophysiology.* Recent developments in neurophysiology suggest the two hemispheres of the brain's cortex may function independently. Investigators have speculated that the *right* brain is concerned with the global, holistic thinking and the *left* brain is concerned with sequential, logical, and analytical thinking. Research in this area may some day help account for personality styles.

5. *Electro-Brain Stimulation.* More than three decades ago, researchers began exploring the functions of different areas of the brain through electronic stimulation. Special interest was given to midbrain areas such as the hypothalamus and thalamus. Today, microelectronics has made it possible to control various aspects of behavior through stimulation of certain brain centers by receivers and transmitters implanted in the brain. These are then operated by computers which send or receive different signals from the brain. These methods are now in use in humans with various neurological impairments like epilepsy and narcolepsy.

6. *Neuroassessment.* New methods for X-raying various parts of the body, including the brain, have provided a new window into the mind (e.g., positron emission tomography—PET Scan). Radioactive elements are injected into the brain and their activity is then

monitored through techniques which provide a vivid and detailed view of brain sites during given tasks such as problem solving, reading, and dreaming. It is the closest scientists have come to watching the brain function *in vivo*. Personality theorists may soon be able to link various personality concepts to specific sites in the brain.

Such advances in biology promise to alter our approaches to personality. They offer new insights into age-old questions of human nature. Personality theorists of the future will require training in physiological as well as psychological aspects of human behavior. The outcome will be the recognition that mind and body are inextricably linked to one another.

Cross-Cultural Research and Personality

Just as biological research is leading personality theorists to look for answers in neurological functioning, cross-cultural research has stimulated theorists to pursue answers about personality through a broader understanding of the role of the social environment. Cross-cultural research has pointed out the ethnocentricity of many of our basic concepts. Increasingly, psychologists are asking how applicable, indeed how ethical, it is to use a theory of personality derived in the Western world to understand the behavior of non-Western people (see Chapters 12 and 11, respectively, by Pedersen and Ziferstein in present volume). Marsella, Tharp, and Ciborowski (1979) and Triandis et al. (1979-1980), among others, have raised questions about our biases.

Cross-cultural research in personality began with the work of Franz Boas. In his classic book, *The Mind of Primitive Man* (1911), Boas called attention to the role of culture in complex human behavior. Boas's students, including Edward Sapir, Margaret Mead, Bronislaw Malinowski, and Ruth Benedict, sought to examine the relationships between culture and personality. Margaret Mead's book, *Coming of Age in Samoa* (1929) and Ruth Benedict's book, *Patterns of Culture* (1934) are classic studies relating personality and culture. Malinowski's book, *Sex and Repression in a Savage Society* (1927), was a direct test and refutation of Freudian concepts of the *Oedipus complex*.

During World War II, cultural anthropologists conducted studies of *national character* or *modal personality*. Ruth Benedict discussed the Japanese personality in *The Chrysanthemum and the Sword* (1946), Geoffrey Gorer discussed the Russians in *The People of Great Russia* (1949), and Margaret Mead discussed the Americans in *And Keep Your Powder Dry* (1942). Reviews of modal personality studies are available in Singer (1961) and Favazza (1974).

Gradually, interest in culture and personality shifted toward studies of specific characteristics such as achievement, authoritarianism, dependency, aggression, locus of control, and Machiavellianism. Western psychologists became involved in the field of cross-cultural psychology, using Western personality scales and assessment measures, including projective techniques such as the Rorschach and Thematic Apperception Test (TAT).

At this point, Western researchers began to recognize their ethnocentricity. For example, dependency is a popular topic of study in the United States; it refers to a tendency to seek excessive social assistance or help. Among Western people, dependency generally is considered an undesirable trait. Healthy people are supposed to be independent, autonomous, self-sufficient, and to avoid needing the care and support of others. But cross-cultural research in Japan (e.g., Doi, 1974) revealed the Japanese culture values dependency. *Amae,* the equivalent Japanese concept for dependency, has a positive connotation. The Japanese encourage dependency among their children. To be independent and assertive is considered to be rude.

Western psychologists have become increasingly aware of the role of culture in influencing behavior, and of the biases that occur when we attempt to apply Western theories and reasearch instruments to non-Western people. Is it sensible to apply a theory like Freud's, developed in 19th-century Vienna, to explain Chinese, Korean, Samoan, or Indian behavior? Isn't it possible that inaccurate conclusions will be reached because of the lack of *conceptual equivalence* in other cultures? Is it meaningful to give a test developed for Americans to Indonesians, Brazilians, Japanese, or Ethiopians?

Cross-cultural studies have had two major impacts: (1) they have highlighted the importance of culture in personality development and dynamics; (2) they have called attention to cultural biases in our personality concepts, theories, and assessment methods. These impacts are likely to become more important in the future as American minority groups begin to assert their discontent with the dominant culture's application of concepts which have no relevance to their experience.

Interactionism

A recent conceptual development in personality theory is *interactionism,* which refers to the growing trend to seek the determinants of behavior in the simultaneous interaction of organismic and environmental variables. Efforts to develop an interaction perspective can be traced to the early 1930s in the work of J. B. Kantor and Kurt Lewin. Only in the last decade, however, has this viewpoint achieved broad popularity.

Personality research during prior decades favored either the organism or the environment as the primary determinant of human behavior. For example, psychodynamic, trait, existential, cognitive, and constitutional theories mainly focused on the organism, while operant conditioning and social learning theories focused on the environment. Theorists within the *interactionist* school of thought (e.g., Lewin, Goldstein, Angyal, Perls, Brunswik) argued both variables are critical since they interact with one another. During the 1930s and 1940s, however, these early interactionists failed to gain much support. To a certain extent this was because of the popularity of other perspectives including psychoanalysis, learning theory, and phenomenological theory.

Interactionism is an outgrowth of field theory in physics. As physics shifted its theoretical perspective from Newtonian, mechanistic models of the universe to Einsteinian relativistic perspectives, many physicists developed an increased interest in the relational properties of phenomena. Causality was no longer considered a simple linear process between two or more directly related variables. Rather, causation was viewed as a complex process of interdependency among force-fields.

Concepts advanced by field theory are actually representative of the much older Galilean conception of causality. Galileo forced a change in previous notions of causality by insisting that the "cause" of an event be sought in relationships among objects and their surroundings.

Early Interactional Theories.   In the early 1930s a number of European psychologists and psychiatrists attempted to apply some conceptualizations in physics to human behavior, construing behavior to be a function of both organismic and environmental forces. In *Principles of Topological Psychology* (1936), Kurt Lewin stated,

> Every psychological event depends upon the state of the person and at the same time on the environment, although their relative importance is different in different cases. Thus we can state our formula $B = f(S)$ for every psychological event as $B = f(PE)$ in which B = behavior; f = function of; S = situation; P = person; and E = environment. The experimental work of recent years shows more and more this twofold relationship in all fields of psychology. Every scientific psychology must take into account whole situations, i.e., the state of both person and environment (Lewin, p. 11).

With these words, Lewin established himself as the first modern interactional theorist. Lewin's efforts were subsequently reinforced by Kurt Goldstein, Fritz Perls, Egon Brunswik, and Andreas Angyal. Andreas Angyal is particularly important because, more than any other theorist, he advanced a new conceptual term for studying the organism and the environment as a holistic unit. He called this unit the *biosphere.* Angyal (1941) stated,

The biosphere includes both the individual and the environment, not as interacting parts, not as constituents which have independent existence, but as aspects
of a single reality which can be separated only by abstraction . . . Every process
which results from the interplay of organismic autonomy or environmental
heteronomy is a part of the life process, irrespective of whether it takes place
within the body or outside of it. The realm in which the life process takes place
has been termed the "biosphere" (pp. 99-100).

While behavior is clearly dependent upon the simultaneous interaction or
organismic and environmental variables, there is a gap between advancing a
theory and having empirical validation methods. In most instances, the concepts posited by these early interactional theorists made good intuitive
sense, but were impossible to investigate empirically. As a result, their
theories were ignored and gradually slipped into the realm of philosophical
speculation rather than scientific findings.

Consistency versus Specificity. By the mid-1960s, Lewin and Angyal had
died, Goldstein had concentrated on brain damage, Perls was developing
Gestalt psychotherapy, and Brunswik's theory of probabilistic functionalism had become mired in theoretical obscurity. A new event gave
rebirth to interactional theory: Walter Mischel's assertion that behavior was
more a function of the situation than of the person. Mischel's position gave
rise to the *consistency versus specificity issue* which subsequently produced
a resurgence of interest in interactionalism.

In 1968, Mischel published *Personality and Assessment* in which he
contended behavior was specific to particular situations rather than to
individual personalities. Mischel's conclusions were challenged by Alker
(1972), Block (1968), Wallach and Leggett (1972), Wachtel (1973), and
Marsella and Murray (1974). They argued that Mischel made numerous
errors in his interpretation of trait research, and that he had failed to credit
research on cited literature which supported the trait position. Marsella and
Murray (1974) published a study concluding behavioral consistency was
itself a personality trait, since some individuals were more consistent than
others. This debate drew a number of Mischel's supporters into the foray
offering data to support the "specificity" position (e.g., Bem, 1972).

At approximately the time Mischel launched his assault on trait psychology, others were rediscovering the virtues of the interactional position.
Endler and Hunt (1968, 1969), for example, conducted a series of studies
designed to assess responses to various anxiety situations. Marsella,
Escudero, and Gordon (1971) and Marsella and Snyder (1981) conducted a
series of studies on psychopathology based on an interactional model in
which psychiatric symptomatology was considered an outcome of the
simultaneous interaction of stresses and resources. These studies
represented a more direct concern with interactional models as posited by
the theorists of the 1930s and 1940s.

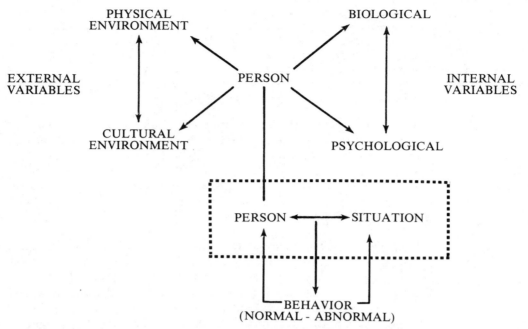

FIGURE 14-1:   INTERACTIONAL MODEL OF BEHAVIOR (MARSELLA & SNYDER 1981)

In 1973, Bowers published a review paper on *situationalism* in which he reported on 11 studies which examined *situation* versus *person* contributions to behavior. Among studies using "behavior observation," three studies favored *person,* and four favored *situation.* In contrast, three studies using "self-ratings" favored *person*, while only one favored *situation.* Among eight studies based on "stimulus-response questionnaires," five favored *person*, while three favored *situation.*

No clear-cut conclusion could be reached favoring either position. In an attempt to resolve the confusion, Bowers cited the importance of the individual's perception in construing the situation to which a person responds. In rebuttal, Mischel (1973) advanced a new social learning theory based on cognition, and contended that his previous reports were misunderstood.

Stability versus Change.   The issue of stability versus change in personality emerged from a growing number of studies about adult development (Brim & Kagan 1980; Rubin, 1981). For years, psychologists and psychiatrists believed personality development halted around the teen years. For example, both Freud and Sullivan stopped their developmental sequences in late adolescence and early adulthood. Carl Jung and Abraham Maslow, Erich Fromm and Erik Erikson, in contrast, advanced theories in which personality development continued until the end of one's life. Levinson (1978), in his book, *The Seasons of Man's Life,* and Gail Sheehy (1976), in her book, *Passages,* also raised arguments regarding the continual growth and change of personality throughout the life cycle.

The "stability" position assumes that there is a considerable amount of constancy in human personality across time. In contrast, the "change" position asserts human beings constantly grow and change. This viewpoint is held by the so-called holistic/humanistic school of personality theory. Zick Rubin (1981) pointed out the unreasonableness of the stability versus change issue. He stated,

> Now that researchers have established beyond a reasonable doubt that there is often considerable stability in adult personality, they may be able to move on to a clearer understanding of how we can grow and change, even as we remain the same people we always were. It may be, for example, that if we are to make significant changes in ourselves, without losing our sense of identity, it is necessary for some aspects of our personality to remain stable. "I'm different now," we can say, "but it's still me." (p. 27.)

Interactionism is a major conceptual trend in personality theory and research. Researchers are attempting to resolve the problems inherent in assessing simultaneous organismic and environmental relationships. Many theorists are advancing models of behavior based on interactional premises. If human behavior is a function of the simultaneous interaction of organismic and environmental variables at a given point in time, this will require a new conceptual language to understand the totality of the organismic-environmental relationship, without separating the various components.

Currently, a "true" interactional theory of behavior represents a hope rather than an actuality. Theorists and researchers are aware of the complexity of the forces that ultimately determine behavior, but they are puzzled about the steps to take to resolve the problem. The problems are conceptual, linguistic, and methodological. In the course of time, as we come to recognize the constraints imposed upon us by our language and previous theories, we will come to develop new frameworks of inquiry which will launch us forward into a new era of understanding of human behavior—an era of interactional theory. When this occurs, personality theory and research will take a quantum step forward and the contents of the present book will be history.

REFERENCES

Alker, H. Is personality situationally specific or intrapsychically consistent? *Journal of Personality,* 1972, *40,* 1-15.

Angyal, A. *Foundations for a science of personality.* Cambridge, Mass.: Harvard University Press, 1941.

Benedict, R. *Patterns of culture*. New York: New American Library, 1934.

Benedict, R. *The chrysanthemum and the sword*. Boston: Houghton Mifflin, 1946.

Bem, D. Constructing cross-situational consistencies in behavior: Some thoughts on Alker's critique of Mischel. *Journal of Personality,* 1972, *40*, 17-26.

Block, J. Some reasons for the apparent inconsistency of personality. *Psychological Bulletin,* 1968, *70*, 210-212.

Boas, F. *The mind of primitive man*. New York: Macmillan, 1930 (rev. ed.). (Original edition, 1911.)

Bowers, K. Situationalism in psychology: An analysis and a critique. *Psychological Review,* 1973, *80*, 307-336.

Brim, O., & Kagan, J. (Eds.). *Constancy and change in human development*. Cambridge, Mass.: Harvard University Press, 1980.

Campbell, D. T., & Stanley, J. C. Stanley experimental and quasi-experimental designs for research on teaching. In N. L. Gage (Ed.) *Handbook on research on teaching*. Chicago: Rand McNally & Co., 1963.

Doi, T. *The anatomy of dependency*. Tokyo, Japan: Kodansha International Press, 1974.

Endler, N., & Hunt, J. McV. S-R inventories of hostility and comparisons of the proportion of variance from persons, responses, and situations for hostility and anxiousness. *Journal of Personality and Social Psychology,* 1968, *9*, 309-315.

Endler, N., & Hunt, J. McV. Generalizability of contributions from sources of variance in the S-R inventories of anxiousness. *Journal of Personality,* 1969, *37*, 1-24.

Favazza, A. A critical review of studies of national character: A psychiatric-anthropological interface. *Journal of Operational Psychiatry,* 1974, *6*, 3-31.

Gorer, G., & Rickman, J. *The people of great Russia: A psychological study*. London, Eng.: Dresset, 1949.

Levinson, *The seasons of a man's life*. New York: Alfred A. Knopf, 1978.

Lewin, K. *Principles of topological psychology*. New York: McGraw-Hill, 1936.

Malinowski, B. *Sex and repression in a savage society*. New York: Harcourt & Brace Co., 1927.

Marsella, A. J., Escudero, M., & Gordon, P. Stresses, resources, and symptom patterns in urban Filipino men. In W. Lebra (ed.), *Transcultural psychiatric research in Asia and the Pacific*. Honolulu, Hawaii: University Press of Hawaii, 1971.

Marsella, A. J., & Murray, M. Diagnostic type, gender, and consistency versus specificity in behavior. *Journal of Clinical Psychology,* 1974, *30*, 484-488.

Marsella, A. J., & Snyder, K. Stress, social supports, and schizophrenic disorders: Toward an interactional model. *Schizophrenia Bulletin,* 1981, *7*, 152-163.

Marsella, A. J., Tharp, R., & Ciborowski, T. (Eds.). *Perspectives on cross-cultural psychology*. New York: Academic Press, 1979.

Mead, M. *Coming of age in Samoa*. New York: Wm. Morrow & Co., 1928.

Mead, M. *And keep your powder dry*. New York: Wm. Morrow & Co., 1942.

Mischel, W. *Personality and assessment*. New York: Wiley, 1968.

Mischel, W. Toward a cognitive social learning reconceptualization of personality. *Psychological Review,* 1973, *80*, 252-283.

Rubin, Z. Does personality really change after 20? *Psychology Today,* 1981, *15* (5), 18-27.

Sheehy, G. *Passages*. New York: E. P. Dutton, 1976.

Singer, M. Culture and personality theory and research. In B. Kaplan (Ed.), *Studying personality cross culturally*. New York: Harper & Row, 1961.

Triandis, H., et al. (Eds.). *The handbook of cross-cultural psychology* (6 vols.). Boston, Mass.: Allyn & Bacon, 1979-1980.

Wachtel, P. Psychodynamics, behavior therapy, and the implacable experimenter: An inquiry into the consistency of personality. *Journal of Abnormal Psychology,* 1973, *82,* 324-334.

Wallach, M., & Leggett, M. Testing the hypothesis that a person will be consistent: Stylistic consistency versus situational specificity in size of children's drawings. *Journal of Personality,* 1972, *40,* 309-330.

CHAPTER XV

Personality Research: Anxiety, Aggression, and Locus of Control

Anthony J. Marsella and
Alan L. Yang

ANXIETY

INTRODUCTION

Types of Anxiety

Anxiety refers to both a transitory state and an enduring pattern of behavior. Exposed to an anxiety-provoking situation (e.g., a tooth extraction, making a speech before a large audience), our hearts pound, our respiration increases, and our muscles tense. These reactions describe the *state* of anxiety. Spielberger (1975) describes this state:

> State anxiety may be conceptualized as a transitory emotional state or condition of the human organism that varies in intensity and fluctuates over time. This condition is characterized by subjective, consciously perceived feelings of tension and apprehension, and activation of the autonomic nervous system (p. 137).

"Anxiety" also describes general characteristics of some people. Statements like "He's really an anxious person" versus "He's feeling anxious" refer to anxiety as an ongoing personality trait.

> Trait anxiety refers to relatively stable individual differences in anxiety proneness, that is, to differences in the disposition to perceive a wide range of stimulus situations as dangerous or threatening, and in the tendency to respond to such threats with A-State reactions. A-Trait may also be regarded as reflecting individual differences in the frequency and intensity which A-States have been manifested in the past, and in the probability that such states will be experienced in the future. (Spielberger, 1975, p. 137)

State anxiety refers to an individual's transient situational anxiety that varies with time and events, while *trait anxiety* refers to a more stable, characteristic level, consistent across time and situations.

Clinical Types of Anxiety

Sometimes, anxiety can become so severe that it assumes the proportion of a clinical problem. In these instances, the problem may be termed *primary anxiety disorder*. It can occur periodically or in specific situations. A *primary anxiety* attack is characterized by feelings of immense panic and fear. Individuals experience extensive confusion and the world appears strange and unreal. At a physiological level, the individual's heart beats rapidly and it is difficult to breathe. There is often a numbness and tingling in the limbs and excessive perspiration even while resting.

Generally, anxiety attacks occur only periodically and may last no longer than a few hours. However, the problem may last for a long time at a lesser level of intensity. If so, the problem is termed *chronic* rather than *acute* primary anxiety disorder. Sometimes individuals are characterologically anxious all their life. These individuals are always tense, fearful, and emotional. Thus, primary anxiety disorders can be acute or chronic; and, in some instances, they may be characterological or lifelong.

In addition to primary anxiety disorder, clinicians also use a separate category for *secondary anxiety disorders*. In these instances, anxiety is considered part of a broader behavioral problem. For example, anxiety attacks can occur in the presence of schizophrenic and depressive disorders. Further, in some instances, anxiety is at the core of some disorders such as the obsessive-compulsive neurosis and various forms of hysteria. In contrast to the primary anxiety disorder, the secondary disorder is not the major problem but rather a part of another disorder.

There are many different theories about the origins and experiences of anxiety to be discussed in the next section.

THEORIES OF ANXIETY

Psychodynamic

1. Freud.   While numerous psychoanalytic theorists discuss anxiety, none have offered as complete a perspective on the topic as Sigmund Freud. Freud (1936) claimed the experience of anxiety is innate, part of an inherited self-preservation instinct. He suggested the actual feelings and responses involved in anxiety may be similar to those of the "birth trauma." Freud also believed anxiety was the fundamental emotion in all types of neurosis. He identified three different types of anxiety: (a) realistic, (b) neurotic, and (c) moral.

Realistic anxiety deals with objective fears of real dangers. Feeling anxious while walking down a dark street in a strange city is an example of realistic anxiety. In realistic anxiety there is an identifiable threat or danger in the external world.

The experience of realistic anxiety serves as the basis for two additional types of anxiety that Freud classified. *Neurotic anxiety* refers to fear that one's inner impulses will get out of control and cause regrettable behavior, the fear of acting on sexual or aggressive impulses to achieve pleasure or gratification.

Moral anxiety refers to fear of one's own conscience. It is the anxiety we associate with guilt out of acts or wishes that violate one's moral codes of right and wrong. Because conscience is part of the superego, moral anxiety can also arise out of acts and wishes which conflict with one's ideal self-image.

The focus of realistic anxiety is outward toward the external world. However, in moral and neurotic anxiety the focus is turned inward toward the internal world of our psyches. There is not objective, external stimuli which we can identify as the source of our anxiety. The source lies within the individual due to the dynamic interplay between conflicting thoughts, emotions, and wishes, often unconscious in nature.

2. Adler. According to Alfred Adler, people can take two positions toward the environment: moving toward or moving away. If one moves closer in a hostile way—that is aggression; and if one moves away in an escaping manner—that is anxiety. Both are seen as neurotic behaviors, having as their purpose the safeguarding of the individual's self-esteem. In 1927, Adler wrote:

> Once a person has acquired the attitude of running away from the difficulties of life, this attitude may be greatly strengthened and safeguarded by the addition of anxiety. . . . In individuals with an attitude of hostility towards their environment we often find traits of anxiety which lend a particular coloring to their character. Anxiety is an extraordinary far-flung phenomenon which accompanies a person from his earliest days, often into his old age . . .

According to Adler, anxiety is only another mechanism to prevent a person from doing what is required. A person in effect is saying: "I can't because I am anxious" and thereby gives himself or herself a kind of excuse, thinking "I can't do it; I am too frightened."

3. Horney and Sullivan. Neo-psychoanalytic theorists who commented on anxiety include Karen Horney and Harry Stack Sullivan. Horney (1942) believed basic anxiety developed in childhood from feelings of isolation, loneliness, and helplessness. Horney thought much of adult life is spent escaping from early feelings of anxiety. Sullivan (1947) agreed much of adult life is spent avoiding or reducing anxiety; however, he believed the child's relationship with its mother was the crucial determinant in anxiety formation. An anxious mother induces anxiety in the child via empathy, thus interferes with the satisfaction of crucial interpersonal needs.

Humanistic

Humanistic personality theorists such as Carl Rogers (1951) consider anxiety as a response to threat to one's self-concept. If scholarship is an important value in a student's self-concept and the student encounters situations which question his/her scholastic abilities (e.g., a D on an examination; not qualifying for a desired scholarship), anxiety results. Thus, incongruity between self-concept and actual experience can elicit anxiety. An individual need not be aware of the incongruity to experience anxiety. On one level, the individual responds to discrepancies in self-concept by experiencing anxiety. However, on another level the individual refuses to consciously acknowledge discrepancies because a painful reevaluation of the self-concept would be necessary.

Thus Rogers views anxiety as a response to threat; if acknowledged, this can create self-concept discrepancies. Anxiety is the tension felt by an individual who recognizes certain discrepancies leading to a reevaluation of the self-concept. From this perspective, anxiety is an emotion that plays an integral role in self-growth, self-exploration, and self-awareness. However, if not handled properly, it can lead to severe maladjustment.

Learning

O. H. Mowrer (1939) based his concept of anxiety on learning theory. He hypothesized anxiety is a conditioned response to perceived dangerous stimuli. A reduction in tension, pain, and discomfort is rewarding to the organism, and therefore behaviors that reduce anxiety are reinforced. Mowrer (1940) stated:

> Anxiety, defined as the anticipation of painfully intense stimuli, appears to exercise an important influence in actually shaping human and infrahuman behavior alike. Just as a reduction of hunger, thirst, sex drive, fatigue, oxygen, or any other organic need or discomfort tends to reinforce behavior which brings about such a reduction or state of relief, so likewise is a reduction in the particular form of discomfort called anxiety effective in fixating behavior that is associated therewith (p. 99).

Other behaviorists (e.g., Skinner, 1938, 1954) agree with Mowrer. Like Mowrer, they believe the primary drive of pain reduction is the basis for understanding anxiety. Most people experience anxiety about an impending visit to the dentist because the dentist's office is associated with pain and discomfort. Because anxiety is uncomfortable, we usually delay visiting the dentist until the last minute or until we convince ourselves that by not going, dire future consequences will occur. Since anxiety is associated with pain and discomfort (primary avoidance drives) the experience of anxiety itself becomes painful and discomforting.

Learning theorists conceive of anxiety as a secondary avoidance drive. Once defined as a secondary avoidance drive, learning theorists can investigate different aspects of anxiety, including how dependent anxiety levels are on the strength of the painful stimulus or the number of times the stimulus has been experienced as painful.

In our example of the dentist's office, we can ask questions about how our level of anxiety varies with: (1) filling a simple cavity versus extracting a tooth, or (2) whether six versus two visits to the dentist proved more painful. The extent anxiety generalizes can also be investigated. For example, would anxiety involving a visit to the dentist generalize to a visit to a physician but not to an optometrist? By defining anxiety within the learning theory perspective, the application of learning theory concepts to the investigation of the experience of anxiety is possible.

Cognitive

From a cognitive perspective, George Kelly (1955) believes people function as scientists, seeking to predict and control their experiential world. To accomplish this, people establish a cognitive construct system. Anxiety occurs when one's construct system is unable to successfully describe, understand, predict, and control an experience.

Existential

From an existential perspective, Rollo May (1950) associates the experience of anxiety with the realization of human mortality—the tenuousness of our existence. Accidents, diseases, and crimes all threaten our physical existence. We are constantly aware of our vulnerability and eventual death. May also believes anxiety arises from threats to the existence of others or of events. An individual can identify so closely with others (parents, spouse, children, relatives, friends, and so on), an occupation (loss of job, professional failure, and so forth), or an event (graduation, marriage, retirement), that the possible loss of the person, occupation, or event would make life meaningless. This potential loss threatens one's psychological existence and causes considerable anxiety. Thus, for May, anxiety arises out of threats to both physical and psychological existence—the vulnerability of body and mind. May (1950) wrote:

> The distinctive quality of human anxiety arises from the fact that man is a valuing animal, who interprets his life and world in terms of symbols and meanings. It is the threat to these values—specifically, to some value that the individual holds essential to him as a self—that causes anxiety (p. 241).

How anxiety is viewed depends upon one's perspective on human nature. We have discussed different views on why anxiety is experienced; however, the actual experience of anxiety—Freud's prototypic birth trauma, Rogers's threats to self-concept, Mowrer's tension and discomfort, and May's realization of physical and psychological mortality—requires consideration of our physiological state.

PHYSIOLOGICAL ASPECTS OF ANXIETY

Early physiological theories of anxiety involved the concept of arousal. Duffy (1951) depicted the continuum of organismic activation as ranging from deep sleep through light sleep, drowsiness, inalert wakefulness, normal wakefulness, finally reaching edginess and hyperactivity. To Duffy, anxiety was just one of many labels that specified an arousal state along the activation continuum. Lader (1966) described this continuum in terms of physiological measures. As activation increased, perspiration, heart rate, blood flow, and muscle tension also increased. Cattell and Scheier (1961) reviewed physiological and neurological studies and noted physiological concomitants, such as an increase in pulse pressure, heart rate, respiration rate, and skin conductance. These are similar to those Darwin described in 1873 as the typical manifestations of fear: rapid palpitation of the heart, trembling, increased perspiration, dryness of the mouth, and a change in voice quality.

Duke and Nowicki (1979) reported the following: increased heart rate, digestive upset, cold sweat, increased respiration, muscle tension and stiffness, butterflies in the stomach, faintness and dizziness, nausea, frequent bowel movements, restlessness, headaches, dry mouth, chills, rashes, and twitches.

In general, it appears anxiety involves: (1) cardiovascular responses (heart rate, blood pressure); (2) respiratory responses (breathlessness, hypertension); (3) gastrointestinal responses (diarrhea, nausea); and more general symptoms of agitation (muscle tension, motor activation, perspiration, sleeplessness).

Psychological and Physiological Relationships

Common experience tells us feelings of anxiety go hand in hand with heart and respiration rate, sweating, muscle tension. A puzzling finding is the failure for psychological and physiological measures to correlate significantly when a person is under specific stress. Reviewing the literature on the physiology of anxiety, Hodges (1976) states:

> From such a consensus of opinion about physiological concomitants of anxiety, one might expect a great deal of research to support the idea that anxiety can be operationalized by either physiological or introspective variables. Yet this area of research is filled with contradictions and inconsistencies. Relationships found in one study are not confirmed in the next . . . (p. 176).

Current research supports this perspective. For example, Crabbs and Hopper (1980) report no relationship between EMG, finger temperature, and state-trait anxiety measures.

Biochemical Theories of Anxiety

Epinephrine and norepinephrine are the major biochemical substances associated with anxiety. When a person is confronted with a stressor, the pituitary gland (the body's master gland) secretes a hormone which activates the body. This activation involves the release of epinephrine (adrenalin) by the adrenals and the release of norepinephrine (noradrenalin) by sympathetic nervous system discharges. However, the circulation of these substances does not account for anxiety by themselves. Other findings elaborate the complex mechanisms involved.

The *nucleus locus coeruleum* located in the midbrain area has been linked to anxiety via the metabolism of norepinephrine. The *nucleus locus coeruleum* has numerous axons branching into all areas of the cerebral cortex and the limbic system of the brain. Thus, its activity has immediate implications for many different brain sites. Some researchers (Huang, Redmond, Snyder, Maas, 1975; Gold & Redmond, 1977; Sweeney, Gold, Pottash & Davies, 1980) have examined urinary and plasma metabolities of norepinephrine of anxious individuals and have speculated that norepinephrine activates *locus coeruleum* axons and this leads to anxiety experiences.

Other researchers (Greenblatt & Shoder, 1978; Hicks, Okonek, & Davis, 1980; Gottschalk, Stone, & Goldine, 1974) think that anxiety is related to beta receptors (adrenergic) associated with heart rate, flushing, dilation of blood vessels, and so forth. These receptors are located largely in the peripheral nervous system, and drugs like propranolol serve to block beta receptor functioning. The research on *beta blockers* supports the notion that the peripheral nervous system may be more important than the central nervous system in anxiety.

Endorphins or opiates which are produced naturally in the brain have also been associated with anxiety (e.g., Extein et al., 1979; Gold et al., 1979). Endorphins have been found in the midbrain areas, especially the *locus coeruleum,* during norepinephrine activity, suggesting some linkage between the norepinephrine and endorphins.

A popular biochemical theory of anxiety is the *sodium lactate hypothesis.* Pitts and McClure (1967) and Pitts (1969) were the first to suggest that decreased amounts of calcium at membrane sites may be related to anxiety. Pitts and his co-workers injected sodium lactate in patients prone to anxiety attacks and found that those prone to attacks experienced severe anxiety, while normals experienced only mild symptoms. They concluded excessive stress leads to an increased flow of adrenalin which increases the amount of lactate. The latter interferes with the availability of ionized calcium at excitable membranes and this leads to many symptoms associated with anxiety such as tingling, numbness, and difficulty in breathing. But, research on this area has been filled with conflicting findings and Levitt (1972) concluded there is little support for this hypothesis.

There are numerous other biochemical hypotheses about anxiety including the *gamma-amino butyric acid (GABA) hypothesis* (see Costa, Guidotti, & Mao, 1976; Haefely, 1978) and the *serotonin hypothesis* (see Sepinwall & Cook, 1978). Kelly (1980), Sepinwall and Cook (1978), and Hicks, Okonek, and Davis (1980) provide excellent reviews of biochemical theories of anxiety. In general, there is no firm support for any biochemical theory; however, there is a growing recognition of the interrelationships across many of the theories. Future research may well reveal specific structural and biochemical correlates of anxiety.

ASSESSMENT

Manifest Anxiety Scale (MAS)

One of the first and most widely used scales to assess trait anxiety is the Taylor *Manifest Anxiety Scale* (MAS) (Taylor, 1953). The *MAS* was developed to measure anxiety, an arousal state, in the context of Hull-Spence learning theory (see Spence, 1960). Briefly, the Hull-Spence theory of learning involves the role of drive reduction in learning. The theory posits the strength of a particular response (R) is a multiplicative function of the total drive state (D) and habit strength (H). The theory also assumes that aversive stimuli arouse a hypothetical emotional response which contributes to the total drive state. The MAS was designed to measure individual differences in the emotional response to aversive or noxious stimuli.

Taylor based the MAS on the Minnesota Multiphasic Personalty Inventory. Sixty-five items from the MMPI were selected as indicative of manifest anxiety, supplemented by 135 buffer (nonanxiety) items. The MAS has undergone revision since its introduction and now contains 50 items used to distinguish individuals according to their level of trait anxiety. An examination of some of the items included on the MAS indicates their character:

I shrink from crisis or difficulty.
I certainly feel useless at times.
I worry quite a bit over possible misfortune.
I have a great deal of stomach trouble.
My sleep is fitful and disturbed.
I cry easily.
It makes me nervous to have to wait.
I am inclined to take things hard.
Life is a strain for me much of the time.
I am easily embarrassed.

(Adapted from Taylor, 1953)

Trait / State Scales

In contrast to the MAS, which seeks to assess enduring characteristics of anxiety, measures of state anxiety attempt to assess situational anxiety or anxiety experienced at particular times. The STAI state anxiety scale consists of 20 items referring to feelings of anxiety at a particular moment in time (e.g., "I feel jittery"). Subjects are asked to respond on a four-point scale consisting of: "not at all," "somewhat," "moderately so," and "very much so."

The *Fear Survey Schedule* (FSS) (Akutagawa, 1956) is the most widely used self-report measure of fear. Some theorists distinguish between fear and anxiety, noting that fear is usually accompanied by avoidance behaviors while state anxiety has no motor element (Bellack & Hersen, 1977). However, other theorists conclude that fear responses and anxiety states are more similar than dissimilar (Marinelli, 1980) and the FSS has been utilized in many studies investigating anxiety. The FSS assesses four types of fear responses: (1) fears related to small animals; (2) fears associated with death and physical pain; (3) fears concerning aggression; and (4) fears concerning interpersonal events.

Behavioral Measures

The behavioral assessment of anxiety involves observations of an individual's overt behavior in anxiety producing situations. Three major observational measures used in the behavioral assessment of anxiety are: (1) timed behavior checklists; (2) behavior avoidance tests; and (3) role playing tests (Marinelli, 1980). Timed behavior checklists involve subjects undertaking an anxiety provoking behavior while observers rate the incidence of observable anxiety indicators on a behavior checklist. Behavior avoidance tests ask subjects progressively to approach a feared stimulus (e.g., a spider) while observers assess distance from or time spent with feared stimulus. Role playing tests require subjects to role play responses to anxiety provoking situations. Observers can identify and assess anxiety responses in a number of categories (e.g., eye contact, physical posture, tone of voice).

Physiological Measures

The physiological assessment of anxiety most often includes cardiovascular and electrodermal measures. Marinelli (1980) reports heart rate is the most consistently used measure of physiological anxiety. Galvanic skin response (GSR) and plethysmography (the measure of muscle blood flow) are two other commonly used measures. The interested reader is referred to Borkovec, Weerts, and Bernstein (1977) for a thorough review of the physiological assessment of anxiety.

AGGRESSION

INTRODUCTION

The Meaning of Aggression

Are humans basically aggressive and hostile, or peaceful and loving? This question has been asked through the centuries by philosophers and theologians, and in more recent decades by social and biological scientists. A good example of our concern for this question can be found in the Bible. The Old Testament is filled with examples of war, murders, suicides, and other aggressive actions. The God of the Old Testament is violent and unforgiving. The Old Testament ends with a curse! In contrast, the New Testament is forgiving, peace loving, and promises good things for the future. It emphasizes love. Appropriately, the New Testament ends with a blessing.

    In modern times, the question of aggression and human nature emerged with the work of Charles Darwin, who argued human beings evolved from lower forms of life and thus possess similar characteristics. The first personality theorist to stress aggression as a major human motive was Alfred Adler. In 1908, in an article called "The Aggressive Drive in Life and Neurosis," Adler stated:

> From early childhood we . . . find the stand of the child toward the environment cannot be called anything but hostile . . . the belligerent position of the individual towards the environment indicates a drive towards fighting for satisfaction which I call the "aggression" drive (p. 23).

Adler was looking for a dynamic underlying principle, a master motive, to explain behavior, and he thought he had found it in aggression. However, Sigmund Freud disagreed. In a paper published a year later, Freud replied:

> Alfred Adler, in a suggestive paper has recently developed the view that anxiety arises from the suppression of what he calls the "aggressive" instinct . . . I am unable to assent to this view . . . I cannot bring myself to assume the existence of a special aggressive instinct (Freud, 1909, vol. III, p. 281).

Incidentally, in reading the above, one may wonder about Adler's use of the word "drive" and Freud's use of the word "instinct." Actually, they both used the German word *Trieb* which Adler's translators translated as *Drive* and Freud's as *Instinct*. So, they were talking about the same thing.

What is fascinating about this little known fact is that subsequently Freud took on the aggressive drive/instinct as a primary explanatory concept about human behavior while Adler rejected it.

There is an important lesson in this bit of history: personality theorists are very unclear about human aggression. Adler first proposed aggression as a master motive, Freud rejected it; then later, Adler rejected it; while Freud, 14 years later, stated, "I have been obliged to assert the existence of an 'aggressive instinct' but it is different from Adler's. I prefer to call it the destructive or death instinct" (Freud, 1924, p. 281).

Some Basic Conceptual Problems

Aggression is a part of our everyday life. Disagreements, fights, arguments are examples of aggression. Annoyance, anger, hostility, resentment are all examples of emotions that often tend to lead to aggressive behavior. The public media such as newspapers and television are constantly filled with accounts of crimes, conflicts, wars, and other overt hostile actions. However, what is or what is not aggression is not easily determined. Take the following incidents as examples.

A couple screaming support for a fighter at a boxing match.

A group of children playing cops and robbers.

A teenager writing obscene phrases on a wall.

A politician voting for a nuclear missile system.

A golfer throwing his clubs into a pond after missing an easy putt.

A child fantasizing injuring a class bully.

A mother spanking her child.

A person laughing at a racial joke.

A person attempting suicide.

A boy throwing stones at a cat.

A driver swearing at a driver who cuts in front.

The list can go on endlessly. What is aggressive behavior to one person may not be aggressive to another. The definition of aggression, the causes of aggressive behavior, and the control of such behavior are areas of great controversy in psychology. Take the following incident as an example.

> Say that you are walking along a sidewalk, minding your own business, perhaps day dreaming, when suddenly, out of nowhere in front of you appears a snarling, menacing dog; his ears back, he is growling, and he shows every sign of being ready to attack you.

Now from your perspective the dog is aggressive. But from the dog's perspective, it is you who are aggressive. You have invaded his territory, and he is prepared to defend it against your aggressive behavior.

This common example is replicated endlessly in human affairs: people see the other person as aggressive and view their own behavior as defensive. We can readily see how wars are started, with each side thinking that it is only defending itself against the aggression of the other side.

Definitions

How can we define aggression? Is simply having hostile intentions an example of aggression, or must actual injurious behavior occur? The child who fantasizes injuring the bully—is he being aggressive? How about a football player who tackles another? Is he being aggressive? Should we make a distinction between justified and unjustified aggression? Is a boxer who wants to knock out an opponent aggressive? Suppose that you attack someone who has threatened you? Are you aggressive? What is aggression? What is defense? Is suicide aggressive? Can one be aggressive against oneself? Not suprisingly, there is little agreement about defining aggression or explaining it.

Let us examine some general views about aggression.

Instinct.   Some people say human nature is instinctually aggressive.

Frustration.   Some authorities see aggression as a reaction to frustration.

Biochemical. Some authorities consider aggression to be a result of various hormones or neurotransmitters.

How we define aggression and how we view its causes determines our view about controlling it. If we adhere to an instinctual view, we might think the thing to do is to channel its expression in socially acceptable ways as William James suggested when arguing for sports as a moral equivalent for wars. If we take a biochemical perspective, we may hope for drug-based control of aggression.

On this issue, Johnson (1972) notes:

> There is not one single kind of behavior which can be called "aggressive" nor is there any single process which represents "aggression." Perhaps this is the most important thing which can be said about defining aggression for it suggests aggression must be understood and analyzed at many different levels (p. 8).

MEASUREMENT

Many assessment instruments measure aggression. Some multidimensional instruments as the *Adjective Checklist* (Gough & Heilbrun, 1965), *Edwards Personal Preference Schedule* (Edwards, 1959), and the *Personality Research Form* (Jackson, 1965) include an aggression scale. The *Minnesota Multiphasic Personality Inventory* has been modified to measure aggression (Magargee, Cook, & Mendelsohn, 1967). Shostrom (1963) developed the *Personal Orientation Inventory* to assess characteristics of self-actualized personalities. Included in the POI is an acceptance of an aggression (A) scale that measures the ability to accept one's own natural aggressiveness as opposed to denying or repressing aggressive behavior.

The *Buss-Durkee Aggression Inventory* (Buss, 1961) and the *Hostility and Direction of Hostility Questionnaire* (Caine, Foulds & Hope, 1967) are designed to assess aggression exclusively. The *Buss-Durkee Aggression Inventory* derives scores on eight aggression-hostility scales. The HDHQ, based on MMPI items, includes both intropunitive (e.g., self-criticism) and extrapunitive (e.g., urge to act out hostility) measures.

Among projective tests that can measure aggression are the *Thematic Apperception Test* (see Lessing, 1957) and the *Holtzman Inkblot Test* (Holtzman & Thorpe, 1958). Olweus (1969) devised a story completion task and reported its ability to predict aggressive behavior in children. Rosenzweig (1945) devised a semi-projective technique utilizing word association and the TAT. The *Rosenzweig Picture-Frustration Test* consists of cartoonlike pictures depicting an interpersonally frustrating situation. One of the characters is making a statement. Another character has a blank caption box (balloon) over his head. The subject's task is to place a reply in the blank balloon. Rosenzweig (1978) reports evidence linking Picture-Frustration Test results to aggressive behavior in subjects.

Measurement Categories

Edmunds (1978) defined four classes of aggressive behavior: (1) initiatory instrumental behaviors (e.g., attacking and robbing innocent victims); (2) reactive instrumental behaviors (defending one's property against an attacker); (3) reactive hostile behaviors (hurting an attacker); and (4) initiatory hostile behaviors (attempts to hurt an innocent victim). In all four classes of behavior there are attempts to hurt others. The prime objective of instrumental acts is to reach a goal and harms inflicted on others generally subserve the purpose of aggressive behavior.

THEORIES AND MODELS

Instinctual Views

1. Sigmund Freud. As we have already seen, although Sigmund Freud first discounted the importance of aggression as an instinct, he later accepted this view. The death and destruction of World War I weighed heavily on Freud. Concern over the welfare of his sons and exposure to the suffering and loss of life caused by the war led Freud to postulate a death instinct which he labeled *Thanatos,* in which he described an organism's wish to return to the original, inert matter from whence it came. Freud came to view life as an external conflict between the destructive force of *Thanatos,* and the creative, growth force of *Eros* (named after the Greek god of love). Both instincts are tension reducing in nature. *Eros* (life instinct) seeks release from sexual tension, and *Thanatos* (death instinct) seeks release from the tension of existence itself. Thus, all life is in a state of constant tension which ultimately ends in death; *Thanatos* eventually predominates.

Freud viewed war and man's inhumanity to fellow man as expressions of *Thanatos.* He believed the urge to destroy others was a redirection of the urge to destroy oneself. Freud thought that from the moment of conception, any living organism carries within it the seeds of its own destruction. Although weak at first, *Thanatos* eventually grows in strength, directing the organism back to its earlier, inert state.

While Freud expressed hope that human reasoning could alter and counteract this destructive tendency, he nevertheless believed destruction and death are integral and inseparable aspects of life. In 1932, the League of Nations (forerunner of the United Nations) arranged for Freud and Albert Einstein to communicate on the topic of war. In response to Einstein's question of why human beings have within them a "lust for hatred and destruction" which can give rise to war and human suffering, Freud in 1932 replied:

You expressed astonishment at the fact that it is so easy to make men enthusiastic about a war and add your suspicion that there is something at work in them—an instinct for hatred and destruction—which goes halfway to meet the effects of the warmongers. I can only express my entire agreement . . .

. . . human instincts are of only two kinds: those which seek to preserve and unite—which we call "erotic" and those which seek to destroy and kill which we class together as the aggressive or destructive instinct. In any case you yourself have remarked, there is no question of getting rid entirely of human aggressive impulses, it is enough to try to divert them to such an extent that they need not find expression in war (E. Jones, 1959, p. 280).

2. Konrad Lorenz. Konrad Lorenz, an ethologist who supports an instinctual basis for aggression, defines aggression as:

. . . the fighting instinct in beast and man which is directed against members of the same species. It is an instinct like any other, and in natural conditions it helps just as much as any other to ensure the survival of the individual and species (Lorenz, 1966, p. ix).

For Lorenz, aggression is one of four major instincts which ensure the survival of the species. The three other instincts are feeding, reproduction, and escape. From Lorenz's perspective, the aggressive instinct helps ensure species survival by fulfilling four main functions:

1. Ensures members of the same species disperse over available territory to increase the opportunity for finding food, escaping predators, establishing a suitable home, etc.
2. Serves the "survival of the fittest" perspective, helping ensure the strongest of the species reproduce.
3. Aids the protection of offspring, whether maternally or paternally.
4. Determines a "pecking" or ranking order among species groups, serving to maintain order and stability.

Lorenz believes civilized man, unlike his more primitive predecessors, does not have the outlets nor the opportunity to express much of his instinctual aggression. Positive and physical health necessitates the release and expression of man's innate, aggressive instincts. Lorenz's views are similar to Freud's, who also emphasized the release of instinctual aggressive energy. Like William James, Lorenz believes human aggression can be redirected toward more constructive activities. Lorenz, as did James, views organized sport as a unique human form of redirected aggression and he believes human enthusiasm in the areas of science, technology, and art can also be seen as a redirection of the human aggressive instinct.

Lorenz notes instances of aggression between infrahuman species members rarely end in fatality. Usually, the earlier one signals submission, the quicker the encounter is terminated. The victor does not inflict additional injury, after surrender. Lorenz believes man has inherited similar inhibitions, but modern long-range weapons of aggression have seriously reduced the effectiveness of such inhibitions. Modern weapons allow humans to kill one another so quickly and so anonymously that gestures of submission have no effect since they are not seen. Thus, for Lorenz, the redirection of the instinctual aggression in humans is of crucial importance in modern society.

The perspective Freud and Lorenz advance defines the cause of aggressive behavior and implies techniques for its control. From the instinctual viewpoint, aggression is inherent in humans. The urge to aggress is an impulse we must live with the best way we can, for it is a part of human nature. What we can hope for is the redirection of this impulse in the least harmful, or perhaps even in constructive ways. Whereas Freud emphasized the negative aspects of this innate impulse (*Thanatos*), Lorenz voices some positive aspects (art, science, creativity) that may arise from aggression. However, the instinctual perspective on aggression is not without its critics.

Various scientists have criticized instinct-based theories of aggression on definitional, methodological, and philosophical issues. Selg (1971) notes that because instincts are species specific, it is incorrect to argue as Lorenz does, from "animal to human instincts," or "to create man in the image of fish and birds" (p. 59). Recent "discoveries" of nonaggressive human societies (e.g., the Tasadays in the Philippines) bring into question the universality of human aggression. A detailed review of the criticisms leveled at instinctual theories of aggression is beyond the scope of the present chapter and the reader is referred to Selg (1971) and Geen and O'Neal (1976) for summaries. We will continue on to a second major perspective on aggression which posits aggressive behaviors are learned.

Social Learning Perspectives

1. Albert Bandura. According to Bandura, aggression is "behavior that results in personal injury and destruction of property" (1973, p. 5). As a behaviorist, Bandura emphasizes observable phenomena in explaining human aggression and de-emphasizes unobservable phenomena such as intention and instinct. From his perspective, the vandalizing of property or an overt physical attack on a person are examples of aggression whereas the wishing of injury or misfortune on another would not be. From the social learning perspective, aggressive behavior is learned as all other learned behavior are acquired—via reinforcement, generalization, extinction, modeling, and so forth.

When aggressive behavior is followed by positive reinforcement, the aggressive behavior will likely reoccur in the future. The neighborhood bully takes pleasure in threatening smaller children, and receives positive reinforcement from their appeasement. The young vandal working with a can of spray paint derives pleasure in viewing the results of his labor on a new subway car. A mugger, finding money in his victim's wallet, decides to "work the same area" again. A boxer, ahead in a bout, hears the crowd roar on the delivery of a solid punch and decides to try for a knockout. All of these are examples of reinforced behavior.

The source of reinforcement for aggressive behavior is varied. Reinforcement may be "intrinsic" (the vandal seeing his name sprayed on a subway car), "concrete" (money to the mugger), "verbal" (the roar of the crowd), or "nonverbal" (the crying of a prospective victim). Various laboratory experiments have confirmed the finding that reinforcement increases aggressive behaviors (Borden, 1975; Buss, 1971, Geen & Stonner, 1971).

If aggressive behavior can be acquired via reinforcement, varied schedules of reinforcement should differentially affect learned aggressive behavior. This appears to be the case. Geen (1972) found it took longer to extinguish aggressive behaviors in subjects rewarded on a *partial (ratio) schedule of reinforcement* than in subjects whose aggressive behaviors were reinforced on all trials.

Aggressive behaviors learned in one situation may also generalize to other similar situations. Both stimulus and response generalization have been demonstrated by Geen and Pigg (1970) and by Parke, Ewall, and Slaby (1972). In Geen and Pigg's study, subjects were either verbally reinforced or not reinforced for aggressing against a fellow subject. Later, they were administered a word association test that had either numerous aggressive connotations (e.g., "hit," "stab") or few aggressive connotations (e.g., "relax," "wash"). Reinforced subjects exhibited more aggressive associations to hostile words than nonreinforced subjects while no differences were found between the two groups in aggressive associations made to neutral words.

Aggressive behaviors may also be acquired through the imitation of aggressive acts by others. Bandura, Ross, and Ross (1963), in a classic experiment, found children who witnessed an adult hitting an inflated "Bobo the Clown" doll were much more inclined to attack the doll when left alone in a toy-filled room than children who witnessed the model playing peacefully in the presence of the doll, or who had not witnessed any model aggressing. Similar results were obtained with a televised model (Liebert & Baron, 1972). In modeling theory (see Bandura, 1969; Flanders, 1968) it has been demonstrated that verbalizing the model's aggressive behavior increases the "influence" of the model on the subject (Bandura, Grusec, & Menlove, 1966) and that stimulus characteristics (similarity of the model to the subject) affects the strength of the aggressive modeling behavior (Bandura, 1970).

The modeling and imitative aspects of learned aggression raises obvious and relevant questions about the role of television in modern society. It has been estimated the average child spends approximately 1,200 hours a year watching television—more time than spent in school. Children witness over 13,000 televised deaths if they watch TV on this schedule of viewing (Skornia, 1965). Important investigations by Bandura (1973) and Berkowitz (1971, 1974) demonstrate the role of television in encouraging violence in our society.

The National Institute of Mental Health released the results of a two and one-half year, million-dollar study concerning the effects of television on aggression and violence (Cisin, Coffin, Janis, Klapper, Mendelsohn, Omwake, Pinderhughes, Pool, Siegel, Wallace, Watson, Wiebe, 1972). While many of the study's findings were inconclusive, the authors concluded that a modest relationship exists between exposure to televised violence and aggressive tendencies. However, the investigators were not sure whether aggressive individuals were simply more predisposed to view violent programs.

The report was criticized for not understanding the problem, for methodological flaws, and even for the membership of the investigative body (Bogart, 1973). Suffice to say that the relationship between television and aggression and violence remains of current interest. For example, while televised violence may provoke violence in some viewers, prosocial television may retard violence. Bankert and Anderson (1979) assessed the impact of prosocial television, "Sesame Street," on the free play of preschool children and found that while it did not increase "rule obedience," it had a strong short-term effect on reducing aggressive acts.

2. Frustration-Aggression Hypothesis. Another social learning perspective is that aggression is linked to feelings of frustration. The frustration-aggression hypothesis (Dollard, Doob, Miller, Mowrer, & Sears, 1939) posits that all aggressive acts are preceded by frustration, and that frustration always leads to aggressive behavior. In an early example of the hypothesis, Barker, Dembo, and Lewin (1941) exposed two groups of children to attractive and desirable toys. One group was allowed immediate access to the toys (nonfrustration condition) while the other group was not allowed into the toy room and could only look at the toys through a window (frustration condition). In later free play, the frustrated group engaged in much more aggressive, destructive behavior than the nonfrustrated group. Similar behavior has been observed in animals. Subsequent research demonstrated not all aggressive acts need be preceded by frustration nor does frustration always lead to some type of aggressive behavior. For example, frustration can lead to withdrawal or regression, but frustration appears to play an important role in determining some aggressive behavior.

Other conditions which induce arousal and increase the probability of aggressive behavior include: *noise, insult, pain, temperature, crowding, erotic stimuli,* and *odor.*

3. Deindividuation.   Another social variable related to aggression is *deindividuation.* Zimbardo (1969) described *deindividuation* as feelings of anonymity, loss of self-awareness, and self-devaluation. One important aspect of *deindividuation* is mob violence. Deindividuation theory posits that two factors facilitate aggression in mob behavior. Studies have shown the mob provides *anonymity* (from other members as well as victims) for the individual, and it increases the *diffusion of responsibility*, making the individual feel less responsible for his own actions. Thus, in certain instances, group membership may encourage aggressive behavior.

Physiological Perspectives

The effects of physiological factors on aggression is a complex area of research. Physiological factors not only interact with one another, but also with a host of environmental variables in exerting an influence on aggressive behavior. In general, the physiological area may·be divided into three subareas: genetic, neurological, and biochemical. The following discussion will present a brief overview of the three areas. For a more detailed treatment, the reader is referred to works by Moyer (1976), Brain (1977), and Sandler (1979).

1. Genetic Approaches.   Genetic differences in animal aggressiveness have long been established. Laboratory studies performed many years ago demonstrated the ability to breed aggressiveness in different rat strains (Hall, 1938; Scott, 1942). However, the evidence of genetic contributions to aggression in humans is not nearly as clear. One of the most investigated areas of genetic factors of aggression in humans is chromosomes. A small segment of the population, approximately 1 in 550 (Shah, 1970), possess an extra Y chromosome and are thus labeled XYY's. While results are by no means definitive, studies suggest the extra Y chromosome may be linked to aggressive behavioral disorders (Baker, 1972; Kessler & Moos, 1970). However, the issue of a direct genetic relationship to aggression in humans is tenuous. Daly (1969) notes XYY males also possess an overabundance of testosterone (male sex hormone) and are statistically taller than normal males. Thus, any increase in aggressiveness may be due to physical size factors. And, many XYY people are not criminals nor aggressive. Further, many criminals are not XYY. Hutchings and Mednick (1975) believe a genetic factor in human aggression exists, but that it is mediated by a host of environmental factors such as conditioning history, social influences, situational cues, and arousal states. While research continues, it is premature to make any definitive statement about the effects of genetic variables on human aggression. Humans are not "fighting cocks"; for one thing, they can think, reason, and remember and they encounter more situations than a cock-fight ring.

2. Neurological Approaches. Research on the neurological bases of aggression has taken many forms. Different areas of the brain, in both animals and humans, have been ablated or stimulated in aggression studies. The *limbic area* of the brain has been considered the most important area involved in the reduction or elicitation of aggression. The *limbic area* is the inner portion of each hemisphere of the brain and is generally considered to be the part of the brain most involved with emotional behavior. Of the many structures which comprise the limbic system, the *hypothalamus* and *amygdala* have been most often linked to aggressive behavior. Lesions in the hypothalamus or amygdala produce different types of aggression. Aggression associated with fear appears to be mediated by the amygdala while aggression associated with *anger* and *impulse* appears to be mediated by specific sections of the hypothalamus (Blanchard & Blanchard, 1981).

In humans, tumors of the frontal and temporal lobes and cingulum and septal regions of the brain have resulted in irritable, aggressive, and destructive behavior. Often when the tumors have been removed and the pressure relieved, behavior has returned to normal. The limbic system's involvement with aggression is further supported by the fact that brain disorders such as encephalitis, rabies, and trauma, resulting in limbic system damage, have produced an increase in aggressive tendencies (Moyer, 1976).

Research in direct brain stimulation in animals has been carried out for over 50 years (Johnson, 1972). Electrodes have been implanted in animals ranging from mice to bulls via stereotaxic surgery (implantation via stereotaxic brain atlas and corresponding reference points on the skull of the animal). A very slight current is then applied (usually a few millionths of an ampere) and resultant behavior changes noted. Very slight differences in electrode implantation often results in characteristically different aggressive responses ranging from "sham rage" (a rage reaction lasting only as long as the electrical stimulation is applied), to "stalking attacks" (relatively unemotional, victim-selective attacks), to "affective attacks" (highly aggressive attacks against any available object or organism). Moyer (1976) notes that in cats certain electrically stimulated sites in the amygdala result in a fear response, while stimulation of an area one millimeter away produces an anger response.

For obvious reasons, similar experimental research has not been undertaken with human subjects except for a few therapeutic cases of chronic psychopathic behavior or intractable pain. Cases in which humans have undergone electrical brain stimulation provide data supporting the connection between hypothalamic stimulation and aggressive reactions (Mark & Ervin, 1970).

The connection between hypothalamic stimulation and aggressive behavior is not conclusive proof that the hypothalamus is the neurological aggression center of the brain. Alternative theories posit aggression may not be a direct result of hypothalamic activity, but rather may be due to the stimulation of predatory behavior in animals and pain-aggression cue interactions in humans (Moyer, 1976).

3. Biochemical Approaches.   The relationship between biochemical factors and aggression is complicated. Testosterone, a male hormone, has been found to increase the probability of aggressive behavior, while estrogen, a female hormone, has been reported to decrease aggressive tendencies in male humans and male animals (Sheard, 1979). Castration has been found to decrease aggressive behavior in both male animals and humans (Strupp, 1972). However, sex differences are evident in aggressive response to hormones. Sheard (1979) notes testosterone and lutenizing hormones inhibited attack behavior in female cats and facilitated it in males.

Various neurotransmitters (e.g., biogenic amines) also have been associated with aggression. Depending on the type of aggression (i.e., predatory versus affective), aggression can be modified in both rats and cats by the modulation of serotonin, norepinephrine, acetylcholine, dopamine, and gamma-aminobutyric acid (GABA) (Eichelman, 1979).

Amphetamines (stimulants) and benzodiazepines (minor tranquilizers) can either increase or inhibit aggressive tendencies. For instance, amphetamines administered in moderate dosages reduce aggressive behavior in children with minimal brain dysfunction; but, when administered in large doses to adults, there is often an increase in violent aggressive behavior. While profound individual differences exist, other drugs are generally known for their antiaggressive action. Phenothiazines (major tranquilizers) have been demonstrated to be effective in reducing violent, aggressive behavior.

One drug whose effect on human aggression has been extensively studied is alcohol. In a 1967 report, the *President's Commission on Law Enforcement and Administration of Justice* stated alcohol is the only drug causally related to violence. Statistics clearly link alcohol consumption with violent, aggressive acts. Wolfgang (1958, 1967) reported alcohol was involved in 72 percent of stabbing homicides, 69 percent of beating homicides, and 55 percent of shooting homicides during a four-year period in a major eastern city in the United States. Other researchers have reported similar findings. One only need scan the pages of the daily newspaper to find reports linking the consumption of alcohol with acts of violent aggression.

Lange, Goeckner, Adesso, and Marlatt (1975) noted personal expectation is an important factor in the relationship of alcohol to aggression. The investigators found when alcoholic and nonalcoholic drunks were randomized, subjects who expected their drinks to be alcoholic, regardless of actual alcoholic content, exhibited more aggressive behavior than subjects who expected to consume nonalcoholic drinks. Schmutte, Leonard, and Taylor (1979) also found alcohol caused individuals to "over-estimate" perceived threats when compared with nondrinking subjects. Other social and cultural variables are also involved. The "macho" image of an individual who can "hold his drinks," and the possible deindividuation factors of drinking in groups must also be considered. The relationship between aggression and drugs is not a direct one; rather, social, cognitive, cultural, and situational intervening variables must be added to the equation.

LOCUS OF CONTROL*

INTRODUCTION

The Meaning of Locus of Control

At the turn of the 20th century, the Western world was undergoing rapid social change as a result of industrialization. Industry's values were gradually rooting themselves in all segments of life. Foremost among these values was a pervasive belief human beings could control their destiny. There was a sense of unlimited optimism in mankind's ability to accomplish anything we wished through proper planning and efficient production. So strong were these values, commentators such as Thorstein Veblen (1857-1929), the famous American social critic, concluded in his book, *The Theory of the Leisure Class* (1899), that only "primitive" societies operated by "luck" or "chance," since this interfered with efficiency.

This distinction between *chance* or *choice* in human destiny recently has emerged as a popular topic of inquiry in personality research under the rubric of "locus of control." As a personality construct, locus of control developed from the research of Julian Rotter, a social learning theorist associated with *Expectancy Reinforcement Theory* (1954).

Within the context of social learning theory, Rotter (1966) defined locus of control as the following:

> The degree to which the individual perceives that a reward follows from or is contingent upon his attributes or behavior versus the degree to which the individual feels the reward is controlled by forces outside of himself (p. 1).

---

*The chapter authors wish to acknowledge the contribution of Ms. Ellen Caringer to the preparation of this section of Chapter 15.

Rotter distinguished between two different locus of control orientations. *Internally oriented* individuals believe events in their life are determined by their own behavior and effort. *Externally oriented* individuals believe events in their life are determined by fate, chance, or other forces over which they have no control. Both of these orientations refer to an individual's perceived locus of causality. Although locus of control was first conceptualized as a "generalized" expectancy for external or internal perceptions of causality, recent modifications in the theory emphasize the specificity of the construct. An individual may have an internal locus of control about one aspect of their life but an external locus of control about others. In addition, locus of control seems to be specific to different situations (Lefcourt, 1981; Phares, 1976).

THE MEASUREMENT OF LOCUS OF CONTROL

The primary method used to assess locus of control has been self-report questionnaires. The first questionnaires to assess the topic were developed in 1957 by Phares (see Rotter, 1966) and James (see James & Rotter, 1958). In 1966, Rotter (1966) published a new scale which emerged as the most popular scale. Rotter's scale consists of 29 items. Six of the items are fillers and the remaining 23 assess locus of control through direct questions regarding an individual's perception of control over. events. Although Rotter attempted to sample locus of control perceptions for different areas of life functioning, he was not successful in developing subscales. But, factor analyses of the Rotter scale by Mirels (1970) and Schneider and Parsons (1970) pointed out its multidimensionality. For example, Mirels found Rotter's scale measured two basic factors: (1) mastery over one's life, and (2) the influence one can exert over political institutions.

The following items reflect typical questions used in locus of control scales:

1. a. In our society, a man's future earning ability is dependent upon his ability (I).
   b. Getting promoted is really a matter of being a little luckier than the next guy (E).
2. a. Getting along with people is a skill that must be practiced (I).
   b. It is almost impossible to figure out how to please some people (E).
3. a. The number of divorces indicates that more and more people are not trying to make their marriages work (I).
   b. Marriage is largely a gamble (E).
4. a. In my experience I have noticed that there is usually a direct connection between how hard I study and the grades I get (I).
   b. Many time the reactions of teachers seem haphazard to me (E).

5. a. I am the master of my fate (I).
   b. A great deal of what happens to me is probably a matter of chance (E).

Nowicki and Duke (1974) developed the Nowicki-Duke Scale for Adults (ANS-IE) in response to what they thought were weaknesses in Rotter's I-E Scale. Nowicki and Duke believed aspects of social desirability were evident in I-E Scale items (i.e., the more socially desirable or acceptable responses of the two alternatives per item is evident). They also concluded the I-E Scale was difficult to read and mixed beliefs of political, ideological, and personal causality were not equivalent. The ANS-IE Scale of 40 yes-no items assesses achievement behavior and does not appear to be related to social desirability or intelligence (Phares, 1976).

Other scales have been developed for more specific uses. For example, Battle and Rotter (1963) developed the *Children's Picture Test of Internal-External Control*. It utilizes six cartoons and asks children what they would say if they were in the cartoon situation. Nowicki and Strickland (1973) developed a simple 40-item, yes-no paper-and-pencil task geared toward 3d-through 12th-grade subjects. It is the most popular children's scale.

THEORETICAL FOUNDATIONS

The concept of locus of control grew from Rotter's *Expectancy Reinforcement Theory* (Rotter, 1954). The central elements of this theory are the concepts of situation, reinforcement, reinforcement value, and expectations. We will briefly discuss each of these elements.

Situations differ, both environmentally and in our psychological perceptions of them. We can be attentive to similar cues in different situations and to different cues in similar situations. Different situations provide different cues. Whether we are attentive to the cues depends upon a variety of personal characteristics.

A reinforcement can be any event that follows a specific behavior. It can be food, money, a loving hug, or an A on an examination. Reinforcement value refers to the degree of preference an individual has for a particular reinforcement. For example, an A on an examination may be reinforcing in terms of an individual's scholastic recognition, status, and self-concept. However, the A may also expose the individual to ridicule from some of his peers for being the "teacher's pet." Thus, reinforcement value is relative for each individual and we can assume relative hierarchies in reinforcement value for different reinforcers given actual behavior. If the student continues to study and obtain good grades, we may conclude that he places the reinforcement value of good grades above the possible alternative reinforcement value of being accepted among a small number of his fellow students.

Expectancy is the belief a specific reinforcement will occur as a result of a particular behavior. Rotter posits two types of expectancies, generalized and specific. There usually is an expectancy by college students that serious studying will result in good grades. Such a belief may be called a generalized expectancy. Generalized expectancies arise out of validated specific expectancies. A student bases a belief that scholastic achievement goes hand in hand with serious studying (generalized expectancy) on specific expectancies he or she had validated in previous, specific situations (e.g., studying English composition, memorizing tenses in French language, and working through equations in physics, all resulted in good grades).

The interaction of situation, reinforcement, reinforcement value, and expectancy is summed up in the formula:

$$BP_x,s_1,R_a = f(E_x,R_a,s_1 \& RV_a,s_1)$$

That is, the probability of behavior x (BP_x) to occur in a particular situation (s_1) with a particular reinforcer (R_a) is a function of the expectancy that behavior x (E_x) will be reinforced by R_a in situation s_1 and the value of that reinforcement in that situation (RV_a,s_1).

For example, John has an important examination tomorrow. What should he do tonight? Should he stay home and study? Should he go back down to the discotheque with his friend? Should he relax and try to sleep early? Being a good student of social learning theory, he analyzes the possibilities. He would enjoy the company of his friend, but that would be countered by the disco's loud music and flashing lights, which, to him, are not particularly enjoyable (overall little reinforcement value). He would like to go to sleep early for a change, but he feels thinking about the exam would probably make sleeping difficult (low expectancy).

Thus, he is left with the third alternative. He knows studying has led to high grades previously and he sees no reason to doubt this (high expectancy). He also desires to graduate with honors and an A on this important exam would certainly mean a lot to him (high-reinforcement value). He decides to stay home and study as we predicted he would.

We have predicted and explained his behavior in a particular situation, with particular expectancies and reinforcement values, in terms of Rotter's theory. Generalized expectancies refer to expectations concerning behavior and reinforcement that are applicable over a wide range of situations over time. Locus of control is one generalized expectancy regarding perceived causes for behavior.

LOCUS OF CONTROL RESEARCH

Probably more than 1,500 publications have been written on locus of control since it was first advanced as a concept in the late 1950s. Locus of control has been shown to affect dozens of variables.

Locus of Control and Emotion

One might expect the less control an individual perceives he has in determining his life outcomes, the more anxiety he would exhibit. Existing evidence supports this position. Archer (1979) reviewed 21 studies relating locus of control to general trait anxiety and concluded externality is related to higher levels of trait anxiety.

However, as Phares (1976) notes, it may be reasonable to assume the relationship may be U-shaped. Both extremely external and internal subjects could experience high levels of anxiety. This perspective agrees with the earlier sentiments of Rotter (1966) who thought extreme "internals" are as maladjusted as extreme "externals." Nonetheless, Rotter noted most internals are better adjusted than externals.

The relationship between state anxiety and locus of control is less clear. Investigations correlating locus of control with state anxiety measures provide conflicting results (Archer & Stein, 1978; Houston, 1972; Manuck et al., 1975). It may be specific expectancies in anxiety-provoking situations overcome more generalized locus of control beliefs brought to the situation (Phares, 1976). Lowery et al. (1975) suggested generalized locus of control expectancies are related to state anxiety only in situations which do not provide explicit control cues; however, further research is needed to support this perspective.

Johnson and Sarason (1979) hypothesized significant life changes would have the greatest effect on subjects who perceive themselves as having little control over life events. The results indicated significant correlations between life change, depression, anxiety, and an external locus of control. Natale (1978) investigated whether depression was associated with an external locus of control and whether elation was related to an internal locus of control. He produced temporary mood states (depression, elation, neutral) through an autosuggestion technique and obtained I-E Scale scores both before and after the autosuggestion procedure. Depression was found to be correlated with significant increase in externality and elation with an increase in internality.

It appears externals are more prone to experience anxiety and depression. A contributing factor is that externals appear to be less able, than internals, to ignore or discount aversive information. Efran (1963) found externals relatively unable to forget failures and personal setbacks.

Social Demands

A popular area of study has been differences in locus of control as a function of social demands in an experimental situation. Investigations have found internals show greater responsiveness to the informational demands of a task, while externals show more orientation to the social requirements of the performance situation, particularly its hidden social demand and evaluations.

Henry, Medway, and Scabro (1979) investigated locus of control and children's responses to peer versus adult praise. They found boys more responsive to peer feedback and girls more responsive to adult feedback. But, children who demonstrated an *external* locus of control orientation were more affected by social reinforcement than were children who demonstrated an *internal* locus of control.

Sex differences in locus of control under competitive and cooperative social demand conditions have also been studied. Nowicki, Duke, and Crouch (1978) asked subjects to complete a digit-symbol task which involved matching appropriate symbols with 100 randomly ordered digits under competitive and cooperative conditions. Results revealed the achievement behavior of *internal* females was more affected by sex of partner and type of competition than that of males. While internal males increased their achievement more than the external males, internal females increased their performance only when competing against males or when cooperating with females. Competition with a male or female makes a difference to an internal female. Thus, locus of control has an effect on the way one performs under conditions of competition versus cooperation, particularly among females.

The tendency to participate in social and political action groups may also be affected by one's locus of control orientation. Sue (1978) discusses the possibility that externality may be a function of a person's opinions about current prevailing social institutions. Because of racism and prejudice, blacks and other minority groups may perceive a discrepancy between their ability and their attainment of status. This perception may be an accurate assessment. However, these perceptions may lead to a more external locus of control. Gurin, Gurin, Lao, and Beattie (1969) concluded externally oriented people are less motivated and perform more poorly in achievement situations; but, this does not hold true for minorities and/or low-income groups. They suggest focusing on external forces may be motivationally healthy if it brings about a more accurate assessment of one's chances for success against the "real" obstacles one encounters.

Cross-Cultural Research

The last area of investigation we will discuss is locus of control orientation across cultures. Hsieh, Shybut, and Lotsof (1969) investigated locus of control among Chinese students from Hong Kong, American-born Chinese, and Anglo-American students. Results revealed Anglo-American scores to be significantly more internal than American-born Chinese; but, the scores of American-born Chinese subjects were significantly more internal than the scores of Chinese from Hong Kong. Thus, there were significant differences in locus of control orientation across these three ethnocultural groups.

Since American society emphasizes independence, self-reliance and autonomy, it is not surprising Anglo-Americans had the highest internal orientation. In contrast, Chinese society emphasizes kinship and status quo, accepting life as full of ambiguity, complexity, and unpredictability. Hsieh et al. concluded cultural orientation may be closely linked with locus of control orientation; societies which value self-reliance and individualism tend to be more internally oriented while individuals from cultures which emphasize interdependence and unpredictability are more externally oriented.

A similar study conducted by Nordholm, Ward, and Bhanthunavin (1974) with 1,500 students from Sweden, Japan, Australia, New Zealand, and the United States revealed the highest external scores were among subjects from Sweden, followed by students from Japan, Australia, the United States, and finally New Zealand. The scores from Australia, New Zealand and the United States did not differ significantly. The fact these scores were more internally oriented was attributed to their common Anglo-Saxon background. The Protestant ethic these countries share emphasizes the virtues of individual initiative and this leads to more internality. The significant difference between these countries and Japan was also expected, since the Japanese value traditions of politeness, deference, self-abasement, acceptance, obedience, and conformity; this leads to a more external orientation.

The most unusual finding was Sweden's high tendency toward externality. The Swedish students' scores were significantly more external than those of the Japanese. The authors speculate this is because the Swedish social system provides a high degree of security for the individual throughout one's lifetime; this may lead to a greater belief in external control.

These findings are similar to those of Hsieh et al.: "Eastern" cultures tend to score externally on locus of control measures, while "Western" cultures (with the exception of Sweden) tend to score internally.

These findings are supported by Parsons and Schneider (1974). They administered the Rotter I-E Scale to students from Eastern and Western societies and found the Eastern students were more externally oriented, while the Western students were internally oriented. They also found women tended to score more externally than males.

Sue (1978) outlined four basic psychological orientations found across different ethnocultural groups. These psychological orientations involve the interaction of locus of control and locus of responsibility, which he defines as the degree of responsibility placed on the individual. Sue describes the first psychological orientation as one of *high* internal personal control and *high* internal locus of responsibility. Individuals who exhibit this orientation believe they are masters of their fate; their actions affect their outcomes. These individuals also attribute their status and position in life to their own unique efforts. They feel success is due to one's own efforts; and a lack of success can only be blamed on one's inadequacies. This orientation is most exemplified in American philosophy and culture.

A second pyschological orientation is an *external* locus of control and an *external* locus of responsibility. In this orientation, individuals feel there is little they can do against obstacles of prejudice and discrimination. Yet, despite their awareness of their plight, these individuals internalize their impotence, which leads to *learned helplessness*. They suffer their inequities in silence for fear of retaliation. In counseling these individuals, the most helpful approach is to teach them new coping strategies.

The third psychological orientation is an *internal* locus of control and an *external* locus of responsibility. These people believe in their ability to shape events in their own life if given a chance. However, they are realistic in assessing the external barriers they face. These barriers generally include discrimination, prejudice, and exploitation. These individuals tend to engage in more civil rights activities, favor group action in dealing with discrimination, and exhibit more innovative coping behavior.

The fourth psychological orientation is an *external* locus of control and an *internal* locus of responsibility. Individuals who fall into this category accept the dominant culture's definition for self-responsibility, but have little real control over how they are defined by others. These individuals find themselves on the margins of two cultures, but not fully accommodated to either of them. In counseling individuals who experience these conflicts, counselors should help the client distinguish between positive attempts to acculturate and rejections of one's own cultural values.

However, it must be remembered locus of control is a "Western" concept, and one must exercise restraint in making generalizations concerning other cultures based on "Western" personality constructs. As Sue points out, an internal locus of control is considered desirable and healthy within Western society but is seen as unhealthy and maladaptive within the context of Eastern cultures. Thus, in cross-cultural counseling this variable must be taken into account. Kuo and Marsella (1977) caution that in cross-cultural personality research one should be certain the constructs being investigated are *conceptually equivalent* across cultures. If there is no conceptual equivalence, the research cannot be comparative.

SUMMARY AND FUTURE DIRECTIONS

Locus of control has generated a voluminous amount of research. Much of the research has involved the construction of various measures. With these measuring instruments, researchers have investigated how locus of control affects behavior in various situations, and how the modification of situational variables alters locus of control orientation. Research with children suggests the development of locus of control proceeds from an external orientation to an internal orientation; but, the extent one shifts toward an internal orientation is influenced by a variety of environmental factors. We have learned we can increase internality through behavior modification, modeling, and learned goal-setting procedures. Cross-cultural research has demonstrated that locus of control is also highly influenced by one's cultural orientation. It has also demonstrated that women tend to score more externally than men within a given culture. Lastly, cross-cultural research has shown an internal locus of control may not be as valued in other cultures as it is in the West.

In the future, investigators need to refine locus of control measures since locus of control is multidimensional; it is not uniform across situations. Since most tests are constructed to give a general measure of locus of control, one must remember the score describes the individual's "average locus of control" orientation across several situations. We must have generalized measures to make predictions about behaviors in unknown situations. But, lack of information concerning an individual's orientation in a specific situation forces us to rely too heavily on generalized scores.

Future research must also pursue the antecedents of locus of control. The information we now have is inadequate. In particular, we need a better understanding of what antecedents are responsible for causing external orientation in women, and why this finding appears across a variety of cultures. If we intend to use our knowledge about locus of control to effect positive changes in behavior we need a thorough understanding of the origins of locus of control.

Also, we need more investigations regarding the consequences of modifying locus of control. The value of an internal orientation is questionable among certain ethnocultural groups. We need more knowledge concerning the appropriateness of certain locus of control orientations within various environmental contexts. This information will benefit those who are involved in counseling individuals who find the acculturation process difficult and painful.

REFERENCES

I. Anxiety

Adler, A. *Understanding human nature.* New York: Fawcett, 1927.

Akutagawa, D. A. *A study of construct validity of the psychoanalytic concept of latent anxiety and a test of projection distance hypothesis.* Unpublished doctoral dissertation, University of Pittsburgh, 1956.

Bellack, A. & Hersen, M. Self-report inventories in behavioral assessment. In J. Cone & R. Hawkins (Eds.), *Behavioral assess-*

ment: New directions in clinical psychology. New York: Brunner, 1977.

Borkovec, T. D., Weerts, T. C., & Bernstein, D. A. Assessment of anxiety. In A. Ciminero, K. Calhoun, & H. Adams (Eds.), *Handbook of behavioral assessment.* New York: Wiley, 1977.

Cattell, R. B. & Scheier, I. H. *The meaning and measurement of neuroticism and anxiety.* New York: Ronald Press, 1961.

Costa, E., Guidotti, A., & Mao, C. A GABA hypothesis for the action of the benzodiazepenes. In E. Roberts, T. Chase, & D. Tower (Eds.), *GABA in nervous function.* New York: Raven Press, 1976.

Crabbs, M., & Hopper, G. The relationship between cognitive and somatic measures in the assessment of anxiety. *Bulletin of the Psychonomic Society,* 1980, *15,* 218-220.

Duke, M., & Nowicki, S. *Abnormal psychology.* Belmont, Calif.: Wadsworth, 1979.

Duffy, E. The concept of energy motivation. *Psychological Review,* 1951, *39,* 30-40.

Extein, I., et al. Behavior and biochemical effects of FK33-824, a parenterally and orally actice enkephalin analogue. In E. Usdin, W. Bunney, Jr., & N. Kline (Eds.), *Endorphins in mental health research.* New York: MacMillan, 1979.

Freud, S. *The problem of anxiety.* New York: Psychoanalytic Quarterly, 1936.

Gold, M., et al. Rapid opiate detoxification: Clinical evidence of antidepressant and antipanic effects of opiate. *American Journal of Psychiatry,* 1979, *136,* 982-983.

Gold, M., & Redmond, D. Pharmacological activation and inhibition of noradrenergic activity behaviors in non-human primates. *Neurosciences Abstracts,* 1977, *3,* 250.

Gottschalk, L., Stone, W., & Goldine, C. Peripheral versus central mechanisms accounting for antianxiety effects of propranolol. *Psychosomatic Medicine,* 1974, *36,* 47-55.

Gray, J. A. Anxiety and the brain: Not by neurochemistry alone. *Psychological Medicine,* 1979, *9,* 605-609.

Greenblatt, D., & Shader, R. Pharmacotherapy of anxiety with benzodiazepines and B-adrenergic blockers. In

M. Lipton, A. DiMascio, & K. Killam (Eds.), *Pharmacotherapy: A generation of progress.* New York: Raven Press, 1978.

Haefly, W. Behavioral and neuropharmacological aspects of drugs used in anxiety and related states. In M. Lipton, A. DiMascio, & K. Killam (Eds.), *Pharmacology: A generation of progress.* New York: Raven Press, 1978.

Hicks, R., Okonek, A., & Davis, J. The pharmacological approach. In I. Kutash, L. Schlesinger, and Associates (Eds.), *Handbook on stress and anxiety.* San Francisco: Jossey-Bass Publishers, 1980.

Hodges, W. F. The psychophysiology of anxiety. In M. Zuckerman & C. Spielberger (Eds.), *Emotions and anxiety.* New York: Wiley, 1976.

Horney, K. *Self-analysis.* New York: Norton, 1942.

Huang, Y., Redmond, D., Snyder, D., & Maas, J., In vivo location and destruction of the locus coeruleus in the Stumptail Macaque. *Brain research,* 1975, *100,* 157-162.

Kelly, D. *Anxiety and emotions: Physiological basis and treatment.* Springfield, Ill.: Thomas, 1980.

Kelly, G. *The psychology of personal constructs* (Vols. 1 & 2). New York: Norton, 1955.

Lader, M. *Physiological measures, sedative drugs, and morbid anxiety.* London: Oxford University Press, 1966.

Levitt, E. A brief commentary on the "psychiatric breakthrough" with emphasis on the hematology of anxiety. In C. Spielberger (Ed.), *Anxiety: Current trends in theory and research* (Vol. 1). New York: Academic Press, 1972.

Marinelli, R. Anxiety. In R. Woods (Ed.), *Encyclopedia of clinical assessment* (Vol. 1). San Francisco: Jossey-Bass, 1980.

May, R. *The meaning of anxiety.* New York: Ronald Press, 1950.

Mowrer, O. H. A stimulus-response analysis of anxiety and its role as a reinforcing agent. *Psychological Review,* 1939, *46,* 553-565.

Pitts, F. The biochemistry of anxiety. *Scientific American,* 1969, *220,* 69-75.

Pitts, F. N., & McClure, J. N. Lactate metabolism in anxiety neurosis. *New England Journal of Medicine,* 1967, *277,* 1329-1336.

Sepinwall, J., & Cook, L. Behavioral pharmacology of anxiety drugs. In L. Iverson, S. Iverson, & S. Snyder (Eds.), *Handbook of psychopharmacology.* New York: Plenum Press, 1978.

Skinner, B. F. *The behavior of organisms: An experimental analysis.* New York: Appleton-Century, 1938.

Skinner, B. F. *Contingencies of reinforcement.* New York: Appleton-Century, 1954.

Spence, K. W. *Behavior therapy and learning: Selected papers.* Englewood Cliffs, N. J.: Princeton-Hall, 1960.

Spielberger, C. D. (Ed.). *Anxiety: Current trends in therapy and research* (Vols. 1 & 2). New York: Academic Press, 1972.

Spielberger, C. D. Anxiety: State-trait-process. In C. Spielberger & I. Sarason (Eds.), *Stress and anxiety* (Vol. 1). Washington, D.C.: Hemisphere, 1975.

Sweeney, D., Gold, M., Pottash, A., & Davies, R. Neurobiological theories. In I. Kutash, L. Schlesinger, and Associates (Eds.), *Handbook on stress and anxiety.* San Francisco: Jossey-Bass Publishers, 1980.

Taylor, J. A. A personality scale of manifest anxiety. *Journal of Abnormal and Social Psychology,* 1953, *48,* 285-290.

II. Aggression

Adler, A. Der aggressionstrieb im leben und in der neurosis. *Fortschritte der medizine,* 1908, *26,* 577-584.

Baker, D. Chromosome errors and antisocial behavior. *CRC Critical Review of Clinical Laboratory Sciences,* 1972, *3,* 41-101.

Bandura, A. *Principles of behavior modification.* New York: Holt, Rinehart, & Winston, 1969.

Bandura, A. An analysis of modeling processes. In A. Bandura (Ed.), *Theories of modeling.* New York: Atherton, 1970.

Bandura, A. *Aggression: A social learning analysis.* Englewood Cliffs, N.J.: Prentice Hall, 1973.

Bandura, A., Ross, D., & Ross, A. A. Initiation of film-mediated aggressive models. *Journal of Abnormal and Social Psychology,* 1963, *66,* 3-11.

Bandura, A., Grusec, J. E., & Menlove, F. L. Observational learning as a function of symbolization of incentive set. *Child Development,* 1966, *37,* 499-506.

Bankert, C. P., & Anderson, C. C. Short term effects of pro-social television viewing on play of preschool boys and girls. *Psychological Reports,* 1979, *44*(3), 935-941.

Barker, R. G., Dembo, T., & Lewin, K. Frustration and aggression: An experiment with young children. *University of Iowa Studies in Child Welfare,* 1941, *18,* 1-314.

Berkowitz, L. The contagion of violence: An S-R mediational analysis of some effects of observed aggression. In W. Arnold & M. Page (Eds.), *Nebraska symposium on motivation.* Lincoln: University of Nebraska Press, 1971.

Berkowitz, L. Some determinants of impulsive aggression: The role of mediated associations with reinforcements for aggression. *Psychological Review,* 1974, *81,* 167-176.

Blanchard, R. & Blanchard, C. Animal aggression and the dyscontrol syndrome. In M. Girges & L. Kiloh (Eds.), *Limbic epilepsy and the dyscontrol syndrome.* New York: Plenum Press, 1981.

Bogart, L. Warning: The Surgeon General has determined that TV violence is moderately dangerous to your child's mental health. *The Public Opinion Quarterly,* Winter, 1973, *36,* 491-521.

Bordon, R. J. Witnessed aggression: Influence of an observer's sex and values on aggressive responding. *Journal of Personality and Social Psychology,* 1975, *31,* 567-573.

Brain, P. F. Hormones and aggression. *Annual Research Review: Hormones and Aggression,* 1977, *1,* 11-126.

Buss, A. H. *The psychology of aggression.* New York: Wiley, 1961.

Buss, A. H. Aggression pays. In J. L. Singer (Ed.), *The control of aggression and violence: Cognitive and physiological factors.* New York: Academic Press, 1971.

Caine, T. M., Foulds, G. A., & Hope, K. *Manual of the HDHQ.* London: University of London Press, 1967.

Cisin, I. H., Coffin, T. E., Janis, I. L., Klapper, J. T., Mendelsohn, D., Omwake, E., Pinderhughes, C. A., Pool, I., Siegel, A. E., Wallace, A., Watson, A. S., & Wiebe, G. D. *Television and growing up: The impact of television violence.* Washington, D. C.: U. S. Government Printing Office, 1972.

Daly, R. F. Neurological abnormalities in XYY males. *Nature,* 1969, *221,* 472-473.

Dollard, J., Doob, L., Miller, N., Mowrer, O. H., & Sears, R. R. *Frustration and aggression.* New Haven, Conn.: Yale University Press, 1939.

Edmunds, G. Judgements of different types of aggressive behavior. *British Journal of Social and Clinical Psychology,* 1978, *17,* 121-125.

Edwards, A. *Edwards personal preference schedule.* New York: Psychological Corporation, 1959.

Eichelman, B. The role of biogenic amines in aggressive behavior. In M. Sandler (Ed.), *Psychopharmacology of aggression.* New York: Raven, 1979.

Flanders, J. P. A review of research on imitative behavior. *Psychological Bulletin,* 1968, *69,* 316-337.

Freud, S. *Collected papers: Volume III.* London, England: Hogarth Press, 1924. (Originally published, 1909.)

Geen, R. G. *Aggression.* Morristown, N. J.: General Learning Corporation, 1972.

Geen, R. G., & O'Neal, E. *Perspectives on aggression.* New York: Academic Press, 1976.

Geen, R. G., & Pigg, R. Acquisition of an aggressive response and its generalization to verbal behavior. *Journal of Personality and Social Psychology,* 1970, *15,* 165-170.

Geen, R. G., & Stonner, D. Effects of aggressiveness habit strength on behavior in the presence of aggression-related stimuli. *Journal of Personality and Social Psychology,* 1971, *17,* 149-153.

Gough, H. G., & Heilbrun, A. B., Jr. *The adjective checklist manual.* Palo Alto, Calif.: Consulting Psychologist's Press, 1965.

Hall, C. S. The inheritance of emotionality. *Sigma Xi Quarterly* 1938.

Holtzman, W. H., & Thorpe, J. *Holtzman inkblot manual.* New York: The Psychological Corporation, 1958.

Hutchings, D. & Mednick, S. A. Registered criminality in the adoptive and biological parents of registered male criminal adoptees. In R. R. Fieve, D. Rosenthal, & H. Brill (Eds.), *Genetic research in psychiatry.* Baltimore: Johns Hopkins University Press, 1975.

Jackson, D. *Personality research form.* New York: Research Psychologist's Press, 1965.

Johnson, R. N. *Aggression in man and animals.* Philadelphia: Saunders, 1972.

Kessler, S., & Moos, R. H. The XYY karyotype and criminality: A review. *Journal of Psychiatric Research,* 1970, *1,* 153-170.

Lange, A. R.: Goeckner, D. J.; Adeso, V. J., & Marlatt, G. A. Effects of alcohol on aggression in male social drinkers. *Journal of Abnormal Psychology,* 1975, *84,* 508-518.

Lessing, G. S. The relation between overt and fantasy aggression as a function of maternal responding to aggression. *Journal of Abnormal and Social Psychology,* 1957, *55,* 218-221.

Liebert, R. M., & Baron, R. A. Some immediate effects of televised violence on children's behavior. *Developmental Psychology,* 1977, *6,* 469-478.

Lorenz, K. *On aggression.* New York: Harcourt, Brace, & World, 1966.

Mark, V. H., & Ervin, F. R. *Violence and the brain.* New York: Harper & Row, 1970.

Margargee, E. I., Cook, P. E., & Mendelsohn, G. A. Development and evaluation of a MMPI scale of assaultiveness in overcontrolled individuals. *Journal of Abnormal Psychology,* 1967, *72,* 519-528.

Moyer, K. E. *The psychobiology of aggression.* New York: Harper & Row, 1976.

Olweus, D. *The prediction of aggression.* Stockholm: Scandinavian Test Corporation, 1969.

Parke, R. D., Ewall, W., & Slaby, R. G. Hostile and helpful verbalizations as regulators of non-verbal aggression. *Journal of Personality and Social Psychology,* 1972, *23,* 243-248.

Rosenzweig, S. The picture association method and its application in a study of reactions to frustration. *Journal of Personality,* 1945, *14,* 3-23.

Sandler, M. *Psychopharmacology of aggression.* New York: Raven, 1979.

Schmutte, G. T., Leonard, K. E., & Taylor, S. P. Alcohol and expectations of attack. *Psychological Reports,* 1979, *45*(1), 163-167.

Scott, J. P. Genetic differences in the social behavior of inbred strains of mice. *Journal of Heredity,* 1942, *33,* 11-15.

Selg, H. *The making of human aggression.* New York: St. Martin's, 1971.

Shah, S. A. Report on the XYY chromosomal abnormality. *NIMH Conference Report.* Washington, D. C.: U. S. Government Printing Office.

Sheard, M. The role of drugs affecting catacholamines on shock-elicited fighting in rats. In E. Usdin (Ed.), *Catacholamines: Basic and clinical frontiers.* New York: Pergammon, 1979.

Shostrom, E. *Personal orientation inventory.* San Diego: Educational & Industrial Testing Service, 1963.

Skornia, H. D. *Television and society: An inquest and agenda for improvement.* New York: McGraw-Hill, 1965.

Strupp, G. K. Castration: The total treatment in sexual behaviors. In H. L. Resnik & M. E. Wolfgang (Eds.), *Sexual behaviors: Social, clinical & legal aspects.* Boston: Little, Brown, 1972.

Wolfgang, M: E. *Patterns in criminal homicide.* New York: Wiley, 1958.

Wolfgang, M.E. (Ed.). *Studies in homicide.* New York: Harper & Row, 1967.

Zimbardo, P. G. The human choice: Individuation, reason and order versus deindividuation, impulse and chaos. *Nebraska symposium on motivation.* Lincoln: University of Nebraska Press, 1969.

III. Locus of Control

Archer, R. Relationship between locus of control and anxiety. *Journal of Personality Assessment,* 1979, *43,* 617-626.

Archer, R., & Stein, D. Personal control expectancies and state anxiety. *Psychological Reports,* 1978, *42,* 551-558.

Battle, E., & Rotter, J. Children's feelings of personal control as related to social class and ethnic groups. *Journal of Personality,* 1963, *31,* 482-490.

Efran, J. *Some personality determinants of memory for success and failure.* Unpublished doctoral dissertation, Ohio State University, 1963.

Gurin, P., Gurin, G., Lao, R., & Beattie, M. Internal-external control in the motivational dynamics of Negro youth. *Journal of Social Issues,* 1969, *25,* 29-53.

Henry, S., Medway, F., & Scabro, H. Sex and locus of control as determinants of children's responses to peer versus adult praise. *Journal of Educational Psychology,* 1979, *71,* 604-612.

Houston, B. Control over stress, locus of control, and response to stress, *Journal of Personality and Social Psychology,* 1972, *21,* 249-255.

Hsieh, T., Shybut, J., & Lotsof, E. Internal versus external control and ethnic group membership: A cross-cultural comparison. *Journal of Consulting and Clinical Psychology,* 1969, *33,* 122-124.

James, W., & Rotter, J. Partial and 100% reinforcement under chance and skill conditions. *Journal of Experimental Psychology,* 1958, *55,* 397-403.

Johnson, J., & Sarason, I. Moderator variables in life stress research. In I. Sarason & C. Spielberger (Eds.), *Stress and anxiety.* Washington, D.C.: Hemisphere Publishing Co., 1979.

Kuo, H., & Marsella, A. J. The meaning and measurement of Machiavellianism in Chinese and American college students. *Journal of Social Psychology,* 1977, *101,* 165-173.

Lefcourt, H. *Research with the locus of control construct.* New York: Academic Press, 1981.

Lowery, B., Jacobsen, B., & Keane, A. Relationships of locus of control to preoperative anxiety. *Psychological Reports,* 1975, *37,* 1115-1121.

Mirels, H. Dimensions of internal versus external control. *Journal of Consulting and Clinical Psychology,* 1970, *34,* 226-228.

Natale, M. Effects of induced elation and depression on internal-external locus of control. *Journal of Psychology,* 1978, *100,* 315-320.

Nordholm, L., Ward, C., & Bhanthunavin, D. Sex and cultural differences in perceived locus of control among students in five different countries. *Journal of Consulting and Clinical Psychology,* 1974, *42,* 451-455.

Nowicki, S., & Duke, M. A pre-school and primary internal-external locus of control scale. *Developmental Psychology,* 1974, *10,* 874-880.

Nowicki, S., Duke, M., & Crouch, M. Sex differences in locus of control and performance under competitive and cooperative conditions. *Journal of Educational Psychology,* 1978, *70,* 482-486.

Nowicki, S., & Strickland, B. A locus of control scale for children. *Journal of Consulting and Clinical Psychology,* 1973, *40,* 148-155.

Parsons, O., & Schneider, J. Locus of control in university students from Eastern and Western societies. *Journal of Consulting and Clinical Psychology,* 1974, *42,* 456-461.

Phares, E. *Locus of control in personality.* New Jersey: General Learning Press, 1976.

Rotter, J. *Social learning and clinical psychology.* Englewood Cliffs, New Jersey: Prentice Hall, 1954.

Rotter, J. Generalized expectancies for internal versus external control of reinforcement. *Psychological Monographs,* 1966, *80* (1, Whole No. 609).

Schneider, J., & Parsons, O. Categories of locus of control scale and cross-cultural comparisons in Denmark and the United States. *Journal of Cross-Cultural Psychology,* 1970, *1,* 131-138.

Sue, D. Eliminating cultural oppression in counseling: Toward general theory. *Journal of Counseling Psychology,* 1978, *25,* 419-428.

Veblen, T. *Theory of the leisure class.* New York: Mentor Press, 1899.

Glossary

Abreaction. Responding emotionally to the memory of a past experience or repressed event.

Accounts. Verbal statements intended to be explanatory relative to problematic behavior.

Actone. Unit of behavior used by H. A. Murray.

Affection. Relating to feelings or emotions. Psychology is sometimes divided into three parts: cognition (knowing), conation (willing) and affection (feeling).

Alpha press. In the personality theory of H. A. Murray, a force in the objective environment which motivates a person.

Amygdala. A section of the limbic area of the brain associated with aggression. Its connection to the hypothalamus has been observed to be related to rage behavior.

Anima. The inherited potential carried by the male to experience the image of woman.

Apersonal. Not relating to a specific individual, such as a phenomenon which affects all people or events over which the individual has no control.

Approach-avoidance conflict. A conflict situation in which the organism simultaneously wants to go in opposite directions. A baby who wants a desired candy offered by a feared stranger is an example of an approach-avoidance conflict.

Archetypal image. An activated, transpersonal nucleus of any emotionally charged complex that is symbolically filled out by collective conscious cultural experience and shared symbolic representations.

Archetype. An innate capacity of the mind to apperceive core emotional human experiences in nearly universal ways accumulated during the experiences of ancestors.

Archetype "as such." Content of the collective unconscious which is the psychological counterpart of instinct; inherited formal property of the human brain to experience typical figures, situations, or behavior patterns.

Authoritarianism. A set of characteristics associated with a preference for an ordered world where everything and everyone has its proper status and function, and authority in relationships is clear and respected. It is an essentially conservative outlook which may include stereotyping and prejudice, rigidity, conventionality, religiosity, intolerance of weakness, cynicism, and a discomfort with ambiguity. Sometimes characterized by a strong desire for servility in others and authority over them. Also it may refer to a style of leadership where assignments and strategies in a group are determined and results evaluated by a detached leader.

Autism. Living and thinking in a self-centered manner, in terms of one's internal aspects, unrelated to reality. Usually used as a synonym for childhood schizophrenia.

Autochthonous. Coming from within; self-generated. See *autogenous*.

Autogenous. Originating from within, self-induced. See *autochthonous*.

Awareness context. Knowledge of self and of others relative to role behavior in any situation.

Behavior modification. A system of changing behavior based on systematic use rewards and punishments.

Behaviorism. The study of behavior without concern for mental contents or introspection. An objective and rigidly controlled system of dealing with organisms to check hypotheses and measure behavior under a variety of conditions.

Beta press. In the personality theory of Henry A. Murray, an individual's perception of forces in the environment which affect his responses.

Biofeedback. The process of informing an individual of the status of some variation of an ordinarily unknown internal event, such as heart rate or brain waves; ordinarily done so that the person can control these events through systematic feedback.

Biogenic amines. An inclusive expression embracing groups of neurotransmitters which mediate behavior.

Biosphere. A concept held by theorists who stress the interaction between the environment and the individual in the determination of the quality or direction of life. All aspects of life, including prevailing social conditions and biological events, are seen to be integral and inseparable in their influence.

Black box. Name given by behaviorally-oriented psychologists to those processes internal to the individual organism (psychological, neurological, and physiological), which they consider unobservable and, therefore, outside the subject matter of psychology.

Career. Relative to an individual, the pattern of movements and thoughts in proceeding through social situations, roughly equivalent to lifestyle and strategies.

Catharsis. Literally, "cleaning out"; the process of emotionally experiencing past events that have been repressed.

Cathexis. An investment of psychic energy in mental representation that may vary in interest or value.

Causality. The relationship between an act and its consequence; the necessary results of the actions of one entity on another.

Cognition. Intellectual functions such as remembering, thinking, planning, recognizing, reasoning. See *affection* and *conation*.

Collective. All psychic contents that belong not to one individual but to the whole group, such as to a society or a race; also the group that is most meaningful to an individual, especially one's gang, the bunch, friends. In Soviet usage, this term implies an enduring community of persons united by common goals.

Collective unconscious. The transpersonal aspect of the psyche, what Jung called the "objective psyche," where archetypes exist but are not necessarily activated by personal life experiences.

Compensation. The tendency of an organ or an individual to make up for a lack by increasing its function or its efforts.

Complex. An emotionally charged group of associated ideas and memories unconsciously organized around an activated archetypal image; always exists in unconscious dynamic relationship to other complexes having bipolar positive and negative emotional significance.

Conation. The "willing" or "wanting" aspect which "pushes" the person onward. See *affection, cognition*

Concurrent validity. Validity of a test established by the comparison of its results with those of a different measure which purports to measure the same variable, and which is taken at the same time as the first.

Constellatory construct. Statement relative to a person with the implication of other associated aspects. See *preemptive construct, propositional construct*.

Construct. Generally, a hypothetical entity (such as Intelligence) treated as though actually in existence. Also, the basic theoretical unit of George Kelly's theory. For the latter, it refers to an emperically evolved bipolar label that develops from experience.

Construct validity. Parallels the wide range of approaches employed in establishing credibility of any abstract property or idea, including experimentation and statistical investigation. The development of a consensus of acceptance is also indicative of the validity of a construct.

Contrasexual. Images, feelings, memories, and behavior patterns associated with the opposite sex; *anima* and *animus* are contrasexual *archetypal images*.

Convergent validity. A test of validity established by the correlation between scores on one measure with the results of a number of other indicators of presumably the same variable as that measured by the first measure. Similar to concurrent validity.

Crèche (French). A child-care nursery.

Cryptomnesia. The unconscious production of something read, heard, or seen at any earlier period of time and then forgotten.

CS. Conditioned stimulus. A stimulus which derives its properties from contiguous pairing with an unconditioned stimulus.

Daseinsanalysis. In German *Daseinsanalyse*. Literally "analysis of existence," a school of psychotherapeutic theory and practice viewing the individual as constantly growing and enfolding, responsible and interactive.

Defectology. The study of human defects, especially relative to aberrations in children.

Defense mechanism. A procedure employed by the ego to protect itself against changes. *Repression* and *idealization* are examples. See *safeguarding tendency*.

Deindividuation. A psychological state in which a person experiences decreased feelings of self-esteem, a lack of individuality as a distinct being, and an unaccountability which derives from a sense of anonymity.

Deintegration. A maturational process, beginning with birth, when a primary self or state of original wholeness and integration is disrupted in the service of growth.

Depressive anxiety. An anxiety derived from the fear of one's own wishes and capacity to destroy, harm, or damage an ambivalently loved object.

Depressive position. Achieved when the infant recognizes his mother as a whole object; an early developmental achievement that peaks around the seventh month of life, resulting in the ego's capacity to tolerate ambivalent feelings of love and hate simultaneously toward the same object.

Depth psychology. Any psychological school of thought which assumes that people operate in terms of unconscious forces.

Determinism. The idea that any event is completely explained or controlled by prior events. This implies perfect prediction of behavior if all antecedent elements were known.

Dialectical materialism. A kind of reasoned argument based on the concept of the priority of the reality of matter, and the philosophy of Hegel that thesis is followed by antithesis and the result is synthesis. See *dialectic process*.

Dialectic process. A method of discovering truth through contrasting arguments, known as the thesis (statement) and antithesis (contrasting or opposing statement), leading to the emergence of a new proposition based on the integration of the two opposing positions.

Discriminant validation. A check of a convergent validation. Established by obtaining a significant negative correlation between a test of a quality which is opposed to the quality intended to be measured by the test being validated and other measures found to be positively correlated with the test being validated.

Dopamine. One of a group of biogenic

unified entity rather than as a summation of parts.

Homeostasis. The tendency of a body to maintain itself in balance; for example, the human body tends to have a constant level of water, salt, and other elements. Also used in terms of psychological balance; the tendency to be in a state of quiet, peaceful rest.

Humoral theory. A theory proposed by Hippocrates that personality is a function of certain body fluids (humors).

Hypothetical-deductive method. A means of attempting to determine the truth of theories by establishing testable hypotheses from theories and then finding evidence for or against the hypotheses.

Id. The part of the psyche that contains instincts; the Unconscious; the seat of pleasure demands. See *ego, superego.*

Idealism. A philosophical position that the ultimate reality is in the mind. See *realism.*

Idealization. A defense mechanism in which the unwanted aspects of person are denied and the individual's own standards are projected onto the person.

Idiographic. Having to do with the lawfulness of individual cases. See *nomothetic.*

Imago. Internal object, frequently an image of a subjective functional complex rather than the external object itself; not identical with the outer object. Created by a combination of an introjected outer object, archetypal fantasies, and instinctual needs.

Impression management. Behavior on the part of an individual designed to generate a particular response or reaction from another.

Indeterminism. The notion that behavior cannot be perfectly predicted or explained, even if all prior events were known.

Individuation. The process of becoming differentiated as an individual.

Interactionism. Concept of reciprocal relations between mind and body, each of which influences the other. Also, a recent theoretical orientation whereby behavior is considered to be a function of the simultaneous interaction of the person and the environment.

Introjection. One of several mental mechanisms. Essentially, it means taking in, absorbing aspects of the outside world, and incorporating them into one's own psyche.

Introspection. Self-analysis; examination of one's internal status; dealing with the conscious mind.

Introvert. A person whose libido tends to turn predominantly inward toward the world of inner objects and subjective reality. See *extravert.*

Labeling theory. Giving names, usually critical, to social behavior of an undesirable sort, thereby often making that behavior deviant by definition.

Libido. Sexual energy.

Limbic system. Part of the brain in which emotional aspects are located.

Locus coeruleum. A section of the midbrain associated with anxiety.

Locus of control. Refers to a person's perception of the point from which one's life is controlled. Internal locus of control implies a belief that one is the master of one's fate. Having an external locus of control would lead one to feel helpless and to claim unaccountability for the results of one's endeavors, characteristically placing their cause on events or conditions outside of one's self over which one has no control.

Longitudinal method. Study of people by following them up over a considerable period of time, such as testing them from infancy through adulthood with intelligence tests.

Looking-glass self. Imagining how another person sees one's self; seeing one's self through the eyes of another.

Machiavellianism. The tenets of Niccolo Machiavelli that any method, however crafty, deceitful, violent or unscrupulous is justified in the obtaining of power. Also a personality trait characterized by exploitative and manipulative interpersonal relationships.

Mandala. A Sanskrit work used by Jung to describe an image representing the self-archetype, a psychic process of centering, and a symbol of a center of the total personality. Also, a formal structure or container in which psychic organization takes place around a center.

Manic defenses. Developed, as the depressive position is achieved, as a protective reaction of the ego against experiencing feelings of guilt and loss that go with depressive anxiety.

Masculine protest. According to A. Adler, a desire to be more powerful or to dominate, to be like a "real man." Can occur in women as well as in men.

Materialism. The view that matter is the only reality. See *idealism, realism*.

Metaphysics. A branch of philosophy which attempts to explain the nature of being and reality.

Metapsychology. Literally "beyond psychology"; any theory that attempts to encompass all the facts of psychology by philosophical generalizations about the nature of reality, the ultimate cause of events, ultimate truth, and so on. Freud used this term to indicate that psychoanalysis went beyond conscious experience to explain behavior.

Modeling. Process of changing someone to someone else's desires. Used mostly in modifying behavior to meet outside specifications.

Molar behavior. Unit of behavior, generally thought of as a completed act.

Molecular behavior. Behavior in terms of units of function within the behavior; seen as the totality of contributing elements to the behavior, physiologically and psychologically.

Monism. The position that life is based on one substance.

Naturwissenschaften (German). Psychology as an objective biological science. See *Geisteswissenschaften*.

Neo-psychoanalytic (or neo-Freudian). Refers to the work of several of Freud's students and later theorists whose ideas, while based on Freudian concepts, have been modified in various directions, often with a more social, rather than biological, bent.

Nomothetic. Relating to general laws, or based on group norms. See *idiographic*.

Norepinephrine. A hormone secreted by the sympathetic nervous system, in particular in the presence of stress. Often used synonomously with noradrenalin, it is closely related to epinephrine (adrenalin). It is found in notable amounts in the hypothalamus of the brain, and it is suspected to be related to some forms of mental illness.

Numinous. Awe-inspiring, overwhelming feeling, thought, sensation, or intuition, related to some thing archetypically experienced as having intense symbolic significance beyond simple, everyday personal concern.

Object. In psychology, this word has a variety of meanings. In personality theory it may refer to another person.

Object relations theory. The complicated interaction of internal objects and archetypal images in psychic reality; emphasizes the original mother–infant relationship in the first two years of life.

Oedipus complex. Psychoanalytic notion that children have a desire for sexual relations with opposite sex parent. This desire is repressed and so is in the Unconscious. In females the analogy is also called the Electra complex.

Ontology. The science of being. A branch of metaphysics relating to the kinds and relations of being.

Operant conditioning. Type of learning whereby the organism's responses are modified by the consequences of the behavior. Essentially, the organism repeats rewarded behavior and discontinues unrewarded or punished behavior.

Operant learning. A process whereby a behavior is reinforced, thus increasing the likelihood of the behavior being repeated. For example, a child's positive behavior is reinforced by his mother's praise, show of affection, or granting of a privilege (or perhaps by the avoidance of a punishment), with the child becoming more strongly disposed to act again in a positive manner. Synonym: operant conditioning, type-R conditioning, reinforcement conditioning, and instrumental conditioning.

Organismic. Pertaining to the organism usually emphasizing an holistic response.

Paradoxical intention. The psychological process in which one chooses to perform behavior which one sees as pathological, as well as out of one's control. By willing to perform it, one regains control, and the undesired behaviors, e.g., perspiring in anticipation of meeting new persons, cease.

Paraphrenia. General term meaning abnormal, insane, psychotic thinking.

Parapraxes. The so-called "Freudian slips," errors one makes in life which are dynamically caused by unconscious wishes, such as forgetting names, slips of the tongue or of the pen.

Parataxic. The second of three successive stages of cognitive development, occurring during the time of early language acquisition. In this stage, relationships are assigned to events on the basis of their proximity in time or space. Followed by syntaxic stage. Suggested by H. S. Sullivan.

Passage. A sequence of steps involved in social movements, a kind of expected protocol of operations regulating how one changes situations.

Pedagogy. Science of teaching.

Pedology. The study of children.

Penis envy. According to Freudian theory, young girls pass through a developmental stage in which they discover with dismay that they do not possess a penis. Their resulting feelings are of deprivation, handicap, and injustice. A repressed wish for a penis is often attributed to the neuroses of women.

Persona. A false self or social mask that represents a facet of the personality turned toward the external world; pathological when the ego rigidly identifies with mask; is unrelated to the reality of the true self and inner world with its unconscious needs and fantasies.

Personal unconscious. Repressed fears, wishes, memories, and emotions of an individual nature; preconscious perceptions of subliminal personal nature that can be recalled.

Personification. A type of projection wherein one attributes characteristics or acts to another person in order to explain the frustration of his wants. Also, the assignment of human qualities to natural forces, inanimate objects, a symbol of a person, or to abstractions. Lastly, one's perception of the qualities of another or of himself which becomes his reality.

Personology. That branch of psychology which addresses the study of the personality as a whole, as it develops and operates within a unique individual. Contrasted to metapsychology, which is concerned with general laws of mental functioning.

Phenotype. The actual appearance of a person, having particular characteristics. See *genotype.*

Phobia. Strong fear of an unreasonable or irrational type.

Phrenology. A spurious conception that personality is based on the contours of the skull which in turn has its shape affected by the brain.

Phylogenetic. Hereditary elements in a group of people, such as what is common for the whole human race.

Physiognomy. The study of the personality as a function of the appearance of the body, especially the face.

Pluralism. The notion that reality consists of more than two ultimate substances. See *monism, dualism.*

Pragmatism. A basically American philosophical movement which finds the meaning of conceptions in their practical implications, the function of thought in the guiding of action, and the test of truthfulness in the practical consequences of belief.

Predictive validity. The accuracy with which the outcome of a test predicts an indicated behavior after a specified interval of time. Synonym: Empirical validity.

Preemptive construct. According to G. Kelly, a statement relative to a person which has the implication that the statement tells all about the individual, all that need be known. See *constellatory construct, propositional construct.*

Press. A term employed by Henry Murray to refer to external forces in life. Alpha press indicates objective forces, while Beta press indicates subjectively seen external forces. The word *press* is singular and plural.

Primary self. The basic psychosomatic unit existing in the infant at birth; an integration disrupted and reestablished again and again at crucial developmental points along the life cycle; precursor of the ego and the archetypes that are derived from deintegration.

Primordial image. Jung's earlier term for archetypal image.

Preconscious. Area of the mind where memories exist which can be brought readily to awareness; in between the unconscious and the conscious.

Prodromic. Tending to predict, an early sign or warning.

Projection. Attributing certain aspects of self to others without awareness.

Projective identification. A state describing fusion characteristic of the earliest mother-infant relationship; referred to by Jung as a state of "participation mystique" or "primary identity" which can be negatively regressive or lead to growth.

Propositional construct. According to G. Kelly, a statement relative to one aspect of an individual among other aspects of the person. See *constellatory construct, preemptive construct.*

Proprioceptive memory. The awareness, facilitated by proprioceptors, of muscle, joint, and tendon sensations.

Proprium. Term suggested by G. Allport as meaning essentially the same as self or ego; one's individuality.

Prototaxic. The first of three successive stages of cognitive development, occurring normally in early infancy. Characterized by an absence of a sense of self as distinct from other people and events. Followed by parataxic and syntaxic stages. Suggested by H. S. Sullivan.

Psychic reality. The experience of one's inner world, including the dynamic relationships between complexes, unconscious fantasies, and archetypal images.

Psychosomatic. Relating to a physical disorder which originates in or is influenced by the emotional state of the person.

Q-sort. Usually a group of cards (perhaps with words or sentences) that are to be sorted according to some preplanned distribution and then mathematically correlated to determine degrees of correspondence.

Range of convenience. The range of events conveniently subsumed by a construct without stretching or distorting it. Suggested by G. Kelly.

Rationalization. A plausible explanation for some behavior that comes after the decision or the act, but not the real reason.

Realism. A philosophical position that the world exists apart from the mind; that it is objectively a fact. *See idealism, materialism.*

Reality testing. Checking out hypotheses relative to people and events; a validation of reality usually done in psychotherapy.

Reciprocal inhibition. Interference of two items with one another.

Reductionism. The view that large events are ultimately explained by elements; the attempt to explain complex units in terms of their constitutent interacting parts.

Reflexology. A system of psychological thought that human behavior can be explained on the basis of reflexes as the fundamental unit, with other processes building on these basics.

Reification. Conceptualizing that something which is abstract is concrete; presupposition of the real existence of concepts.

Reinforcement. Strengthening various behavioral responses through rewards.

Reliability. An indication of the degree of stability of results which a test will yield over repeated administrations, its consistency or dependability. Also, the extent to which a sample under study is representative of the underlying population from which it was taken.

Replication. Repeating an experiment to check the accuracy of prior conclusions.

Repression. Unconscious exclusion of events: also includes such events as instinctual drives, and conflicts between such drives and defense mechanisms. A *defense mechanism* or a *safeguarding tendency.* More or less equivalent to the term *blocking.*

Respondent. Relating to behavior that is the effect of, or identified with, a particular stimulus.

Role playing. This word has four meanings: (1) theatrical acting, (2) social role taking, (3) dissembling, and (4) acting a part for educational-therapeutic reasons, such as psychodrama.

Role taking. Imagining another's point of view; a kind of empathy.

Rorschach test. Best-known of the projective personality tests; consists of ten standard inkblots, black-and-white and chromatic plates, which people observe and report what they see in them.

Safeguarding tendency. Means used by individuals without awareness or intention to preserve self-esteem, through such processes as distortion, repression, and regression. See *defense mechanisms.*

Schedule of Reinforcement. Planned program, used mostly in terms of behavior modification, experiments in which predetermined intervals and rewards and/or punishments are given to various behaviors.

Self. The archetype of order, centering, and integration; also the totality of the personality.

Self-reflexivity. Process whereby a person defines his own behavior rather than simply responding to stimuli.

Serotonin. One of a group of biogenic amines (neurotransmitters). See *biogenic amines.* A synaptic agent which is involved in the control of various autonomic functions.

Set. A determining tendency; a kind of preparation to behave in particular ways; a habitual kind of response preparation.

Shadow. The unconscious "natural" instinctual dark side of a person, often guilt-laden. Suggested by C. G. Jung.

Shaping. A type of behavior modification wherein a subject is conditioned to respond to a stimulus in a new way by the reinforcement of increasingly close approximations of the desired response.

Sign. Expression that stands for a known thing, created from known associations, in contrast to a living symbol pregnant with ambiguous, hidden, unconscious meanings.

Social interactionism. Doctrine that people do not interact with others in terms of themselves as individuals but as members of groups.

Soft determinism. Acknowledgment of the influences of both the individual (indeterminism) and the environment (determinism) to generate consequences.

Social stimulus value. How the person is generally seen by others.

Solipsism. A theory which states that the self is the only existent thing; and that the self can know nothing but its own creations.

Somatotype. Classification of body structure. There are a variety of systems in use, all arbitrary in nature.

Splitting. Dichotomizing, such as the distinction between the good and bad self.

Structuralism. School of thought relative to elements or structure in the mind, such as the quality of cold. In sociology, behavior in reference to social entities. See *functionalism*.

Subception. Perception without awareness.

Superego. Psychoanalytic term referring to the incorporation of social standards within the mind of the individual more-or-less corresponds to the term "conscience." See *ego, id*.

Symbol. Distinguished from a sign; a "living" symbol expresses something relatively unknown to consciousness that is pregnant with meaning which cannot be characterized in any other way; formulates an essential, unconscious factor, not something already conventionally known.

Syntaxic. The last of three successive stages of cognitive development, beginning at approximately age two years. The outstanding feature of this stage is the increasing use of linear logic, extending into maturity. Suggested by H. S. Sullivan.

Tabula rasa (Latin). A blank slate, referring to John Locke's concept that children are born with no experiences and their minds are like a clean piece of paper.

Teleology. Purposive; the concept that behavior is best understood in terms of the organism's prediction of or orientation to the future; goal orientation.

Thanatos. The death instinct; opposed to *Eros*, the life instinct.

Thema. The unifying "plot" behind behavior in H. A. Murray's system; a constant general aim of the individual. Also, the relationship between a press and a need.

Thematic Apperception Test (TAT). A projective technique of personality assessment wherein subjects are presented with a set of social situations depicted by pictures on cards. The stories woven by the subject as descriptions of what is happening in the pictures are thought to be expressions of the nature of the interpersonal relations in the subject's life.

Thermodynamic theory. Relationship between energy and heat.

Third-force psychology. Term referring to a group of psychological schools of thought distinguished from depth psychologies, such as psychoanalysis and behaviorism; generally humanistic in tone, best represented by A. Maslow.

Token economy. Method of training organisms by teaching them first that tokens can be used to obtain various gratifications and then that tokens can be obtained by a variety of behaviors.

Trait. Any more-or-less permanent aspect or characteristic of an individual; a person's reliably consistent ways of operating.

Transaction. A relationship event depending on the transfer of forces between participating parties.

Transcendental. Going beyond normal understanding and human potentialities.

Transcendent function. Cognitive process which unites two psychological opposites in

Subject Index

Book Manufacture

PERSONALITY THEORIES, RESEARCH, AND ASSESSMENT
was typeset at Printech Inc., Schaumburg, Illinois. Printing and binding
was at Kingsport Press, Inc., Kingsport, Tennessee. Cover design was by
Quarto, Inc., Morton Grove, Illinois. Internal design was by F.E. Peacock
Publishers art department. The typeface is Times Roman, various sizes.